Cognitive-Behavior Therapy for Children

Treating Complex and Refractory Cases

Dean McKay, PhD, ABPP, is Associate Professor, Department of Psychology, Fordham University. He currently serves on the editorial boards of *Behaviour Research and Therapy*, *Journal of Clinical Psychology,* and *Journal of Anxiety Disorders,* and is Associate Editor of *Journal of Cognitive Psychotherapy.* He has published over 120 journal articles and book chapters, is editor or co-editor of 8 published or forthcoming books, and has given over 150 conference presentations. Dr. McKay has been a member of the Obsessive Compulsive Cognitions Working Group since 1995. He is Board Certified in Behavioral and Clinical Psychology by the American Board of Professional Psychology (ABPP), is a Fellow of the American Board of Behavioral Psychology and the Academy of Clinical Psychology as well as a Clinical Fellow of the Behavior Research and Therapy Society. His research has focused primarily on obsessive-compulsive disorder (OCD), body dysmorphic disorder, and health anxiety and their link to OCD and the role of disgust in psychopathology. His research has also focused on mechanisms of information-processing bias for anxiety states. Dr. McKay is also director and founder of the Institute for Cognitive Behavior Therapy and Research, a private treatment and research center in Westchester County, New York. He resides in Port Washington, New York, with his wife, Dawn, and daughter, Rebecca.

Eric A. Storch, PhD, earned his BA in Psychology from Binghamton University in 1997, followed by his MS, MPhil, and PhD degrees in Child-Clinical Psychology from Teachers College, Columbia University. At the University of South Florida, he is currently an Associate Professor of Clinical Psychology in the Department of Pediatrics and holds joint appointments in the Departments of Psychiatry and Psychology. Dr. Storch is a licensed clinical psychologist and serves as the Director of the University of South Florida Obsessive Compulsive Disorder Program.

Dr. Storch specializes in the cognitive behavioral treatment of adult and childhood obsessive-compulsive disorder (OCD), as well as other obsessive-compulsive spectrum disorders (e.g., trichotillomania, tic disorders, body dysmorphic disorder, skin picking) and anxiety disorders. He is highly regarded for the psychological treatment of OCD, particularly with regard to treatment-refractory cases. He also has a special interest in the dissemination of effective psychological treatment approaches for OCD and tics as well as in the development and validation of OCD assessment measures. Dr. Storch has published over 150 peer-reviewed articles. He is the lead editor on a text entitled *Handbook of Child and Adolescent Obsessive-Compulsive Disorder.* Dr. Storch has received grant funding from the National Institute of Mental Health, Obsessive Compulsive Foundation, National Alliance for Research on Schizophrenia and Depression (NARSAD), Foundation for Prader-Willi Research, and numerous other foundations for his research on OCD and related topics. He resides in Tampa, Florida, with his wife, Jill, and their daughter, Maya.

Cognitive-Behavior Therapy for Children

Treating Complex and Refractory Cases

DEAN McKAY, PhD, ABPP

ERIC A. STORCH, PhD

Editors

SPRINGER PUBLISHING COMPANY
New York

Springer Publishing Company, LLC
11 West 42nd Street
New York, NY 10036
www.springerpub.com

Acquisitions Editor: Sheri W. Sussman
Production Editor: Pamela Lankas
Cover design: Mimi Flow
Composition: International Graphic Services

Ebook ISBN: 978-0-8261-1687-1

09 10 11 12 / 5 4 3 2 1

Printed in the United States of America by Hamilton Printing.

Library of Congress Cataloging-in-Publication Data

Cognitive-behavior therapy for children : treating complex and refractory cases / Dean McKay, Eric A. Storch, editors.
p. ; cm.
Includes bibliographical references and index.
ISBN 978-0-8261-1686-4 (alk. paper)
1. Cognitive therapy for children. 2. Cognitive therapy for teenagers. 3. Child psychotherapy. I. McKay, Dean, 1966. II. Storch, Eric A.
[DNLM: 1. Cognitive Therapy—methods. 2. Adolescent. 3. Child. 4. Mental Disorders—therapy. WS 350.6 C67625 2009]
RJ505.C63C646 2009
618.92'891425—dc22

2009017312

This book is dedicated to my family, Dawn and Rebecca, for their support and encouragement and for being such fun travel partners, both on vacation and in life. And for the children whom I have worked with, for creating a sense of importance in determining effective means of alleviating distress.

—Dean McKay

With much love this book is dedicated to my mother and father, who instilled in me both the joy of learning and the importance of helping others. And to my daughter, Maya—thank you for being the perfect reason to come home from work early.

—Eric Storch

Contents

Contributors

Anne Marie Albano, PhD, Department of Psychiatry, Columbia University College of Physicians and Surgeons, New York, New York

Renae Beaumont, BSc (Hons), PhD, School of Psychology, University of Queensland, Brisbane, Australia

Sara J. Becker, MA, Department of Psychology and Neuroscience, Duke University, Durham, North Carolina

Elissa J. Brown, PhD, Department of Psychology, St. John's University, Queens, New York

Tymesha Buckner, MA, Applewood Centers, Elyria, Ohio

Carole L. Campbell, PhD, Department of Psychiatry, Children's Hospital of the King's Daughters, Norfolk, Virginia

Bruce F. Chorpita, PhD, Department of Psychology, University of California–Los Angeles, Los Angeles, California

Christine A. Conelea, MS, Department of Psychology, University of Wisconsin–Milwaukee, Milwaukee, Wisconsin

John F. Curry, PhD, Professor and Director of Clinical Psychology, Department of Psychology and Neuroscience, Duke University, Durham, North Carolina

Carla Kmett Danielson, PhD, Assistant Professor, Department of Psychiatry, Medical University of South Carolina, Charleston, South Carolina

Thompson E. Davis III, PhD, Department of Psychology, Louisiana State University, Baton Rouge, Louisiana

Angela Celio Doyle, PhD, Department of Psychiatry, University of Chicago, Chicago, Illinois

Norah Feeny, PhD, Associate Professor, Department of Psychiatry, Case Western Reserve University, Cleveland, Ohio

Clint E. Field, PhD, Director, Psychology Community Clinic, Department of Psychology, Utah State University, Logan, Utah

Sarah Fischer, PhD, Assistant Professor, Department of Psychology, University of Georgia, Athens, Georgia

Gary R. Geffken, PhD, Department of Psychiatry, University of Florida, Gainesville, Florida

Erin L. Girio, MA, Department of Psychology, Ohio University, Athens, Ohio

Daniel le Grange, PhD, Department of Psychiatry, University of Chicago, Chicago, Illinois

Paulo Graziano, MA, Department of Clinical and Health Psychology, University of Florida Health Center and Department of Psychology, University of North Carolina at Greensboro, Greensboro, North Carolina

Wendy N. Gray, MS, Department of Clinical and Health Psychology, University of South Florida, Gainesville, Florida

David M. Janicke, PhD, Department of Clinical and Health Psychology, University of South Florida, Gainesville, Florida

Mary L. Keeley, MS, Department of Clinical and Health Psychology, University of Florida Health Center and Department of Psychiatry and Behavioral Sciences, Emory University, Atlanta, Georgia

Alyssa M. Marder, PhD, Department of Psychology, University of California–Los Angeles, Los Angeles, California

Lisa J. Merlo, PhD, Assistant Professor, Department of Psychiatry, University of Florida, Gainesville, Florida

Miguel Morales, MD, Child Psychiatrist, Departments of Pediatrics and Psychiatry, University of South Florida, Gainesville, Florida

Melanie W. Moretz, PhD, Department of Psychology, Fordham University, Bronx, New York

Brett Nelson, MD, Departments of Pediatrics and Psychiatry, University of South Florida, Gainesville, Florida

Thomas H. Ollendick, PhD, Department of Psychology, Child Study Center, Virginia Polytechnic Institute and State University, Blacksburg, Virginia

Julie Sarno Owens, PhD, Department of Psychology, Ohio University, Athens, Ohio

Tara Peris, PhD, Department of Psychiatry, University of California–Los Angeles School of Medicine, Los Angeles, California

John Piacentini, PhD, Department of Psychiatry, University of California–Los Angeles School of Medicine, Los Angeles, California

Jennifer Regan, BA, Department of Psychiatry, Columbia University College of Physicians and Surgeons, New York, New York

Thomas M. Reimers, PhD, Clinic Director, Boys Town Pediatric and Family Services Clinic, Clinical Associate Professor, Creighton University School of Medicine, Omaha, Nebraska

Lauren Richerson, PhD, Department of Psychology, Ohio University, Athens, Ohio

Connie J. Schnoes, PhD, Boys Town Pediatric and Family Services Clinic, Boys Town, Nebraska

Cristian Sirbu, MD, PhD, Charleston Area Medical Center Health Education and Research Institute and West Virginia University School of Medicine–Charleston Division, Charleston, South Carolina

Heather L. Smith, PhD, Department of Psychiatry, Montefiore Hospital and Albert Einstein School of Medicine, Bronx, New York

Kate Sofronoff, PhD, School of Psychology, University of Queensland, Brisbane, Australia

Amanda M. Stone, MA, Department of Psychiatry, University of Florida, Gainesville, Florida

Sharon C. Sung, PhD, Department of Psychiatry, Montefiore Hospital and Albert Einstein School of Medicine, Bronx, New York

Cydney J. Van Dyke, MA, Department of Psychology, Fordham University, Bronx, New York

Michael R. Walther, BS, Department of Psychology, University of Wisconsin-Milwaukee, Milwaukee, Wisconsin

Douglas W. Woods, PhD, Department of Psychology, University of Wisconsin-Milwaukee, Milwaukee, Wisconsin

Eric A. Youngstrom, PhD, Department of Psychology, University of North Carolina–Chapel Hill, Chapel Hill, North Carolina

Jen Kogos Youngstrom, PhD, Department of Psychology, University of North Carolina–Chapel Hill, Chapel Hill, North Carolina, and Applewood Centers, Elyria, Ohio

Foreword

Readers of *Cognitive-Behavior Therapy for Children: Treating Complex and Refractory Cases* are likely drawn to this book to learn more about how to alleviate most effectively the distress of children and adolescents who suffer from psychiatric disorders. The development and evaluation of psychological treatments has yielded an array of interventions with scientific documentation to help affected youth. Mental health professionals, as a consequence, have at their disposal many available methods by which to reduce child and adolescent disorders. Most of these methods rely on cognitive-behavioral treatment procedures. Although the probability is high that other treatments currently in use in the field, as well as treatments under development or interventions yet to be developed, are also effective, one cannot deny that cognitive-behavioral therapy (CBT) has advanced most significantly over the past decades.

In this context, the current volume is significant because it addresses head-on an issue that has been generally neglected in the literature. Namely, despite the availability of effective CBTs to address key child and adolescent disorders, including those that are covered in this book (e.g., depression, separation anxiety disorder), substantial proportions of youth treated with evidence-based CBT protocols fail to show symptomatic improvement at posttreatment evaluations. This book does not sweep this fact under the rug, neither does it transmit a sense of hopelessness and helplessness to a subset of child and adolescent clients. Instead, the editors have brought together leading experts to synthesize and analyze a body of research on treatment outcome predictors and barriers of treatment for the different disorders. Chapter authors cogently describe barriers to treatment implementation and recommend systematic adjustments to help improve the outcomes of formerly refractory child and adolescent clients.

The current volume is significant on another level. This book highlights the fact that the sharp distinctions often drawn in the literature between efficacy and effectiveness can be misleading. “Efficacy” refers to whether a particular CBT has been found to “work” by means of experimental procedures. “Effectiveness” refers to whether a particular CBT has been found to “work” in settings and under conditions in which the treatment will typically be delivered, such as in private practice and community mental health clinics. The chapters contained herein highlight the notion that the child and adolescent psychological treatment research literature is better characterized as falling along a continuum with respect to efficacy and effectiveness. Many so-called efficacy studies are high in external validity and many so-called effectiveness studies use rigorous internal validity or controls. It is this continuum between efficacy and effectiveness that made it possible for the chapters' authors to blend lessons learned from both areas to formulate recommendations about the handling of complex and refractory cases. These recommendations are not only empirically informed but are also richly illustrated through case examples that showcase the authors' clinical acumen and skills.

Cognitive-Behavior Therapy for Children: Treating Complex and Refractory Cases thus represents an important effort in narrowing the gap between research and practice. The reluctance of many clinicians to adopt evidence-based treatments in their practices often occurs because they have found that these treatments may help some of their clients, but, for other clients, the treatments did not help or helped only partially. Families dropped out, children could not become engaged, debilitating comorbid symptoms interfered with the CBT procedures, and other extant factors were operating. The chapters in hand delineate these factors for each of the disorders covered. Clinicians can turn to these chapters when faced with the challenge of treating clients whose manifestations do not permit application of evidence-based CBT protocols as described in the literature. Having an understanding of these issues provides the clinician in practice with the flexibility to be adaptable to variations in problem, context, or condition.

The chapters also provide a valuable guide that researchers can turn to in their efforts to expand the current evidence base for child and adolescent psychological treatments. The chapters' coverage of which subgroups of child and adolescent patients show optimal response to current intervention strategies, and which subgroups do not, is essential to “get at” moderators of treatment outcome. The chapters' coverage of how treatments need to be adjusted for certain cases is also essential to get at mediators of treatment outcome.

Consequently, the chapters suggest avenues for future study designs that might include comprehensive and systematic assessments to measure hypothesized moderating and mediating variables. Such designs might also include the assessment of why child and adolescent clients do not adhere to CBT protocols. Such designs, which move beyond the "basic" pre–post randomized clinical trial design, will ultimately lead to significant theoretical advances about child and adolescent psychosocial treatments and, concomitantly, lead to more effective and better treatments for these debilitating child and adolescent disorders.

The result, I hope, of *Cognitive-Behavior Therapy for Children: Treating Complex and Refractory Cases* is that it will help to optimize the mental health interventions that children and adolescents deserve to receive—treatments that have, at their core, the theory and methods of CBT. It is also my hope that this important volume will reduce the barriers that currently exist in the implementation of evidence-based CBTs in clinical and community practice settings.

Wendy K. Silverman, PhD, ABPP
Professor of Psychology
Florida International University
Miami, Florida

PART I

General Issues in Refractory Cases

1

The Challenge of Difficult Cases

DEAN McKAY AND ERIC A. STORCH

At the present time, there are empirically supported treatments for most of the major psychiatric diagnoses that may be identified in children and adolescents. The advent of these empirically supported approaches has been critical in providing a heuristic for developing treatment plans for affected youth. No client neatly fits into the ideal template for any empirically supported treatment program, however. There are innumerable client-specific factors that may alter the nature and outcome of even the most carefully conducted therapy program.

A sign of maturity for any treatment research program is the ability to move beyond interventions for specific diagnoses and address, systematically, prognostic limitations that might interfere with standard delivery of care. Cognitive-behavioral therapy (CBT) has advanced significantly over the past quarter century. When refractory cases were first systematically discussed for adult clients, there were two important distinctions that occurred. First, many clinicians were resigned to the notion that nonresponders were "treatment failures" often directly or indirectly conveying a sense of hopelessness to a subset of clients (Foa & Emmelkamp, 1983). Second, 25 years ago there was a limited body of literature on empirically supported treatment and virtually no data available on outcome predictors. Instead, CBT-oriented clinicians were refining individual techniques and only beginning to see CBT's widespread applicability to diagnoses (Franks & Wilson, 1973).

As is so often the case, many of the empirically supported approaches for major psychiatric diagnoses were developed with adults in mind. To this end, the ability to describe barriers to treatment implementation and the inclusion of empirically supported modification to these therapies has progressed faster for adults and has recently been summarized (McKay, Abramowitz, & Taylor, in press). Nonetheless, there appears a widespread reluctance to consider refractory cases, perhaps because of the inherent difficulty associated with the term. Fortunately, as more researchers endeavor to address poor prognostic signs, the ability to address these problems will help move formerly refractory clients into a different category, perhaps merely referenced by the diagnosis with special modifiers.

Whereas there are now two texts that deal directly with refractory cases in adult disorders (Foa & Emmelkamp, 1983; McKay et al., in press), this book is the first to cover this topic in children and adolescents. The importance of addressing such cases may serve the purpose of bridging the gap between laboratory and controlled treatment outcome results and applicability in the clinic. For example, Weisz and colleagues (Weisz, Donenberg, Han, & Weiss, 1995) found that outcomes with children and adolescents were generally poorer for specific diagnoses when treated in community clinic settings when compared with protocols for empirically supported treatments. On the one hand, this may simply reflect the variations and unreliability of uncontrolled treatment implementation. On the other hand, it also likely reflects the variety of known complicating factors that often lead to exclusion from clinical trials, particularly in the early stages of treatment development.

EMPIRICALLY SUPPORTED TREATMENTS VERSUS EMPIRICALLY SUPPORTED PRACTICE

In some respects, the movement to identify factors that may interfere with standard delivery of empirically supported treatment packages is a movement back to the early days of behavior therapy. At that time, there was limited reliance on diagnosis, and instead a focus on functional analyses of behavior that allowed for identification of theory-driven empirically supported techniques. The approach of empirically supported practice (McKay & Tryon, 2002) or, in a nod to classification, the transdiagnostic approach (Harvey, Watkins, Mansell, & Shafran, 2004), is consistent with the broader approach to training clinicians based on principles of psychological clinical science (for a historical perspective, see Bootzin, 2007). A comparison that summarizes this distinction is in order. Engineers building a bridge do not rely on a manual for bridge building, but are daunted by limitations such as variations in river width or tidal changes that deviate from the originally empirically supported approach to building a bridge. Instead, there are a set of theoretically derived principles that guide bridge building, with limitations coming also from that same theory (i.e., water depth combined with width of expanse). Psychological science may be entering a similar phase of treatment development.

With respect to childhood disorders, we are perhaps better positioned to use previously empirical support than for adult disorders. Many empirically supported treatments for children are age-downward extensions of the same protocol for adults. A notable example is the treatment of childhood obsessive-compulsive disorder (OCD). The early empirically supported treatment involves exposure with response prevention. This approach, even with modifications drawn from cognitive therapy, remains the key therapeutic element in treatment for adults with the disorder (Abramowitz, Taylor, & McKay, 2005). However, in the case of children with OCD, it is not necessarily the case that there will be good insight into the disorder. In adults, poor insight is also a poor prognostic indicator for the disorder (McKay & McKiernan, 2005). In such instances, exposure-based treatments are not necessarily advised. This would suggest a modified approach, or one that does not rely at all on previously successful approaches used with adults. In the case of diagnoses first identified in childhood (e.g., attention-deficit/hyperactivity disorder [ADHD]; separation anxiety disorder), treatments may be developed specifically with children in mind, an unusual scenario in psychological interventions. In fact, it is in this arena that there may be age-upward extensions to adult presentations of similar problems. Such is the case with ADHD, where at least in the case of psychopharmacological management, there are now numerous trials of stimulant medication for attention problems in adults (Davidson, 2008).

SCOPE OF THIS VOLUME

This book has been developed with both researchers and clinicians in mind. We considered researchers as we sought to identify prognostic signs that would be the source of future research into developing and refining treatment for a wide range of childhood disorders. We bore clinicians in mind as they face the challenge of treating clients who present with what immediately may fit neatly into a diagnostic category, but whose specific manifestation of the condition does not permit application of the standard protocols as described in the published literature.

The book is organized into three major sections. The first provides an overview of general considerations that may lead to barriers in treatment for children and adolescents. As noted earlier, many empirically supported approaches are age-downward extensions of previously validated approaches for adults. However, childhood and adolescence are complex developmental periods. When psychopathology intrudes on youth, there are specific considerations in developing treatments, and special barriers to implementation that must be addressed. Should one fail to contend with these special considerations, treatment may fail before one even reaches a prognostic barrier that is unique to the diagnosis in question.

The second section deals with issues involving internalizing disorders, or those related to inner emotional disturbance. Oftentimes, these children present with problems that are a source of disturbance for parents and child alike, but do not necessarily rise to the attention of school personnel. Many of the disorders in this section conform to the age-downward extension model of treatment development. The final section addresses externalizing disorders. Most of these conditions are ones initially identified in childhood. Clinicians treating these disorders must often devote significant energy working with other personnel (i.e., school personnel, other providers) as well as parents, and perhaps spend more time with these individuals than with the identified child client. In both sections on internalizing and externalizing disorders, case illustrations are provided detailing ways in which treatment was modified from the original approach to address complicating factors.

It is our hope that this text will inform researchers and clinicians alike as they provide services to children and adolescents with a wide range of psychopathology. In light of the advances in the delivery of CBT, we feel that this is a timely occasion to consider the wide range of psychotherapy modifications available to address factors that may negatively impact outcome.

REFERENCES

Abramowitz, J. S., Taylor, S., & McKay, D. (2005). Potentials and limitations of cognitive treatments for obsessive-compulsive disorder. *Cognitive Behaviour Therapy, 34*, 140–147.

Bootzin, R. R. (2007). Psychological clinical science: Why and how we got to where we are. In T. A. Treat, R. R. Bootzin, & T. B. Baker (Eds.), *Psychological clinical science: Papers in honor of Richard M. McFall* (pp. 1–28). New York: Taylor & Francis.

Davidson, M. (2008). ADHD in adults: A review of the literature. *Journal of Attention Disorders, 11*, 628–641.

Foa, E. B., & Emmelkamp, P. M. G. (1983). *Failures in behavior therapy*. New York: Wiley.

Franks, C. M., & Wilson, G. T. (1973). *Annual review of behavior therapy*. Oxford, UK: Brunner/Mazel.

Harvey, A., Watkins, E., Mansell, W., & Shafran, R. (2004). *Cognitive behavioural processes across psychological disorders: A transdiagnostic approach to research and treatment*. Oxford, UK: Oxford University Press.

McKay, D., Abramowitz, J.S., & Taylor, S. (in press). *Cognitive behavior therapy for refractory cases: Turning failure into success*. Washington, DC: American Psychological Association.

McKay, D., & McKiernan, K. (2005). Information processing and cognitive behavior therapy for obsessive-compulsive disorder: Comorbidity of delusions, overvalued ideas, and schizophrenia. *Cognitive and Behavioral Practice, 12*, 390–394.

McKay, D., & Tryon, W.W. (2002). Behavior therapy: Theoretical bases. In W. Sledge & M. Hersen (Eds.), *Encyclopedia of psychotherapy* (Vol. 1, pp. 277–291). San Diego, CA: Academic Press.

Weisz, J. R., Donenberg, G. R., Han, S. S., & Weiss, B. (1995). Bridging the gap between laboratory and clinic in child and adolescent psychotherapy. *Journal of Consulting and Clinical Psychology, 63*, 688–701.

2

Adjustments in Treatment for Limited or Nonresponding Cases in Contemporary Cognitive-Behavioral Therapy With Youth

ALYSSA M. MARDER AND BRUCE F. CHORPITA

The field of cognitive-behavioral therapy (CBT) has influenced and produced numerous treatment programs for youth and families that have demonstrated robust, positive outcomes. Cognitive-behavioral therapy has been demonstrated as an effective approach for youth with both internalizing disorders (Cartwright-Hatton, Roberts, Chitsabesan, Fothergill, & Harrington, 2004; Harrington, Whittaker, Shoebridge, & Campbell, 1998) and externalizing disorders (Brestan & Eyberg, 1998; Kazdin, 2000). Nevertheless, a close examination of the wealth of accumulated quantitative and qualitative observations reveals that these interventions do not always result in an uncomplicated, ideal downtrend in symptoms for every youth. For example, commenting on the relatively large evidence base for CBT approaches for the treatment of anxiety disorders in children, Ollendick (2000) noted that although CBT treatments yield superior success rates relative to waitlist control groups, significant proportions of children treated with these protocols fail to show significant symptomatic improvement at posttreatment assessments.

Indeed, findings from clinical trials for CBT-based child anxiety treatments over the last decade have demonstrated nonresponder rates (as defined by continued presence of diagnosis at posttreatment) that range from 5% to 61%, with a mean of 34% across university-based trials (Barrett, 1998; Barrett, Healy-Farrell, & March, 2004; Biedel, Turner, & Morris, 2000; Cobham, Dadds, & Spence, 1998; Flannery-Schroeder & Kendall, 2000; King et al., 1998; Last, Hansen, & Franco, 1998; March, Amaya-Jackson, Murray, & Schulte, 1998; Nauta, Scholing, Emmelkamp, & Minderaa, 2003; Pediatric OCD Treatment Study [POTS] Team, 2004; Rapee, Abbot, & Lyneman, 2005; Shortt, Barrett, & Fox, 2001; Silverman, Kurtines, Ginsburg, Weems, Lumpkin, & Carmichael, 1999; Silverman et al., 1999; Spence, Donovan, & Brechman-Toussaint, 2000). Community-based trials within this same time period include nonresponder rates from 21% to 46%, with a mean of 38% (Barrington, Prior, Richardson, & Allen, 2005; Berstein, Layne, Egan, & Tennison, 2005; Cohen, Deblinger, Mannarino, & Steer, 2004; Hayward et al., 2000; King et al., 2000; Lyneham & Rapee, 2006; Masia-Warner et al., 2005; Masia-Warner, Fisher, Shrout, Rathor, & Klein, 2007). This means that across contexts, more than a third of the youth tested in these treatment studies maintained symptoms severe enough to warrant diagnoses at posttreatment.

Such proportions of nonresponse likely come as no surprise to community clinicians who continually witness the challenges facing treatment in the real world. These statistics on lack of response in clinical trials may in part serve as quantitative data to support the plentiful anecdotal reports of frustrations that occur with the implementation of evidence-based treatments (Nelson & Steele, 2007). In practice, it is common to witness the plateaus of progress and rise in symptoms in the presence of acute stressors. A youth's symptoms may rise and fall because of the nature of his or her disorder, or during periods of developmental change during childhood and adolescence (Holmbeck, Greenley, & Franks, 2003). The practice of therapy is obviously not always an uncomplicated path to symptom remittance. There are copious factors contributing to stagnancy in treatment that vary across particular treatment approaches or disorder types, and many of these factors are discussed elsewhere in this book. Although some treatment protocols offer specific suggestions for altering the therapy course based on the implementation experiences of the treatment development team, most are far less explicit in making such recommendations. This is unfortunate, and our experience working with a span of different evidence-based protocols for youth suggests that there are several universal considerations in treatment adjustment applicable to contemporary cognitive-behavioral treatment of youth and families (see Chorpita, 2007).

Using a sailing metaphor to consider therapy, the waters where therapies are delivered are often choppy, murky, and uncharted. Our work with evidence-based practice in the state of Hawaii has demonstrated that successful navigation of refractory conditions in such waters benefits from a well-formulated map such as a treatment manual or structured protocol. However, any map is easier to interpret when paired with a compass, and thus we have often recommended an explicit clinical decision flowchart to help keep us headed in the right direction. This guiding compass includes consideration of factors such as the therapeutic relationship and level of engagement with youth and their families, the formulation of clinical problems that informs ongoing selection of treatment strategies, and the integrity with which we deliver those strategies.

This chapter aims to provide a structured, hypotheses-testing framework for navigating limited or nonresponding cases in contemporary CBT protocols for children and adolescents. This decision-making map is an adaptation of other similar models (see Chorpita, 2007; Daleiden & Chorpita, 2005), though the starting point of the model at hand is situated at the assessment of treatment progress rather than at initial referral (see Figure 2.1). Our discussion will begin with considerations of the initial determination of a case's refractory status. We will provide guidance in the systematic examination of factors that may influence treatment gains, including family and child engagement, therapeutic integrity, case formulation, and external interference. For each of these factors, we will present (a) sources of information that may be helpful in their evaluation and (b) practical suggestions for working through obstacles at each factor level that may be inhibiting potential progress.

STEP 1: ASSESSMENT OF SYMPTOMS AND REFLECTION ON TREATMENT COURSE

Any adjustments in one's approach to treatment will require thoughtful reflection and rigorous evaluation of the therapy course taken so far. In the initial stage of treatment, we would have conducted a thorough assessment of the youth's presenting problem area(s) using standardized methods, which would help us understand the relative breadth and

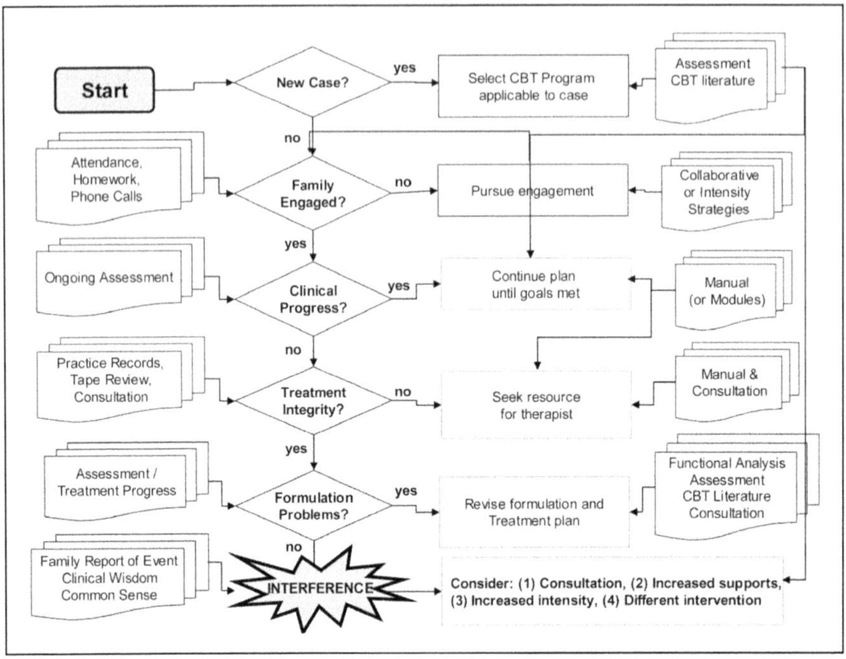

Figure 2.1 Clinical decision framework: Navigation of refractory conditions.

severity of his or her symptoms. This initial assessment would also have served to inform what standardized measures might be most appropriate and useful in tracking symptom progress over future serial measurements. Further, this initial assessment would have served to inform any ideographic measures that we might plan to use during treatment to gauge progress. For example, we might measure specific behaviors noted to be problematic in the view of youth or parent, or may even track a rating of motivation to change if this is deemed to be a particular area of concern in the case. The initial choices made regarding our assessment tools are vital to establishing a reliable and accurate means of determining treatment progress. Before moving forward, we must feel confident in our assessment so that if our tools indicate poor response later in treatment, we can assume that the phenomenon is "real" and not an artifact of inaccurate measurement (see Chorpita, Bernstein, & Daleiden, 2008; Daleiden & Chorpita, 2005).

The initial assessment and resultant formulation are important information sources in the first clinical decision within our framework: Treatment Protocol Selection (see Figure 2.1). As discussed by Daleiden and Chorpita (2005), the three common models of treatment selection include the evidence-based services model, the individualized case conceptualization model, and the practice-based evidence model. The evidence-based services model relies on the broadest base of information, and is most relevant to high-level treatment decisions when generalizations from the research literature are clear. The individualized case conceptualization and practice-based evidence models often apply to decisions for which the evidence-based services model may be less relevant. Examples of such decisions include agency or program selection based on local aggregate performance data (e.g., should the child receive CBT at clinic A or clinic B?) or highly specific adjustments to treatment course based on client response (e.g., is the child ready for termination, or are more sessions needed?). The information gleaned from the initial assessment would be our first resource in determining which problems are interfering most with functioning and warrant the most immediate clinical attention.

Once we have narrowed the scope of treatment by identifying primary problems, we would turn to the treatment outcome literature to determine our options. Currently, the vast majority of cognitive-behavioral treatment programs for youth is diagnosis or problem driven, and typically addresses one primary problem area at a time. However, as mentioned by Daleiden and Chorpita (2005), this practice may not be consistent with the philosophy or practical structure of most service systems. An approach of matching treatment strategies based on "treatment targets" rather than diagnoses or broad problems may be preferable or more realistic for some practice settings. Indeed, many of the early behavioral and cognitive-behavioral treatments on which the current collection of evidence-based practices were more commonly prescribed were determined by the level of behaviors rather than broad problems or disorders. Of course, the validity of prescription at different levels of specificity remains a controversial matter, and is beyond the scope of this chapter (see Beutler & Clarkin, 1990; Beutler & Harwood, 2000). In either case, the results of initial assessment would indicate the problem areas/diagnoses that would serve to inform selection of a treatment program on a broad scale. Within this chapter, we present our decision-making framework to CBT as traditionally practiced; however, we will also provide commentary on how this framework would look different if applied to more recently proposed "unified" or "modular" treatment approaches as well (Chorpita, Daleiden, & Weisz, 2005), which may prove to have some unique utility in dealing with multiple treatment targets/diagnoses.

As stated previously, results of the initial assessment provide a baseline of symptoms and functioning to serve as a comparison when gauging treatment progress and accurately identifying refractory status later in treatment. Building on that foundation, ongoing assessment has the potential to serve as a valuable feedback mechanism to clinicians. The Child and Adolescent Mental Health Division of the State of Hawaii Department of Health has employed a computerized, on-demand, user-friendly, clinical reporting system for summarizing and displaying ongoing assessment data for clinicians (Daleiden & Chorpita, 2005). Such a system allows for early detection of refractory risk by providing plots representing symptom change over time and scatter plots to indicate the history of implemented therapeutic practices. The "clinical dashboards" that contain this data can be manipulated by the clinician as she or he uses it to navigate treatment decisions such that he or she can more closely examine scale scores, ideographic ratings, level of care, or interagency involvement (see also Chorpita et al., 2008).

These clinical dashboard reports can be useful tools in identifying refractory status and tracking information that may aid in troubleshooting an observed lack of progress. In general, provision of feedback to clinicians regarding client progress has been shown to improve therapeutic outcomes (for a review, see Sapyta, Riemer, & Bickman, 2005), particularly for those cases in which treatment is identified as eliciting minimal response in symptoms (Lambert, Hansen, & Finch, 2001; Lambert et al., 2001). Lambert and colleagues (2003) discussed flagging those clients whose response is less than a standardized, normative treatment response to provide in a "signal-alarm" feedback process. Feedback comparing client response with an expected response based on aggregate data or a normative "standard" has been theorized to be the most powerful feedback for clinicians (Sapyta et al., 2005). Within the system we have described from Hawaii, such feedback is achieved by plotting client symptoms in comparison with pooled treatment responses from regional centers for the relevant population. In other settings, most therapists may not have such normative data at their fingertips; however, they may be able to create an aggregate of their cases or those from their agency over time to serve as a reference point.

Riemer, Rosof-Williams, and Bickman (2005) outlined their Contextual Feedback Intervention Theory, which considers the source, content, sign (positive or negative), and format of how feedback is provided to clinicians regarding their specific behaviors ("performance") and client outcomes. This model is valuable and pertinent to the "clinical dashboard" system mentioned previously, as it underscores the need to be mindful in the delivery of feedback so it can be received and integrated by therapists. For ongoing assessment to be useful in making therapeutic changes to target outcome, its feedback system should be made as relevant as possible to the environment of treatment delivery. Although work examining the effectiveness of the use of feedback via "dashboards" or other reporting mechanisms is yet to be published for youth-focused treatments, research movement in this direction represents an acknowledgement that ongoing assessment has the potential to provide important information, particularly in determining refractory status.

STEP 2: EVALUATION OF YOUTH AND FAMILY ENGAGEMENT

The work of therapy necessarily requires the involvement of both therapist and client, and therefore youth and family engagement represents our first area of consideration when achieving limited treatment response. Engagement may be particularly important within CBT, which considers active client participation and rehearsal of skills both within and outside of the therapy room to be essential agents of change. It is important to note at this point that in describing engagement, we are specifically addressing behaviors that indicate treatment involvement and investment and are not attempting to quantify the broader phenomenon of the "therapeutic relationship." Further, although there is growing evidence to support commonly held beliefs regarding the valuable role of relationship variables in outcomes for childhood CBT treatments (Hughes & Kendall, 2007), recommendations regarding the bolstering of these common factors will not be discussed here. This section of the chapter will present specific indicators of poor involvement in treatment and potential remediating interventions.

Families with children suffering from mental health problems are typically faced with obstacles on a daily basis that go beyond the already daunting challenges of routine parenthood. Furthermore, many families seeking treatment are further burdened by stressors related to meeting basic needs such as providing a stable home and healthy nutrition, sometimes for numerous children. Research on therapeutic engagement has demonstrated that, indeed, families who struggle with the stress of lower socioeconomic status (Kazdin, Mazurick, & Bass, 1993) and have children with higher levels of psychopathology (Evans, Radunovich, Cornette, Wiens, & Roy, 2008) and those who report higher levels of perceived stress (Kazdin, Mazurick, & Siegel, 1994; Kazdin & Wassell, 1999) have lower levels of participation in treatment.

The act of seeking treatment is in and of itself a significant step toward engagement, though families may be unaware of the commitment they will be asked to make to manifest change in their children's behavior. Making changes is difficult for anyone and, above all, families who have taken the brave step to seek help are in need of genuine support. Without suitable investment in the relationship, we cannot expect parents to join with us to implement interventions. Active participation from both youth and parents is considered valuable in making efficient, effective changes for families and, in fact, both youth and parental willingness to participate in therapy have been shown through meta-analyses to have a moderate relationship with therapeutic outcomes (Karver, Handelsman, Fields, & Bickman, 2006). Further, interventions aimed at bolstering engagement have shown promise. For example, Santisteban et al. (1996) evaluated an intensity-based strategy designed to enhance engagement in families whose children were at risk for drug use and found that families receiving higher levels of engagement efforts were associated with a 21% greater attendance rate than those who received low levels of engagement effort. Santisteban et al.'s (1996) engagement strategies are based on family systems theory and involved providing pretreatment phone-call support to primary caregivers and other supportive family members to establish alliance, problem-solve barriers to attendance at treatment, and bolster confidence that therapy will have a positive impact for the youth and family. Other valuable and successful efforts at increasing engagement will be discussed within the "proposed solutions" provided in this section.

The effects of engagement problems can manifest in at least two important forms: *impaired collaboration* and *attrition risk* (Chorpita,

2007). *Impaired collaboration* is present when youth and families do the necessary work to keep therapy moving, but lack fully present engagement and reciprocity in taking responsibility for the tasks of making change. This type of engagement problem is evidenced as a lack of participation in the tasks of therapy, such as homework completion, role plays, or scheduled weekly check-in assessments. The youth or family might regularly attend sessions, call when needing to cancel, and appear to be "going through the motions" though their assignments or in-session actions may be haphazard or completed with minimal attention or effort.

Attrition risk represents a more severe situation wherein the work of therapy can hardly be conducted or cannot happen at all because of the low level of youth or family involvement. This type of engagement problem is frequently characterized by appointments missed without notice, and may include differential attendance, such as a lack of parental involvement or an unwillingness to attend any portion of treatment sessions despite consistent child attendance. Within this step in our decision-making process, we are on the lookout for behaviors such as these, which may indicate evidence of either a slow-to-develop or waning engagement processes.

Once we have identified whether either of these engagement problems may be at play, we come to the first compass-led decision. Should we find that our youth and family are suitably engaged, we might simply move forward and consider the next step. On the other hand, if we identify engagement problems, we may need to turn to the treatment manual or accompanying materials for initial guidance. Many treatment protocols contain initial sessions aimed at establishing engagement, though the content of these sessions varies widely. For example, some manuals may include specific session content aimed at motivational interviewing interventions for use in low-engagement situations (e.g., "The Family Check Up"; Dishion, Nelson, & Kavanagh, 2003), whereas others may include engagement sessions simply focused on treatment orientation and "get to know you" activities (e.g., "Coping Cat"; Kendall & Hedtke, 2006). Although revisiting these previous sessions may be valuable at this juncture, what universal efforts may we take to intervene and support engagement? First, let us take a closer look at potential sources of an engagement problem.

The first helpful step may be considering the sources of poor engagement. For example, youth and families with low engagement may be acting on a sense that the "costs" of therapy outweigh the potential value. In such a scenario, "costs" may include the literal amount they must pay for therapy (particularly relative to their weekly income), but also relate to the mental and emotional energy necessary to face complex and difficult therapy tasks, the interference that therapy participation may cause in addressing competing demands for the family (such as getting time off of work, finding babysitters for other children in the household, missing out on extracurricular events), and/or a feeling that therapy commitment compounds other family stressors ("It's just too much!").

Another consideration is that families are likely viewing potential benefits from a different vantage point than the therapist. Therapists have the benefit of a broader perspective, often having witnessed many courses of difficult though eventually successful treatment. When families are new to therapy, they may be easily discouraged by slow initial progress or obstacles that arise to complicate the course. It is important to recognize that therapy often asks families to change behaviors and operate in new ways that may feel unnatural or uncomfortable at first. For these reasons, a careful inventory of a family's engagement is the first remedial step in adjusting treatment. In the following section, we will discuss both *collaborative strategies* (those aimed at improving treatment progress by increasing the collaborative style of the therapist) and *intensity strategies* (those that attempt to improve progress by increasing the effort of the therapist).

Collaborative Solution 1: Weigh the Cost–Benefit Ratio

Interventions aimed at understanding the costs and benefits of therapy participation for youths and their families and exploring means to improve this ratio represent an important first step in the engagement process. Such interventions are akin to techniques involved in the motivation enhancement family of techniques (W. R. Miller & Rollnick, 2002). One excellent example is Nock and Kazdin's (2005) Participation Enhancement Intervention. This strategy includes a discussion of the benefits associated with participation in therapy, elicits motivational statements in regard to participation, and helps parents identify and overcome barriers to treatment engagement. Results of a randomized trial testing treatment for youth with conduct problems demonstrated that the inclusion of this intervention was associated with higher levels of parental motivation, parental adherence to treatment assignments, and attendance when compared with a similar treatment group that did not receive the intervention (Nock & Kazdin, 2005). This type of intervention goes hand in hand with problem solving, as an examination of costs and benefits allows for the identification of barriers. Skillful clinicians may be able to use the identification of barriers as an opportunity to develop a plan of action to clarify how the family can move forward to reaching their valued goals.

Collaborative Solution 2: Use Informed Consent

As highlighted previously, CBT work requires practice and usually requires at least some minimal observation or documentation of thoughts, feelings, or behaviors. At the beginning of work with a family, it may prove helpful to be upfront and realistic about the expectations and minimum input necessary for the treatment program. This information can be presented as a short-term/long-term tradeoff in that the work and stress might temporarily increase, but in exchange the problems should get better overall and have a positive lasting impact on the youth and family. Informing families of both the expectations of the program as well as the common experience of initial frustration may serve as an inoculation by framing these challenges as predictable and time-limited (Chorpita, 2007). Normalizing early struggles within treatment may help prevent families from feeling that the limited response to symptoms or feelings of being overwhelmed are unique to their situation and therefore evidence that the treatment is not likely to be helpful to them.

Collaborative Solution 3: Simplify

Participation in therapy necessarily involves work, and the emotional and practical expenditure required may be more than significantly stressed families have available to contribute. If the youth or family's poor engagement is determined to stem from dissonance between the demands of therapy work versus the amount of energy or time available, it may be an appropriate move to examine in which ways the treatment program can be scaled back so as to not overwhelm the family. For example, when conducting CBT-based exposures with an anxious youth, it might be advisable to target one fear area rather than discussing how treatment will eventually tackle the possibly complicated web of different anxiety-inducing situations in the youth or family's life. Homework assignments can be limited in their scope or level of demand for the individual (Chorpita, 2007).

One relevant case we have recently supervised involved treatment of a second-grader with primary problems involving generalized worry and anxiety who also struggled with weaknesses in written language. In this case, the youth demonstrated limited engagement in therapy homework assignments, which unfortunately happened to require considerable writing in the treatment practice book. To lessen the demand of the task, his therapist removed the pages requiring written work and instead had the youth draw pictures to represent situations that he would typically have written about on those pages. In this way, the youth was less overwhelmed by the task and yet still received the benefits of the homework. Similar adjustments could be made in terms of expectations of parental monitoring or involvement in sessions in an effort to meet families at their available level of engagement.

Collaborative Solution 4: Go for High Impact

For families that have been struggling mightily and for long periods with the youth's symptoms, slow initial progress may be a factor limiting their engagement. In some cases, maximizing initial improvement in therapy may help to bolster family engagement. One means of increasing the impact of initial treatment is to choose treatment targets that are the highest priority for the family (Chorpita, 2007). Research has demonstrated that greater consistency between parent's expectations for therapy and the therapeutic interventions or activities is related to higher levels of engagement (G. E. Miller & Prinz, 2003; Nock & Kazdin, 2001). For example, in treating a youth with conduct problems, the first items included in a home point system to track and reinforce behaviors should involve behaviors that are salient and important for the family to feel progress. If a parent reports that life is made terribly problematic by the child's refusal to brush his teeth and subsequent tooth decay, dental bills, and perhaps dentist-related anxiety on the part of the child, this would be an appropriate high-impact target with which to start. In another example, a youth with separation anxiety may present with a number of different ways in which fears manifest. One common manifestation may be co-sleeping arrangements in which the youth is sleeping with his or her caretakers during the night. Some parents may not mind having the child in their bed, whereas others might see this as intrusive or disruptive to their sleep or relationship with his or her spouse or partner. In cases where this was considered a major intrusion, focusing initial interventions on ameliorating such a sleeping pattern might bring caretakers some much-needed relief and personal space.

Collaborative Solution 5: Accept Partial Engagement

It may be possible to achieve treatment progress and some positive outcomes without full engagement from both youth and family. As others have noted (Nock & Kazdin, 2005), working with youth is characteristically different than working with adults, as the parent is largely responsible for the referral and for assuring the youth shows up to appointments. In this way, the identified client may or may not be inherently engaged in the treatment progress. There may be times when engagement with the youth is very limited, such as when the youth is chronically and severely depressed. Swartz et al. (2007) have proposed an initial session aimed at enhancing engagement through meeting depressed adolescents at their current level of motivation to change. This treatment session involves using techniques derived from motivational and ethnographic interviewing specifically adapted for youth with depression, and acknowledges a need to accept—and even expect—ambivalence related to the diagnosis of and treatment for depression. Although evidence supporting the efficacy of this intervention is still being collected, Swartz and colleagues present an interesting and innovative application of techniques that have been shown to increase engagement when used with other populations.

Alternatively, there may be cases in which the youth is highly involved in treatment and the family is not willing or able to participate to any degree beyond the waiting room. In either case, progress may still be achieved by accepting the partial engagement of the party who is most involved. Such a result was found in an investigation by Chorpita and colleagues (Chorpita, Taylor, Francis, Moffitt, & Austin, 2004), in which no parent was willing to see or speak to the therapist yet the youth's symptoms significantly improved.

Intensity Solution 1: Increase Reminders for Participation

One simple means of supporting engagement and participation in treatment can involve providing appointment reminders to families. As we have previously discussed, families that are at the most risk for low engagement are those that have the most perceived stress going into treatment. Reminders may serve as a supportive means of helping to organize the family and get them into sessions. A number of interventions related to providing reminder phone calls and letters have demonstrated that this method is an effective means of increasing session attendance (for a review, see McKay & Bannon, 2004).

Intensity Solution 2: Go to the Problem

Although leaving the therapy room may run counter to treatment as usual in outpatient therapy, taking this step may provide valuable lessons regarding barriers to treatment and the relevancy of the interventions to the family's everyday life. As Chorpita (2007) suggests, going to a family's home environment may have the effect of decreasing the social distance of the therapist and thus increasing his or her relevance or credibility to the family. Such techniques are not uncommon elements of family therapy protocols (e.g., Minuchin & Fishman, 1981).

In cases in which outpatient therapists have constraints on their ability to "go to the problem" (e.g., lack of time, insurance reimbursement issues, etc.), it may be helpful to engage families by including other helping professionals who may already be working in the home. For example, in North Carolina there has been a transition to increasingly privatized service provision and a shift toward providing more services "in the community" (North Carolina Department of Health & Human Services, 2007). In this system, many youth and families receive case management services that include the assignment of "community support workers" (typically Bachelor's or Master's degree-level mental health workers) who spend anywhere from 5 to 20 hours in the home to implement treatment plans. In this context, outpatient CBT therapists have a unique opportunity to partner with these service providers to optimize treatment. For example, community support workers can be helpful in providing transportation for youth and families to therapy appointments, assisting youth (and parents) with therapy homework tasks, and providing insight for outpatient therapists into challenges from the home environment that may be contributing to a lack of engagement in therapy. Work by Koroloff, Elliott, Koren, and Friesen (1994, 1996) provides evidence of the utility of collaborative efforts with other professionals in increasing and sustaining participation in mental health services. In this study, the use of family associates (paraprofessionals who provided emotional support and problem solving) was significantly related to initiating and continuing contact with the mental health system. Similar results were found by Burns and colleagues (Burns, Farmer, Angold, Costello, & Behar, 1996), who employed a randomized controlled design to demonstrate the added benefit of case management services in keeping families engaged in mental health services.

Intensity Solution 3: Whatever It Takes

Practitioners of multisystemic therapy (Henggeler, Schoenwald, Borduin, Rowland, & Cunningham, 1998) use the phrase "whatever it takes" to describe their commitment to problem solving in challenging situations with youth and families. Research has demonstrated that CBT works best in the context of an engaged and motivated family, and thus it is ultimately worth our effort as clinicians to employ all the talent, creativity, discipline, and wisdom that we have accumulated in our experience in our work with youth. This is particularly true for those cases in which low engagement is a sign of the magnitude of obstacles that the family faces in improving the child's mental health.

In some cases, doing "whatever it takes" may mean that clinicians take on roles to which they are unaccustomed, such as home-based worker or case manager. In other cases it may mean working diligently in cooperation with existing helping professionals to help families work through obstacles to engagement, as described in Intensity Solution 2. In other cases, this may mean attending not solely to CBT interventions with the child, but also to parents' perceived stress levels and ecological-level variables affecting engagement. Kazdin and Whitley (2003) demonstrated that CBT-oriented therapy for youth and families that was supplemented by an intervention aimed at problem-solving parental stress and barriers to participation resulted in superior therapeutic outcomes when compared with the CBT treatment on its own. Although this intervention and others (e.g., Prinz & Miller, 1994) have shown evidence for families with children who have conduct problems, it would be interesting to see how it might also benefit families that have children with internalizing disorders.

STEP 3: EVALUATION OF TREATMENT INTEGRITY

In our previous step, we examined a central client-level variable (engagement) and its potential contribution to the problem of limited treatment response. Within our framework, we have now either (a) identified sources of poor engagement and then implemented strategies to improve this problem or (b) found no evidence of poor engagement. In the first case, we have addressed this variable and are in a place to continue our treatment and continuous assessment of progress. If we encounter further evidence that treatment progress is limited, or if we never encountered engagement issues (as in the second case), our compass would guide us to consider a central therapist-level variable—treatment integrity.

The child psychotherapy literature has recently started to examine more closely the issue of treatment integrity as it applies to implementation in clinical trials. The thrust to assess and document integrity was initially born out of a desire to ensure proper internal validity; that is, to demonstrate that the active ingredients assumed to affect clinical outcomes were in fact the variables being manipulated between groups. Treatment integrity has been shown to assist in the interpretation of outcomes in several studies across both the adult (DeRubeis & Feeley, 1990; Shaw et al., 1999) and youth (Forgatch, Patterson, & DeGarmo, 2005; Huey, Henggeler, Brondino, & Pickrel, 2000) psychotherapy literatures. Relatively less has been written with regard to the application of treatment integrity analysis as it applies to everyday clinical experiences. Research considering the relationships between integrity and outcomes suggests the potential value of this pursuit (Forgatch et al., 2005; Huey et al., 2000). This section provides a brief background on the research on treatment integrity and discusses some potential considerations related to the domains of integrity within the practice of evidence-based cognitive-behavioral treatment approaches with youth.

Background on Treatment Integrity

Treatment integrity encompasses a number of different constructs, all of which are important in assessing therapist fidelity to a manual or protocol. *Adherence*, *competence*, and *differentiation* have been identified as the primary domains within integrity (McGlinchy & Dobson, 2003). In psychotherapy research, *treatment adherence* has been defined as the extent to which the delivered treatment includes techniques prescribed by the particular model or manual and excludes or avoids proscribed techniques (Waltz, Addis, Koerner, & Jacobson, 1993; Yeaton & Sechrest, 1981). Therefore, the term "adherence" reflects whether the treatment was delivered as outlined in the protocol. Researchers have proposed specific recommendations for the definition and corresponding measurement of adherence (Waltz et al., 1993). Such recommendations include the measurement of (a) therapist behaviors unique to the treatment of interest, (b) therapist behaviors essential but not unique to the treatment of interest, (c) therapist behaviors compatible with the specified treatment though not prescribed or unique, and (d) therapist behaviors prohibited within the treatment of interest (Waltz et al., 1993) (see Figure 2.2). This definition is most readily applicable to the measurement of therapist adherence to a particular therapeutic orientation. For example, in a study of cognitive-behavioral therapy one would examine (a) therapist behaviors unique to behavioral therapy (e.g., exposures to a feared stimulus), (b) general therapist behaviors present in behavioral therapy and other orientations (e.g., functional analysis of problem behaviors), (c) therapist behaviors compatible with behavior therapy though not prescribed or unique (e.g., reflective listening), and (d) proscribed behaviors (e.g., psychodynamic interpretations).

In cases for which the treatment in question is more akin to a curriculum, with prescribed activities and tasks for each session, the methods of adherence measurement may differ from those suggestions previously described. This is particularly relevant for adherence measurement within the child psychotherapy domain, where treatments meet their clients at their developmental level by taking a more concrete approach reminiscent of a school-based curriculum. The question of adherence may ask whether the therapist performed all of the prescribed activities, including assigning and checking homework. Adherence mea-

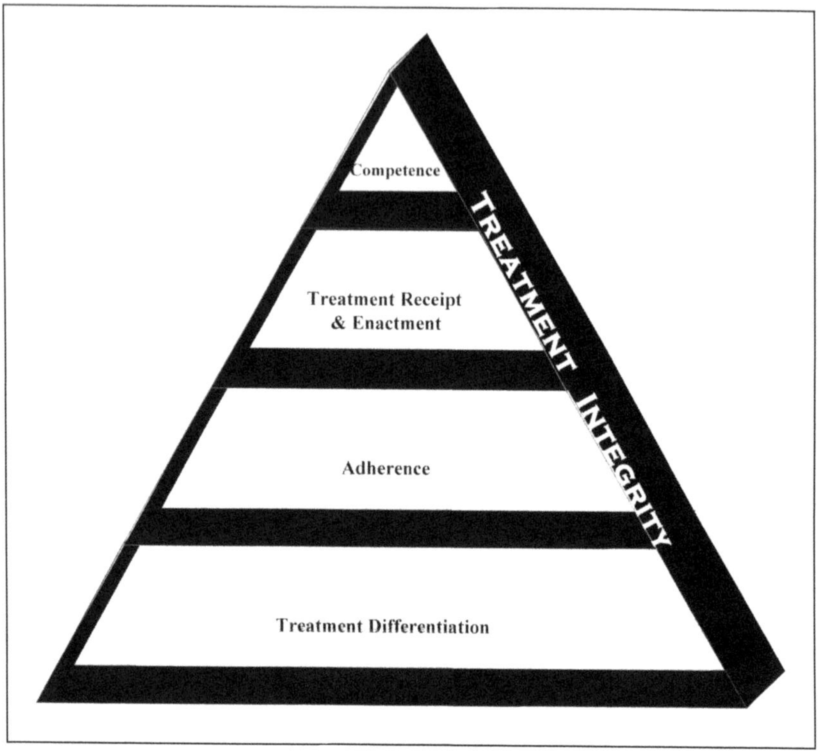

Figure 2.2 The components of treatment integrity.

surement looks at the base level of treatment delivery; that is, did the therapist perform the therapeutic tasks as directed by the protocol? Adherence may also be rated for extensiveness to determine if the delivery of the intervention was a cursory overview or involved significant review and assessment of comprehension. More detailed questions of the quality of the delivery, such as whether the intervention was adapted for the client or performed with interpersonal flexibility falls within the next domain of integrity—therapist competence.

Waltz and colleagues (1993) assert that successful investigation of adherence must also include measurement of therapist competence. Returning to our sailing metaphor, adherence is akin to properly following the path laid out by a map, whereas competence represents a therapist's ability to coordinate the crew, assess the ship, and use the compass to find direction. Without the navigation of a skilled therapist, protocol-driven therapy runs the risk of appearing as a monotonous journey void of personal relevance to the client. Competence has been defined as the therapist's skill level as she/he recognizes, considers, and responds to contextual factors surrounding the delivery of a treatment protocol (Waltz et al., 1993).

Competence has been described as a "state" variable that changes with time (i.e., experience as a therapist, experience with a particular protocol, stage in therapy) and circumstance (i.e., working with a particular client or presenting problem) (Kazantzis, 2003). Several authors (Elkin, 1999; McGlinchy & Dobson, 2003) have noted that definitions of competence have varied in the literature in terms of their breadth. For example, some assessment of competence has focused on therapist training or preparedness variables, whereas others have focused on variables akin to therapist flexibility in adapting treatments to meet the needs of individual clients.

Within integrity research, many researchers have struggled with the considerable overlap between adherence and competence. In fact, adherence and competence measures have demonstrated high correlations in several studies of addiction treatment (Barber, Mercer, Karkauer, & Calvo, 1996; Carroll et al., 2000). Some have suggested that within integrity research, competence carries an implicit association with adherence (Kazantzis, 2003). This association is clear: in working with a treatment protocol, one must be adherent before one can become competent. The therapist providing the intervention must be well versed in the protocol, to the point that that s/he is able to adapt the sessions to use examples from the client's life and communicate the intervention in a way that reaches the client without sacrificing the integrity of the protocol. Extreme levels of flexibility in delivery could arguably sacrifice adherence to the protocol, and thus the boundaries surrounding competent delivery need to be closely considered within the context of each treatment package.

Kendall and Chu (2000) discussed *therapist flexibility* in the delivery of manualized treatment as a construct that is related to yet distinct from competence. They offer a working definition of flexibility as "a therapist's adaptiveness to the situation at hand while he or she is adhering to the instructions and suggestions in the manual" (Kendall & Chu, 2000, p. 11). There is overlap between therapist flexibility and competence. They both refer to the skill with which a therapist adapts a treatment to fit an individual client. However, flexibility does not imply the same evaluative component as competence. That is, within this current definition, flexibility accounts for therapist adaptations or deviations from the manual but does not refer to whether these behaviors were done "skillfully/competently" or "poorly/incompetently." As mentioned earlier, extreme flexibility may sacrifice adherence and the overall integrity of the intended treatment delivery. Thus, whereas competence is expected to enhance outcomes, the correlation between outcome and flexibility is not necessarily presumed to be positive (Kendall & Chu, 2000). As we will discuss in the sections to come, well-formulated flexibility as applied by a competent therapist may assist in ameliorating refractory conditions.

McGlinchy and Dobson (2003) underscored the need for consistent terminology when discussing adherence and competence, given the considerable overlap between the two constructs. They suggested that the Waltz et al. (1993) definitions be held as a standard, and that more studies are needed to sort out the individual and combined contributions of these constructs to treatment outcomes.

Treatment differentiation is a term used to describe whether the treatment under study is sufficiently unique from other treatment conditions. The treatment protocol in question must be distinct from its comparisons so as to assure that the independent variable (treatment type) was manipulated properly and in the intended fashion (Kazdin, 1986). Differentiation is an important element of fidelity research because the treatment may be delivered as intended (good integrity) but may be too similar to comparison treatments to draw conclusions about its relative effectiveness (Kazdin, 1986). When it comes to assessing refractory case scenarios and examination of treatment, differentiation allows for consideration of whether the treatment being provided is sufficiently different from other interventions that have been attempted in the past with limited result. Detecting such differences may prove useful in determining the best-matched treatment for a case based on symptom changes that correlate with changes in treatment approach.

On the other end of the therapy relationship, *treatment receipt* has been described as the level at which clients demonstrate working knowledge and accurate understanding of skills learned while working with their therapist (Lichstein, Riedel, & Grieve, 1994). A related concept, *treatment enactment*, is the level at which the client integrates and practices therapy-learned skills in his or her daily life (Lichtenstein et al., 1994). These two domains of treatment integrity are the most recent to emerge within this literature, and recognize the need to assess whether the properly delivered techniques reached the client. In refractory cases, assessment of treatment receipt may play a valuable role in determining whether the treatment has been fully comprehended and enacted by the client, as a lack of receipt may be one reason for a lack of symptom response.

To date, there is no universally accepted method of measuring any of these components of treatment integrity in the practice of CBT with youth. Therefore, our guidance will not include recommendation of particular assessment tools, but will instead discuss domains of consideration within this area based on our experience in both supervision of clinical trials and general clinical practice in the community. After discussing potential pitfalls within treatment integrity, we will discuss means of assessing these problems and finding solutions that are applicable to each.

Problem Area 1: Novice Implementation

Although research has yet to demonstrate any effect of therapist practice or rehearsal with a protocol on the integrity of subsequent treatment delivery, we can hypothesize that as with most skills, one's competence is likely to improve with practice. The first aim when examining our delivery of a treatment protocol should be an honest look at our experience and training within the relevant model. Is this the first time we are taking this boat out on the water? If this is our first time implementing the treatment, we may be at risk of "less than elegant" technique. For example, one may be more likely to stringently adhere to the protocol during early learning and may lack some reasonable flexibility to address possible crises that arise, or one may not individualize the protocol sufficiently to the youth. A therapist new to the treatment approach may lack the breadth of examples or metaphors that a seasoned therapist may have at her or his disposal and therefore may rely too heavily on "cookie cutter" examples presented in the manual. It is certainly understandable that anyone starting out with a new protocol may be more reliant on outlines or deliver the material in a less natural manner—this is a part of developing competence. We make note of these pitfalls not to discourage novice therapists, but to serve as a reminder that these characteristics may interfere with the youth's engagement or comprehension of the material. As new methods of approaching treatment are continually developed and disseminated, even veteran therapists may encounter novel experiences, and we should all be mindful of our potential contributions to less-than-desired treatment response.

Problem Area 2: Integrity Fatigue

Even the oldest hand in cognitive-behavioral practice can encounter problems with treatment integrity. One matter for reflection relevant to those with strong familiarity with a protocol may be potential "drift" from the protocol. Such drift may arise from a level of comfort with the protocol to the point that one has not reviewed the materials very recently and may have forgotten some components within sessions that may prove helpful. Also, someone very familiar with a particular treatment may have gathered a weighty load of anecdotal data that may inform his or her clinical decisions. Such a process may bias clinical decisions in an unintentional manner that nonetheless may be harmful to integrity.

For example, after many years of implementing a relaxation protocol, a therapist may have observed that their elementary-age clients appear to be "growing up more quickly" than cohorts in the past and have become increasingly "mature" in their interests. He or she might have noticed that current clients listen to music or watch television with mature themes and seem to shrug off approaches or topics in therapy that they perceive to be "kid stuff." In this case, the therapist may have fallen out of the practice of using metaphorical deep-breathing instructions or relaxation scripts (e.g., "Imagine you are squeezing a lemon..."; Koeppen, 1974) and instead is relying on more literal descriptions during these procedures. In this example, the therapist may notice that his or her young client appears bored or is unable to attend to literal scripts ("Now tighten your hand and hold for 10 seconds"); the therapist then attributes this to engagement issues and moves forward without sufficiently teaching these skills. This is a situation wherein a closer examination of treatment integrity might highlight the tendency to use a single script for relaxation, and one solution might be to approach the client with a more metaphorical script, which the therapist had not used in several years, but that is compatible with the treatment program. In fact, some research suggests that children may prefer metaphorical scripts (Heffner, Grego, & Eifert, 2003). There is always a chance that the initial hypothesis is supported, and the child rejects this new approach; however, a close look at these basic fundamentals is important in making sure that we have made our best attempt at delivering the prescribed intervention.

Another example of integrity fatigue might include a therapist's use of particular examples or props in his or her delivery (e.g., videos, comics, etc.) that may have become out of date or no longer salient to the client population with whom she or he is working. Therapists in practice are busy and subject to increasing pressures for clinical productivity. Once a therapist has collected a number of props, it may be hard to find time to supplement these as they become less relevant to current popular culture. For example, a therapist may rely on clips from television shows or cartoons that are no longer widely appreciated, and thus the lessons they are trying to impart are less salient to the youth. Keeping the integrity of the model includes maintaining the integrity of the examples we use to deliver the model. The examples and props used in cognitive-behavior therapy can be quite valuable in bringing the material to life and helping the child to encode the lessons and practice the skills effectively.

Problem Area 3: Lack of Assessment of Treatment Receipt

A third potential problem area within treatment integrity is treatment receipt; that is, whether or not the youth has comprehended the material presented. This variable of integrity serves as a reminder that we can be didactic until we are "blue in the face," but if the youth has not encoded or learned to apply the skills then s/he is not likely to appreciate change in symptoms. Treatment protocols may have valuable embedded practices that facilitate an assessment of treatment receipt, including structured previous session review, homework review, or in-session practice. For a variety of reasons, such as limited session time, therapists may fall into a habit of covering didactic information on skills without allowing sufficient time for practice or review. Homework review and in-session practice can be tricky elements of cognitive-behavioral practice in that youth may be reluctant to report on or rehearse skills because of fear of embarrassment. Further, it is arguably a more difficult task for therapists to motivate, engage, and support youth in practicing skills than simply discussing them in theory. In a recent community-based study examining a cognitive-behavioral treatment for depression in youth, it was found through process coding for adherence that therapists rarely provided a comprehensive review of the previous session and that they performed significantly more didactic than in-vivo practice intervention elements in most sessions (even when the manual called for predominantly in-vivo content) (Marder et al., 2006). This finding may suggest that therapists may fall into patterns of uneven distribution of "learning" versus "practice" in sessions. Practice within session is a precious opportunity for a therapist to assess whether the youth has received the messages and lessons of therapy. Patterns of limited in-session practice are potential threats to the integrity of the treatment and may result in movement through skills without the comprehension necessary to afford alleviation of symptoms.

Problem Area 4: Integrity of Parental Collaboration

Another potentially difficult area in implementation may be involving parents or caregivers as much as is recommended in the treatment manual. Although caregiver engagement was evaluated and (we hope) addressed in our initial step of clinical decision making, this current problem represents less-than-ideal efforts on the part of the therapist to involve parents in treatment implementation. Making sure that parents are debriefed on skills learned or practiced in sessions is highly valuable in assuring that practice assignments are carried out to their full therapeutic potential in the home. It is also essential to be mindful of parental treatment receipt; that is, assuring that parents understand therapist expectations regarding their role in treatment delivery. In some instances, the manual may provide handouts for therapists to give parents to keep them up-to-date on the treatment process. Some therapists may not feel they have the time to meet with a parent postsession and instead provide the handout to them as a default method of communication. However, what happens if the parent has limited reading abilities or loses the handout before reading it? For these reasons, an appraisal of how consistently and thoroughly one has worked with the parent as intended by the manual is important when encountering lack of progress.

Problem Area 5: Pitfalls in Basic Structure of Delivery

Other more general aspects of treatment integrity should be considered as one evaluates this problem and its possible impact on lack of progress in treatment. Basic structural elements, such as the duration of weekly sessions, may vary from the intended treatment delivery. For example, our work in Hawaii often involves collaboration with therapists working within the school system. In such an environment, a traditional 50–60-minute session may be impossible because of scheduling restraints, and therapists may split sessions up into 20–30-minute segments. Although this is not necessarily a negative situation for outcome, it may be important to consider how the time distribution is affecting the structure of sessions. Some therapists may have two or three short sessions per week and quite effectively budget time in each session for material coverage, whereas others might struggle with how to divide tasks most effectively across sessions within the scenario. For example, therapists may find themselves spending the bulk of short sessions in homework review or in review of the previous session, with little time left to move on to new skills or cover them in depth.

Problem Area 6: Cautions on Competence

Although competence may be defined differently across treatments with youth, there may be some factors worth reflection relevant to general technique in the delivery of cognitive-behavioral interventions. For example, work in the adult arena of cognitive therapy has suggested that competence within structuring therapy sessions is related to outcomes (Shaw et al., 1999), which supports similar findings regarding adherence to agenda-setting and homework tasks (DeRubeis & Feeley, 1990). This research may imply that in looking at competency in clinical practice, we should consider how thoroughly and consistently we structure and attend to somewhat "universal" techniques such as these.

Two other dimensions of delivery may be worth consideration, including (a) the relative level of expectations set for youth within their work in therapy and (b) the degree of therapist perseverance in working toward youth skill acquisition and application. These areas are purposefully described as "dimensions"—they are concepts that are perhaps not easily quantified though experience impresses on us that these factors may affect treatment outcome. Setting expectations too low, even if out of concern that one might intimidate or overwhelm clients, may subsequently limit the amount of symptom change. Conversely, setting the bar too high may result in hopelessness or feelings of disappointment if expectations go unmet within therapy. Expectations may be expressed within the complexity or difficulty level of therapy tasks presented or in the level of participation demanded by verbal cues. They may also be expressed in more dynamic features of the relationship, such as therapist reactions to situations like incomplete homework. Therapist perseverance represents how intensely and persistently one attempts to engage the youth, present and practice skills until comprehended, and evaluate factors that may inhibit those processes. Poor perseverance may be the "chicken or the egg" in situations of refractory status, but regardless of its role as contributor or outcome it warrants reflection as an area that may be altered to increase treatment response.

Solutions: Seeking Integrity in Practice

In evaluating the fundamentals of treatment integrity, one has several sources of information with varying degrees of bias and expertise. The treatment manual offers perhaps the most direct resource, as it is readily available for review. For therapists new to the treatment, oversights in implementation would be perfectly normal, as manuals often present a wealth of information and instruction that may require multiple implementations to reach full comprehension and familiarity. For veteran therapists, oversights or "manual drifting" would also be reasonable, as their strong familiarity with the model may mean that they have not sat down and directly read the text in some years. Beyond examination of the manual or any accompanying materials, a therapist can always increase the rigor of his or her self-assessment by recording and listening to sessions to avoid relying on retrospective memory of the course of therapy during this process of self-evaluation. Thoughtful listening of one's own recording is always a good initial step and may reveal indications of integrity breakdown that were not apparent previously. The next step up might involve peer supervision wherein one could present the case conceptualization and treatment course to date and receive feedback from a less biased though equally experienced party. This might be followed by consultation with a clinical supervisor, who might also benefit from listening to tape, to better understand the material covered and the quality of implementation. In cases that present particular clinical conundrums, consultation with an expert in the treatment model or manual may be warranted to assure that all resources of advice have been exhausted.

STEP 4: EVALUATION OF CASE FORMULATION

At this point in our framework, we have examined the integrity of our treatment delivery and have either (a) found it to be intact and of sound quality or (b) identified areas of poor integrity and addressed them through protocol review, rigorous self-examination, and consultation with knowledgeable others. If a lack of treatment progress persists, we are now in a position to question whether we have a sound case formulation. A revisitating of our formulation is a dramatic step, as it involves evaluation of the factor that has most directly shaped the direction of treatment. However, if the youth and family are engaged, the treatment has strong integrity, and we remain stagnant in progress it is an appropriate time to question whether we are on a course appropriate for the youth's symptoms.

Sources of information in examining the case formulation include (a) the initial assessment materials, (b) the youth and family's current report of symptoms, and (c) evidence regarding the nature of the youth's problems gleaned from experiences in therapy. Initial assessment materials are necessary as they serve as a reference point for where the youth started in treatment, and the problem areas as perceived and reported by the family at that time. A revisiting of formulation necessarily involves a formal reassessment of symptoms and interview with all primary reporters (e.g., youth, parents, teachers, other caretakers, etc.) involved to determine whether the symptoms have qualitatively changed, or whether new information might change the interpretation of these symptoms. For example, treatment to this point may have involved youth and parent psychoeducational components that may have led to the family having a better understanding of the youth's presenting problem in such a way that would alter treatment. The parents may have initially viewed their child as predominantly oppositional, but with greater psychoeducation regarding factors influencing misbehavior they may now report that they see significant evidence of depression with irritable mood. In the case in which the initial formulation led to the selection of a parent training model and little treatment response has occurred, such evidence may indicate that the child would best be served by a treatment targeting depression. Similarly, the course of therapy may have allowed for greater observation of the youth's behavior (or a wider collection of observations from multiple informants), which may lend itself to a different interpretation of symptoms than originally applied. Working in communities in Hawaii, we certainly appreciate through our own observations what others (Southam-Gerow, Chorpita, Miller, & Gleacher, 2008; Southam-Gerow, Silverman, & Kendall, 2006; Southam-Gerow, Weisz, & Kendall, 2003) have documented: youth seeking community treatment frequently present with multiple problems and diagnoses. The full clinical picture of a typical community-treated youth may not be fully appreciated until therapy has been underway for some time and a larger collection of observations has been gathered to inform the conceptualization.

Because most documented, efficacious treatments within CBT for youth are single-problem focused, a reevaluation of formulation with significant findings might mean a complete abandonment of the current protocol in favor of one that might more directly address the most intense problem behavior. Such a decision, although presumably "evidence based," may run counter to clinical intuition for practitioners, as prioritizing treatment targets can be a complicated and sometimes ethically demanding process. Multiple problem areas (e.g., conduct problems and depression) can be intertwined within the case conceptualization and may be assessed to be at similar levels of severity across reports. In such cases, the selection of a treatment target runs the risk of becoming a subjective "best-guess" within manual-driven treatments as traditionally practiced. In sum, the oft-cited issue of mismatch between narrowly focused treatments and the clinical needs of youth with multiple problems presents one of the most difficult clinical decisions in a refractory case scenario.

Research has not yet demonstrated the potential costs and benefits of addressing multiple problems through the application of serial protocols for each issue. Our experiences working with diverse communities has fueled our appreciation for concerns, expressed across the field of psychotherapy, that such a "serial-delivery" approach does not sit well with therapists and families within the community. Proposals across varying literatures have called for greater individualization within cognitive-behavioral therapy with youth. Persons and colleagues (Persons, 1989; Persons & Tompkins, 1997) have advocated for an approach born of the behavioral assessment literature wherein the therapist develops a working model of the youth's primary problems and the drivers behind them, to act as a guide for systematically addressing treatment targets. "Prescriptive models, " or protocols tailored specifically to target problems, have been applied to treatments of anxious school-refusing children (Burke & Silverman, 1987; Kearney & Silverman, 1990) as well as those with generalized anxiety disorder (Eisen & Silverman, 1998).

Formal Models for a Flexible Treatment

In recognition of the need for structured flexibility within the application of interventions, modular treatments have been suggested as a means to strike a balance between individualization and integrity within delivery (Chorpita et al., 2005; Liberman, Mueser, & Glynn, 1988). A modular approach affords the advantage of selecting discrete therapeutic interventions (or skill sets) to apply in a flexible sequence. The order, frequency, duration, pace, setting of delivery, and other such factors are seen as flexible, though decisions regarding these variables are made by following a structured framework akin to that presented in this chapter (see Figure 2.1). It is important to note that the "flexibility" inherent in modular treatment is different from the within-manual individualization described by Kendall and Beidas (2007). The latter approach acknowledges the breadth of different techniques and forms in which manualized CBT treatment interventions can be applied so as to adapt to a wide range of youth. This type of flexibility is guided by the internal compass of the clinician as she or he molds the established manual to fit the youth. This type of flexibility is important and, as Kendall and Beidas (2007) have elegantly described, it can exist within fidelity to the spirit of the manual. However, this flexibility is conceptually different from flexibility in the context of modular treatment in two ways: (1) modularity can specify the orchestrated use of strategies across multiple evidence based-CBT treatment manuals rather than within a single manual, and (2) choices within modular flexibility are made using an explicit, decision-making framework rather than a clinician's intuition (see Chorpita et al., 2005).

Initial tests of the modular approach have yielded promising outcomes (Chorpita et al., 2004), and a large-scale investigation of their effectiveness is currently under way (Research Network on Youth Mental Health, 2003). It is our hope that these current efforts will provide knowledge as to whether modular approaches to cognitive-behavioral therapy with youth hold advantages over standard, serially applied manuals. The framework offered in this chapter provides navigation for assessing variables that may contribute to a lack of treatment progress regardless of whether a modular or traditional, integral approach is adopted.

STEP 5: INTERFERENCE—"THE REAL WORLD"

As practitioners know too well, therapy out in what we have described previously as the murky, choppy waters of "the real world" tends to be wrought with interference. During the course of therapy, events occur that are simply not accounted for in manuals for cognitive-behavioral, evidence-based treatments. Family members die. Children develop chronic medical illnesses. Hurricanes hit. Parents lose their jobs. There is no "evidence base" that informs us as therapists as to how to navigate these situations while remaining on course within treatment. Intense interference with treatment goals requires that we be doubly diligent in our assessment and bolster the variables that kept us on track before—namely, engagement, integrity, and fundamental conceptualization of the problem. Life teaches us that crises occur and will continue to occur, and as such we must learn to cope to move forward. The task of a therapist is to channel these crises and use them for fodder in practicing the very skills that cognitive-behavioral therapy teaches. In essence, interference can be seen as an opportunity to bring detrimental behaviors and thoughts into the light and work with families and youth in the most demanding moments of their lives to practice therapy skills and rise above these challenges.

CONCLUSIONS

When working with youth and families, poor response with symptoms can feel like a heavy weight to both therapist and client. There are few explicit, universally applicable words of suggestion to use when we are faced with these situations. This chapter has offered a structured, systematic means of assessing potential contributing variables to limited response in an effort to guide navigation with a cognitive-behavioral map. This framework includes careful consideration of the following factors: (a) course of treatment and symptom trends to date, (b) level of youth and family engagement, (c) treatment integrity, and (d) case formulation. Within this navigational tool, we have presented possible sources of information informing us of the status of each factor and have provided suggestions for finding solutions to identified problems within these domains. Interestingly, the variables that we presented overlap significantly with those proposed as factors defining therapist competence within cognitive therapy. Padesky (1996) has suggested that collaboration, guided discovery/empiricism, and structure are the fundamental therapeutic processes within cognitive therapy and, along with case conceptualization, are essential components of competence. We have discussed competence within our framework as it applies to the specific integrity of technique delivery. Padesky's conceptualization highlights the point that a therapist's competency lies not only within the technicalities of intervention delivery, but also within her or his ability to navigate the course of therapy using such a framework as is proposed here. Thus, we hope that our suggestions on successful navigation support broad-based competency for therapists faced with daily challenges in their efforts to implement evidence-based practice in often uncharted waters.

ACKNOWLEDGMENT

Preparation of this chapter was supported in part through the Research Network on Youth Mental Health, sponsored by the John D. and Catherine T. MacArthur Foundation.

REFERENCES

Barber, J. P., Mercer, D., Krakauer, I., & Calvo, N. (1996). Development of adherence/competence rating scale for individual drug counseling. *Drug & Alcohol Dependence, 43,* 125–132.

Barrett, P. M. (1998). Evaluation of cognitive-behavioral group treatments for childhood anxiety disorders. *Journal of Clinical Child Psychology, 27,* 459–468.

Barrett, P. M., Healy-Farrell, L., & March, J. S. (2004). Cognitive behavioral family treatment of obsessive compulsive disorder: A controlled trial. *Journal of the American Academy of Child and Adolescent Psychiatry, 43,* 46–62.

Barrington, J., Prior, M., Richardson, M., & Allen, K. (2005). Effectiveness of CBT versus standard treatment for childhood anxiety disorders in a community clinic setting. *Behaviour Change, 22,* 29–43.

Bernstein, G. A., Layne, A. E., Egan, E. A., & Tennison, D. A. (2005). School-based interventions for anxious children. *Journal of the American Academy of Child and Adolescent Psychiatry, 44,* 1118–1127.

Beutler, L. E., & Clarkin, J. F. (1990). *Systematic treatment selection: Toward targeted therapeutic interventions.* New York: Brunner/Mazel.

Beutler, L. E., & Harwood, T. M. (2000). *Prescriptive psychotherapy: A practice guide to systematic treatment selection.* Oxford, UK: Oxford University Press.

Biedel, D. C., Turner, S. M., & Morris, T. L. (2000). Behavioral treatment of childhood social phobia. *Journal of Consulting & Clinical Psychology, 68,* 1072–1080.

Brestan, E. V., & Eyberg, S. M. (1998). Effective psychosocial treatment of conduct-disordered children and adolescents: 29 years, 82 studies, and 5,272 kids. *Journal of Clinical Child Psychology, 27,* 180–189.

Burke, A. E., & Silverman, W. K. (1987). The prescriptive treatment of school refusal. *Clinical Psychology Review, 7,* 353–362.

Burns, B. J., Farmer, E. M., Angold, A., Costello, E. J., & Behar, L. (1996). A randomized trial of case management for youths with serious emotional disturbance. *Journal of Clinical Child Psychology, 25,* 476–486.

Carroll, K. M., Nich, C., Sifry, R. L., Nuro, K., Frankforter, T. L., Ball, S. A., Fenton, L., & Rouansville, B. J. (2000). A general system for evaluating therapist adherence and competence in psychotherapy research in the addictions. *Drug & Alcohol Dependence, 57,* 225–238.

Cartwright-Hatton, S., Roberts, C., Chitsabesan, P., Fothergill, C., & Harrington, R. (2004). Systematic review of the efficacy of cognitive behaviour therapies for childhood and adolescent anxiety disorders. *British Journal of Clinical Psychology, 43,* 421–436.

Chorpita, B. F. (2007). *Modular cognitive-behavioral therapy for childhood anxiety disorders.* New York: Guilford Press.

Chorpita, B. F., Bernstein, A., & Daleiden, E. L. (2008). Driving with roadmaps and dashboards: Using information resources to structure the decision models in service organizations. *Administration and Policy in Mental Health and Services Research, 35,* 114–123.

Chorpita, B. F., Daleiden, E. L., & Weisz, J. R. (2005). Modularity in the design and application of therapeutic interventions. *Applied and Preventative Psychology, 11,* 141–156.

Chorpita, B. F., Taylor, A. A., Francis, S. E., Moffitt, C. E., & Austin, A. A. (2004). Efficacy of modular cognitive behavior therapy for childhood anxiety disorders. *Behavior Therapy, 35,* 263–287.

Cobham, V. E., Dadds, M. R., & Spence, S. H. (1998). The role of parental anxiety in the treatment of childhood anxiety. *Journal of Consulting and Clinical Psychology, 66,* 893–905.

Cohen, J. A., Deblinger, E., Mannarino, A. P., & Steer, R. A. (2004). A multisite, randomized controlled trial for children with sexual abuse–related PTSD symptoms. *Journal of the American Academy of Child & Adolescent Psychiatry, 43,* 393–402.

Daleiden, E. L., & Chorpita, B. F. (2005). From data to wisdom: Quality improvement strategies supporting large-scale implementation of evidence-based services. *Child and Adolescent Psychiatric Clinics of North America, 14,* 329–349.

DeRubeis, R. J., & Feeley, M. (1990). Determinants of change in cognitive therapy for depression. *Cognitive Therapy and Research, 14,* 469–482.

Dishion, T. J., Nelson, S. E., & Kavanagh, K. (2003). The Family Check-Up with high-risk young adolescents: Preventing early-onset substance use by parent monitoring. *Behavior Therapy, 34,* 553–571.

Eisen, A. R., & Silverman, W. K. (1998). Prescriptive treatment for generalized anxiety disorder in children. *Behavior Therapy, 29,* 105–121.

Elkin, I. (1999). A major dilemma in psychotherapy outcome research: Disentangling therapists from therapies. *Clinical Psychology: Science and Practice, 6,* 10–32.

Evans, G. D., Radunovich, H. L., Cornette, M. M., Wiens, B. A., & Roy, A. (2008). Implementation and utilization characteistics of a rural, school-linked mental health program. *Journal of Child and Family Studies, 17,* 84–97.

Flannery-Schroeder, E. C., & Kendall, P. C. (2000). Group and individual cognitive-behavioral treatments for youth with anxiety disorders: A randomized clinical trial. *Cognitive Therapy & Research, 24,* 251–278.

Forgatch, M. S., Patterson, G. R., & DeGarmo, D. S. (2005). Evaluating fidelity: Predictive validity for a measure of competent adherence to the Oregon Model of Parent Management Training. *Behavior Therapy, 36,* 3–13.

Harrington, R., Whittaker, J., Shoebridge, P., & Campbell, F. (1998). Systematic review of efficacy of cognitive behaviour therapies in childhood and adolescent depressive disorder. *British Medical Journal, 316,* 1559–1563.

Hayward, C., Varady, S., Albano, A. M., Thienemann, M., Henderson, L., & Schatzberg, A. F. (2000). Cognitive-behavioral group therapy for social phobia in female adolescents: Results of a pilot study. *Journal of the American Academy of Child and Adolescent Psychiatry, 39,* 721–726.

Heffner, M., Greco, L. A., & Eifert, G. H. (2003). Pretend you are a turtle: Children's responses to metaphorical versus literal relaxation instructions. *Child and Family Behavior Therapy, 25,* 19–33.

Henggeler, S. W., Schoenwald, S. K., Borduin, C. M., Rowland, M. D., & Cunningham, P. B. (1998). *Multisystemic treatment of antisocial behavior in children and adolescents.* New York: Guilford Press.

Holmbeck, G. N., Greenley, R. N., & Franks, E. A. (2003). Developmental issues and considerations in research and practice. In A. E. Kazdin & J. R. Weisz (Eds.), *Evidence-based psychotherapies for children and adolescents* (pp. 21–41). New York: Guilford Press.

Huey, S. J., Henggeler, S. W., Brondino, M. J., & Pickrel, S. G. (2000). Mechanisms of change in multisystemic therapy: Reducing delinquent behavior through therapist adherence and improved family and peer functioning. *Journal of Consulting and Clinical Psychology, 68,* 451–467.

Hughes, A. A., & Kendall, P. C. (2007). Prediction of cognitive behavior treatment outcome for children with anxiety disorders: Therapeutic relationship and homework compliance. *Behavioural and Cognitive Psychotherapy, 35*, 487–494.

Karver, M. S., Handelsman, J. B., Fields, S., & Bickman, L. (2006) Meta-analysis of therapeutic relationship variables in youth and family therapy: The evidence for different relationship ariables in the child and adolescent treatment outcome literature. *Clinical Psychology Review, 26*, 50–65.

Kazantzis, N. (2003). Therapist competence in cognitive-behavioural therapies: Review of the contemporary empirical evidence. *Behaviour Change, 20,* 1–12.

Kazdin, A. E. (1986). Comparative outcome studies in psychotherapy: Methodological issues and strategies. *Journal of Consulting and Clinical Psychology, 46,* 629–642.

Kazdin, A. E. (2000). *Psychotherapy for children and adolescents: Directions for research and practice.* New York: Oxford University Press.

Kazdin, A. E., Mazurick, J., & Bass, D. (1993). Risk for attrition in treatment of antisocial children and families. *Journal of Clinical Child Psychology, 22*, 2–16.

Kazdin, A. E., Mazurick, J. L., & Siegel, T. C. (1994). Treatment outcome among children with externalizing disorder who terminate prematurely versus those who complete psychotherapy. *Journal of the American Academy of Child and Adolescent Psychiatry, 33,* 549–557.

Kazdin, A. E., & Wassell, G. (1999). Barriers to treatment participation and therapeutic change among children referred for conduct disorder. *Journal of Clinical Child Psychology, 28,* 162–172.

Kazdin, A. E., & Whitley, M. K. (2003). Treatment of parental stress to enhance therapeutic change among children referred for aggressive and antisocial behavior. *Journal of Consulting and Clinical Psychology, 71*, 504–515.

Kearney, C. A., & Silverman, W. K. (1990). A preliminary analysis of a functional model of assessment and treatment for school refusal behavior. *Behavior Modification, 14*, 340–366.

Kendall, P. C., & Beidas, R. S. (2007). Smoothing the trail for dissemination of evidence-based practices for youth: Flexibility within fidelity. *Professional Psychology: Research & Practice, 38,* 13–20.

Kendall, P. C., & Chu, B. C. (2000). Retrospective self-reports of therapist flexibility in a manual based treatment for children with anxiety disorders. *Journal of Clinical Child Psychology, 29,* 209-220.

Kendall, P. C., & Hedtke, K. A. (2006). *The coping cat workbook* (2nd ed.). Ardmore, PA: Workbook Publishing.

King, N. J., Tonge B. J., Heyne, D., Pritchard, M., Rollings, S., Young, D., Myerson, N., & Ollendick, T. H. (1998). Cognitive-behavioral treatment of school-refusing children: A controlled evaluation. *Journal of the American Academy of Child and Adolescent Psychiatry, 37*, 375–403.

King, N. J., Tonge, B. J., Mullen, P., Myerson, N., Heyne, D., Rollings, S., Martin, R., & Ollendick, T. (2000). Treating sexually abused children with posttraumatic stress symptoms: A randomized clinical trial. *Journal of the American Academy of Child & Adolescent Psychiatry, 39,* 1347–1355.

Koeppen, A. S. (1974). Relaxation training for children. *Elementary School Guidance and Counseling, 9,* 14–21.

Koroloff, N. M., Elliott, D. J., Koren, P. E., & Friesen, B. J. (1994). Connecting low-income families to mental health services: The role of the family associate. *Journal of Emotional & Behavioral Disorders, 2*, 240–246.

Koroloff, N. M., Elliott, D. J., Koren, P. E., & Friesen, B. J. (1996). Linking low-income families to children's mental health services: An outcome study. *Journal of Emotional & Behavioral Disorders, 4*, 2–11.

Lambert, M. J., Hansen, N. B., & Finch, A. E. (2001). Patient-focused research: Using patient outcome data to enhance treatment effects. *Journal of Consulting & Clinical Psychology, 69*, 159–172.

Lambert, M. J., Whipple, J. L., Hawkins, E. J., Vermeersch, D. A., Nielsen, S. L., & Smart, D.V. (2003). Is it time for clinicians to routinely track patient outcome? A meta-analysis. *Clinical Psychology: Science and Practice, 10*, 288–301.

Lambert, M. J., Whipple, J. L., Smart, D. W., Vermeersch, D. A., Nielsen, S. L., & Hawkins, E. J. (2001). The effects of providing therapists with feedback on patient progress during psychotherapy: Are outcomes enhanced? *Psychotherapy Research, 11*, 49–68.

Last, C. G., Hansen, C., & Franco, N. (1998). Cognitive-behavioral treatment of school phobia. *Journal of the American Academy of Child and Adolescent Psychiatry, 37*, 404–411.

Liberman, R. P., Mueser, K., & Glynn, S. (1988). Modular behavioral strategies. In I. R. H. Falloon (Ed.), *Handbook of behavioral family therapy* (pp. 27–50). New York: Guilford Press.

Lichstein, K. L., Riedel, B. W., & Grieve, R. (1994). Fair tests of clinical trials: A treatment implementation model. *Advances in Behavior Research and Therapy, 16*, 1–29.

Lynehan, H., & Rapee, R. M. (2006). Evaluation of therapist-supported parent-implemented CBT for anxiety disorders in rural children. *Behaviour Research and Therapy, 44*, 1287–1300.

Masia-Warner, C., Fisher, P., Shrout, P. E., Rathor, S., & Klein, R. G. (2007). Treating adolescents with social anxiety disorder in school: An attention control trial. *Journal of Child Psychology and Psychiatry and Allied Disciplines, 48*, 676–686.

Masia-Warner, C., Klein, R. G., Dent, H. C., Fisher, P. H., Alvir, J., Albano, A. M., & Guiardino, M. (2005). School-based intervention for adolescents with social anxiety disorder: Results of a controlled study. *Journal of Abnormal Child Psychology, 33*, 707–722.

March, J. S., Amaya-Jackson, L., Murray, M. C., & Schulte, A. (1998). Cognitive-behavioral psychotherapy for children and adolescents with posttraumatic stress disorder after a single-incident stressor. *Journal of the American Academy of Child & Adolescent Psychiatry, 37*, 585–593.

Marder, A. M., Bettencourt, A., Brown, R., McLeod, B., Southam-Gerow, M. A., & Weisz, J. (2006, November). *The PASCET program: An investigation of treatment adherence.* Poster presentation at the Association for Behavioral and Cognitive Therapies Conference, Chicago, IL.

McGlinchey, J. B., & Dobson, K. S. (2003). Treatment integrity concerns in cognitive therapy for depression. *Journal of Cognitive Psychotherapy, 17*, 299–318.

McKay, M. M., & Bannon, W. M. (2004). Engaging families in child mental health services. *Child & Adolescent Psychiatric Clinics of North America, 13,* 905–921.
Miller, G. E., & Prinz, R. J. (2003). Engagement of families in treatment for childhood conduct problems. *Behavior Therapy, 34,* 517–534.
Miller, W. R., & Rollnick, A. (Eds.). (2002). *Motivational interviewing: Preparing people for change* (2nd ed.). New York: Guilford Press.
Minuchin, S., & Fishman, H. (1981). *Family therapy techniques*. Cambridge, MA: Harvard University Press.
Nauta, M. H., Scholing, A., Emmelkamp, P., & Minderaa, R. B. (2003). Cognitive-behavioral therapy for children with anxiety disorders in a clinical setting: No additional effect of a cognitive parent training. *Journal of the American Academy of Child & Adolescent Psychiatry,* 42, 1270–1278.
Nelson, T. D., & Steele, R. G. (2007). Predictors of practitioner self-reported use of evidence-based practices: Practitioner training, clinical setting, and attitudes toward research. *Administration and Policy in Mental Health & Mental Health Research Services, 34,* 319–330.
Nock, M. K., & Kazdin, A. E. (2001). Parent expectancies for child therapy: Assessment and relation to participation in treatment. *Journal of Child and Family Studies, 10,* 155–180.
Nock, M. K., & Kazdin, A. E. (2005). Randomized controlled trial of a brief intervention for increasing participation in parent management training. *Journal of Clinical & Consulting Psychology, 73,* 872–879.
North Carolina Department of Health & Human Services. (2007). *Transformation of North Carolina system of services for mental health, developmental disabilities, and substance abuse: The State Strategic Plan 2007–2010, July, 2007*. Raleigh, NC: Author.
Ollendick, T. H. (2000, November). Discussant in T. L. Morris (Chair), *Innovative approaches to the treatment of child anxiety: Conceptual issues and practical constraints*. Symposium conducted at the meeting of the Association for the Advancement of Behavior Therapy, New Orleans, LA.
Padesky, C. (1996). Developing cognitive therapist competence: Teaching and supervision models. In P. M. Salkovskis (Ed.), *Frontiers of cognitive therapy* (pp. 266–292). New York: Guilford Press.
The Pediatric OCD Treatment Study (POTS) Team. (2004). Cognitive-behavior therapy, sertraline, and their combination for children and adolescents with obsessive-compulsive disorder: The Pediatric OCD treatment study (POTS) randomized controlled trial. *Journal of the American Medical Association, 292,* 1969–1976.
Persons, J. B. (1989). *Cognitive therapy in practice: A case formulation approach*. New York: Norton.
Persons, J. B., & Tompkins, M. A. (1997). Cognitive-behavioral case formulation. In T. D. Eells (Ed.), *Handbook of psychotherapy case formulation* (pp. 314–339). New York: Guilford Press.
Prinz, R. J., & Miller, G. E. (1994). Family-based treatment for childhood antisocial behavior: Experimental influences on dropout and engagement. *Journal of Consulting and Clinical Psychology, 62,* 645–650.
Rapee, R., Abbot, M. J., & Lyneman, H. J. (2005). Bibliotherapy for children with anxiety disorders using written materials for parents: A randomized control trial. *Journal of Consulting & Clinical Psychology, 74,* 436–444.

Research Network on Youth Mental Health. (2003). *Linking science and practice to improve youth mental health care: II. Evidence-based practice in clinics and systems.* Unpublished grant proposal.

Riemer, M., Rosof-Williams, J., & Bickman, L. (2005). Theories related to changing clinical practice. *Child and Adolescent Psychiatric Clinics of North America, 14*, 241–254.

Santisteban, D. A., Sazpocznik, J., Perez-Vidal, A., Kurtines, W. M., Murray, E. J., & LaPerriere, A. (1996). Efficacy of intervention for engaging youth and families into treatment and some variables that may contribute to differential effectiveness. *Journal of Family Psychology, 10*, 35–44.

Sapyta, J., Riemer, M., & Bickman, L. (2005). Feedback to clinicians: Theory, research, and practice. *Journal of Clinical Psychology, 61*, 145–153.

Shaw, B. F., Elkin, I., Yamaguchi, J., Olmsted, M., Vallis, T. M., Dobson, K. S., Lowery, A., Sotsky, S. M., Watkins, J. T., & Imber, S. D. (1999). Therapist competence ratings in relation to clinical outcomes in cognitive therapy for depression. *Journal of Consulting and Clinical Psychology, 67*, 837–846.

Shortt, A. L., Barrett, P. M., & Fox, T. L. (2001). Evaluating the FRIENDS Program: A cognitive-behavioral group treatment for anxious children and their parents. *Journal of Clinical Child Psychology, 30*, 525–535.

Silverman, W. K., Kurtines, W. M., Ginsburg, G. S., Weems, C. F., Lumpkin, P. W., & Carmichael, D. H. (1999). Treating anxiety disorders in children with group cognitive-behavior therapy: A randomized clinical trial. *Journal of Consulting and Clinical Psychology, 67*, 995–1003.

Silverman, W. K., Kurtines, W. M., Ginsburg, G. S., Weems, C. F., Rabian, B., & Serafini, L. T. (1999). Contingency management, self-control, and education support in the treatment of childhood phobic disorders: A randomized clinical trial. *Journal of Clinical & Consulting Psychology, 67*, 675–687.

Southam-Gerow, M. A., Chorpita, B. F., Miller, L. M., & Gleacher, A. A. (2008). Are children with anxiety disorders privately referred to a university clinic like those referred from the public mental health system? *Administration and Policy in Mental Health and Mental Health Services Research, 34*, 168–180.

Southam-Gerow, M. A., Silverman, W. K., & Kendall, P. C. (2006). Client similarities and differences in two childhood anxiety disorders research clinics. *Journal of Clinical Child and Adolescent Psychology, 35*, 528–538.

Southam-Gerow, M. A., Weisz, J. R., & Kendall, P. C. (2003). Youth with anxiety disorders in research and service clinics: Examining client differences and similarities. *Journal of Clinical Child and Adolescent Psychology, 32*, 375–385.

Spence, S. H., Donovan, C., & Brechman-Toussaint, M. (2000). The treatment of childhood social phobia: The effectiveness of a social skills training-based, cognitive-behavioural intervention, with and without parental involvement. *Journal of Child Psychology and Psychiatry and Allied Disciplines, 41*, 713–726.

Swartz, H., Zuckoff, A., Grote, N., Spielvogle, H., Beldsoe, S., Shear, M. K., & Frank, E. (2007). Engaging depressed patients in psychotherapy: Integrating techniques from motivational interviewing and ethnographic interviewing to improve treatment participation. *Professional Psychology: Research & Practice, 38*, 430–439.

Waltz, J., Addis, M. E., Koerner, K., & Jacobson, N. S. (1993). Testing the integrity of psychotherapy protocol: Assessment of adherence and competence. *Journal of Consulting and Clinical Psychology, 61*, 620–630.

Yeaton, W. H., & Sechrest, L. (1981). Critical dimensions in the choice and maintenance of successful treatments: Strength, integrity, and effectiveness. *Journal of Consulting & Clinical Psychology, 49*, 156–167.

3

Adjustments in Treatment for Limited or Nonresponding Adolescents in Contemporary CBT

TARA PERIS AND JOHN PIACENTINI

Evidence-based psychosocial treatments are now available to treat a range of adolescent mental health conditions (Brown et al., 2008; Silverman & Hinshaw, 2008). Supported by both controlled clinical trials and meta-analytic research, these treatments provide clear benefit to many youth and their families (Kazdin, Bass, Eyers, & Rodgers, 1990; Weisz, McCarty, & Valeri, 2006). At the same time, however, enthusiasm for current evidence-based treatments (EBTs) is dampened by the fact that a substantial number of youth demonstrate less than optimal responses to treatment. Indeed, across numerous clinical trials targeting a variety of child and adolescent psychiatric conditions (Dumas, 1984; Kendall, 1994; Pediatric OCD Treatment Study [POTS] Team, 2004), rates of nonresponse are relatively high, even for treatments that have been found to be otherwise efficacious. Moreover, even among youth who do respond to treatment, a significant number continue to experience lingering symptoms and functional impairment. Thus, a central task for the field is the elucidation of factors associated with treatment nonresponse in adolescents and the development of strategies for intervening with these youth.

There are several reasons to examine treatment-resistant mental illness. First, identification of factors that may undermine treatment response can guide adaptation and modification of existing treatments. Second, understanding the factors that influence treatment response (and nonresponse) enables empirically guided strategies for designating which intervention strategies are to be used with different subsets of youth. This may mean, for example, prescribing adjunctive family-based treatments to youngsters living in homes with high levels of family stress or conflict or specialized multicomponent interventions for youth presenting with comorbid mental health conditions. Finally, examining factors related to poor treatment response is important for establishing the limits of given treatments with regard to acceptability, feasibility, and efficacy (Southam-Gerow, Kendall, & Weersing, 2001). For example, poor response to primarily cognitive interventions by very young or cognitively delayed youths might suggest a greater reliance on behavioral strategies with these individuals in future interventions (Southam-Gerow et al., 2001).

In this chapter, we discuss the correlates of nonresponse to cognitive-behavioral therapy (CBT) and provide a preliminary discussion of potential strategies for addressing this important clinical problem. We begin by defining treatment nonresponse and by providing a brief overview of treatment nonresponse rates across multiple psychiatric phenotypes. We then discuss adolescence as a developmental period worthy of particular attention among intervention researchers. Finally, we provide a general overview of the individual, family, and treatment-process-related variables associated with CBT nonresponse in adolescents. Every effort is made to discuss treatment resistance across a range of adolescent disorders. However, given that the bulk of the treatment literature on attention-deficit and disruptive behavior disorders centers on school-age children (e.g., Eyberg, Nelson, & Boggs, 2008; Pelham & Fabiano, 2008), an age range covered elsewhere in this volume, the emphasis of this chapter is primarily on internalizing disorders.

DEFINING TREATMENT RESPONSE

The term "treatment resistant" is defined as a failure to respond to an adequate dose of treatment (Brent & Birmaher, 2006). Thus, the classification captures both the degree of change (i.e., treatment response) and the amount of intervention that was provided. Clearly these two concepts overlap to the extent that treatment response is linked to the dosing, intensity, or number of interventions that are administered. Yet, it is important to recognize that individuals who do not respond to a single adequate treatment trial typically are labeled treatment resistant (Brent & Birmaher, 2006; Souery et al., 1999; Thase, 2003). The measurement of treatment response is itself a tricky task, as responses occur on a continuum and are relative to the specific outcome measure employed (e.g., symptom severity, functional impairment). Indeed, it is worth noting that treatment response may embody both decreases in symptom severity and related functional impairment, although symptom reduction tends to be the primary focus.

Most treatment studies use multiple methods or measures for documenting treatment response that can also be conceptualized as either a dichotomous or continuous variable (or sometimes both). The most common dichotomous measure of treatment response in the psychiatric literature is the Clinical Global Impression-Improvement scale (CGI-I; Guy, 1976), a clinician-rated, ordinal scale on which ratings of 1 ("very much" improved) and 2 ("much" improved) reflect responder status and ratings of 3 and higher indicate suboptimal or worse response. Although less popular in the psychological treatment literature (e.g., Barkley, Edwards, Laneri, Fletcher, & Metevia, 2001; Barrett, Healy-Farrell, & March, 2004; Clarke, Rohde, Lewinsohn, Hops, & Seely, 1999; Kendall et al., 1997), the CGI-I has been used as the primary outcome measure for most of the major pediatric multisite randomized controlled comparative trials employing CBT, medication, and/or combined approaches (e.g., Child and Adolescent Multimodal Treatment Study [CAMS]; Walkup et al., 2008; POTS study group, 2004; Treatment of Adolescent Depression Study [TADS], 2004). Other treatment outcome measurement approaches employ dimensional child- and parent-report symptom scales (Scahill, Vitulano, Brenner, Lynch, & King, 1996; Silverman et al., 1999) or change in diagnostic status on a structured diagnostic interview such as the Schedule for Affective Disorders and Schizophrenia–School Age Version (K-SADS; Jayson, Wood, Kroll, Fraser, & Harrington, 1998) or Anxiety Disorders Interview Schedule (ADIS; Silverman & Albano, 1996; e.g., Kendall, 1994; Kendall et al., 1997; Silverman et al., 1999). Finally, some studies evaluate treatment outcome in terms of the percentage of youth who no longer meet criteria for their primary diagnosis, while still allowing for other symptoms and conditions to remain (e.g., Kendall, 1994; Rapee, Abbott, & Lyneham, 2006). Clearly these different measurement approaches have implications for who is deemed a responder as well as the overall level of improvement that is captured by that classification.

Definitions of adequate treatment dose are also quite variable and depend on the type of intervention (pharmacological vs. psychosocial) implemented and the condition being treated. For example, 8 to 16 sessions of treatment is considered appropriate for both cognitive-behavioral therapy and interperson therapy (IPT) for adolescents with major depressive disorder (MDD; Brent & Birmaher, 2006). The literature on child and adolescent anxiety reflects still further variation, with 12 to 14 sessions considered adequate for obsessive-compulsive disorder (OCD; Barrett et al., 2004; Piacentini, Bergman, Jacobs, McCracken, & Kretchman, 2002; Storch et al., 2007) and 12 to 20 sessions considered adequate for child and adolescent anxiety (Kendall, 1994; Kendall et al., 1997). The broad variation in treatment length for anxiety protocols is similar to treatments for adolescent delinquency and antisocial behavior, which typically employ 12 to 20 sessions (e.g., multisystemic therapy, MST; Henggeler & Lee, 2003). Thus, the determination of an adequate treatment trial relies to some degree on clinical judgment rather than empirical criteria.

THE SCOPE OF THE PROBLEM: EXAMINING RATES OF NONRESPONSE

Whether outcomes are measured continuously (using dimensional measures) or categorically (using the CGI-I or change in diagnostic status), findings from the treatment literature indicate that large numbers of adolescents fail to evince sufficient improvement to be considered a treatment responder. To be sure, therapy is helpful to most youth. Meta-analytic work separating child and adolescent samples suggests that, on average, psychosocial therapy produces effect sizes ranging from .58 (Weisz, Weiss, Alicke, & Klotz, 1987) to .82 (Weisz, Donenberg, Han, & Weiss, 1995). At the same time, other findings suggest that more than 20% of youth receiving treatment may exhibit worse outcomes than their counterparts assigned to no-treatment control conditions (Weisz et al., 1995). Although this work also suggests a clear advantage of behavioral interventions over nonbehavioral treatments, findings regarding nonresponse rates can be sobering.

In subsequent years, CBT has emerged as the most widely studied form of psychosocial treatment across the spectrum of child and adolescent psychopathology, including depression (Weisz, Jensen-Doss, & Hawkley, 2006), anxiety (Kendall & Suveg, 2006; Silverman, Pina, & Viswesvaran, 2008), and obsessive-compulsive disorder (Barrett, Farrell, Pina, Peris, & Piacentini, 2008). Indeed, the literature on psychosocial interventions has produced over 80 clinical trials for youth depression (David-Ferdon & Kaslow, 2008; Weersing & Brent, 2006; Weisz et al., 2006), 32 for phobic and anxiety disorders (Silverman et al., 2008), and 21 for OCD (Barrett et al., 2008), the vast majority of which employ some variant of CBT. However, although CBT is the most widely studied psychosocial treatment, it is important to note that other interventions have garnered enough empirical support to be designated as "well established" according to the criteria set forth by Chambless and Hollon (1998), albeit with rates of suboptimal response similar to that for CBT (e.g., IPT for adolescent MDD; Brent & Birmaher, 2006).

In the realm of adolescent depression, Brent and Birmaher (2006) report that, across clinical trials of CBT, the average response rate is 60% with the remaining 40% of youth designated as partial or nonresponders. Likewise, studies of IPT for teens with depression produce suboptimal responses for between 18% and 50% of youth (Mufson et al., 2004; Mufson, Weissman, Moreau, & Garfinkel, 1999). Some of the most striking findings regarding treatment response for child and adolescent MDD, however, emanate from recent meta-analytic work by Weisz et al. (2006), who conducted a rigorous meta-analysis of treatment trials from 1965 to 2004 and found average effect sizes of .34 (small to medium by Cohen's 1988 criteria) and no difference in treatment outcome for youth receiving CBT versus non-CBT treatments. Critically, this effect size did not hold up over time, and at 1-year follow-up there was no evidence of lasting treatment effects. Thus, it seems that even for youth designated as treatment responders, treatment-related changes may be relatively modest.

Adolescent depression is not unique in this regard. Studies of CBT for child and adolescent anxiety reveal nonresponse rates of 36% to 37% when diagnostic status is used as the primary outcome measure (Kendall, 1994; Kendall et al., 1997). Likewise, group CBT with a parent component has produced nonresponse rates between 36% and 39% (Rapee et al., 2006; Silverman et al., 1999). Notably, these studies tend to pool youth with social phobia (SOP), generalized anxiety disorder (GAD), and separation anxiety (SAD) and to rate outcome in terms of the percentage of youth who no longer meet criteria for their primary anxiety diagnosis following treatment. As a result, youth designated as responders may still present with multiple anxiety symptoms, and indeed, may still meet criteria for having an anxiety disorder provided it is not the diagnosis rated as most impairing at study entry.

Within the sphere of child and adolescent OCD, the picture is similar. Although CBT remains the treatment of choice for pediatric OCD according to both expert consensus (March, Frances, Carpenter, & Khan, 1997) and scientific literature review (Barrett et al., 2008), nonresponse rates demonstrate considerable variability across studies depending on the level of methodological rigor employed and the specific outcomes measures used. Indeed, nonresponse rates range from 14% (Storch et al., 2006) to 31% (March, Mulle, & Herbel, 1994) when CGI ratings are used as primary outcome measures, and several studies indicate that at least a third of all youth do not respond to CBT treatment (see Barrett et al., 2008).

Some of the most striking findings regarding treatment-resistant illness come from multisite randomized treatment trials comparing the relative efficacy of CBT, pharmacotherapy, combined treatment, and pill placebo for each of these conditions. Clinical trials testing multiple active treatments represent a significant advancement in the field of treatment outcome research, as they control not only for the passage of time (as in waitlist control designs), but for multiple other variables including placebo effects, treatment expectancy, as well as nonspecific therapeutic process variables (Weisz et al., 2006). This more rigorous approach may account for the well-documented finding that clinical trials comparing two active interventions produce smaller effect sizes compared to those employing waitlist or no treatment controls (Baskin, Tierney, Minami, & Wampold, 2003). Certainly, this trend is evident in two of the major multisite treatment studies conducted to date, studies that point to high rates of nonresponse for both CBT and pharmacotherapy.

Specifically, the Treatment for Adolescent Depression Study (TADS) (TADS Team, 2004) found a response rate of 43% for depressed youth receiving 12 weeks of CBT, a rate that did not differentiate this treatment from placebo and that is markedly lower than the 60% CBT response rate reported elsewhere in the literature (Reinecke, Ryan, & DuBois,

1998). In the Pediatric Obsessive Compulsive Disorder Treatment Study (2004) trial, only 39% of youngsters showed an excellent response to CBT and only 54% to CBT plus sertraline. In contrast to the TADS study, CBT emerged as the preferred treatment for youth with OCD, particularly because the difference between CBT and combined treatment was not significant. However, it is striking to note that fully 60% of youth did not achieve optimal response to current state-of-the-art psychosocial treatment.

ADOLESCENTS AS NONRESPONDERS

The study of adolescent nonresponse rates in particular has been impeded by a relative dearth of research on this specific patient population. To be sure, advances in treatment outcome research have been matched by growing sensitivity to the need for developmentally sensitive interventions. Budding interest in this area has resulted in numerous book chapters and journal issues devoted specifically to the topic of intervening with adolescent psychopathology (e.g., Holmbeck, O'Mahar, Abad, Colder, & Updegrove, 2006). Nonetheless, treatment development for adolescent psychopathology has lagged. Indeed, one review found nearly twice as many published clinical trials for children versus adolescents (Weisz & Hawley, 2002). Worse still, studies with adolescent participants tended to focus on a narrower range of mental illness compared to studies with other age groups, despite the fact that many forms of mental illness are relatively common in adolescence or emerge during this timeframe (Weisz & Hawley, 2002).

Until relatively recently, it has been the norm for clinical trials to collapse youth of widely varying ages into a single sample (e.g., Muris, Merckelbach, Holdrinet, & Sijsenaar, 1998; POTS Team, 2004; Silverman et al., 1999). Although this approach suggests that treatment is more or less a one-size-fits-all proposition and that children and adolescents are more similar than they are different (i.e., the "developmental uniformity myth"; Kendall, 1984), a growing body of research debunks this myth (see Holmbeck et al., 2006). However, debate continues with regard to how adolescence should be defined and which specific age cut-offs to use in treatment outcome research. For example, in their meta-analysis of child and adolescent treatment outcomes, Weisz and Hawley (2002) defined adolescent samples as those averaging 11.0 to

17.9 years of age. Although this decision was based on research suggesting that the physical changes associated with puberty have commenced by age 11 years for most youngsters (Arnett, 2000; Jaffe, 1998), it is problematic in that studies reporting a mean participant age of 11 or 12 years may have subjects well outside the puberty window. Moreover, given the variability in the timing of puberty as well as the distinct transitions that occur during the early and late stages of adolescence (Steinberg, 2005), broad classifications of this age group may mask important within-group developmental differences. These differences likely have important implications for treatment, but they have yet to be addressed in the treatment outcome literature. Instead, current adolescent treatments tend to be adaptations of adult or child treatment protocols, a strategy that obscures understanding of the factors that contribute to treatment response (and nonresponse) in adolescents.

At the same time, converging strands of developmental and neurobiological research provide ample evidence that adolescents may require a unique treatment approach. Although the transition to adulthood is no longer viewed as a period of stress and upheaval that conveys distinct risk for psychopathology (Steinberg & Morris, 2001), adolescence is second only to infancy in terms of the scope and velocity of developmental change (Holmbeck et al., 2000). Change occurs across numerous domains (e.g., social, familial, physiological) and demonstrates marked variation with regard to onset, degree, and duration (Holmbeck, O'Mahar, et al., 2006). Thus, efforts to intervene with adolescents are likely to be more efficacious when they are grounded in a biopsychosocial framework that recognizes the interplay of multiple factors in contributing to the development and maintenance of youth psychopathology.

Developmental Processes in Adolescence and Their Implications for Treatment

From a biological perspective, adolescence ushers in dramatic hormonal changes that are linked to heightened arousal and emotional reactivity (Dahl, 2004). As puberty begins, activation of the endocrine system may result in increases in negative affect and aggression (Angold, Costello, Erkanli, & Worthman, 1999; Finkelstein et al., 1997). These hormonal changes may be further confounded by neurodevelopmental processes that elicit increased risk-taking and reward-motivated behavior at a time when self-regulatory skills have yet to mature (Casey, Getz, & Galvan, 2008). Indeed, neurodevelopment during adolescence centers on brain regions associated with motivation, impulsivity, and novelty-seeking, and changing neurocircuitry in these areas may place youth at risk for vulnerability to addiction (Chambers, Taylor, & Potenza, 2003), anxiety, and depression (Hare et al., 2008). Finally, considerable literature implicates the timing of puberty in the development and maintenance of adolescent mental illness, with precocious development linked to a wide range of psychopathology in both the internalizing and externalizing spectra (see Mendle, Turkheimer, & Emery, 2007, for a review).

These basic biological changes are accompanied by numerous shifts in social roles, including increased autonomy in interpersonal, economic, political, and legal domains (Steinberg, 2005). The capacity to adjust to new freedoms (e.g., driving) and to meet new responsibilities (e.g., first jobs) varies, and is no doubt influenced by broader interpersonal contexts. For example, adolescence is marked by decreased time spent with parents and increased emotional distancing (Larson, Richards, Moneta, Holmbeck, & Duckett, 1996). At the same time, peer relationships take on greater importance, and the nature of these relationships carries significant implications for long-term adult functioning (Parker & Asher, 1987). Finally, adolescence is accompanied by pursuit of more intimate relationships, including friendships marked by greater self-disclosure and romantic relationships that may involve initial experiences with sexual activity (Holmbeck et al., 2006).

Changes in biological, social, and interpersonal domains are likely to be interrelated, and when unfolding biological processes are teamed with challenging social contextual factors, the risk for mental illness in adolescence is likely to increase. For example, early pubertal development (a biological change) may hasten pursuit of romantic relationships (an interpersonal change), which in turn may influence key developmental outcomes including psychosocial adjustment, sense of identity, and views of sexuality (Holmbeck et al., 2006). Alternatively, the link between pubertal change and youth outcomes may be moderated by family and peer responses such that early developers fare poorly only when others respond unfavorably toward their maturation (Holmbeck et al., 2006). The dynamic interplay of these variables calls for multidimensional assessment of youth functioning as well as treatment approaches that recognize the multiple systems within which adolescents operate.

This is a tall order, and it is perhaps not surprising that adolescents can be particularly difficult to engage in treatment (Oetzel & Scherer, 2003). At the broadest level, problems may arise from the use of interventions that are either downward extensions of adult treatments or upward extensions of child protocols. These treatment strategies may have limited utility with adolescents, either because teens may lack the cognitive and emotional maturity to respond to adult-oriented adaptations or because they are put off by a child-targeted manual adaptation that appears to baby them. Moreover, the shortcomings of developmentally insensitive treatment approaches may be compounded by numerous other factors, including the stigma associated with mental illness, a perceived lack of choice about whether to pursue treatment, and disagreement about the very problems that brought them to treatment. Indeed, recent research indicates that willingness to participate in treatment is one of the most robust predictors of youth outcomes (Karver, Handelsman, Fields, & Bickman, 2006), a factor we discuss along with other therapeutic process variables later in this chapter.

Treatment Studies With Adolescent Populations

Which treatments are designed specifically for adolescent populations? Although this is a growing area of research interest, progress has been uneven. In their review of evidence-based treatments for child and adolescent MDD, Devid-Ferdon and Kaslow (2008) identified 12 randomized controlled trials (RCTs) for adolescent depression conducted since 1998 (using age 13 as the cut-off for adolescent status). Of these studies, eight were deemed methodologically rigorous (Type 1) RCTs as defined by Nathan and Gorman (2002). Likewise, a recent review of treatments for disruptive and delinquent behavior identified seven studies employing adolescent samples (Eyberg et al., 2008), with six of these trials meeting criteria for Type 1 status. Critically, these studies not only employed adolescent samples, but administered treatments developed specifically for this age group (e.g., multisystemic therapy [MST] for adolescent conduct disorder). By contrast, however, Kendall and Suveg (2006) note that the study of adolescents with anxiety disorders remains strikingly limited, with few treatment packages specifically formulated for this subset of youth such as Group CBT for Adolescents (Albano, Marten, Holt, Heimberg, & Barlow, 1995) and Coping Cat (Kendall, Hudson, Choudhury, Webb, & Pimental, 2005). Likewise, there are currently no interventions specifically designed to address the unique needs of adolescents with OCD.

Given the current state of the adolescent intervention literature, it is difficult to examine factors related to treatment-resistant illness in adolescents with much precision. Because age ranges vary in studies published to date and because many major forms of mental illness have yet to amass a literature base focused specifically on teens, we devote the next section of this chapter to discussing predictors of nonresponse as they emerge in the general child and adolescent literature. Where possible, we highlight findings that apply specifically to adolescent populations.

PREDICTORS OF NONRESPONSE IN ADOLESCENTS

Symptom Severity

Baseline symptom severity has emerged as one of the most robust predictors of poor response to CBT for adolescent psychiatric disorders, including MDD (Brent et al., 1998; Clarke et al., 1992; Curry et al., 2006; Jayson et al., 1998) and OCD (Keeley, Storch, Merlo, & Geffken, 2008; Piacentini et al., 2002). Moreover, baseline symptom severity appears to predict long-term outcome for youth with OCD (Barrett, Farrell, Dadds, & Boulter, 2005). Although baseline severity has been shown to predict response to CBT for childhood anxiety disorders (Silverman et al., 2008), predictors of CBT response for adolescent depression remain unstudied. Findings from treatment studies for adolescents with externalizing disorders are mixed, with some studies suggesting that pretreatment symptom severity is linked to poor outcome (Patterson & Forgatch, 1995) and others failing to find this link using similar treatment approaches (Fleischman, 1981).

Age

The relationship between age and treatment response is less consistent and appears to vary as a function of both the psychiatric condition being treated and the nature of the intervention itself. For example, for youth with conduct disorder, higher age is associated with poorer treatment outcome following parent training (Patterson & Chamberlain, 1994). Likewise, for youth with MDD, older age has been linked to poorer outcome as indicated by a categorical rating of remission on the K-SADS (Jayson et al., 1998). Findings from the TADS study also suggest that older adolescents may not respond as well to acute treatment compared to their younger counterparts (Curry et al., 2006).

By contrast, the limited work on predictors of response for pediatric OCD suggests that age is not a factor in treatment response (Piacentini et al., 2002), although further research is needed with adolescent populations. With regard to other forms of youth anxiety, research has yielded mixed results. Barrett, Dadds, and Rapee (1996) found that older anxious youth (age 11 to 14 years) fared more poorly in response to individual cognitive behavioral therapy (ICBT) plus family involvement compared to younger children (age 7 to 10 years). By contrast, a study of anxious-depressed adolescents (age 12 to 18 years) with school refusal found that age did not predict treatment response to CBT plus imipramine or CBT plus placebo (Layne, Bernstein, Egan, & Kushner, 2003). Thus, it may be the case that age does not influence adolescent response to individual CBT treatment or medication management, but that it poses problems for youth pursuing family-based treatments at a time when there is an increased developmental pull for autonomy.

Cognitive Factors

Among adolescents with MDD, higher levels of cognitive distortion and hopelessness have been associated with poor response to treatment (Brent et al., 1998; Curry et al., 2006). These findings are consistent with those reported by Clarke et al. (1992), who found that, among depressed teens treated with group CBT, self-reported irrational thoughts at baseline predicted poorer treatment outcome. Likewise, Treadwell and Kendall (1996) found that anxious self-talk and negative self-statements predicted poorer treatment outcome for anxious youth, with some evidence for a mediating role. This work was recently replicated on a sample of youth aged 9 to 13 years, providing further evidence for the mediating role of anxious self-talk in child anxiety treatment, and modest evidence for the role of states of mind in predicting outcome

(Kendall & Treadwell, 2007). Interestingly, although considerable research elucidates cognitive factors linked to adult OCD (Keeley et al., 2008), the literature on children and adolescents with OCD is much more limited (Farrell & Barrett, 2006) and these variables have yet to be examined in relation to treatment outcome.

Comorbidity

Although clinical experience suggests that youth who present to treatment with comorbid conditions may be more difficult to treat, a consistent pattern of findings has yet to emerge both within and across disorders. In the realm of child and adolescent anxiety, several studies suggest that comorbidity does not predict treatment outcome. For example, Kendall, Brady, and Verduin (2001) found that youth with co-occurring anxiety and/or externalizing disorders evinced more severe internalizing symptomatology at baseline but that pretreatment comorbidity did not predict treatment outcome. Similarly, Flannery-Schroeder, Suveg, Safford, Kendall, and Webb (2004) found no difference in long-term outcome among anxious youth with and without comorbid externalizing disorders. However, other research has found that comorbid internalizing, but not comorbid externalizing, symptomatology is associated with poorer treatment outcome for anxious youth following 12 weeks of individual CBT (Southam-Gerow et al., 2001). Notably, several studies have indicated that there is no link between the number of comorbid diagnoses and treatment outcome for anxiety (Kendall et al., 1997, 2001; Shortt, Barrett, Dadds, & Fox, 2001; Southam-Gerow et al., 2001).

With regard to adolescent depression, findings from the TADS study (Curry et al., 2006) indicate that the presence of comorbid conditions is associated with poorer treatment outcome. In addition, Brent et al. (1998) found that comorbid dysthymia was linked to increased rates of dropout during psychosocial treatment. However, comorbid externalizing and substance abuse problems do not appear to dampen response to group CBT for adolescent depression (Rohde, Clarke, Lewinsohn, Seeley, & Kaufman, 2001; Rohde, Clarke, Mace, Jorgensen, & Seeley, 2004).

The literature on pediatric OCD indicates that comorbid depression is linked to poor outcomes, a finding that parallels work in the adult

OCD arena (Keeley et al., 2008). Interestingly, the presence of comorbid tic disorder does not appear to predict treatment outcome for adolescents with OCD (Himle, Fischer, Van Etten, Janeck, & Hanna, 2003). However, Storch et al. (2008) reported that nonanxiety comorbid conditions predicted poorer outcome in a sample of children and adolescents with OCD. Indeed, among youth aged 7 to 19 years receiving either individual or weekly CBT, treatment response rates were substantially lower for youth with comorbid attention-deficit/hyperactivity disorder (ADHD) or disruptive behavior disorder compared to youth without a comorbid diagnosis.

FAMILY-LEVEL PREDICTORS OF TREATMENT OUTCOME

Whereas studies of clinical and demographic features associated with treatment-refractory illness have produced a somewhat muddy picture to date, ample literature implicates the role of dysfunctional family dynamics in undermining treatment response for a range of psychiatric conditions.

Family Dynamics

Across nearly every major category of child and adolescent mental illness, family conflict emerges as a salient risk factor for poor outcomes (Berman, Weems, Silverman, & Kurtines, 2000; Brent & Birmaher, 2006; Dadds, Schwartz, & Sanders, 1987). Among youth with conduct disorder, higher levels of family conflict including interparental and familial discord are associated with poorer treatment response (Dadds et al., 1987). Similarly, family conflict has been shown to lead to slower treatment response, less complete remission, and more frequent recurrence of symptoms for youth seeking both pharmacotherapy and CBT treatment for depression (Birmaher et al., 2000; Emslie et al., 1998). Finally, family dysfunction also predicts poor response to the treatment of child anxiety (Berman et al., 2000).

Parental Psychopathology

Parental mental illness may pose problems for adolescent treatment to the extent that it puts practical constraints on treatment attendance and adherence and creates a home environment that undercuts treatment-related gains. Certainly, it is likely to challenge the ability to parent effectively, a task that may itself have direct implications for how youth respond to treatment. For example, baseline parental management skills predicted outcome for a sample of 53 adolescents following treatment for antisocial behavior (Chamberlein & Reid, 1998).

Regardless of the specific mechanisms by which parental psychopathology interacts with the treatment process, it has been linked to poor outcomes for youth with a range of clinical presentations (Berman et al., 2000; Brent et al., 1998; Patterson & Chamberlain, 1994). In particular, parental depression appears to be especially problematic, and in some studies it has emerged as the strongest predictor of outcome (Berman et al., 2000).

THERAPEUTIC PROCESS AND TREATMENT RESPONSE

Beyond child and family characteristics that may contribute to treatment-resistant mental illness, specific features of the therapeutic process are likely to shape outcomes for adolescents seeking mental health treatment. Given the unique developmental issues with which youth in this age group contend, issues of attendance, motivation, and therapeutic relationship are likely to rise to the fore.

Attendance, Adherence, and Involvement

It is estimated that as many as one third of all treatment-seeking youth do not show up for their initial treatment session (Carr, McDonnell, & Owen, 1994; McKay, McCadam, & Gonzales, 1996). Thereafter, patterns of attendance remain spotty for many families, with missed sessions occurring approximately once every three visits (Conduit, Byrne, Court, & Stefanovic, 2004). Indeed, nearly half of the families that pursue mental health treatment will terminate prematurely (Baekeland & Lundwall, 1975; Pekarik & Stephenson, 1988), a factor that no doubt carries detrimental consequences for youth outcomes (see Armbruster & Kazdin, 1994 for a review).

This pattern exists across psychiatric phenotypes and is likely to hold for both child and adolescent patients. For example, Layne et al. (2003) found that higher levels of baseline attendance predicted better outcome for anxious-depressed adolescents receiving CBT. Similarly, in their community sample of 1,422 youth aged 9 to 13 years, Angold, Costello, Burns, Erkanli, and Farmer (2000) found that higher rates of attendance were linked to higher levels of symptom reduction.

Beyond weekly attendance, however, youth involvement in therapy is also important. Most psychosocial treatments for children and adolescents are collaborative approaches predicated on active participation and involvement. Thus, youth who sit passively in treatment or exhibit poor engagement may fare more poorly compared to youth who take a more assertive stance. Recent research supports this idea such that child involvement midway through treatment predicts later treatment gains for anxious youth (Chu & Kendall, 2004).

Therapeutic Relationship

The therapeutic relationship is also likely to play a central role in adolescent treatment, particularly given the fact that youth typically do not refer themselves to treatment and may not acknowledge or agree with their parents about the problems in need of treatment (Russell & Shirk, 1998; Shirk & Karver, 2003; Shirk & Saiz, 1992). Indeed, work by Kendall and Southam-Gerow (1996) documents the emphasis placed on a favorable therapeutic relationship by treatment-completing child clients themselves. Thus, it is not surprising that in their meta-analysis of 23 treatment outcome studies, Shirk and Karver (2003) found that the therapeutic relationship is associated with outcomes across a range of psychopathology and psychosocial treatment approaches.

This finding has been well replicated in subsequent research, with evidence for the role of therapeutic alliance in predicting posttreatment and follow-up outcomes for youth with anxiety (Hughes & Kendall, 2007), externalizing (Hogue, Dauber, Stambaugh, Cecero, & Liddle, 2006; Kazdin, Whitley, & Marciano, 2006) and substance abuse disorders (Diamond et al., 2006). Critically, parent–therapist and child–therapist alliance are likely to have distinct but equally important roles in the treatment process. Hawley and Weisz (2005) found that parent–therapist alliance was associated with increased attendance and participation, whereas child–therapist alliance predicted both child and parent ratings of symptom improvement. Similarly, research on the use of multidimensional family therapy for adolescent substance abuse suggests that observations of parent–therapist alliance predict premature dropout, whereas observations of adolescent–therapist alliance predict improvement in substance-abuse symptoms at posttreatment and 3-month follow-up (Shelef, Diamond, Diamond, & Little, 2005).

STRATEGIES FOR INTERVENING WITH TREATMENT-RESISTANT MENTAL ILLNESS

In light of these issues, how must clinicians proceed when intervening with adolescents who respond poorly to treatment? In their discussion of this issue, Brent and Birmaher (2006) note the importance of revisiting the measurement issues discussed earlier in this chapter. That is, clinicians should begin by evaluating the adequacy of outcome measures as well as the sufficiency of the initial treatment trial. Highly distressed patients may have difficulty recognizing or acknowledging their progress, a problem that may be heightened in the absence of standardized measures that provide clear markers of progress. Moreover, progress may be uneven, with significant improvement in some areas and slower gains in others. This in turn may result in global ratings that do not capture clinically significant changes. Likewise, in cases in which symptoms linger, there may be marked improvements in functional impairment that are obscured by focusing solely on symptom severity. Thus, it is important to conduct a careful, systematic, and multidimensional assessment of patient outcomes prior to assigning nonresponse status.

ASSESSING THE TREATMENT TRIAL

The quality of the trial must also be evaluated with particular attention to issues of treatment adherence (Brent & Birmaher, 2006). This in cludes not only how well the therapist applied the designated intervention, a variable that may be assessed via chart review and case conference, but process variables as well. Indeed, patient and family attendance should be evaluated to determine how much of the intervention was actually administered. In addition, in-session compliance and rates of homework completion provide clear indicators of how much practice was obtained during treatment. Assessment of these factors will inform subsequent treatment steps ranging from efforts to enhance motivation for treatment to the addition of extra sessions to allow sufficient exposure to intervention material.

Increasing Dose and Intensity

A review of these factors may point to the need to adjust the dose or intensity of the intervention. Certainly, there has been growing interest in of the use of these strategies for youngsters who demonstrate suboptimal response to psychosocial treatment (Weisz et al., 2006). In many cases a review of the treatment trial reveals gradual but noteworthy progress, suggesting that the patient simply needs more time to attain responder status. In this case, the treatment strategy would involve the provision of additional sessions. Alternatively, refractory youth may need the same treatment in a more intensive form to achieve clinically significant symptom reduction. A growing number of interventions support the efficacy of intensive interventions for a range of psychiatric illnesses (Blomgren, Roy, Callister, & Merrill, 2005; Moffitt, Chorpita, & Fernandez, 2003; Pelham & Hoza, 1996; Storch et al., 2007; Whiteside, Brown, & Abramowitz, 2008). These interventions may involve home visits, bi-weekly sessions, or camp program formats designed to increase therapist contact; these interventions may be viable solutions for addressing suboptimal response.

Assessing Developmentally Appropriate Intervention

In addition to assessing the adequacy of a trial's dose and intensity, it is crucial to evaluate the degree to which it was developmentally sensitive. As noted, adolescents comprise a heterogeneous group that presents a unique and complex set of treatment issues. Historically, these issues have been overlooked in treatment outcome research despite their clear relevance for shaping youth outcomes. Following a failed trial, it is therefore especially important to revisit these issues, paying attention both to the nuts and bolts of the treatment approach that was employed and to broader developmental issues that may have intersected with the treatment process.

Critically, it is not enough to rely on a treatment packaged as an "adolescent" intervention (where such treatments exist), as developmental variations within this age group may call for adaptation of and flexibility with an adolescent treatment (Kendall, 2002). Indeed, it is important to recognize that developmental research summarizes trends for a particular age group, whereas therapy is conducted with an individual who may or may not align with the group norm (Weisz & Hawley, 2002). With this in mind, therapists must evaluate for themselves how key developmental tasks are brought to bear on the patient's presenting symptoms. In the early stages of treatment, this may mean assessing social perspective-taking skills for a patient with social phobia or evaluating impulsivity and risk-taking activity within the context of developmental norms for a youngster with oppositional behavior. Following poor response to treatment, however, this assessment may involve taking stock yet again of whether the specific strategies employed during the treatment trial were adequately matched to the child's developmental level and attempting to determine whether the youngster's needs have shifted over the course of treatment (e.g., school transitions, dissolution of romantic relationships, emergence of new family issues).

With regard to matching treatment to the adolescent's developmental status, Holmbeck and colleagues (Holmbeck, Friedman, et al., 2006) have emphasized the importance of considering developmental level as a moderator of treatment outcome. A patient's developmental status, particularly in cognitive spheres, may determine whether he or she achieves responder status at the end of treatment. Cognitive maturity may interact with treatment in multiple ways by either increasing (or decreasing) the participant's ability to participate in specific treatment tasks (e.g., cognitive restructuring, perspective-taking during role play) or by worsening of certain symptoms (e.g., the capacity to ruminate; Holmbeck, Friedman, et al., 2006). Therefore, therapists should evaluate an adolescent patient's ability to reflect on future consequences, participate in meta-cognitive tasks, and demonstrate perspective taking and social problem-solving skills. Although this is clearly a task to be conducted at the start of treatment, a patient's level of skill with these types of exercises may not become fully evident until treatment unfolds, making it worthwhile to revisit this informal assessment when strategizing about how to address suboptimal treatment response.

Assessing the developmental sensitivity of a failed therapy course provides valuable information that can inform subsequent treatment steps. First, it can help to prioritize therapy goals in as much as it alerts therapists to key issues that might be interfering with treatment (e.g., a teenager who is increasingly drawn to deviant peers). Second, it can help therapists identify specific strategies for revamping subsequent treatment sessions. For example, an adolescent who lacks proficiency with the abstract-reasoning tasks described previously is likely to struggle with insight-oriented techniques or with role-play tasks that require perspective taking. By contrast, he or she may benefit from strategies that are more behavioral in nature (e.g., an emphasis on exposure or scheduling pleasant events). The therapist may also want to consider modifying strategies to adapt to the child's cognitive developmental level. For example, he or she might choose to talk aloud during role play as a method of illustrating recursive reasoning techniques in a more concrete fashion (Piacentini & Bergman, 2001). Finally, assessment of an intervention's developmental fit can help to address process issues that also interfere with treatment. This may mean bolstering behavioral rewards to increase motivation for a patient with little intrinsic desire to pursue treatment. Alternatively, for youth who demonstrate emerging cognitive flexibility, therapists may benefit from prompting consideration of the future benefits of treatment as a method of harnessing motivation and compliance with treatment.

Comorbidity

Given the high rates of comorbidity reported in the adolescent psychopathology literature as well as links between comorbidity and poor outcomes (Southam-Gerow et al., 2001), an additional strategy for intervening with treatment-resistant mental illness may involve treating co-occurring conditions. These comorbid conditions may be present at the start of treatment, as in the case of a teenager who presents with both ADHD and comorbid tics. Alternatively, additional conditions may emerge over the course of treatment as in situations in which depression develops secondary to an anxiety disorder or OCD. Because of this and because adolescence is a peak period of onset for many types of psychiatric illness, it is important for therapists to assess regularly for the presence of additional illnesses. When present, these conditions may call for strategic pharmacotherapy for the comorbid symptoms, or for reprioritizing of treatment goals.

One strategy for addressing comorbid mental illness among treatment-refractory youth involves the use of modular treatments. There has been growing emphasis on the value of identifying the common elements across treatment protocols and using them to match treatment techniques to various presenting problems (i.e., the distilling and matching model [DMM]; Chorpita, 2007). Approaches such as these may provide valuable guidance when it comes to helping therapists mix and match evidence-based techniques in the service of treating comorbid illness.

Family Intervention

Family interventions also hold promise for treating refractory youth (Miklowitz et al., 2007; Peris et al., 2008), particularly in light of research linking family dysfunction to poor treatment outcomes for several forms of adolescent psychopathology (see preceding review). Notably, factors that contribute to family dysfunction (e.g., conflict, parental psychopathology, marital discord) are likely to wax and wane over the course of treatment. As such, they may not be immediately evident or may worsen over the course of treatment. In addition, adolescent patients may be particularly reluctant to talk about challenging family issues, making detection and assessment of family issues an especially daunting enterprise.

Despite these obstacles, family-focused interventions have demonstrated efficacy for treating refractory bipolar disorder in adolescents (Fristad & Goldberg-Arnold, 2003; Miklowitz, 2008) and adolescents with depression (Asarnow, Tompson, & Berk, 2005). In addition, clinical trials employing mixed child and adolescent samples point to the value of family-focused intervention for OCD (Barrett et al., 2004) and anxiety (Barmish & Kendall, 2005). As such, they may well prove to be valuable adjuncts to individual treatment. However, it is important to recognize that many current family interventions will need to be retooled for adolescent populations. For example, Shirk (1999) has emphasized the importance of tailoring behavioral parent training for parents of adolescents to be less unilateral and more collaborative compared to standard child programs. Likewise, issues of limit setting, problem solving, and negotiating may need to be recast in a new light when working with youth who are exploring newfound autonomy. Given developmental and familial variation, family treatments are unlikely to be a one-size-fits-all proposition. However, implementing strategies to foster greater stability and improved conflict management in the home environment is likely to bolster outcomes for refractory youth.

Multimodal Intervention

In addition to making treatment adjustments based on an adolescent's changing developmental and psychosocial needs, therapeutic response may be enhanced by the use of multimodal intervention. Indeed, in each of the major multisite RCTs conducted to date, combined treatments integrating well-regimented pharmacotherapy with psychosocial intervention have yielded the highest response rates. Although algorithms have yet to be developed specifically for adolescent psychopathology, one viable solution for addressing suboptimal treatment response is to augment an initial psychosocial treatment trial with the use of medication or adjunctive family therapy.

SUMMARY

The last decade has seen enormous gains in evidence-based psychosocial treatment for adolescent psychopathology (Silverman & Hinshaw, 2008). Numerous clinical trials have established the efficacy of cognitive-behavioral interventions for the most common disorders in this developmental period, and a series of large-scale, controlled multisite trials has provided information regarding the comparative efficacies of monotherapy CBT, monotherapy medication, and combination treatment (CBT plus medication) versus pill placebo (Brown et al., 2008). In spite of this progress, however, a substantial number of treated youngsters do not evidence a clinically significant response, and a majority of treated youngsters, including a proportion of those rated as treatment responders, continue to evidence some level of symptoms following the completion of treatment (Brown et al., 2008; Silverman & Hinshaw, 2008). A particular concern for treatment-seeking adolescents is the evidence suggesting that older youths tend to fare more poorly in some treatments than their younger counterparts (Barrett et al., 1996; Curry et al., 2006; Patterson & Chamberlain, 1994).

Although treatments designed specifically for adolescent populations are limited, the biological, cognitive, and social changes associated with this period underscore the importance of developmentally sensitive approaches to optimize outcomes. In addition to the need for developmentally tailored approaches, other strategies for addressing treatment-resistant adolescents include careful re-evaluation of the target and any comorbid problems and associated maintaining factors, change in treatment dose or intensity, greater involvement of family or other ecologically relevant systems (e.g., school) in treatment, and consideration of concurrent psychopharmacological intervention. Although efforts to develop systematic and evidence-based protocols for addressing treatment-resistant mental illness in adolescents have garnered increased attention over the past decade (e.g., Brent, Emslie, et al., 2008), considerable work remains to be done and the field is ripe for further research.

REFERENCES

Albano, A. M., Marten, P. A., Holt, C. S., Heimberg, R. G., & Barlow, D. H. (1995). Cognitive-behavioral group treatment for social phobia in adolescents: A preliminary study. *Journal of Nervous and Mental Disease, 183*, 649–656.

Angold, A., Costello, E. J., Burns, B. J., Erkanli, A., & Farmer, E. M. (2000). Effectiveness of nonresidential specialty mental health services for children and adolescents in the "real world." *Journal of the American Academy of Child and Adolescent Psychiatry, 39*, 154–160.

Angold, A., Costello, E. J., Erkanli, A., & Worthman, C. H. (1999). Pubertal changes in hormone levels and depression in girls. *Psychological Medicine, 29*, 1043–1053.

Armbruster, P., & Kazdin, A. (1994). Attrition in child psychotherapy. *Advances in Clinical Child Psychology, 16*, 81–108.

Arnett, J. J. (2000). Emerging adulthood: A theory of development from the late teens through the twenties. *American Psychologist, 55*, 469–480.

Asarnow, J. R., Tompson, M. R., & Berk, M. (2005). Adolescent depression: Family-focused treatment strategies. In W. M. Pinsof & J. L. Lebow (Eds.), *Family psychology: The art of the science* (pp. 425–450). New York: Oxford University Press.

Baekeland, F., & Lundwall, L. (1975). Dropping out of treatment: A critical review. *Psychological Bulletin, 82*, 738–783.

Barkley, R. A., Edwards, G., Laneri, M., Fletcher, K., & Metevia, L. (2001). The efficacy of problem-solving communication training alone, behavior management training alone, and their combination for parent–adolescent conflict in teenagers with ADHD and ODD. *Journal of Consulting and Clinical Psychology, 69*, 926–941.

Barmish, A. J., & Kendall, P. J. (2005). Should parents be co-clients in cognitive-behavioral therapy for anxious youth? *Journal of Clinical Child and Adolescent Psychology, 34*, 569–581.

Barrett, P. M., Dadds, M. M., & Rapee, R. (1996). Family treatment of childhood anxiety: A controlled trial. *Journal of Consulting and Clinical Psychology, 64*, 333–342.

Barrett, P. M., Farrell, L. J., Dadds, M., & Boulter, N. (2005). Cognitive-behavioral family treatment of childhood obsessive-compulsive disorder: Long-term follow-up and predictors of outcome. *Journal of the American Academy of Child and Adolescent Psychiatry, 44*, 1005–1014.

Barrett, P. M., Farrell, L. M., Pina, A., Peris, T. S., & Piacentini, J. (2008). Evidence-based psychosocial treatments for child and adolescent obsessive-compulsive disorder. *Journal of Clinical Child and Adolescent Psychology, 37,* 131–155.

Barrett, P. M., Healy-Farrell, L. J., & March, J. S. (2004). Cognitive-behavioral family treatment of childhood obsessive-compulsive disorder: A controlled trial. *Journal of the American Academy of Child and Adolescent Psychiatry, 43,* 46–62.

Baskin, T. W., Tierney, S. C., Minami, T., & Wampold, B. E. (2003). Establishing specificity in psychotherapy: A meta-analysis of structural equivalence of placebo controls. *Journal of Consulting and Clinical Psychology, 71,* 973–979.

Berman, J., Weems, C. F., Silverman, W. K., & Kurtines, W. M. (2000). Predictors of outcome in exposure-based cognitive and behavioral treatments for phobic and anxiety disorders in children. *Behavior Therapy, 31,* 713–731.

Birmaher, B., Brent, D. A., Kolko, D., Baugher, M., Bridge, J., & Holder, D. (2000). Clinical outcome after short-term psychotherapy for adolescents with major depressive disorder. *Archives of General Psychiatry, 57,* 29–36.

Blomgren, M., Roy, N., Callister, T., & Merrill, R. (2005). Intensive stuttering modification therapy: A multidimensional assessment of treatment outcomes. *Journal of Speech, Language, and Hearing Research, 48,* 509–523.

Brent, D., Emslie, G., Clarke, G., Wagner, K. D., Asarnow, J. R., Keller, M., et al. (2008). Switching to another SSRI or to venlafaxine with or without cognitive behavioral therapy for adolescents with SSRI-resistant depression: The TORDIA randomized controlled trial. *Journal of the American Medical Association, 299,* 901–913.

Brent, D. A., & Birmaher, B. A. (2006). Treatment-resistant depression in adolescents: Recognition and management. *Child and Adolescent Psychiatric Clinics of North America, 15,* 1015–1034.

Brent, D. A., Kolko, D., Birmaher, B., Baugher, M., Bridge, J., Roth, C., & Holder, D. (1998). Predictors of treatment efficacy in a clinical trial of three psychosocial treatments for adolescent depression. *Journal of the American Academy of Child and Adolescent Psychiatry, 37,* 906–914.

Brown, R., Antonuccio, D., DuPaul, G., Fistad, M., King, C., Leslie, L., McCormick, G., Pelham, W., Piacentini, J., & Vitiello, B. (2008). *Childhood mental health disorders: Evidence base and contextual factors for psychosocial, psychopharmacological, and combined interventions* (pp. 3–14). Washington, DC: American Psychological Association.

Carr, A., McDonnell, D., & Owen, P. (1994). Audit and family systems consultation: Evaluation of practice at a child and family centre. *Journal of Family Therapy, 16,* 143–157.

Casey, B. J., Getz, S., & Galvan, A. (2008). The adolescent brain. *Developmental Review, 28,* 62–77.

Chamberlain, P., & Reid, J. B. (1998). Comparison of two community alternatives to incarceration for chronic juvenile offenders. *Journal of Consulting and Clinical Psychology, 66,* 624–633.

Chambers, R. A., Taylor, J., & Potenza, M. N. (2003). Developmental neurocircuitry of motivation in adolescence: A critical period of addiction vulnerability. *American Journal of Psychiatry, 160,* 1041–1052.

Chambless, D. L., & Hollon, S. L. (1998). Defining empirically supported therapies. *Journal of Consulting and Clinical Psychology, 66,* 7–18.

Chorpita, B. F. (2007). *Modular cognitive-behavioral therapy for childhood anxiety disorders.* New York: Guilford Press.

Chu, B. C., & Kendall, P. C. (2004). Positive association of child involvement and treatment outcome within a manual-based cognitive-behavioral treatment for children with anxiety. *Journal of Consulting and Clinical Psychology, 72,* 821–829.

Clarke, G. N., Hops, H., Lewinsohn, P. M., Andrews, J. A., Seeley, J. R., & Williams, J. (1992). Cognitive behavioral group treatment of adolescent depression: Prediction of outcome. *Behavior Therapy, 23,* 341–354.

Clarke, G. N., Rohde, P. N., Lewinsohn, P. M., Hops, H., & Seeley, J. R. (1999). Cognitive-behavioral treatment of adolescent depression: Efficacy of acute group treatment and booster sessions. *Journal of the American Academy of Child and Adolescent Psychiatry, 38,* 272–279.

Conduit, T., Byrne, S., Court, J., & Stefanovic, S. (2004). Non-attendance at a university-based psychology clinic: Telephone appointment reminders versus no reminders. *Australian Psychologist, 39,* 68–75.

Curry, J., Rohde, P., Simons, A., Silva, S., Vitiello, B., Kratochvil, C., et al. (2006). Predictors and moderators of acute outcome in the treatment for adolescents with depression study (TADS). *Journal of the American Academy of Child and Adolescent Psychiatry, 45,* 1427–1439.

Dadds, M. R., Schwartz, S. R., & Sanders, M. (1987). Marital discord and treatment outcome in behavioral treatment of child conduct disorders. *Journal of Consulting and Clinical Psychology, 55,* 396–403.

Dahl, R. E. (2004). Adolescent brain development: A period of vulnerabilities and opportunities. In *Adolescent brain development: Vulnerabilities and opportunities* (pp. 1–22). New York: New York Academy of Sciences.

David-Ferdon, C., & Kaslow, N. (2008). Evidence-based psychosocial treatments for child and adolescent depression. *Journal of Clinical Child and Adolescent Psychology, 37,* 62–104.

Diamond, G., Panichelli-Mindel, S., Shera, D., Dennis, M., Tims, F., & Ungemack, J. (2006). Psychiatric syndromes in adolescents with marijuana abuse and dependency in outpatient treatment. *Journal of Child and Adolescent Substance Abuse, 15,* 37–54.

Dumas, J. E. (1984). Child, adult-interactional, and socioeconomic setting events as predictors of parent training outcome. *Education and Treatment of Children, 7,* 351–363.

Emslie, G. J., Rush, A. J., Weinberg, W. A., Kowatch, R. A., Carmody, T., & Mayes, T. L. (1998). Fluoxetine in child and adolescent depression: Acute and maintenance treatment. *Depression and Anxiety, 7,* 32–39.

Eyberg, S. M., Nelson, M. M., & Boggs, S. (2008). Evidence-based psychosocial treatments for children and adolescents with disruptive behavior. *Journal of Clinical Child and Adolescent Psychology, 37,* 215–237.

Farrell, L., & Barrett, P. (2006). Obsessive-compulsive disorder across developmental trajectory: Cognitive processing of threat in children, adolescents and adults. *British Journal of Psychology, 97,* 95–114.

Finkelstein, J. W., Susman, E. J., Chinchilli, V. M., Kunselman, S. J., D'Arcangelo, M. R., Schwab, J., et al. (1997). Estrogen or testosterone increases self-reported aggressive behavior in hypogonadal adolescents. *Journal of Clinical Endocrinology and Metabolism, 82,* 2423–2438.

Flannery-Schroeder, E., Suveg, C., Safford, S., Kendall, P. C., & Webb, A. (2004). Comorbid externalizing disorders and child anxiety treatment outcomes. *Behavior Change, 21,* 14–25.

Fleischman, M. J. (1981). A replication of Patterson's "Intervention for boys with conduct problems." *Journal of Consulting and Clinical Psychology, 49,* 342–351.

Fristad, M. A., & Goldberg-Arnold, J. S. (2003). Family interventions for early-onset bipolar disorder. In B. Geller & M. P. DelBello (Eds.), *Bipolar disorder in childhood and early adolescence* (pp. 295–313). New York: Guilford Press.

Guy, W. (1976). *Clinical global improvement scale: Assessment manual of psychopharmacology*. Rockville, MD: National Institute of Mental Health.

Hare, T. A., Tottenham, N. A., Galvan, A., Voss, H., Glover, G. H., & Casey, B. J. (2008). Biological substrates of emotional reactivity and regulation in adolescence during an emotional go-no go task. *Biological Psychiatry, 63,* 927–934.

Hawley, K. M., & Weisz, J. M. (2005). Youth versus parent working alliance in usual clinical care: Distinctive associations with retention, satisfaction, and treatment outcome. *Journal of Clinical Child and Adolescent Psychology, 34,* 117–128.

Henggeler, S. W., & Lee, T. W. (2003). Multisystemic treatment of serious clinical problems. In Kazdin, A. E. & Weisz, J. R. (Eds.), *Evidence-based psychotherapies for children and adolescents* (pp. 301–322). New York: Guilford Press.

Himle, J. A., Fischer, D. A., Van Etten, M. L., Janeck, A. S., & Hanna, G. L. (2003). Group behavioral therapy for adolescents with tic-related and non-tic-related obsessive-compulsive disorder. *Depression and Anxiety, 17,* 73–77.

Hogue, A., Dauber, S., Stambaugh, L. F., Cecero, J. J., & Liddle, H. A. (2006). Early therapeutic alliance and treatment outcome in individual and family therapy for adolescent behavior problems. *Journal of Consulting and Clinical Psychology, 74,* 121–129.

Holmbeck, G. N., Colder, C. N., Shapera, W., Westhoven, V., Kenealy, L., & Updegrove, A. (2000). Working with adolescents: Guides from developmental psychology. In P. C. Kendall (Ed.), *Child and adolescent therapy: Cognitive-behavioral procedures* (3rd ed., pp. 334–385). New York: Guilford Press.

Holmbeck, G. N., Friedman, D. N., Abad, M., & Jandasek, B. (2006). Development and psychopathology in adolescence. In D. A. Wolfe & E. J. Mash (Eds.), *Behavioral and emotional disorders in adolescents: Nature, assessment, and treatment* (pp. 21–55). New York: Guilford Press.

Holmbeck, G. N., O'Mahar, K. N., Abad, M., Colder, C. N., & Updegrove, A. (2006). Cognitive-behavioral therapy with adolescents: Guides from developmental psychology. In P. C. Kendall (Ed.), *Child and adolescent therapy: Cognitive-behavioral procedures* (3rd ed., pp. 419–464). New York: Guilford Press.

Hughes, A. A., & Kendall, P. C. (2007). Prediction of cognitive behavior treatment outcome for children with anxiety disorders: Therapeutic relationship and homework compliance. *Behavioral and Cognitive Psychotherapy, 35,* 487–494.

Jaffe, M. L. (1998). *Adolescence*. New York: Wiley.

Jayson, D., Wood, A., Kroll, L., Fraser, J., & Harrington, R. (1998). Which depressed patients respond to cognitive-behavioral treatment? *Journal of the American Academy of Child and Adolescent Psychiatry, 37,* 35–39.

Karver, M. S., Handelsman, J. S., Fields, S., & Bickman, L. (2006). Meta-analysis of therapeutic relationship variables in youth and family therapy: The evidence for different relationship variables in the child and adolescent treatment outcome literature. *Clinical Psychology Review, 26,* 50–65.

Kazdin, A. E., Bass, D. E., Ayers, W., & Rodgers, A. (1990). Empirical and clinical focus of child and adolescent psychotherapy research. *Journal of Consulting and Clinical Psychology, 58,* 729–740.

Kazdin, A. E., Whitley, M. E., & Marciano, P. (2006). Child– and parent–therapist alliance and therapeutic change in the treatment of children referred for oppositional, aggressive, and antisocial behavior. *Journal of Child Psychology and Psychiatry and Allied Disciplines, 47,* 436–445.

Keeley, M. L., Storch, E. L., Merlo, L., & Geffken, J. R. (2008). Clinical predictors of response to cognitive-behavioral therapy for obsessive-compulsive disorder. *Clinical Psychology Review, 28,* 118–130.

Kendall, P. C. (1984). Cognitive-behavioral self-control therapy for children. *Journal of Child Psychology and Psychiatry and Allied Disciplines, 25,* 173–179.

Kendall, P.C. (1994). Treating anxiety disorders in children: Results of a randomized clinical trial. *Journal of Consulting and Clinical Psychology, 62,* 100–110.

Kendall, P.C. (2002). Toward a research-practice-community partnership: Goin' fishing and showing slides. *Clinical Psychology: Science and Practice, 9,* 214–216.

Kendall, P. C., Brady, E. C., & Verduin, T. (2001). Comorbidity in childhood anxiety disorders and treatment outcome. *Journal of the American Academy of Child and Adolescent Psychiatry, 40,* 787–794.

Kendall, P. C., Flannery-Schroeder, E., Panichelli-Mindel, S. M., Southam-Gerow, M., Henin, A., & Warman, M. (1997). Therapy for youths with anxiety disorders: A second randomized clinical trial. *Journal of Consulting and Clinical Psychology, 65,* 366–380.

Kendall, P. C., Hudson, J. L., Choudhury, M., Webb, A., & Pimental, S. (2005). Cognitive-behavioral treatment for childhood anxiety disorders. In E. D. Hibbs & P. S. Jensen (Eds.), *Psychosocial treatments for child and adolescent disorders: Empirically based strategies for clinical practice* (2nd ed., pp. 47–73). Washington, DC: American Psychological Association.

Kendall, P. C., & Southam-Gerow, M. A (1996). Long-term follow-up of a cognitive-behavioral therapy for anxiety-disordered youth. *Journal of Consulting and Clinical Psychology, 64,* 724–730.

Kendall, P. C., & Suveg, C. C. (2006). Treating anxiety disorders in youth. In P. C. Kendall (Ed.), *Child and adolescent therapy: Cognitive-behavioral procedures* (3rd ed., pp. 243–294). New York: Guilford Press.

Kendall, P. C., & Treadwell, K. C. (2007). The role of self-statements as a mediator in treatment for youth with anxiety disorders. *Journal of Consulting and Clinical Psychology, 75,* 380–389.

Larson, R. W., Richards, M. W., Moneta, G., Holmbeck, G., & Duckett, E. (1996). Changes in adolescents' daily interactions with their families from ages 10 to 18: Disengagement and transformation. *Developmental Psychology, 32,* 744–754.

Layne, A. E., Bernstein, G. A., Egan, E. A., & Kushner, M. G. (2003). Predictors of treatment response in anxious-depressed adolescents with school refusal. *Journal of the American Academy of Child and Adolescent Psychiatry, 42*, 319–326.

March, J. S., Frances, A., Carpenter, D., & Kahn, D. (1997). Expert consensus guidelines: Treatment of obsessive-compulsive disorder. *Journal of Clinical Psychology, 58*, (Suppl. 4).

March, J. S., Mulle, K. S., & Herbel, B. (1994). Behavioral psychotherapy for children and adolescents with obsessive-compulsive disorder: An open trial of a new protocol-driven treatment package. *Journal of the American Academy of Child and Adolescent Psychiatry, 33*, 333–341.

McKay, M. M., McCadam, K. M., & Gonzales, J. (1996). Addressing the barriers to mental health services for inner city children and their caretakers. *Community Mental Health Journal, 32*, 353–361.

Mendle, J., Turkheimer, E., & Emery, R. (2007). Detrimental psychological outcomes associated with early pubertal timing in adolescent girls. *Developmental Review, 27*, 151–171.

Miklowitz, D. J. (2008). Bipolar disorder. In D. H. Barlow (Ed.), *Clinical handbook of psychological disorders: A step-by-step treatment manual* (4th ed., pp. 421–462). New York: Guilford Press.

Miklowitz, D. J., Otto, M. J., Frank, E., Reilly-Harrington, N. A., Kogan, J. N., Sachs, G. S., et al. (2007). Intensive psychosocial intervention enhances functioning in patients with bipolar depression: Results from a 9-month randomized controlled trial. *American Journal of Psychiatry, 164*, 1340–1347.

Moffitt, C. E., Chorpita, B. E., & Fernandez, S. (2003). Intensive cognitive-behavioral treatment of school refusal behavior. *Cognitive and Behavioral Practice, 10*, 51–60.

Mufson, L., Dorta, K., Wickramaratne, P., Nomura, Y., Olfson, M., & Weissman, M. M. (2004). A randomized effectiveness trial of interpersonal psychotherapy for depressed adolescents. *Archives of General Psychiatry, 61*, 577–584.

Mufson, L., Weissman, M., Moreau, D., & Garfinkel, R. (1999). Efficacy of interpersonal psychotherapy for depressed adolescents. *Archives of General Psychiatry, 56*, 573–579.

Muris, P., Merckelbach, H., Holdrinet, I., & Sijsenaar, M. (1998). Treating phobic children: Effects of EMDR versus exposure. *Journal of Consulting and Clinical Psychology, 66*, 193–198.

Nathan, P. E., & Gorman, J. E. (2002). *A guide to treatments that work* (2nd ed.). New York: Oxford University Press.

Oetzel, K. B., & Scherer, D. B. (2003). Therapeutic engagement with adolescents in psychotherapy. *Psychotherapy: Theory, Research and Practice, 40*, 215–225.

Parker, J. G., & Asher, S. G. (1987). Peer relations and later personal adjustment: Are low-accepted children at risk? *Psychological Bulletin, 102*, 357–389.

Patterson, G. R., & Chamberlain, P. (1994). A functional analysis of resistance during parent training therapy. *Clinical Psychology, 1*, 53–70.

Patterson, G. R., & Forgatch, M. S. (1995). Predicting future clinical adjustment from treatment outcome and process variables. *Psychological Assessment, 7*(3), 275-285.

Pediatric OCD Treatment Study [POTS] Team. (2004). Cognitive-behavior therapy, sertraline, and their combination for children and adolescents with obsessive-compulsive disorder. *Journal of the American Medical Association, 292*, 1969–1976.

Pekarik, G., & Stephenson, L. (1988). Adult and child client differences in therapy dropout research. *Journal of Clinical Child Psychology, 17,* 316–321.

Pelham, W. E., & Fabiano, G. E. (2008). Evidence-based psychosocial treatments for attention-deficit/hyperactivity disorder. *Journal of Clinical Child and Adolescent Psychology, 37,* 184–214.

Pelham, W. E., & Hoza, B. E. (1996). Intensive treatment: A summer treatment program for children with ADHD. In E. D. Hibbs & P. S. Jensen (Eds.), *Psychosocial treatments for child and adolescent disorders: Empirically based strategies for clinical practice* (pp. 311–340). Washington, DC: American Psychological Association.

Peris, T. S., Bergman, R. L., Langley, A., Chang, S., McCracken, J. T., & Piacentini, J. (2008). Correlates of family accommodation of childhood obsessive-compulsive disorder: Parent, child, and family characteristics. *Journal of the American Academy of Child and Adolescent Psychiatry, 47,* 1173–1181.

Piacentini, J., & Bergman, R. (2001). Developmental issues in cognitive therapy for childhood anxiety disorders. *Journal of Cognitive Psychotherapy, 15,* 165–182.

Piacentini, J., Bergman, R. L., Jacobs, C., McCracken, J., & Kretchman, J. (2002). Cognitive-behavior therapy for childhood obsessive-compulsive disorder: Efficacy and predictors of treatment response. *Journal of Anxiety Disorders, 16,* 207–219.

Rapee, R. M., Abbott, M. M., & Lyneham, H. (2006). Bibliotherapy for children with anxiety disorders using written materials for parents: A randomized controlled trial. *Journal of Consulting and Clinical Psychology, 74,* 436–444.

Reinecke, M. A., Ryan, N. A., & DuBois, D. (1998). Cognitive-behavioral therapy of depression and depressive symptoms during adolescence: A review and meta-analysis. *Journal of the American Academy of Child and Adolescent Psychiatry, 37,* 26–34.

Rohde, P., Clarke, G., Lewinsohn, P., Seeley, J. R., & Kaufman, N. K. (2001). Impact of comorbidity on a cognitive-behavioral group treatment for adolescent depression. *Journal of the American Academy of Child and Adolescent Psychiatry, 40,* 795–802.

Rohde, P., Clarke, G., Mace, D., Jorgensen, J. S., & Seeley, J. R. (2004). An efficacy/effectiveness study of cognitive-behavioral treatment for adolescents with comorbid major depression and conduct disorder. *Journal of the American Academy of Child and Adolescent Psychiatry, 43,* 660–668.

Russell, R. L., & Shirk, S. L. (1998). Child psychotherapy process research. *Advances in Clinical Child Psychology, 20,* 93–124.

Scahill, L., Vitulano, L. A., Brenner, E. M., Lynch, K. A., & King, R. A. (1996). Behavioral therapy in children and adolescents with obsessive-compulsive disorder: A pilot study. *Journal of Child and Adolescent Psychopharmacology, 6,* 191–202.

Shelef, K., Diamond, G. M., Diamond, G. S., & Liddle, H. A. (2005). Adolescent and parent alliance and treatment outcome in multidimensional family therapy. *Journal of Consulting and Clinical Psychology, 73,* 689–698.

Shirk, S. R. (1999). Developmental therapy. In W. K. Silverman & T. H. Ollendick (Eds.), *Developmental issues in the clinical treatment of children* (pp. 60–73). Boston: Allyn & Bacon.

Shirk, S. R., & Karver, M. R. (2003). Prediction of treatment outcome from relationship variables in child and adolescent therapy: A meta-analytic review. *Journal of Consulting and Clinical Psychology, 71,* 452–464.

Shirk, S. R., & Saiz, C. R. (1992). Clinical, empirical, and developmental perspectives on the therapeutic relationship in child psychotherapy. *Development and Psychopathology, 4*, 713–728.

Shortt, A. L., Barrett, P. L., Dadds, M., & Fox, T. L. (2001). The influence of family and experimental context on cognition in anxious children. *Journal of Abnormal Child Psychology, 29*, 585–598.

Silverman, W. K., & Albano, A. M. (1996). *Anxiety Disorders Interview Schedule for DSM-IV: Parent version.* San Antonio, TX: Graywing.

Silverman, W. K., & Hinshaw, S. P. (2008). The second special issue on evidence-based psychosocial treatments for children and adolescents: A 10-year update. *Journal of Clinical Child & Adolescent Psychology, 37*, 1–7.

Silverman, W. K., Kurtines, W. K., Ginsburg, G. S., Weems, C. F., Lumpkin, P. W., & Carmichael, D. H. (1999). Treating anxiety disorders in children with group cognitive-behavioral therapy: A randomized clinical trial. *Journal of Consulting and Clinical Psychology, 67*, 995–1003.

Silverman, W. K., Pina, A. K., & Viswesvaran, C. (2008). Evidence-based psychosocial treatments for phobic and anxiety disorders in children and adolescents. *Journal of Clinical Child and Adolescent Psychology, 37*, 105–130.

Souery, D., Amsterdam, J., de Montigny C., Lecrubier Y., Montgomery, S., Lipp, O., Racagni, G., Zohar, J., & Mendlewicz, J. (1999). Treatment resistant depression: Methodological overview and operational criteria. *European Neuropsychopharmacology, 9*, 83–91.

Southam-Gerow, M. A., Kendall, P. C., & Weersing, V. R. (2001). Examining outcome variability: Correlates of treatment response in a child and adolescent anxiety clinic. *Journal of Clinical Child Psychology, 30*, 422–436.

Steinberg, L. (2005). Cognitive and affective development in adolescence. *Trends in Cognitive Sciences, 9*, 69–74.

Steinberg, L., & Morris, A. (2001). Adolescent development. *Annual Review of Psychology, 52*, 83–110.

Storch, E. A., Geffken, G. R., Merlo, L. J., Mann, G., Duke, D., Munson, M., et al. (2007). Family-based cognitive-behavioral therapy for pediatric obsessive-compulsive disorder: Comparisons of intensive and weekly approaches. *Journal of the American Academy of Child and Adolescent Psychiatry, 46*, 469–478.

Storch, E. A., Merlo, L. J., Larson, M. J., Geffken, G. R., Lehmkuhl, H. D., Jacob, M. L., et al. (2008). Impact of comorbidity on cognitive-behavioral therapy response in pediatric obsessive-compulsive disorder. *Journal of the American Academy of Child and Adolescent Psychiatry, 47*, 583–592.

Storch, E. A., Murphy, T. A., Geffken, G. R., Mann, G., Adkins, J., Merlo, L. J., et al. (2006). Cognitive-behavioral therapy for PANDAS-related obsessive-compulsive disorder: Findings from a preliminary waitlist controlled open trial. *Journal of the American Academy of Child and Adolescent Psychiatry, 45*, 1171–1178.

Thase, M. E. (2003). Therapeutic alternatives for difficult-to-treat depression: A narrative review of the state of the evidence. *CNS Spectrums, 9*, 808–821.

Treadwell, K. R., & Kendall, P. R. (1996). Self-talk in youth with anxiety disorders: States of mind, content specificity, and treatment outcome. *Journal of Consulting and Clinical Psychology, 64*, 941–950.

Treatment for Adolescent Depression Study (TADS) Team. (2004). Fluoxetine, cognitive-behavioral therapy, and their combination for adolescents with depression: Treatment for Adolescents with Depression Study (TADS) randomized controlled trial. *Journal of the American Medical Association, 292,* 807–820.

Walkup, J., Albano, A. M., Birmaher, B., Kendall, P., March, J., Piacentini, J., Compton, S., & Sherrill, J. (2008, May). *Child/Adolescent Anxiety Multimodal Study (CAMS): Acute phase efficacy and safety results.* Presented at NIMH New Clinical Drug Evaluation Unit (NCDEU) Conference, Phoenix, AZ.

Weersing, V. R., & Brent, D. A. (2006). Cognitive behavioral therapy for depression in youth. *Child and Adolescent Psychiatric Clinics of North America, 15,* 939–957.

Weisz, J. R., Donenberg, G. R., Han, S. S., & Weiss, B. (1995). Bridging the gap between laboratory and clinic in child and adolescent psychotherapy. *Journal of Consulting and Clinial Psychology, 63,* 688–701.

Weisz, J. R., & Hawley, K. R. (2002). Developmental factors in the treatment on adolescents. *Journal of Consulting and Clinical Psychology, 70,* 21–43.

Weisz, J. R., Jensen-Doss, A., & Hawkley, K. M. (2006). Evidence-based youth psychotherapies versus usual clinical care: A meta-analysis of direct comparisons. *American Psychologist, 61,* 671–689.

Weisz, J. R., McCarty, C. A., & Valeri, S. M. (2006). Effects of psychotherapy for depression in children and adolescents: A meta-analysis. *Psychological Bulletin, 132,* 132–149.

Weisz, J.R., Weiss, B., Alicke, M.D., & Klotz, M.L. (1987). Effectiveness of psychotherapy with children and adolescents: A meta-analysis for clinicians. *Journal of Consulting and Clinical Psychology, 55,* 542–549.

Whiteside, S. P., Brown, A. P., & Abramowitz, J. (2008). Five-day intensive treatment for adolescent OCD: A case series. *Journal of Anxiety Disorders, 22,* 495–504.

Internalizing Disorders

PART II

4

Obsessive-Compulsive Disorder in Children and Adolescents: Treating Difficult Cases

DEAN McKAY, ERIC A. STORCH, BRETT NELSON, MIGUEL MORALES, AND MELANIE W. MORETZ

Once considered rare among children and adolescents, pediatric obsessive-compulsive disorder (OCD) is now recognized as one of the most common childhood psychiatric illnesses. Estimates suggest that between 1% and 3% of youth meet diagnostic criteria for OCD at any given time (Douglass, Moffitt, Dar, McGee, & Silva, 1995; Rapoport & Inoff-Germain, 2000; Valleni-Basile et al., 1994; Zohar, 1999). Most patients with OCD initially experience symptoms during childhood (DeVeaugh-Geiss et al., 1992) and, without treatment, endure a protracted yet fluctuating clinical course (Murphy et al., 2004). The symptoms of OCD are quite debilitating (Piacentini, Bergman, Keller, & McCracken, 2003) to both the affected patient and his or her family.

As in adults, pediatric OCD is heterogeneous in clinical presentation, with many patients experiencing multiple obsessions and compulsions at a given time (Leonard, Goldberger, Rapoport, Cheslow, & Swedo et al., 1990; Rettew, Swedo, Leonard, Lenane, & Rapoport, 1992). Common obsessions (i.e., repetitive thoughts, images, or impulses that are distressing to the person, difficult to control, and recognized as irrational [at least to a degree]) include contamination fears; worries about harm to self or others; the need for symmetry, exactness, and order; religious/moralistic concerns; forbidden thoughts (e.g., sexual or aggressive); or desires to collect unneeded items. Common compulsions (i.e., repetitive overt or mental behaviors that are linked to obsessional anxiety and serve to reduce associated distress/anxiety or the chance of a feared outcome taking place) include washing and cleaning rituals, checking, counting, repeating, straightening, confessing, praying, reassurance seeking, touching, tapping or rubbing, hoarding, and avoidance (Swedo, Rapoport, Leonard, Lenane, & Cheslow, 1989). The distinct and varied presentation of OCD often makes accurate diagnosis challenging and symptoms are often mistaken for other forms of psychopathology (e.g., a person with harm obsessions is considered homicidal).

ETIOLOGY

Biological Model

Several biological models of OCD have been advanced. Evidence has accumulated for dysfunction in brain structure, neurochemistry, and neurocircuitry. These models have all led to specific pharmacological approaches that have been promising in the treatment of OCD.

Neurobiology of OCD

Well-researched cortical and subcortical circuits deliver sensory and motor information via the striatum and thalamus to and from the prefrontal cortex for processing (Alexander, DeLong, & Strick, 1986). There is growing evidence to implicate anatomical and functional abnormalities in these regions as the neurobiological basis for OCD (Baxter et al., 1988; Rauch et al., 1997; Saxena, Brody, Schwartz, & Baxter, 1998). It has been theorized that abnormal gating of sensory information from the cortex by the basal ganglia produces an abnormal cortico–striatal–thalamic–cortical circuit and thus obsessive-compulsive symptoms (Rauch et al., 1997; Rosenberg, Keshevan, O'Hearn, et al., 1997; Szeszko, MacMillan, McMeniman, Chen, et al., 2004) (see Figure 4.1). Historically, the research regarding the neurobiological pathology of OCD in the pediatric population has been an extension of the adult literature. Researchers are now focusing more on children and adoles-

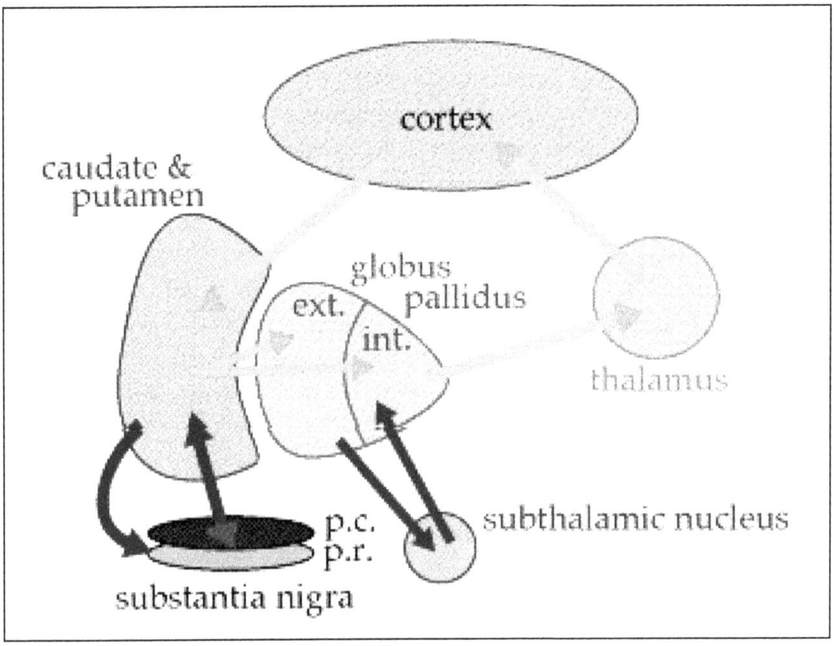

Figure 4.1 Basal ganglia and cerebellum.
Adapted from Molavi, D. (1997). *Basal ganglia and cerebrum.* http://thalamus.wustl.edu/course

cents as most OCD patients have had a pediatric presentation of obsessive-compulsive symptoms (King, Leonard, & March, 1998).

Numerous reports have supported the cortical/subcortical circuitry malfunction theory of formation and propagation of OCD in adults. A meta-analysis of functional neuroimaging studies identified abnormally functioning areas of the orbitofrontal cortex, anterior cingulate, caudate, striatum, and thalamus in adults with OCD (Saxena & Rauch, 2000). Specific abnormalities in these areas identified in a further meta-analysis included the head of the caudate nucleus as well as the orbital gyrus (Whiteside, Port, & Abramowitz, 2004).

Abnormally functioning cortical and subcortical regions in adult brains with OCD have been correlated with different phenotypic expressions of OCD symptoms (Mataix-Cols et al., 2004). It was shown by functional magnetic resonance imaging (fMRI) in one study that washing- and hoarding-related symptoms appear to have the most CNS activation in the ventromedial prefrontal cortex and paralimbic regions.

Patients with primarily checking-related symptoms exhibited increased activation in the dorsolateral prefrontal cortex, thalamus, and striatum. Symptom severity was noted to directly correlate with the degree of cerebral activation (Mataix-Cols et al., 2004).

One piece of evidence supporting the malfunctioning of cortico–striatal–thalamic–cortical circuitry in children with OCD includes the differences in volume measurements of the thalamus, the primary center for the handling of sensory and motor information for the cerebral cortex (Gilbert et al., 2000) (see Figure 4.2). In a study of 56 psychotropic-naive children and adolescents with OCD, thalamic volumes were measured by MRI. Paroxetine was prescribed to 28 subjects with the others receiving placebo. There was a significant reduction in thalamic volume noted in the subjects taking paroxetine after 12 weeks. The increased thalamic volume in psychotropic-naive children with OCD was concluded to be parallel to the abnormalities seen in the functional imaging of the thalamus of adult patients (Gilbert et al., 2000).

Numerous other neurobiological abnormalities have been described in pediatric OCD patients. These include decreased pituitary volumes (MacMaster et al., 2006), enlarged left amygdala volumes (Szeszko et al., 2004), and increased volume and myelination in the corpus callosum (MacMaster, Keshavan, Dick, & Rosenberg, 1999; Rosenberg et al., 1997). An fMRI study by Viard and colleagues (2005) evaluated cerebral activation in response to repetitive visual stimuli in 12 children with OCD and compared them to healthy controls. Subjects with OCD displayed more metabolic activity in the anterior cingulate cortex and left parietal lobe (Viard et al., 2005). Patients with OCD who were unable to resist obsessions using cognitive techniques had increased activity in the bilateral precuneus, pulvinar, and paracentral lobules (Viard et al., 2005). When the cortical–striatal–thalamic–cortical circuits do not function properly in children, the precuneus regions of the parietal lobe, the pulvinar nucleus of the thalamus, and the paracentral lobules of the superior frontal gyrus apparently attempt to compensate (Viard et al., 2005). Finally, the density of cerebral gray matter structures are altered in children with OCD as reduced gray matter density was present in the left anterior cingulate cortex and bilateral medial superior frontal gyrus, whereas increased gray matter density was noted in the right putamen (Gilbert et al., 2008).

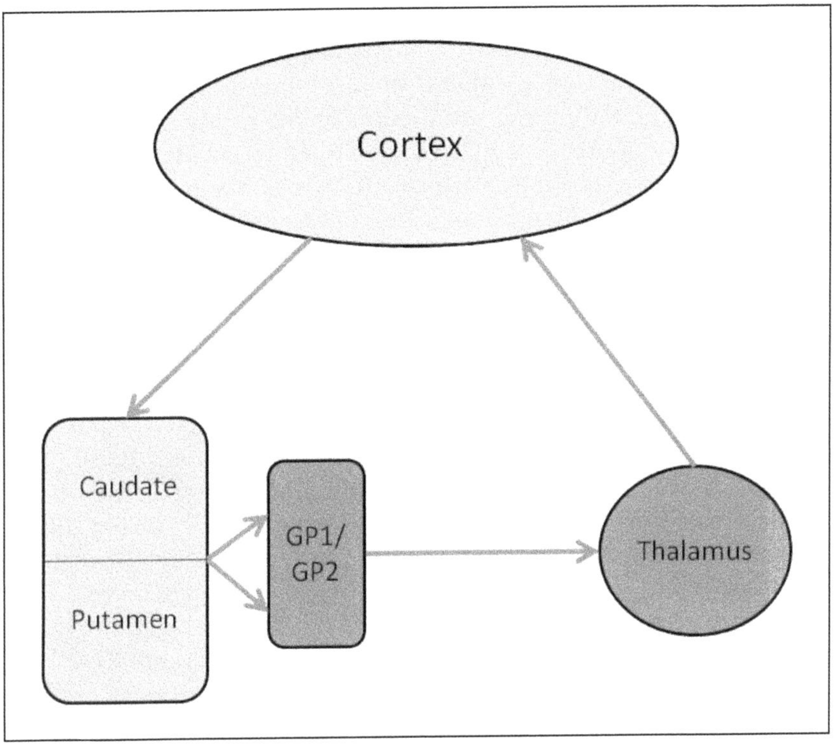

Figure 4.2 Cortical–striatal–thalamic–cortical circuit.

Neurochemistry of OCD

Abnormally functioning serotonin, dopamine, and glutamate neurotransmitter systems have been implicated in the neurochemistry of OCD (Grados & Riddle, 2001). Serotonin plays a key role in the pathology of OCD and this is empirically evident when considering the effectiveness of serotonin reuptake inhibitors in the treatment of OCD (King, Leonard, & March, 1998). Several studies have indicated that a decreased amount of available serotonin transporter proteins (5-HTTT) exist in subjects with OCD (Goddard, Shekhar, Whiteman, & McDougle, 2008). One study using single photon emission computed tomography (SPECT) imaging showed decreased availability of 5-HTTT in the thalamus, hypothalamus, midbrain, and brainstem of patients with OCD (Hesse et al., 2005). Serotonin reuptake inhibitors (SRIs) are associated with improved symptoms of OCD through the mechanism of increasing the available amount of serotonin in the synaptic cleft and then by stimulating the production of these serotonin transport proteins there (Goddard et al., 2008). Other recent data supporting serotonin's role in the formation of OCD includes mixed results in genetic studies showing a complicated connection between 5-HTTT, HT2A, and 5-HT1D gene mutations and OCD symptoms (Denys, Van-Nieuwerburgh, Deforce, & Westenberg, 2006; Grados, Walkup, & Walford, 2003). As stated, changes are observed in the gross morphology of key cerebral structures in patients with OCD after treatment with SRIs. This suggests that altering cerebral serotonin transmission in patients with OCD leads to altered cerebral morphology, which usually correlates with symptomatic improvement (Gilbert et al., 2000).

The regulatory system of dopamine has been implicated in the production of OCD. OCD symptoms are often worsened with the administration of dopamine agonists such as psychostimulant medication used to treat attention-deficit/hyperactivity disorder (ADHD) or certain disorders of arousal (Goddard et al., 2008). On the other side, dopamine transmission inhibitors such as antipsychotic medications have been shown to be effective as augmentating agents in treatment-resistant OCD (Bloch et al., 2006). A recent SPECT study has also shown altered availability of dopamine transport proteins in patients with OCD in important sections of the basal ganglia (Hesse et al., 2005).

Glutamate hyperactivity has been proposed as a potential factor in the production of OCD symptoms. This theory is supported by the fact that glutamate levels are elevated in the cerebrospinal fluid of patients with untreated OCD (Chakrabarty, Bhattacharyya, Christopher, & Khanna, 2005). Excessive glutaminergic activity found by magnetic resonance spectroscopy in the prefrontal cortex, striatum, and thalamus has been suggested as evidence supporting this theory as well (Whiteside, Port, Deacon, & Abramowitz, 2006). In studies on children with OCD, Rosenberg (Rosenberg et al., 2000, 2004) has described altered glutamate concentrations in the caudate and anterior cingulated gyrus in these children.

Pharmacological Approaches

There are limited double-blind, placebo-controlled studies to guide the pharmacological management of treatment-resistant OCD in adolescents. Few studies have yet to even evaluate the differential efficacy of the first-line agents used in this population (Geller et al., 2003). Obsessive-compulsive disorder in adolescents is generally categorized as treatment-resistant using the same standard as in adults, which is a failure of two adequate trials of a serotonin reuptake inhibitor (Goodman, McDougle, Barr, Aronson, & Price, 1993). An adequate trial consists of a maximal dose (or highest tolerated dose) for 10 to 12 weeks, which includes consideration of the child's weight and tolerance (American Academy of Child and Adolescent Psychiatry [AACAP], 1998; Goodman et al., 1993). After two adequate SRI trials, as many as 60% of patients fail to have a satisfactory response (Goodman et al., 1993; Hollander et al., 2002; March, Frances, Carpenter, & Kahn, 1997). Further, symptom remission with SRI monotherapy is quite rare, occurring in only about 20% of instances (Pediatric OCD Treatment Study [POTS], 2004). Though a number of adult studies exist (see Bloch et al., 2006, for a review) that address treatment-resistant OCD, the literature in pediatric OCD lags substantially. Given this, findings from adults must be extrapolated to this younger population.

Limited data exists to guide the choice of an initial agent to treat pediatric OCD. Of the SRIs (i.e., clomipramine, citalopram, fluoxetine, fluvoxamine, paroxetine, and sertraline), clomipramine is used as a second-line agent, given its higher side-effect profile and greater toxicity in overdose (DeVeaugh-Geiss et al., 1992; Stoner et al., 1997). Though few if any rigorous studies exist comparing the efficacy of the SSRIs in adolescents, a meta-analysis indicates that the SSRIs (fluoxetine, fluvoxamine, paroxetine, and sertraline) are comparably effective (Geller et al., 2003). Furthermore, as with several meta-analytic reviews in the adult literature (Ackerman & Greenland, 2002; Piccinelli, Pini, Bellantuono, & Wilkinson, 1995), this analysis shows that clomipramine has superior efficacy when compared to the SSRIs (Geller et al., 2003). Of the SRIs, only four have U.S. Food and Drug Administration (FDA) approval for treatment of OCD in the pediatric population: clomipramine for children beginning at age 10 (DeVeaugh-Geiss et al., 1992), fluoxetine for children beginning at age 7 (Geller et al., 2001), fluvoxamine beginning at age 8 (Riddle et al., 2001), and sertraline beginning at age 6 (March et al., 1998; POTS, 2004). There are limited studies of citalopram in the adolescent population (Grados, Scahill, & Riddle, 1999). Paroxetine does not have any FDA indication for those younger than age 18. Furthermore, along with carrying a black box warning since 2004 (as do all antidepressants), paroxetine has the highest risk ratio among the SSRIs for suicidal behavior (FDA, 2004a, 2004b). Venlafaxine, a combined serotonergic and noradrenergic reuptake blocker, has no FDA indications in the pediatric population and shows an increase in both suicidal behavior and suicidal ideations (FDA, 2004a, 2004b). The use of either paroxetine or venlafaxine in the pediatric population must therefore be undertaken with explicit consent, extremely close monitoring, and only after the patient has not responded to other appropriate treatment options.

Dose-response data for treatment of OCD in adolescents is limited. Clinic consensus and extrapolation from the adult data has guided treatment. Fixed-dose studies in adults have demonstrated a response to lower doses than those used in multicenter trials (Greist et al., 1995; Tollefson et al., 1994). Of note is that the results of some adult studies suggest that higher SSRI doses correlate with a higher response rate and greater symptom relief. For example, an adult fluoxetine trial showed response at 13 weeks, with a mean decrease in Yale-Brown Obsessive-Compulsive Scale (Y-BOCS; Goodman, Price Rasmussen, & Mazure, 1989) score of 32% (3.4 points) at a 20-mg daily dose, 32% (4.6 points) at a 40-mg daily dose, and 35% (5.9 points) at a 60-mg daily dose (Tollefson et al., 1994). Similar results were seen with sertraline, paroxetine, and citalopram (Greist et al., 1995; Hollander et al., 2003; Montgomery et al., 2001). See Table 4.1 for SRI dosing guidelines (Clinical Pharmacology, 2008; Grados et al., 1999).

Augmentation of Nonresponse or Partial Response

Once a pediatric patient has not responded to an adequate trial of two SRIs, treatment options are guided by a limited number of studies in treatment-resistant adolescents and a limited but larger number of studies in treatment-resistant adults. A case series of 17 treatment-resistant adolescents, whose SSRI treatment regimen was augmented with risperidone 1–2 mg daily over a 12-week period, shows some promise that risperidone may be an effective augmentation agent (Thomsen, 2004) ($\text{Y-BOCS}_{\text{Baseline}} = 24.2 \pm 2.6$, $\text{Y-BOCS}_{\text{Posttreatment}} = 19.9 \pm 2.9$).

Much of the evidence base on augmentation is derived from double-blind, placebo-controlled adult studies (Bystritsky et al., 2004; Denys, de Geus, van Megen, & Westenberg, 2004; McDougle, Epperson, Pelton,

Wasylink, & Price, 2000). One olanzapine trial showed a Y-BOCS reduction in the intent-to-treat (ITT) group versus placebo of 17% versus 2%, with 46% of the olanzapine patients showing a 25% reduction in symptoms (Bystritsky et al., 2004). One quetiapine trial showed a Y-BOCS reduction in the ITT group versus placebo of 32% versus 7%, with 40% of quetiapine patients showing a 35% reduction in symptoms (Denys et al., 2004). One risperidone trial showed a Y-BOCS reduction in the ITT group versus placebo of 27.4 ±5.4 to 18.7 ±8.3 (31.8%) versus 27.6 ±3.7 to 25.0 ±4.4 (9%), with 45% of risperidone patients showing a 35% reduction in symptoms (McDougle et al., 2000).

A number of other agents or approaches have limited data in adults but have yet to be systematically investigated in youngsters. These include intravenous (IV) clomipramine, augmentation of an SSRI with clomipramine, venlafaxine, monoamine oxidase inhibitors (i.e., phenelzine), bupropion, mirtazapine, haloperidol, aripiprazole, ziprasidone, pindolol (beta-blocker and 5-HT_{1A} presynaptic receptor antagonist), alprazolam, clonazepam, buspirone, inositol (precursor in phosphatidylinositol cycle), lithium, carbamazepine, topiramate, riluzole, oral morphine, and D-amphetamine (Koran et al., 2007). There have been numerous open trials examining individual and combined psychopharmacological agents. Although it is beyond the scope of this chapter to review all the results of these medication trials, there has been no single medication with clearly superior efficacy in reducing symptoms.

Summary of Medication Approaches for the Treatment-Resistant Adolescent

Limited treatment strategies exist for adolescents after failure of two SRIs. Further treatment strategies should consider comorbid diagnosis and what part the symptoms and possibly their treatment may play in the current therapy of the patient. If the patient has not responded successfully to two of the approved SSRIs, she or he is unlikely to respond to a trial of the third. If a trial of clomipramine was not initially implemented, then its use may be appropriate, after considering the greater side-effect profile. Though both typical and atypical antipsychotics have shown benefit, the atypicals should likely be favored secondary to a safer side-effect profile; risperidone and possibly aripiprazole are most likely to show benefit. A combination of clomipramine and an

Table 4.1

DOSE RANGES FOR SRIs IN CHILDREN AND ADOLESCENTS WITH OBSESSIVE-COMPULSIVE DISORDER

DRUG	STARTING DOSE (MG)	TYPICAL DOSE	CHILD/ADOLESCENT MAX FDA
Clomipramine	25	50-200	≥ 10 yo (smaller of) 3 mg/kg/day or 200 mg/day
Fluoxetine	5–10	5–50	≥ 7 yo 60 mg; younger/lower weight 20–30 mg
Fluvoxamine	12.5–25	50–200	8–11 yo 200 mg; adolescents 300 mg
Sertraline	12.5–25	50–200	≥ 6 yo 200 mg
Citalopram*	10	10–40	≥ 9 yo 40 mg (suggested)
Paroxetine*	10–20	10–40	≥ 8 yo 20–40 mg (suggested)

*Neither citalopram nor paroxetine has any pediatric FDA indication.

SSRI that will inhibit its metabolism, such as fluvoxamine, may be considered with close monitoring of the clomipramine level as the level may show a significant increase. If after other options have been exhausted, significant symptoms still remain, then agents with only limited support in children may be considered. These might include other atypical antipsychotics (olanzapine or quetiapine), typical antipsychotics (haloperidol), riluzole, mirtazapine or D-amphetamine.

Cognitive-Behavioral Model

Several decades ago, OCD was considered to be resistant to psychological treatment, as varied forms of psychotherapy (e.g., insight-oriented therapy, client-centered therapy, family therapy, or play therapy) showed little efficacy in decreasing symptoms, with some going as far as to suggest that clinicians should not treat these clients as they only worsen with intervention (Kringlen, 1965). A meta-analysis later confirmed that traditional psychotherapy tended to worsen symptoms

(Christensen, Hadzi-Pavlovic, Andrews, & Mattick, 1987), most likely by increasing doubting symptoms based on the functional relation between efforts at improving insight and methods at producing it. However, behavior therapy in and of itself is not adequate, as several traditional behavioral interventions also produce limited or nonresponse (i.e., relaxation training, thought stopping). Yet, with the introduction of exposure and response prevention (E/RP) to treat anxiety disorders in the 1960s and its expansion to OCD in the following decades (e.g., Foa & Kozak, 1986), it became apparent that E/RP is one effective manner of treating OCD. What follows is a synopsis of the cognitive-behavioral theory for the etiology and maintenance of OCD.

Behavioral Components

Exposure and response prevention is based on the premise that there is a functional relationship between obsessional anxiety and compulsive behavior. Fear and anxiety emerge when associations develop between neutral and aversive stimuli vis-à-vis classical conditioning processes. The neutral (conditioned) stimulus takes on the anxiety-producing qualities of the original aversive (unconditioned) stimulus. To contend with anxiety linked to the conditioned stimulus, patients with OCD engage in compulsive behavior or avoidance of anxiety-provoking stimuli to reduce distress and anxiety. Through this operant mechanism of negative reinforcement, ritualistic behavior is rewarded and strengthened, resulting in an increased likelihood of continued avoidant and ritualistic behavior.

Given this theoretical perspective, effective treatment (i.e., E/RP) involves progressive exposures to situations that elicit obsessional anxiety and associated rituals, while refraining from ritual engagement. When the patient endures the initial anxiety, the natural conditioning processes of anxiety habituation and fear extinction occur, which weaken the association between the conditioned stimulus and response. Empirically, E/RP has been shown to be the single most effective treatment for adult and pediatric OCD, with superiority relative to serotonergic medication and psychotherapeutic control conditions (e.g., Abramowitz, Whiteside, & Deacon, 2005; Foa et al., 2005).

Cognitive Components

Cognitive models of OCD highlight the role of dysfunctional beliefs and interpretations and normally occurring intrusive thoughts to understand the maintenance of obsessions and compulsions (Rachman, 1997; Salkovskis, 1985, 1989). It is thought that obsessive-compulsive symptoms arise from inaccurate beliefs about the potential dangers posed by stimuli, negative predictions about the outcomes of these situations, and doubt or uncertainty about one's actions (Salkovskis, 1996, 1999). When a person appraises an otherwise normally occurring thought (e.g., "This behavior is sinful") as highly meaningful (e.g., "This means I will not go to heaven"), distress ensues that motivates efforts to remove the intrusion (i.e., compulsions) and prevent the feared consequences from taking place. Paradoxically, such efforts increase the frequency of intrusions and associated anxiety, escalating the symptom into persistent and distressing clinical obsessions.

The cognitive model of OCD has become dominant in the treatment literature. Recent research has suggested that, in adults, cognitive interventions focusing on altering situational appraisals, particularly those involving inflated responsibility, show the greatest benefit (see, for example, Fama & Wilhelm, 2005). There are some notable limitations in this model as it applies to adults. First, it has recently been shown that OCD is largely comprised of subtypes (Abramowitz, McKay, & Taylor, 2008; McKay et al., 2004), which are heterogeneous among each other. Second, although responsibility appraisals are relevant for some individuals with OCD, there are also substantial proportions of sufferers who do not endorse significantly higher levels of the theoretically specific cognitions (Taylor et al., 2006). Third, the response among individuals with the various types of symptom presentation do not respond equally well to CBT specifically formulated for OCD (Abramowitz, Franklin, Schwartz, & Furr, 2003). And finally, although cognitive therapy has gained prominence in the literature as an acceptable and efficacious approach to treatment, the central therapeutic element remains exposure-based treatment, with the corresponding cognitive intervention "behavioral experiment" (Abramowitz, McKay, & Taylor, 2005). It appears that, to date, there has not been an adequate model developed that describes the mechanisms associated with OCD, whether psychosocial or biomedical (Taylor, McKay, & Abramowitz, 2005).

Application to Children

Given the success of CBT with E/RP in adult OCD patients, this intervention has been adapted for use with children and adolescents with OCD.

Dr. John March pioneered this movement with the publication of the first treatment manual oriented toward children (March & Mulle, 1998), which was later validated in a number of rigorous treatment studies (e.g., POTS, 2004; Storch et al., 2007). Developmental considerations in adapting this intervention include considering the cognitive level of children, integrating family members into treatment, and tailoring the treatment components to appeal to youngsters (e.g., Freeman et al., 2007). Cognitive-behavioral treatment for children, similar to that for adults, is a time-limited, present-oriented approach that teaches children and family members the cognitive and behavioral competencies needed to adaptively respond to obsessive-compulsive symptoms. Treatment is a collaborative effort among the therapist, patient, and relevant family members to develop the skills needed to respond to symptoms. Although the literature is not yet as extensive as that for adults, the results have been encouraging. A recent meta-analysis (Watson & Rees, 2008) shows large effect sizes for randomized and nonrandomized trials of CBT in children (*d* range from 0.95 to 2.56). These findings are similar to those obtained in meta-analyses of the adult literature on CBT (i.e., Abramowitz, 1998).

TREATMENT-INTERFERING FACTORS

Whereas the aforementioned meta-analyses suggest positive treatment response for CBT for childhood OCD, there are a number of complicating factors that can potentially limit treatment response. Among these are comorbid conditions, scrupulosity and overvalued ideation, biological factors (i.e., pediatric autoimmune neurolopsychiatric disorders associated with streptococcus, or PANDAS), developmental cognitive functioning, and stimulus-environment and stimulus-outcome relations.

Comorbid Conditions

As in the adult literature on OCD, it appears that comorbid conditions adversely affect treatment outcome in pediatric OCD. This has been shown in medication trials (i.e., Masi et al., 2005) where it appears that disruptive behavior disorders adversely affect treatment outcome. One recent study examining the impact of comorbid conditions on treatment outcome with CBT also suggests that comorbidity in general negatively affects treatment outcome (Storch, Merlo, et al., 2008). This study specifically pointed to the adverse effects of disruptive behavior disorders (such as oppositional defiant disorder, attention-deficit/hyperactivity disorder) and major depression as particularly poor prognostic indicators, as well as the number of comorbid diagnoses at baseline.

Although the role of comorbidity appears to suggest that the old adage in psychiatry of "more is worse, " this is not uniformly the case. For example, it appears that the presence of comorbid tics does not affect CBT (March et al., 2007). Further complicating the picture, children with OCD and comorbid tics or Tourette's syndrome tend to have more severe behavior problems and other psychiatric disturbance (Termine et al., 2006). One possibility is that OCD in children is a specific expression of a tic disorder (Eichstedt & Arnold, 2001), making a diagnosis of tics redundant rather than comorbid, leaving outcome based only on the disorder per se rather than based on the presence of additional conditions.

Scrupulosity and Overvalued Ideation

At the present time, there is very little in the published literature that describes problems in treatment caused by excessive scrupulosity in children. The problem is, however, well documented in adults and is generally seen as a significant barrier to treatment (Abramowitz, 2008). The essential features of scrupulosity revolve around specific standards of conduct and moral codes for which rigid adherence are demanded. This could include, but is not limited to, compulsions related to religious and value-driven beliefs. What makes these kinds of problems so difficult to treat is the fine line that therapists must walk between engaging the client in activities that will diminish rigidity on the one hand, with the risk of offending the client on the other.

Whereas scrupulosity in children with OCD has not been investigated to the extent it has in adults, there is one report on the phenomena. Weisner and Riffel (1960) described 23 cases of children with compulsive behavior referred for treatment because of chronic scrupulosity. In general, the children did not respond well to treatment (the nature of which was not described), and the article is primarily descriptive in nature. It does, however, highlight the phenomenal features of scrupulosity. Further, the descriptions mirror that of contemporary case presentations of OCD in youth.

As with scrupulosity, overvalued ideation is an understudied but highly salient aspect of OCD that can seriously impact treatment outcome. Overvalued ideation goes by a few different names in the literature, including: obsessive-compulsive psychosis, belief fixidity, and poor insight. The limited literature available suggests that when overvalued ideas are present, treatment outcome is poorer (Carmin, Wiegartz, & Wu, 2008; Neziroglu, Stevens, Yaryuya-Tobias, & McKay, 2001). In the case of childhood OCD, the *Diagnostic and Statistical Manual of Mental Disorders, Fourth Edition, Text Revision* (*DSM-IV-TR*; American Psychiatric Association, 2000) indicates the insight may not be present in children. Overvalued ideation (and the variants) describes occasions in which the client fails to recognize the senselessness of the rituals. In the case of children, the loss of insight is often the result of developmental cognitive factors, similar to any problem related to avoidance, whereby the feared outcome may come to be viewed as more realistic. Nonetheless, some children can view their symptoms as senseless, and it is possible that when these symptoms are viewed as reasonable, the ability to implement treatment will be impaired.

Biological Factors

The previous discussion regarding localized brain regions and neural circuitry relates to generalities of OCD. There are, however, special circumstances that can result in obsessive-compulsive symptoms caused by biological events. The one that has received the most attention by far in the pediatric OCD literature relates to PANDAS. Unlike other presentations of OCD, PANDAS occurs suddenly following streptococcal infection. Further, there are characteristic signs associated with the PANDAS form of OCD. Aside from sudden OCD onset following streptococcal infection, there are typically other neurological signs such as excessive motor activity (not related to tics or compulsions) or other movement-related signs (see detailed description in Larson, Storch, & Murphy, 2007).

If PANDAS is suspected as part of the clinical presentation of OCD in a child, the presence of a streptococcal infection can be verified and, if present, treated as clinically appropriate. Currently, there are no set guidelines on the most appropriate manner of treatment for OCD of the PANDAS subtype, although some data support antibiotic treatment (e.g., Snider, Lougee, Slattery, Grant, & Swedo, 2005), whereas other data indicate that CBT may be effective (Storch et al., 2004, 2006). One preliminary report suggests that youth with PANDAS may be at risk for developing other behavior problems following SSRI initiation (Murphy, Storch, & Strawser, 2006). Aside from the reports by Storch and colleagues, as yet there are no controlled published trials of CBT for children with the PANDAS presentation of OCD.

Developmental and Cognitive Functioning

There has been little empirical attention paid to the role of developmental and cognitive functioning on treatment outcome. However, in some cases, developmental and cognitive considerations can exert a significant role. Developmentally, chronological age can affect a child's ability to understand key therapeutic constructs and independently engage in therapeutic tasks (e.g., E/RP exercises). On balance, younger children are often more responsive to tangible and social rewards, which can positively impact outcome.

Developmental disabilities such as autism and Asperger's disorder, which often co-occur with OCD (Leyfer et al., 2006), can also exert an effect on treatment course. Youth with these comorbid conditions often display limited insight into their symptoms, a marked resistance to change, and frequently do not exhibit obsessions linked to their compulsive behaviors. Besides several case reports (e.g., Lehmkuhl, Storch, Bodfish, & Geffken, 2007), methodologically rigorous outcome trials examining the role of autism spectrum disorders on CBT outcome are lacking.

Family Accommodation and Environment

Despite the importance of the family in the treatment process, relatively little empirical attention has been directed to family factors and their impact on treatment outcome. One of the most studied variables is family accommodation (e.g., Calvocoressi et al., 1995, 1999; Storch et al., 2007). Family accommodation consists of actions taken by family members to facilitate rituals, provide symptom-related reassurance, acquiesce to the child's symptom-related demands, or decrease the child's day-to-day responsibility (Waters & Barrett, 2000). Accommodating behaviors are often fueled by family members' efforts to reduce the child's ritual engagement, distress, or functional impairment. Yet, such efforts are essentially rituals and result in reinforcing the child's symptoms, and also negatively affect family members' lives (Steketee & Van Noppen, 2003). This process is counter to the therapeutic goals and theoretical mechanism of E/RP. Only one study has examined the predictive effects of family accommodation on CBT outcome. Merlo, Lehmkuhl, Geffken, and Storch (in press) found that decreases in family accommodation during treatment predicted a more positive treatment outcome. Together with other data indicating its high frequency, these data indicate that the level of family accommodation may be a salient barrier to CBT outcome.

In addition to family accommodation, expressed emotion has received empirical attention in adults. For example, Chambless and Steketee (1999) found that emotional overinvolvement and hostility was linked to higher treatment dropout, whereas hostility and perceived criticism were inversely linked to adjustment outcomes at posttreatment. Although comparable data are not yet available for children with OCD, our clinical experience also suggests that expressed emotion is linked to negative treatment outcome by virtue of decreased child adherence, motivation, generalization of skills, and overall higher levels of family chaos.

Stimulus-Environment and Stimulus-Outcome Relations

Central to the effective application of exposure-based interventions for OCD is the ability to access stimuli that will provoke obsessions, or the urge to engage in compulsions. In adults, the symptoms of OCD that have the best response to treatment (symmetry/ordering, washing; Abramowitz et al., 2003) are associated with relative ease of stimuli access for exposure. Other symptoms of OCD tend to have stimuli that are more difficult to access, making direct therapeutic exposure in session difficult to complete. In children, there are several symptom domains that have been identified, namely: compulsions, sexual and aggressive obsessions, superstitions, and hoarding/ordering/somatic concerns (McKay et al., 2006). Some of these dimensions (superstitions, sexual/aggressive obsessions) can be accessed in session readily, whereby the therapist can deliberately violate the rules governing the superstitious behavior. Alternatively, obsessions related to somatic concerns may be more difficult to access during sessions.

In addition to the need to readily access stimuli that would provoke obsessions or compulsions, the relation between exposure to the stimuli and the feared consequence is also a critical component in successful treatment. For example, many children with OCD experience religious obsessions (i.e., the devil will get me if I don't pray properly, confess my actions to my parents, etc.). This is a difficult obsession to treat because the feared outcome may or may not occur until after death. Alternatively, children with OCD also frequently report concerns about aggressive urges, usually toward their parents or friends. Stimuli that might provoke these obsessions include knives or other sharp objects. This creates an opportunity for clinicians whereby the ability to access stimuli for exposure (or behavioral experiments) is readily available and the consequences known in a short period.

CASE PRESENTATION

Margaret (not her real name) was referred for treatment by a local pediatric neurologist and was treated by one of the authors (DM). At the time of treatment, she was 9 years old, with a recent onset of severe obsessive-compulsive symptoms, although her parents thought that she developed attention problems. It was the apparent attention difficulty that prompted the visit to the pediatric neurologist, a local authority on attention deficit disorder. She had no developmental delays, was a very good student with the exception of the prior 3 months when her symptoms were most acute, and lived with both of her parents. Her parents were professionals, and there was one other child in the home, a younger brother (age 7 years). Upon examining her, the neurologist felt that, although she might have had attention deficit, it was difficult to discern in light of the obsessive-compulsive behaviors. He withheld prescribing medication pending a psychological evaluation.

During the initial evaluation, Margaret would only meet with the therapist accompanied by her mother. Margaret reported, and her mother concurred, that her symptoms involved excessive concerns with cleanliness. Margaret had begun washing extensively, and felt the need to complete at least 25 washings of each hand when she felt "contaminated." Unlike typical contamination, Margaret was primarily concerned that contamination would lead to evil spirits invading her home, ruining her parents' marriage, and potentially lead to their death. When asked to clarify whose death, she indicated that anyone in her family, including herself, was potentially at risk of dying if she was not clean. She was also concerned that she might invite evil forces into her life, even if accidentally. For example, keeping books in the house that had titles involving evil (i.e., *Midnight in the Garden of Good and Evil*) could not be tolerated because, as she put it, "You might not be deliberately calling the evil spirit, but you are leaving the door open and he can just walk right in." Margaret expressed good insight into this problem, noting that "most other kids don't worry about this stuff, and I doubt they are all going to hell." She reported a strong interest in working on this problem. Her mother noted that Margaret had also begun to show signs of minor tics, mostly rapid blinking, but also some finger twitching and occasionally a shoulder shrug. Because her symptoms had such an apparently sudden onset, and she had the accompanying tics (observed during the initial session), she was referred to her pediatrician for an evaluation for PANDAS.

During the initial evaluation, the therapist met with the mother while the child waited in the waiting room. It was during this time that the mother indicated that, in addition to the concerns revolving around evil, Margaret often asked questions regarding whether she might harm someone, even if accidentally. For example, if the family went out to dinner and a family member ordered food that would be served with a sharp knife, she would ask if there was any risk of her taking it and hurting someone with it. Margaret would ask frequently where the knives were stored in the home, even if she had just opened the drawer where they were kept. She also expressed concerns over the location of all sharp objects (razors, box cutters) and potentially sharp objects (i.e., any objects that are sharp when broken such as glasses or plates) when going to bed. The mother or father, when putting Margaret to bed, had developed a short-hand for dealing with this by simply stating "All objects are away, and we are all safe, " which seemed to satisfy Margaret so long as it was stated nightly. In addition to this, Margaret was concerned about sexually aggressive acts such as rape, and could not tolerate being in the room if the news was on, even if it was the weather report, for fear that the report might at some point turn into a rape case. Whereas her concerns over evil spirits were areas Margaret indicated directly that she wanted to overcome, the concerns over aggression and sex were not, and Margaret was concerned that her mother would report these to the therapist.

During the second session, Margaret continued to express concerns over the risk of evil entering her life, and was washing extensively. Potential immunological variables were screened via blood testing with negative results. Around the time of her symptom onset, there were two potential stressors reported by the mother. One was a news report of a serious rape, in which the victim then sought retribution and killed her attacker. The victim was described in the news as someone who was otherwise mild mannered and seemed to be on an upward professional trajectory. The second was an accident in the home just shortly after this news report, in which her brother was playing with a toy truck and inadvertently cut himself, badly enough that it required stitches. Following each of these incidents, Margaret was highly distressed, and showed sleeplessness and considerable daytime agitation.

Additional questioning revealed that the Margaret showed signs of the tics only when anxious, and that if she was fully reassured and did not feel contaminated at all (a state she was capable of achieving at home), she did not have any tics. Further, the mother revealed that prior to the acute onset, Margaret tended to be "anxious, " and would ask questions "with a worried tone." Asked to clarify, the mother indicated that Margaret would often ask questions out of curiosity, but invariably the direction of the conversation would turn to risk of harm, either to herself or to others. The mother noted several of these discussions, such as discussions about: fatty foods and heart attack risk for her parents; risk to all members of the family of deep vein thrombosis if they flew somewhere on vacation; auto accident risk when traveling around the region; why the sky is blue and does the shade of blue mean that she might be at increased risk of skin cancer; and whether the pilot light on the gas stove would poison the entire family someday. These concerns were not as prominent when Margaret started treatment, primarily because she was more consumed by her acute symptoms, and the mother noted a sharp decrease in her curiosity. Assessment of symptom severity was completed with the Children's Yale-Brown Obsessive-Compulsive Scale (Scahill et al., 1997). Her scores were in the moderately severe range, with an obsession score of 11, and a compulsion score of 12.

General Treatment Plan

Because Margaret was both motivated for treatment and exhibited low overvalued ideation regarding her concerns over contamination by evil, treatment began with exposure for this component of her symptoms. As an additional element of treatment, a star chart was developed whereby Margaret would receive "stars" (or other stickers) for each day she could engage in treatment-related activities. At the end of each week she could redeem these "stars" for some small reinforcer, typically not exceeding $5 in cost.

It appeared that her symptoms related to concerns over harming were not going to be easily addressed. In discussing this with Margaret, she objected strongly. When pressed a bit further, she said that "this is not really a problem. I don't know why my mother would tell you I am afraid of the news." Given this reaction, in a separate discussion with the mother, it was agreed that this symptom would be dealt with after reducing her contamination concerns.

Readily Treated Symptoms

Margaret engaged in exposure for her contamination concerns. During sessions, treatment began by drawing pictures of "the devil" in which the therapist participated. To offset the intensity of the initial exposures, Margaret was instructed to draw the pictures with the devil "smiling, but not devilishly." Margaret's mother was instructed to practice this exercise with Margaret each day, but while also restricting her hand washing to meal times. Further, the mother was instructed to begin bringing a few books into the home in which images of evil might be provoked. One of the starting points for this component was the inclusion of religious books, where evil is mentioned, but sanctioned by the family's religious orientation. Margaret responded well to these initial exercises, and earned "stars" for successful engagement in treatment.

Treatment of her contamination symptoms proceeded well until it came time to pursue more advanced exposure exercises. One in particular, in which Margaret was to read a satirical article in *The Onion* depicting the conversion of Jesus to Islam, created significant distress. Margaret reported a strong urge to wash, and struggled to habituate. The exercise was conducted with the mother present in light of the content of the satirical newspaper and to allay any concerns the mother might have regarding the content of therapy sessions. By the end of the session, Margaret had recovered, although she continued to report a high level of washing urge. Her primary concern was that she "had gone too far. This is really too much, and now God may not forgive me." The mother was asked to try only to reassure Margaret that she worked hard during the session, but to avoid reassuring her regarding the outcome from the exposure. By the next session, Margaret and her mother both reported that, although the evening following the prior session was difficult, she felt fine at this point. In light of the difficulty of the prior session, Margaret was instructed to re-read the satirical piece, which provoked anxiety, but not as severely as it had during the prior session.

Difficult-to-Treat Symptoms

Margaret's symptoms related to harming obsessions were not approached until her contamination concerns were significantly reduced, which occurred after following six sessions of treatment (or the eighth meeting). Until this point, she was permitted to continue avoiding stimuli that might provoke anxiety regarding harm such as news reports and Web sites in general. Web sites were avoided because Margaret became fearful that a "pop-up" ad might show up for "some sex things." On several occasions, she went online on her parent's computer and pop-up ads for various pharmaceutical products appeared (i.e., Viagra, Levitra), which prompted her sexual obsessions. She therefore would not send e-mail to friends, play video games on a computer (although television video games were acceptable), and did not go to Web sites that were popular among children her age.

Although Margaret felt strongly that her concerns over harm were not something she was prepared to work on in therapy, she did agree to two interventions that were meaningfully related. One was that she would discuss and draw pictures related to the ostensible stressful events that marked the onset of symptoms. The other was that, although she did not want to engage in direct exposure of news and media information in which there was a risk of exposure to violent crime stories, she would not object to the newspaper being in the home if her parents wanted to read it. On hearing this, the mother began by purchasing the local community newspaper, in which most of the stories were neutral and the risk of violent crime stories was extremely low. Because Margaret was agreeable to these terms, this was also added to her "star" chart.

A week after initiating this approach to treatment, Margaret indicated that she was not happy about having the newspaper in the house, that she tried not to look at it, and struggled when eating breakfast before school because it was often on or near the table. It was at this point that the therapist met with the mother to discuss some options for the next steps. It was agreed that the following session would include a trip to the nearby mall, where we (Margaret, mother, therapist) would walk into many stores to "browse." Any time a newspaper, magazine, or other media materials were present, the mother would say, "Well, we might need to leave since there are newspapers/magazines/etc. present. I know you would like to stay here, but it seems that we may not be able to manage it." This approach is consistent with motivational interviewing methods (Miller & Rollnick, 2002). The session ended at the mall, with the mother instructed to keep the local newspaper, and to purchase the next published issue as well, but not to pursue it further until the next session.

For the next session, Margaret appeared depressed when she arrived. She reported that it was getting harder to avoid all the news information, and that there was an assignment in school that required her to gather some current-events materials. Margaret reported extreme anxiety, but reluctantly agreed that she would need to overcome her fear of harming. We agreed to start with the local newspaper, which was now regularly in her home, and to read articles that were neutral based on the title, and some of the letters to the editor. During the session, the therapist visited several children-themed Web sites with Margaret.

The following three sessions were all focused on Margaret's concerns with harming, and although she progressed rapidly, she remained reluctant to complete several important exercises. For example, she could not handle a steak knife, still refused to read certain news articles related to harm, such as articles related to the Iraq war, other national news involving aggression, as well as news reports regarding animal attacks. She was, however, able to read the daily newspaper and tolerate the televised news, as well as visit Web sites that were frequented by her friends. Her mother noted that Margaret appeared much happier at this point, did not express as many concerns over danger when she asked questions out of curiosity, and appeared completely recovered from her contamination fears. At treatment termination, her CY-BOCS score was 4 for obsessions, and 3 for compulsions. These gains remained at 6-month follow-up. A summary of her treatment progress is provided in Figure 4.3.

Summary of Treatment of Margaret

Although Margaret can be considered a treatment success, it is noteworthy that she exhibited a dichotomy between symptoms that could be

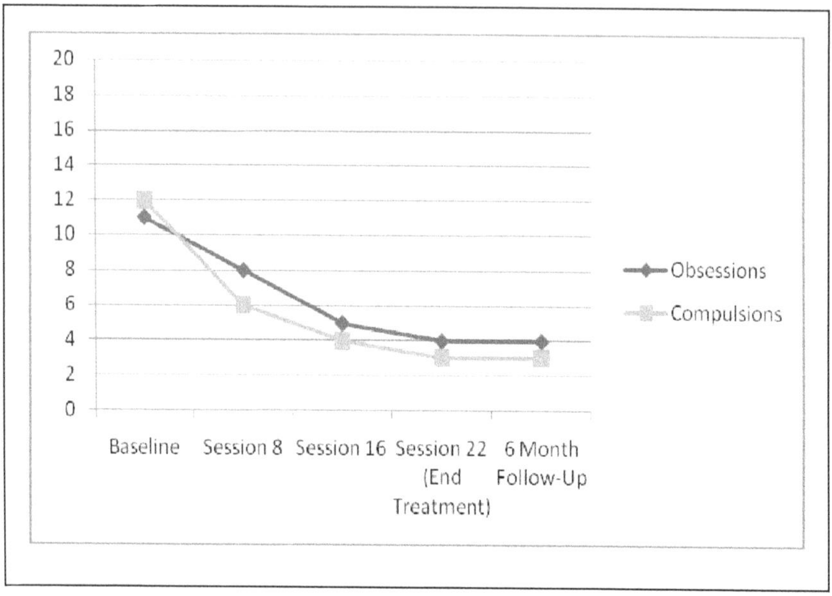

Figure 4.3 Treatment progress for Margaret.

initially treated and those that could not. In this case these were neatly divided between those in which she was insightful and those for which she was less so. However, this arrangement represents a common challenge for clinicians treating OCD. Namely, making decisions regarding symptoms that can be targeted versus those that, although debilitating, cannot be approached until the client is ready. Readiness is a difficult variable to assess for clients generally, and for children in particular. In this case, Margaret was able to be prepared for treatment of more difficult symptoms through a straightforward motivational intervention. Other children may not respond so easily to such an intervention.

It is also noteworthy that Margaret's symptoms did not completely remit, and that some of her concerns over harming remained at the end of treatment. This poses a challenge for clinicians. Namely, what constitutes a desirable outcome? Treatment in this case terminated because the primary presenting symptoms had diminished, and the family and child appeared satisfied with the outcome. It is in this way that the goals of the therapist may not match those of the client.

SUMMARY AND FUTURE DIRECTIONS

Obsessive-compulsive disorder, in both children and adults, is a complex and heterogeneous condition marked by substantial functional impairment. The research shows that a number of significant barriers may negatively impact the provision of effective treatment. Although CBT has shown great promise in the treatment of the disorder, there are numerous exceptions that make treatment difficult to successfully implement.

In surveying complicating factors in the disorder, it appears that one area that requires additional investigation is the role of overvalued ideas. The presence of insight is not presently a requirement for the diagnosis in children, and the qualified "with poor insight" is available for adults. However, it appears that the means of treating those with an understanding of the senselessness of symptoms, compared to those who do not, is substantially different. The case illustration provided suggests this, and in light of the fact that a substantial number of OCD sufferers fail to respond to treatment, this seems a fruitful area of additional investigation.

In addition to overvalued ideation, there are other areas that warrant empirical attention. Several, in no particular order, include treatment augmentation and/or enhancement. Regarding augmentation, the question of the best augmenting strategy for youth who have not responded to prior interventions has yet to be examined. There is currently a study under way examining the efficacy of various CBT intensities for youth who have had a partial SSRI response, but, to date, there are no data that compare the efficacy of CBT relative to atypical antipsychotic treatment for those who have failed two medication trials. Regarding treatment enhancement, d-cycloserine has shown promise in enhancing treatment outcomes in adult patients with OCD and anxiety disorders (see Norberg, Krystal, & Tolin, 2008).

REFERENCES

Abramowitz, J. S. (1998). Does cognitive-behavioral therapy cure obsessive-compulsive disorder? A meta-analytic evaluation of clinical significance. *Behavior Therapy, 29*, 339–355.

Abramowitz, J. S. (2008). Scrupulosity. In J.S. Abramowitz, D. McKay, & S. Taylor (Eds.), *Clinical handbook of obsessive-compulsive disorder and related problems* (pp. 156–172). Baltimore: Johns Hopkins Press.

Abramowitz, J. S., Franklin, M. E., Schwartz, S. A., & Furr, J. M. (2003). Symptom presentation and outcome of cognitive-behavioral treatment for obsessive-compulsive disorder. *Journal of Consulting and Clinical Psychology, 71*, 1049–1057.

Abramowitz, J. S., McKay, D., & Taylor, S. (2005). Potentials and limitations of cognitive treatments for obsessive-compulsive disorder. *Cognitive Behaviour Therapy, 34*, 140–147.

Abramowitz, J. S., McKay, D., & Taylor, S. (2008). *Obsessive-compulsive disorder: Subtypes and spectrum conditions*. Amsterdam: Elsevier.

Abramowitz, J. S., Whiteside, S. P., & Deacon, B. J. (2005). The effectiveness of treatment for pediatric obsessive-compulsive disorder: A meta-analysis. *Behavior Therapy, 36*, 55–63.

Ackerman, D. L. & Greenland, S. (2002). Multivariate meta-analysis of controlled drug studies for obsessive-compulsive disorder. *Journal of Clinical Psychopharmacology, 22*, 309–317.

Alexander, G., DeLong, M., & Strick, P. (1986). Parallel organization of functionally segregated circuits linking basal ganglia and cortex. *Annual Review of Neuroscience, 9*, 357–381.

American Academy of Child and Adolescent Psychiatry: Practice Parameters for the Assessment and Treatment of Children and Adolescents with Obsessive-Compulsive Disorder. (1998). *Journal of the American Academy of Child and Adolescent Psychiatry, 37* (Suppl.), 27–45.

American Psychiatric Association. (2000). *Diagnostic and statistical manual of mental disorders* (4th ed., text rev.). Washington, DC: American Psychiatric Press.

Baxter, L. R., Schwartz, J., Mazziotta, J., Phelps, M. E., Pahl, J. J., Guze, B. H., et al. (1988). Cerebral glucose metabolic rates in nondepressed patients with obsessive-compulsive disorder. *American Journal of Psychiatry*, 1560–1563.

Bloch, M. H., Landeros-Weisenberger, A., Kelmendi, B., Coric, V., Bracken, M. B., & Leckman, J. F. (2006). A systematic review: Antipsychotic augmentation with treatment refractory obsessive-compulsive disorder. *Molecular Psychiatry, 11*, 622–632.

Bystritsky, A., Ackerman, D. L., Rosen, R. M., Vapnik, T., Gorbis, E., Maidment, K. M., & Saxena, S. (2004). Augmentation of serotonin reuptake inhibitors in refractory obsessive-compulsive disorder using adjuvant olanzapine: A placebo-controlled trial. *Journal of Clinical Psychiatry, 65*, 565–568.

Calvocoressi, L., Lewis, B., Harris, M., Trufan, S. J., Goodman, W. K., McDougle, C. J., & Price, L. H. (1995). Family accommodation in obsessive compulsive disorder. *American Journal of Psychiatry, 152*, 441–443.

Calvocoressi, L., Mazure, C., Kasl, S. V., Skolnick, J., Fisk, D., Vegso, S. J., Van Noppen, B. L., & Price, L. H. (1999). Family accommodation of obsessive-compulsive symptoms: Instrument development and assessment of family behavior. *Journal of Nervous and Mental Disease, 187*, 636–642.

Carmin, C., Wiegartz, P. S., & Wu, K. (2008). Obsessive-compulsive disorder with poor insight. In J. S. Abramowitz, D. McKay, & S. Taylor (Eds.), *Clinical handbook of obsessive-compulsive disorder and related problems* (pp. 109–125). Baltimore, MD: Johns Hopkins Press.

Chakrabarty, K., Bhattacharyya, S., Christopher, R., & Khanna, S. (2005). Glutamatergic dysfunction in OCD. *Neuropsychopharmacology, 30*, 1735–1740.

Chambless, D. L., & Steketee, G. (1999). Expressed emotion and behavior therapy outcome: A prospective study with obsessive-compulsive and agoraphobic outpatients. *Journal of Consulting and Clinical Psychology, 67*, 658–665.

Christensen, H., Hadzi-Pavlovic, D., Andrews, G., & Mattick, R. (1987). Behavior therapy and tricyclic medication in the treatment of obsessive-compulsive disorder: A quantitative review. *Journal of Consulting and Clinical Psychology, 55*, 701–711.

Clinical Pharmacology [database online]. (2008). Tampa, FL: Gold Standard, Inc. Available at http://www.clinicalpharmacology.com

Denys, D., de Geus, F., van Megen, H. J., & Westenberg, H. G. (2004). A double-blind, randomized, placebo-controlled trial of quetiapine addition in patients with obsessive-compulsive disorder refractory to serotonin reuptake inhibitors. *Journal of Clinical Psychiatry, 65*, 1040–1048.

Denys, D., VanNieuwerburgh, F., Deforce, D., & Westenberg, H. (2006). Association between serotonergic candidate genes and specific phenotypes of obsessive compulsive disorder. *Journal of Affective Disorders, 91*, 39–44.

DeVeaugh-Geiss, J., Moroz, G., Biederman, J., Cantwell, D., Fontaine, R., Greist, J. H., et al. (1992). Clomipramine hydrochloride in childhood and adolescent obsessive-compulsive disorder: A multicenter trial. *Journal of the American Academy of Child and Adolescent Psychiatry, 31*, 45–49.

Douglas, H. M., Moffitt, T. E., Dar, R., McGee, R., & Silva, P. (1995). Obsessive-compulsive disorder in a birth cohort of 18-year-olds: Prevalence and predictors. *Journal of the American Academy of Child and Adolescent Psychiatry, 34*, 1424–1431.

Eichstedt, J. A., & Arnold, S. L. (2001). Childhood-onset obsessive-compulsive disorder: A tic-related subtype of OCD? *Clinical Psychology Review, 21*, 137–157.

Fama, J., & Wilhelm, S. (2005). Formal cognitive therapy: A new treatment for OCD. In J. S. Abramowitz & A. C. Houts (Eds.), *Concepts and controversies in obsessive-compulsive disorder* (pp. 263–281). New York: Springer Publishing Company.

Foa, E. B., & Kozak, M. J. (1986). Emotional processing of fear: Exposure to corrective information. *Psychological Bulletin, 99*, 20–35.

Foa, E. B., Liebowitz, M. R., Kozak, M. J., Davies, S., Campeas, R., Franklin, M. E., et al. (2005). Randomised, placebo-controlled trial of exposure and ritual prevention, clomipramine, and their combination in the treatment of obsessive-compulsive disorder. *American Journal of Psychiatry, 162*, 151–161.

Food and Drug Administration Center for Drug Evaluation and Research. (2004a). *Summary comments on antidepressants and suicidality in pediatric patients and questions/topics for comment*. Washington, DC: FDA.

Food and Drug Administration Center for Drug Evaluation and Research. (2004b). *FDA statement on recommendations of the Psychopharmacologic Drugs and Pediatric Advisory Committee*. Washington, DC: FDA.

Freeman, J. B., Choate-Summers, M. L., Moore, P. S., Garcia, A. M., Sapyta, J. J., Leonard, H. L., et al. (2007). Cognitive behavioral treatment for young children with obsessive-compulsive disorder. *Biological Psychiatry, 61*, 337–343.

Geller, D. A., Biederman, J., Stewart, S. E., Mullin, B., Martin, A., Spencer, T., & Faraone, S. V. (2003). Which SSRI? A meta-analysis of pharmacotherapy trials in pediatric obsessive-compulsive disorder. *American Journal of Psychiatry, 160*, 1919–1928.

Geller, D. A., Hoog, S. L., Heiligenstein, J. H., Ricardi, R. K., Tamura, R., Kluszynski, S., et al. (2001). Fluoxetine treatment for obsessive-compulsive disorder in children and adolescents: A placebo-controlled clinical trial. *Journal of the American Academy of Child and Adolescent Psychiatry, 40*, 773–779.

Gilbert, A. R., Keshavana, M. S., Diwadkar, V., Nutche, J., MacMaster, F., Easter, P.C., et al. (2008). Gray matter differences between pediatric obsessive-compulsive disorder patients and high-risk siblings: A preliminary voxel-based morphometry study. *Neuroscience Letters, 435*, 45–50.

Gilbert, A. R., Moore, G. J., Keshavan, M. S., Paulson, L. A., Narula, V., Master, F. P., et al. (2000). Decrease in thalamic volumes of pediatric patients with obsessive-compulsive disorder who are taking paroxetine. *Archives of General Psychiatry, 57*, 449–456.

Goddard, A., Shekhar, A., Whiteman, A., & McDougle, C. (2008). Serotoninergic mechanisms in the treatment of obsessive-compulsive disorder. *Drug Discovery Today, 13*, 325–332.

Goodman, W. K., McDougle, C. J., Barr, L. C., Aronson, S. C., & Price, L. H. (1993). Biological approaches to treatment-resistant obsessive compulsive disorder. *Journal of Clinical Psychiatry, 54* (Suppl.), 16–26.

Goodman, W. K., Price, L. H., Rasmussen, S. A., & Mazure, C. (1989). The Yale-Brown Obsessive-Compulsive Scale: I. Development, use and reliability. *Archives of General Psychiatry, 46*, 1006–1011.

Grados, M. A., & Riddle, M. A. (2001). Pharmacological treatment of childhood obsessive-compulsive disorder: From theory to practice. *Journal of Clinical Child Psychology, 30*, 110–113.

Grados, M., Scahill, L., & Riddle, M. A. (1999). Pharmacotherapy in children and adolescents with obsessive-compulsive disorder. *Child and Adolescent Psychiatric Clinics of North America, 8*, 617–634.

Grados, M. A., Walkup, J., & Walford, S. (2003). Genetics of obsessive-compulsive disorders: New findings and challenges. *Brain and Development, 25*, S55–S61.

Greist, J., Chouinard, G., DuBoff, E., Halaris, A., Kim, S.W., Koran, L., et al. (1995). Double-blind parallel comparison of three dosages of sertraline and placebo in outpatients with Obsessive-Compulsive Disorder. *Archives of General Psychiatry, 52*, 289-295.

Greist, J.H., Jefferson, J.W., Kobak, K.A., Chouinard, G., DuBoff, E., Halaris, A., et al. (1995). A 1 year double-blind placebo-controlled fixed dose study of sertraline in the treatment of obsessive-compulsive disorder. *International Clinical Psychopharmacology, 10*, 57–65.

Hesse, S., Müller, U., Lincke, T., Barthel, H., Villmann, T., Angermeyer, M. C., et al. (2005). Serotonin and dopamine transporter imaging in patients with obsessive–compulsive disorder. *Psychiatry Research: Neuroimaging, 140*, 63–72.

Hollander, E., Allen, A., Steiner, M., Wheadon, D. E., Oakes, R., & Burnham, D.B. (2003). Acute and long-term treatment and prevention of relapse of obsessive-compulsive disorder with paroxetine. *Journal of Clinical Psychiatry, 64*, 1113–1121.

Hollander, E., Bienstock, C.A., Koran, L.M., Pallanti, S., Marazziti, D., Rasmussen, S.A., et al. (2002). Refractory obsessive-compulsive disorder: State-of-the-art treatment. *Journal of Clinical Psychiatry, 63* (Suppl. 6), 20–29.

King, R. A., Leonard, H., & March, J. (1998). Summary of the practice parameters for the assessment and treatment of children with obsessive-compulsive disorder. *Journal of the American Academy of Child and Adolescent Psychiatry, 37*, 1110–1116.

Koran, L. M., Hanna, G. L. Hollander, E., Nestadt, G., Simpson, H. B., & American Psychiatric Association. (2007). Practice guideline for the treatment of patients with obsessive-compulsive disorder. *American Journal of Psychiatry, 164* (Suppl. 7), 5–53.

Kringlen, E. (1965). Obsessional neurotics: A long-term follow-up. *British Journal of Psychiatry, 111*, 709–722.

Larson, M. J., Storch, E. A., & Murphy, T. K. (2007). Pediatric autoimmune neuropsychiatric disorders associated with streptococcal infections. In E. A. Storch, G. R. Geffken, & T. K. Murphy (Eds.), *Handbook of child and adolescent obsessive-compulsive disorder* (pp. 163–174). Mahwah, NJ: Erlbaum.

Lehmkuhl, H. D., Storch, E. A., Bodfish, J. W., & Geffken, G. R. (2007). Brief report: Exposure and response prevention for obsessive compulsive disorder in a 12-year-old with autism. *Journal of Autism and Developmental Disorders*. Epub ahead of print retrieved July 28, 2008, from http://www.springerlink.com/content/e501122800266323/fulltext.html

Leonard, H. L., Goldberger, E. L., Rapoport, J. L., Cheslow, D. L., & Swedo, S. E. (1990). Childhood rituals: Normal development or obsessive-compulsive symptoms? *Journal of the American Academy of Child and Adolescent Psychiatry, 29*, 17–23.

Leyfer, O. T., Folstein, S. E., Bacalman, S., Davis, N. O., Dinh, E., Morgan, J., et al. (2006). Comorbid psychiatric disorders in children with autism: Interview development and rates of disorders. *Journal of Autism and Developmental Disorders, 36*, 849–861.

MacMaster, F. P., Keshavan, M. S., Dick, E. L., & Rosenberg, D. R. (1999). Corpus callosal signal intensity in treatment-naive pediatric obsessive compulsive disorders. *Progress in Neuro-Psychopharmacology and Biological Psychiatry, 23*, 601–612.

MacMaster, F. P., Russell, A., Mirza, Y., Keshavan, M. S., Banerjee, S. P., Bhandari, R., et al. (2006). Pituitary volume in pediatric obsessive-compulsive disorder. *Biological Psychiatry, 59*, 252–257.

March, J. S., Biederman, J., Wolkow, R., Safferman, A., Mardekian, J., Cook, E. H., et al. (1998). Sertraline in children and adolescents with obsessive-compulsive disorder: A multicenter randomized control trial. *Journal of the American Medical Association, 280*, 1752–1756.

March, J. S., Frances, A., Carpenter, D., & Kahn, D. A. (1997). Expert consensus guideline series: Treatment of obsessive-compulsive disorder. *Journal of Clinical Psychiatry, 58* (Suppl. 4), 2–72.

March, J. S., Franklin, M. E., Leonard, H., Garcia, A., Moore, P., Freeman, J., et al. (2007). Tics moderate treatment outcome with sertraline but not cognitive-behavior therapy in pediatric obsessive-compulsive disorder. *Biological Psychiatry, 61*, 344–347.

March, J. S., & Mulle, K. (1998). *OCD in children and adolescents: A cognitive-behavioral treatment manual*. New York: Guilford Press.

Masi, G., Perugi, G., Millipiedi, S., Toni, C., Mucci, M., Pfanner, C., et al.(2005). Bipolar comorbidity in pediatric obsessive-compulsive disorder: Clinical and treatment implications. *Journal of Child and Adolescent Psychopharmacology, 17*, 475–486.

Mataix-Cols, D., Wooderson, S., Lawrence, N., Brammer, M.J., Speckens, A., & Phillips, M. L. (2004). Distinct neural correlates of washing, checking, and hoarding symptom dimensions in obsessive-compulsive disorder. *Archives of General Psychiatry*, 564–576.

McDougle, C. J., Epperson, C. N., Pelton, G. H., Wasylink, S., & Price, L. H., (2000). A double-blind, placebo-controlled study of risperidone addition in serotonin reuptake inhibitor-refractory obsessive-compulsive disorder. *Archives of General Psychiatry, 57*, 794–801.

McKay, D., Abramowitz, J., Calamari, J., Kyrios, M., Radomsky, A., Sookman, D., et al. (2004). A critical evaluation of obsessive-compulsive disorder subtypes: Symptoms versus mechanisms. *Clinical Psychology Review, 24*, 283–313.

McKay, D., Piacentini, J., Greisberg, S., Graae, F., Jaffer, M., & Miller, J. (2006). The structure of childhood obsessions and compulsions: Dimensions in an outpatient sample. *Behaviour Research and Therapy, 44*, 137–146.

Merlo, L. J., Lehmkuhl, H., Geffken, G. R., & Storch, E. A. (in press). Decrease in family accommodation is associated with improved cognitive-behavioral therapy outcome in pediatric obsessive-compulsive disorder. *Journal of Consulting and Clinical Psychology*.

Miller, W. R., & Rollnick, S. (2002). *Motivational interviewing* (2nd ed.). New York: Guilford Press..

Montgomery, S. A., Kasper, S., Stein, D. J., Bang, H. K., & Lemming, O. M. (2001). Citalopram 20 mg, 40 mg and 60 mg are all effective and well tolerated compared with placebo in obsessive-compulsive disorder. *International Clinical Psychopharmacology, 16*, 75–86.

Murphy, T. K., Sajid, M., Soto, O., Shapira, N., Edge, P., Yang, M., et al.. (2004). Detecting pediatric autoimmune neuropsychiatric disorders associated with streptococcus in children with obsessive-compulsive disorder and tics. *Biological Psychiatry, 55*, 61–68.

Murphy, T. K., Storch, E. A., & Strawser, M. (2006). SSRI-induced behavioral activation in the PANDAS subtype. *Primary Psychiatry, 13*, 87–89.

Neziroglu, F., Stevens, K. P., Yaryura-Tobias, J. A., & McKay, D. (2001). Predictive validity of the Overvalued Ideas Scale: Outcome in obsessive-compulsive and body dysmorphic disorders. *Behaviour Research and Therapy, 39*, 745–756.

Norberg, M. M., Krystal, J. H., & Tolin, D. F. (2008). A meta-analysis of D-cycloserine and the facilitation of fear extinction and exposure therapy. *Biology Psychiatry, 63*, 1118–1126.

Pediatric OCD Treatment Study (POTS) Team. (2004). Cognitive-behavior therapy, sertraline, and their combination for children and adolescents with obsessive-compulsive disorder: The Pediatric OCD Treatment Study (POTS) randomized controlled trial. *Journal of the American Medical Association, 292*, 1969–1976.

Piacentini, J., Bergman, R. L., Keller, M., & McCracken, J. (2003). Functional impairment in children and adolescents with obsessive compulsive disorder. *Journal of Child and Adolescent Psychopharmacology, 13*, S61–S69.

Piccinelli, M., Pini, S., Bellantuono, C., & Wilkinson, G. (1995). Efficacy of drug treatment in obsessive-compulsive disorder: A meta-analytic review. *British Journal of Psychiatry, 166*, 424–443.
Rachman, S. (1997). A cognitive theory of obsessions. *Behavior Research and Therapy, 35*, 793–802.
Rapoport, J. L., & Inoff-Germain, G. (2000). Update on childhood-onset schizophrenia. *Current Psychiatry Reports, 2*, 410–415.
Rauch, S. L., Savage, C. R., Alpert, N. M., Dougherty, D., Kendrick, A., Curran, T., et al. (1997). Probing striatal function in obsessive-compulsive disorder: A PET study of implicit sequence learning. *Journal of Neuropsychiatry Clinical Neurosciences*, 568–573.
Rettew, D. C., Swedo, S. E., Leonard, H. L., Lenane, M. C., & Rapoport, J. L. (1992). Obsessions and compulsions across time in 79 children and adolescents with obsessive-compulsive disorder. *Journal of the American Academy of Child and Adolescent Psychiatry, 31*, 1050–1056.
Riddle, M. A., Reeve, E. A., Yaryura-Tobias, J. A., Yang, H. M., Claghorn, J. L., Gaffney, G., et al. (2001). Fluvoxamine for children and adolescents with obsessive-compulsive disorder: A randomized, controlled, multicenter trial. *Journal of the American Academy of Child and Adolescent Psychiatry, 40*, 222–229.
Rosenberg, D. R., Keshavan, M. S., Dick, E. L., Bagwell, W. W., MacMaster, F. P., & Birmaher, B. (1997). Corpus callosal morphology in treatment-naive pediatric obsessive compulsive disorder. *Progress in Neuro-Psychopharmacology and Biological Psychiatry, 21*, 1269–1283.
Rosenberg, D. R., Keshavan, M. S., O'Hearn, K. M., Dick, E. L., Bagwell, W. W., Seymour, A. B., et al. (1997). Frontostriatal measurement in treatment-naive children with obsessive-compulsive disorder. *Archives of General Psychiatry, 54*, 824–830.
Rosenberg, D. R., MacMaster, F., Keshavan, M., Fitzgerald, K., Stewart, C., & Moore, G. (2000). Decrease in caudate glutamatergic concentrations in pediatric obsessive-compulsive disorder patients taking paroxetine. *Journal of the American Academy of Child and Adolescent Psychiatry, 39*, 1096–1103.
Rosenberg, D. R., Mirza, Y., Russell, A., Tang, J., Smith, J., Banerjee, S., et al. (2004). Reduced anterior cingulate glutamatergic concentrations in childhood OCD and major depression versus healthy controls. *Journal of the American Academy of Child and Adolescent Psychiatry, 43*, 1146–1153.
Salkovskis, P. M. (1985). Obsessional-compulsive problems: A cognitive-behavioural analysis. *Behavioral Research and Therapy, 23*, 571–581.
Salkovskis, P. M. (1989). Cognitive-behavioural factors and the persistence of intrusive thoughts in obsessional problems. *Behaviour Research and Therapy, 23*, 571–583.
Salkovskis, P. M. (1996). The cognitive approach to anxiety: Threat beliefs, safety-seeking behavior, and the special case of health anxiety and obsessions. In P. M. Salkovskis (Ed.), *Frontiers of cognitive therapy* (pp. 48–74). New York: Guilford Press.
Salkovskis, P.M. (1999). Understanding and treating obsessive-compulsive disorder. *Behavioral Research and Therapy, 37*, S29–S52.
Saxena, S., & Rauch, S. L. (2000). Functional neuroimaging and the neuroanatomy of obsessive-compulsive disorder. *Psychiatric Clinics of North America, 23*, 563–586.

Saxena, S., Brody, A. L., Schwartz, J. M., & Baxter, L. R. (1998). Neuroimaging and frontal-subcortical circuitry in obsessive-compulsive disorder. *British Journal of Psychiatry, 35*(Suppl.), 26–37.

Scahill, L., Riddle, M. A., McSwiggin-Hardin, M., Ort, S. L., King, R. A., Goodman, W. K., et al. (1997). Children's Yale-Brown Obsessive-Compulsive Scale: Reliability and validity. *Journal of the American Academy of Child and Adolescent Psychiatry, 36*, 844–852.

Snider, L. A., Lougee, L., Slattery, M., Grant, P., & Swedo, S. E. (2005). Antibiotic prophylaxis with azithromycin or penicillin for childhood-onset neuropsychiatric disorders. *Biological Psychiatry, 57*, 788–792.

Steketee, G., & Van Noppen, B. (2003). Family approaches to treatment for obsessive compulsive disorder. *Revista Brasileira de Psiquiatria, 25*, 42–50.

Stoner, S. C., Marken, P. A., Watson, W. A., Switzer, J. L., Barber, M. F., Meyer, V.L., et al. (1997). Antidepressant overdoses and resultant emergency department services: The impact of SSRIs. *Psychopharmacology Bulletin, 33*, 667–670.

Storch, E. A., Gerdes, A., Atkins, J., Geffken, G. R., Star, J., & Murphy, T. (2004). Behavioral treatment of child with pediatric autoimmune neuropsychiatric disorder associated with group A streptococcal infection. *Journal of the American Academy of Child and Adolescent Psychiatry, 43*, 510–511.

Storch, E. A., Kaufman, D. A., Bagner, D., Merlo, L. J., Shapira, N. A., Geffken, G. R., et al. (2007). Florida Obsessive-Compulsive Inventory: Development, reliability, and validity. *Journal of Clinical Psychology, 63*, 851–859.

Storch, E. A., Merlo, L., Larson, M. J., Geffken, G. R., Lehmkuhl, H. D., Jacob, M. L., et al. (2008). Impact of comorbidity on cognitive-behavioral therapy response in pediatric obsessive-compulsive disorder. *Journal of the American Academy of Child and Adolescent Psychiatry, 47*, 583–592.

Storch, E. A., Murphy, T. K., Geffken, G. R., Mann, G., Adkins, J., Merlo, L. J., et al. (2006). Cognitive behavioral therapy for PANDAS related obsessive-compulsive disorder: Findings from a preliminary wait-list controlled open trial. *Journal of the American Academy of Child and Adolescent Psychiatry, 45*, 1171–1178.

Swedo, S. E., Rapoport, J. L., Leonard, H., Lenane, M., & Cheslow, D. (1989). Obsessive-compulsive disorder in children and adolescents. Clinical phenomenology of 70 consecutive cases. *Archives of General Psychiatry, 46*, 335–341.

Szeszko, P. R., MacMillan, S., McMeniman, M., Chen, S., Baribault, K., Lim, K.O., et al. (2004). Brain structural abnormalities in psychotropic drug-naive pediatric patients with obsessive-compulsive disorder. *American Journal of Psychiatry*, 1049–1056.

Szeszko, P. R., MacMillan, S., McMeniman, M., Lorch, E., Madden, R., Ivey, J., et al. (2004). Amygdala volume reductions in pediatric patients with obsessive-compulsive disorder treated with paroxetine: Preliminary findings. *Neuropsychopharmacology*, 826–832.

Taylor, S., Abramowitz, J., McKay, D., Calamari, J., Sookman, D., Kyrios, M., et al. (2006). Do dysfunctional beliefs play a role in all types of obsessive-compulsive disorder? *Journal of Anxiety Disorders, 20*, 85–97.

Taylor, S., McKay, D., & Abramowitz, J. (2005). Is obsessive-compulsive disorder a disturbance of security motivation? Comment on Szechtman & Woody (2004). *Psychological Review, 112*, 650–656.

Termine, C., Ballotin, U., Rossi, G., Maisano, F., Salini, S., DiNardo, R., & Lanzi, G. (2006). Psychopathology in children and adolescents with Tourette's syndrome: A controlled study. *Brain and Development, 28*, 69–75.

Thomsen, P.H. (2004). Risperidone augmentation in the treatment of severe adolescent OCD in SSRI-refractory cases: A case-series. *Annals of Clinical Psychiatry, 16*, 201–207.

Tollefson, G. D., Rampey, A. H. Jr., Potvin, J. H., Jenike, M. A., Rush, A. J., Kominguez, R. A., et al. (1994). A multicenter investigation of fixed-dose fluoxetine in the treatment of obsessive-compulsive disorder. *Archives of General Psychiatry, 51*, 559–567.

Valleni-Basile, L. A., Garrison, C. Z., Jackson, K. L., Waller, J. L., McKeown, R. E., Addy, C. L., et al. (1994). Frequency of obsessive-compulsive disorder in a community sample of young adolescents. *Journal of the American Academy of Child and Adolescent Psychiatry, 33*, 782–791.

Viard, A., Flament, M., Artiges, E., Dehaene, S., Naccache, L., Cohen, D., et al. (2005). Cognitive control in childhood-onset obsessive-compulsive disorder: A functional MRI study. *Psychological Medicine, 35* (7), 1007–1017.

Waters, T. L. & Barrett, P. M. (2000). The role of the family in childhood obsessive-compulsive disorder. *Clinical Child and Family Psychology Review, 3*, 173–184.

Watson, H. J. & Rees, C. S. (2008). Meta-analysis of randomized, controlled treatment trials for pediatric obsessive-compulsive disorder. *Journal of Child Psychology and Psychiatry, 49*, 489–498.

Weisner, W. M., & Riffel, A. (1960). Scrupulosity: Religion and obsessive compulsive behavior in children. *American Journal of Psychiatry, 117*, 314–318.

Whiteside, S. P., Port, J. D., & Abramowitz, J. S. (2004). A meta–analysis of functional neuroimaging in obsessive–compulsive disorder. *Psychiatry Research: Neuroimaging, 132* (1), 69–79.

Whiteside, S. P., Port, J. D., Deacon, B. J., & Abramowitz, J. S. (2006). A magnetic resonance spectroscopy investigation of obsessive–compulsive disorder and anxiety. *Psychiatry Research: Neuroimaging, 132*, 1096–1103.

Zohar, A. H. (1999). The epidemiology of obsessive-compulsive disorder in children and adolescents. *Child and Adolescent Psychiatric Clinics of North America, 8*, 445–460.

5

Separation Anxiety Disorder

CYDNEY J. VAN DYKE, JENNIFER REGAN, AND
ANNE MARIE ALBANO

Pathological anxiety has been recognized for decades as a commonly occurring psychiatric condition of childhood and adolescence (Albano, Chorpita, & Barlow, 2003). Among the anxiety disorders defined in the latest revision of the *Diagnostic and Statistical Manual of Mental Disorders, Fourth Edition, Text Revision* (*DSM-IV-TR*; American Psychiatric Association [APA], 2000), separation anxiety disorder (SAD) is the only anxiety disorder preserved in the section on disorders of childhood or adolescence. The central feature of SAD is excessive, developmentally inappropriate anxiety or fear concerning separation from the child's home or major attachment figures. It is important to note that the fear or anxiety must be inappropriately severe based on the child's age, as separation anxiety is a normal developmental experience of early childhood (Albano et al., 2003). This fear includes cognitive (e.g., excessive worry that a catastrophic event will result in loss of or harm to the parent), behavioral (e.g., avoidance of school for fear of being separated from the parent), and physical (e.g., vague somatic complaints) components. Recurrent nightmares characterized by separation themes are also common in youngsters with SAD. Table 5.1 presents the diagnostic criteria (including the necessary number and duration of symptoms) for SAD based on the *DSM-IV-TR* (APA, 2000).

Table 5.1

DIAGNOSTIC CRITERIA FOR SEPARATION ANXIETY DISORDER (SAD) BASED ON THE *DSM-IV-TR*

I. Based on the individual's developmental level, inappropriate or excessive anxiety concerning separation from the home or major attachment figures, as evidenced by three (or more) of the following symptoms:
   a) Recurring excessive distress when anticipating or experiencing a separation from the home or major attachment figures
   b) Persistent and extreme worry about the possibility of losing or of harm befalling major attachment figures
   c) Persistent and extreme worry that an adverse event will result in a separation from major attachment figures
   d) Persistent reluctance or refusal to go to school or other places due to separation fears
   e) Persistent and extreme fear or avoidance of being alone or without major attachment figures or other significant adults
   f) Persistent reluctance or refusal to go to sleep without being near major attachment figures
   g) Recurrent nightmares involving separation themes
   h) Frequent physical complaints (such as headaches, stomachaches, nausea, or vomiting) when anticipating or experiencing separation from major attachment figures

II. The symptoms must last for at least 4 weeks.

III. The onset occurs before the age of 18.

IV. The disturbance causes clinically significant distress or impairment in social, academic (occupational), or other important domains of functioning.

V. The symptoms do not occur solely during the course of a pervasive developmental disorder or psychotic disorder and, in adolescents and adults, is not better explained by Panic Disorder With Agoraphobia.

VI. The specifier of *early onset* is appropriate if symptoms occur before the age of 6.

From: American Psychiatric Association. (2000). *The Diagnostic and Statistical Manual of Mental Disorders, Fourth Edition, Text-Revision,* Washington, DC: American Psychiatric Press.

In addition to these core diagnostic indicators, there are several associated symptoms and features common to SAD. When separated from their home or parents, children with SAD might exhibit social withdrawal with accompanying apathy or sadness (Albano et al., 2003; APA, 2000; Silverman & Dick-Niederhauser, 2004). For example, these youngsters may experience distress when dropped off for a classmate's birthday party or exhibit a general reluctance to leave home. This social avoidance can lead to difficulties with establishing and maintaining friendships and with achieving full academic potential (e.g., trouble concentrating in class because of preoccupying separation concerns or having to repeat a grade due to poor school attendance; Eisen & Schaefer, 2007). School refusal behaviors, in particular, tend to contribute further to social difficulties, as these children forgo valuable opportunities to engage socially with their peers (Kearney, 2001). It is also common for children with SAD to develop specific fears of stimuli or situations that are perceived to be threatening to the self or the family (e.g., monsters, animals, the dark, burglars, car accidents; APA, 2000; Last, 1989). Finally, children with SAD may threaten to hurt themselves to prevent separations from parents; however, serious suicidality in this population is rare (Last, 1989). On the contrary, concerns or fears of death and dying are not uncommon (APA, 2000).

High rates of psychiatric comorbidity are reported among youngsters with SAD. Verduin and Kendall (2003) found children with primary SAD to have a higher number of comorbid diagnoses than those with primary generalized anxiety disorder (GAD) or social phobia. In particular, it was common for children with primary SAD to have a comorbid diagnosis of GAD, specific phobia, attention-deficit/hyperactivity disorder (ADHD), social phobia, oppositional defiant disorder (ODD), and sleep terror disorder. Shear, Jin, Ruscio, Walters, and Kessler (2006) retrospectively studied comorbid psychiatric diagnoses among adults diagnosed with SAD during childhood or adolescence. In addition to other anxiety disorders, participants commonly met criteria for comorbid mood disorders (e.g., major depressive disorder, bipolar I or II disorders), impulse-control disorders (e.g., ADHD, conduct disorder), and substance abuse disorders. Given these common comorbidities, important rule-out diagnoses in the assessment of SAD include: GAD, panic disorder with or without agoraphobia, ODD, conduct disorder, social phobia, mood disorders, and pervasive developmental disorders (APA, 2000; Eisen & Schaefer, 2007).

Prevalence estimates suggest that SAD occurs in about 3% to 13% of children (Anderson, Williams, McGee & Silva, 1987), and upwards of 2.4% of adolescents (Bowen, Offord, & Boyle, 1990; McGee, Feehan, Williams, & Anderson, 1992). Although it can occur at any age, SAD is most commonly diagnosed in prepubertal children (Bowen et al.,

1990; Kashani & Orvaschel, 1988) and must be present before the age of 18 years (APA, 2000). Age-related differences in symptom presentation have been explored. One study reported nightmares, school refusal, and fears of harm befalling parents to be most common among children ages 5 to 8 years; anxiety and distress upon separation to be most common among children ages 9 to 12 years; and somatic complaints and school refusal to be most common among adolescents ages 13 to 16 years (Francis, Last, & Strauss, 1987). Gender differences in the rate of SAD also have been explored, but with mixed results. Although Francis et al. (1987) found no prevalence differences, Compton, Nelson, and March (2000) found self-reported separation anxiety symptoms to occur more frequently in females in a community sample and more frequently in males in a clinical sample. The researchers interpreted these findings as possibly resulting from differential rates of mental health treatment referral and use between girls and boys in the clinical sample.

The onset of SAD is typically acute, occurring during early to middle childhood (Shear et al., 2006). At times, SAD develops following a major life stressor (e.g., the death of a parent, divorce, relocation to a new school) or during a time of developmental change (e.g., starting elementary school; Last, 1989). In a longitudinal study of SAD symptoms at ages 3 and 6 years, Kearney, Sims, Purcell, and Tillotson (2003) found that most diagnoses of SAD were not stable during this period of development, as many children experienced a dissipation of symptoms on reassessment. Other studies (Cantwell & Baker, 1989; Keller et al., 1992) have suggested the variable course of SAD as the "waxing and waning" (Masi, Mucci, & Millepiedi, 2001, p. 96) of symptom severity often coinciding with major life changes such as an extended school holiday, a prolonged illness, or a change in residence. Furthermore, Last, Perrin, Hersen, and Kazdin (1996) reported that, among the anxiety disorders examined, children with SAD demonstrated the highest rate of recovery (95.7%), regardless of whether they received treatment. Still, a small subgroup of youngsters suffer a more chronic and persistent course (Kearney et al., 2003).

Various etiological models of SAD have been considered in the literature. Some theorists (e.g., Weems & Carrion, 2003) suggest the utility of attachment theory in explaining the development of SAD. Attachment theory proposes that youngsters with insecure attachment styles have had caregiver experiences characterized by inconsistencies in the availability and responsiveness to their needs. These children—much like those with SAD—exhibit significant distress upon separation from their caregivers and, even upon the caregiver's return, are difficult to console (Ainsworth, Blehar, Waters, & Wall, 1978). Given the striking similarities in symptom presentation, Weems and Carrion (2003) argue that the same processes underlie the development of both an insecure attachment style and SAD.

Similarly, parenting style seems to play a role in the development and maintenance of SAD. Parents of youngsters with SAD might not teach their children adequate coping skills to manage feelings of anxiety and insecurity in the parents' absence (Jurbergs & Ledley, 2005). For example, parents of anxious children tend to grant them less autonomy than do parents of nonanxious children (Silverman & Dick-Niederhauser, 2004). Parents of children with SAD also display higher rates of anxiety and mood disorders, as well as psychopathology in general (Kearney et al., 2003), than parents of nonanxious children. These parents may avoid fearful situations in their own lives, thereby modeling or reinforcing similar behavior in their children (Poulton, Milne, Craske, & Menzies, 2001). Youngsters with SAD may also make excessive demands on their parents' limited emotional resources, leading parents to quickly acquiesce or rescue the child with overprotectiveness or overindulgence (Kearney et al., 2003). This pattern of parental overinvolvement was studied by Wood (2006), who found that "parental intrusiveness" (i.e., the tendency to assume tasks that children could perform independently) correlated significantly with symptoms of separation anxiety. This pattern of parent–child interaction might serve to limit the child's development of a sense of mastery, foster excessive dependence on the caregivers, and ultimately maintain symptoms of SAD beyond the limits of developmental normalcy.

Finally, the role of temperament in the development of child anxiety disorders has been described at length in the literature (see Albano et al., 2003, for a review). Briefly, a temperament characterized by avoidance and withdrawal in new or unfamiliar situations—termed "behavioral inhibition" (Kagan, 1997)—has been linked to anxiety disorders during youth (e.g., Biederman et al., 1993). Jurbergs and Ledley (2005) further suggest that a difficult temperament during infancy and early childhood may exhaust parents' emotional resources, thereby contributing to the inconsistent or unresponsive parenting styles described previously.

In addition to the above-mentioned etiological models, several environmental and genetic risk factors for SAD have been identified in the literature. Life events such as exposure to a natural disaster or other trauma (Hoven et al., 2004), a prolonged separation from or loss of a parental figure (Cronk, Slutske, Madden, Bucholz, & Heath, 2004), a significant life change (Last, 1989), or a prolonged illness suffered by the self or a close other (Last, 1989) are associated with the development of SAD. Genetic risk factors have received empirical attention as well, with studies of identical twins suggesting a clear genetic component to child anxiety disorders in general and SAD in particular. Feigon, Waldman, Levy, and Hay (2001) found both genetic and shared environmental (e.g., prenatal conditions, parental health, divorce, socioeconomic status) risk factors to underlie the development of SAD in twins ages 3 to 18 years. Such genetic influences were moderated by age and gender, with a greater magnitude found among girls and older adolescents. Interestingly, one study by Ehringer, Rhee, Young, Corley, and Hewitt (2006) suggested that different genes may play a role in mediating SAD in males and females and that the heritability of SAD may be greater for girls than for boys.

EFFECTIVE TREATMENTS

Cognitive-Behavioral Interventions

A review of the literature on effective treatments for child anxiety disorders strongly supports the use of cognitive behavioral interventions. Although few trials have solely focused on treatment for SAD, most of the trials reported here included a significant portion of children with a primary diagnosis of SAD. Individual cognitive-behavioral therapy (ICBT) in particular has shown superiority to wait-list control groups in treating child anxiety disorders (Barrett, Dadds, & Rapee, 1996; Kendall, 1994; Kendall et al., 1997), with treatment gains maintained at long-term follow-up (Barrett, Duffy, Dadds, & Rapee, 2001; Kendall & Southam-Gerow, 1996). CBT manuals such as Kendall's "Coping Cat" (Kendall et al., 1992) are flexible and can be modified to accommodate for age, developmental level, and diagnostic status (e.g., SAD; Grover, Hughes, Bergman, & Kingery, 2006). Historically in CBT (i.e., before the development of manuals) the therapist developed an empirically informed treatment plan based on the functional analysis, with identified treatment targets (i.e., goals for specific symptoms) and criteria for outcomes specified in a collaboration with the child and parents. In clinical practice, as opposed to randomized controlled studies, manuals that are empirically supported in the treatment of certain conditions such as SAD can facilitate the selection of treatment components following a careful diagnostic evaluation and functional analysis.

Using criteria set forth by the American Psychological Association's Task Force on the Promotion and Dissemination of Psychological Procedures, Ollendick and King (1998) considered CBT a "probably efficacious" treatment for child anxiety disorders. Although some techniques may differ by protocol, CBT usually consists of psychoeducation, somatic management, cognitive restructuring, problem solving, exposure, and relapse prevention (Velting, Setzer, & Albano, 2004). To date, the most well-studied and empirically established CBT manual is the "Coping Cat" (Kendall et al., 1992), which emphasizes identification of anxious thoughts, coping skills, rewards, and graded exposure to anxiety-provoking situations. In monotherapy trials comparing CBT to a psychosocial control or wait-list condition, this program and others like it have been largely successful in improving diagnostic and clinical status for anxiety-disordered children, although a significant portion of these children remain symptomatic posttreatment, thus necessitating improved interventions (Ollendick & King, 1998).

Over the past few years, research on CBT for anxiety disorders has focused on maximizing treatment gains by examining the effectiveness of added emotional components, family involvement, and group treatment formats. In line with this call for innovative treatments, Suveg, Kendall, Comer, and Robin (2006) recently evaluated (using a multiple baseline design) and found initial support for emotion-focused CBT (ECBT), a traditional CBT program that integrates emotion-related concepts. Children participating in the trial improved diagnostically on anxiety measures and showed the added benefit of gains in understanding and regulating emotions. These promising, yet preliminary, results indicate the need for future trials comparing ECBT to traditional CBT.

Research investigating family involvement in CBT for anxiety disorders has also reported encouraging findings, particularly among treatments in which the family intervention is wholly integrated with the child's therapy. Such findings may be especially important for treating SAD, given that parental psychopathology is often a contributing factor, that high rates of family accommodation of symptoms have been reported among parents of anxious children (Storch et al., 2007), and that SAD has a high incidence among young females (Albano & Krain, 2005). For example, child-focused CBT (CCBT) with added family management has demonstrated increased efficacy on anxiety measures when compared to CCBT without family management (Barrett et al., 1996; Cobham, Dadds, & Spence, 1998). However, these added benefits were not maintained long-term (Barrett et al., 2001). Of note, treatment gains in these studies were greater for children with one or more anxious parents as well as for younger children and females.

Wood, Piacentini, Southam-Gerow, Chu, and Sigman (2006) recently compared family-focused CBT (FCBT), which emphasizes communication training, to CCBT. Following treatment, independent evaluator ratings indicated significantly greater improvements in global functioning and decreased anxiety severity in the FCBT group, as compared to the CCBT group. Parent ratings also indicated a more rapid decrease in anxiety symptoms in the FCBT group over the course of treatment. Yet, comparable findings were not evident in child self-reports. As the absence of treatment differences in child self-reports is common across studies, the authors argue that, from a child's perspective, the treatments may be equally efficacious. However, given the significant decreases in observable anxiety symptoms and the improved global functioning in the FCBT condition, further research in this area is encouraged.

Research on group CBT (GCBT) with family involvement has similarly demonstrated significant treatment effects, but with some limitations. Mendlowitz et al. (1999) found that children randomized to a combined parent-and-child group intervention used more active coping strategies and evidenced greater improvement in parent-reported emotional well-being, as compared to those in the parent-only and child-only groups. In addition, Shortt, Barrett, and Fox (2001) reported that children who completed family-focused GCBT improved on assessment measures significantly more than children in a wait-list control group. However, because there was no GCBT comparison group, it is unclear whether these gains were the result of family involvement. Barrett (1998) also reported improvements on parent self-report measures in a GCBT-plus-family management group as compared to a GCBT group; however, these improvements were only marginal and necessitate replication. Further support for GCBT-plus-family intervention was also indicated in a recent school-based intervention trial (Bernstein, Layne, Egan, & Tennison, 2005).

The research on GCBT without added family interventions also shows promise (Barrett, 1998; Silverman et al., 1999), but more studies are needed to determine whether GCBT is equally as efficacious as ICBT across anxiety disorders. In one trial, Flannery-Schroeder and Kendall (2000) found that children in both ICBT and GCBT conditions improved on diagnostic measures compared to wait-list controls; yet, only children receiving ICBT showed improved self-reported state anxiety. Given that there were pretreatment group differences on this measure and that there may have been insufficient opportunity to detect differences between the two active treatments, the authors suggest that these findings be interpreted with caution.

In a related trial, Manassis et al. (2002) reported that, although children in both ICBT and GCBT conditions showed significant improvements on parent, child, and clinician measures, the few significant group differences on these measures mostly favored individual treatment. However, given that both treatments included parental involvement, it is possible that the positive effects are attributable to this additional factor. Future research should focus on comparing ICBT and GCBT to inactive treatments in larger sample sizes.

Investigations of psychosocial treatments specifically geared toward younger children have also reported preliminary support for their use in treating anxiety disorders. Friedberg et al. (2003) assessed outcomes for a cognitive-behaviorally based skills training program in a small group of elementary school children with anxious and depressive symptoms. Results showed that children reported fewer symptoms at posttreatment and follow-up and perceived the program to be modestly helpful and somewhat fun. However, further long-term outcomes remain unclear, as parents and children lessened their use of coping skills following treatment.

Additionally, Choate, Pincus, Eyberg, and Barlow (2005) investigated the use of parent–child interaction therapy (PCIT) in a multiple-baseline study of three children diagnosed with SAD. Results indicated clinically significant change in separation anxiety on all measures, as well as maintenance of treatment gains at a 3-month follow-up. This adapted treatment is noted for being the only treatment to specifically target SAD, and an upcoming randomized clinical trial will study its efficacy further.

Pharmacological Interventions

In addition to these psychosocial treatments, pharmacological treatments, particularly selective serotonin reuptake inhibitors (SSRIs), have shown efficacy in treating child anxiety disorders. The Research Unit on Pediatric Psychopharmacology Anxiety Study Group (2001) found that children randomized to receive fluvoxamine demonstrated a greater reduction in anxiety symptoms and a superior clinical response as compared to children in the placebo group, thus supporting its short-term use in treating child anxiety. Birmaher et al. (2003) also reported that children (ages 7 to 17 years) with GAD, SAD, or SP (social phobia) receiving fluoxetine showed more improvement on main outcome measures than those in the placebo group. However, following this 12-week trial, approximately 50% of children continued to remain symptomatic. Although SP was a moderator of clinical and functional response, severity of illness at intake and family history of anxiety predicted poorer outcome in this study.

Combined CBT and Pharmacotherapy

The Child/Adolescent Anxiety Multimodal Study (CAMS; Walkup et al., 2009), a 6-year, six-site, multimodal randomized controlled trial, evaluated the comparative short-term efficacy of cognitive-behavioral therapy, medication (sertraline), combination treatment, and pill placebo in 488 youth ages 7 to 17 years diagnosed with SAD, social phobia, and generalized anxiety disorder. Funded by the National Institutes of Mental Health (NIMH), the primary aims of CAMS were to compare the relative efficacy of the active treatments to pill placebo, while also comparing the efficacy of combination treatment to CBT and sertraline. In addition, CAMS allowed for the systematic assessment of the relative safety of the medication, prescribed as the sole treatment or in combination with CBT, as compared with the nonactive medication conditions (CBT, placebo). The investigators hypothesized that all three active treatments would be superior to placebo and that combination treatment would prove superior to CBT or medication alone. At the time of this writing, the CAMS authors are embargoed from reporting the primary outcomes in print form until the journal publication is published. Suffice it to say that after 12 weeks of acute treatment, all the active treatments proved superior to pill placebo, indicating that children with SAD, SP, and GAD benefit from active intervention. Moreover, examination of side effects and adverse events were consistent with prior studies of the use of SSRI medications for pediatric mood and anxiety disorders, suggesting these medications are safe and well tolerated by pediatric patients.

Given these findings, the unknown potential of negative effects of long-term SSRI use (Pine, 2002) and the results from studies of combination treatments (Bernstein et al., 2000; Walkup et al., 2009), pharmacological treatments may be most beneficial for child anxiety disorders when used in the short term and in conjunction with cognitive-behavioral therapy.

FACTORS ASSOCIATED WITH POOR RESPONSE TO CBT

Child Factors

Despite recent advances in the empirical validation of treatments for SAD, various psychological, behavioral, cultural, and family factors tend to be associated with a poor response to traditional cognitive-behavioral therapies. As previously noted, SAD is accompanied by high rates of psychiatric comorbidity in childhood (Albano et al., 2003; Eisen & Schaefer, 2007) that extends into adulthood (Shear et al., 2006). Perhaps unsurprisingly, comorbidity is often associated with severity of functional impairment over the long term (e.g., Shear et al., 2006). Furthermore, most patients with comorbid conditions fail to receive psychological treatment for SAD symptoms; rather, other emotional or behavioral problems often become the reported focus of treatment (Shear et al., 2006). This finding suggests that clinicians may have difficulty effectively recognizing and targeting SAD symptoms in the context of a comorbid anxiety, mood, or externalizing disorder. For example, a study by Berman, Weems, Silverman, and Kurtines (2000) found comorbid depression in children with phobic and anxiety disorders to be correlated with a poorer response to exposure-based cognitive and behavioral treatments.

Likewise, accompanying school-refusal behavior has been related to a refractory course in the treatment of SAD. In addition to limiting opportunities for social interactions with peers, research suggests serious short- and long-term consequences of school-refusal behavior, including academic decline, family conflict, financial and legal problems, social isolation, and school dropout (Buitelaar, van Andel, Duyx, & van Strien, 1994; Kearney, 2001). Given the severity of such consequences, school-refusal behavior has the potential to seriously complicate the course of treatment and therefore demands specific attention from clinicians.

Several demographic factors have been identified as contributing to a poor treatment response. Older age has been associated with less favorable outcomes in the treatment of child and adolescent anxiety disorders, including SAD (Southam-Gerow, Kendall, & Weersing, 2001). It may be that older youth have more chronic or "non-normative" (developmentally speaking) conditions, suggesting the likelihood of greater symptom severity or intransigence. The presence of gender differences in SAD treatment response has also been studied, but with mixed results. Layne, Bernstein, Egan, and Kushner (2003) found anxious-depressed male adolescents to respond more positively than females to CBT for SAD; however, Southam-Gerow et al. (2001) found no gender differences in CBT outcomes among anxious youth ages 7 to 15.

Few studies have examined potential cultural differences in SAD treatment response during youth (Albano et al., 2003). However, it is generally accepted that a child or family's cultural frame of reference (including beliefs about mental illness and appropriate forms of emotional expression) can affect initial entry into treatment, as well as subsequent treatment compliance, course, and outcome. Socioeconomic disadvantages can further hinder treatment response among ethnic and cultural minority populations by limiting access to appropriate services because of financial or transportation constraints or a lack of effective outreach and psychoeducation programs (Aponte & Johnson, 2000). The importance of considering such cultural and socioeconomic factors in the treatment of SAD is highlighted by findings of greater frequency of SAD symptoms among African American children than European American children in community and clinical samples (Compton et al., 2000).

Finally, learning disabilities and other deficits in intellectual functioning can affect a youngster's understanding of and subsequent response to psychosocial treatment for SAD. More specifically, research has identified several limitations to the effectiveness of CBT with cognitively or learning-disabled populations in general. For example, Kroese

(1998) suggested that CBT can only be effective with clients who can (a) provide reliable and valid self-reports, (b) understand abstract concepts (such as anxiety and fear) through psychoeducation, and (c) engage in some form of self-regulation so as to enable the generalization and maintenance of treatment gains over time and across situations. Depending on the extent of the youngster's cognitive limitations, deficits in such abilities may reduce the effectiveness of traditional CBT techniques and therefore necessitate a more novel, client-specific approach.

Parent Factors

Parental psychopathology has been associated with poor treatment response among youth with SAD. Berman et al. (2000) studied predictors of treatment outcomes in exposure-based cognitive and behavioral therapies for youth with phobic and anxiety disorders in general; results showed that symptoms of parental psychopathology—such as depression, fear, hostility, and paranoia—predicted a poorer treatment response. Studies of SAD in particular tend to corroborate these findings. Southam-Gerow et al. (2001) found higher levels of maternal self-reported depressive symptoms to predict a less favorable response to CBT among youth ages 7 to 15. Likewise, Kearney et al. (2003) reported parental psychopathology (i.e., depressive symptoms, obsessive-compulsive behaviors, general distress, and phobic anxiety) to predict the maintenance of SAD symptoms in young children over 3 years' time.

These findings suggest the need for clinicians to equally target symptoms of parental psychopathology and distress, as they may lead to the modeling or reinforcement of avoidant behavior and attachment problems and ultimately impact the generalizability of treatment gains to other settings. A parent's response to his or her child's fearful or avoidant behavior, in particular, has been identified as contributing to poor treatment response. As noted earlier, Wood (2006) studied the relationship between "parental intrusiveness" and SAD symptoms; results showed that parental intrusiveness or overinvolvement (e.g., invasions of privacy, infantilizing behavior, unnecessary assistance with the child's tasks of daily living) correlated with SAD symptoms but not with symptoms of GAD or social phobia. This specific link suggests that parents of children with SAD may be differentially inclined to acquiesce or rescue their children from anxiety-provoking separations, thus reinforcing the avoidant behavior and sacrificing valuable opportunities for their children to develop a sense of autonomy and mastery over separation experiences (Kearney et al., 2003; Wood, 2006).

CASE PRESENTATION

Presenting Complaint and History

Jason, a 12-year-old Caucasian child, was referred for an evaluation and cognitive behavioral treatment following 3 months of school-refusal behavior. In November, during the weekend prior to Thanksgiving, Jason developed a streptococcal throat infection necessitating his staying home from school. These absences necessitated by illness led into the holiday, after which Jason complained, cried, begged and threw tantrums, in response to having to return to school. His parents cajoled, bribed, begged, and threatened, but to no avail, as Jason remained steadfast in his refusal to dress for school and remained in his room until his father and younger brother left the house each day, leaving him with his mother. He "agreed" to go back to school after the New Year, but this did not occur. Jason's parents were given referrals by the school at the beginning of February, when it was apparent that Jason was not budging.

During the intake process, a long-standing pattern of separation anxiety symptoms and disorder emerged, dating back to Jason's preschool days. According to his parents, Jason was never able to stay alone in a room for any reasonable length of time, such as to play by himself while his mother was in another room of the house, nor was he able to sleep alone at night. They described Jason as temperamentally anxious as a baby and toddler, one who "always had to be held" and "never having slept through the night." He slept with his parents until his brother, who was 3 years younger than he, reached the age of 3 and the boys were moved into one bedroom together. Still, Jason insisted on keeping a bedside light on throughout the night, despite his brother's protests. Jason's mother sat outside his preschool classroom for the 3-hour morning sessions, and he constantly checked to see if she was there. Once he entered kindergarten, and the public school took a harder line on parents staying through the session, Jason was "forced" to stay in school without his mother. She reported being "torn to pieces" by his wailing when dropping him off each day. According to the teachers, Jason did not settle into a routine for the first several months of school but instead watched out the window and waited for his mother's return. By first grade, he was more accustomed to being left at school but began a pattern of complaining about somatic symptoms, resulting in trips to the school nurse and calls to his mother. His father described an escalating pattern of calls from the nurse throughout each school year, with Jason's mother picking him up from school early more days than not. At the time of referral, Jason was in the 6th grade and according to his father, had probably never had a full week of school during which he stayed all day, every day. He reportedly was "not surprised" that Jason finally stood his ground and refused to leave the house. Jason's father added that "if she {mother} had let him toughen up, we wouldn't be here."

Diagnostic Evaluation

Jason and his parents were administered the Anxiety Disorders Interview Schedule for *DSM-IV*, Child and Parent Versions (Silverman & Albano, 1996), a semi-structured, reliable interview format covering the *DSM* diagnoses and related behavioral disturbances in children. At the time of the evaluation, Jason refused to leave home without his mother or allow his mother to leave home without him. He tolerated staying home with his father or grandparents, if his mother left for a brief period, such as to run an errand. She admitted that she was never gone for more than 2 hours at a time, and hadn't left him for longer than that since he was at least 8 years of age. Both Jason and his parents reported that he feared something terrible happening to either him or his mother, less so for his father, that would then result in their not seeing each other again. Jason refused to attend any activities without his mother present, such as birthday parties, sports events, or even playing outside his home with friends. He reported having nightmares that revolved around themes of loss or separation. Jason recognized that his fear was extreme, and admitted to feeling embarrassed about his separation anxiety, but he felt helpless to change. Both Jason and his parents also admitted that Jason has lost friends because of his anxiety, as he stopped going outside to play ball with friends or to play over at their homes. Initially, his parents bought him bigger and better toys, computer games, televisions, and all sorts of "things" to entice his friends to keep coming to their home to hang out with Jason. However, Jason's parents realized that the reinforcement value of these items are very time limited and wear thin fast, hence, the kids stopped coming to visit. Jason and his parents agreed that this separation anxiety was exerting a significant negative impact on his life and it impaired his functioning severely, across several domains. In addition to school problems, loss of friendships, continued dependence on his mother rather than advancing toward adolescence, Jason's parents also admitted to severe discord because of their disagreement in how to handle Jason. His mother reported an ingrained belief that if she "left him alone for days, to cry this out as his father wished her to do, " then Jason would be permanently scarred by the separation trauma. Based on the history and presenting problem, Jason met criteria for separation anxiety disorder at a very severe and disabling level.

Also, Jason and his parents endorsed a variety of specific phobias that were present for many years and also impaired his functioning. For example, his fear of thunderstorms, birds, and insects hampered Jason's ability to enjoy the outdoors. His family stopped having picnics and taking vacations in the mountains because of his distress. He often stayed inside during the warmer months for fear of encountering an insect. Jason also had a phobia of choking, hence he would eat only smoothies and softer foods and needed to have any solids such as meat or chicken cut into tiny pieces. He did not eat any food not prepared by his parents, for fear that "something hard could get into the food" and become stuck in his throat. Jason also met criteria for generalized anxiety disorder, and was called a "50-year-old man" by his parents. That is, he worried about the family finances, whether they had enough health insurance, the potential for war to break out in the United States, the potential for a natural disaster, burglars breaking into his family's home, and whether he would be homeless one day. His parents reported that "he's always fretting" over one thing or another and was never reassured for any length of time. When worrying, Jason reported feeling on edge, being unable to relax, and complained of headaches and stomach aches. Hence, similar to other children with SAD, Jason met criteria for additional anxiety disorders of GAD and phobias. Of note, there was no significant history of loss in Jason's family. Whereas the father denied any personal or family history of mental illness, Jason's mother admitted to a long history of worry, occasional panic attacks, and a strong history of depression with repeated hospitalizations in her mother.

Treatment and Course

Jason's parents were strongly opposed to medication treatment and specifically sought psychosocial therapy. Given the comorbidity pattern and severe degree of disability and distress evidenced in this child, which included school refusal, impairment in peer relationships, disruption in activities of daily living, and family stress, among other concerns, a combined psychosocial and medication approach was offered to the family. Taking their treatment preference into account, Jason and his parents agreed to cognitive-behavioral therapy. In the initial treatment session, specific, well-defined treatment goals were identified in collaboration with Jason and his parents (Table 5.2). Jason understood from the outset of treatment that our overall goals were to return him to school on a full-time basis, increase his ability to be comfortable in settings and situations without his mother, and increase his skills in managing anxiety in a wide range of situations involving separation, worry, and specific fears. Because of the complexity of this case, initial treatment goals were defined with reasonable time-courses for when treatment gains should be expected. For example, the goal after the first week of treatment was to have Jason engage with his teacher by e-mail to access assignments. During the second week, this contact increased to Jason talking to the teacher on the phone and, by the end of this week, visiting her at school to pick up his work and have his academic work reviewed by her. The third week of treatment involved setting the goal for Jason to be attending selected classes for part of the school day. These stepwise goals, aimed at returning Jason to school, were accompanied by home-based behavioral goals of allowing his mother to leave him for increasing periods of time. An agreement between Jason and the therapist was developed whereby if these goals were not met within a reasonable time frame, plus or minus 7 to 10 days of the target, we would have to revisit the issue of medication treatment.

Jason's school refusal was at a critical level as the school officials were discussing holding him back if he did not catch up in his work and attend a sufficient number of school days to pass for the year. Historically, Jason was a good, solid student who made average to above average grades in all areas. The idea of holding him back was troublesome for Jason, as he had already lost some friends because of his anxieties and he was concerned about what other kids would think

Table 5.2

TREATMENT GOALS AND TARGET TIME FRAME

SCHOOL-BASED GOALS	TARGET TIME PERIOD FOR ACHIEVEMENT
1. Connect with homeroom teacher/advisor via email and complete assignments	End of treatment week 1
2. Talk to teacher/advisor by telephone	End of treatment week 1 to beginning of treatment week 2
3. Visit teacher at school, after school hours to receive homework and feedback on completed assignments	End of treatment week 2
4. Attend 1 or 2 class periods each day	Treatment week 3
5. Increase attendance in school to full days	Treatment week 4
HOME-BASED GOALS	**TARGET TIME PERIOD FOR ACHIEVEMENT**
1. Mother leaves during home-based tutoring sessions (1 hour), Jason stays on task without disruption	End of treatment week 1
2. Mother leaves for unspecified short periods and calls home during these separations, Jason allows these separations to occur without begging or crying	End of week 1 to beginning of treatment week 2
3. Mother leaves, does not call or respond to phone calls, and is gone for unspecified periods of time (15 minutes to 2-3 hours) while Jason remains on-task or engages in relaxation/breathing practice (note, father or sitter at home during this time but not interacting with Jason)	End of treatment week 2, beginning of week 3
4. Jason continues to practice his skills and otherwise engage in self-directed or school-based activity while his mother is away from him for increasingly longer time periods	Treatment week 4
5. Jason stays with a sitter in the evenings while his parents go out, and by the end of this week he goes to bed before they return home for the night.	End of treatment week 4 and treatment week 5

of him. Hence, treatment was initiated on a twice-weekly basis to provide a concentrated, more intensive intervention approach in the initial stage of therapy. During the first week, psychoeducation about the nature of anxiety, identification of and normalization of feelings, the three components of anxiety and related feelings, and tracking of triggers to anxiety were taught and emphasized. Concurrently, Jason was instructed in deep, diaphragmatic breathing as a basic relaxation and focusing technique. Also, situational exposures to contacting the school teacher and allowing his mother to separate for brief periods were implemented. All of this was implemented while also getting Jason on a regular school-day schedule (awake by 7, dressed and fed by 7:45; initiating schoolwork by 8:15), even though he was still at home. The importance of maintaining school routines for an easier re-entry was emphasized. Most important, Jason was assisted in understanding the role of avoidance in maintaining and increasing anxiety. Not keeping to a school schedule, talking to his teacher, and falling behind in his school work, were identified as subtle avoidance behaviors that build on one another and contribute to an overall pattern of "hiding" from any situations or triggers to school-related stimuli. Incentives were tied to the new school-day schedule, with computer and television time used as reinforcement for compliance with the new routines. Much to his credit, Jason was motivated to address these problems so he responded well to the school-day routine and increase in expectations for completing academic tasks.

Although the treatment plan was implemented with all good intentions by Jason and his parents, difficulties quickly arose over the expectation for Jason to spend increasing amounts of time away from his mother. The difficulties centered on Jason's expected and natural reactions of increasing anxiety and some tearfulness at the initiation of the separations. These reactions are not unusual, even in highly motivated children, as the reality of the situation sets in as the child confronts his or her fear. The complication in this case was evident in Jason's mother's inability to remove herself as planned, as she became overwhelmed with her own anxieties and feelings of guilt for causing upset in her child. In response, the therapist conducted a home-based observation to assist with a separation. Left on their own, a clear cycle was evident whereby Jason's mother presented her intended departure with trepidation: "Son, I know this will be hard for you but I have to go to the store while you stay with the tutor. I will only be at the store so I know you worry about me and that something bad can happen, but I will call you and you can call me." As Jason's mother continued to infuse anxiety into her departure, Jason's tears began along with trembling and other panic-like symptoms. Accompanying these reactions were his pleas to stay at home: "I can't do this. I'm not ready and won't be able to do this. Please don't leave me!" The process continued with Jason's mother validating his lack of readiness and pleading with the therapist to slow down the separation exposures.

Once this cycle of parental reinforcement of the child's anxious behavior and avoidance was realized, the therapist and parents met separately to evaluate his mother's concerns, make suggestions for concurrent therapy for the mother to address her anxiety, and plan for the father to assist in the separation exposures. Time lines for meeting goals were adjusted at this point, as it was evident that a strong environmental component was contributing to the ongoing anxiety, and so the medication treatment was again put on hold to provide Jason's mother with skills to manage her own anxieties and those related to doing psychological damage to her child. At the same time, parent training sessions to assist both parents with reasonable limit-setting, use of ignoring of complaints and whining, appropriate use of tangible reinforcement for proactive/coping-focused behavior, and labeled praise for confronting his fears were taught via role play, rehearsal, and feedback. The treatment schedule was therefore adjusted to one full child session per week plus an addition session split into half for Jason and half for the parent training.

Jason remained in CBT for a full year, with a return to school full time at the end of the 9th week of treatment. At that point, his parents were consistent with the parenting, with his father mainly administering any treatment components at home. Sessions were then scaled back to one per week, focused on Jason, with a parent session occurring every 6 weeks. His mother continued in her own therapy and interestingly, began medication treatment plus CBT for long-standing anxiety issues. Once the school refusal was addressed, a plan for relapse prevention was enacted whereby Jason attended day camp throughout the summer, while also working on addressing his specific phobias of insects and environmental situations. This continued "out of the house" structured activity was meant to prevent old habits from spontaneous recovery. At the start of the summer, Jason's fear of the dark and sleeping away from home (at relatives' and friends' houses) was addressed with a similar graded exposure approach. Concurrently, the therapy also focused on activity scheduling of pleasant, peer-focused situations that did not involve parents. With impending adolescence and pubertal changes, Jason's independent functioning became paramount. Age-appropriate independent activity was therefore made a priority toward the end of the treatment year, as Jason had turned 13 and was attending 8th grade. He continued in therapy on a monthly basis for an additional 6 months. Of note, treatment was provided by a graduate student therapist at a university clinic, making this intensive and longer term treatment affordable for the family. At the conclusion of treatment, Jason continued to evidence occasional episodes of heightened worry, usually triggered by challenging events (e.g., high school entrance exam; illness in grandparent) and often accompanied by somatic complaints. These GAD symptoms were discussed as a vulnerability for increased anxiety sensitivity and the potential for setting him up for avoidance behavior. A book of relapse prevention strategies was made in treatment by Jason and his therapist. This book outlined the strategies learned in therapy and upcoming challenges that will be faced over the next several years (e.g., start of high school; dating; college-entrance exams; grandparents' aging; learning to drive). Plans were developed to address these various challenges in realistic, reasonable ways, along with a plan for deciding when to call the therapist for help.

CONCLUSIONS AND FUTURE DIRECTIONS

Separation anxiety disorder is one of the most common anxiety disorders affecting children and adolescents. The current state of the literature clearly supports the efficacy of both individual and group CBT for SAD. Furthermore, medication trials have garnered evidence for the efficacy of certain pharmacological agents (particularly SSRIs) in the treatment of childhood anxiety disorders in general. However, despite these recent clinical advances, a subset of youth remains clinically impaired by their symptoms, warranting the consideration of a combination treatment approach incorporating both CBT and medication treatments in tandem. As such, several child and parent factors have been identified empirically as contributing to a more refractory disease course and a poorer response to treatment with traditional CBT. These findings suggest the need for continued research and clinical trials with refractory cases in particular.

Such research may reveal novel treatment techniques that can be used in tailoring more client-specific treatment plans and ultimately improving treatment outcomes for these youngsters.

Future clinical investigations of both psychosocial and pharmacological interventions should also focus their efforts on the study of youngsters with SAD in particular (as opposed to anxiety disorders in general). Although many of the studies described in this chapter included in their samples a sizeable proportion of youth with a primary diagnosis of SAD, children and adolescents with primary diagnoses of GAD or major depressive disorder, for example, often are included as well. The overall findings of such research may obscure the need for interventions that target the unique clinical needs of children and adolescents with SAD in particular. For example, compared with other anxiety and mood disorders, successful treatment of SAD may require increased parental involvement or consultation with the child's school. Large-scale research programs of youngsters with SAD in particular are therefore needed to assess the appropriateness and efficacy of such additional treatment components.

REFERENCES

Ainsworth, M. D., Blehar, M. C., Waters, E., & Wall, S. (1978). *Patterns of attachment: A psychological study of the strange situation.* Hillsdale, NJ: Erlbaum.

Albano, A. M., Chorpita, B. F., & Barlow, D. H. (2003). Childhood anxiety disorders. In E. J. Mash & R. A. Barkley (Eds.), *Child psychopathology* (pp. 279–329). New York: Guilford Press.

Albano, A. M., & Krain, A. (2005) Anxiety and anxiety disorders in girls. In D. J. Bell, S. L. Foster, & E. J. Mash (Eds.), *Handbook of behavioral and emotional problems in girls* (pp. 79–116). New York: Academic/Plenum Publishers.

American Psychiatric Association. (2000). *Diagnostic and statistical manual of mental disorders* (4th ed., text revision). Washington, DC: American Psychiatric Press.

Anderson, J. C., Williams, S. M., McGee, R., & Silva, P. A. (1987). DSM-III disorders in preadolescent children: Prevalence in a large sample from the general population. *Archives of General Psychiatry, 44,* 69–76.

Aponte, J. F., & Johnson, L. R. (2000). The impact of culture on the intervention and treatment of ethnic populations. In J. F. Aponte & J. Wohl (Eds.), *Psychological intervention and cultural diversity* (2nd ed.; pp. 18–39). Needham Heights, MA: Allyn & Bacon.

Barrett, P. M. (1998). Evaluation of cognitive-behavioral group treatments for childhood anxiety disorders. *Journal of Clinical Child Psychology, 27,* 459–468.

Barrett, P. M., Dadds, M. R., & Rapee, R. M. (1996). Family treatment of childhood anxiety: A controlled trial. *Journal of Consulting and Clinical Psychology, 64,* 333–342.

Barrett, P. M., Duffy, A. L., Dadds, M. R., & Rapee, R. M. (2001). Cognitive-behavioral treatment of anxiety disorders in children: Long-term (6-year) follow-up. *Journal of Consulting and Clinical Psychology, 69*, 135–141.

Berman, S. L., Weems, C. F., Silverman, W. K., & Kurtines, W. M. (2000). Predictors of outcome in exposure-based cognitive and behavioral treatments for phobic and anxiety disorders in children. *Behavioral Therapy, 31*, 713–731.

Bernstein, G. A., Borchardt, C. M., Perwien, A. R., Crosby, R. D, Kushner, M. G., Thuras, P. D. & Last, C. G. (2000). Imipramine plus cognitive-behavioral therapy in the treatment of school refusal. *Journal of the American Academy of Child and Adolescent Psychiatry, 39*, 276–283.

Bernstein, G. A., Layne, A. E., Egan, E. A., & Tennison, D. M. (2005). School-based interventions for anxious children. *Journal of the American Academy of Child and Adolescent Psychiatry, 44*, 1118–1127.

Biederman, J., Rosenbaum, J. F., Boldue-Murphy, E. A., Faraone, S., Chaloff, J., Hirschfield, D. R., et al. (1993). Behavioral inhibition as a temperamental risk factor for anxiety disorders. *Child and Adolescent Psychiatric Clinics of North America, 2*, 667–684.

Birmaher, B., Axelson, D. A., Monk, K., Kalas, C., Clark, D. B., Ehmann, M., et al. (2003). Fluoxetine for the treatment of childhood anxiety disorders. *Journal of the American Academy of Child and Adolescent Psychiatry, 42*, 415–423.

Bowen, R. C., Offord, D. R., & Boyle, M. H. (1990). The prevalence of overanxious disorder and separation anxiety disorder: Results from the Ontario Child Health Study. *Journal of the American Academy of Child and Adolescent Psychiatry, 29*, 753–758.

Buitelaar, J. K., van Andel, H., Duyx, J. H. M., & van Strien, D. C. (1994). Depressive and anxiety disorders in adolescence: A follow-up of adolescents with school refusal. *Acta Paedopsychiatrica: International Journal of Child and Adolescent Psychiatry, 56*, 249–253.

Cantwell, D. P., & Baker, L. (1989). Stability and natural history of DSM-III childhood diagnoses. *Journal of the American Academy of Child and Adolescent Psychiatry, 29*, 691–700.

Choate, M. L., Pincus, D. B., Eyberg, S. M., & Barlow, D. H. (2005). Parent-child interaction therapy for treatment of separation anxiety disorder in young children: A pilot study. *Cognitive and Behavioral Practice, 12*, 126–135.

Cobham, V. E., Dadds, M. R., & Spence, S. H. (1998). The role of parental anxiety in the treatment of childhood anxiety. *Journal of Consulting and Clinical Psychology, 66*, 893–905.

Compton, S. N., Nelson, A. H., & March, J. S. (2000). Social phobia and separation anxiety symptoms in community and clinical samples of children and adolescents. *Journal of the American Academy of Child and Adolescent Psychiatry, 39*, 1040–1046.

Cronk, N. J., Slutske, W. S., Madden, P. A. F., Bucholz, K. K., & Heath, A. C. (2004). Risk for separation anxiety disorder among girls: Paternal absence, socioeconomic disadvantage, and genetic vulnerability. *Journal of Abnormal Psychology, 113*, 237–247.

Ehringer, M. A., Rhee, S. H., Young, S., Corley, R., & Hewitt, J. K. (2006). Genetic and environmental contributions to common psychopathologies of childhood and adolescence: A study of twins and their siblings. *Journal of Abnormal Child Psychology, 34,* 1–17.

Eisen, A., & Schaefer, C.A. (2007). *Separation anxiety in children and adolescents: An individualized approach to assessment and treatment.* New York: Guilford Press.

Feigon, S. A., Waldman, I. D., Levy, F., & Hay, D. A. (2001). Genetic and environmental influences on separation anxiety disorder symptoms and their moderation by age and sex. *Behavior Genetics, 31,* 403–411.

Flannery-Schroeder, E. C. & Kendall, P. C. (2000). Group and individual cognitive-behavioral treatments for youth with anxiety disorders: A randomized clinical trial. *Cognitive Therapy and Research, 24,* 251–278.

Francis, G., Last, C. G., & Strauss, C. C. (1987). Expression of separation anxiety disorder: The roles of age and gender. *Child Psychiatry and Human Development, 18,* 82–89.

Friedberg, R.D., McClure, J. M., Wilding, L., Goldman, M.L., Long, M. P., Anderson, L., et al. (2003). A cognitive-behavioral skills training group for children experiencing anxious and depressive symptoms: A clinical report with accompanying descriptive data. *Journal of Contemporary Psychotherapy, 33,* 157–175.

Grover, R. L., Hughes, A. A., Bergman, R. L., & Kingery, J. N. (2006). Treatment modifications based on childhood anxiety diagnosis: Demonstrating the flexibility in manualized treatment. *Journal of Cognitive Psychotherapy, 20,* 275–286.

Hoven, C. H., Duarte, C. S., Wu, P., Erickson, E. A., Musa, G. J., & Mandell, D. J. (2004). Exposure to trauma and separation anxiety in children after the WTC attack. *Applied Developmental Science, 8,* 172–183.

Jurbergs, N., & Ledley, D. R. (2005). Separation anxiety. *Psychiatric Annals, 35,* 728–735.

Kagan, J. (1997). Temperament and the reactions to unfamiliarity. *Child Development, 68,* 139–143.

Kashani, J. H., & Orvaschel, H. (1988). Anxiety disorders in mid-adolescence: A community sample. *American Journal of Psychiatry, 145,* 960–964.

Kearney, C. A. (2001). *School refusal behavior in youth: A functional approach to assessment and treatment.* Washington, DC: American Psychological Association.

Kearney, C. A., Sims, K. E., Pursell, C. R., & Tillotson, C. A. (2003). Separation anxiety disorder in young children: A longitudinal and family analysis. *Journal of Clinical Child and Adolescent Psychology, 32,* 593–598.

Keller, M. B., Lavori, P., Wunder, J., Beardslee, W. R., Schwartz, C. E., & Roth, J. (1992). Chronic course of anxiety disorders in children and adolescents. *Journal of the American Academy of Child and Adolescent Psychiatry, 31,* 595–599.

Kendall, P. C. (1994). Treating anxiety disorders in children: Results of a randomized clinical trial. *Journal of Consulting and Clinical Psychology, 62,* 100–110.

Kendall, P. C., Chansky, T. E., Kane, M., Kim, R., Kortlander, E., Ronan, K., et al. (1992). *Anxiety disorders in youth: Cognitive-behavioral interventions.* Needham Heights, MA: Allyn & Bacon.

Kendall, P. C., Flannery-Schroeder, E., Panichelli-Mindel, S., Southam-Gerow, M., Henin, A., & Warman, M. (1997). Therapy for youths with anxiety disorders: A second randomized clinical trial. *Journal of Consulting and Clinical Psychology, 65,* 366–380.

Kendall, P. C., & Southam-Gerow, M. A. (1996). Long-term follow-up of cognitive-behavioral therapy for anxiety-disordered youth. *Journal of Consulting and Clinical Psychology, 64,* 724–730.

Kroese, B. S. (1998). Cognitive-behavioral therapy for people with learning disabilities. *Behavioural and Cognitive Psychotherapy, 26,* 315–322.

Last, C. G. (1989). Anxiety disorders of childhood or adolescence. In C. G. Last & M. Hersen (Eds.), *Handbook of child psychiatric diagnosis* (pp. 156–169). New York: Wiley.

Last, C. G., Perrin, S., Hersen, M., & Kazdin, A. E. (1996). A prospective study of childhood anxiety disorders. *Journal of the American Academy of Child and Adolescent Psychiatry, 35,* 1502–1510.

Layne, A. E., Bernstein, G. A., Egan, E. A., & Kushner, M. G. (2003). Predictors of treatment response in anxious-depressed adolescents with school refusal. *Journal of the American Academy of Child and Adolescent Psychiatry, 42,* 319–326.

Manassis, K., Mendlowitz, S. L., Scapillato, D., Avery, D., Fiksenbaum, L., Freire, M., et al. (2002). Group and individual cognitive-behavioral therapy for childhood anxiety disorders: A randomized trial. *Journal of the American Academy of Child and Adolescent Psychiatry, 41,* 1423–1430.

Masi, G., Mucci, M., & Millepiedi, S. (2001). Separation anxiety disorder in children and adolescents. *CNS Drugs, 15,* 93–104.

McGee, R., Feehan, M., Williams, S., & Anderson, J. (1992). DSM-III disorders from age 11 to age 15 years. *Journal of the American Academy of Child & Adolescent Psychiatry, 31,* 50–59.

Mendlowitz, S. L., Manassis, K., Bradley, S., Scapillato, D., Miezitis, S., & Shaw, B. F. (1999). Cognitive-behavioral group treatments in childhood anxiety disorders: The role of parental involvement. *Journal of the American Academy of Child and Adolescent Psychiatry, 38,* 1223–1229.

Ollendick, T. H., & King, N. J. (1998). Empirically supported treatments for children with phobic and anxiety disorders: Current status. *Journal of Clinical Child Psychology, 27,* 156–167.

Pine, D. S. (2002). Treating children and adolescents with selective serotonin reuptake inhibitors: How long is appropriate? *Journal of Child and Adolescent Psychopharmacology, 12,* 189–203.

Poulton, R., Milne, B. J., Craske, M. G., & Menzies, R. G. (2001). A longitudinal study of the etiology of separation anxiety. *Behavior Research and Therapy, 39,* 1395–1410.

The Research Unit on Pediatric Psychopharmacology Anxiety Study Group. (2001). Fluvoxamine for the treatment of anxiety disorders in children and adolescents. *New England Journal of Medicine, 334,* 1279–1285.

Shear, K., Jin, R., Ruscio, A. M., Walters, E. E., & Kessler, R. C. (2006). Prevalence and correlates of estimated DSM-IV child and adult separation anxiety disorder in the National Comorbidity Survey replication. *American Journal of Psychiatry, 163,* 1074–1083.

Shortt, A. L., Barrett, P. M., & Fox, T. L. (2001). Evaluating the FRIENDS program: A cognitive-behavioral group treatment for anxious children and their parents. *Journal of Clinical Child Psychology, 30,* 525–535.

Silverman, W. K., & Albano, A. M. (1996). *Anxiety Disorders Interview Schedule for DSM-IV, Child/Parent Version*. New York: Oxford University Press.

Silverman, W. K., & Dick-Niederhauser, A. (2004). Separation anxiety disorder. In T. L. Morris & J. S. March (Eds.), *Anxiety disorders in children and adolescents* (2nd ed., pp. 164–188). New York: Guildford Press

Silverman, W. K., Kurtines, W. M., Ginsburg, G. S., Weems, C. F., Lumpkin, P. W., & Carmichael, D. H. (1999). Treating anxiety disorders in children with group cognitive-behavioral therapy: A randomized clinical trial. *Journal of Consulting and Clinical Psychology, 67*, 995–1003.

Southam-Gerow, M. A., Kendall, P. C., & Weersing, V. R. (2001). Examining outcome variability: Correlates of treatment response in a child and adolescent anxiety clinic. *Journal of Clinical Child Psychology, 30*, 422–436.

Storch, E. A., Geffken, G. R., Merlo, L. J., Jacob, M. L., Murphy, T. K., Goodman, W. K., et al. (2007). Family accommodation in pediatric obsessive-compulsive disorder. *Journal of Clinical Child and Adolescent Psychology, 36*, 207–216.

Suveg, C., Kendall, P. C., Comer, J. S., & Robin, J. (2006). Emotion-focused cognitive-behavioral therapy for anxious youth: A multiple-baseline evaluation. *Journal of Contemporary Psychotherapy, 36*, 77–85.

Velting, O. N., Setzer, N. J., & Albano, A.M. (2004). Update on and advances in assessment and cognitive–behavioral treatment of anxiety disorders in children and adolescents. *Professional Psychology: Research and Practice, 35*, 42–54.

Verduin, T. L., & Kendall, P. C. (2003). Differential occurrence of comorbidity within childhood anxiety disorders. *Journal of Clinical Child and Adolescent Psychology, 32*, 290–295.

Walkup, J., Albano, A. M., March, J. S., Piacentini, J. C., Birmaher, B., Compton, S., et al. (2009). *The Child/Adolescent Multimodal Study (CAMS): Primary outcomes and safety results*. Manuscript submitted for publication.

Weems, C. F., & Carrion, V. G. (2003). The treatment of separation anxiety disorder employing attachment theory and cognitive behavior therapy techniques. *Clinical Case Studies, 2*, 188–198.

Wood, J. J. (2006). Parental intrusiveness and children's separation anxiety in a clinical sample. *Child Psychiatry and Human Development, 37*, 73–87.

Wood, J. J., Piacentini, J. C., Southam-Gerow, M., Chu, B., & Sigman, M. (2006). Family cognitive behavioral therapy for child anxiety disorders. *Journal of the American Academy of Child and Adolescent Psychiatry, 45*, 314–321.

6

Cognitive-Behavioral Therapy for Refractory Selective Mutism

SHARON C. SUNG AND HEATHER L. SMITH

Selective mutism (SM) is a childhood condition marked by a persistent failure to speak in certain social settings where speech is expected. Children and adolescents with selective mutism are unable to, or only rarely do, speak around their peers or in public, though they speak normally around their immediate family and people they know very well. *Diagnostic and Statistical Manual of Mental Disorders, Fourth Edition, Text Revision* (*DSM-IV-TR*; American Psychiatric Association, 2000) criteria for selective mutism include an ongoing failure to speak in specific social situations in which there is an expectation for speech despite speaking in other situations, in addition to some evidence of impairment in psychosocial functioning. The mutism must last at least 1 month, so children who show transient mutism during the first month of school are excluded. Selective mutism should not be diagnosed if the behavior can be better accounted for by a communication disorder or by lack of knowledge of, or comfort with, the spoken language required in the social situation. Additional rule-outs include the presence of a pervasive developmental or psychotic disorder that could account for the mutism. Associated features may include "excessive shyness, fear of social embarrassment, social isolation and withdrawal, clinging, compulsive traits, negativism, temper tantrums, or controlling or oppositional behavior, particularly at home" (American Psychiatric Association, 2000, p. 126).

The terminology used to describe selective mutism has changed over the years, reflecting different conceptualizations of the nature of the child's nonspeaking behavior. For example, Kussmaul (1877) initially described what he termed *aphasia voluntaria*, a disorder in which individuals made a voluntary decision not to speak. This conceptualization was supported by Tramer (1934), who used the term *elective mutism* to describe children who stubbornly refused to speak in certain situations. More recent conceptualizations of selective mutism place less emphasis on the oppositional nature of the behavior, focusing more on the situational specificity of the child's mutism. Research and clinical evidence suggest that children with selective mutism are not willfully refusing to speak, but that they feel as though they are unable to engage in spontaneous speech in certain settings (Dow, Sonies, Scheib, Moss, & Leonard, 1995). This position is reflected in the fourth edition of the *Diagnostic and Statistical Manual of Mental Disorders'* nomenclatural shift from *elective* to *selective* mutism (American Psychiatric Association, 1994).

Parents often describe children with selective mutism as being extremely talkative at home and in other family settings. In contrast, when observed outside of the home environment these same children typically appear very shy, timid, and withdrawn and they do not interact verbally with others. The extent to which a child with selective mutism will speak can vary greatly. The majority of children with selective mutism converse freely at home and some children will also speak in other specific settings that are deemed "safe zones" (e.g., a relative's home). Most children with selective mutism have a distinct hierarchy of people and places that are considered safe for speech (Freeman, Garcia, Miller, Dow, & Leonard, 2004). For example, some children will speak to family members and peers outside of school, but will not speak to these same individuals on school grounds. Children with selective mutism may interact nonverbally with peers, teachers, store clerks, neighbors, and other adults, depending on their level of comfort in a given setting. Research indicates that these children are most likely to speak in the home environment, somewhat less likely to speak in public settings such as restaurants or supermarkets, and least likely to speak in school settings (Black & Uhde, 1995; Cunningham, McHolm, Boyle, & Patel, 2004). School is typically the first setting in which significant functional impairment is evident, even if the child did not speak in other settings prior to school entry (Giddan, Ross, Sechler, & Becker, 1997; Standart & Le Couteur, 2003).

ETIOLOGY, PHENOMENOLOGY, AND PREVALENCE RATES

Although the etiology and phenomenology of selective mutism have yet to be fully elucidated, the existing literature suggests that it is a heterogeneous and multifactorial condition (Cohan, Price, & Stein, 2006; Freeman et al., 2004; Kristensen, 2000). Early psychodynamic theorists viewed the disorder as a manifestation of unresolved conflict (e.g., a child who is orally or anally fixated and wishes to punish his parents by speaking only in certain situations; Meijer, 1979; Parker, Elsen, & Throckmorton, 1960), a response to familial neurosis (e.g., domineering mother and strict or avoidant father; Youngerman, 1979), or a reaction to trauma (e.g., sexual abuse, early hospitalization, parental divorce; Browne, Wilson, & Laybourne, 1963). More recent conceptualizations of selective mutism have focused on links between the condition and shyness, behaviorally inhibited temperament, and social anxiety (Bergman, Piacentini, & McCracken, 2002; Dummit, Klein, Tancer, & Asche, 1997; Ford, Sladeczek, Carlson, & Kratochwill, 1998). High rates of social phobia have consistently been found among children with selective mutism and their family members (Black & Uhde, 1995; Chavira, Shipon-Blum, Hitchcock, Cohan, & Stein, 2007; Kristensen, 2000; Vecchio & Kearney, 2005), suggesting a strong relationship between the two conditions. Moreover, recent research indicates that children with selective mutism may present with a variety of clinical profiles, all of which are characterized by high levels of social anxiety (Cohan et al., in press). Other studies have reported elevated rates of speech and language problems (Manassis et al., 2003, 2007), oppositional behavior (Yeganeh, Beidel, & Turner, 2006; Yeganeh, Beidel, Turner, Pina, & Silverman, 2003), and neurodevelopmental delays (Kristensen, 2000, 2001) among children with selective mutism. However, these problems are rarely present in the absence of significant social anxiety or temperamental inhibition and the majority of the current literature supports the notion that selective mutism is best viewed as an anxiety spectrum disorder (Anstendig, 1999; Sharp, Sherman, & Gross, 2007).

Data from community-based studies place the population prevalence of selective mutism between .71% and 1.9% (Bergman et al., 2002; Elizur & Perednik, 2003; Kumpulainen, Räsänen, Raaska, & Somppi, 1998). Some studies have found a slightly higher prevalence in girls (Black & Uhde, 1995; Cunningham et al., 2004; Karakaya et al., 2007), while others found no evidence of gender differences (Bergman et al., 2002; Elizur & Perednik, 2003). Higher rates have also been found for immigrant children (Elizur & Perednik, 2003; Steinhausen & Juzi, 1996) and language-minority immigrants may be at greater risk for developing selective mutism (Toppelberg, Tabors, Coggins, Lum, & Burger, 2005). Lower prevalence rates were found in a recent study of primary care patients (.50%; Chavira, Stein, Bailey, & Stein, 2004) and in a survey of practicing child and adolescent psychiatrists (.11%; Carlson, Kratochwill, & Johnson, 1994). These findings suggest that children with selective mutism are not typically seen for treatment in child psychiatry or primary care settings, which may have led to the widespread belief that selective mutism is a rare condition (Standart & Le Couteur, 2003).

AGE OF ONSET, COURSE, AND OUTCOMES

The age of onset for selective mutism ranges from 2 to 5 years, with an average age of onset of approximately 3.5 years (Black & Uhde, 1995; Cunningham et al., 2004; Dummit et al., 1997; Steinhausen & Juzi, 1996). Unfortunately, there have been no well-controlled longitudinal epidemiological studies and the natural history of the disorder has not been well described. In a recent community-based case-control study, Bergman et al. (2002) found that 27% of elementary school children with selective mutism at baseline showed some improvement at 6-month follow-up, but the majority of children with selective mutism remained impaired relative to children without the disorder. The three children who did show spontaneous improvement over the study period were all female, had relatively mild cases of selective mutism, and were in the youngest age group studied.

Results from clinically referred samples also indicate that some children will experience a chronic course of mutism or will have marked difficulty in speaking situations even after remission of the disorder (Kolvin & Fundudis, 1981). In a more recent follow-up study, Steinhausen, Wachter, Laimböck, and Metzke (2006) found a total remission rate of 57.6% by young adulthood. An additional 24.2 % of the sample was markedly improved, whereas the remaining 18.2% was only slightly improved at follow-up. Data from this and other studies suggests that many children with selective mutism will continue to experience social withdrawal, communication deficits, high rates of anxiety and phobic disorders, and impairment in psychosocial functioning well into young adulthood (Ford et al., 1998; Remschmidt, Poller, Herpertz-Dahlmann, Hennigause, & Gutenbunner, 2001; Steinhausen et al., 2006). High rates of taciturnity and/or selective mutism within the family have been shown to predict poor long-term outcome for children with selective mutism (Remschmidt et al., 2001; Steinhausen et al., 2006), although the genetic and/or environmental (e.g., parental modeling) mechanisms for this finding warrant further study.

TREATMENT FOR SELECTIVE MUTISM

Unfortunately, up to 40% of children with selective mutism are never referred for evaluation or treatment, possibly because of professional and parental beliefs that many cases will remit spontaneously over time (Black & Uhde, 1995; Dummit et al., 1997; Kumpulainen, Räsänen, Raaska, & Somppi, 1998). Several studies indicate that despite the fact that symptoms of selective mutism are typically present before age 5 years, the average age of referral to specialty treatment varies between age 6 and 9 years (Ford et al., 1998; Kumpulainen et al., 1998; Standart & Le Couteur, 2003). Historically, pediatricians and other helping professionals took a "wait and see" approach to selective mutism, with the expectation that the majority of children would "outgrow" the behavior (Freeman et al., 2004). This approach may help to explain the large time lag between identification and treatment for children with selective mutism. However, contrary to clinical lore, a growing body of evidence suggests that early interventions may be particularly important for these children (Bergman et al., 2002; Pionek Stone, Kratochwill, Sladezcek, & Serlin, 2002). For example, in a follow-up study of 24 treatment-seeking children with selective mutism, Kolvin and Fundudis (1981) found that almost all of the children who improved did so before age 10 years. Clinicians should be encouraged to intervene early, rather than waiting for the disorder to remit spontaneously.

There has also been a long-standing misconception that selective mutism is a treatment-refractory or "intractable" condition (Dow et al., 1995). However, this idea is not well supported in the clinical literature and there is a growing evidence base for the effectiveness of both psychosocial (Cohan, Chavira, & Stein, 2006) and psychopharmacological interventions (Kaakeh & Stumpf, 2008). In a recent meta-analysis of the existing treatment literature, Pionek Stone and colleagues (2002) concluded that some treatment was better than no treatment, behaviorally oriented treatment approaches were better than no treatment, and two different behavioral models (i.e., strictly behavioral treatments vs. combined cognitive-behavioral treatments) were not differentially effective in treating children with selective mutism. Several types of combination or "multimodal" treatments have been reported in the literature, but there is little evidence for the benefit of play therapy, art therapy, supportive psychotherapy, or family therapy that does not also include behavioral techniques (Bergman & Piacentini, 2005). Behavioral and cognitive behavioral interventions have received the most research support (Anstendig, 1998; Labbe & Williamson, 1984; Leonard & Topol, 1993) and they are considered to be first-line treatments for selective mutism (Freeman et al., 2004; Kaakeh & Stumpf, 2008; Mendlowitz & Monga, 2007).

BEHAVIORAL TREATMENTS

From a behavioral perspective, selective mutism is conceptualized as a learned pattern of avoidant behavior. In this model, when a child responds to speech requests through mutism, these requests are often removed. This anxious avoidance reinforces the child's lack of speech and reduces his or her anxiety. Over time, the mutism is negatively reinforced by the withdrawal of repeated requests to speak (and the associated reduction in anxiety) and positively reinforced by secondary gains such as increased attention from parents and peers (Labbe & Williamson, 1984). Therefore, the major goals of behavioral treatment for selective mutism are to improve the child's self-confidence, decrease his or her anxiety, extinguish reinforcement for the mutism, and develop skills to achieve positive reinforcement via more effective means (Reed, 1963). The specific behavioral strategies that have been effective in treating selective mutism include contingency management (Amari,

Slifer, Gerson, Schenk, & Kane, 1999; Porjes, 1992; Powell & Dalley, 1995; Russell, Raj, & John, 1998), stimulus fading (Giddan et al., 1997; Watson & Kramer, 1992), systematic desensitization or graded exposure (Jackson, Allen, Boothe, Nava, & Coates, 2005; Rye & Ullman, 1999; Vecchio & Kearney, 2007), shaping (Masten, Stacks, Caldwell-Colbert, & Jackson, 1996; Sluckin, Foreman, & Herbert, 1991), and self-modeling (Blum et al., 1998; Kehle, Madaus, Baratta, & Bray, 1998; Kehle, Owen, & Cressy, 1990).

Direct contingency management interventions involve positive reinforcement for speaking and lack of reinforcement for mute behavior. Because many children will not speak at all in certain settings at the outset of treatment, contingency management is frequently combined with other interventions such as shaping and stimulus fading to increase verbalizations in problematic settings. Shaping involves reinforcement for successive approximations of behaviors that resemble speech (e.g., mouthing words, whispering) with the goal of working toward normal spontaneous speech. Once speech has been achieved in a given setting, stimulus fading can be used to gradually increase the number of people and places in which speech is rewarded. Self-modeling interventions that involve having the child review video or audiotapes of him or herself speaking can also be implemented concurrently to improve self-confidence and to facilitate the transfer of speaking behaviors into the classroom. Most behavioral treatment packages include several of these strategies to increase speech across home, school, and other social settings.

COGNITIVE-BEHAVIORAL TREATMENTS

Behavior modification approaches are the most established treatments for selective mutism, but newer cognitive-behavioral interventions have also been developed (Bergman & Keller, 2007; Fung, Manassis, Kenny, & Fiskenbaum, 2002; Mendlowitz & Monga, 2007). These treatments were designed based on similarities between selective mutism and social phobia, and they typically take an anxiety-management approach to treatment (e.g., relaxation training, graded exposure, cognitive restructuring). For example, Mendlowitz and Monga (2007) have developed a cognitive-behavioral treatment package that included graded exposure, anxiety management and social skills training, contingency management, shaping, and use of speech/language games. An earlier version of this intervention (Fung et al., 2002) was modeled after traditional anxiety-management treatments (e.g., Kendall, Hudson, Choudhury, Webb, & Pimentel, 2005) that teach the child to identify his or her emotional, physiological, cognitive, and behavioral responses to anxiety-provoking situations and to develop alternative nonavoidant coping strategies. However, after pilot testing the anxiety management treatment package in their clinic, the authors concluded that the anxiety-management approach alone was not effective for many children with selective mutism. This led to the addition of social skills and language training modules.

The literature supporting behavioral and cognitive-behavioral interventions for selective mutism consists largely of case studies and single-subject experiments, but a larger randomized controlled trial evaluating a 20-session integrated modular behavioral treatment package is currently underway (Bergman & Keller, 2007). This treatment consists of parent, child, and teacher psychoeducation regarding selective mutism; relaxation training; graduated exposure exercises implemented in therapy sessions, at home, at school, and in other public settings; shaping strategies; and self-modeling skills. Sessions take place over a 6-month period, with the therapist initially taking responsibility for implementing the behavioral program and eventually shifting greater and greater responsibility to the child, parents, and teacher.

TREATMENT CHALLENGES

Because of the heterogeneous clinical profiles of selectively mute children, it is unlikely that a single manual-based approach to treatment will be effective (McInnes & Manassis, 2005). Instead, individualized cognitive-behavioral interventions based on the child's presenting problems appear to be among the most successful treatments for this population (Cohan et al., 2006). Clinicians working with selectively mute children are likely to find heterogeneity in associated features (e.g., comorbid conditions, presence of genetic/environmental risk factors) to be the norm in this population, and it may be necessary to consider adjunctive interventions to tailor treatment to more complicated clinical presentations. Treatment manuals that take a module-based approach may be more effective with this group of children. For example, preliminary evidence suggests that children with selective mutism who have behavior problems do not initially respond as well to cognitive-behavioral treatments as do children with a predominantly anxious presentation (Bergman & Keller, 2007). Children who present with oppositional behavior in addition to selective mutism may respond better to interventions that focus on parent management training in addition to managing anxiety symptoms (e.g., Pincus, Choate, Eyberg, & Barlow, 2005). However, this type of intervention has yet to be rigorously evaluated. Preliminary evidence from a recent case study indicates that a modified social skills training program for social anxiety disorder plus parent management training may be effective in treating selective mutism (Fisak, Oliveros, & Ehrenreich, 2006).

Interventions specifically targeting expressive language skills may also be needed to augment the standard behavioral and anxiety-management approaches for children exhibiting comborbid speech and language problems. Speech therapy focused on articulation and language training has been used successfully to treat selectively mute children with coexisting speech/language difficulties (Dow et al., 1995), and integrated psychosocial and speech/language approaches are likely to be the most effective with this group of children (McInnes & Manassis, 2005). Integrated interventions that are designed to be implemented concurrently by psychologists and speech pathologists have been developed (e.g., Schum, 2002), as have models focused on improving speech/language skills and pragmatic aspects of social communication (Hungerford, Edwards, & Iantosca, 2003; Trembley, 2005). When specific expressive and/or receptive language impairments are a treatment target, the speech/language pathologist may work individually with the child to improve phonology, pronunciation, grammar, vocabulary, or processing of verbal information. For this type of child, the standard cognitive-behavioral interventions can also be implemented concurrently in the classroom to address anxiety and social-communication issues.

For treatment to be successful, it is also essential to enlist the help of parents, peers, school personnel, and other treating professionals. Therapists working individually with the child may elicit some change in session, but without consistent implementation of a cognitive-behavioral program across settings, these gains will be minimal and likely not generalize (Mendlowitz & Monga, 2007; Vecchio & Kearney, 2006). Successful outcomes are possible when working with selectively mute children, but clinicians must be willing to devote substantial time and energy to this process. Out-of-office travel for in vivo exposures and frequent consultation to parents and schools is necessary, and the duration of treatment is likely to be much longer than for other anxiety spectrum disorders. For example, Mendlowitz and Monga (2007) reported that children with more severe selective mutism required more than five times as many treatment sessions as children with generalized anxiety, separation anxiety, or social anxiety.

Although cognitive-behavioral therapy is considered the first-line treatment for selective mutism, some children will still remain symptomatic even after several sessions. For those who do not initially respond, adjunct psychopharmacological interventions may be considered to reduce the child's situational anxiety and to allow him or her to more effectively engage in exposure-based treatment (Freeman et al., 2004; Kaakeh & Stumpf, 2008; Mendlowitz & Monga, 2007). The evidence base for pharmacotherapy is fairly limited, but there have been a few controlled and noncontrolled trials of selective serotonin reuptake inhibitors (SSRI) (fluoxetine, sertraline, & fluvoxamine; Black & Uhde, 1994; Carlson, Kratochwill, & Johnson, 1999; Dummit, Klein, Tancer, Asche, & Martin, 1996; Lafferty & Constantino, 1998) and monamine oxidase inhibitors (phenelzine; Golwyn & Sevlie, 1999). Results from a small number of case studies and single-subject experiments also indicate that the combination of psychosocial and psychopharmacological interventions have been useful for treating selective mutism (Russell et al., 1998; Wright, Cuccaro, Leonhardt, Kendall, & Anderson, 1995). These studies generally support the efficacy of antidepressant medications for reducing mutism and social anxiety, but larger controlled trials are still needed to evaluate a combined treatment approach. Based on their clinical experience, Mendlowitz and Monga (2007) recommend a medication consultation if no measurable progress has been made by the sixth session of stand-alone cognitive-behavioral therapy. The decision to add medication should be based on the severity of the child's mutism, poor response to other treatment methods, and the presence of comorbid conditions that might also benefit from antidepressant treatment (Kaakeh & Stumpf, 2008). Still, parents may be reluctant to consider this type of treatment, particularly given recent concerns regarding behavioral activation among children receiving antidepressant treatment. Although there is little data addressing this issue among children with SM, parents and clinicians should be alert for any signs of SSRI-induced activation syndrome (e.g., increased irritability, agitation, anxiety, aggressive behavior, panic attacks, restlessness, hostility, disinhibition, emotional lability, impulsivity, mania, or paranoia; Goodman, Murphy, & Storch, 2007).

PRETREATMENT CONSIDERATIONS

Several authors have recommended a broad assessment battery to properly evaluate and diagnose children with selective mutism (Dow et al., 1995; Schwartz & Shipon-Blum, 2005), but this approach has yet to be widely adopted in clinical practice. A typical battery should include information from multiple informants; an extensive history of developmental, medical, psychiatric, temperamental, and speech/language issues; standardized speech/language assessments; and a family history of psychiatric and communication disorders (McInnes & Manaassis, 2005). Structured diagnostic interviews such as the Anxiety Disorders Interview Schedule for Children (Albano & Silverman, 1996), dimensional measures of internalizing/externalizing symptoms, and behavioral observations across settings are also highly recommended in this population (Vecchio & Kearney, 2006). Clinicians are also likely to encounter difficulty treating selective mutism because of the long history of secondary gain that is typically associated with speech avoidance. By the time children with selective mutism are referred for treatment, this behavior has typically been reinforced for years, and it is essential to conduct a thorough functional analysis of the variables maintaining the child's mutism across home, school, and other social settings prior to initiating treatment (Kearney & Vecchio, 2006; Schill, Kratochwill, & Gardner, 1996).

A number of standardized tests are available to evaluate nonverbal cognitive and receptive language abilities (Dow et al., 1995; Manassis et al., 2003), and new techniques that do not require verbal responses have been specifically developed for evaluating expressive narrative abilities in selectively mute children (McInnes et al., 2004). Other assessments may need to be adapted to evaluate expressive language skills. For example, some authors have modified standardized batteries by allowing the child to be tested by a familiar adult in the home environment (McInnes et al., 2004), allowing the family to choose the most comfortable environment for testing (Kristensen & Oerbeck, 2006), using audiotapes to evaluate expressive language and phonological skills (Dow et al., 1995), or using videotapes of the child communicating in a comfortable setting to rule out pervasive developmental disorder or language delays (Schwartz & Shipon-Blum, 2005). Schill et al. (1996) have also developed an analogue assessment protocol in which parents evaluate the factors that maintain a child's mutism and select the most promising behavioral interventions based on the functional assessment. A comprehensive assessment that attends to psychological, behavioral, social, and speech/language issues, in addition to the factors maintaining the mutism will help clinicians to tailor their interventions to the particular strengths and weaknesses of the individual child.

Although the literature suggests that behavioral and cognitive-behavioral strategies (i.e., contingency management, shaping, stimulus fading, systematic desensitization) are effective in the treatment of selective mutism, many clinicians have found it difficult to treat selectively mute children who present with multiple risk factors (Dow et al., 1995). This will be highlighted in the case of our composite patient "Maria" (not her real name), a 9-year-old Hispanic female who was referred for cognitive-behavioral treatment following an unsuccessful course of play therapy.

CASE PRESENTATION

At the time of referral Maria lived with her biological parents and 11-year-old sister, Jane, in a small two-bedroom house in the Bronx. She was enrolled in a regular education class at a public elementary school several blocks from her family's home. Her sister Jane attended the same school and was a sixth-grade honor-roll student. In the fall of her third-grade year Maria was referred for treatment at the child outpatient program of our community-based catchment area clinic. Maria's parents, Mr. and Mrs. J., and her school counselor, Ms. P. made the referral.

At the onset of treatment, Maria had not spoken to her teachers, school faculty, or her classmates for over 3 years, including kindergarten. Mrs. J. described Maria as "clingy" and reported that her daughter had difficulty separating when she started school and spent her entire first year in silence. She stated that Maria refused to eat during school hours and was finally referred for a special education evaluation at the end of her first-grade year.

Results from the evaluation indicated that Maria's cognitive ability, as measured by nonverbal subtests of the Wechsler Intelligence Scale for Children-Fourth Edition (WISC-IV; Weschler, 2003), was within the average to high average range. Maria showed no evidence of any learning disability as suggested by her performance on the Wechsler Individual Achievement Test-Second Edition (WIAT-II; Wechsler, 2001) and her strong report card. Results from a speech and language evaluation conducted by her school's speech pathologist were used to rule out a communication disorder and any other speech pathology. Her parents denied any history of trauma and/or delays in Maria's growth and development. Mr. and Mrs. J. denied any familial psychiatric history. Mr. J. described himself as "introverted" as a child and stated that he still occasionally became nervous when giving presentations at work; however, he denied any history or experience of anxiety-related functional impairment. Mrs. J. described herself as "extroverted" and stated that she found socializing to be her "greatest strength."

Mr. and Mrs. J. reported that Maria began to receive school counseling in the first grade and she also attended weekly individual play-therapy sessions with an outside treatment provider. Of note, Mr. and Mrs. J. could not describe any changes in Maria's verbal or nonverbal behaviors since she began therapy and they were unsure as to what her goals were in session. After 2 years of play therapy, Maria's parents refused a referral for a medication evaluation as recommended by her therapist. They stated that therapy was discontinued shortly after the referral was made. The decision was reportedly mutual and her parents felt that "Maria didn't respond to therapy as we hoped. She still hasn't said a word in school."

Prior to initiating cognitive-behavioral therapy, Maria reported to her parents daily that she "loved" school, her classmates, and her teacher. On the way to school each morning, she eagerly told her father, "Today's the day I'm going to talk Daddy." Every day Maria's verbal communication stopped at the gates of the school playground, or even earlier if she saw a classmate on the way to school. On the way home from school, Maria would run to her mother, rush into their car, and chat feverishly chronicling the events of her school day, who said what, and what she had learned. Maria's older sister, Jane would frequently roll her eyes, sigh, and say to Maria, "Stop talking already, it's my turn." Prior to starting treatment in September, Maria would speak only to immediate family members and she would not participate in class verbally or nonverbally. Maria strongly believed that "everyone would think her voice was funny and laugh at her" and she had not spoken out loud to anyone inside the school building for over 3 years.

DIAGNOSTIC PROFILE

Informal and structured clinical interviews were administered to Maria and her parents. The Kiddie Schedule for Affective Disorders and Schizophrenia (K-SADS, Kaufman et al., 1997) resulted in only a diagnosis of selective mutism, with no other comorbid conditions. Maria teacher's and parents' ratings on the Behavior Assessment Scale for Children, Second Edition (BASC-2; Reynolds & Kamphaus, 2004), and the Children's Global Assessment Scale (CGAS; Shaffer et al., 1983) indicated that Maria experienced clinically significant levels of anxiety and functional impairment at school.

PRETREATMENT GOALS AND FUNCTIONAL ASSESSMENT

The therapist's essential goals of pretreatment were (a) to establish a therapeutic alliance with Maria, her parents, and her classroom teacher; (b) to assess the functionality of Maria's nonspeaking behavior; (c) to obtain the child's and parents' agreement on goals (e.g., feel less scared at school, improve relationships with friends and teachers, get better participation grades); and (d) to link these to the primary goals of cognitive-behavioral therapy for selective mutism (e.g., decrease symptoms of anxiety that interfered with speaking, change the response of not speaking to a response of verbal communication, and subsequently improve her academic and her social functioning).

According to functional assessment and Maria's parents' and teacher's reports, Maria's mutism in school appeared to be a learned pattern of avoidant behavior. When Maria responded to speech requests by her teachers and peers through mutism and other avoidant behaviors (i.e., diverting her gaze to the floor, flushing, shrugging her shoulders), requests for her verbal behavior were removed. The removal of the request reduced Maria's anxiety and reinforced her lack of speech. Maria's mutism was thereby negatively reinforced by withdrawal of repeated requests to speak and positively reinforced by the secondary gains of parental and peer attention.

A complicating feature in this case was the fact that Maria's classroom teacher, Ms. S., was also negatively reinforced by this interaction. Ms. S. stated that she felt "so relieved" when she called on another student after Maria failed to respond because, "I felt very bad making a student feel so uncomfortable in front of others. That's not my job." Thus, in addition to rapport building, goal development, and functional analysis, the pretreatment phase required orientation and role induction: Maria, and particularly Maria's parents and classroom teacher, needed to understand the importance of consistent treatment structure, rationalization, and the expectation that they would work very hard and would have to be active participants in Maria's treatment for significant progress to be made.

COGNITIVE-BEHAVIORAL FORMULATION AND TREATMENT

This case presented several challenges at the outset, including Maria's previous poor response to treatment, chronic course of nonspeaking behavior, and the failure of her parents and teacher to enforce behavioral contingencies. Maria's marked display of discomfort when asked to speak in school and the subsequent pattern of negative reinforcement with secondary gain set the stage for a challenging course of treatment. Because Maria did not engage in any verbal responses in school, direct contingency management and positive reinforcement of speech could not be used. Further complicating the clinical picture was the fact that demand situations were uncomfortable for both Maria and her teacher. Therefore, when Maria did not respond, requests of her were withdrawn and she was inadvertently rewarded for her avoidance of language by her reduction in anxiety. Based on this formulation, a comprehensive cognitive-behavioral treatment package was designed specifically to fit Maria's more complex clinical presentation and to address the mechanisms maintaining her behaviors. Conventional cognitive-behavioral strategies were creatively modified and a parent and teacher skills-training component was added in an effort to strengthen and promote speaking behavior in school.

PSYCHOEDUCATION

Following pretreatment and functional assessment sessions, Maria's therapist met with her parents and her classroom teacher (a) to provide psychoeducation regarding the conceptualization of selective mutism as an anxiety response and as a learned behavior that has been conditioned through negative reinforcement and secondary gain, (b) to set up a schedule for treatment and intensive collaboration among all members of the treatment team, and (c) to provide validation and support regarding the difficult task of asking Maria to engage in behaviors that would undoubtedly make her feel uncomfortable.

To demonstrate the principle of negative reinforcement, Maria's therapist identified numerous chains of events that were described by Maria's parents and her teacher in the assessment phase of treatment. Her therapist highlighted the interaction effects of each person's behavior and proposed how the adult's responses increased the likelihood that Maria would engage in avoidant behaviors.

> Ms. S, you most recently described a situation in which you asked Maria to come to the board to solve a math problem. You stated that you asked, "Maria, could you please come to the board and show how you solved Math homework #5?" You then remarked that Maria diverted her gaze to the floor, turned red, and began to shake her leg back and forth. You stated that you said to yourself, "Back off, you were clearly too harsh on her; she looks so embarrassed," and remarked that you began to feel sad and guilty for "making Maria feel uncomfortable." Rather than repeating the directive, you stated that you then quickly called on another student and reported that Maria sighed, smiled at you, and raised her back up. Based on our discussion of negative reinforcement, what did Maria just learn and how were you both reinforced from this interaction?

Maria's therapist explicitly defined the transactional nature of these interactions and explained how the removal of her teacher's request negatively reinforced Maria's silence. The behavioral analysis helped Maria and her parents to identify and understand the contingencies that had been maintaining Maria's mutism at school and set the stage for new treatment strategies that would reinforce Maria's behaviors that more closely approximated speech.

COGNITIVE-BEHAVIORAL SKILLS TRAINING AND PARENT/TEACHER COACHING

In an effort to set the stage for treatment compliance and commitment from Maria, her therapist made clear from the outset that these skills would be specifically for Maria to "feel stronger and take charge of her difficult feelings." Her therapist identified each cognitive and behavioral strategy as a tool that Maria would use to "stay strong" and referred to Maria's skills holistically as her "Scooby Powers." (Scooby Doo was Maria's favorite cartoon character, whom she proudly described to her mother as having "really cool powers.") Maria's therapist also developed a reinforcement menu in collaboration with Maria in which they identified numerous small, medium, and large Scooby Doo prizes that she would earn for engaging in behaviors that approximated speech.

Maria's parents and her teacher were taught each skill simultaneously with Maria. Maria's therapist taught these skills via parent and teacher training sessions and/or phone consultation. Although Maria appeared to understand each skill, she had a great deal of difficulty applying these skills at school and in her community when she felt anxious. Maria's therapist assisted her parents and her teacher in starting to view themselves as skills coaches and they gradually began to coach Maria to use her skills when she or they observed her to be anxious. This greatly increased Maria's ability to generalize her skills from her therapy sessions to her school and promoted her sense of self-efficacy and control of her body and her feelings.

SYSTEMATIC DESENSITIZATION WITH RELAXATION TRAINING

In addition to rapport building, initial therapy sessions with Maria consisted of constructing a detailed graded hierarchy of feared speaking situations at school. Items were generated and ranked accordingly using feedback from Maria's parents, her teacher's behavioral observations, and Maria's written feedback and nonverbal gestures (see Table 6.1). Concurrently, Maria received psychoeducation regarding her experience of anxiety. She was taught how to self-monitor her feelings and how to use relaxation skills to increase her behavioral control over her anxiety. Maria's therapist developed a relaxation script by detailing a scene from Scooby Doo in which Scooby had to stretch and relax each major muscle group to walk through the dense woods of a forest. She also developed a similar diaphragmatic breathing exercise in which Scooby had to use his abdominal muscles to blow out the many candles on his very large birthday cake. Maria's therapist taped these scripts for Maria and her parents agreed to practice these skills at home nightly so Maria would be able to use them when she experienced symptoms of anxiety at school and later during her exposure sessions.

COGNITIVE STRATEGIES

Maria had previously informed her mother that she did not want her classmates or school faculty members to hear her speak because she believed that her voice sounded funny and that people would hear her voice, laugh, and then make fun of her. During individual therapy sessions Maria's therapist was able to coach Maria to identify her anxious cognitions (e.g., "I know everybody will laugh at me when they hear how weird my voice sounds. I'll die of embarrassment."), challenge her negative thoughts, and subsequently restructure and replace her thought processes with more realistic expectations (e.g., "I've spoken to other people outside of school and they didn't laugh at my voice. No one has ever really told me that my voice sounds funny before. If it hasn't happened before, what makes me think it will happen now? If people do start to laugh at me, I may turn red, but that's it. I've turned red before and I know I can't die from my red face. I can always use my Scooby Doo powers to help me feel strong if I get nervous.") Maria also began to practice positive self-talk via the use of role-plays and behavioral scripts with her family members. With repeated practice, she began to develop more confidence in her ability to speak to others outside of her family.

SHAPING AND CONTINGENCY MANAGEMENT

At the start of Maria's treatment, she did not engage in any verbal behaviors at school, in close proximity to the schoolyard, or in her community. Therefore, her parents and teacher were taught to prompt

Table 6.1

MARIA'S FEAR HIERARCHY

RANK	ITEM	FEAR RATING (0–100)
1	Speaking spontaneously in front of the class and my teacher.	100
2	Answering my teacher's open-ended questions by looking at my friend and responding to my teacher.	95
3	Answering my teacher's "yes" or "no" questions in front of class.	90
4	Talking in a regular speech volume to friends in class.	90
5	Saying "hi" to the janitor in the classroom.	85
6	Speaking spontaneously in school to the janitor.	80
7	Whispering to close friends in class.	70
8	Laughing out loud in front of class.	70
9	Playing an audiotape of my voice to my class.	65
10	Letting my teacher hear my voice on audiotape.	60
11	Writing my teacher a Good Morning note.	55
12	Speaking to my best friends in my Girl Scouts meeting.	55
13	Saying "yes" or "no" to my mother or sister in a Girl Scout meeting.	50
14	Saying "hi" to the janitor in different areas of the school.	50
15	Nodding my head "yes" or "no" in front of the Girl Scout members during a meeting.	50
16	Going to the board during class when class is in session.	50
17	Standing up in front of the class when class is in session.	45
18	Raising my hand in class when class is in session.	45
19	Reading a book out loud in the classroom with the janitor present and Mom is in the room.	40
20	Going to the pencil sharpener during class time.	40
21	Mouthing words to Mom in the classroom when the janitor is present.	35
22	Speaking to Mom in the classroom when no one was present.	35
23	Speaking to Mom and Dad in the schoolyard when no one was present.	30
24	Laughing out loud without sound.	25
25	Breathing loudly or sighing in class.	25

Maria to engage in behaviors that gradually or more closely approximated "normal" speech. Initially, Maria's parents and teacher were taught to reinforce Maria with Scooby stickers, Scooby pencils, and labeled praise for her lower rated fear/communication behaviors (i.e., breathing, laughing, mouthing words, standing in class, going to the board, whispering, passing a note). Over time, her parents and teacher were taught to allow her nonverbal behaviors, but to no longer provide reinforcement for them. Instead, her parents and teacher were taught to reinforce only Maria's higher order behaviors (those that more closely approximated speech). The end goal was to gradually shape Maria's behavior until she was only rewarded for speaking in a normal tone and at an appropriate volume.

STIMULUS FADING AND GRADED EXPOSURE

Stimulus fading and graded exposure strategies provided for the transfer of "language" to "nonlanguage" situations using the comfort cues that promote speech. At the start of treatment, Maria's mother and father were the comfort cues or the discriminative stimuli for Maria to speak. Because Maria typically stopped speaking as soon as she arrived on the school grounds if she was in the proximity of a peer or school faculty member, Maria's therapist gave Maria and her parents the assignment of going to school in the early mornings, later in the evenings, and on the weekends. Maria was encouraged to use her relaxation skills with identification of anxious feelings, and over time Maria forgot that she was anxious and began to speak freely to her parents as she did when they were at home or with her sister. Maria's parents were granted permission by the school principal to enter her classroom on Saturday afternoons with Maria while the school janitor was cleaning the building. Maria's parents asked Maria to read her books aloud inside the classroom and to tape her stories so her favorite 3-year-old cousin, who Maria frequently spoke to and saw on the weekends, could listen to them as her nightly bedtime story. Maria agreed, and every week they taped her reading.

The therapeutic challenge was for Maria to use her behavioral and cognitive skills while gradually broadening the spectrum of her comfort zone (the discriminative stimuli) by introducing more people and more variables into the setting. On one occasion, unbeknownst to Maria, her parents asked the janitor to walk into the classroom and begin to sweep while Maria was reading. Although Maria's reading immediately stopped, her parents continued the demand situation and requested that the janitor continue to enter the room each week. At the recommendation of Maria's therapist, her parents asked the janitor to acknowledge Maria's reading. The janitor agreed and he informed Maria that he heard her voice and commented on her strong reading ability. From that point forward, Maria was able to tolerate reading in front of the janitor in her classroom and was even able to say "hi" to him if he was in other areas of the school building and no one else was present.

As Maria's mother was also her Girl Scout Troop leader, Mrs. J. requested that the Girl Scout meetings be transferred from the school cafeteria to Maria's classroom in an effort to promote Maria's speech by adding more people to the context of Maria's comfort cue (her mother) in the desired setting of the classroom. Maria's sister (another discriminative stimulus for speech) was also a Girl Scout member and Maria had a difficult time inhibiting her verbal behavior in the presence of her sister. Mrs. J. also began to insist that Maria either nod her head or answer "yes" or "no" to questions; otherwise Maria wouldn't be allowed to engage in meeting privileges such as being the "line leader" or "helper." Maria began to speak minimally in the classroom to her mother and her sister, and after 2 weeks she was willing to speak to her best friends who were also Girl Scout members.

At the recommendation of Maria's therapist, Maria's classroom teacher, Ms. S., began to "accidentally forget various belongings" in her classroom on Girl Scout meeting days and on one occasion came to the classroom to decorate her bulletin board on a weekend in which Maria "happened" to be taping a reading for her younger cousin. Maria's teacher did not acknowledge the reading. However, the next school day, she asked Maria and her mother if she could have a copy of the tape of Maria reading the book as Ms. S. was considering purchasing the book for her own daughter and would like to play it for her. Maria agreed and from that point forward she allowed Ms. S. to hear her voice on audiotape. Concurrently, Ms. S. continued to increase the demands on Maria by writing her a Good Morning note and asking her to reply. She then gave Maria firm directives to go to the board while coaching her to use her skills and providing reinforcement, including labeled praise and tangible Scooby Doo items. Eventually, Ms. S. only allowed Maria to go to the bathroom if she wrote her request down and began to reinforce her with classroom privileges only if she wrote her responses or nodded her head. A few weeks following the start of Maria's book tapings, Ms. S. requested that Maria audiotape her class assignments. Over time, Maria agreed that Ms. S. could play her work in front of the class.

END-OF-ACADEMIC-YEAR CASE SUMMARY

By the end of June Maria had progressed toward the most feared item on her treatment hierarchy (i.e., speaking spontaneously in front of her entire class and Ms. S.). Subsequently, she was also close to achieving her most desired item on her reinforcement survey (i.e., a family puppy that she'd be allowed to name Scooby). Maria whispered and sometimes spoke to her close girl friends and fellow Girl Scout members in the classroom, laughed out loud in class, wrote her teacher daily "hello" notes, and requested if she wanted a privilege or needed something. By the end of her grade-school year, Maria consistently raised her hand in class, allowed the teacher and her classmates to listen to audiotapes of her class assignments, verbally answered her teacher's "yes" or "no" questions, answered her teacher's open-ended questions by looking at her friend and responding to Ms. S., and engaged in spontaneous speech with the school janitor. Table 6.2 presents a comparison of Maria's pre- and posttreatment functioning.

RELAPSE-PREVENTION PLANNING

Maria's parents had planned a 1-month family vacation to Puerto Rico to visit her maternal grandparents the weekend following the last day of school, and therapy was intermittently stopped with the goal of resuming in July. In an effort to maintain therapeutic gains over the course of the summer, Maria's therapist discussed the importance of continuing therapy and of implementing cognitive and behavioral strategies consistently during the summer. Maria's parents requested permission from her school principal for Maria to meet her new fourth-grade teacher and the teacher agreed to e-mail or speak to Maria on the phone at least once a week to foster a relationship and to decrease Maria's anticipatory anxiety. Mrs. J. also asked permission from the school

Table 6.2

PRE- AND POSTTREATMENT COMPARISON FOR MARIA

PRETREATMENT (SEPTEMBER)	POSTTREATMENT (JUNE)
Whispered to immediate family members and a friend outside of school.	Whispered and sometimes spoke spontaneously to her girlfriends outside of school.
No one truly heard her voice for 3 years inside the school building.	Laughed out loud inside school building.
Would not participate in class nonverbally or verbally.	Wrote the teacher "hello" notes daily and if she needed/wanted something.
	Went to the board when asked.
	Raised her hand in class.
	Answered her teacher's questions by looking at her friend and responding to the teacher.
Thought everyone would think her voice was funny and would laugh at her.	Let the janitor hear her voice in school. Read books for tape recorder and let class hear her voice.

principal to continue bi-weekly Girl Scout meetings in Maria's new fourth-grade classroom. Maria's parents also agreed to take Maria and two school peers to the school playground at least three times a week until school resumed in September.

Maria's therapist discussed the possibility of a setback in speaking behaviors when Maria started school in the fall and explained how compliance with the aforementioned therapeutic recommendations over the summer would decrease the likelihood of a setback. Maria's parents were again encouraged to reconsider the referral for a medication evaluation a few months into next year's school year if Maria's symptoms worsened. When her treatment was briefly stopped at the end of June, Maria and her parents were proud of Maria's accomplishments and agreed to follow through with all of the aforementioned recommendations. Maria reported a significant decrease in her feelings of anxiety and was functioning more effectively in her social and academic environments.

CONCLUSIONS AND FUTURE DIRECTIONS

As this case illustrates, there are many factors that must be taken into consideration in designing an effective cognitive-behavioral protocol for treatment-refractory selective mutism. Although research supports the application of conventional behavioral and cognitive-behavioral treatment strategies for children with SM (Cohan, Chavira, et al. 2006; Labbe & Williamson, 1984; Pionek Stone et al., 2002), children who have multiple risk factors or who have been refractory to standard modes of cognitive-behavioral therapy are likely to require the development of more individualized and tailored treatment packages. Different treatment components may be needed to supplement the skills deficits that are underlying or further exacerbating selective mutism symptoms (e.g., behavior problems, social skills deficits, language delays). Therapists working with these children must be willing to spend additional time conducting a thorough pretreatment evaluation, including a detailed functional assessment of the child's mutism. A great deal of time is also needed to engage parents, siblings, teachers, peers, and other significant individuals in the child's treatment. Some children with SM may also require adjunct medication treatment to engage in cognitive-behavioral treatment. It is likely that this sort of comprehensive, individualized approach will lead to improved outcomes for selectively mute children.

The selective mutism treatment literature is still extremely small and consists mainly of retrospective reviews, case studies, and single-subject experiments. There is currently a reasonable evidence base for the use of behavioral techniques such as contingency management, shaping, stimulus fading, and graded exposure, and a smaller evidence base for the use of anxiety management and social skills/language training interventions. However, large, well-controlled treatment-outcome studies are clearly needed to determine the optimal treatment package or packages for children with selective mutism. This presents a challenge for researchers, as flexible or module-based protocols will likely be needed to effectively address the varied clinical profiles of children with selective mutism. There has been an increase in research in this area over the past decade, and it is likely that we will continue to make significant advances in the treatment of a disorder that was long considered to be "intractable."

REFERENCES

Albano, A.M. & Silverman, W.K. (1996). *Clinician manual for the Anxiety Disorders Interview Schedule for DSM-IV: Child version*. New York: Psychological Corporation.

Amari, A., Slifer, K. J., Gerson, A. C., Schenck, E., & Kane, A. (1999). Treating selective mutism in a paediatric rehabilitation patient by altering environmental reinforcement contingencies. *Pediatric Rehabilitation, 3*, 59–64.

American Psychiatric Association. (1994). *Diagnostic and statistical manual of mental disorders* (4th ed.) Washington, DC: American Psychiatric Press.

American Psychiatric Association. (2000). *Diagnostic and statistical manual of mental disorders* (4th ed., text rev.). Washington, DC: American Psychiatric Press.

Anstendig, K. (1998). Selective mutism: A review of the treatment literature by modality from 1980-1996. *Psychotherapy: Theory, Research, Practice, Training, 35*, 381–391.

Anstendig, K. (1999). Is selective mutism an anxiety disorder? Rethinking its DSM-IV classification. *Journal of Anxiety Disorders, 13*, 417–434.

Bergman, R. L., & Keller, M. L. (2007, January). *Research on selective mutism: Past findings, current focus, and future directions*. Paper presented at Selective Mutism Conference, Los Angeles, CA.

Bergman, R. L., & Piacentini, J. (2005). Selective mutism. In B. Sadock & V. Sadock (Eds.), *Comprehensive textbook of Psychiatry VIII*. Baltimore, MD: Williams & Wilkins.

Bergman, R. L., Piacentini, J., & McCracken, J. T. (2002). Prevalence and description of selective mutism in a school-based sample. *Journal of the American Academy of Child & Adolescent Psychiatry, 41*, 938–946.

Black, B., & Uhde, T. W. (1994). Treatment of elective mutism with fluoxetine: A double-blind, placebo-controlled study. *Journal of the American Academy of Child & Adolescent Psychiatry, 33*, 1000–1006.

Black, B., & Uhde, T. W. (1995). Psychiatric characteristics of children with selective mutism: A pilot study. *Journal of the American Academy of Child & Adolescent Psychiatry, 34*, 847–856.

Blum, N. J., Kell, R. S., Starr, H. L., Lender, W. L., Bradley-Klug, K. L., Osbourne, M. L. et al. (1998). Case study: Audio feedforward treatment of selective mutism. *Journal of the American Academy of Child & Adolescent Psychiatry, 37*, 40–43.

Browne, E., Wilson, V., & Laybourne, P. C. (1963). Diagnosis and treatment of elective mutism in children. *Journal of the American Academy of Child & Adolescent Psychiatry, 2*, 605–617.

Carlson, J. S., Kratochwill, T. R., & Johnston, H. (1994). Prevalence and treatment of selective mutism in clinical practice: A survey of child and adolescent psychiatrists. *Journal of Child and Adolescent Psychopharmacology, 4*, 281–291.

Carlson, J. S., Kratochwill, T. R., & Johnson, H. F. (1999). Sertraline treatment of 5 children diagnosed with selective mutism: A single-case research trial. *Journal of Child and Adolescent Psychopharmacology, 9*, 293–306.

Chavira, D. A., Shipon-Blum, E., Hitchcock, C., Cohan, S. L., & Stein, M. B. (2007). Selective mutism and social anxiety disorder: All in the family? *Journal of the American Academy of Child & Adolescent Psychiatry, 46*, 1464–1472.

Chavira, D. A., Stein, M. B., Bailey, K., & Stein, M. T. (2004). Child anxiety in primary care: Prevalent but untreated. *Depression & Anxiety, 20*, 155–164.

Cohan, S. L., Chavira, D. A., Shipon-Blum, E., Hitchcock, C., Roesch, S., & Stein, M. B. (in press). Refining the classification of children with selective mutism: A Latent Profile Analysis. *Journal of Clinical Child and Adolescent Psychology*.

Cohan, S. L., Chavira, D. A., & Stein, M. B. (2006). Psychosocial treatments for children with selective mutism: A critical evaluation of the literature from 1990-2005. *Journal of Child Psychology and Psychiatry, 47*, 1085–1097.

Cohan, S. L., Price, J. M., & Stein, M. B. (2006). Suffering in silence: Why a developmental psychopathology perspective on selective mutism is needed. *Journal of Developmental & Behavioral Pediatrics, 27*, 341–355.

Cunningham, C. E., McHolm, A., Boyle, M. H., & Patel, S. (2004). Behavioral and emotional adjustment, family functioning, academic performance, and social relationships in children with selective mutism. *Journal of Child Psychology and Psychiatry, 45*, 1363–1372.

Dow, S. P., Sonies, B. C., Scheib, D., Moss, S. E., & Leonard, H. L. (1995). Practical guidelines for the assessment and treatment of selective mutism. *Journal of the American Academy of Child & Adolescent Psychiatry, 34*, 836–846.

Dummit, E. S., Klein, R. G., Tancer, N. K., & Asche, B. (1997). Systematic assessment of 50 children with selective mutism. *Journal of the American Academy of Child & Adolescent Psychiatry, 36*, 653–660.

Dummit, E. S., Klein, R. G., Tancer, N. K., Asche, B., & Martin, J. (1996). Fluoxetine treatment of children with selective mutism: An open trial. *Journal of the American Academy of Child & Adolescent Psychiatry, 35*, 615–621.

Elizur, Y., & Perednik, R. (2003). Prevalence and description of selective mutism in immigrant and native families: A controlled study. *Journal of the American Academy of Child & Adolescent Psychiatry, 42*, 1451–1459.

Fisak, B. J., Oliveros, A., & Ehrenreich, J. T. (2006). Assessment and behavioral treatment of selective mutism. *Clinical Case Studies, 5*, 382–402.

Ford, M. A., Sladeczek, I. E., Carlson, J., & Kratochwill, T. R. (1998). Selective mutism: Phenomenological characteristics. *School Psychology Quarterly, 13*, 192–227.

Freeman, J. B., Garcia, A. M., Miller, L. M., Dow, S. P., & Leonard, H. L. (2004). Selective mutism. In T. L. Morris & J. S. March (Eds.), *Anxiety disorders in children and adolescents* (2nd ed., pp. 280–301). New York: Guilford Press.

Fung, D. S., Manassis, K., Kenny, A., & Fiskenbaum, L. (2002). Web-based CBT for selective mutism. *Journal of the American Academy of Child & Adolescent Psychiatry, 41*, 112–113.

Giddan, J. L., Ross, G. J., Sechler, L. L., & Becker, B. R. (1997). Selective mutism in elementary school: Multidisciplinary interventions. *Language, Speech, and Hearing Services in Schools, 28*, 127–133.

Golwyn, D. H., & Sevlie, C. P. (1999). Phenelzine treatment of selective mutism in four prepubertal children. *Journal of Child and Adolescent Psychopharmacology, 9*, 109–113.

Goodman, W. K., Murphy, T. K., & Storch, E. A. (2007). Risk of adverse behavioral effects with pediatric use of antidepressants. *Psychopharmacology, 191,* 87–96.

Hungerford, S., Edwards, J., Iantosca, A. (2003, November). *A socio-communication model for selective mutism.* Paper presented at the meeting of the American Speech-Language-Hearing Association, Chicago, IL.

Jackson, M. F., Allen, R. S., Boothe, A. B., Nava, M. L., & Coates, A. (2005). Innovative analyses and interventions in the treatment of selective mutism. *Clinical Case Studies, 4,* 81–112.

Kaakeh, Y., & Stumpf, J. L. (2008). Treatment of selective mutism: Focus on selective serotonin reuptake inhibitors. *Pharmacotherapy, 28,* 214–224.

Karakaya, I., Sişmanlar, Ş. G., Öç, Ö. Y., Memik, N. Ç., Coşkun, A., Ağaoğlu, B., & Yavuz, C. I. (2007). Selective mutism: A school-based cross-sectional study from Turkey. *European Child & Adolescent Psychiatry, 17,* 114–117.

Kaufman, J., Birmaher, B., Brent, D., Rao, U., Flynn, C., Moreci, P., et al. (1997). Schedule for affective disorders and schizophrenia for school-aged children—Present and lifetime (K-SADS-PL): Initial reliability and validity data. *Journal of the American Academy of Child & Adolescent Psychiatry, 36,* 980–988.

Kearney, C. A., & Vecchio, J. (2006). Functional analysis and treatment of selective mutism in children. *Journal of Speech-Language Pathology and Applied Behavior Analysis, 1,* 141–148.

Kehle, T. J., Madaus, M. R., Baratta, V. S., & Bray, M. A. (1998). Augmented self-modeling as a treatment for children with selective mutism. *Journal of School Psychology, 36,* 247–260.

Kehle, T. J., Owen, S. V., & Cressy, E. T. (1990). The use of self-modeling as an intervention in school psychology: A case study of an elective mute. *School Psychology Review, 19,* 115–121.

Kendall, P. C., Hudson, J. L., Choudhury, M., Webb, A., & Pimentel, S. (2005). Cognitive-behavioral treatment for childhood anxiety disorders. In E. D. Hibbs & P. S. Jensen (Eds.), *Psychosocial treatments for child and adolescent disorders: Empirically based strategies for clinical practice* (2nd ed., pp. 47–73). Washington, DC: American Psychological Association.

Kolvin, I., & Fundudis, T. (1981). Elective mute children: Psychological development and background factors. *Journal of Child Psychology and Psychiatry, 22,* 219–232.

Kristensen, H. (2000). Selective mutism and comorbidity with developmental disorder/delay, anxiety disorder, and elimination disorder. *Journal of the American Academy of Child & Adolescent Psychiatry, 39,* 249–256.

Kristensen, H. (2001). Multiple informants report of emotional and behavioural problems in a nation-wide sample of selective mute children and controls. *European Child & Adolescent Psychiatry, 10,* 135–142.

Kristensen, H., & Oerbeck, B. (2006). Is selective mutism associated with deficits in memory span and visual memory? An exploratory case control study. *Depression and Anxiety, 23,* 71–76.

Kumpulainen, K., Räsänen, E., Raaska, H., & Somppi, V. (1998). Selective mutism among second-graders in elementary school. *European Child & Adolescent Psychiatry, 7,* 24–29.

Kussmaul, A. (1877). *Handbuch speciellen pathologie und therapie (Handbook of Speech Pathology and Therapy)*. Leipzig: Verlag.

Labbe, E. E., & Williamson, D. A. (1984). Behavioral treatment of elective mutism: A review of the literature. *Clinical Psychology Review, 4*, 273–292.

Lafferty, J. E., & Constantino, J. N. (1998). Fluvoxamine in selective mutism. *Journal of the American Academy of Child & Adolescent Psychiatry, 37*, 12–13.

Leonard, H. L., & Topol, D. A. (1993). Elective mutism. *Child and Adolescent Psychiatric Clinics of North America, 2*, 695–707.

Manassis, K., Fung, D., Tannock, R., Sloman, L., Fiksenbaum, L., & Mclnnes, A. (2003). Characterizing selective mutism: Is it more than social anxiety? *Depression & Anxiety, 18*, 153–161.

Manassis, K., Tannock, R., Garland, E. J., Minde, K., Mclnnes, E., & Clark, S. (2007). The sounds of silence: Language, cognition, and anxiety in selective mutism. *Journal of the American Academy of Child & Adolescent Psychiatry, 46*, 1187–1195.

Masten, W. G., Stacks, J. R., Caldwell-Colbert, A. T., & Jackson, J. S. (1996). Behavioral treatment of a selectively mute Mexican-American boy. *Psychology in the Schools, 33*, 56–60.

Mclnnes, A., Fung, D., Manassis, K., Fiksenbaum, L., & Tannock, R. (2004). Narrative skills in children with selective mutism: An exploratory study. *American Journal of Speech-Language Pathology, 13*, 304–315.

Mclnnes, A., & Manassis, K. (2005). When silence is not golden: An integrated approach to selective mutism. *Seminars in Speech & Language, 26*, 201–210.

Meijer, A. (1979). Elective mutism in children. *Israeli Annals of Psychiatry & Related Disciplines, 17*, 93–100.

Mendlowitz, S. L., & Monga, S. (2007). Unlocking speech where there is none: Practical approaches to treatment of Selective Mutism. *Behavior Therapist, 30*, 11–15.

Parker, E.B., Elsen, T.F., & Throckmorton, M.S. (1960.) Social casework with elementary school children who do not talk in school. *Social Work, 5*, 64–70.

Pincus, D.B., Choate, M.L., Eyberg, S.M., & Barlow, D.H. (2005). Treatment of young children with separation anxiety disorder using parent-child interaction therapy. *Cognitive and Behavioral Practice*, 12, 126–135.

Pionek Stone, B., Kratochwill, T. R., Sladezcek, I., & Serlin, R. C. (2002). Treatment of selective mutism: A best-evidence synthesis. *School Psychology Quarterly, 17*, 168–190.

Porjes, M. D. (1992). Intervention with the selectively mute child. *Psychology in the Schools, 29*, 367–376.

Powell, S., & Dalley, M. (1995). When to intervene in selective mutism: The multimodal treatment of a case of persistent selective mutism. *Psychology in the Schools, 32*, 114–123.

Reed, G. F. (1963). Elective mutism in children. *Journal of Child Psychology & Psychiatry, 4*, 99–107.

Remschmidt, H., Poller, M., Herpertz-Dahlmann, B., Hennigause, K., & Gutenbunner, C. (2001). A follow-up study of 45 patients with elective mutism. *European Archives of Psychiatry & Clinical Neuroscience, 251*, 284–296.

Reynolds, C. R., & Kamphaus, R. W. (2004). *Behavior Assessment System for Children—Second edition (BASC-2)*. Circle Pines, MN: American Guidance Service.

Russell, P. S., Raj, S. E., & John, J. K. (1998). Multimodal intervention for selective mutism in mentally retarded children. *Journal of the American Academy of Child & Adolescent Psychiatry, 37*, 903–904.

Rye, M. S., & Ullman, D. (1999). The successful treatment of long-term selective mutism: A case study. *Journal of Behavior Therapy and Experimental Psychiatry, 30*, 313–323.

Schill, M. T., Kratochwill, T. R., & Gardner, W. I. (1996). An assessment protocol for selective mutism: Analogue assessment using parents as facilitators. *Journal of School Psychology, 34*, 1–21.

Schum, R. L. (2002). Selective mutism: An integrated treatment approach. *ASHA Leader, 7*, 4–6.

Schwartz, R.H., & Shipon-Blum, E. (2005). 'Shy' child? Don't overlook selective mutism. *Contemporary Pediatrics, 22*, 30–34.

Shaffer, D., Gould, M. S., Brasic, J., Ambrosini, P., Fisher, P., Bird, H., et al. (1983). A children's global assessment scale. *Archives of General Psychiatry, 40*, 1228–1231.

Sharp, W. G., Sherman, C., & Gross, A. M. (2007). Selective mutism and anxiety: A review of the current conceptualization of the disorder. *Journal of Anxiety Disorders, 24*, 568–579.

Sluckin, A., Foreman, N., & Herbert, N. (1991). Behavioural treatment programs and selectivity of speaking at follow-up in a sample of 25 selective mutes. *Australian Psychologist, 26*, 132–137.

Standart S., & Le Couteur, A. (2003). The quiet child: A literature review of selective mutism. *Child and Adolescent Mental Health, 8*, 154–160.

Steinhausen, H., & Juzi, C. (1996). Elective mutism: An analysis of 100 cases. *Journal of the American Academy of Child & Adolescent Psychiatry, 35*, 606–614.

Steinhausen, H. C., Wachter, M., Laimböck, K., & Metzke, C. W. (2006). A long-term outcome study of selective mutism in childhood. *Journal of Child Psychology and Psychiatry, 47*, 751–756.

Toppelberg, C. O., Tabors, P., Coggins, A., Lum, K., & Burger, C. (2005). Differential diagnosis of selective mutism in bilingual children. *Journal of the American Academy of Child & Adolescent Psychiatry, 44*, 592–595.

Tramer, M. (1934). Elektiver mutismus bei kinder (Selective mutism of children). *Zeitschrift fur Kinderpsychiatrie, 1*, 30-35.

Trembley, J. F. (2005). *Selective mutism in the public school setting: A case study*. Paper presented at the meeting of the American Speech-Language-Hearing Association, San Diego, CA.

Vecchio, J. L., & Kearney, C. A. (2005). Selective mutism in children: Comparison to youths with and without anxiety disorders. *Journal of Psychopathology & Behavioral Assessment, 27*, 31–37.

Vecchio, J. L., & Kearney, C. A. (2006). Selective mutism in children: A synopsis of characteristics, assessment, and treatment. *Behavior Therapist, 29*, 102–104.

Vecchio, J. L., & Kearney, C. A. (2007). Assessment and treatment of a Hispanic youth with selective mutism. *Clinical Case Studies, 6*, 34–43.

Watson, T. S., & Kramer, J. J. (1992). Multimethod behavioral treatment of long-term selective mutism. *Psychology in the Schools, 29*, 359–366.

Wechsler, D. (2001). *Wechsler Individual Achievement Test, second edition*. San Antonio, TX: Psychological Corporation.

Wechsler, D. (2003). *Wechsler Intelligence Scale for Children, fourth edition*. San Antonio, TX: Psychological Corporation.

Wright, H. H., Cuccaro, M. L., Leonhardt, T. V., Kendall, D. F., & Anderson, J. H. (1995). Case study: Fluoxetine in the multimodal treatment of a preschool child with selective mutism, *Journal of the American Academy of Child & Adolescent Psychiatry, 34*, 857–862.

Yeganeh, R., Beidel, D. C., & Turner, S. (2006). Selective mutism: More than social anxiety? *Depression and Anxiety, 23*, 117–123.

Yeganeh, R., Beidel, D. C., Turner, S. M., Pina, A. A., & Silverman, W. K. (2003). Clinical distinctions between selective mutism and social phobia: An investigation of childhood psychopathology. *Journal of the American Academy of Child & Adolescent Psychiatry, 42*, 1069–1075.

Youngerman, J. K. (1979). The syntax of silence: Electively mute therapy. *International Review of Psycho-Analysis, 6*, 283–295.

7

Specific Phobias

THOMAS H. OLLENDICK, THOMPSON E. DAVIS III,
and CRISTIAN SIRBU

Fear is a normal, adaptive emotion essential to human development and everyday life. For example, infants show a healthy wariness of heights, loud noises, and unexpected, novel stimuli. Moreover, fears are common in toddlers, children, and adolescents and follow a developmental progression that parallels increasingly greater cognitive-developmental gains from concrete to abstract thought (Davis, in press; Muris, Merckelbach, Meesters, & van den Brand, 2002; Ollendick, Hagopian, & King, 1997). More specifically, children progress from concrete fears in infancy and toddlerhood to increasingly abstract fears such as ghosts, the supernatural, and social situations in childhood and adolescence. As a result, parents and physicians have understandably come to expect fears to emerge, progress, and fade over time, attributing them to the worn-out adage of it just being "a phase."

These fears, however, may not be just a phase for some children; when fears are intense, persistent, and result in significant distress or interference, they are indicative of a severe problem with fear and are best viewed as a phobia. Based on parental report, 17.6% of children with "childhood fears" meet full criteria for a specific phobia (Muris & Merckelbach, 2000). Moreover, based on child report, 22.8% of youngsters who report "childhood fears" also meet criteria for a phobic disorder (Muris, Merckelbach, Mayer, & Prins, 2000). In fact, the mean age of onset for specific phobias is in middle childhood, at about 9 to 10 years of age (Ollendick et al., 1997); however, it is disturbing that the mean duration of specific phobia in adults is over 20 years and that only 8% of adults with specific phobia have ever sought treatment for their phobias (Stinson et al., 2007). Upon becoming adults with specific phobia, these grown children going through "a phase" access medical care at a rate second only to those with panic disorder—and significantly more often than those with more pervasive difficulties such as obsessive-compulsive disorder (Deacon, Lickel, & Abramowitz, 2008). As a result, it is unfortunate that these enduring fears from childhood are frequently overlooked, left untreated, and allowed to potentially become intractable as accommodation and avoidance become a common part of their developmental course.

PHENOMENOLOGY

When a specific, identifiable fear becomes a persistent and intense part of a child's developmental experience, it is labeled a "specific phobia." According to the *Diagnostic and Statistical Manual of Mental Disorders, Fourth Edition, Text Revision* (*DSM-IV-TR*; American Psychiatric Association 2000), a child's fear must meet seven criteria to be classified as a disorder (pp. 443–450). The child's fear must be intense, enduring, and cued by exposure (or anticipated exposure) to the feared stimulus (criterion A). Exposure must provoke an anxiety response (which can be a panic attack; criterion B), and the source of the fear must be avoided or, if avoidance is not possible, endured with considerable distress (criterion D). In turn, the avoidance must interfere significantly with the child's academic, social, and family functioning (criterion E). Finally, the child must have had the fear for at least 6 months (criterion F), and the fear cannot be better subsumed under another mental disorder (criterion G). Of importance, the *DSM-IV-TR* incorporates the tenets of developmental psychopathology in its diagnostic structure. A child with specific phobia must have the fear for a duration long enough to suggest it is not "just a phase" and not a part of normal development (criterion F), and the child need not realize the fear is excessive or unreasonable (criterion C), as is required for adults. If a child meets these criteria, then the diagnosis can be further specified as being of the animal, natural environment, situational, blood/injection/injury, or other type.

Specific phobia involves three response systems—behavioral, cognitive, and physiological—all of which are based on the cued activation of a memory (Davis & Ollendick, 2005; Lang, 1979). A child with specific phobia is avoidant (i.e., behavior), thinks (and sometimes verbalizes) scary thoughts or expectations about the stimulus (i.e., cognition), and frequently experiences various bodily changes or sensations including increased heart rate, sweating, and trembling (i.e., physiological). As a result, a specific phobia is more than a simple list of diagnostic criteria; rather, it is a highly integrated network of memories and learning histories based on the observable characteristics of the feared stimulus, the meaning assigned to the stimulus, and the potentiated responses that follow from activation of the memorial network (Davis & Ollendick, 2005; Lang 1977, 1979). The challenge to the clinician is to create new learning and memories that are not as pathologized and that compete with the fear across various stimulus contexts (Bouton, 2004; Davis, in press). The total elimination of a fear of dogs, for example, is not the ultimate goal; rather, the goal is to develop a more adaptive and healthy association to dogs. To fear dogs that pose a risk to one's health is adaptive; however, it is not adaptive to stay indoors because of a fear that a dog might be present.

EPIDEMIOLOGY AND ETIOLOGY

Specific phobias occur in approximately 5% of children in community samples and 15% of children in mental health settings (Ollendick et al., 1997). Typically, girls and younger children report more fears than boys (Muris, Schmidt, & Merckelbach, 1999; Ollendick, King, & Frary, 1989), with fears of spiders, the dark, death, being kidnapped, and thunderstorms being among the more common concerns reported both by children and the parents of children (Muris & Merckelbach, 2000; Muris et al., 2000). Although the mean age of onset is 9 to 10 years of age, a developmental progression in the onset of specific phobia type is similar to that of typically developing fears. For example, animal phobias typically have an onset around 7 years of age, followed by blood-injection-injury phobias at about 9 years, situational fears around 13 years of age, and claustrophobia at 20 years of age (Öst, 1987a).

Specific phobias are thought to emerge from four potential pathways that can be grouped broadly into associative and nonassociative accounts (Rachman, 1977, 2002). Phobias can be created through associative means by classical conditioning (i.e., having a negative experience with the stimulus), modeling (i.e., seeing someone else have a negative experience or evince fearful behaviors), and negative information (i.e., receiving information that interaction with the stimulus is dangerous or scary). In addition, a nonassociative path has been suggested to account for factors related to not knowing the origin of the fear, or possibly having a genetic or biological predisposition to be fearful (Rachman, 2002). In all likelihood, a more accurate etiological account acknowledges that although any one path is sufficient to create a specific phobia, most children acquire a specific phobia through the additive effects of various combinations of associative experiences interacting with other predisposing, perhaps nonassociative factors (cf. Ollendick & King, 1991; Ollendick, King, & Muris, 2002).

EFFECTIVE TREATMENTS FOR SPECIFIC PHOBIA IN CHILDREN AND ADOLESCENTS

The effective treatment of specific phobia in children begins with a comprehensive, evidence-based assessment. The adequacy of this assessment is an especially important consideration when selecting a treatment, as poor assessment can lead to inaccurate diagnosis and selection of a treatment that might be less efficacious. Although more detailed descriptions of evidence-based assessment can be found in Ollendick, Davis, and Muris (2004) and Silverman and Ollendick (2005), an assessment for specific phobia in children should include instruments and procedures that examine the diagnostic criteria as well as the three components of the fear response (i.e., *DSM-IV-TR* guidelines *and* measures of behavior, cognition, and psychophysiology; Davis & Ollendick, 2005). This assessment should ideally include a semistructured diagnostic interview, child self-report, a behavioral avoidance task, physiological measurement, and a functional assessment of the fear (cf. Ollendick et al., 2004). Currently, researchers and clinicians are encouraged to use the Anxiety Disorders Interview Schedule for *DSM-IV* Child/Parent version as the diagnostic interview of choice (ADIS-IV-C/P; Silverman & Albano, 1996) and the Multidimensional Anxiety Scale for Children

(MASC; March, Parker, Sullivan, Stallings, & Conners, 1997) and the Fear Survey Schedule for Children-Revised (FSSC-R; Ollendick, 1983) as their child self-report measures (Ollendick et al., 2004; Silverman & Ollendick, 2005). They are also encouraged to use a behavioral avoidance task to observe the behavioral, cognitive, and physiological components of the fear response. Based on this information and the confirmation of a diagnosis of specific phobia, one of several empirically supported treatments for specific phobia can be selected. The information obtained from such a comprehensive assessment extends beyond the diagnostic process by aiding in the planning of treatment and preparing for the child's and family's responses during treatment—which will almost always involve some form of exposure to the feared stimulus.

Currently, there are several efficacious treatments for specific phobias in children based on the original guidelines put forth by the Task Force on Promotion and Dissemination of Psychological Procedures created by APA Division 12 (Task Force, 1995). These guidelines assign treatments into "well-established, " "probably efficacious, " and "experimental" categories based on the level of empirical support available for them. At this time, some differences exist in the literature on the application of these guidelines. Differences range from a more lenient standard for the inclusion of studies (e.g., including those with extreme fears as well as phobias; Davis & Ollendick, 2005) to a very strict standard for the inclusion of studies (e.g., including only those with specific phobia diagnoses; Chambless & Ollendick, 2001; Davis, in press). For purposes of this chapter on phobias that are refractory to change, both approaches should be considered. Clinicians treating difficult-to-treat phobias will need to make an informed treatment selection based on an understanding of what is efficacious for children with specific phobias as well as what is effective for the treatment of children with fears that are not of a phobic proportion.

EVIDENCE-BASED TREATMENTS

Based on the most recent reviews of the evidence-based treatment of specific phobias (Davis, in press; Davis & Ollendick, 2005; Ollendick et al., 2004), there are four treatments that have at least some empirical support for their use with children—systematic desensitization, reinforced practice, participant modeling, and cognitive-behavioral therapy.

Each of these treatments will be briefly described prior to our discussion of factors associated with poor treatment response to these and other interventions. The componential approach to treatment evaluation (i.e., examining the evidence for the behavioral, cognitive, and physiological response components of fear; cf. Davis & Ollendick, 2005) will also be reviewed to highlight which symptoms treatments have the strongest evidence for change.

Systematic Desensitization

Systematic desensitization (SD) is one of the earliest treatments used for phobias in children. Wolpe (1958) developed this treatment as a way of counterconditioning fear through use of an incompatible response, typically muscular relaxation. SD evolved out of classical conditioning theory in that problematic fears were thought to be the result of direct negative experiences with an unconditioned stimulus, leading to the stimulus becoming a conditioned stimulus and causing a conditioned fear response. For example, an attack by a dog would cause the physiological aspects of fear (previously an unconditioned response) to become a conditioned response on exposure to any dog (i.e., now a conditioned stimulus). It then follows that the goal of treatment would be to extinguish the conditioned response by having the conditioned stimulus no longer predict the unconditioned stimulus, and according to Wolpe (1958), thereby use "particular responses that, through inhibiting anxiety, weaken neurotic habits" (p. 112). As a result, treatment begins with the initial creation of a graduated fear hierarchy—a list of increasingly fearful exposures to the conditioned stimulus. Next, a counterconditioning agent is selected and the child is taught to perform it. Typically, progressive muscle relaxation and diaphragmatic breathing are used and recommended; however, Wolpe (1958) indicated that a variety of appetitive behaviors could also be used, including food and humor. Finally, treatment begins by slowly using the counterconditioning agent to induce a state hedonically incompatible with fear and then exposing the child to a step in the fear hierarchy either imaginally or *in vivo*. Ideally, the client should not become afraid during the exposures, as one is trying to condition a new response on exposure to the conditioned stimulus—experiencing fear during the exposure would essentially strengthen the fear association. As a result, clinicians frequently assess fear levels during exposure and will often develop a signal that the client can use when the exposure becomes too intense and begins to elicit fear (Ollendick & Cerny, 1981).

SD has been influential in the treatment of fears and phobias; however, its theory and procedures have been increasingly scrutinized. The process of "counterconditioning" is generally considered now to be a process of learning competing, context-specific information instead of overwriting the fear conditioning itself (Bouton, 2004). Clinicians must also consider treatment generalization to combat spontaneous recovery (i.e., return) of fear in situations not encountered during treatment (Davis, in press). Unexpectedly, SD has not been shown to robustly affect the physiology of fear—a finding that runs counter to the primary claim that a clinician is conditioning a different, competing physiological state (Davis & Ollendick, 2005). Even so, both imaginal and *in vivo* SD have been found to be probably efficacious for the treatment of fears—especially at reducing fearful behavior (Davis & Ollendick, 2005; Ollendick & King, 1998). In a more stringent review involving diagnosed specific phobia, SD is considered experimental for the alleviation of the diagnosis and the various components of the fear response (Davis, in press; Davis & Ollendick, 2005).

Reinforced Practice

Reinforced practice (RP) or "contingency management" uses operant conditioning techniques to encourage increasing amounts and degrees of exposure. This approach conceptualizes "fear [as] not only a response of glands and smooth muscles, [but as] a reduced probability of moving toward a feared object and a heightened probability of moving away from it" (Skinner, 1988, p. 172). As a result, the goal of RP is to use operant principles to increase the probability that a fearful child will approach the feared stimulus (Davis & Ollendick, 2005). To accomplish this, a clinician must first conduct a thorough functional assessment to determine what variables are currently maintaining the avoidance behavior and also administer a reinforcement survey schedule to identify increasingly potent reinforcers for use with increasingly more intense exposures. RP then involves progressing through graduated hierarchical exposures using shaping, reinforcement, extinction, and verbal feedback from the clinician (Ollendick et al., 2004). The clinician must focus on grading the exposure, providing clear, succinct directions, and contingently providing reinforcement and verbal feedback about the child's performance. Over time and repeated practices, the schedule of reinforcement can be thinned and eventually faded out.

At present, RP has not been used alone to treat specific phobia in children, though it has been used productively as part of an integrated behavioral treatment (cf. Davis, in press; Silverman, Kurtines, Ginsburg, Weems, Lumpkin, et al., 1999). In the treatment of subclinical fears, however, RP procedures have been found to be effective and have garnered well-established support (Davis & Ollendick, 2005). In addition, RP has been found to be probably efficacious for altering the cognitive component of the fear response in individuals with a phobia (Davis & Ollendick, 2005; cf. Silverman, Kurtines, Ginsburg, Weems, Lumpkin, et al., 1999).

It is important to note that RP and SD often become confused in the literature and, at other times, are misconstrued as "distractors" or "safety behaviors, " especially when techniques other than progressive muscle relaxation are used (e.g., allowing a child to have some "security" object such as a teddy bear during an exposure; Davis, in press). At the crux of the issue is precisely when a competing response (as in SD) is initiated or when a reinforcer (as in RP) is delivered. Specifically, the reinforcement in RP should be delivered as soon as possible *after* the approach behavior occurs (i.e., temporal contiguity); conversely, SD involves the initiation of a competing response *before* the fear occurs and is enacted in an attempt to prevent the fear response from occurring. Confusion occurs when another form of a competing response (other than relaxation) is delivered before or during an exposure, but is then incorrectly labeled by some as a "reinforcer" (Davis, in press). Conversely, if the "reinforcer" were administered after the completion of a step in the hierarchy, then it is aptly applied and reinforces the approach behavior. For example, the teddy bear described earlier could be used for both RP and SD. If the bear were provided contingent on approach behavior, then the procedure would be best viewed as RP; however, if the teddy bear were provided before the exposure and the child were allowed to keep it throughout, then it would act in competition to the fear and would best be viewed as SD.

Participant Modeling

Participant modeling (PM) has been found to be an efficacious treatment for childhood fears since its inception in the mid- to late 1960s (Ritter,

1965, 1968). Observing another person interact skillfully with a feared stimulus and without evincing fear is thought to weaken the associations between the unconditioned and conditioned stimuli in the observer as new context-specific inhibitory learning begins to compete with fear (Bandura, 1969; Bouton, 2004; Myers & Davis, 2002). PM takes this one step further by encouraging the observer to interact with the model and the feared stimulus. As such, PM incorporates a significant skill-building component as the model not only serves to demonstrate successful interactions with the stimulus, but also guides the observer through interactions with the stimulus. The model typically demonstrates the successful negotiation of a step in the fear hierarchy, then physically and verbally guides the child observer through the step and, finally, slowly fades the amount of physical and verbal guidance the child requires to complete the step until he or she is able to master the task without assistance.

Similar to RP, PM has not been evaluated in a strict randomized controlled trial with children diagnosed with specific phobia (Davis, in press). For example, many classic studies of PM have either used samples composed of both adults and adolescents (e.g., Bandura, Blanchard, & Ritter, 1969) or used children who were fearful and not necessarily phobic (e.g., Murphy & Bootzin, 1973). Even so, using Davis and Ollendick's (2005) broader evidence-based approach, including studies like those just mentioned, PM has been found to be well-established for the treatment of fearful behavior and probably efficacious for the alteration of fearful cognition.

Cognitive-Behavioral Therapy

Cognitive-behavior therapy (CBT) makes use of many of the behavioral techniques already described to alter dysfunctional behaviors and the physiology associated with those behaviors, but also focuses on altering the schemas, attentional biases, and cognitive distortions that have come to create an automatic and negatively biased interpretation of the world (Beck, 1993; Beck & Clark, 1997; Kendall, 1993). CBT for specific phobia frequently involves reinforcement, graduated exposure, and participant modeling, but also incorporates psychoeducation about the feared stimuli; behavioral skills with which to interact with the feared stimuli; and cognitive techniques with which to alter distortions, automatic thoughts, and catastrophic thinking. As a result, CBT requires the clinician to obtain a detailed description of the child's catastrophic thinking prior to treatment. Determining these cognitions allows for the testing of catastrophic thoughts during exposure and helps the clinician prevent cognitive as well as behavioral avoidance during the tasks.

A particular combination of cognitive-behavioral techniques into a massed session—one-session treatment—has proven to be an effective treatment for specific phobias (Öst, 1987b, 1989; for a recent review see Zlomke & Davis, 2008). One-session treatment includes many of the standard cognitive-behavioral techniques—psychoeducation, graduated exposure, reinforcement, cognitive challenges, participant modeling—but masses the exposure into a single therapy session typically lasting up to 3 hours. This unique alteration to the typical treatment-session format may contribute to the treatment's impressive results (Davis, in press). Moreover, these massed sessions are well tolerated by children and typically progress as per their expectations (Svensson, Larsson, & Öst, 2002)

According to Davis and Ollendick (2005), CBT probably merits efficacious status for the treatment of both fearful behavior and cognition. Even when using stricter study inclusion and exclusion criteria, Davis (in press) found CBT likely to be efficacious for the treatment of phobic behaviors. Also, the unique massed combination of behavioral and cognitive techniques into one-session treatment has itself been found to be probably efficacious in children (Zlomke & Davis, 2008).

FACTORS THAT LEAD TO POOR TREATMENT RESPONSE

Although behavioral and cognitive-behavioral treatments have enjoyed considerable success in the treatment of fears and specific phobias, a significant minority of youth do not respond favorably to these treatments. Unfortunately, and somewhat surprisingly, only two large randomized control trials have examined predictors of treatment outcome with carefully diagnosed children with specific phobias and are able to inform us about those factors associated with poor treatment response. In the first clinical trial, Silverman and her colleagues (Silverman, Kurtines, Ginsburg, Weems, Rabian, et al., 1999) evaluated the relative efficacy of two exposure-based treatments (contingency management or RP and self-control CBT treatments) to an education-support control condition. Eighty-one children and adolescents between 6 and 16 years of age and their parents participated in the trial; 72% of the sample had at least one comorbid diagnosis, including additional specific phobias, separation anxiety disorder, overanxious disorder, and attention deficit-hyperactivity disorder. Treatments were manualized and consisted of a 10-week program in which children and their parents were seen in separate treatment sessions with the same therapist, followed by a brief conjoint meeting (90 minutes' duration). Although the results were somewhat mixed on self-report and parent-report measures, Silverman, Kurtines, Ginsburg, Weems, Rabian, et al. (1999) reported significant differences among treatment conditions on "clinically significant" measures of change. Composite diagnoses from the structured diagnostic interview (ADIS-IV C/P) at posttreatment revealed that 88% of the children in the exposure-based, self-control CBT condition were recovered, compared to 55% in the exposure-based RP condition and 56% in the education-support condition (a difference that was statistically significant favoring the exposure-based CBT condition over the other two conditions). In addition, a criterion-referenced measure of outcome, a Fear Thermometer, showed clinically significant improvement (defined as a change that eliminated or substantially reduced children's reported level of distress and behavioral avoidance) for both the CBT and RP groups (80% each), but not the education-support group (25%). Subsequently, Berman, Weems, Silverman, and Kurtines (2000) examined variables potentially associated with successful outcomes in the two exposure-based CBT treatment groups: child sociodemographics, severity of the disorder, comorbidity, parental psychopathology, and family functioning. Treatment success was defined as no longer meeting diagnostic criteria for specific phobia at posttreatment. For these analyses the two exposure-based treatment groups were combined because both were superior to the education-support condition on some of the measures (the education support group participants were not included in these analyses). There were no significant differences between the treatment success and treatment failure groups in terms of age, gender, ethnicity, or family income. Moreover, and unexpectedly, there were no significant differences between the treatment success and failure groups in terms of total number of diagnoses, severity of diagnosis, or comorbidity of diagnoses. However, as hypothesized, children's report of their own depression and generalized anxiety were higher in the treatment failure group, as were parents' ratings of their own depression and anxiety. Thus, depression and generalized anxiety, as endorsed by both the children and their parents, signaled a poor treatment response.

In the second large randomized trial, Öst, Svensson, Hellstrom, and Lindwall (2001) compared the relative efficacy of one-session CBT treatment to a wait-list control condition. Sixty children and adolescents between 7 and 17 years of age and their parents participated in the trial; 42% of the children had at least one comorbid diagnosis, including additional specific phobias, separation anxiety disorder, generalized anxiety disorder, social phobia, and major depressive disorder. Treatment was manualized and consisted of one intensive 3-hour session as described previously. Treatment outcomes indicated that 85% of the treated youth were free of diagnosis at posttreatment, compared to 0% in the wait-list condition. In addition, children in the treatment condition completed a higher percentage of steps on a behavioral-avoidance task and reported less subjective anxiety while completing this task than did those in the wait-list control condition. No differences in physiology, however, were obtained. As with Silverman Kurtines, Ginsburg, Weems, Lumpkin, et al. (1999), a host of measures were examined as potential predictors of successful outcome in the one-session CBT treatment condition. Like Silverman et al., age and number of diagnoses did not predict treatment outcome. Contrary to what Silverman et al. found, self-report of depression in the treated youth did not predict poor treatment response, whereas gender and type of phobia did predict differential outcomes: girls responded better than boys and youth with animal phobias responded better than youth with other phobias, including situational, environmental, and blood-injection-injury phobias. Unfortunately, parental psychopathology and family environment were not explored in this study.

Thus, conclusions about factors related to poor treatment response are difficult to draw from these two studies. Age and number of comorbid diagnoses did not differentially predict poor outcome in either study. However, the findings were mixed for gender and presence of co-occurring depression. Moreover, although Silverman, Kurtines, Ginsburg, Weems, Lumpkin, et al. (1999) found parental psychopathology and family functioning to be related to poor outcome, these variables were not examined by Öst et al. (2001). Although findings are inconclusive, it seems prudent to continue to explore all of these variables in subsequent clinical trials to more firmly rule on them and their potential role in treatment response. At this time, for specific phobias, it appears that youth who are comorbid with depression *may* be less responsive to treatment than *might* children from more dysfunctional families. Boys *might* also be less responsive to these efficacious treatments than girls. And, the treatment *might* be more effective for animal phobias than situational or environmental ones.

In these two well-controlled treatment outcome studies, as well as others in the broader anxiety disorders area, it is evident that only the selection and evaluation of initial treatments have been examined (Ollendick & March, 2004). That is, in the published clinical trials, an initial treatment was implemented and response to treatment was determined—no attempt was made to address partial responders or individuals who might have been refractory to change. Ollendick and March (2004) suggest that partial responders are those who improve on a number of variables but still retain their pretreatment diagnoses. For example, clinician severity ratings on the ADIS-IV C/P might be reduced significantly as a result of treatment, but the individual still meets criteria for diagnosis and shows avoidance on a behavioral avoidance task and high scores on relevant self-report measures. In the Silverman, Kurtines, Ginsburg, Weems, Lumpkin, et al. (1999) and Öst et al. (2001) studies, most of the poor responders fit into this category; that is, they showed partial response to some outcome measures but not all. According to Ollendick and March (2004), these individuals might respond to a greater dose of treatment (i.e., more sessions), a modification in the delivery of the intervention (i.e., inclusion of parents), or a "fine-tuning" of the intervention itself (i.e., re-examination of the fear hierarchy). In many instances, adjustments in the exposure activities that are so central to effective change might be necessary for the poor responders (see Bouchard, Mendlowitz, Coles, & Franklin, 2004). For example, it might be the case that the purpose of exposure was not sufficiently explained to the child or the child simply did not understand fully the explanation provided by the therapist. It might also be the case that the fear hierarchy was not sufficiently graduated to address the fears expressed by the child and a new fear hierarchy needs to be developed. Finally, it might be the case that the therapist did not adequately or fully address the faulty cognitions associated with the phobic object. For exposure to work effectively, corrective information that is incompatible with the dysfunctional associations stored in memory must be provided and new and more functional associations need to be made (Lang, 1979; Rachman, 1991). In other cases, a strong therapeutic alliance may not have been developed with the child and his or her family and the family may not have been engaged fully in therapy activities (see Chu et al., 2004). In still other situations, it might be the case that comorbidity or some other factor is interfering with treatment progress (Ginsburg & Walkup, 2004; Ollendick et al., 2004). In any event, the primary assumption with the partial responders is that the "problem" does not reside solely with the child or his or her family; rather, the problem resides in the selection and implementation of the intervention itself (Ollendick & March, 2004). Based on the componential analysis of the fear response (Davis & Ollendick, 2005), it is probable that the selected treatment did not address the "complete" phobic response and hence the dose of treatment was insufficient to produce more complete and lasting change. For example, Öst et al. (2001) failed to show significant change in the disrupted physiology of the phobic children in their study and Silverman, Kurtines, Ginsburg, Weems, Lumpkin, et al. (1999) did not assess for such a component nor report on changes in this domain. It is conceivable that the 12% who did not respond in the Silverman, Kurtines, Ginsburg, Weems, Lumpkin, et al. (1999) trial and the 15% who did not respond in the Öst et al. (2001) trial would have done so had this dimension of fear been more effectively treated. Unfortunately, these studies do not report additional treatment for these partial responders and so we do not know whether they would have responded or not. Indeed, some of them may have been refractory even to additional intervention of the same type.

In contrast, for those individuals refractory to treatment, the assumption is that the treatment itself simply does not work with these children and their families (Ollendick & March, 2004). In these cases, the child and his or her family show minimal to no change following what is thought to be efficacious treatment. Ollendick and March (2004) suggest that a child should not be viewed as refractory to treatment until any one treatment of adequate dose and duration has been attempted for at least two trials but no more that three trials. If the child shows an inadequate response after two to three trials, then alternate treatments including other psychosocial or pharmacological treatments should be tried. Figure 7.1, found in the Treatment section, illustrates a flow chart of a treatment algorithm for specific phobia in children with emphasis on the distinction between partial responders and refractory cases.

Thus, in our experience, most individuals who do not respond fully to treatment are "partial responders" and respond more fully to variations in the delivery, dose, or structure of the implemented treatment. In those cases in which the individual is truly refractory to change, the identified treatment might need to be abandoned and alternate treatments considered. In the section that follows, we present the case of a partial responder to one-session treatment and speculate on what we would try if the child were truly refractory to change.

CASE PRESENTATION

Billy (not his real name), a 10-year-old Caucasian boy, lived with his parents and 6-year-old brother. His mother (age 39) was a business woman and his father (age 38) was a skilled craftsman. Billy was referred to our clinic for a phobia of dogs. Although he appeared physically normal and healthy for his age, he was shy and seemed somewhat lethargic and "depressed" during the assessment session. Based on his parents' report, Billy's fear of dogs interfered significantly with his own and their lives. His mother reported that whenever she had to take her son to school, she had to avoid driving in neighborhoods where dogs might be present; if she did not do so, Billy would frequently panic and become so upset that he refused to get out of the car and go into school. On one school day, he refused to go to school even before leaving home because everyone was supposed to bring their pets and he was afraid that his classmates would bring their dogs. In addition, when Billy and his parents visited his grandparents (who had a dog) Billy secluded himself in a bathroom and refused to come out until his parents decided to return home. His fear had become worse in recent months, precipitating his appointment, after their neighbor bought a dog. Billy refused to go outside to play in his own yard and asked his parents to keep the doors to their home locked to make sure that the dog could not somehow get into their house. Billy's parents indicated they tried to listen to their son's complaints and concerns but they had become increasingly frustrated with him. They also indicated they tried to make him "happy" by avoiding situations where dogs might be present.

Billy's parents reported they had taken him to a play therapist when he was 6 years of age because of his fear of dogs and because he was reluctant to try new things and to meet new people. They saw this therapist for 25 sessions and reported that Billy really liked his therapist and enjoyed going to see her; however, they reported that he did not "really change very much." He continued to have his fear of dogs and to be shy around others.

ASSESSMENT

A comprehensive assessment was conducted. Two separate clinicians interviewed Billy and his parents simultaneously using the Anxiety Disorders Interview Schedule for *DSM–IV* Child/Parent version (ADIS-IV-C/P; Silverman & Albano, 1996). His mother indicated that Billy's fear started when he was 5 years of age and the family lived in a nearby neighborhood where a neighbor had a "really mean-looking dog" penned in the backyard. However, she could not recall any incident in which Billy was hurt or attacked by the dog, nor, to her knowledge, did Billy ever witness anyone else being hurt or attacked by this dog or any other dog. She did report, however, that the neighbor's dog often barked and growled at children and others when they passed the home. Based on the diagnostic interview, Billy was diagnosed with a specific phobia of dogs with a clinician severity rating (CSR) of 8 (maximum score on a scale from 0 to 8). Additionally, he endorsed criteria for a diagnosis of social phobia (a clinical severity rating of 6), and a subclinical diagnosis of major depressive disorder (clinician severity rating of 2). Billy's fear of dogs was most pronounced and troubling and was viewed as the primary diagnosis.

A separate evaluation of Billy's mother and father using the ADIS-IV-Client version (Brown, DiNardo, & Barlow, 1994) (the adult version of the interview) indicated that his mother endorsed symptoms of clinical depression (CSR = 4). She mentioned feeling overwhelmed by trying to help Billy and also take care of her other son, as well as responsibilities associated with her full-time job. She wished her husband would be more involved in helping her deal with Billy and his problems. His father, on the other hand, endorsed symptoms consistent with a subclinical diagnosis of panic disorder without agoraphobia (CSR = 3). He reported his symptoms were long-standing. He acknowledged his low level of involvement with Billy, but indicated he spent more time with his younger son who was more outgoing and liked to play various sports. He indicated that Billy was a major source of frustration for him, that Billy was not the son he thought he would be, and that he thought Billy just needed "to grow up and get over it."

A behavioral avoidance task (BAT) was administered in which Billy was asked to enter a room where a dog was being held on a leash by an assistant and to pet the dog for 10 seconds. Billy refused to enter the room and reported his subjective anxiety to be an 8 (on a scale ranging from 0 to 8). Throughout this task, his heart rate was monitored. Although his heart rate had been relatively stable prior to this task (beats per minute [BPM] = 80), it rose dramatically to 117 BPM while standing outside the door of the room where the dog was located. While standing in front of the closed door, he became extremely agitated, stating "I cannot go into the room... no way can I go in that room... the dog might jump on me and hurt me."

A cognitive-behavioral functional analysis was conducted to establish (a) the antecedents and consequences of Billy's avoidant behavior, (b) his catastrophic cognitions about dogs, and (c) a hierarchy of his fear (a rating from 0 to 8 for different situations that might trigger his fear). He indicated he fears any and all dogs and that if his family is watching a program on TV and a dog appears, he asks them to turn the TV off immediately. He also indicated that he checks the doors at home throughout the day to see if they are locked and shuts the blinds on the windows to avoid seeing their neighbor's dog. When asked if the fear of dogs prevented him from doing things he wanted to do, he indicated he was okay as long as his parents did not make him go outside or do things where dogs might be present. He had a keen awareness of his fears and their impact on him. Billy's cognitions associated with dogs and his ratings for danger, outcome, and self-efficacy in dealing with his fears are displayed in Table 7.1. As can be seen, his danger expectancies were very high, he was very sure negative things would happen to him if he was around dogs, and he was quite sure that he could not cope with them if they did occur.

On the fear hierarchy, Billy indicated that seeing a dog on the street or in the park without a leash would result in a fear level of 8 (on 0–8 scale) and that seeing a dog being walked on the street with a leash would result in a fear level of 7. Looking at a dog from his home or some other safe place would result in a fear level of 6 and just seeing a dog on TV would produce a fear level of 5. Moreover, even just looking at pictures of dogs would increase his fear level to a 2. Various steps in between these were also determined to construct a full fear hierarchy that could be used in therapy. At the end of the cognitive-behavioral functional analysis, the treatment rationale for one-session

Table 7.1

BILLY'S COGNITIONS AND EXPECTANCIES*

CATASTROPHIC COGNITION	DANGER EXPECTANCY (How bad would it be if it really occurred?)	OUTCOME EXPECTANCY (How likely is it to happen?)	SELF-EFFICACY (How sure are you that you will be able to cope with it if it does occur?)
I will bleed and die if the dog bites me.	8	8	0
The dog will chase me and I won't be able to run away.	7	7	0
If I see a dog outside, I will panic and not be able to breathe.	7	7	1
The dog will bark at me and try to bite me.	6	7	2
The dog will jump on me.	5	8	3

* Scale = 0–8; 8 being the worst, most likely, and most certain.

intensive exposure treatment was offered to Billy and his parents. The therapist indicated that the key to the one-session treatment is gradual but intensive exposure to the phobic object rather than avoidance of it and the active testing of his cognitions associated with dogs. The exposure activities were explained as behavioral experiments that were set up to test and challenge his thoughts and beliefs. Billy's parents were asked to help out with treatment by arranging situations that would help their son be exposed to dogs following treatment. Billy's parents appeared to understand the treatment and the need for in vivo exposure to help Billy overcome his fears, though they expressed some skepticism as to how well such a brief treatment would work.

CASE CONCEPTUALIZATION

Billy's phobia of dogs was severe. The origin of his fear could not be clearly identified, but was seemingly related to experiences that occurred while he lived in the neighborhood with a "vicious-looking dog." We hypothesized that he learned over time that dogs might be dangerous; moreover, his avoidance appeared to be reinforced and maintained by his mother's overprotective parenting style and his father's reluctance to become involved in more effective parenting with him. Behaviorally, he appeared to be a somewhat introverted and inhibited child. In addition he was subclinically depressed; also, his mother was clinically depressed and his father had a subclinical anxiety disorder. His motivation for treatment appeared reduced, likely because of the family's accommodation of his avoidance behavior and because his fear had become entrenched. His parents, however, expressed interest in helping him and Billy was willing to come in for the treatment because of the disruption his fear was causing him. Even though his parents expressed interest in helping their son, they did not seem to know how to do so.

Based on what we know about treatment in this young population, one-session treatment was chosen based on a tentative consideration of several factors: (a) one-session treatment is potentially less influenced by the child's comorbid depression compared to RP or a self-control CBT treatment (based on the findings from Öst et al., 2001, in contrast to those obtained by Silverman, Kurtines, Ginsburg, Weems, Rabian, et al., 1999); (b) RP and the self-control CBT treatment have been associated with poorer outcomes when the parents themselves are symptomatic with either depression or anxiety—both of which were present in this family (Silverman, Kurtines, Ginsburg, Weems, Rabian, et al., 1999); (c) the brief, single session of treatment was preferred, as it was thought multiple sessions over an extended period of time might create attendance issues, given the father's poor understanding of the disorder and the mother's distress over her son's symptoms; and (d) given the high level of behavioral avoidance and one-session treatment's successful outcomes with the behavioral component of the fear response (Davis & Ollendick, 2005; Öst et al., 2001), it was thought this rapid treatment might impart the quickest change in the most severe aspects of Billy's symptoms. It was anticipated that this treatment would also reduce his heightened physiological arousal and his distorted and dysfunctional cognitions.

TREATMENT

The single session followed the format of one-session treatment (3 hours of gradual exposure, modeling, reinforcement of approach behavior, and testing of faulty cognitions; see Zlomke & Davis, 2008, for a detailed description). Billy was seen alone and his parents were not directly involved in treatment. Initially, Billy was reluctant to even talk about dogs or to look at pictures of dogs in a colorful book. After repeated encouragement, however, he agreed to talk and to look at the pictures. The therapist provided information about dogs and their behavior (e.g., why they bark, why and when they wag their tails, how to approach them, etc.). Next, Billy was asked to watch a brief videotape depicting the information provided by the therapist. While watching the videotape, Billy initially indicated that his fear level was a 7 (on a 0-to-8 scale). His catastrophic cognitions about the possibility of having a panic attack while watching dogs in the video were tested and partially disconfirmed. He learned that he could be exposed to a dog on the video screen without developing a panic attack. This exercise, as with other exercises, was repeated three times. Following the third viewing, his fear level had dropped to a level of 2. After talking more about dogs and their behavior, he agreed to look outside the clinic window at a dog held on a leash by an assistant. Again, after the third trial, his fear had dropped from an 8 to a 3. Gradually, over the course of 3 hours, he was asked to do the following activities: allow the dog that was outside the clinic to be brought into the clinic waiting room and to look at it from the hallway; have the dog brought into the far end of the therapy room; and then to increasingly approach the dog, feed it some dog biscuits, and then pet it on the head for a few seconds. Throughout, his faulty cognitions were tested and disconfirmed and he practiced his skills about approaching and interacting with dogs. The therapist engaged in extensive modeling (demonstrating the various steps), participant modeling (having Billy touch his shoulder, then arm, and then hand while interacting with the dog), and profuse praise (for approaching the dog with the therapist slightly behind him). A playful, supportive, and trusting relationship was developed. Although considerable progress was made during the session, Billy still displayed considerable fear and reticence to interact more "naturally" with the dog. Billy and his parents were reassured that this was "only the beginning" of treatment and, if the treatment were to work fully, it would be important for them to continue exposure activities outside of therapy for several months.

Upon posttesting 1 week later, Billy's fear was reduced considerably from his pretreatment levels, but his phobia of dogs was still clinically significant, as evident in a CSR rating of 5 on the ADIS-IV C/P and his inability to open the door, approach, and then pet a tethered dog in a BAT similar to that used at pretreatment. Although his catastrophic cognitions (danger and outcome expectancies) had been reduced to a subclinical level of 3 (from an 8 at pretreatment), his heart rate remained high during the behavioral task (BPM = 122). Moreover, his social anxiety disorder (CSR = 6) and his subclinical level of depression (CSR = 2) remained. Thus, although there was evidence of change in his catastrophic cognitions, his heightened physiological arousal and behavioral avoidance—though reduced—remained at high levels. Although still symptomatic overall, the therapist suggested waiting an additional month to see if other changes might occur with the requested exposures outside of treatment, per the one-session treatment protocol.

One month later, Billy and his parents were re-evaluated. Not much progress had been made, even though his parents and Billy had arranged several opportunities to work on his fears (e.g., renting Scooby-Doo videotapes, visits to grandparents' home, leaving the blinds in the home pulled to be able to look outside and view the neighbor's dog, playing a game with dad and brother in the front yard, etc.). At that time his CSR for his phobia of dogs was a 6. It had increased some since posttreatment assessment, but had not fully returned to its pretreatment level. Consistent with our view (Ollendick & March, 2004) on the distinction between partial responders and those refractory to change, we viewed him as a partial responder and decided to provide him a second intensive one-session treatment rather than attempt some other psychosocial or pharmacological approach. This time, however, we decided to "tweak" our one-session treatment by adding a parental involvement component and by attempting to expose him to more than one dog in anticipation of greater generalization of treatment gains.

A 3-hour re-treatment session was scheduled 1 week later. We began this session where we left off with the initial treatment, with the primary exception that we arranged to have his parents observe the session and then enter the therapy room during the last hour to assist with therapy and learn skills to work with their son firsthand. The following in-session activities were arranged with three different dogs (starting with the same dog used in the first session): looking at the dog in the waiting room; being in the same room with the dog, which was leashed and held by an assistant at the far end of the therapy room; gradually approaching and feeding the dog; petting the dog; and taking the leash and walking the dog in the clinic and then outside the clinic. During the last hour and with the third dog in the room, his parents were brought into the therapy room to assist with training and to foster a transfer of control from therapist to parents (see Silverman, Kurtines, Ginsburg, Weems, Lumpkin, et al., 1999). Treatment seemed to go well and Billy seemed to have fun with the dogs and to be more "naturalistic" in his interactions with them. He beamed with excitement when his parents entered the room and they were profuse with their praise about him and his accomplishments (e.g., "Look at you... you are so brave and courageous... think of what granny will say... we are really proud of you"). As before, they were encouraged to practice what they had learned in therapy and asked to return for a posttreatment assessment in 1 week and then again in 1 month.

On posttesting a week later, his CSR ratings on the ADIS-IV C/P were a 2 and in the behavioral task he opened the door, looked inside the room, saw the dog, approached it, and petted it for about 10 seconds. Moreover, his catastrophic cognitions (danger and outcome expectancies) were now nonexistent (rating of 0, with a statement of "who would ever think that?"), and his heart rate was 88 BPM. In addition, a CSR of 4 (still clinical) on the ADIS-IV C/P Social Phobia module and a CSR of 1 on the Major Depression Module were obtained. One-month later his ADIS-IV C/P CSR rating for a specific phobia of dogs was a 0; for Social Phobia, a 2; and for MDD, a 0. During the behavioral test, he approached and petted the dog and even requested to take it on a walk. His formerly catastrophic cognitions remained at a 0 and his heart rate during the exposure task was 84 BPM. At this time, we requested the parents and Billy return 6 months later for an extended follow-up session to let us know how they were doing. They did so and by all indications Billy continued to have little or no fear of dogs and to be more socially engaged. His mother said he seemed "like a different boy" and his father reported how much he enjoyed outdoor activities with Billy and his brother. Moreover, his mother reported that she felt more in control of her own emotions and that she was less depressed herself (although a formal ADIS-IV: Client was not administered) and his father reported that he was much more engaged with the family. The father still reported occasional panic attacks but with less severity. Although Billy was a partial responder initially, he was a full responder following the second intensive treatment session, which was modified to address issues of parental involvement and generalization of treatment gains (see Figure 7.1).

What would we have done had Billy not been responsive to our second attempt at single-session treatment? Although we have no firm empirical findings to support our clinical decisions, we likely would have fine-tuned our approach even further and proceeded in the following manner (see Figure 7.1). Consistent with strategies recommended in Stage 2 of our model for partial responders and those individuals refractory to change, we likely would have continued our CBT approach with additional sessions but for an extended period of time and delivered on a weekly basis (spaced weekly over a 2 to 3 month period). This approach too has received strong empirical support (Ollendick et al., 2004). In addition, if his social phobia persisted, we likely would have considered Social Effectiveness Therapy (Beidel, Turner, & Morris, 2000) for the treatment of his social phobia, as it is possible that the presence of social phobia might be compromising the effectiveness of treatment for his specific phobia. Finally, we might have considered evidence-based treatments for his mother's depression and his father's subclinical panic disorder, inasmuch as parents' own psychopathology can serve as barriers to treatment response (Berman et al., 2001). As is evident, this third attempt at psychosocial treatment would have been an "all-out" attempt to address not only his specific phobia but also his social phobia and depression as well as the anxiety in his parents. Rarely, however, have we had to take such extensive actions in working with phobic children and adolescents. The clear majority respond with one or two trials of the evidence-based interventions.

If, however, these treatments did not work and his dog phobia and social phobia remained, we likely would view Billy as a "refractory" case and consult with our child psychiatric consultant and initiate a trial of selective serotonin reuptake inhibitors as recommended by Albano and Hayward (2004). However, we likely would not have selected some other psychosocial treatment such as play therapy or family therapy because there is little to no evidence for the efficacy of such approaches in the treatment of specific phobias in children (Ollendick et al., 2004; Ollendick & Davis, 2004). It is important to note that from our standpoint, we would not have considered Billy and his family

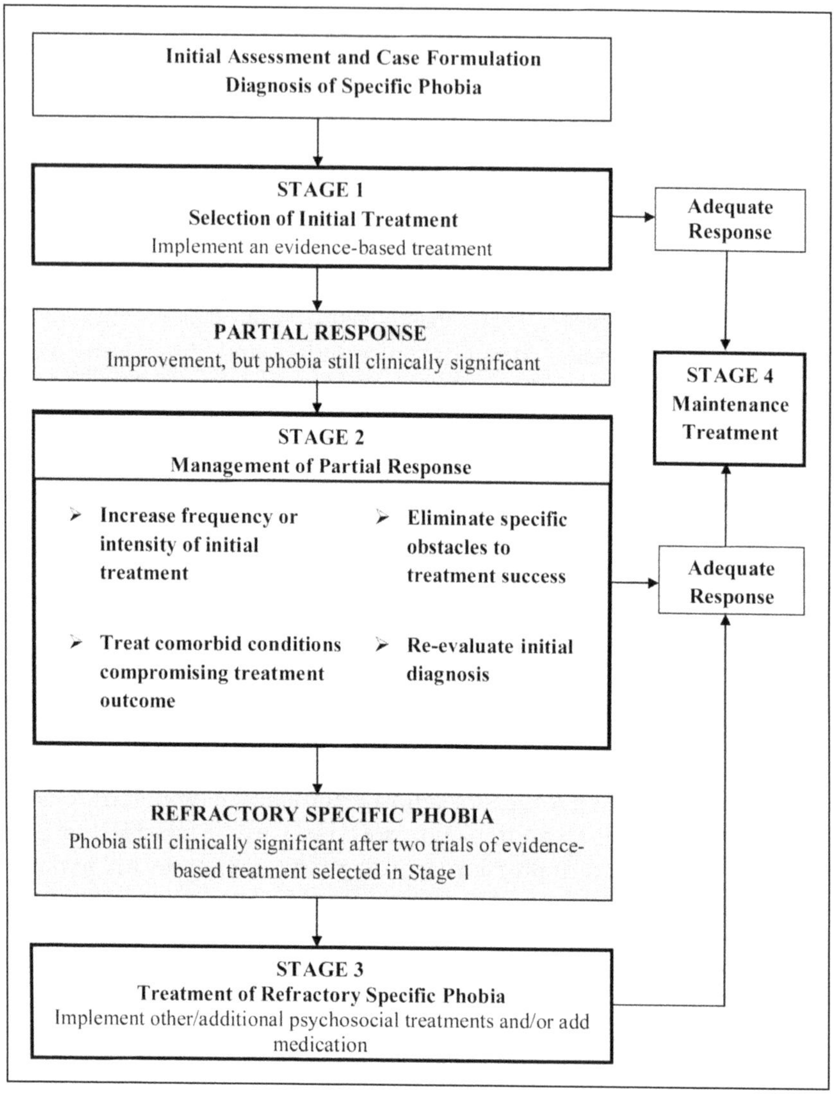

Figure 7.1 Treatment algorithm for children with specific phobia.
Adapted from Ginsburg and Walkup (2004) and Ollendick and March (2004).

"resistant" to change, even at this latter stage; rather, we would view their inadequate response to treatment as our "failure" to conduct an adequate cognitive-behavioral functional analysis and to provide them evidence-based treatments based on that assessment and case conceptualization.

SUMMARY

The use of behavioral and cognitive-behavioral techniques for treating fear and specific phobias in children has led to impressive results, with a clear majority of children and adolescents benefitting from these efficacious procedures. These treatments have even been successfully used to treat specific phobias in intellectually disabled populations. For example, Davis, Kurtz, Gardner, and Carman (2007) successfully treated a boy with a pervasive developmental disorder and specific phobias of heights and water using CBT (i.e., one-session treatment). Even so, these evidenced-based treatments do not help a significant minority of children with phobic disorders (e.g., ranging from 12% to 30%). In these cases, most of the youth are partial responders and a few are refractory to change. As we have noted, there may be a host of factors that predict poor treatment response, including the type of phobia, the child's gender, and comorbid depression and anxiety in the individual child and his or her parents. There may be other factors as well, but, if so, they are poorly understood. Still, as we illustrated in our case study, we have many evidence-based tools to use with such youth and their families. In our opinion, we must move away from the notion that those who do not respond are "resistant" to change. Still, a great deal more research and refinement of our evidence-based practices need to be realized before we can conclude that we have an "evidence-informed" strategy to help those children who are more difficult to treat and seemingly unresponsive to our initial efforts. We must move beyond acute care of these youth and their families and extend our reach to those who are partial responders and seemingly refractory to change.

REFERENCES

Albano, A. M., & Hayward, C. (2004). Social anxiety disorder. In T. H. Ollendick & J. S. March (Eds.), *Phobic and anxiety disorders in children and adolescents: A clinician's guide to effective psychosocial and pharmacological interventions* (pp. 175–197). New York: Oxford University Press.

Bandura, A. (1969). *Principles of behavior modification.* New York: Holt, Rinehart, & Winston.

Bandura, A., Blanchard, E. B., & Ritter, B. (1969). Relative efficacy of desensitization and modeling approaches for inducing behavioral, affective, and attitudinal changes. *Journal of Personality and Social Psychology, 13,* 173–199.

Beck, A. T. (1993). Cognitive therapy: Past, present, and future. *Journal of Consulting and Clinical Psychology, 61,* 194–198.

Beck, A. T., & Clark, D. A. (1997). An information processing model of anxiety: Automatic and strategic processes. *Behavioral Research Therapy, 35,* 49–58.

Beidel, D. C., Turner, S. M., & Morris, T. L. (2000). Behavioral treatment of social phobia. *Journal of Consulting and Clinical Psychology, 68,* 1072–1080.

Berman, S. L., Weems, C. F., Silverman, W. K., & Kurtines, W. M. (2000). Predictors of outcome in exposure-based cognitive and behavioral treatments for phobic and anxiety disorders in children, *Behavior Therapy, 31,* 713–731.

Bouchard, S., Meldlowitz, S. L., Coles, M. E., & Franklin, M. (2004). Considerations in the use of exposure with children. *Cognitive and Behavioral Practice, 11,* 56–65.

Bouton, M. (2004). Context and behavioral processes in extinction. *Learning and Memory, 11,* 485–494.

Brown, T. A., Di Nardo, P. A., & Barlow, D. H. (1994). *Anxiety Disorders Interview Schedule for DSM-IV (ADIS-IV).* San Antonio, TX: Psychological Corporation/Graywind Publications.

Chambless, D. L., & Ollendick, T. H. (2001). Empirically supported psychological interventions: Controversies and evidence. *Annual Review of Psychology, 52,* 685–716.

Chu, B. C., Choudhury, M. S., Shortt, A. L., Pincus, D. B., Creed, T.A., & Kendall, P.C. (2004). Alliance, technology, and outcome in the treatment of anxious youth. *Cognitive and Behavioral Practice, 11,* 44–55.

Davis III, T. E. (in press). PTSD, anxiety, and phobias. In J. Matson, F. Andrasik, & M. Matson (Eds.), *Treating childhood psychopathology and developmental disorders.* New York: Springer Science and Business Media.

Davis III, T. E., Kurtz, P., Gardner, A., & Carman, N. (2007). Cognitive-behavioral treatment for specific phobias with a child demonstrating severe problem behavior and developmental delays. *Research in Developmental Disabilities, 28,* 546–558.

Davis III, T. E., & Ollendick, T. H. (2005). A critical review of empirically supported treatments for specific phobia in children: Do efficacious treatments address the components of a phobic response? *Clinical Psychology: Science and Practice, 12,* 144–160.

Deacon, B., Lickel, J., & Abramowitz, J. S. (2008). Medical utilization across the anxiety disorders. *Journal of Anxiety Disorders, 22,* 344–350.

Ginsburg, G. S., & Walkup, J. T. (2004). Specific phobia. In T. H. Ollendick & J. S. March (Eds.), *Phobic and anxiety disorders in children and adolescents: A clinician's guide to effective psychosocial and pharmacological interventions* (pp. 175–197). New York: Oxford University Press.

Kendall, P. C. (1993). Cognitive-behavioral therapies with youth: Guiding theory, current status, and emerging developments. *Journal of Consulting and Clinical Psychology, 61*, 235–247.

Lang, P. J. (1977). Imagery in therapy: An information processing analysis of fear. *Behavior Therapy, 8*, 862–886.

Lang, P. J. (1979). A bio-informational theory of emotional imagery. *Psychophysiology, 16*, 495–512.

March, J., Parker, J., Sullivan, K., Stallings, P., & Conners, C. K. (1997). The Multidimensional Anxiety Scale for Children (MASC): Factor structure, reliability, and validity. *Journal of the American Academy of Child and Adolescent Psychiatry, 36*, 554–565.

Muris, P., & Merkelbach, H. (2000). How serious are common childhood fears? II. The parent's point of view. *Behaviour Research and Therapy, 38*, 813–818.

Muris, P., Merkelbach, H., Mayer, B., & Prins, E. (2000). How serious are common childhood fears? *Behaviour Research and Therapy, 38*, 217–228.

Muris, P., Merkelbach, H., Meesters, C., & van den Brand, K. (2002). Cognitive development and worry in normal children. *Cognitive Therapy and Research, 26*, 775–787.

Muris, P., Schmidt, H., & Merckelbach, H. (1999). The structure of specific phobia symptoms among children and adolescents. *Behaviour Research and Therapy, 37*, 863–868.

Murphy, C. M., & Bootzin, R. R. (1973). Active and passive participation in the contact desensitization of snake fear in children. *Behavior Therapy, 4*, 203–211.

Myers, K. & Davis, M. (2002). Behavioral and neural analysis of extinction. *Neuron, 36*, 567–584.

Ollendick, T.H. (1983). Reliability and validity of the Revised Fear Survey Schedule for Children (FSSC-R). *Behaviour Research and Therapy*, 21, 685–692.

Ollendick, T. H., & Cerny, J. A. (1981). *Clinical behavior therapy with children*. New York: Plenum Press.

Ollendick, T. H., & Davis III, T. E. (2004). Empirically supported treatments for children and adolescents: Where to from here? *Clinical Psychology: Science and Practice, 11*, 289–294.

Ollendick, T. H., Davis, T. E., & Muris, P. (2004). Treatment of specific phobia in children and adolescents. In P. Barrett, & T. H. Ollendick (Eds.), *The handbook of interventions that work with children and adolescents: From prevention to treatment* (pp. 273–299). West Sussex, UK: John Wiley.

Ollendick, T. H., Hagopian, L. P., & King, N. J. (1997). Specific phobias in children. In G. C. L. Davey (Ed.), *Phobias: A handbook of theory, research and treatment* (pp. 201–223). London: John Wiley.

Ollendick, T. H., & King, N. J. (1991). Origins of childhood fears: An evaluation of Rachman's theory of fear acquisition. *Behaviour Research and Therapy, 29*, 117–123.

Ollendick, T. H., & King, N. J. (1998). Empirically supported treatments for children with phobic and anxious disorders: Current status. *Journal of Clinical Child Psychology, 27*, 156–167.

Ollendick, T. H., King, N. J., & Frary, R. B. (1989). Fears in children and adolescents: Reliability and generalizability across gender, age, and nationality. *Behaviour Research and Therapy, 27*, 19–26.

Ollendick, T. H., King, N. J., & Muris, P. (2002). Fears and phobias in children: Phenomenology, epidemiology, and aetiology. *Child and Adolescent Mental Health, 7*, 98–106.

Ollendick, T. H., & March, J. S. (2004). *Phobic and anxiety disorders in children and adolescents: A clinician's guide to effective psychosocial and pharmacological interventions*. New York: Oxford University Press.

Öst, L. G. (1987a). Age of onset in different phobias. *Journal of Abnormal Psychology, 96*, 223–229.

Öst, L. G. (1987b). One-session treatments for a case of multiple simple phobias. *Scandinavian Journal of Behavior Therapy, 16*, 175–184.

Öst, L. G. (1989). One-session treatment for specific phobias. *Behaviour Research and Therapy, 27*, 1–7.

Öst, L. G., Svensson, L., Hellstrom, K., & Lindwall, R. (2001). One-session treatment of specific phobias in youth: A randomized clinical trial. *Journal of Consulting and Clinical Psychology, 69*, 814–824.

Rachman, S. (1977). The conditioning theory of fear acquisition: A critical examination. *Behavior Research and Therapy, 15*, 375–387.

Rachman, S. (1991). Neo-conditioning and the classical theory of fear acquisition. *Clinical Psychology Review, 11*, 155–173.

Rachman, S. (2002). Fears born and bred: Non-associative fear acquisition? *Behaviour Research and Therapy, 40*, 121–126.

Ritter, B. (1965). *The treatment of a dissection phobia*. Unpublished manuscript, Queens College.

Ritter, B. (1968). The group desensitization of children's snake phobias using vicarious and contact desensitization procedures. *Behaviour Research and Therapy, 6*, 1–6.

Silverman, W. K., & Albano, A. M. (1996). *Anxiety Disorders Interview Schedule for DSM-IV, Child and Parent versions*. San Antonio, TX: Psychological Corporation.

Silverman, W., Kurtines, W., Ginsburg, G., Weems, C., Lumpkin, P., & Carmichael, D. (1999). Treating anxiety disorders in children with group cognitive-behavioral therapy: A randomized clinical trial. *Journal of Consulting and Clinical Psychology, 67*, 995–1003.

Silverman, W., Kurtines, W., Ginsburg, G., Weems, C., Rabian, B., & Serafini, L. T. (1999). Contingency management, self-control, and education support in the treatment of childhood phobic disorders: A randomized clinical trial. *Journal of Consulting and Clinical Psychology, 67*, 675–687.

Silverman, W., & Ollendick, T. H. (2005). Evidence-based assessment of anxiety and its disorders in children and adolescents. *Journal of Clinical Child and Adolescent Psychology, 34*, 380–411.

Skinner, B. F. (1988). The operant side of behavior therapy. *Journal of Behavior Therapy and Experimental Psychiatry, 19*, 171–179.

Stinson, F. S., Dawson, D. A., Chou, S. P., Smith, S., Goldstein, R. B., Ruan, W. J., et al. (2007). The epidemiology of DSM-IV specific phobia in the USA: Results from the National Epidemiologic Survey on Alcohol and Related Conditions. *Psychological Medicine, 37*, 1047–1059.

Svensson, L., Larsson, A., & Öst, L. G. (2002). How children experience brief exposure treatment of specific phobias. *Journal of Clinical Child and Adolescent Psychology, 31*, 80–89.

Task Force on Promotion and Dissemination of Psychological Procedures. (1995). Training in and dissemination of empirically validated psychological treatments: Report and recommendations. *Clinical Psychologist, 48,* 3–23.

Wolpe, J. (1958). *Psychotherapy by reciprocal inhibition.* Stanford, CA: Stanford University Press.

Zlomke, K., & Davis III, T. E. (2008). One-session treatment of specific phobias: A detailed description and review of treatment efficacy. *Behavior Therapy, 39,* 207–223.

8

Children's Refractory Posttraumatic Stress Disorder: An Ecological, Evidence-Based Perspective

ELISSA J. BROWN AND CAROLE L. CAMPBELL

POSTTRAUMATIC STRESS DISORDER IN YOUTH

Posttraumatic stress disorder (PTSD) is a significant public health problem for children and adolescents, and is characterized by symptoms that develop after exposure to a traumatic event (*Diagnostic and Statistical Manual of Mental Disorders, Fourth Edition, Text Revision* [*DSM-IV-TR*]; American Psychiatric Association, 2000). As currently defined, the symptoms of PTSD fall into three clusters: re-experiencing (e.g., recurrent and intrusive thoughts of the event, dreams/nightmares about the event, flashbacks), avoidance and numbing (e.g., efforts to avoid thoughts, feelings, people, places, or activities that remind the person of the trauma), and hyperarousal (e.g., difficulty falling or staying asleep, hypervigilance, exaggerated startle response). A person must have a minimum of one re-experiencing, three avoidance/numbing, and two hyperarousal symptoms to meet criteria for the diagnosis. Researchers have argued that the *DSM-IV-TR* criteria, developed based on research with combat veterans, do not adequately capture the presentation of traumatized youth. It is clear that developmental factors play a role in the expression of posttraumatic stress reactions (Amaya-Jackson & March, 1995; Kerig, Fedorowicz, Brown, & Warren, 2000). Studies suggest that older children, and particularly adolescents, show more adult-like symptoms (i.e., *DSM-IV-TR*) than younger children. As a result, experts have suggested alternate criteria for diagnosing PTSD in young children (Scheeringa, Zeanah, Myers, & Putnam, 2003). Proposed adjustments to the *DSM-IV-TR* criteria of PTSD for children include generalized nightmares, new fears, loss of previously acquired developmental skills, reenactment of trauma in behavior or play, and self-destructive or aggressive behavior (Cook et al., 2005; Courtois, 2004; Margolin & Vickerman, 2007). Although debate on this issue remains, what is clear is that, in addition to presenting with symptoms of hypervigilence, hyperarousal, numbing, and intrusive thoughts, traumatized youth often present with complex symptoms and/or comorbid symptoms of depression, defiance, conduct problems, and substance abuse (Kerig et al., 2000; Margolin & Vickerman, 2007; Spitzer, Chevalier, Gillner, Freyberger, & Barnow, 2006). Consequently, the most researched treatment for trauma symptoms in youth, to date, has addressed problems in these areas.

THEORETICAL ARGUMENT FOR AND DESCRIPTION OF TRAUMA-SPECIFIC COGNITIVE-BEHAVIORAL THERAPY

Lang (1977, 1979) developed a bio-informational theory of emotions in which he hypothesized that an emotional experience is mapped as a cognitive schema containing information about the stimulus, its meaning, and responses to the stimulus. Applying this work to traumatic events, Foa and Kozak (1986) argued that schemas related to the emotion of fear must include information that the stimuli and/or responses are dangerous. Because a traumatic event is a psychological, physical, and/or moral violation that disrupts previous concepts of safety (Herman, 1992; Janoff-Bulman, 1992), numerous stimuli and responses in the victim's daily life that previously signaled safety become associated with danger. Ehlers and Clark (2000) have proposed that, among those who develop persistent PTSD, this has a cumulative effect on the individual, creating a sense of ongoing, current threat. Moving beyond the sole emotion of fear, Resick and Schnicke (1992, 1993) argue that intrusive recollections and avoidance may be activated by complex emotions such as anger, humiliation, and guilt. Drawing from cognitive theory, they argue that these strong emotional reactions to trauma may arise because of conflicts between prior schemata and the current event (Resick & Schnicke, 1993). For example, people believe in a "just-world," in which good things happen to good people and bad things happen to bad people (Lerner & Miller, 1978). In traumatic circumstances, a conflict emerges because the new information ("*I have been abused*") is inconsistent with preexisting beliefs ("*I am a good kid*" and "*Abuse doesn't happen to good kids*"). Ehlers and Clark propose that PTSD is maintained by these attributions about the traumatic event, as well as by negative appraisals about initial trauma reactions. For example, although a majority of individuals experience sequelae such as numbing, irritability, and intrusive recollections shortly after a traumatic event, maladaptive appraisals (*"I've been permanently changed"*) contribute to and maintain PTSD.

Exposure therapy and cognitive restructuring are the core elements of trauma-specific cognitive-behavioral therapy (TS-CBT; Nikulina et al., 2008). Exposure to the traumatic memory in the absence of aversive consequences results in habituation to feared consequences (Foa, Steketee, & Rothbaum, 1989). Cognitive restructuring involves the direct confrontation of conflicts, misattributions, and expectations (Resick & Schnicke, 1992). Additional coping skills (e.g., relaxation training) are used to help patients cope with their physiological responses to the trauma memory.

For preschoolers, children, adolescents, and their caregivers, additional components are included in TS-CBT to address developmental factors, such as affect dysregulation and parenting deficits. Evidence-based TS-CBT for children typically consists of individual sessions for children and caregivers, followed by family work (Brown, 2002; Cohen, Mannarino, & Deblinger, 2006; Kolko & Swenson, 2002). Children's sessions involve psychoeducation, affect awareness and regulation, coping skills (e.g., relaxation training and cognitive restructuring), exposure therapy, safety planning, and creating a reminder for skills learned.

Psychoeducation is introduced immediately in the first session of TF-CBT and continues throughout treatment. Psychoeducation involves defining relevant terms, including the trauma (e.g., "*Physical abuse is when someone taking care of a child goes too far with discipline, causing bruises or scratches*"). Psychoeducation also consists of: discussion of common emotional and behavioral reactions to trauma exposure (with emphasis on conflicting reactions; for example, feeling love for the abuser, but hate for the abuser's behavior), description of the cognitive-behavioral model, and provision of rationales for specific treatment components. The goals of psychoeducation are to reinforce accurate cognitions, normalize reactions to the trauma(s), and engage patients in treatment.

Affect awareness and coping skills are designed to help children identify emotions and use skills to ameliorate upsetting and overwhelming emotions. Behavioral approaches, such as modeling, behavioral rehearsal, and feedback, are used to teach the skills. Affect awareness is conducted through role-playing different emotions, during which children learn to explain their internal experiences and describe their observations of their therapist's emotional expression. Relaxation techniques, including diaphragmatic breathing, mindfulness, meditation, and progressive muscle relaxation are taught for management of anger and anxiety. Cognitive skills are used to address maladaptive thoughts (e.g., self-blame, perception that the world is dangerous) and processes (e.g., rumination) related to the trauma. Cognitive skills include cognitive restructuring, social problem solving, and worry time. For younger or delayed children with less sophisticated cognitive development, cognitive restructuring and other complex cognitive techniques may not be appropriate. Instead, positive self-talk, thought stopping, and positive imagery may be helpful. The techniques are taught before discussing the trauma in a comfortable, safe, and positive environment. The goal is for children to master the relaxation and cognitive skills before using them in later sessions to cope with the stress of trauma reminders and exposure therapy. Children develop a "tool box reminder," an artistic expression of the various skills learned that they will present during graduation (to ensure their understanding) and take home as a preventive intervention for future stressful life events (Brown, 2002).

Exposure therapy (termed "conducting a trauma narrative" by Cohen et al., 2006) involves the repeated writing, rewriting, and reading of details of the trauma(s) to habituate children and their caregivers to memories of the event(s). Children create a trauma narrative over the course of several sessions, and include in the narrative as many details as possible regarding what happened before, during, and after the trauma(s). Children are encouraged to incorporate their affective, physiological, and cognitive reactions during the trauma(s). While writing and reading the narrative, children's level of anxiety/anger are monitored and recorded. If anxiety does not decline through habituation, previously learned coping skills are implemented to facilitate coping and challenge inaccurate beliefs about the trauma. If appropriate, children prepare to share their trauma narratives with their caregivers in conjoint parent–child sessions.

In parallel sessions, caregivers are taught the coping skills to address their own trauma-related symptoms and to be a "coach" for their children as they are learning skills. Caregivers also receive parent training (McMahon & Forehand, 2003) to help them with children who are responding to trauma with anger and behavior problems like aggression. The five main skills taught during this component are child-directed play, praise/positive attention, selective attention (including ignoring), time-out procedures, and contingency reinforcement.

Conjoint child–parent sessions are conducted to review skills and improve communication about the trauma, specifically, and family functioning, generally. For PTSD associated with abuse, children and caregivers may participate in clarification (e.g., Lipovsky, Swenson, Ralston, & Saunders, 1998). Clarification is a process that includes four steps: (a) caregivers draft a letter acknowledging their role in the violence, apologizing for it, and explaining how they will keep their children safe in the future; (b) therapists and caregivers edit the letter over a period of weeks or months until content and tone are supportive and accurate; (c) therapists and children prepare for the clarification session (e.g., develop a list of questions for the caregiver, decide on set-up of room); and (d) a clarification session is conducted in which the letter is read to the child(ren), who then ask questions of the caregiver, resulting in open, adaptive communication about the trauma. Family problem-solving and graduation are then conducted.

EFFICACY OF TRAUMA-SPECIFIC COGNITIVE-BEHAVIORAL THERAPY

TS-CBT is the most widely studied psychosocial intervention for PTSD in preschoolers, children, and adolescents. The majority of investigations studied TS-CBT conducted using individual therapy, with parallel child and caregiver sessions. Individual psychotherapy may be the more common modality because of clinical concerns regarding: (a) conducting exposure therapy in a group format (e.g., fear of secondary traumatization); (b) being able to organize groups based on developmental level; and (c) needing to begin treatment immediately, rather than having patients wait for the group to fill. What follows is a summary of the treatment-outcome literature, with an emphasis on randomized controlled trials (for comprehensive literature reviews, see Cohen, Mannarino, Murray, & Ingelman, 2006; Nikulina et al., 2008; Skowron & Reinemann, 2005).

The first randomized controlled trial that evaluated psychosocial treatments for pediatric PTSD compared trauma-focused CBT (TF-CBT, a form of TS-CBT for Childhood Sexual Abuse [CSA] related PTSD) to routine community care (Deblinger, Lippman, & Steer, 1996). The CBT conditions included: (a) children only, (b) caregivers only, and (c) children and caregivers. Children who received CBT (with and without caregiver involvement) experienced a greater reduction in symptoms of PTSD than those in the control condition (routine community care). Children of caregivers who participated in CBT (with and without children's involvement) showed more significant improvements in symptoms of depression and externalizing behaviors than those in the control group. This seminal study not only provided empirical support for TS-CBT, but suggested the importance of child and caregiver involvement for adequate treatment of internalizing and externalizing trauma-related psychopathology.

In addition to routine community care, TF-CBT has been found to be superior to nondirective supportive therapy (NST), a commonly used intervention with children and families (Cohen & Mannarino, 1996a, 1998). NST incorporated active listening, reflection, and empathy, with the goal of encouraging children and caregivers to generate their own solutions to abuse-related emotional and behavioral difficulties. In a randomized clinical trial of preschoolers, TF-CBT was found to be more efficacious then NST in reducing PTSD symptoms, internalizing symptoms, and externalizing behavioral problems (Cohen & Mannarino, 1996b). These differences were maintained at a 1-year follow-up (Cohen & Mannarino, 1997). In a parallel randomized trial of sexually abused school-aged children, TF-CBT was superior to NST in reducing symptoms of depression, behavior problems, and social competence (Cohen & Mannarino, 1998). In a 6-month follow-up study, Cohen, Mannarino, and Knudsen (2005) found that children in the TF-CBT condition evidenced greater improvement on state and trait anxiety, depression, sexual problems, and dissociation than those in the NST condition. At 12-month follow-up, children who received TF-

CBT showed greater improvement in PTSD symptoms and dissociation than those who received NST.

To address the sample size limitation of the aforementioned studies, Cohen, Deblinger, Mannarino, and Steer (2004) conducted the first multisite, randomized trial for children with PTSD. Two hundred twenty-nine children, ages 8 to 14 years, and their primary caregivers received TF-CBT or child-centered therapy (CCT). CCT was a manualized treatment focused on establishing trust between the child and parent, while the family directs their own treatment. The CCT intervention differed from the NST condition described previously in that CCT allowed for invitational, nondirective prompts (e.g., to discuss the traumatic experience). CCT also allowed for limited psychodynamic interpretations of child and parent feelings. Interpretive statements about thoughts were not allowed, so as to distinguish CCT from cognitive processing (J. A. Cohen, personal communication March 26, 2008). Although participants were referred for CSA exposure, 70% had experienced at least one other trauma, including witnessing domestic violence, serious accident, and/or child physical abuse. At posttreatment, children assigned to TF-CBT evinced greater improvement in PTSD symptoms, depression, behavioral problems, and attributions regarding their abuse than those assigned to CCT. Parents assigned to TF-CBT reported greater improvement on symptoms of depression, distress related to abuse, child support, and parenting effectiveness.

Treatment gains were maintained at 6- and 12-month follow-up assessments for families who received TF-CBT (Deblinger, Mannarino, Cohen, & Steer, 2006). Children continued to experience fewer symptoms of PTSD and shame related to abuse when compared to those in the CCT condition, and caregivers continued to report reductions in abuse-specific distress. Based on this investigation and the aforementioned studies, TF-CBT is viewed by experts (such as the National Child Traumatic Stress Network, 2008) as a best practice for the treatment of children with PTSD. Subsequent randomized controlled trials, such as that conducted by Smith and colleagues (2007), which examined the efficacy of TS-CBT (based on Ehlers and Clark's model of PTSD) with children who had histories of multiple types of single-incident traumatic events, lend further support to this intervention.

In the only randomized trial of a psychopharmacological intervention for children with PTSD, Cohen, Mannarino, Perel, and Staron (2007), conducted a 12-week pilot double-blind trial comparing TF-

CBT plus sertraline to TF-CBT plus placebo. Twenty-four children, ages 10 to 17 with CSA-related PTSD participated. TF-CBT was implemented as discussed earlier and sertraline was titrated to a maximum dose of 200 mg per day with a mean of 173 mg per day. There were no significant differences between conditions in the reduction of PTSD symptoms. Children who received TF-CBT plus sertraline had a significantly higher global functioning score at posttreatment than those in the TF-CBT alone condition. No differences in side effects between the two groups were reported, suggesting that sertraline is a safe short-term treatment for PTSD in children. However, because no added improvement in PTSD symptoms can be attributed to sertraline, it appears that TF-CBT alone remains the best initial treatment for children with trauma-related symptoms.

FACTORS RELATED TO TREATMENT OUTCOME

As research in the field moves beyond efficacy studies, researchers have become more sophisticated in their examination of factors that are correlated with treatment outcome. Individual-level variables, including children's pretreatment symptom severity and cognitive processing of the trauma, have been examined as predictors. Microsystemic variables are characteristics of those systems in close proximity to the child, or with whom the child interacts regularly, such as teachers, parents, siblings, and clinicians. In addition to individual and microsystemic factors, broader macrosystemic (e.g., cultural, socioeconomic, legal, social service) factors are incorporated in clinical evaluations because they may influence treatment course and response. Race and ethnicity are considered macrosystemic because they represent cultural beliefs and practices. The studies that have examined factors related to treatment outcome will first be described, followed by a discussion of those factors found to be related to or predictive of treatment outcome, putting them within an ecological framework (i.e., Bronfenbrenner, 1979).

Studies of Factors Related to Treatment Outcome

Four studies were conducted to extend the aforementioned randomized trials of children with PTSD to examine correlates of treatment outcome (Cohen & Mannarino, 1996b, 2000; Deblinger et al., 2006; Smith et al.,

2007). For preschoolers and school-age children, Cohen and Mannarino examined the following correlates: demographic variables (age, gender, race, socioeconomic status, and household composition), abuse-related variables (number of abusive episodes, type of sexual abuse, parents' and school-age children's attributions and perceptions related to the abuse incident, and parental emotional responses to their children having been abused), levels of family cohesion and adaptability, levels of social support available to mothers, and levels of parental support for and blame of their children regarding the abuse. Deblinger and colleagues (2006) conducted a preliminary study of the potential influence of pretreatment demographic and trauma characteristics (child's sex, race, age, total number of traumas experienced before treatment, having a parent as a perpetrator) and symptom severity on posttreatment symptoms. Smith and colleagues (2007) examined whether the effect of treatment on PTSD symptoms was mediated by cognitive appraisals.

Individual-Level Variables Associated With Treatment Response

Children's attributions related to abuse appear to be important correlates of internalizing and externalizing problems. Cohen and Mannarino (2000) found that children's self-blame for negative events, lack of perceived credibility, perception of being different from their peers, and belief that others are not to be trusted were strongly associated with symptoms of anxiety, depression, and anger at posttreatment. Smith and colleagues' (2007) findings suggest that cognitive processing changes may be the mechanism of action that accounts for symptom reduction in treatment. Consistent with a mediational model, after controlling for the effect of changes in cognitive appraisals, the direct effect of therapy was significantly reduced.

Interestingly, trauma characteristics were associated with poorer treatment response only for those participants in the control (CCT) condition (Deblinger et al., 2006). In the CCT group, the total number of traumas reported by children at pretreatment was positively associated with posttreatment PTSD symptoms. CCT children's pretreatment depression was predictive of PTSD symptoms at both posttreatment and 12-month follow-up. Pretreatment trauma exposure and depression were not significant predictors of posttreatment functioning for children in the CBT condition. Regardless of treatment approach, individual-level demographic characteristics (e.g., age, gender) have not been found to be predictive of treatment response.

Microsystemic Variables Associated With Treatment Response

To date, studies that have included microsystemic variables have focused exclusively on parental factors. In preschoolers (Cohen & Mannarino, 1996b), parents' emotional responses to the abuse were associated with children's parent-reported behavior problems, whereas in school-age children (Cohen & Mannarino, 2000), parents' emotional responses were associated with children's self-reported internalizing symptoms (i.e., anxiety, depression) following treatment. This distinction might be the result of methodological (e.g., parent-report on preschoolers versus self-report by school-age children) and/or developmental differences (e.g., children at different ages responding in different ways to parents' distress); nevertheless, the findings highlight the importance of parental functioning and emotional response to the abuse. Similarly, the degree to which rules and boundaries shift in families was associated with social skills deficits and behavior problems in preschoolers, and associated with children's anxiety and posttraumatic stress symptoms in school-age children. In contrast to their findings related to children's own self-blame, parents of children high (versus low) on self-blame for the abuse evidenced greater improvements on parental anger (Cohen & Mannarino, 2000). In this case, children's blaming themselves may remove responsibility from the parent and result in decreased resentment and anger. Parents of children who scored high on global assessment of functioning showed more improvement in violent behavior toward their child. With treatment, these parents may have been able to recognize (potentially, for the first time) the effect their behavior has on their children. Overall, these findings highlight the importance of the family system, including the interaction of the child and parent, on both the child's and the parent's response to treatment. Further research is needed to examine other microsystemic factors, such as sibling, peer, teacher, and clinician attributions and support.

Macrosystemic Variables Associated With Treatment Response

Studies have yet to examine a majority of macrosystemic variables. Extant research on race and ethnicity is mixed. In their two-site study of TS-CBT for children who had experienced traumatic bereavement, Cohen et al. (2007) found no differences in outcome based on racial/ethnic group. However, in their studies of TS-CBT with sexually abused preschoolers, racial/ethnic group was predictive of change on one variable, social competence, with non-Latino White children showing greater improvement (Cohen & Mannarino, 1996b, 1998). Further research on the impact of cultural beliefs on symptom development and treatment response is needed.

Macrosystemic Variables Associated With Treatment Participation

One limitation of treatment outcome research is that findings can be generalized only to those who would be willing to participate in randomized trials. Traumatized families may not only be unwilling to participate in research, but they may be unwilling to participate in mental health care at all (Davis, Ressler, Schwartz, Stephens, & Bradley, 2008).

Families of color, the most likely to be traumatized and develop serious mental health consequences, are the least likely to access services (Office of the Surgeon General, 2001). Once they access services, they are more likely to drop out and less likely to be satisfied with services received. Concrete challenges to participation include language problems, lack of transportation, lack of insurance coverage, and long waiting lists. Other barriers include the stigmatization of mental health, low acculturation, delays in seeking treatment until patients are in crisis, and use of non-evidence-based alternative therapies (e.g., faith healers): these factors may influence access of services. For the Latino community (represented in the case study that follows), cultural values and beliefs that might influence participation in mental health care include the emphasis on family (i.e., familismo) and personal, informal relationships (personalismo), respect for elder members of the community (respeto), enactment of traditional gender roles (machismo), and spirituality (Bernal, Bonillo, & Bellido, 1995). The impact these factors might have on treatment access and/or response is not yet known.

As research practitioners working to affect dissemination of TS-CBT, our experience is consistent with the literature indicating that the aforementioned barriers impede the implementation of evidence-based practices in real-world settings. Apart from patient characteristics, issues such as billing requirements, scheduling difficulties, and case management time involved in treating multistressed, traumatized families are added barriers (Addis, 2002). Therapist resistance, limited access to research, and training costs are cited by department directors as barriers to implementing best-practice approaches (Proctor et al., 2007). Although macrosystemic factors are understudied within randomized controlled trials, their influence on trauma exposure and access to services suggest a growing need for innovative ways to include them in treatment outcome and service delivery research. The following case of refractory PTSD reflects these challenges.

CASE PRESENTATION

JaQuan Lopez (all names are pseudonyms to protect the identify of actual clients) was a 13-year-old Hispanic/Latino male adolescent referred by child protective services (CPS) to the Prevention of Adverse Reactions To Negative Events and Related Stress (PARTNERS) Program, a specialized outpatient mental health clinic for traumatized youth. As is typical for PARTNERS Program referrals, the first step was to initiate contact with the referring agency.

The CPS caseworker reported that she had concerns about JaQuan related to a history of sexual abuse by a maternal uncle when JaQuan was 10 years of age. According to the caseworker, JaQuan was placed in foster care 2 months prior to the referral because of allegations of physical abuse by his stepfather and neglect (failure to protect) by his mother. Since the initial placement, he had been moved to a second foster home as a result of oppositional behavior in the first foster home, coupled with the fact that he ran away from that home. When asked about mental health symptoms, the CPS caseworker stated that she was concerned that JaQuan had "unresolved issues" related to his history of abuse, and that he was defiant, angry, and verbally aggressive toward authority figures. According to the worker, he had been physically aggressive with a teacher who touched him on his arm. When questioned by the worker about the incident, JaQuan reportedly justified this behavior, stating, "I don't like to be touched." Otherwise, JaQuan stated that he "[got] along okay" with his peers in his urban high school. Reportedly, his primary peer group included youth who frequently "acted out" and received suspensions.

On entry to the program, JaQuan and his foster mother completed an evidence-based clinical evaluation, which included standardized measures of PTSD, other internalizing symptoms (e.g., depression), and externalizing behavior problems (e.g., aggression). In addition, a detailed psychosocial history, including trauma exposure, parenting practices, and substance use was gathered. A list of recommended measures with demonstrated reliability and validity for use with traumatized youth in clinical settings is provided in Table 8.1. As is common among children in foster care, JaQuan's biological parents (and stepfather) did not participate in the pretreatment evaluation. During the course of the evaluation, the CPS worker contacted the therapist to inform her that a family court review of the case had been conducted, in which reunification of the family was anticipated for the next case review, scheduled for approximately 10 weeks later.

Evaluation measures were scored, summarized, and presented to JaQuan and his foster parents in a feedback session. Validity indices on the self- and parent-report forms of the Behavioral Assessment System for Children, second edition (Reynolds & Kamphaus, 2004) suggested that JaQuan was "at-risk" for underreporting, whereas his foster parents were in the normal range. JaQuan and his caregivers endorsed significant symptoms of PTSD, including intrusive thoughts of the abuse, nightmares, avoiding thinking or talking about the abuse, hypervigilence, increased startle response, and irritability. According to his CPS worker, teacher, and foster mother, JaQuan also exhibited significant behavior problems, meeting criteria for oppositional defiant disorder (APA, 2000). His symptoms included truancy, defiance, arguing with adults, mild aggression, and breaking rules (such as talking out of turn in class and not performing chores in his foster home). JaQuan denied all of these symptoms. Substance use, suicidal ideation, and self-harm behaviors were denied by all sources.

Based on the evaluation results, the PARTNERS Program recommended treatment for JaQuan, his foster parents, and his biological mother and stepfather. Specifically, the evaluators recommended individual sessions of TS-CBT for JaQuan, to teach affection regulation and coping skills and develop a trauma narrative for emotional and cognitive processing. Parallel caregiver sessions with his foster parents were recommended so that they would learn coping skills and ways to manage/monitor his behavior. Parallel caregiver sessions with his mother and stepfather, conducted separately from the foster parents' and JaQuan's sessions, were planned in accordance with the best-practice model for working with physically abusive caregivers if reunification is anticipated (Kolko & Swenson, 2002). In addition to learning the same skills as the

Table 8.1

RECOMMENDED MEASURES FOR USE IN EVALUATING TRAUMATIZED YOUTH

MEASURE	DOMAIN	AUTHOR(S) AND PSYCHOMETRIC PAPERS
Schedule for Affective Disorders and Schizophrenia for School-Age Children, Present and Lifetime Version	*Psychiatric diagnosis* *Trauma history*	Kaufman et al. (1997)
Things I Have Seen and Heard: An Interview for Young Children About Exposure to Violence	*Community violence exposure*	Richters & Martinez (1990)
Conflict Tactics Scales	*Interpersonal violence exposure*	Archer (1999); Straus (1990); Straus et al. (1998)
Child PTSD Symptom Scale (CPSS)	*PTSD* *Functional impairment*	Foa, Johnson, Feeny, & Treadwell (2001)
The Behavioral Assessment System for Children–Second Edition (BASC-2), Parent, Child, and Teacher Reports	*Internalizing symptoms (general)* *Behavior problems* *Adaptive functioning*	Reynolds & Kamphaus (2004)
Children's Inventory of Anger	*Anger*	Nelson & Finch (2000)
Form 90	*Substance use*	Miller & Del Boca (1994)
Extended Grief Inventory	*Children's traumatic grief*	Layne, Steinberg, Savjak, & Pynoos (1998)

Table 8.1 (continued)

MEASURE	DOMAIN	AUTHOR(S) AND PSYCHOMETRIC PAPERS
Characteristics, Attributions, and Responses After Exposure to Death, Youth and Parent versions	*Characteristics of bereavement due to traumatic circumstances*	Brown, Cohen, Amaya-Jackson, Handel, & Layne (2003)
Alabama Parenting Questionnaire	*Parenting practices*	Frick, Christian, & Wootton (1999)
PERceptions of Children Exposed to Interpersonal ViolencE (PERCEIVE)	*Children's violence-specific attributions*	Brown (2006)
Brief Symptom Inventory	*Caregivers' psychiatric symptoms*	Derogatis & Melisaratos (1983)
Posttraumatic Stress Disorder Symptom Scale	*Caregivers' PTSD*	Foa, Riggs, Dancu, & Rothman (1993)
Barriers to Treatment Participation Scale	*Barriers to treatment*	Kazdin, Holland, Crowley, & Breton (1997)

foster parents, JaQuan's parents were to participate in the clarification process, during which they would acknowledge their roles in his maltreatment and write a letter of clarification to JaQuan. Although the coping skills and behavioral monitoring sessions were planned to include both parents, it was recommended that JaQuan's mother and stepfather complete the clarification sessions separately. Initial family sessions were planned to include JaQuan and his foster parents to reinforce the skills learned. Later family sessions with JaQuan, his mother, and his stepfather were planned to begin with the clarification process and continue through the reunification transition, with an emphasis on easing this transition (via developing a behavioral monitoring system and reducing anticipatory anxiety triggered by entry into the environment where the physical abuse occurred).

JaQuan and his foster parents arrived on time for the first seven sessions. Individual sessions with JaQuan focused on psychoeducation about physical and sexual abuse, affective expression, psychoeducation about the cognitive behavioral model, and presentation of relaxation and cognitive coping skills. Psychoeducation and skill building were successful with JaQuan. For example, despite demonstrating a nonchalant attitude toward treatment, JaQuan reported in the fourth session that he had implemented diaphragmatic breathing after becoming irritated at a peer the previous week. At the end of the seventh session, the therapist introduced the idea of the trauma narrative to JaQuan and informed him that they would begin the narrative during the next session.

During the parallel caregiver sessions, his foster parents received psychoeducation about children's responses to abuse and began skills training. They participated in sessions and were cooperative in engaging JaQuan in home-based practice of the skills. After learning about behavior management, his foster parents implemented a token economy at home that allowed JaQuan to earn television privileges and telephone time for completing desired activities (i.e., chores). Additional rewards (for example, an appropriate allowance) and natural and logical consequences (for example, cleaning up messes, losing time outside when returning home late) were introduced as the behavioral management plan developed.

After the seventh session (prior to starting the trauma narrative), JaQuan and his foster parents completed a brief mid-treatment evaluation, which included measures of PTSD, internalizing symptoms, and externalizing behavior problems. Results indicated that JaQuan's defiant behaviors (truancy, aggression, and verbal outbursts) had significantly decreased. His foster parents also reported that he had been completing his chores at home, earning many of the identified rewards each week. Nevertheless, JaQuan's symptoms of PTSD, including avoidance, re-experiencing, and arousal, had increased mildly.

JaQuan's mother and stepfather, Lena and Antonio Hernandez, were inconsistent in attending their parallel caregiver sessions. They attended the first session together, arriving 20 minutes late. His mother appeared overwhelmed, as indicated by her shortness of breath on arrival, and reported that she had worked a 9-hour day and forgotten the appointment until leaving work. JaQuan's stepfather appeared disengaged, as indicated by his silence and gazing out the window as his wife answered the therapist's questions. When the therapist attempted to engage him in a discussion about his goals for therapy, he stated that he was attending the session "because [he had] to." He disagreed with the psychoeducation provided on physical abuse and corporal punishment, reporting that his parents "beat [him] and [he] turned out pretty good."

JaQuan's parents did not call to cancel, nor did they attend the second session. The therapist attempted to contact JaQuan's mother via telephone, leaving one message and reaching her on the second attempt. Mrs. Hernandez reported that they "forgot" about the session. The therapist incorporated engagement strategies found to increase likelihood of session attendance (McKay, McCadam, & Gonzales, 1996). The therapist praised Mrs. Hernandez's efforts to support the family financially (through her demanding work) as well as emotionally (by attending the first session). The therapist linked Mrs. Hernandez's session attendance to her stated goal of having her son return home. They then discussed how to overcome the barriers to session attendance.

Mrs. Hernandez attended the third session without her husband. Rather than continue with treatment aims, the therapist addressed her husband's noncompliance. Mrs. Hernandez reported that he had told her repeatedly that "therapy doesn't work." In addition, she stated that he was working full time, so he was unable to attend at the scheduled time. The therapist and Mrs. Hernandez agreed that treatment would be more effective if conducted with both parents. They planned to meet for treatment only when both parents were able to attend, and a time chosen that was more convenient for Mr. Hernandez.

Mr. and Mrs. Hernandez arrived promptly for the next two sessions. The therapist continued skill building, focusing on relaxation and cognitive coping. The rationale for learning the coping skills was twofold: (a) helping JaQuan manage his behaviors and (b) helping Mr. and Mrs. Hernandez modulate their own emotional reactions. Both caregivers participated in the skill-building sessions.

During the sixth week, a model for behavioral management was introduced, including the concepts of rewarding positive behaviors and using natural and logical consequences when rules are broken. The therapist encouraged Mr. and Mrs. Hernandez to practice effective parenting strategies in preparation for reunification. Mrs. Hernandez was attentive during this session, and indicated she had used the progressive muscle relaxation technique the previous week at work. Although Mr. Hernandez expressed understanding of the model, he indicated uncertainty of its efficacy with adolescents, stating, "It just seems like it's for little kids. JaQuan is old enough to know better, and he should respect us enough to follow the rules without us *buying* [his compliance]." Mrs. Hernandez rebutted him, noting that she was rewarded for good behavior growing up, and never considered her compliance as "bought." Mr. Hernandez acknowledged her comment and agreed to try, but maintained that he believed it would work better with younger children. His viewpoint was acknowledged by the therapist, who suggested that they discuss methods for making the behavioral management plan applicable to JaQuan in the following session. Although they arrived 5 minutes late to that session, the therapist was able to work with the parents to identify activities relevant to JaQuan as "rewards, " and engage both parents in developing a list of desired and nondesired behaviors.

During the week between the seventh and eighth sessions, a court hearing (unannounced to the therapist) was held, in which physical custody of JaQuan was returned to his parents. The family did not attend the following session. Despite several telephone calls to the family, the therapist could not reach Mrs. Hernandez, nor did she return the therapist's telephone calls. A message was left for the ongoing case worker to inform her of the status of the case. The next day, Mrs. Hernandez called the therapist to reschedule the session and an appointment was scheduled for the following day.

JaQuan, Mr. Hernandez, and Mrs. Hernandez arrived on time for the eighth session. JaQuan's initial subjective units of discomfort (SUDS) ratings were low, and his affect was noticeably flatter than in previous sessions. When this observation was noted by the therapist, JaQuan admitted that he had anticipatory anxiety about conducting the trauma narrative, thinking "I won't be able to handle it." He also stated that he had been feeling "really antsy since [he'd] gotten home." He reported that his nightmares were more frequent and vivid, he was aroused constantly, and he had poor concentration. He then admitted that he had smoked marijuana earlier in the day, "to help [him] relax." JaQuan was reminded that one purpose of his trauma narrative was to master his trauma-related anxiety through habituation. He was invited to return to therapy when prepared to do the narrative without substance use. With the understanding that a safety plan would be developed with his parents, his session was discontinued.

In the parallel caregiver session, the therapist reported JaQuan's substance use. Mrs. Hernandez indicated that she had suspected that JaQuan had smoked marijuana earlier in the week, based on his odor when he returned from school. Mr. Hernandez was angry that the therapist had discontinued JaQuan's session. He exclaimed, "This is ridiculous! You call our worker to get us here, and now you won't see him! If this actually worked, he probably wouldn't be high in the first place. What do you expect us to do to control his behavior? I can't hit him or social services will take him away, but you won't work with him because he's high." He stood up during this exclamation, waving his arms, and spoke in a loud, agitated tone. Mr. Hernandez was allowed to voice his frustration without interruption. He repeated that his parents had used corporal punishment with him, and this was an effective method of discipline. "How dare you tell me how to discipline my kid" he yelled; "Do you have children?" Conceptualizing the situation as Mr. Hernandez feeling criticized and helpless, the therapist used verbal and nonverbal methods (e.g., leaning over, lowering her tone of voice, slowing her voice) to empathize with his frustration and provide a sense of control. Problem solving and challenging maladaptive statements were avoided to prevent repeated escalation. When Mr. Hernandez began to communicate in a calmer tone, the therapist praised both parents for their willingness to schedule and attend the session, despite continued frustration with child protective services and disbelief about the effectiveness of therapy.

Once Mr. Hernandez had re-engaged with the therapist and Mrs. Hernandez, the therapist revisited the need to address JaQuan's substance abuse. Mr. Hernandez expressed a plan to use physical discipline. The therapist, having used psychoeducation and cognitive restructuring to address beliefs about corporal punishment, recognized that she needed an alternative treatment approach to address parenting methods. Motivational Interviewing (Miller & Rollnick, 2002), an evidence-based treatment that has been applied with caregivers of abused children (Chaffin et al., 2004; Corcoran, 2002), was used to help Mr. and Mrs. Hernandez identify the pros and cons of using corporal punishment with a teenage boy. The therapist asked about the potential consequences of the typical progression from spanking on the bottom over clothes, used by about 94% of Americans (Straus & Stewart, 1999), to more severe forms of discipline. The therapist also asked whether corporal punishment had been successful with JaQuan, and how it might have affected his relationship with his stepfather. The therapist asked about Mr. Hernandez's reactions to his childhood discipline versus Mrs. Hernandez's reactions to her childhood experience with positive reinforcement. Lastly, the therapist asked Mr. and Mrs. Hernandez to consider a potential link between JaQuan's fears (including of his stepfather) and symptoms (including substance use).

Through Motivational Interviewing, JaQuan's parents were able to link his substance use to his desire to reduce his anxiety. Mr. Hernandez conceded that the structure of the behavioral management plan might help JaQuan's anxiety decrease because he would be able to anticipate consequences—he made an association between knowing his work schedule and feeling calm because he can anticipate his day. Mrs. Hernandez expressed understanding that, given changes in JaQuan's environment and the fact that she and Mr. Hernandez had yet to begin behavioral management, it was possible that progress could yet be seen.

The therapist and Mr. and Mrs. Hernandez were then able to problem-solve ways to address JaQuan's substance use. The intervention plan was based on Multisystemic Therapy (MST; Henggeler, Schoenwald, Borduin, Rowland, & Cunningham, 1998), an efficacious treatment for adolescent substance abuse and conduct disorder (Henggeler et al., 1999) that has been used conjoint to TS-CBT (Danielson et al., 2006). As is central to MST, treatment built on the strengths of JaQuan, his parents, school, and community. The immediate plan focused on monitoring JaQuan during and after school. Given their strong communication skills, the therapist worked with Mr. and Mrs. Hernandez to identify goals and methods for contacting the school. A role-play was conducted in which Mrs. Hernandez rehearsed requesting a point of contact for monitoring JaQuan's behavior during school hours and for 1 hour after school (on the days that the parents could not identify another person to monitor behavior). Mr. Hernandez was encouraged to provide feedback and support. A day and time (end of academic day) was selected for making the telephone call. Mr. and Mrs. Hernandez agreed to speak to their supervisors to ensure that at least one of them was home each night for supervision.

Positive activities with their family, peers, and community also were promoted (Henggeler et al., 1998). Mr. and Mrs. Hernandez reported that JaQuan had been involved with the church youth group prior to being placed in foster care. They also described his athletic prowess with pride. Lastly, they discussed JaQuan's cousins, who lived locally and were positive role models, especially a boy who was a few years older than JaQuan. The therapist used problem solving to help Mr. and Mrs. Hernandez brainstorm how to mobilize these resources given their schedules and transportation challenges (e.g., asking Mr. Hernandez's mother to drive JaQuan to church with her). Mr. and Mrs. Hernandez left the session holding hands.

The therapist called Mrs. Hernandez a few days later to check in. She reported having a successful conversation with the school counselor, who was identified as a contact person and agreed to call JaQuan's parents immediately if he was found to be truant at any point during the school day. JaQuan was enrolled in after-school services (study session) on the days in which supervision was needed. Reportedly, Mr. and Mrs. Hernandez were able to monitor JaQuan during the evening hours. Mrs. Hernandez expressed gratitude for the therapist's help and reported feeling "calm for the first time in a while." The therapist reinforced her successes.

JaQuan and his parents arrived on time for the next session. Individually, JaQuan reported that he wanted to continue with treatment, expressing understanding that this was possible only if he abstains from substance use. His recent marijuana use and its link to trauma exposure and PTSD were discussed in more detail. JaQuan and his therapist downloaded information from the Internet about marijuana and other drug use (including alcohol), including their impact on the nervous system (i.e., as depressants). Motivational Interviewing (Miller & Rollnick, 2002) was applied to substance use, and JaQuan was able to generate both positive and negative consequences of smoking marijuana. One such positive consequence was that, "Smoking [helped him] not feel upset about what happened." JaQuan admitted that he had been having considerable problems sleeping since returning to his parents' home. He also stated that he was, "so jumpy [he could] hardly stand it" when around his stepfather. According to JaQuan, he had difficulty remaining in the same room with Mr. Hernandez if he was wearing a belt. Psychoeducation was conducted about types of trauma cues (e.g., place where physical abuse occurred, instrument used during physical abuse) and tendency of cues to elicit PTSD symptoms. One of the identified negative consequences of substance use was avoidance of the trauma narrative, which might alleviate his symptoms. Another identified negative consequence was his parents' removal of his privileges and their distress. Following Motivational Interviewing, JaQuan iterated that he would like to continue with treatment.

The following four individual sessions (weeks 10–13) with JaQuan consisted of his creating a trauma narrative about the abuse. Separate narratives were created related to JaQuan's physical abuse and sexual abuse. For each type of maltreatment, he began by describing the disclosure of maltreatment and child protective services' investigation. Subsequent sessions included descriptions of the abuse, adding more detail over time. During these sessions, JaQuan manipulated a "stress ball" in his hands while dictating the narrative. The therapist transcribed the narrative to review in subsequent sessions. SUDS ratings were gathered during each narrative session, until the exposure to the narrative no longer elicited distress (i.e., SUDS ratings elevated only to a 2 on a 0–10 scale). JaQuan was provided the option of sharing all, or part, of his trauma narrative with his parents. He chose to share his physical abuse narrative with both parents, and selected parts of his sexual abuse narrative to share with his mother.

Although not consistently on time, the family was consistent in communicating with the therapist about tardiness or missing a session for the remainder of treatment. In parallel parent sessions, JaQuan's parents developed a behavioral management/monitoring system. He was able to earn back desired rewards for following the rules (e.g., no truancy, no breaking of the monitoring system). One home-based session was planned in which the therapist helped the parents identify barriers to the system's success (Henggeler et al., 1999). The therapist observed that JaQuan had a television and computer in his room (making it impossible to remove privileges when he was in his room). These were moved to a common area.

The clarification letter and process were described and initiated in the 10th week of treatment. Mr. and Mrs. Hernandez were instructed to complete separate letters, in which each wrote a description of the abuse, took full responsibility for his or her role (e.g., for Mrs. Hernandez, failure to protect JaQuan from the abuse), apologized to JaQuan, and described how they would keep him safe in the future (Lipovsky et al., 1998). Letters were drafted, reviewed, and edited by the therapist and each parent in separate sessions. Mr. Hernandez incorporated lessons learned in therapy about managing JaQuan's behavior, stating, "I know now that the way I disciplined you wasn't working. I should have looked for another way. I am glad that we have found something that is working now."

Joint sessions followed in which the clarification letters and JaQuan's selected trauma narratives were shared. JaQuan prepared for the clarification sessions by listing questions he had for each parent. Each parent was prepared, in advance, to hear these questions to ensure appropriate responses. Similarly, Mr. and Mrs. Hernandez were prepared to hear JaQuan's trauma narratives by anticipating their own reactions to his thoughts, behaviors, and feelings. Supportive responses were modeled and practiced. In each of these joint sessions, JaQuan was given authority to determine where participants sat and who would share his or her letter/narrative first. The joint sessions offered an opportunity for honest sharing of thoughts and feelings about this traumatic family experience. Each family member showed moderate anxiety at the start of his/her narrative, and both JaQuan and his mother were tearful after her clarification letter was shared. Mr. Hernandez, as well, was tearful as he described his attachment to JaQuan and regret for the impact his behavior had on him. In the final sessions, family-level problem solving was conducted (e.g., timing of JaQuan's curfew). JaQuan presented a review of his coping skills to his parents, which he took with him to use in the case of future trauma/stress.

A posttreatment evaluation was conducted 2 weeks after termination. JaQuan no longer met criteria for PTSD; there were no re-experiencing and avoidance symptoms, and only one arousal symptom (hypervigilance). Depression and anxiety scores were in the normal range on the BASC. Although JaQuan reported intermittent irritability and anger related to his parents' rules, he no longer met criteria for oppositional defiant disorder, and the BASC-Parent report of conduct problems was in the normal range. Grades and peer relations were improved.

CONCLUSIONS AND FUTURE DIRECTIONS

Based on the literature review and case presentation, there are several important clinical and research implications for refractory PTSD. Given that PTSD is often a result of exposure to multiple traumas, the diagnostic picture of traumatized children may be severe and comorbid, including PTSD and many other clinical problems (e.g., depression, aggression, substance abuse). These other clinical problems may be maintaining or worsening the PTSD; as a result, they need to be assessed and addressed in treatment.

The aforementioned research on treatment outcome and its correlates, and the clinical case example illustrate the value of comprehensive evaluations. There is a need for multimethod, multiinformant assessment to ensure identification of internalizing and externalizing problems. Use of standardized measures allows for comparisons across clinical and traumatized samples. Validity indices provide guidance on the degree to which conclusions should be based on the report. Lastly, the treatment outcome research and case vignette highlight the value of mid-treatment (between-components) evaluations in our understanding of a particular client's progress and link between intervention component and symptom reduction.

Another lesson learned related to the complexity of the clinical picture of refractory PTSD is the limitations of TS-CBT and need to incorporate other relevant evidence-based interventions. TS-CBT has excellent results when conducted with engaged families in which the primary caregiver is not the offender (e.g., Cohen et al., 2004). In the presented case, one of the primary caregivers was the perpetrator (as is more common with physical than sexual abuse; Kolko & Swenson, 2002) and the client experienced substance abuse and conduct problems that maintained his PTSD. Once the challenges were identified, the therapist accessed the treatment outcome literature. Engagement strategies were used to increase likelihood of session attendance. Motivational Interviewing was used to increase readiness for change, both in the case of the parenting strategies of the father and substance use of the client. Lastly, Multisystemic Therapy was used to promote relationships between primary caregivers and other systems (e.g., schools), build on strengths of family and community, and identify barriers to the efficacy of TS-CBT.

Also related to the complexity of refractory PTSD is the need to include caregivers in assessment and treatment. Traumatized children, as in the presented case, commonly underreport their symptoms, making collateral report particularly meaningful. Regarding treatment, Deblinger et al. (1996) provide empirical evidence that inclusion (versus absence) of parents in TS-CBT results in greater improvements in children's depression and externalizing behavior problems. Studies of microsystem correlates of treatment outcome provide further support for the importance of family participation. The presented case illustrates the value of involving both current (i.e., foster parents) and future (i.e., biological parents) family in treatment. Foster parents need to be educated about traumatic stress, efficacious parenting, and coping skills for traumatized youth. Biological parents, especially when responsible for the maltreatment, need to alter their own coping and parenting strategies. Linares, Montalto, Li, and Oza (2006) have successfully used evidence-based parent training (Webster-Stratton, 2001) with biological and foster parents of maltreated children.

Another implication for the treatment of refractory PTSD is the need to educate the systems working with these children on the mental health impact of their decisions. In the aforementioned case, a legal decision, reunification, was implemented with no warning or preparation. When judges, attorneys, and law guardians (who represent the children's best interests in court) engage the therapist in making such decisions, the therapist can inform the system about the family's readiness and prepare the family for reunification.

A last lesson learned from the presented case and literature on conducting trauma treatment (e.g., self-care; Azar, 2000; Pearlman, 1995) is the importance of supervision. The severity and complexity of psychopathology in trauma survivors requires education on multiple areas of assessment and treatment. In addition, trainees need modeling of expeditious problem solving. Lastly, self-care is particularly important when hearing narratives of repeated violence and attempting to engage anxious and angry caregivers. The father in the presented case became irate when he felt trapped by the demands of his son, his wife, the therapist, child protective services, and other systems serving his son. He expressed his frustration to the therapist, a safe figure. Although his ability to do so might be seen as a breakthrough in the therapeutic relationship because he was then able to engage in treatment, being the recipient of such anger is upsetting and, at times, frightening. Trainees need to be prepared for this experience, both in terms of their attributions (e.g., misattribution that they did something wrong or deserve it) and reactions (e.g., using verbal and nonverbal responses to calm the client, mobilizing social support to address feelings after the session).

REFERENCES

Addis, M. E. (2002). Methods for disseminating research products and increasing evidence-based practice: Promises, obstacles, and future directions. *Clinical Psychology: Science and Practice, 9*, 367–378.

Amaya-Jackson L., & March J. S. (1995). Posttraumatic stress disorder. In J. S. March (Ed.), *Anxiety disorders in children and adolescents* (pp. 276–300). New York: Guilford Press.

American Psychiatric Association. (2000). *Diagnostic and statistical manual of mental disorders* (4th ed., text rev.). Washington, DC: American Psychiatric Press.

Archer, J. (1999). Assessment of the reliability of the Conflict Tactics Scales: A meta-analytic review. *Journal of Interpersonal Violence, 14*, 1263–1289.

Azar, S. T. (2000). Preventing burnout in professionals and paraprofessionals who work with child abuse and neglect cases: A cognitive behavioral approach to supervision. *In Session: Psychotherapy in Practice, 56*, 643–663.

Bernal, G., Bonilla, J., & Bellido, C. (1995). Ecological validity and cultural sensitivity for outcome research: Issues for the cultural adaptation and development of psychosocial treatments with Hispanics. *Journal of Abnormal Child Psychology, 23*, 67–82.

Bronfenbrenner, U. (1979). *The ecology of human development*. Cambridge, MA: Harvard University Press.

Brown, E. J. (2002). *Comprehensive treatment of child physical abuse*. Unpublished manuscript.

Brown, E. J. (2006). *PERceptions of Children Exposed to Interpersonal ViolencE (PERCEIVE)*. Unpublished manuscript.

Chaffin, M., Silovsky, J. F., Funderburk, B., Valle, L. A., Brestan, E. V., Balachova, T., et al. (2004). Parent-child interaction therapy with physically abusive parents: Efficacy for reducing future abuse reports. *Journal of Consulting and Clinical Psychology, 72*, 500–510.

Cohen, J. A., Deblinger, E., Mannarino, A. P., & Steer, R. A. (2004). A multisite randomized controlled trial for children with sexual abuse-related PTSD symptoms. *Journal of the American Academy of Child and Adolescent Psychiatry, 43*, 393–402.

Cohen, J. A., & Mannarino, A. P. (1996a). A treatment outcome study for sexually abused preschool children: Initial findings. *Journal of the American Academy of Child and Adolescent Psychiatry, 35*, 42–50.

Cohen, J. A., & Mannarino, A. P. (1996b). Factors that mediate treatment outcome of sexually abused preschool children. *Journal of the American Academy of Child and Adolescent Psychiatry, 35*, 1402–1410.

Cohen, J. A., & Mannarino, A. P. (1997). A treatment study for sexually abused preschool children: Outcome during a one-year follow-up. *Journal of the American Academy of Child and Adolescent Psychiatry, 36*, 1228–1235.

Cohen, J. A., & Mannarino, A. P. (1998). Interventions for sexually abused children: Initial treatment outcome findings. *Child Maltreatment, 3*, 17–26.

Cohen, J. A., & Mannarino, A. P. (2000). Predictors of treatment outcome in sexually abused children. *Child Abuse and Neglect, 24*, 983–994.

Cohen, J. A., Mannarino, A. P., & Deblinger, E. (2006). *Treating trauma and traumatic grief in children and adolescents*. New York: Guilford Press.

Cohen, J. A., Mannarino, A. P., & Knudsen, K. (2005). Treating sexually abused children: 1 year follow-up of a randomized controlled trial. *Child Abuse & Neglect, 29*, 135–145.

Cohen, J. A., Mannarino, A. P., Murray, L. K., & Ingelman, R. (2006). Psychosocial interventions for maltreated and violence-exposed children. *Journal of Social Issues, 62*, 737–766.

Cohen, J. A., Mannarino, A. P., Perel, J. M., & Staron, V. (2007). A pilot randomized controlled trial of combined trauma-focused CBT and setraline for childhood PTSD symptoms. *Journal of the American Academy of Child & Adolescent Psychiatry, 46*, 811–819.

Cook, A., Spinnazola, J., Ford, J., Lanktree, C., Blaustein, M., & Cloitre, M. (2005). Complex trauma in children and adolescents. *Psychiatric Annals, 35*, 390–398.

Corcoran, J. (2002). The transtheoretical stages of change model and motivational interviewing for building maternal supportiveness in cases of sexual abuse. *Journal of Child Sexual Abuse, 11*, 1–17.

Courtois, C. A. (2004). Complex trauma, complex reactions: Assessment and treatment. *Psychotherapy: Theory, Research, Practice, Training, 41*, 412–425.

Danielson, C. K., de Arellano, M. A., Ehrenreich, J. T., Suarez, L. M., Bennett, S. M., Cheron, D. M., et al. (2006). Identification of high-risk behaviors among victimized adolescents and implications for empirically supported psychosocial treatment. *Journal of Psychiatric Practice, 12*, 364–383.

Davis, R. G., Ressler, K. J., Schwartz, A. C. Stephens, K. J., & Bradley, R. G. (2008). Treatment barriers for low-income, urban African Americans with undiagnosed posttraumatic stress disorder. *Journal of Traumatic Stress, 21*, 218–222.

Deblinger, E., Lippmann, J., & Steer, R. (1996). Sexually abused children suffering posttraumatic stress symptoms: Initial treatment outcome findings. *Child Maltreatment, 1*, 310–321.

Deblinger, E., Mannarino, A. P., Cohen, J. A., & Steer, R. A. (2006). A follow-up study of a multisite, randomized, controlled trial for children with sexual abuse-related PTSD symptoms. *Journal of the Academy of Child and Adolescent Psychiatry, 45*, 1474–1484.

Derogatis, L., & Melisaratos, N. (1983). The brief symptom inventory: An introductory report. *Psychological Medicine, 13*, 595–605.

Ehlers, A., & Clark, D. M. (2000). A cognitive model of posttraumatic stress disorder. *Behavior Research and Therapy, 38*, 319–345.

Foa, E. B., & Kozak, M. J. (1986). Emotional processing of fear: Exposure to corrective information. *Psychological Bulletin, 99*, 20–35.

Foa, E. B., Steketee, G., & Rothbaum, B. O. (1989). Behavioral/cognitive conceptualizations of post-traumatic stress disorder. *Behavior Therapy, 20*, 155–176.

Henggeler, S. W., Rowland, M.D., Randall, J., Ward, D. M., Pickrel, S. G., Cunningham, P. B., et al. (1999). Home-based multisystemic therapy as an alternative to the hospitalization of youths in psychiatric crisis: Clinical outcomes. *Journal of the American Academy of Child and Adolescent Psychiatry, 38*, 1331–1339.

Henggeler, S. W., Schoenwald, S. K., Borduin, C. M., Rowland, M. D., & Cunningham, P. B. (1998). *Multisystemic treatment of antisocial behavior in children and adolescents*. New York: Guilford Press.

Herman, J. L. (1992). *Trauma and recovery*. New York: Basic Books.

Janoff-Bulman, R. (1992). *Shattered assumptions*. New York: Free Press.

Kaufman, J., Birmaher, B., Brent, D. A., Rao, U., Flynn, C., Moreci, P., Williamson, D., et al. (1997). Schedule for Affective Disorders and Schizophrenia for School-Age Children-Present and Lifetime Version (K-SADS-PL): Initial reliability and validity data. *Journal of the American Academy of Child and Adolecent Psychiatry, 36*, 980–988.

Kerig, P. K., Fedorowicz, A. E., Brown, C. A., & Warren, M. (2000). Assessment and intervention for PTSD in children exposed to violence. *Journal of Aggression, Maltreatment and Trauma*, 3, 161–184.

Kolko, D. J., & Swenson, C. C. (2002). *Assessing and treating physically abused children and their families: A cognitive behavioral approach*. Thousand Oaks, CA: Sage.

Lang, P. J. (1977). Imagery in therapy: An information processing analysis of fear. *Behavior Therapy, 8*, 862–886.

Lang, P. J. (1979). A bio-informational theory of emotional imagery. *Psychophysiology, 16*, 495–512.

Lerner, M. J., & Miller, D. T. (1978). Just world research and the attribution process: Looking back and ahead. *Psychological Bulletin, 85*, 1030–1051.

Linares, L. O., Montalto, D., Li, M., & Oza, V. S. (2006). A promising parenting intervention in foster care. *Journal of Consulting and Clinical Psychology, 74*, 32–41.

Lipovsky, J. A., Swenson, C. C., Ralston, M. E., & Saunders, B. E. (1998). The abuse clarification process in the treatment of intrafamilial child abuse. *Child Abuse & Neglect, 22*, 729–741.

Margolin, G., & Vickerman, K. A. (2007). Posttraumatic stress in children and adolescents exposed to family violence: I. Overview and issues. *Professional Psychology: Research and Practice, 38*, 613–619.

McKay, M. M., McCadam, K., & Gonzales, J. J. (1996). Addressing the barriers to mental health services for inner city children and their caretakers. *Community Mental Health Journal, 32*, 353–361.

McMahon, R. R., & Forehand, R. L. (2003). *Helping the noncompliant child*. New York: Guilford Press.

Miller, W.R., & Rollnick, S. (2002). *Motivational interviewing, second edition: Preparing people for change*. New York: Guilford Press.

National Child Traumatic Stress Network. (2008). *Treatments that work*. Retrieved February 28, 2008, from http://www.nctsnet.org/nccts/nav.do?pid=ctr_top_trmnt

Nikulina, V. Hergenrother, J. M., Brown, E. J., Doyle, M. E., Filton, B. J., & Carson, G. S. (2008). From efficacy to effectiveness: The trajectory of the treatment literature for children with PTSD. *Neurotherapeutics*.

Office of the Surgeon General. (2001). *Mental health: Culture, race, ethnicity supplement*. Retrieved April 5, 2005, from http://www.mentalhealth.org/cre/default.asp

Pearlman, L. A. (1995). Self-care for trauma therapists: Ameliorating vicarious traumatization. In B. H. Stamm (Ed.), *Secondary traumatic stress: Self-care issues for clinicians, researchers, and educators* (pp. 51–64). Baltimore, MD Sidran Press.

Proctor, E. K., Knudsen, K. J., Fedoravicius, N., Hovmand, P., Rosen, A., & Perron, B. (2007). Implementation of evidence-based practice in community behavioral health: Agency director perspectives. *Administration and Policy in Mental Health and Mental Health Services Research, 34*, 479–488.

Resick, P. A., & Schnicke, M. K. (1992). Cognitive processing therapy for sexual assault victims. *Journal of Consulting and Clinical Psychology, 60*, 748–756.

Resick, P. A., & Schnicke, M. K. (1993). *Cognitive processing therapy for rape victims: A treatment manual*. Newbury Park, CA: Sage.

Reynolds, C. R., & Kamphaus, R. W. (2004). *The Behavior Assessment Scale for Children, 2nd ed.* Circle Pines, MN: American Guidance Service.

Richters, J. E., & Martinez, P. E. (1990). *Things I have seen and heard: An interview for young children about exposure to violence.* Rockville, MD: National Institute of Mental Health.

Scheeringa, M. S., Zeanah, C. H., Myers, L., & Putnam, F. W. (2003). New findings on alternative criteria for PTSD in preschool children. *Journal of the American Academy of Child and Adolescent Psychiatry, 42,* 561–570.

Skowron, E., & Reinemann, D. H. S. (2005). Effectiveness of psychological interventions for child maltreatment. *Psychotherapy: Theory, Research, Practice, Training, 42,* 52–71.

Smith, P., Yule, W., Perrin, S., Tranah, T., Dalgleish, T., & Clark, D. M. (2007). Cognitive-behavioral therapy for PTSD in children and adolescents: A preliminary randomized controlled trial. *Journal of the Academy of Child and Adolescent Psychiatry, 46,* 1051–1061.

Spitzer, C., Chevalier, C., Gillner, M., Freyberger, H. J., & Barnow, S. (2006). Complex posttraumatic stress disorder and child maltreatment in forensic inpatients. *Journal of Forensic Psychiatry and Psychology, 17,* 204–216.

Straus, M. A., & Stewart, J. H. (1999). Corporal punishment by American parents: National data on prevalence, chronicity, severity, and duration, in relation to child and family characteristics. *Clinical Child and Family Psychology Review, 2,* 55–70.

Webster-Stratton, C. (2001). *Incredible years: The parents, teachers, and children training series.* Seattle, WA: Author.

9

Better But Not Well: Strategies for Difficult-to-Treat Youth Depression

JOHN F. CURRY AND SARA J. BECKER

Depression among children and adolescents is a common and impairing condition with major social and economic costs. Epidemiological studies suggest that depressive disorders affect approximately 2% of elementary-school-aged children and 4 to 8% of adolescents (Anderson, Williams, McGee, & Silva, 1987; Kessler & Walters, 1998). Estimates of the lifetime prevalence rates of depression among adolescents range from 15 to 20% (Kessler & Walters, 1998; Oldehinkel, Wittchen, & Schuster, 1999). Depression causes significant impairment in social, academic, and family functioning. Among youth, depression is also associated with elevated risk of substance use and other psychiatric disorders (Angold & Costello, 1993; Deykin, Levy, & Wells, 1987).

Depression is diagnosed using the same criteria across the lifespan, with only slight exceptions. A major depressive episode (MDE) occurs when a significantly low mood and/or loss of interest or pleasure (anhedonia) endures for most of the time for at least 2 weeks, marking a notable decline in a person's functioning and accompanied by characteristic associated symptoms (American Psychiatric Association, 2000). The depressed person may describe her or his mood as sad, down, or blue, although in youth, depressed mood may be exhibited as persistent irritability. Anhedonia can range from the loss of interest in a few of the person's typical activities to complete inability to enjoy life. Biological symptoms of an MDE may include significant decreases or increases in sleep, a marked increase or decrease in appetite or weight, fatigue or low energy, and a marked increase or decrease in motor activity and speed (psychomotor agitation or retardation). Psychomotor retardation would be manifested by very slow walking, slow tempo of speech, or marked delays when responding in a conversation. By contrast, psychomotor agitation would be indicated by pacing restlessly, by having great difficulty sitting still because of emotional discomfort (not because of a consistent trait of hyperactivity), or by picking at clothing or skin. Observations of parents and of others can supplement the self-report of adolescents or children, especially for such behaviors as crying (depressed mood), irritability, decreased participation in activities (anhedonia), inability to sit still, or markedly slow walking or speech (agitation or retardation).

Cognitive symptoms of an MDE can include unrealistic guilt or a sense of worthlessness; difficulty concentrating or making decisions; or recurrent thoughts of death, dying, or suicide. Feelings of worthlessness are qualitatively more extreme and more painful than low self-esteem. Unrealistic guilt can occasionally reach psychotic proportions and manifest in delusions (Maj, Pirozzi, Magliano, Fiorillo, & Bartoli, 2007). Recurrent thoughts of death or suicide represent a particularly alarming symptom, especially when associated with a suicide plan or attempt, and require immediate clinical management. Formal diagnosis of a major depressive episode requires the presence of five symptoms, one of which must be depressed mood or anhedonia (American Psychiatric Association, 2000). Episodes of MDE range from mild to severe, but all are characterized by functional impairment or significant distress. Most young people who experience an MDE will be diagnosed with major depressive disorder (MDD), although approximately 15 to 20% will experience a manic or hypomanic episode during his or her lifetime, and will then be diagnosed with a bipolar disorder (Frank, 2007; also see chapter 12).

In contrast to MDD, dysthymic disorder (DD) is a less severe, but typically more prolonged depressive mood disorder. The duration of a dysthymic episode must be at least 1 year in children or adolescents, during which depressed (or irritable) mood is present more than half of the time. Two additional symptoms are required for the diagnosis, from among the following six: appetite disturbance, sleep disturbance, low energy or fatigue, low self-esteem, difficulty concentrating or making decisions, feelings of hopelessness (American Psychiatric Association, 2000).

Relative to depression among adults, depression in youth tends to be more chronic and persistent. Naturalistic studies of clinically referred samples suggest that the median duration of a major depressive episode in youth is 7 to 9 months (Birmaher et al., 1996), whereas the median duration of a dysthymic episode is 3.9 years (Kovacs, Obrosky, Gatsonis, & Richards, 1997). The chronicity of depression is compounded by high rates of recurrence, defined as the emergence of depressive symptoms after a sustained period of recovery. Rates of recurrence among adolescents have been estimated as approximately 40% at 2 years and 70% at 5 years (Birmaher et al., 1996; Kovacs, 1996). Of particular concern in this cohort is the association with depression and increased risk of suicidal ideation, suicidal behavior, and completed suicide (Brent, 1995; Shaffer et al., 1996). Moreover, suicidal ideation during one episode of depression tends to predict the occurrence of suicidal ideation in subsequent episodes (Williams, Crane, Barnhofer, Van der Does, & Segal, 2006), highlighting the urgency of effective treatment for these at-risk youth.

EFFECTIVE TREATMENTS FOR YOUTH DEPRESSION

Effective interventions for depression in children and adolescents include both specific psychotherapies (Curry, 2001) and antidepressant medications (ADM) (Hughes et al., 2007). Among the psychotherapies, cognitive-behavior therapy (CBT) has been tested and supported the most extensively. Interpersonal psychotherapy has also demonstrated effectiveness for adolescent depression (Mufson, Weissman, Moreau, & Garfinkel, 1999; Mufson et al., 2004). Among ADMs, fluoxetine has the most empirical support and is the only drug approved by the FDA for the indication of depression in children and adolescents, ages 8 through 17 (Hughes et al., 2007). Recently, combined CBT and fluoxetine has proven effective for moderately to severely depressed adolescents (The Treatment for Adolescents with Depression Study [TADS] Team, 2004, 2007), and is acutely more effective than either monotherapy. In this chapter we will review the evidence in support of CBT interventions for youth depression, attending also to the evidence in support of combined CBT and ADM.

CBT for Youth Depression

Both children and adolescents with depression have demonstrated benefit from CBT. Published studies of CBT for depressed prepubertal children have shown that it can reduce depressive symptoms in children treated in school-based groups (Stark, Reynolds, & Kaslow, 1987; Stark, Rouse, & Livingston, 1991; Weisz, Thurber, Sweeney, Proffitt, & Legagnoux, 1997). Two small sample studies by Stark and colleagues (1987, 1991) demonstrated superiority of twice-weekly group CBT, first compared to a wait-list control and then to counseling as usual. In another school-based study, Weisz and his colleagues (1997) demonstrated that group CBT was more effective than a no-treatment condition for children in reducing both self-reported and clinician-rated symptoms, and that effects endured at 9-month follow-up. An ongoing study by Stark is an evaluation of group CBT for 9- to 13-year old girls with MDD or DD (Stark et al., 2006). Elements of the treatment include coping skills, problem solving, and cognitive restructuring, as well as parent psychoeducation, parent training, family communication, and conflict-resolution skills. At the same time, Weisz's model of group CBT, which includes increasing pleasant activities, problem solving, and cognitive restructuring, is being compared to treatment-as-usual in community clinics (J. R. Weisz, personal communication).

Several different models of CBT have been used to treat MDD among adolescents, aged 13 to 18 years. In contrast to studies of childhood depression, the adolescent studies have required that participants meet formal diagnostic criteria for MDD and have compared CBT to a broader range of control or comparison conditions. The first type of CBT developed for adolescents diagnosed as depressed was based on the multifactorial model of depression formulated by Lewinsohn and colleagues (Lewinshohn, Clarke, Hops, & Andrews, 1990). According to this model, both thoughts and behaviors, particularly a lack of behaviors that lead to positive reinforcement, are major maintaining variables in depression. Consequently, both areas are targeted in treatment. Clarke, Lewinsohn, and Hops (1990) adapted the original model for adolescents and designed the Adolescent Coping with Depression Course (CWD-A), which is delivered in a psychoeducational group format that emphasizes skills training. A typical course of CWD-A consists of highly structured groups of 2 hours' duration that convene biweekly for 7 to 8 weeks. Multiple skills are covered in the course, including mood monitoring, relaxation, cognitive restructuring, problem solving, communication, and social skills. Two studies have shown that this treatment is more effective than a waiting-list control condition (Clarke, Rohde, Lewinsohn, Hops, & Seeley, 1999; Lewinsohn et al., 1990).

The second model developed for adolescents was based on the cognitive therapy (CT) for MDD established by Beck and colleagues (Beck, Rush, Shaw, & Emery, 1979). Brent and his colleagues (1997) adapted this model of CT for adolescents. Consistent with the traditional cognitive model, cognitive processes are viewed as the major maintaining variables associated with depression. Treatment emphasizes the importance of identifying and modifying maladaptive thoughts, assumptions, and distortions to promote behavioral and emotional change. Although behavioral techniques such as activity scheduling are a component of the model, they are viewed as a means to an end (discovering and modifying cognitions) rather than as primary change agents.

Similarities between CT for adolescents and for adults include the duration and frequency of sessions, the nature of the therapeutic alliance, and the strategies used to modify maladaptive thought patterns. A typical course of CT for teens consists of 12 to 16 weekly sessions delivered in individual psychotherapy format. The relationship between the therapist and patient in these sessions is one of collaborative guided discovery. As in adult CT, techniques used to challenge and modify negative cognitions include: identification of mood shifts experienced in session and the specific thoughts that preceded the shifts, Socratic questioning, and evaluating the evidence in support of a specific thought or belief. The primary adaptations to the adult CT protocol were the addition of parent and adolescent psychoeducation, social skills training, affect regulation, and relatively increased emphasis on problem-solving techniques. In an intent-to-treat analysis of all participants randomized to treatment, Brent and colleagues (1997) demonstrated that CT was more effective than nondirective supportive psychotherapy and systems behavioral family therapy in the acute (first 12 to 16 weeks) treatment of adolescent MDD.

A third model of CBT that synthesized the two preceding approaches was developed by Curry and colleagues for the Treatment for Adolescents with Depression Study (Curry et al., 2003). The TADS was a 13-site trial with 439 subjects, funded by the National Institutes of Mental Health, comparing CBT, fluoxetine, clinical management with a pill placebo, and the combination of CBT and fluoxetine for the acute (12 weeks) and longer term (36 weeks) treatment of adolescent MDD (The TADS Team, 2003). TADS CBT was designed for use by clinicians with training in CBT, but not necessarily specialized postdoctoral expertise, who were seeing the full range of depressed adolescents. Adolescents in TADS had at least moderately severe MDD, with dysphoric mood of at least 6 weeks' duration and impairment in two or more settings. Comorbidity was common, with approximately 50% of adolescents having at least one co-occurring condition (The TADS Team, 2005). Consequently, TADS CBT was designed to be more flexible than the highly structured group CBT in the Lewinsohn and Clarke (1990) studies, which used more stringent exclusion criteria. At the same time, to assure that the same essential treatment was delivered across 13 sites, it was designed to be more structured than the CT used in Brent et al.'s (1997) study. In essence, skills training modules were embedded within individual therapy sessions. Core (required) skills were mood monitoring, goal-setting, increasing pleasant activities, problem solving, and cognitive restructuring. Use of other modules was driven by an individualized case formulation. Each treatment session included agenda setting, homework review, skills training, work on agenda items, and formulating new homework assignments. Pace and content of skills training could be adjusted by clinicians to meet the needs of individual adolescents and families. Parent and family sessions included psychoeducation, family communication, family problem solving, and contingency management.

Results of the TADS study, which analyzed all participants randomized to treatment, indicated that the combination of CBT and fluoxetine was the most effective treatment acutely (week 12), and was the only treatment significantly better than clinical management with pill placebo on the study's primary outcome measure, namely, slope of change in scores on the Children's Depression Rating Scale-Revised (CDRS-R; Poznanski & Mokros, 1996) administered by independent evaluators (The TADS Team, 2004). Fluoxetine alone was superior to placebo on some of the secondary measures, whereas CBT alone was not significantly different from the placebo condition. During longer term treatment, adolescents receiving all three active interventions experienced significant benefit (placebo was discontinued at week 12) such that there were no significant differences among the conditions by week 36 (The TADS Team, 2007). CBT alone was equivalent to fluoxetine alone on response rate by week 18. Treatment responders were those rated as "much improved" or "very much improved" since baseline by the independent evaluator who completed the CDRS-R. By week 18, 69% of fluoxetine-treated adolescents and 65% of CBT-treated adolescents were rated as responders. Combined treatment remained the most effective, with an 85% response rate by week 18.

Most recently, TADS CBT was modified and expanded for adolescents with ADM-resistant depression as part of the Treatment Of selective serotonin reuptake inhibitor-Resistant Depression in Adolescents (TORDIA) trial, a six-site study funded by the National Institute of Mental Health (Brent et al., 2008). Participants in this trial were 334 adolescents aged 12 to 18 years with a diagnosis of MDD, who had not responded to an adequate course of an initial selective serotonin reuptake inhibitor (SSRI). Adolescents were randomized to one of four conditions: (a) switch to a second, different SSRI; (b) switch to venlafaxine, a selective serotonin and noradrenergic reuptake inhibitor; (c) switch to a second SSRI plus CBT; or (d) switch to venlafaxine plus CBT. The trial focused on nonresponse to SSRI medications rather than nonresponse to psychotherapy, because SSRI medications have been the predominant method of treatment for adolescent depression in community settings over the past decade (Ma, Lee, & Stafford, 2005). Similar to other recent adolescent studies, analyses used an intent-to-treat approach that included all adolescents randomized to treatment.

The CBT model used in the TORDIA protocol augmented TADS CBT by including a greater emphasis on emotion regulation (Bonner, 2002). In addition, TORDIA used a more flexible method of CBT delivery by eliminating the requirement to use certain core skills, which was an element of TADS. Components of TORDIA CBT included cognitive restructuring, behavioral activation, emotion regulation, social skills, and problem solving for participants, as well as parent–child sessions intended to increase parental support, family communication, and family problem solving. Similar to TADS CBT, the TORDIA CBT protocol used a modular approach in which the therapist selected different modules on the basis of the specific needs of the adolescent and family, feedback from onsite and external supervisors, and input from team members during a biweekly review of case conceptualizations. Results of TORDIA were particularly encouraging in light of the difficulties inherent in intervention with treatment-resistant MDD. The combination of CBT and switching to a different medication (either venlafaxine or a different SSRI) resulted in a higher rate of clinical response than did a medication switch alone (Brent et al., 2008).

Summary of CBT Depression-Outcome Studies

For depressed children under the age of 13 years, group CBT has been shown to be superior to no treatment, wait list, and counseling as usual (Stark et al., 1987, 1991; Weisz et al., 1997). In studies of this age group, sample sizes have been small, depression has been symptomatic rather than diagnosed (although at least some of the children would almost certainly have met diagnostic criteria), and treatment has been delivered in school-based groups for less than 3 months. Ongoing work is expanding evaluation of CBT to diagnosed samples and to comparisons against community treatment as usual. For depressed adolescents, CBT has proven superior to wait list and to certain alternative psychotherapies (Brent et al., 1997; Clarke et al., 1999; Lewinsohn et al., 1990), but not to clinical management with pill placebo (The TADS Team, 2004). Combining CBT and ADM has proven quite effective for moderately to severely depressed adolescents, including those who have previously not responded to ADM (Brent et al., 2008; The TADS Team, 2004). However, most treatments last only 12 to 18 weeks in duration.

A recent meta-analysis by Weisz, McCarty, and Valeri (2006) found that the mean effect size across trials of psychotherapy for youth depression is .34, with effect size defined as the posttherapy difference between the control and treatment groups, divided by the control group standard deviation. Cognitive methods of intervention were not significantly different from noncognitive methods of intervention. CBT therefore appears to have a significant but modest effect on youth depression when all available studies are reviewed. However, earlier studies were generally associated with larger effect sizes than more recent investigations. Differences between earlier and more recently reported effect sizes are likely the result of several key factors: (a) more recent studies have involved more seriously depressed young people; (b) more recent studies have tended to use active rather than passive comparison conditions (e.g., clinical management with pill placebo versus no treatment or wait list); (c) more recent studies have used intent-to-treat statistical analyses, which include data from all subjects who entered the trial in the analysis, rather than analyses that include only those who complied with treatment sessions (completer analyses) or with research appointments (available case analysis); (d) more recent studies have treated adolescents across multiple sites, rather than restricting participants to the site that developed the CBT protocol.

ASSESSMENT OF TREATMENT RESPONSE IN CLINICAL RESEARCH

Outcome Variables Used in Clinical Trials

Application of treatment outcome research by clinicians and other researchers requires familiarity with the outcome variables most frequently used in clinical depression trials. One construct is "symptom reduction," often measured as the slope of change during and after acute treatment. One treatment is superior to another (or to a control) if it demonstrates a steeper slope during and/or after acute treatment than does its counterpart. In TADS, for example, the slopes of scores on the Children's Depression Rating Scale–Revised (Poznanski & Mokros, 1996), which was the primary outcome measure, declined more steeply for CBT + fluoxetine than for any other treatment (The TADS Team, 2004). Symptom reduction is a continuous measure, suitable for assessing mean differences among treatments and for more sophisticated statistical analyses, such as random regression analyses and growth curve analyses. However, measures of symptom reduction do not necessarily reveal the absolute level of depression or whether the adolescent has returned to the normal range.

A second outcome variable is "loss of diagnosis," defined as no longer meeting diagnostic criteria for the target condition. Loss of diagnosis is probably the most frequently used measure of treatment outcome in psychotherapy trials (Compton et al., 2004). However, it is virtually always a less stringent measure of outcome than "remission" and usually less stringent than "response," both of which are described in the text that follows. The clinical utility of "loss of diagnosis" is also highly dependent on the specific diagnosis under consideration. For example, substance abuse is a diagnosis that requires only one (or more) symptom(s) (American Psychiatric Association, 2000). Therefore, loss of diagnosis implies the end of any active symptoms associated with the disorder. By contrast, MDD requires five (or more) symptoms. Therefore, loss of diagnosis could technically be attained when an adolescent still has several active symptoms. In TADS, for example, there were very high rates of loss of diagnosis after acute treatment: 85% for CBT + fluoxetine; 79% for fluoxetine alone; 61% for CBT alone, and 60% for placebo (The TADS Team, 2004). However, as will be discussed, rates of "response" and "remission" were considerably more conservative.

A third construct that has historically been used more often in psychopharmacology studies than in psychotherapy studies is "treatment response." Treatment response is typically measured in one of three ways: (a) by a global evaluator judgment that the youngster's condition is "much improved" or "very much improved," (b) by a specific percentage of decline in symptoms (often 50%) on a rating scale, or (c) by a combination of these two components (M. Fava & Davidson, 1996; Rush, Thase, & Dube, 2003). It is also possible to differentiate among youth based on the level of treatment response, as indicated by the specific percentage of reduction in depressive symptoms. Treatment response indicates the extent to which the youth has benefited from the treatment and gotten significantly "better," but not whether the youth has become "well." Because treatment response indicates the extent to which treatment is having a positive effect, it has significant implications for decisions about whether to continue the same intervention, augment the dose, add an additional treatment, or switch to a different intervention.

Finally, a fourth treatment outcome variable is "remission." Remission refers to the absence of any significant symptoms of the target disorder, and is the most stringent criterion for outcome. It is typically defined by absence of any symptoms of depression on a diagnostic interview or by a very low score on a rating scale. Although remission is assessed at a single time point, true "recovery" from a depressive episode requires the absence of any significant symptoms for a reasonably long period of time, typically 8 weeks. A new episode that occurs following remission is termed "relapse," whereas one that follows full recovery is termed "recurrence" (Frank et al., 1991).

Although important advances have been made in recent years in understanding and treating depression during childhood and adolescence, a significant number of youths are not treatment "responders" and even fewer are "remitted." Follow-up studies of psychotherapy and pharmacotherapy trials have found that over 40% of adolescents with depression do not show a sufficient clinical response to monotherapy, whereas one third or fewer show full symptomatic remission following acute treatment (Brent et al., 1997; Emslie et al., 1997; Kennard et al., 2006; The TADS Team, 2004). For example, in TADS, at the end of 12 weeks of acute treatment (The TADS Team, 2004), "response" rates on the primary outcome measure were 71% with CBT + fluoxetine, 61% with fluoxetine alone, 43% with CBT alone, and 35% with clinical management and pill placebo, all considerably lower than the "loss of diagnosis" rates listed previously. Moreover, corresponding "remission" rates were only 37%, 23%, 16%, and 17%, respectively. Clearly, then, 12 weeks of acute treatment for moderate to severe MDD in adolescents is not sufficient to reach a point where symptoms are essentially absent for the vast majority of these teens.

Studies indicate that, of those who do experience acute treatment "response," approximately 25 to 50% will experience a depressive relapse or recurrence over a period of 6 months to 2 years of follow-up care. Similar findings have been documented in the adult treatment literature (Belsher & Costello, 1998; Elkin et al., 1989), highlighting the challenges associated with treating depression across the life span.

Although "response" is currently the most common indicator of treatment outcome in pharmacotherapy trials or in trials comparing psychotherapy to ADM, there is growing consensus that "remission" should be the primary outcome used to evaluate interventions delivered to depressed youth or adults (Depression Guideline Panel, 1993; Keller, 2004; Kennard et al., 2006). Treatment guidelines for MDD have cited sustained remission as the strongly preferred goal of treatment (American Academy of Child and Adolescent Psychiatry, 1998), because of the recognition that response without remission is often associated with mild but chronic residual symptoms, which in turn are associated with continued distress and worse daily functioning. In addition, residual symptoms are associated with poorer long-term outcomes and increased risk of relapse and recurrence (G. A. Fava, 1999; G. A. Fava, Fabbri, & Sonino, 2002; Thase & Ninan, 2002).

The substantial proportion of youth with nonresponsive, treatment-resistant, or refractory depression highlights the need for continued pursuit and delivery of effective interventions for childhood and adolescent depression. In the following sections of this chapter, we discuss factors contributing to nonresponse or treatment resistance among youth and review guidelines for assessing treatment response in clinical practice. We conclude with a case example illustrating how cognitive-behavioral treatment can be effectively tailored to youth with a history of inadequate treatment response.

Factors Contributing to Nonresponse or Treatment Resistance

The majority of literature on non-responsive or treatment-resistant depression in youth and adult populations has focused on failure to attain remission following treatment with ADM (Birmaher et al., 1996). However, the definition of non-responsive or treatment-resistant depression can be applied to any patient who has failed to attain and sustain remission with adequate treatment, which may include medication, psychotherapy, or combined treatment approaches. For instance, in TADS (The TADS Team, 2003), adolescents who were rated by independent evaluators as "much improved" or "very much improved" were considered "full responders," whereas those who were "somewhat or minimally improved" were considered "partial responders." Full responders were continued on the same dose of fluoxetine or began a tapered dose of CBT, to continue their process toward remission. Partial responders were given a higher dose of fluoxetine or continued weekly CBT or both. Only adolescents who showed no improvement or worsening symptoms were considered "non-responders" or acutely treatment resistant. In this context, "nonresponders" were referred for alternative treatment(s) because they had not benefited appreciably from 12 weeks of intervention with study treatments.

Adequacy of treatment is a central issue when evaluating the response to intervention. Classification as nonresponsive or treatment resistant should be reserved for patients whose depression does not resolve after intervention of adequate intensity or dosage and over a sufficient time period, based on currently accepted treatment standards and guidelines. Indeed, Nierenberg and Amsterdam (1990) described nonresponse to inadequate treatment as "pseudoresistance" to the extent that the patient appears to be resistant to treatment, but may actually respond if given treatment of appropriate duration and dosage. In studies of ADM, adequate treatment is often defined as one ADM trial of satisfactory dose and duration, although a more conservative definition requires two appropriate trials of different classes of ADM (M. Fava, 2003). An appropriate trial typically entails standard dosage of ADM administered continuously for at least 6 weeks (G. A. Fava & Fabbri, 2008). Definitions of adequate dosage and intensity are somewhat more elusive in psychotherapy trials, although randomized trials containing behavioral interventions for depression often consist of approximately 12 to 18 sessions delivered over the same number of weeks.

A number of other factors have been found to contribute to inadequate treatment response among youth and adults with depression, including misdiagnosis, comorbid conditions, and severity of depression. Accurate diagnosis of unipolar depression requires careful differentiation from bipolar disorder, as effective treatment approaches differ for these conditions (Nierenberg & Amsterdam, 1990). Differentiation of depression and bipolar disorder is often facilitated by an evaluation of the patient's history to determine whether there is a family history of mania, a history of spontaneous or ADM-induced episodes of elevated mood, and a relatively acute onset or cessation of symptoms (Bowden, 2001). Medical illness must also be ruled out, because a number of conditions (e.g., anemia, mononucleosis, thyroid problems, inflammatory bowel disease, and vascular disorders) may cause symptoms that overlap with depression (Brent & Birhmaher, 2002).

Inadequate management of co-occurring conditions has also been documented as a corollary of non-responsive or treatment-resistant depression. Among adolescents, the conditions that most frequently co-occur with depression include substance use, anxiety disorders, and disruptive behavior disorders (Lewinsohn, Hops, Robert, Seeley, & Andrews, 1993; The TADS Team, 2005). Naturalistic and clinical studies indicate that comorbid conditions are associated with increased severity of depression and poorer outcomes following treatment. In addition, treatment studies suggest that co-occurring conditions may predict differential response to treatment. For instance, in Brent's randomized controlled trial of CBT and two alternate psychotherapy interventions for adolescent depression (Brent et al., 1997, 1998), the presence of a co-occurring anxiety disorder predicted better response to CBT than to the other forms of psychotherapy.

A final factor that has been related to increased treatment resistance is depression severity. In an analysis of Brent's randomized control trial (Brent et al., 1998), severity variables that were found to predict continued depression following psychotherapy included higher levels of cognitive distortion and hopelessness. Severity of self-reported depression at baseline was also found to predict lack of recovery, chronicity, and recurrence. In the two randomized trials by Lewinsohn, Clarke, and colleagues (Clarke et al., 1999; Lewinsohn et al., 1990), higher levels of irritational (depressive) thinking at baseline were found to predict poorer treatment outcomes across treatment conditions. Another randomized controlled trial by Rohde and colleagues (Rohde, Clarke, Mace, Jorgensen, & Seley, 2004; Rohde, Seeley, Kaufman, Clarke, & Stice, 2006) identified severity variables that predicted time to recovery over a 1-year period following treatment. Measures of depression severity that were associated with slower recovery time included higher levels of negative thoughts, hopelessness, functional impairment, and suicidal ideation. Other predictors of slower time to recovery included earlier onset of MDD, attention-deficit/hyperactivity disorder (ADHD) low family cohesion, low coping skills, and parental report of problem behaviors. In the analysis of the trial by Rohde and colleagues (2006), there was also evidence that depression severity predicted differential response to treatment: among adolescents with recurrent major depression, the receipt of CBT was associated with significantly faster time to recovery than the receipt of a life skills control condition.

In the TADS, relatively poorer response to acute treatment was predicted by several of the aforementioned factors. Predictors of poor response included the presence of melancholic features; the duration of the presenting episode of MDD; and several measures of severity, including more severe hopelessness, suicidal ideation, and poorer global functioning (Curry et al., 2006). Those with more than one other diagnosis, in addition to MDD, had poorer response, as did adolescents with lower initial expectations for improvement with treatment. In addition, there was evidence that child characteristics were associated with differential response to treatment. CBT was as effective as combined treatment for youths from higher income families with greater parental education, whereas adding CBT to fluoxetine improved outcome for youths with high levels of cognitive distortions, but not for those with low cognitive distortions or for severely depressed adolescents (Curry et al., 2006).

ASSESSMENT AND TREATMENT OF DEPRESSION IN CLINICAL PRACTICE

Assessment of Treatment History

In clinical practice, the first step in treating childhood or adolescent depression is conducting a careful diagnosis of current depressive symptoms. Even though the child or adolescent may have a history of prior diagnosis and intervention, it is important to treat a patient who has remitted or relapsed as a new patient (G. A. Fava & Fabbri, 2008). The evaluation should begin with an emphasis on the youth's symptoms in recent weeks, with careful differentiation from other medical and psychiatric conditions that are commonly associated with symptoms of depressed or irritable mood.

Once a current diagnosis of MDD or DD is confirmed by a careful diagnostic interview, a thorough treatment history should be gathered to assess prior response to treatment. Youth and their parents should be asked to provide information about any previous ADM trials, including the duration, initial dosage, and any changes in the dosing schedule. As noted by M. Fava (2003), it is also important to ask patients whose depression has not responded to ADM whether they actually took the ADM as prescribed and in a consistent manner. This information can be used to gauge the adequacy of prior treatment and differentiate true resistance from "pseudoresistance" (Nierenberg & Amsterdam, 1990).

In the same vein, the adequacy of previous psychotherapy trials should be assessed. As well as assessing the duration and approximate number of sessions, clinicians should query youth and parents about the specific elements of psychotherapy they received. Direct questions about whether the intervention included agenda setting, skills training, homework assignments, and identification of negative thoughts can help to establish whether the youth has previously received CBT or an alternate psychotherapy such as nondirective supportive psychotherapy. Regardless of the specific type of intervention, it is important to interview the youth and his/her parents about any benefits and adverse effects associated with prior treatment.

An important issue facing clinicians evaluating prior response to treatment is the inherent inaccuracy of retrospective assessments. Youth and their parents may underestimate the level of improvement experienced with prior intervention, particularly if the youth is currently symptomatic (M. Fava, 2003). Review of the youth's medical records can be used to supplement youth and parent reports, although variability in how clinicians track and record treatment response can make it difficult to gauge the specific effects of treatment.

Establishing the youth's diagnosis and prior response to treatment sets the foundation for the creation of a treatment plan. Given the results of existing clinical trials, clinicians treating adolescents and children with MDD, particularly those with a history of nonresponse, should share reasonable expectations with youths and parents about an expected time to response and remission. Families should be informed that longer duration of treatment will be needed for youth with more chronic and severe depression, more severe levels of hopelessness or suicidal thinking, more comorbid diagnoses, and more global functional impairment (Curry et al., 2006). Moreover, if the adolescent is moderately to severely depressed, combining ADM with CBT should be recommended, with this recommendation being particularly advisable for severely depressed youths (Brent et al., 2008; The TADS Team, 2004). Finally, helping youths and parents to develop reasonable expectations includes establishing the expectation that treatment will be helpful. Youth and parents should be assured that, even if the first treatment provided is not sufficiently effective, alternatives exist and can be used after an adequate trial of initial treatment.

Psychoeducation

Youth and parents should also be educated about depression and about the treatment model, using a collaborative process of repeated dialogue. Information about depression should include a description of the youth's current symptoms, the nature of MDD as a disorder, and an explanatory model of factors that led to or are maintaining MDD for this particular child or adolescent. A CBT or combined CBT and ADM model of treatment should be explained to youth and parents, including how the treatments are delivered and how they are hypothesized to work. For CBT, it is important to set the expectation of active, collaborative involvement and to clarify the typical structure of sessions. Printed handouts are helpful to many youths and parents, but they do not substitute for careful and attentive dialogue. Therapist sensitivity to questions and to signs of puzzlement or doubt is also essential for establishing rapport. It is particularly important to help parents understand that MDD is a disorder that is not under the voluntary control of the young person or something she or he can "snap out of." On the other hand, over time there are skills that all parties can learn, so as to reduce depression and prevent relapse.

Monitoring Treatment Response

Once treatment has been initiated and education has been provided, the clinician should encourage the collaborative and continuous monitoring of treatment response. There are a number of reliable and valid instruments that can be used to assess systematically the youth's depressive symptoms. One well-established clinician-rating scale is the Children's Depression Rating Scale-Revised (Poznanski & Mokros, 1996). Additionally, self- and parent report scales such as the Beck Depression Inventory (Beck, Steer, & Brown, 1996) or the Reynolds Child/Adolescent Depression Rating Scales (Reynolds, 1986, 1989) can provide a valuable source of information. Factors that may influence treatment outcome should also be routinely assessed, such as the youth's current level of stress, level of social support, and severity of co-occurring medical or psychiatric conditions (M. Fava, 2003). It is particularly important to evaluate the adolescent's home environment for indication of abuse, neglect, or discord because these family factors are associated with worse treatment outcomes and might contribute to treatment resistance (Brent et al., 1998; Birmaher et al., 2000; Emslie et al., 1998).

CASE PRESENTATION

Presenting Problem

Anthony was a 14-year-old Caucasian male ninth-grader who was referred for treatment after a suicide gesture, in which he had threatened to take a handful of Tylenol pills. He reported that the attempt had been precipitated by his girlfriend breaking up with him; and cited poor academic performance as an additional stressor. The gesture occurred in the early evening, while his parents and sister were at home with him. He was reportedly distressed about poor grades and the loss of his relationship with his girlfriend, and made a threatening comment to his father about taking pills. His parents became very concerned and took him to the local emergency room for an evaluation. He denied imminent suicidal intent, but was admitted for inpatient care because of continued suicidal ideation with inability to agree to a safety plan. Following 4 days of inpatient care, during which he began treatment with 20 mg per day of fluoxetine, his suicidal ideation improved, and he was referred for outpatient treatment.

Initial Assessment

On a semi-structured diagnostic interview administered directly to Anthony and a collateral interview administered to his mother, he met criteria for MDD and for attention-deficit/hyperactivity disorder, inattentive type. Both disorders were of long duration, with the onset of ADHD in first grade and the first episode of MDD in third grade. He reported prior periods of improvement in depression but was unable to recall sufficient detail about his symptoms to determine whether he had ever had significant periods of time that were completely symptom-free. During fourth grade, Anthony was diagnosed with a learning disability (LD) in mathematics by a school psychologist. Depressive symptoms at the beginning of the current treatment included depressed and irritable mood, pervasive anhedonia, initial insomnia, fatigue, poor concentration (beyond that attributable to ADHD), decreased appetite, feelings of worthlessness, and morbid and suicidal ideation. The current episode had apparently begun about 5 months prior to his suicide gesture and had worsened as pressure mounted in school as a result of his poor grades and failure to complete work.

To augment the diagnostic interview, Anthony was administered two well-validated clinician-rating scales and interviewed about his prior treatment. On the Children's Depression Rating Scale–Revised (Poznanski & Mokros, 1996), he obtained a score of 64, which falls at the lower end of the severely depressed range. On the Children's Global Assessment Scale (CGAS), Anthony obtained a rating of 46, indicating moderate functional impairment, with difficulties in school and family. Anthony had previously received both ADM and supportive counseling, often at separate times and, even when simultaneous, not in a coordinated fashion. He reported multiple experiences of frustration with treatment. Whether these represented treatment nonresponse, inadequate treatment regimens, or noncompliance could not be conclusively determined based on Anthony and his mother's retrospective reports. Nevertheless, it was clear from the duration of his depression and his experience of ineffective previous treatments that it was best to proceed on the assumption that he had not previously responded fully and had not attained sustained remission.

Risk Factors for Poor Response

Anthony had MDD of long duration, two comorbid conditions (ADHD and LD), elevated suicidal ideation with a recent suicide attempt, and moderately impaired global functioning, all of which are risk factors for less than full response to acute treatment for depression (Curry et al., 2006). On the other hand, he exhibited several factors associated with positive response. He did not demonstrate hopelessness and had surprisingly positive expectations for improvement with the recommended treatment. In addition, his parents were supportive and willing to be involved in treatment.

Psychoeducation

Given the severity of his depression, the presence of a suicide gesture, and several other negative predictors of treatment response, Anthony and his parents were informed that treatment would probably involve 5 to 6 months of regular CBT, beginning with weekly and then possibly tapering to biweekly sessions at some point. Similarly, the recommendation was given to combine CBT and fluoxetine to maximize the chances for a response to treatment, while attending carefully to safety issues (The TADS Team, 2007). It was further recommended that Anthony receive both treatments at the same medical center, so that his psychologist and psychiatrist could meet regularly, at least briefly, to discuss his case. The possibility of adding booster sessions after the 6-month period was introduced at the outset of treatment.

Because Anthony's parents were familiar with the symptoms of depression from his earlier efforts to obtain treatment, little psychoeducation was required in this domain. Psychoeducation about CBT involved an explanation of the expected phases of treatment and of the typical structure of sessions (e.g., agenda setting, skills training, homework). Parent sessions were scheduled for the second and fourth week of treatment, to give parents time to express their concerns, to explain to them how the early phase of treatment was progressing, and to formulate plans to select modules for skills training.

Case Formulation

Anthony's family had a history of MDD on his father's side, suggesting possible biological vulnerability. In addition, several environmental factors appeared to contribute to his depression. His history of ADHD and LD led to a great deal of frustration in school, and he tended to compare himself unfavorably to his sister, who was a strong student. The immediate precipitant to his suicide attempt was a breakup with a girl friend, which led to automatic thoughts that he would never find another satisfying relationship and that he had somehow failed in relationships as well as in school. This triggered what was hypothesized to be his underlying core belief of worthlessness. Another risk factor for Anthony was a history of using avoidance as a coping mechanism. For example, when faced with an academic challenge, he would not seek help or work harder, but rather would avoid assignments, which in turn led to his eventually becoming overwhelmed by an accumulation of work. He had frequent experiences in school of "giving up" on courses, and was experiencing a similar urge to "give up" on relationships with girls. In terms of protective factors, he felt supported by his family and had several good friends. He had experienced loss of interest and pleasure in activities, but had a history of several areas of extracurricular interests.

Early Phase of CBT

For an adolescent with previous experiences of treatment nonresponse, setting realistic goals is critically important. Anthony was able to articulate a clear set of goals. Although his primary goal was to avoid future episodes of depression, his secondary goal was to tolerate such episodes, should they occur, and to maintain control over his life if faced with an episode. Negative automatic thoughts evident during early sessions included "When things are difficult, I give up," and "I am not smart enough to do well in school." These suggested an underlying core belief of worthlessness or helplessness, representing an overgeneralized and extreme response to frustration, especially in the academic domain.

Because of his suicide threat, it was critically important to develop a safety plan at the outset of outpatient treatment. In Anthony's case, this involved generating a short list of people he could contact if he started to experience thoughts of hopelessness or urges to harm himself. In addition to his therapist, the list included his parents and a counselor at school. As treatment progressed, the plan was expanded to include specific skills he could use on his own to counter negative thoughts.

Middle Phase of CBT

In collaboration with Anthony and his parents, the therapist chose three key skills to include in the middle phase of his treatment. To counter anhedonia and his tendency to avoid and withdraw, the first proposed skill was increasing his involvement in pleasant activities. To counter his tendency to "give up" and his hopeless/helpless automatic thoughts, the second proposed skill was problem solving. To build on his ability to identify and articulate negative automatic thoughts, the final proposed skill was cognitive restructuring. As a supplement to individual CBT, Anthony's parents were given psychoeducation about these three core skills, and also joined him in several sessions in the middle phase of treatment to improve family communication, particularly focused on enhancing Anthony's ability to ask for help when needed.

The first skill addressed was increasing his involvement in pleasant activities. Anthony was able to generate an initial list of 10 potential activities and then focus on 3 as targets for the next several weeks. Two of these were social activities with friends (phone calls and visits to friends' homes), whereas one was a skill he could do alone (listening to music). Despite the ease with which he generated potential pleasant activities, he reported participating in these activities less than once per week over the month prior to treatment. As he began to engage in them more frequently, his mood improved and he was able to appreciate the connection between his activities and mood. He eventually expanded his target activities to include a few small-group and self-improvement activities (e.g., regular exercise).

The second skill area addressed was problem solving. This skill was more challenging to implement because it directly confronted Anthony's long-standing tendency to use avoidant coping. For instance, in the early stages of treatment his psychologist noted that he never brought in items to put on the agenda. Despite efforts to directly target this area during the middle phase of treatment and discover associated cognitions, it remained difficult for Anthony to come up with agenda items. Anthony also struggled to apply problem-solving skills to his academic life. Although he did not have difficulty applying problem-solving skills to hypothetical situations in session, he became overwhelmed when attempting to apply them to real academic problems. Consequently, his psychologist worked with him on breaking down subject material into manageable segments and studying for tests over a sustained period of time. Eventually, problem solving became a skill that Anthony could use effectively to prepare for a test or to ask teachers for help with material he did not understand.

The final skill of cognitive restructuring focused on identifying and challenging two key thoughts. First, Anthony had developed a long-standing belief that school performance was totally attributable to ability and not at all related to effort. Discovering and articulating this belief represented a breakthrough in the middle phase of treatment, and he was able to modify it during the middle and final phases of CBT. Second, his core belief of worthlessness, which had been stimulated by the breakup with his girlfriend, was challenged by helping him to articulate evidence that he was a worthwhile person, who was loved by others. He was able to recognize the support of his parents and sister, as well as his close friendships, as evidence for his own worth. Furthermore, he was able to identify several life goals for himself, such as having a job, having his own family, and making a difference in the world, all of which contributed to his sense of being a worthwhile person.

Ending Phase of Treatment

During the middle phase of treatment, the CBT skills that proved most helpful to Anthony were increasing positive activities, cognitive restructuring, and, to a lesser extent, problem solving. Although his mood fluctuated somewhat during acute treatment, by week 12 he was considered to be partially responsive to treatment. His CDRS-R had reduced to 46, and his CGAS had improved to 54. Weekly sessions were therefore continued for another 6 weeks and then tapered around week 18. Content of these sessions consisted of practice with restructuring hopeless/helpless thinking, and applying coping skills in the event of either poor grades or problems with romantic relationships. Anthony did receive poor grades for several courses during the middle and end phases of treatment, but was able to respond more flexibly, realizing that these indicated not that he was incapable of the work, but rather that he had been unsure of how to prepare for tests. Over time, his academic performance improved as he began to seek help from teachers and work with a tutor in mathematics.

Around week 18, Anthony began to feel better and was generally more responsive to treatment (i.e., engaged in sessions and demonstrated greater change) and asked to end his treatment sessions prematurely. Several additional conjoint family sessions were held to support his efforts to pass his courses and to enable him to let his parents know of the skills he had learned in individual sessions. These sessions helped to highlight the benefits he had experienced in treatment and reduced some of his avoidant behavior during meetings. By the end of 24 weeks of treatment, Anthony was free of any significant symptoms of depression. On the CDRS-R, his score had been reduced to 28, a score often considered a marker for remission (Kennard et al., 2006), and his CGAS was elevated to 62. Continued monthly CBT booster sessions were recommended to sustain this level of response, because his mood had fluctuated considerably across the middle phase of treatment and because he still had minimal levels of irritability and low self-esteem. However, Anthony declined this recommendation, expressing confidence in his ability to apply the skills he had learned in therapy. Continued fluoxetine was also recommended and Anthony was willing to follow this recommendation. He and his parents were encouraged to contact their psychologist if further support was desired in the future.

CONCLUSIONS

Much of the existing research on CBT for youth depression focuses on acute treatment and uses "loss of diagnosis" or "response" as outcome variables. Even with these outcomes, many young people do not respond adequately to CBT delivered weekly over 12 to 16 weeks, the typical duration of acute treatment. When "remission" is used as the outcome variable, as recommended by recent guidelines, rates of adequate response are even lower. Thus, it appears that a great deal of child or adolescent depression would be considered "difficult to treat" using only the existing acute treatment protocols. There remains a need for innovative treatment strategies, for combining CBT with medication, for integrating well-validated outcome measures into clinical practice, and for making greater use of tailored case formulation and psychoeducation in working with difficult-to-treat depressed youth. Conveying to parents and young people treatment expectations that are realistic, formulating flexible multilevel goals, continuing treatment over a longer duration, and intending to treat to remission with appropriate tapering and dose adjustment over time are recommended to optimize treatment response among depressed youth.

REFERENCES

American Academy of Child and Adolescent Psychiatry. (1998). Practice parameters for the assessment and treatment of children and adolescents with depressive disorders. *Journal of the American Academy of Child and Adolescent Psychiatry, 37* (Suppl. 10), 63S–83S.

American Psychiatric Association. (2000). Practice guidelines for the treatment of patients with major depressive disorder. *American Journal of Psychiatry, 157*(Suppl. 4), 1–45.

Anderson, J. C., Williams, S., McGee, R., & Silva, P. A. (1987). DSM-III disorders in preadolescent children. Prevalence in a large sample from the general population. *Archives of General Psychiatry, 44*, 69–76.

Angold, A., & Costello, E. (1993). Depressive comorbidity in children and adolescents: empirical, theoretical, and methodological issues. *American Journal of Psychiatry, 150*, 1779–1791.

Beck, A., Steer, R., & Brown, G. (1996). *Manual for the Beck Depression Inventory—II*. San Antonio, TX: Psychological Corporation.

Beck, A. T., Rush, A. J., Shaw, B. F., & Emery, G. (1979). *Cognitive therapy of depression*. New York: Guilford Press.

Belsher, G., & Costello, C. (1988). Relapse after recovery from unipolar depression: A critical review. *Psychological Bulletin, 104*, 84–96.

Birmaher, B., Brent, D., Kolko, D., Baugher, M., Bridge, J., Holder, D., et al. (2000). Clinical outcome after short-term psychotherapy for adolescents with major depressive disorder. *Archives of General Psychiatry, 57*, 29–36.

Birmaher, B., Ryan, N. D., Williamson, D., Brent, D., Kaufman, J., Dahl, R., et al. (1996). Childhood and adolescent depression: A review of the past 10 years: Part I. *Journal of the American Academy of Child and Adolescent Psychiatry, 35*, 1427–1439.

Bonner, C. W. (2002). *Emotion regulation, interpersonal effectiveness, and distress tolerance skills for adolescents: A treatment manual*. Pittsburgh, PA: Star Center—University of Pittsburgh Medical Center.

Bowden, C. L. (2001). Strategies to reduce misdiagnosis of bipolar depression. *Psychiatry Service, 52*, 51–55.

Brent, D., Emslie, G., Clarke, G., Wagner, K., Asarnow, J., Keller, M., et al. (2008). Switching to another SSRI or to venlafaxine with or without cognitive behavioral therapy for adolescents with SSRI-resistant depression: The TORDIA randomized controlled trial. *Journal of the American Medical Association, 299*, 901–913.

Brent, D., Kolko, D., Birmaher, B., Baugher, M., Bridge, J., Roth, C., et al. (1998). Predictors of treatment efficacy in a clinical trial of three psychosocial treatments for adolescent depression. *Journal of the American Academy of Child and Adolescent Psychiatry, 37*, 906–914.

Brent, D. A. (1995). Risk factors for adolescent suicide and suicidal behavior: Mental and substance abuse disorders, family environmental factors, and life stress. *Suicide and Life-Threatening Behavior, 25*(Suppl.), 52–63.

Brent, D. A., & Birmaher, B. (2002). Adolescent depression. *New England Journal of Medicine, 347*, 667–671.

Brent, D. A., Holder, D., Kolko, D., Birmaher, B., Baugher, M., Roth, C., et al. (1997). A clinical psychotherapy trial for adolescent depression comparing cognitive, family, and supportive treatments. *Archives of General Psychiatry, 54*, 877–885.

Clarke, G. N., Lewinsohn, P.M., & Hops, H. (1990). *Adolescent coping with depression course*. Eugene, OR: Castalia Press.

Clarke, G. N., Rohde, P., Lewinsohn, P. M., Hops, H., & Seeley, J. R. (1999). Cognitive-behavioral treatment of adolescent depression: Efficacy of acute group treatment and booster sessions. *Journal of the American Academy of Child and Adolescent Psychiatry, 38*, 272–279.

Compton, S. N., March, J. S., Brent, D., Albano, A. M., Weersing, R., & Curry, J. F. (2004). Cognitive-behavioral psychotherapy for anxiety and depressive disorders in children and adolescents: An evidence-based medicine review. *Journal of the American Academy of Child and Adolescent Psychiatry, 43*, 930–959.

Curry, J., Rohde, P., Simons, A., Silva, S., Vitiello, B., Kratochvil, C., et al. (2006). Predictors and moderators of acute outcome in the Treatment for Adolescents with Depression Study (TADS). *Journal of the American Academy of Child and Adolescent Psychiatry, 45*, 1427–1439.

Curry, J., Wells, K., Brent, D., Clarke, G., Rohde, P., Albano, A., et al. (2003). Treatment of Adolescents with Depression Study (TADS) cognitive behavior therapy manual: Introduction, rationale, and adolescent sessions. *Unpublished manual.*

Curry, J. F. (2001). Specific psychotherapies for childhood and adolescent depression. *Biological Psychiatry, 49*, 1091–1100.

Depression Guideline Panel. (1993). *Clinical practice guideline. Depression in primary care. Volume 2. Treatment of major depression* (AHCPR publication no. 93-0551). Rockville, MD: U.S. Department of Health and Human Services, Public Health Service, Agency for Health Care Policy and Research.

Deykin, E. Y., Levy, J. C., & Wells, V. (1987). Adolescent depression, alcohol and drug abuse. *American Journal of Public Health, 77*, 178–182.

Elkin, I., Shea, M., Watkins, J., Imber, S., Sotsky, S., Collin, J., et al. (1989). National Institute of Mental Health Treatment of Depression Collaborative Research Program: General effectiveness of treatments. *Archives of General Psychiatry, 46*, 971–982.

Emslie, G., Rush, A., Weinberg, W., Kowatch, R., Carmody, T., & Mayes, T. (1998). Fluoxetine in child and adolescent depression: Acute and maintenance treatment. *Depression and Anxiety, 7*, 32–39.

Emslie, G., Rush, A., Weinberg, W., Kowatch, R., Hughes, C., Carmody, T., et al. (1997). A double-blind, randomized, placebo-controlled trial of fluoxetine in children and adolescents with depression. *Archives of General Psychiatry, 54*, 1031–1037.

Fava, G. A. (1999). Subclinical symptoms in mood disorders: Pathophysiological and therapeutic implications. *Psychological Medicine, 29*, 47–61.

Fava, G. A., & Fabbri, S. (2008). Drug-resistant and partially remitted depression. In M. A. Whisman (Ed.), *Adapting cognitive therapy for depression* (pp. 110–131). New York: Guilford Press.

Fava, G. A., Fabbri, S., & Sonino, N. (2002). Residual symptoms in depression: An emerging therapeutic target. *Progress in Neuro-Psychopharmacology & Biological Psychiatry, 26*, 1019–1027.

Fava, M. (2003). Diagnosis and definition of treatment-resistant depression. *Biological Psychiatry, 53*, 649–659.

Fava, M., & Davidson, K. G. (1996). Definition and epidemiology of treatment-resistant depression. *Psychiatric Clinics of North America, 19*, 179–200.

Frank, E. (2007). Bipolar disorder. In F. Bloom, M. F. Beal, & D. J. Kupfer (Eds.), *The Dana guide to brain health: A practical family reference from medical experts*. New York: Dana Press.

Frank, E., Prien, R. F., Jarrett, R. B., Keller, M. B., Kupfer, D. J., Lavori, P. W., et al. (1991). Conceptualization and rationale for consensus definitions of terms in major depressive disorder: Remission, recovery, relapse, and recurrence. *Archives of General Psychiatry, 48*, 851–855.

Hughes, C. W., Emslie, G. J., Crismon, M. L., Posner, K., Birmaher, B., Ryan, N., et al. (2007). Texas Children's Medication Algorithm Project: Update from Texas Consensus Conference Panel on medication treatment of childhood major depressive disorder. *Journal of the American Academy of Child and Adolescent Psychiatry, 46*, 1442–1454.

Keller, M. (2004). Remission versus response: The new gold standard of antidepressant care. *Journal of Clinical Psychiatry, 65*, 53–59.

Kennard, B., Silva, S., Vitiello, B., Curry, J., Kratochvil, C., Simons, A., et al. (2006). Remission and residual symptoms after short-term treatment in the treatment of adolescents with depression study (TADS). *Journal of the American Academy of Child and Adolescent Psychiatry, 45*, 1404–1411.

Kessler, R. C., & Walters, E. E. (1998). Epidemiology of DSM-III-R major depression and minor depression among adolescents and young adults in the national comorbidity survey. *Depression & Anxiety, 7*, 3–14.

Kovacs, M. (1996). Presentation and course of major depressive disorder during childhood and later years of the life span. *Journal of the American Academy of Child and Adolescent Psychiatry, 35*, 705–715.

Kovacs, M., Obrosky, D., Gatsonis, C., & Richards, C. (1997). First-episode major depressive and dysthymic disorder in childhood: Clinical and sociodemographic factors in recovery. *Journal of the American Academy of Child and Adolescent Psychiatry, 36*, 777–784.

Lewinsohn, P. M., Clarke, G. N., Hops, H., & Andrews, J. (1990). Cognitive-behavioral treatment for depressed adolescents. *Behavior Therapy, 21*, 385–401.

Lewinsohn, P. M., Hops, H., Roberts, R. E., Seeley, J. R., & Andrews, J. A. (1993). Adolescent psychopathology: I. Prevalence and incidence of depression and other DSM-III-R disorders in high school students. *Journal of Abnormal Psychology, 102*, 133–144.

Ma, J., Lee, K., & Stafford, R. (2005). Depression treatment during outpatient visits by U.S. children and adolescents. *Journal of Adolescent Health, 37*, 434–442.

Maj, M., Pirozzi, R., Magliano, L., Fiorillo, A., & Bartoli, L. (2007). Phenomenology and prognostic significance of delusions in major depressive disorder: A 10-year prospective follow-up study. *Journal of Clinical Psychiatry, 68*, 1411–1417.

Mufson, L., Dorta, K. P., Wickramaratne, P., Nomura, Y., Olfson, M., & Weissman, M. M. (2004). A randomized effectiveness trial of interpersonal psychotherapy for depressed adolescents. *Archives of General Psychiatry, 61*, 577–584.

Mufson, L., Weissman, M. M., Moreau, D., & Garfinkel, R. (1999). Efficacy of interpersonal psychotherapy for depressed adolescents. *Archives of General Psychiatry, 56*, 573–579.

Nierenberg, A., & Amsterdam, J. D. (1990). Treatment-resistant depression: Definition and treatment approaches. *Journal of Clinical Psychiatry, 51*(Suppl.), 39–47.

Oldehinkel, A. J., Wittchen, H. U., & Schuster, P. (1999). Prevalence, 20-month incidence and outcome of unipolar depressive disorders in a community sample of adolescents. *Psychological Medicine, 29*, 655–668.

Poznanski, E. O., & Mokros, H. B. (1996). *Children's Depression Rating Scale—Revised manual*. Los Angeles, CA: Western Psychological Services.

Reynolds, W. M. (1986). *Reynolds Adolescent Depression Scale*. Odessa, FL: Psychological Assessment Resources.

Reynolds, W. M. (1989). *Reynolds Child Depression Scale*. Odessa, FL: Psychological Assessment Resources.

Rohde, P., Clarke, G. N., Mace, D. E., Jorgensen, J. S., & Seeley, J. R. (2004). An efficacy/effectiveness study of cognitive-behavioral treatment for adolescents with comorbid major depression and conduct disorder. *Journal of the American Academy of Child and Adolescent Psychiatry, 43*, 660–668.

Rohde, P., Seeley, J. R., Kaufman, N. K., Clarke, G. N., & Stice, E. (2006). Predicting time to recovery among depressed adolescents treated in two psychosocial group interventions. *Journal of Consulting and Clinical Psychology, 74*(1), 80–88.

Rush, A., Thase, M. E., & Dube, S. (2003). Research issues in the study of difficult-to-treat depression. *Biological Psychiatry, 53*, 743–753.

Shaffer, D., Gould, M. S., Fisher, P., Trautman, P., Moreau, D., Kleinman, M., et al. (1996). Psychiatric diagnosis in child and adolescent suicide. *Archives of General Psychiatry, 53*, 339–348.

Stark, K. D., Hargrave, J., Sander, J., Custer, G., Schnoebelen, S., Simpson, J., et al. (2006). Treatment of childhood depression: The ACTION Treatment Program. In P. C. Kendall (Ed.), *Child and adolescent therapy, third edition: Cognitive-behavioral procedures* (pp. 169–216). New York: Guilford Press.

Stark, K. D., Reynolds, W. M., & Kaslow, N. J. (1987). A comparison of the relative efficacy of self-control therapy and a behavioral problem-solving therapy for depression in children. *Journal of Abnormal Child Psychology, 15*, 91–113.

Stark, K. D., Rouse, L., & Livingston, R. (1991). Treatment of depression during childhood and adolescence: Cognitive-behavioral procedures for the individual and family. In P. Kendall (Ed.), *Child and adolescent therapy* (pp. 165–206). New York: Guilford Press.

Thase, M., & Ninan, P. (2002). New goals in the treatment of depression: Moving toward recovery. *Psychopharmacology Bulletin, 36*(Suppl. 2), 24–35.

The Treatment for Adolescents with Depression Study (TADS) Team. (2003). Treatment for Adolescents With Depression Study (TADS): Rationale, design, and methods. *Journal of the American Academy of Child and Adolescent Psychiatry, 42*, 531–542.

The Treatment for Adolescents with Depression Study (TADS) Team. (2004). Fluoxetine, cognitive-behavioral therapy, and their combination for adolescents with depression. *Journal of the American Medical Association, 292*, 807–820.

The Treatment for Adolescents with Depression Study (TADS) Team. (2005). The Treatment for Adolescents With Depression Study (TADS): Demographic and clinical characteristics. *Journal of the American Academy of Child and Adolescent Psychiatry, 44*, 28.

The Treatment for Adolescents with Depression Study (TADS) Team. (2007). The Treatment for Adolescents with Depression Study (TADS): Long-term effectiveness and safety outcomes *Archives of General Psychiatry, 64*, 1132–1143.

Weisz, J. R., McCarty, C. A., & Valeri, S. M. (2006). Effects of psychotherapy for depression in children and adolescents: A meta-analysis. *Psychological Bulletin, 132*, 132–149.

Weisz, J. R., Thurber, C. A., Sweeney, L., Proffitt, V. D., & LeGagnoux, G. L. (1997). Brief treatment of mild to moderate child depression using primary and secondary control enhancement training. *Journal of Consulting and Clinical Psychology, 65*, 703–707.

Williams, J., Crane, C., Barnhofer, T., Van der Does, A., & Segal, Z. (2006). Recurrence of suicidal ideation across depressive episodes. *Journal of Affective Disorders, 91*(2–3), 189–194.

10

Cognitive-Behavior Therapy for Eating Disorders in Childhood and Adolescence

SARAH FISCHER, ANGELA CELIO DOYLE, AND DANIEL LE GRANGE

The purpose of this chapter is to review the use of cognitive-behavioral therapy (CBT) for the treatment of child and adolescent eating disorders, with a focus on using cognitive-behavioral techniques in difficult-to-treat cases. Although this task seems fairly straightforward, a number of issues in the current state of research and treatment of child and adolescent eating disorders present several stumbling blocks. First, there are three primary diagnostic categories subsumed under the diagnosis of eating disorder: anorexia nervosa (AN), bulimia nervosa (BN), and eating disorder not otherwise specified (EDNOS). In fact, the primary diagnosis of an adolescent presenting for treatment in an outpatient setting is likely to be EDNOS (Eddy, CelioDoyle, Hoste, Herzog, & le Grange, 2008). Symptoms of AN versus BN may necessitate different approaches to treatment; this is certainly true in adults. Second, if a clinician were to search the available literature for randomized controlled trials (RCTs) for treatment of eating disorders in children and adolescents, he or she would find relatively little guidance. For example, to date, there are only two published RCTs that examine the treatment of BN in adolescents (le Grange, Crosby, Rathouz, & Levanthal, 2007;

Schmidt et al., 2007). Adolescents with EDNOS are often excluded from trials. And only one of the trials with BN participants used a form of CBT as a treatment condition. Thus, there is a dearth of well-controlled research on treatment of adolescents with eating disorders, on CBT in particular. This is both surprising and a matter of concern because the age of onset of BN, AN, and EDNOS is typically in adolescence.

In this chapter we briefly review the etiology, symptoms, and incidence of eating disorders in adolescents. We present information about the *treatment* of AN and BN separately, as empirical literature suggests some differences in the effectiveness of various treatments for the two disorders. For both of these disorders, however, it was necessary to review literature on treatment and outcome predictors in adults as well as adolescents, as there are so few studies that used child and adolescent samples. Thus, we provided information on how the data on adult samples may or may not be extrapolated to child and adolescent samples.

We review the current state of CBT in AN and the current status of evidence-based treatment of AN in children and adolescents. In this section, it is noted that family-based treatment (FBT) is the treatment with the most evidence supporting its effectiveness in AN. A case example is presented of a child with AN who received FBT. However, in this case, the therapist used behavioral techniques in treatment, illustrating how behavior modification and management techniques can be implemented within this treatment. We then review empirical literature on the use of CBT in adults with BN, to guide our review of what is known regarding the use of these techniques in children and adolescents. In contrast to the literature on AN, there is ample evidence to support the use of CBT for adults with BN, and an accumulating base of evidence indicating that it may be effective in adolescents as well. We next review any RCTs and pilot data involving children and adolescents with BN, to highlight what seems to be effective and what we still have yet to learn. We conclude with a case example of an adolescent with BN.

SYMPTOMS

Eating disorders most typically begin during adolescence and have been diagnosed in children as young as 7 years old (Bostic, Muriel, Hack,

Weinstein, & Herzog, 1997). *The Diagnostic and Statistical Manual of Mental Disorders, Fourth Edition, Text Revision* (*DSM-IV-TR*; American Psychiatric Association [APA], 2000) provides three diagnoses for eating disorders: anorexia nervosa, bulimia nervosa, and eating disorder not otherwise specified (EDNOS). Binge-eating disorder is described as a criterion set that requires further study in the *DSM-IV-TR* and is presently best captured diagnostically as EDNOS.

The *DSM-IV-TR* defines AN as a refusal to maintain weight (or lack of weight gain at a time of growth) at 85% of expected weight for height (ideal body weight). This is accompanied by an intense fear of gaining weight or becoming fat, despite a low body weight. Individuals with AN also experience a disturbance in the way they perceive their body shape or weight, assign undue influence of body shape or weight on their self-evaluation, or deny the seriousness of their low body weight. Finally, in postmenarchal females, a diagnosis of AN is made only when menstrual cycles are absent for 3 consecutive months (amenorrhea; note: a woman is considered to be amenorrheic if her periods only occur while using hormones, e.g., through oral contraceptives). Two subtypes further describe AN: restricting type, in which the individual purely restricts her or his caloric intake, and binge-eating/purging type, which is characterized by regular binge eating and purging behaviors (i.e., self-induced vomiting or the misuse of laxatives or diuretics) during the current episode of AN.

Bulimia nervosa is characterized by a pattern of binge eating coupled with inappropriate compensatory methods intended to prevent weight gain and overvaluation of body weight and shape (APA, 2000). Binge eating is defined as consuming an objectively large amount of food (e.g., more than what most people would eat during a discrete period of time under similar circumstances) accompanied by a feeling of loss of control. Compensatory behaviors can include self-induced vomiting, misuse of laxatives, misuse of diuretics, excessive exercise, and fasting. To meet criteria for BN, binge eating and compensatory behaviors occur at least twice per week over a 3-month period. Two subtypes further describe BN: purging type and non-purging type. Purging type of BN is marked by purging behaviors, such as self-induced vomiting, laxative or diuretic misuse; non-purging type is marked by compensatory behaviors such as excessive exercise or fasting. Body weight in individuals with BN tends to be in the normal range. For those who meet BN diagnostic criteria in the presence of AN (i.e., low weight with high frequency of binge eating and purging), a diagnosis of AN is given.

The diagnosis of EDNOS captures several common variations on AN and BN in addition to binge-eating disorder (BED) and more rare presentations (e.g., chewing and spitting out large quantities of food). For instance, EDNOS would be diagnosed when an individual meets all criteria for AN except that she has a regular menstrual cycle. In addition, EDNOS would be diagnosed when all of the criteria for BN are met, but the duration of illness has been less than 3 months or the frequency of binge eating/purging is less than two times per week. Although EDNOS was originally conceived as a category for exceptions to more common presentations, the diagnosis of EDNOS is particularly prevalent within the younger population. In fact, when following the strict criteria provided by the *DSM-IV-TR*, the majority of all adolescents with eating disorders are considered EDNOS. Clinicians are typically guided in their treatment of EDNOS by what is effective for AN or BN, depending on presentation.

AGE OF ONSET AND PREVALENCE IN ADOLESCENTS

Anorexia Nervosa

Onset of anorexia nervosa occurs most commonly during adolescence, with a point prevalence rate of 0.48% in adolescent females (Lucas et al., 1991). Rates of AN are lower in boys, estimated at a 19:2 female to male ratio in adults (Hoek, 1993), but some have identified increased referral rates for males with eating disorders. The peak age of onset is estimated to be between age 14 and 18 years (APA, 2000), but AN has been diagnosed in children as young as 7 years old (Bostic et al., 1997). Although AN occurs in individuals of all racial/ethnic backgrounds, it is more commonly found in Caucasian, Hispanic, and Asian American women, compared with African American women, and is most prevalent in industrialized societies. In terms of prognosis, adolescent-onset AN tends to be associated with better outcome than prepubertal or adult-onset AN; prepubertal AN may be associated with a more severe psychiatric profile (Bryant-Waugh & Lask, 1995). This may be caused by several factors. First, there is some evidence that adolescents with AN present to physicians multiple times in the years prior to the recognition of the disorder, increasing the likelihood of the diagnosis (Lask et al., 2005). Children may not be diagnosed because they may not meet the diagnostic criteria of being at 85% or below the ideal body weight. In children and adolescents, continuous growth is expected. Thus, it is important to note the appearance of slowed growth or halted growth; in determining pathological weight status it is necessary to use several data points plotted on a growth chart over time rather than a single point in time. Additionally, length of illness predicts poor outcome, with individuals with illness of less than 3 years having a better outcome than those with more protracted length (Eisler et al., 2000). These factors may interact. Illness may be protracted in early-onset AN because of failure to recognize slow growth as a symptom, leading to entrenchment of the illness and associated behaviors over several years, which may then make it more difficult to treat.

Bulimia Nervosa

Estimates show that 1 to 5% of adolescent girls in the United States meet criteria for BN (American Academy of Pediatrics, 2003) and one fifth of adolescents with BN are male (Steiner & Lock, 1998), compared with one tenth of adults with BN (Steiger & Seguin, 1999). Bulimia nervosa in premenarchal youth is relatively rare (Kent, Lacey, & McClusky, 1992). BN is more likely to be diagnosed in adolescents between the ages of 13 and 20 years than in those younger than 13 years (Peebles, Wilson, & Lock, 2006). The peak age of onset is estimated to be between 15.7 and 18.1 years old (Fairburn, Cooper, Doll, Norman, & O'Connor, 2000; Herzog, Keller, Sacks, Yeh, & Lavori, 1992). In a recent study of 80 adolescents with BN and subthreshold BN, 62.5% of the sample had a comorbid diagnosis (Fischer & Le Grange, 2007), with the majority of these presenting with a major mood disorder. In addition, 25% of the sample had previously attempted suicide or self-harmed, 65.8% had consumed alcohol, and 30% had used illegal drugs Medical complications occurring in individuals with BN are largely related to binge/purge behaviors and include hypokalemia, esophageal tears, gastric disturbances, dehydration, and severe changes in blood pressure or heart rate when standing or sitting (orthostasis), which may require intermittent hospitalization.

ETIOLOGY AND COGNITIVE-BEHAVIORAL MODELS OF THE DEVELOPMENT OF EATING DISORDERS

Current consensus in the field is that the etiology of AN and BN has multiple components, with both genetic and nonshared environmental influences. The etiology of AN has historically been described in terms of maladaptation of typical adolescent development (Lock, le Grange, Agras, & Dare, 2001). Psychodynamically oriented theorists tended to describe the development of starvation as a response to feeling overwhelmed by the developmental demands of adolescence and puberty (Bruch, 1973, 1995). Precursors to the development of AN include negative attitudes toward the body during puberty, teasing by peers, and maternal food restriction (Attie & Brooks-Gunn, 1989; Fabian & Thompson, 1989; Hill, Weaver, & Blundell, 1990). Recent research indicates that the heritability of AN symptoms is over 50% (Bulik et al., 2006). Parallel to earlier conceptualizations of AN, recent research indicates that genetic influences on disordered eating emerge during pubertal development. Klump and colleagues found that there were very little, if any, genetic influences on disordered eating symptoms in a twin sample aged 11 years, but substantial genetic heritability for symptoms at age 17 years (Klump, McGue & Iacono, 2000). A recent longitudinal study indicates that disordered eating symptoms increased in a twin cohort from ages 11 to 18 years and that the genetic influence on disordered eating also increased during these years. Shared environmental influences, accounting for the most variance in disordered eating in the early years, decreased over time (Klump, Burt, McGue, & Iacono, 2007). Although these studies examined a range of disordered eating symptoms, they highlight the importance of the transition from childhood to older adolescence in the development of eating disorders.

The cognitive behavioral model of the development of binge eating and purging has received much research support, and will be briefly described here. Recent studies indicate, however, that a large portion of the variability in BN symptoms is also caused by genetically heritable influences (Bulik, Sullivan, & Kendler, 2003). The cognitive-behavioral model of the development of bulimia nervosa outlines several steps that lead to dieting and then binge-eating behavior (Fairburn, Marcus, & Wilson, 1993). These pathways are as follows: Weight and shape concerns are thought to result from low self-esteem. Attempts to change weight and shape as a result lead to food restriction, strict food rules, and dieting. Breaking these food rules then results in binge eating, often through the abstinence violation effect or because of the physiological need for caloric intake (Fairburn et al., 1993) (see Figure 10.1). Purging is thought to arise as an attempt to compensate for binge eating. Individuals who attempt to modify their shape and weight through self-initiated dieting in the form of undereating may be most at risk. These individuals are described as "cognitively restrained" eaters, or persons who have rigid rules for eating and dieting (Larsen, van Strien, Eisinga, Herman, & Engels, 2007). These individuals may have differential responses to food cues in the environment than low-restrained eaters (Coelho, Polivy, Herman, & Pliner, 2008). Several prospective, longitudinal studies indicate that weight concerns and self-initiated dieting influence the development of bulimic symptoms (Fairburn, Welch, Doll, Davies, & O'Connor, 1997; Killen et al., 1994, 1996; Patton, Selzer, Coffey, Carlin, & Wolfe, 1999). Additionally, examination of specific effects of CBT for BN using adult samples provide support for the hypothesis that extremely restrictive dieting leads to binge eating. Specifically, reducing dietary restraint and eating three prescribed meals and two snacks per day leads to greater abstinence and reduction in binge–purge symptoms at the end of treatment (Shah, Passi, Bryson, & Agras, 2005; Wilson, Fairburn, Agras, Walsh, & Kraemer, 2002). In sum, although the etiology of both AN and BN is influenced by multiple determinants, there is more evidence accumulated for the cognitive-behavioral model of the development of BN specifically.

ADAPTATION OF CBT FOR ADOLESCENTS WITH EATING DISORDERS: ADOLESCENT DEVELOPMENT AND THE ROLE OF THE FAMILY

A number of issues related to adolescent development have been outlined when considering the adaptation of CBT for this population (Holmbeck et al., 2000) An overall goal of the use of any therapy with adolescents is adapting the treatment to fit the child's stage of development. Adolescence is typically a time of major developmental changes in physiology, cognitive abilities, interpersonal relationships, and the development of an autonomous identity, more so than any other developmental period except growth during infancy (Feldman & Elliot, 1990). Thus, there are several developmental changes occurring

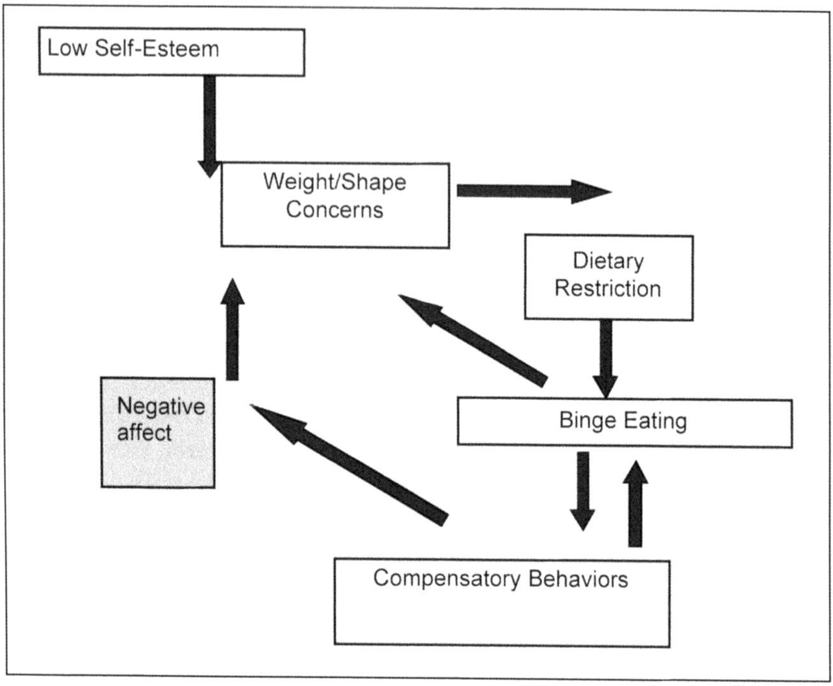

Figure 10.1 The cognitive-behavioral model of the development of bulimia nervosa. Adapted from Fairburn et al. (1993).

during which psychopathology or successful resolution of psychopathology cold lead one on a trajectory to health or maladaptation (Rutter, 1990). Eating disorders have an impact in all of these areas of development. First, by their nature both AN and BN affect physiological development. Extreme weight loss leads to amenhorrea, which, in addition to causing detrimental effects on physical health later, also impedes the successful transition of an adolescent girl through puberty. Starvation also affects brain structure and functioning. Although structural and functional changes during a period of starvation associated with AN are well documented, the evidence concerning the prolonged impact of starvation on neuropsychological functioning is mixed (Tchanturia, Campbell, Morris, & Treasure, 2005). There is also little known about how weight loss or starvation caused by EDs affect the development of more advanced cognitive skills during adolescence. However, evidence suggests that the omission of breakfast may have a deleterious impact on certain cognitive tasks, and that consistent glucose intake is important in brain functioning in children and adolescents (Bellisle, 2004). It may be safe to assume that an adolescent in a state of starvation is not able to engage fully in the cognitive activities of typical psychotherapy, which is one of the many reasons that a focus on weight gain and refeeding during the initial phase of treatment is so important.

Several aspects of social development may be affected secondarily by symptoms of the eating disorder as well. Individuals with both AN and BN often attempt to follow strict dietary rules and feel shame or other negative emotions when eating in front of others. Thus, an adolescent with an eating disorder may have several cognitions and emotions that deter her or him from socializing with friends in situations that involve food. This could include going out before a dance, participating in slumber parties, or eating with friends in the cafeteria. Distorted cognitions that may be present certainly include thoughts about appearance, but also may include thoughts that others are judging the individual for what she or he is eating. Other distorted thoughts may be that eating a certain food will cause an immediate change in appearance. Additionally, the impact of weight and shape on self-esteem may inhibit a child or adolescent from engaging in normative social activities. For example, an adolescent who believes that no one will want to date her because of her weight may cause her to disengage from social activities because she is a "lost cause" or "not worth trying." Shame may often prevent an adolescent from engaging in normative activities. For example, an adolescent who purges may not attend sleepovers because of temptations to eat junk food and embarrassment about the desire to vomit after eating.

The major psychological developmental task of adolescence is forming a separate identity from one's family of origin and the development of autonomy (Erikson, 1968). This stage of psychological development may affect the adolescent's ability to collaborate with the therapist, who is likely to be another adult associated with one's parents (Lock, 2005). Additionally, many aspects of eating disorders are ego syntonic, meaning that the individual feels that some part of the disorder is part of one's identity. Although this is most true of individuals with anorexia, dieting and restriction may also develop into an ego-syntonic behavior in adolescents with BN. Thus, it is important for the therapist to constantly separate the eating disorder from the client's own identity and personality (Lock et al., 2001; le Grange, Lock, & Dymek, 2003) as she moves through this transition. On the other hand, adolescents are also quite dependent on their families. Additionally, as we have described, family involvement can be critical in the successful management of adolescent eating disorders. It is also important for therapists to be aware of the significant stress associated with being a caregiver for someone with an eating disorder.

WHAT IS KNOWN ABOUT CBT FOR ANOREXIA NERVOSA?

In contrast to what is known regarding the efficacy of specific treatments for adults with BN (described in the text that follows), there is very little evidence to support any one particular method of psychotherapy more than another in the treatment of adults with AN (Fairburn, Cooper, & Shafran, 2002). Randomized controlled trials of adults with AN are often compromised by high dropout rates and small sample sizes (Halmi et al., 2005), making the establishment of an evidence-based treatment for adults with AN difficult. Several studies have compared CBT and other specialized therapies in the treatment of adult AN and the findings are generally equivocal (Dare, Eisler, Russell, Treasure, & Dodge, 2001; Serfaty, Turkington, Heap, Ledsam, & Jolley, 1999). In a study of 24 adults with AN, CBT was no more effective than treatment as usual or behavior therapy (Channon, de Silva, Hemsley, & Perkins, 1989). In this study, the primary focus of CBT was described as restructuring dysfunctional thoughts about the value of weight and shape that were hypothesized to influence symptoms. The primary focus of behavior therapy was exposure to feared foods through construction of a hierarchy. One study found that CBT was more effective than a comparison treatment, but the participants in the study were weight recovered (Pike, Walsh, Vitousek, Wilson, & Bauer, 2003). A more recent trial that compared CBT to interpersonal therapy and a control condition found that the control condition was more effective than IPT in the entire sample, and more effective than both CBT and IPT in the treatment completers (McIntosh et al., 2005). The focus of AN inpatient treatment is weight restoration, but CBT is often used as a therapy component in this milieu (Bowers & Ansher, 2008). One recent study followed patients for 1 year after discharge from an inpatient unit that used CBT and found maintained reduction of symptoms (Bowers &

Ansher, 2008). However, this was not a randomized controlled trial. In sum, there is not sufficient evidence to support CBT, let alone any one type of outpatient therapy, as a first line of treatment in adults with anorexia nervosa.

Treatment of Adolescents With AN

In contrast to the empirical data for treatment of adults with AN, the accumulated evidence to date suggests that FBT is the treatment of choice for adolescents with AN. FBT remains one of the only empirically supported treatments for adolescent AN (Eisler et al., 1997, 2000; le Grange, Binford, & Loeb, 2005; le Grange, Eisler, Dare, & Russell, 1992; Lock, le Grange, Forsberg, & Hewell, 2006; Loeb et al., 2007; NCCMH, 2004; Russell, Szmukler, Dare, & Eisler, 1987). The therapeutic rationale of FBT is that an adolescent's family is seen as a significant resource for helping the adolescent normalize his/her eating and return to health. Family-based treatment is problem focused, and behavioral change directed by unified parents is the main strategy. Family-based treatment is agnostic as to the etiology of the disorder and families are assured that they are not the cause of the eating disorder. Family-based treatment also aims to externalize and separate the AN pathology from the affected adolescent to promote parental action and encourage adolescent cooperation. There are three phases that span 6 months of treatment (15 to 20 sessions). The focus of FBT for AN in the first phase is to develop and support parental management of restrictive dieting, and any other pathologic weight-control behaviors in the adolescent to disrupt these behaviors. Once disordered eating has been mostly resolved, the second phase of treatment aims to return control over eating to the adolescent and discussions of independence and autonomy take place. Finally, the third phase of FBT addresses the ways that the AN has affected healthy adolescent development and the family determines how to get the adolescent "back on track" with age-appropriate normal development (e.g., autonomy as seen through dating, moving out of the home) (Lock et al., 2001). A thorough understanding of behavioral principles will likely be very beneficial to a therapist treating adolescents with AN. Therapists often must explain principles of reinforcement and punishment to families of adolescents with AN when coaching them on refeeding.

Factors That Predict Poor Treatment Response

Some specific factors that predict poor treatment response in adolescents with anorexia nervosa have been identified. These factors highlight the need for a thorough understanding of behavioral principles when working with families to refeed the adolescent. In a sample of adolescents and families participating in a trial of FBT, several factors predicted remission of symptoms at follow-up (Lock, Couturier, Bryson, & Agras, 2006). Weight gain by session 2 and session 9 increased odds of remission at follow-up. In FBT, successful weight gain could be influenced by the family's ability to encourage the adolescent to eat successfully and consistently despite tantrums, other negative emotions, and behavioral difficulties. Additionally, reduction in behavior problems by the adolescent increased odds of remission at follow-up, again indicating that a family and therapist need to use skills to consistently refrain from reinforcing tantrums or other acting-out behaviors associated with refeeding. The presence of comorbid psychiatric conditions indicates less likelihood of remission (Lock et al., 2006). Finally, high levels of expressed emotion, particularly hostility, on the part of the parents indicate poor response to treatment (Eisler, et al. 2000). This may be because these parents have difficulty separating the child or adolescent's identity from the illness, or because these families are typically more likely to drop out of treatment (Eisler et al., 2000).

The following case example illustrates the use of behavioral therapy principles within the paradigm of FBT. In this case example, we focus on the behavioral problems that emerged when parents attempted to refeed their child with AN, and the solutions that were generated to these problems. As stated earlier, failure to manage behavioral difficulties is often a poor prognostic indicator in FBT.

CASE PRESENTATION—TREATMENT OF ANOREXIA WITH CBT

History and Presenting Problems

Katie was a 9-year-old Caucasian female from an intact family. She had a 2-month history of symptoms of AN when she was brought to treatment by her parents. At the onset of Katie's eating concern, she had been cutting out snacks, looking at herself in the mirror after meals, and checking her body during meals. She had lost 5.5 lbs over the previous 4 months, during a time of expected consistent growth. According to Katie's parents, Katie feared "the thoughts that tell me I'm fat" and that these thoughts also compelled her to eat less. During this same period of time, Katie's parents noticed her acting "very nervous" and getting into more fights with her one younger sibling.

After a month of these symptoms, the family had sought a referral from their pediatrician for psychological treatment. Katie received individual psychotherapy from a master's-level therapist for "anxiety and body dysmorphic disorder" for 4 weekly sessions. The family was discouraged by a lack of progress and, after a month, Katie "had a meltdown" during which she became violent and extremely agitated. She was admitted for a weekend to an inpatient psychiatric hospital, where she was given regular meals, but was discharged at a slightly lower weight than her intake weight. (This inpatient facility did not specialize in eating-disorder treatment, but rather disruptive behavior problems). At that point, Katie presented to our clinic for an evaluation and outpatient treatment.

Katie was administered the Eating Disorder Examination (EDE) (Fairburn & Cooper, 1993) and the Schedule of Affective Disorders and Schizophrenia for School Age Children (K-SADS) (Ambrosini, 2000). Both are structured clinical interviews. The EDE is considered the "gold standard" of interview-based assessment in the eating disorders field. Additionally, Katie's parents were given a semistructured clinical interview assessing growth and treatment history. Finally, she was given a physical examination by a pediatrician who specializes in eating-disorder treatment. At the time of the evaluation, Katie's eating habits were quite restrictive, although she had been eating breakfast and dinner with her family. She claimed that she was eating lunch at school, but this was unconfirmed. Katie had cut out all snacks and "junk food." She resisted eating cheese on pizza and would eat smaller portions at family meals. Katie reported being preoccupied with her weight and shape, a fear of weight gain, feeling fat, and a desire for a flat stomach. She also identified her weight and shape as the most important components of her self-esteem. Katie's weight, height, and age placed her at 88.5% of her ideal body weight. Given that Katie had not only stalled in growth, but had lost weight, she was deemed low weight. Katie denied all forms of purging and binge eating. Katie was prepubertal, so the criterion of amenorrhea was not applicable. Through this evaluation with Katie and her parents, Katie was diagnosed with anorexia nervosa, restricting subtype.

Phase 1 of Treatment

FBT for AN was initiated with Katie and her family. At the first appointment, Katie was seen for 5 minutes alone, during which time she was weighed. Her parents and younger sibling then joined the session to discuss the efforts, to date, to treat the eating disorder. The family was quite anxious and perplexed regarding the onset and symptoms of the eating disorder, saying that Katie was not the cheerful, funny girl who they once knew. After reviewing how each person in the family had been negatively affected by the eating disorder—not Katie, herself—the parents were given the task of reversing Katie's starvation by taking charge of refeeding Katie. Her younger sibling was asked to be supportive of Katie and to help her feel better when she was feeling down or upset. He was very willing to do this, saying that he could make jokes to cheer her up. A second appointment, a family meal, was scheduled for the next evening. The purpose of the family meal was to observe and shape Katie's parents' behavior during meals so that they could begin to refeed their daughter at home.

At the second meeting, Katie was weighed alone at the beginning of the session, after which she became very upset and cried. She had a great deal of difficulty refocusing on the session. Her family brought pizza, breadsticks, and milk and Katie's parents served her and her sibling appropriate amounts. Food preparation and mealtimes were discussed. Her parents were given strategies on how to help Katie eat enough at meals and were instructed to feed her three meals plus three snacks, amounting to approximately 3,000 to 5,000 kcal/day. At the end of the meal, Katie had eaten only her pizza and milk. Her parents were instructed to ask her to eat the breadsticks, which Katie resisted vehemently. She cried, pounded the table, and yelled at her parents. Her parents were reassured by the therapist that this was normal to see, but that Katie's health depended on their firm and loving resolve to get her to eat more food. With persistent, repetitive, and firm requests her parents were successful in having Katie eat another breadstick before the session ended.

Behavioral Problems and Solutions

Over the following seven sessions, several behavioral challenges arose that impeded the family's ability to successfully refeed Katie. One was Katie's tendency to have tantrums around mealtimes. If parents stopped encouraging Katie to eat while she was at the height of a tantrum, this would reinforce the behavior and make the next meal even more difficult. However, this was a difficult task for parents as they had to encourage Katie to eat through a tantrum several times per day. The parents were reinforced when they stopped encouraging Katie to eat because her behavior became much easier to manage. Second, when Katie presented for treatment, her parents were encouraged to be present at meals, but her lunch was being unobserved at school. This made her food refusal intermittently reinforced in that she did not "have to" eat at one meal, but was encouraged to eat at all the other meals. A solution to this problem was that Katie's mother temporarily ate with her at school. As treatment progressed, the family moved to having a lunch supervisor check-in with Katie. Third, during this first phase of treatment, it became apparent that the parents were not always "on the same page." Katie found her mother was more lax with certain expectations about food, and so would engage in behaviors around her mother to "get out of" eating as much she could. Once this was identified, it was pointed out to her parents. This pattern again intermittently reinforced Katie's food refusal, as she was "rewarded" for resisting eating at some times but not at others. Her parents were consistently guided by the therapist to "be on the same page," meaning that they discussed Katie's food preparation and meal targets together while Katie was not present, and that they did not relax meal targets when one parent was not present.

At session 10, Katie's family was still in Phase I of treatment and certain eating-disordered behaviors were still quite problematic for the parents. Specifically, Katie demanded to check her appearance in the mirror following every snack and meal, which would make her distressed. However, when her parents did not allow her to do so, she had a tantrum. Additionally, Katie also argued with family members, engaged in name-calling, and sometimes hit other family members. At this point, the therapist worked with the parents to create a chart targeting these behaviors and choose rewards for not engaging in those behaviors. When this was successfully implemented, her parents were able to engage in refeeding Katie more consistently and successfully.

COGNITIVE–BEHAVIORAL TREATMENT OF BULIMIA NERVOSA

To date, there is ample evidence available to support the use of CBT for the treatment of bulimia nervosa and binge/purge behaviors in adults

(Mitchell, Agras, & Wonderlich, 2007). Almost 50 RCTs have been conducted to compare treatments for BN in adults (Shapiro et al., 2007). In general, RCTs comparing CBT to other forms of treatment indicate that individuals who receive CBT reduce binge eating and purging symptoms, as well as cognitive symptoms, to a greater extent than those who receive other treatments. Individuals who receive CBT also have higher abstinence rates at the end of treatment and at follow-up points than those who receive other forms of treatment (Fairburn, Kirk, O'Connor, & Cooper, 1985; Fairburn, Jones, Peveler, & Hope, 1993). One exception to this finding is that two RCTs have also demonstrated that interpersonal psychotherapy has similar long-term effects on symptoms of BN, but may take a slower course (Agras, Walsh, Fairburn, Wilson, & Kraemer, 2000). In sum, CBT is considered the first line of treatment for adults with BN (Wilson & Shafran, 2005).

Cognitive-behavioral therapy for bulimia nervosa consists of three main elements: behavior modification to regulate eating, cognitive restructuring to identify and change distorted thoughts regarding weight and shape, and relapse prevention. More recent investigations of treatment of BN in adults have also emphasized the management of emotion dysregulation and associated co-occurring behaviors (Fairburn, Cooper, & Shafran, 2002; Safer, Telch, & Agras, 2001; Wonderlich, Mitchell, Peterson, & Crow, 2001). In the first phase of treatment, clients are encouraged to eat three regular meals and two snacks per day. If regular eating is implemented successfully, then binge eating and subsequent purging behavior is often significantly reduced in the first phase of treatment. In the second phase of treatment, clients begin to identify distorted thoughts regarding their weight, shape, and food. These thoughts are challenged through behavioral experiments and are restructured. Relapse prevention consists of tapering treatment and practicing skills learned over longer periods of time, as well as outlining a maintenance plan.

CBT for Adolescents With Bulimia Nervosa

In contrast to the many RCTs for adults with BN, to date there have been only two published RCTs of treatment of BN in adolescents. One of those studies compared guided self-help CBT to family-based treatment (Schmidt et al., 2007) and the other study compared family-based treatment to supportive individual psychotherapy (le Grange et al., 2007). The limited number of RCTs is in sharp contrast to the strong need for effective treatments in this age group. First, as described earlier, symptoms of BN often emerge in adolescence. Symptoms of BN in and of themselves present medical risk, including low potassium (hypokalemia), esophageal tears, gastric disturbances, dehydration, and severe changes in blood pressure or heart rate when standing or sitting (orthostasis). Medical complications occurring in individuals with BN are largely related to weight-control behaviors and malnutrition. Among individuals with BN, as many as 25% may require hospitalization for medical reasons (Kreipe et al., 1995). It is not uncommon to observe fluid imbalances and electrolyte disturbances such as hypokalemia, hyponatremia, and hypochloremia, which can result from purging and may lead to cardiac arrhythmias (Rome & Ammerman, 2003). Gastro-esophageal reflux disease, Mallory-Weiss tears, periodontal disease, and dental caries caused by excessive vomiting are also seen in individuals with BN, as well as irregular menses and swelling of the parotid glands (Rome & Ammerman, 2003). These physiological impairments, as well as the psychological impairments, occur at a critical time of emotional and physical development in adolescents with BN. This in and of itself warrants effective and timely intervention.

Second, having BN in adolescence is a risk factor for the development of disordered eating in adulthood. In a longitudinal study following adolescents with full-syndrome eating disorders over a 17-year interval, it has been found that adolescent BN that is left untreated predicts a 20-fold (younger adolescents) to 35-fold (older adolescents) increase in the risk for BN in adulthood (Kotler, Cohen, Davies, Pine, & Walsh, 2001), highlighting the significance of BN in adolescents and the need to intervene early. Additionally, one longitudinal study with a large sample found that having BN in adolescence was associated with a number of psychiatric problems in adulthood, including mood disorders and suicide attempts (Johnson, Cohen, Kasen, & Brook, 2002). Thus, effectively treating symptoms of BN in adolescence will likely have a long-term effect on the individual's emotional and physical health in adulthood.

Because of the efficacy of CBT for adults with BN, and the need for timely interventions described earlier, many researchers have advocated adapting CBT for BN for adolescents (Wilson & Sysko, 2006). One case series using CBT for 34 adolescents with BN, and one RCT comparing the effectiveness of FBT to guided CBT self-help, have been published (Lock, 2005; Schmidt et al., 2007). An additional case series using CBT for binge-eating disorder, which is currently classified as EDNOS in the *DSM-IV*, has also been published (Schapman-Williams, Lock, & Couturier, 2006). All demonstrated reductions in binge-eating and purging symptoms comparable to the results of studies with adult samples. Lock (2005) reported a 78% reduction of binge–purge symptoms and a 56% abstinence rate. Schmidt and colleagues (2007) reported abstinence rates of 41.4% for the FBT group and 36% for the guided-CBT group at 12-month follow-up, and the differences between the two treatment groups were not statistically significant. Although these results are encouraging, more research is needed. Given the relative success of CBT with adults, applying the CBT model to the treatment of BN in adolescents is a logical next step (le Grange & Schmidt, 2005).

The two published RCTs compared FBT to another form of treatment. As described earlier, guided CBT self-help was equally as effective as FBT in one trial (Schmidt et al., 2007). In the other trial, adolescents in the FBT group had significantly greater reductions in binge-eating and purging symptoms and significantly higher abstinence rates than the supportive psychotherapy condition, both at end of treatment and at 6-month follow-up (le Grange et al., 2007). Thus, although published reports of the use of CBT in adolescence are encouraging, available research suggests that FBT is also effective in the treatment of BN in adolescence. Clinicians who desire to be guided by empirical evidence should note that the role of the family in the implementation of treatment for adolescents appears to be very important.

Factors Predicting Poor Response to Treatment

Two studies in adult women with BN indicate that early decreases in binge-eating or purging behavior predict increased chances of remission (Bulik, Sullivan, Carter, McIntosh, & Joyce, 1999; Fairburn, Agras, Walsh, Wilson, & Stice, 2004). Bulik and colleagues (1999) found that abstinence of binge eating by session eight predicted sustained abstinence of symptoms at an 8-month follow-up. Thus, in the adult literature, it appears that early reduction of binge and purge symptoms increases chances of remission. Similar results have been published in studies on adolescents. One study examining mediators of outcome in the RCT of FBT versus Supportive Psychotherapy (SPT) found that reduction in distorted cognitions mediated the effect of FBT on outcome (Lock, le Grange, & Crosby, 2008). Additionally, in all treatment conditions, having fewer binge/purge episodes and lower scores on a measure of depression predicted greater chances of remission (le Grange, Crosby, & Lock, 2008).

Additionally, family characteristics can have a negative effect on eating-disorder treatment outcome in adolescence. A meta-analysis of specific mental disorders and expressed emotion found a large effect of high expressed emotion levels on poor outcome in eating-disorder treatment (weighted mean effect size = .51) (Buzlaff & Hooley, 1998). Individual studies of both AN and BN patients indicate that parents of adolescent patients who drop out of treatment express significantly more critical comments about their child than those who remain (Szmukler, Eisler, Russell, & Dare, 1985). For example, parents may become increasingly frustrated with an adolescent who eats large amounts of food and then vomits, and may assign blame to the individual for this behavior as opposed to viewing the behavior as a mental illness (Hodges & le Grange, 1993). Additionally, adolescents with bulimia nervosa tend to have more unpredictable behavior and engage in more delinquent types of behaviors, such as use of illegal substances (Fischer & le Grange, 2007; Hodges & le Grange, 1993).

The following case example describes the adaptation of CBT for BN for an older adolescent. This adolescent had experienced symptoms of BN and comorbid depression for several years, typically a poor predictor of outcome. The case example describes ways in which the therapist enhanced motivation for behavior change, especially for behaviors that were ego syntonic to the adolescent. Additionally, the case illustrates ways in which the family can be incorporated into CBT for adolescents with eating disorders. Finally, this case is used to discuss factors that may uniquely affect relapse prevention in adolescence.

CASE PRESENTATION—TREATMENT OF ADOLESCENT BN WITH CBT

History and Presenting Symptoms

Maria was a 17-year-old Hispanic female from an intact family. She had a 3-year history of symptoms of bulimia nervosa at the time that she presented for treatment. Her previous treatment consisted of individual supportive psychotherapy in combination with 60 mg fluoxetine per day. At the start of her previous treatment, she was diagnosed with bulimia nervosa, major depressive disorder, and had been having some problems with grades and truancy in school. Maria was referred to individual therapy after a follow-up appointment with her psychiatrist 6 months after her previous treatment had ended. At that appointment, Maria was given the EDE and participated in a semistructured interview of other Axis I symptoms with her psychiatrist. At the time that she started individual cognitive-behavioral therapy, she engaged in binge eating and purging approximately once per day and endorsed distorted cognitions regarding her appearance and the importance of her weight and shape. Thus, she met full diagnostic criteria for bulimia nervosa. However, her depressive symptoms had remitted and she was improving her grades and behavior in school. Lingering symptoms of depression primarily centered on feelings of distress regarding her eating-disordered behavior and hopelessness regarding her ability to change her weight.

During the first meeting with Maria, an assessment was conducted and history gathered regarding the start of the eating disorder and her previous treatment. Maria reported that she believed that the eating disorder had been triggered by a breakup with an older adolescent boy when she was 14. She stated that she "used to be so thin and pretty," and went on to describe the way that she looked at that time in detail. She believed that the older boy had been attracted to her appearance and that is why they started dating. Maria reported that she had not been able to see the boy very much on dates, because her parents did not allow her to travel far outside of her neighborhood to go out with other adolescents whom they did not know. Thus, Maria believed that they developed an intense emotional connection via their telephone conversations, and became convinced that he had genuine feelings for her. She reported that she did not see him in person for several months, during which time she gained weight and changed her hairstyle. Maria reported that when she saw him in person again, he broke up with her. She attributed this entirely to his "shock" at her weight gain and the fact that she "wasn't pretty anymore." She was subsequently devastated as she had believed that they had developed genuine feelings for each other. Maria reported that at that point, she became determined to lose weight to return to the appearance that she had in the summer before she started high school and began dieting intensely. She successfully lost some weight and was able to maintain a restricted caloric intake for several months. She also reported that she began to look at "pro-ana" Web sites (Web sites that promote behaviors symptomatic of anorexia nervosa) for tips on how to maintain weight loss and lose more weight. Eventually, however, she began to binge eat after periods of restriction and then started purging after binges by self-induced vomiting.

Stage 1 of Treatment

Enhancing Motivation and Psychoeducation

Maria was motivated to reduce her binge eating and purging symptoms as they caused her distress and shame. However, as is often the case in adolescents with eating disorders, she was not motivated to stop restricting her eating. She was convinced that she could return to her pre-high school weight if she only had enough will power. She also expressed some feelings of shame that she could not manage her urges to eat in the same way that some of the individuals posting on the "pro-ana" Web sites were able to do.

First, the cognitive-behavioral model of BN was presented to Maria in a collaborative fashion. The basic model was outlined and the therapist asked Maria to fill in which parts of the model fit with her experience. Maria was able to identify links in her own experience that were similar to the hypothesized model in which feelings of low self-esteem led to concerns about weight and shape, which led to dieting. She was also able to identify links in her own experience in which purging followed binge eating, which caused feelings of shame and reinforced low self-esteem. However, she had difficulty understanding that restricted eating actually increased her chances of engaging in binge eating, and did not endorse this aspect of the model. At this point, to enhance motivation and collaboration, the therapist expressed willingness to entertain the idea with Maria that her restriction did not cause binge eating, and asked her to keep a detailed food record for the next week so that they could examine the evidence confirming or disconfirming this point together. Additionally, psychoeducation was provided regarding the effects of purging on the body and evidence that purging did not rid the body of the majority of the calories consumed during a binge.

To enhance motivation to engage in regulated eating behavior, pros and cons of binge eating, purging, and restriction were discussed in the next session. Additionally, the CBT model was reviewed again, with added information from the food diary. Maria had successfully kept a food diary over the previous week. On review of the food diary, it was evident that Maria attempted to engage in fairly severe caloric restriction throughout the day. She did not eat breakfast, and also skipped lunch at school. She then attempted to eat a salad and soup after school, without other food intake. Late in the evening, she tended to engage in objective binge episodes followed by purging. Through examination of food diary patterns with the client, Maria acknowledged that it appeared as though restriction might be linked to binge eating. She was able to generate several "cons" for binge eating and purging behaviors. However, she still expressed ambivalence regarding food restriction. Thus, she appeared horrified when the therapist introduced the idea of eating three regular meals and two snacks on a schedule. The therapist was able to enhance her motivation for eating regular meals by pointing out that she was likely to consume more calories during a binge than during a regular meal, and by reviewing her pros and cons list for binge eating and purging. Maria agreed to experiment with eating breakfast over the ensuing week.

Regulation of Eating and Incorporation of the Family

At the following session, Maria reported that she had eaten breakfast all 7 days of the week. She stated that once she had tried it, she realized that it had helped her feel less hungry. Thus, she was much more willing to incorporate additional meals and snacks into her schedule over the ensuing weeks. Additionally, her motivation was enhanced by the fact that her binge eating, and subsequent purging, had decreased dramatically as she added meals and snacks into her day.

As Maria began eating more regularly, she also noted that she began to feel increased hunger at specific time points in the day. She became increasingly concerned in this first treatment phase regarding her ability to control her eating as she felt hunger. She especially felt concerned regarding the time of day that she returned from school to her parents' home until her family's evening meal. At this point, the therapist and Maria engaged in problem solving together to generate solutions for regulating her eating after school. With therapist prompting, a solution was generated to ask Maria's mother for help on her return from school in the afternoon. Maria agreed to ask her mother for help by asking her to help prepare one specific snack after school for her to eat.

The family was further incorporated into treatment in week 8. At this point, Maria had dramatically reduced her binge-eating and purging symptoms. The therapist and Maria invited her parents and siblings to come in to discuss the CBT model of BN, Maria's treatment to date, and further ways in which the family could help her solidify her progress. Maria presented the model to her parents and explained how her own thoughts, feelings, and behaviors fit into the model. She also explained what she worked on in treatment up to that point and showed her parents a graph of her reduction in binge–purge symptoms. Maria expressed excitement about this aspect of the meeting, as she felt guilt regarding the length of time that she had eating-disorder symptoms and the distress that this caused her family. The family meeting also provided an opportunity for the therapist to observe the height, weight, and appearance of Maria's family members. It appeared that Maria's current weight and height were consistent with the appearance of her other family members, and that her expectations regarding her ability to significantly change her shape and weight were not realistic. These observations provided useful evidence to be incorporated into cognitive restructuring activities.

Cognitive Restructuring and Incorporation of Age-Appropriate Activities

After Maria had significantly reduced her binge eating and purging, cognitive restructuring was introduced. In this phase of treatment, the therapist also attempted to help Maria participate in typical adolescent activities that she had been avoiding because of her distorted thoughts regarding her appearance and her shame regarding eating-disorder symptoms. At this phase of treatment, her psychiatrist began to taper off the use of fluoxetine as well, with no problems noted.

Maria noted several automatic negative thoughts about her appearance, including that she was fat, that because she was fat romantic partners would not be interested in her, and that everyone at school had noticed how much her appearance had changed over the years and thought less of her for this. Further probing revealed that Maria also generated negative automatic thoughts regarding her intellectual abilities and guilt about how much "trouble she had caused her family." Finally, she endorsed automatic thoughts that were judgments about her eating disorder. On one hand, she felt that the eating disorder was an illness and that she wanted to fight against it. On the other hand, she endorsed beliefs that she didn't have the willpower to "succeed" in her eating disorder, because she had bulimia nervosa instead of anorexia nervosa. She initially endorsed several thoughts that she would feel much better about herself if she could make herself anorexic. The therapist used traditional cognitive restructuring activities incorporating behavioral experiments in treatment. However, behavioral experiments were tailored to typical activities in late adolescence. For example, the therapist encouraged Maria to participate in extracurricular activities that fit her interests. She participated in a school science fair and won, which caused her to move on to a science fair competition involving other local schools. This experience yielded several behavioral samples that were incorporated into restructured thoughts. First, Maria was able to engage in a different kind of social comparison than she had previously, which caused her to reframe her thoughts about herself. When she saw the resources available to adolescents in other parts of the city that were not available at her school, she was able to generate new thoughts about her own intelligence. Essentially, she was able to generate thoughts that she had strong intellectual abilities but had not had the wide range of resources available to her, compared to other students in wealthier parts of the city. Additionally, several students from different schools approached her to ask her for her phone number and ask her on dates. This allowed her to restructure thoughts about how her appearance may not have caused students at her own school to look down on her, but perhaps her withdrawal and low mood had caused some of her friends to be less active in pursuing social activities with her.

Spike in Binge Eating and Purging and Behavior-Chain Analysis

Prior to session 18, Maria had been abstinent from binge eating and purging for approximately 9 weeks and had been moving toward termination of therapy. However, her food diary revealed that she had suddenly experienced several binge and purge episodes. A cursory review of her food diary revealed that she had also experienced a spike in negative emotions around that time. The therapist attempted to engage

Maria in problem solving involving the causes of negative moods that appeared to be related to the resurgence of binge eating and purging. Maria left the session agreeing to implement solutions that had been generated. However, at the next session, she had again experienced binge and purge episodes. At this point, the therapist conducted a detailed behavior-chain analysis of the most recent purging episode. Although her food logs indicated that she had continued to experience an increase of negative emotions on days during which a binge occurred, the chain analysis revealed that Maria had attempted to ameliorate her affect by restricting her eating and viewing material on "pro-ana" Web sites for support. The negative affect had been followed by the thought, "I would probably feel better if I were thinner," which led to the attempts at restriction, which were reinforced by viewing the pro-ana material, which led to binge eating and subsequent purging. At this point, therapist and client were able to challenge and restructure remaining distorted thoughts surrounding the value of being thin. Additionally, they were able to incorporate targeting viewing of Internet material that encouraged eating-disordered behavior into relapse-prevention planning.

Relapse Prevention and Termination

After the brief resurgence of binge/purge episodes, Maria remained abstinent from behavioral eating-disorder symptoms. At this point, she had made plans to attend a community college located in the same city as her family, yet not in the same neighborhood. Relapse prevention focused on possible triggers that she may encounter in the transition from high school to college, and ways to use skills she had learned in therapy to cope with those triggers. Maria also planned to attend follow-up visits with the therapist to check in every few months during the first semester of school. Possible triggers for urges to restrict eating included social comparisons between herself and other women she met in the new environment, the emotional stress of a new workload and new intellectual challenges, environmental contexts that may have made it difficult to continue eating on a regular schedule, and relapse of depressive symptoms. Maria agreed to not look at Web material that promoted eating-disorder behavior, and decided to live at home with her parents for the first year of school. During follow-up visits, she noted that she had made new friends, one of whom she had told about her eating-disorder history. This friend normalized the emotional stress by sharing that she had also experienced an eating disorder. She also began discussing more and more differences between her identity and that of her parents, and decided to move out of the home after her first year to pursue her own independent interests further.

SUMMARY

As previously described, there are very few methodologically rigorous studies examining the effectiveness of treatments for eating disorders in adolescents. Evidence to date suggests that FBT is the most effective treatment for anorexia nervosa in children and adolescents. As the case example used here illustrates, however, therapists who implement FBT must often explain behavioral principles of reinforcement and punishment to the parents of a child with AN. Management of potential behavior problems that arise when parents start to engage in treatment with their child appears to be very important for the morale of the family and the quick return to healthy weight that is so necessary for full recovery from AN.

Only two published studies have evaluated the effectiveness of any treatment at all for BN in adolescents. In these studies, FBT was more effective than supportive psychotherapy but equally as effective as guided self-help CBT. Additionally, two case series have been published using CBT for adolescents with BN and BED. In all studies, recovery rates in adolescents were comparable to recovery rates in adults participating in randomized trials of CBT. These results indicate that CBT is a promising approach for adolescents with BN, but therapists should also note that family participation and involvement also appears to be crucial for adolescent recovery. The case example used here was that of an older adolescent who had suffered from BN for several years. This adolescent had the cognitive capabilities needed to fully participate in CBT. Although her family was incorporated into treatment, she was able to do a great deal of it on her own. Thus, important points to consider when examining the research evidence and planning treatment for an adolescent with BN are age and cognitive development. Parents may need to be more active and involved in meal planning with a younger adolescent than with an older adolescent, or with an adolescent who has not fully developed abstract thinking skills. Additionally, family environment needs to be considered, as expressed hostility toward an adolescent appears to be a poor prognostic indicator for therapy in general.

The case example of an adolescent with BN also illustrates the tendency of this age group to use technology and the Internet in healthy and unhealthy ways. Therapists working with adolescents with eating disorders should be aware of how the Internet is being used by their clients. Most individuals who post on pro-ana Web sites are females between the ages of 13 and 25 (Bardone-Cone & Cass, 2007). Experimental manipulations of viewing images of extremely thin people and the pro-anorexia messages typical of these Web sites indicate that viewing increases negative affect, body dissatisfaction, and desires to exercise and be thinner (Bardone-Cone & Cass, 2007; Groesz, Levine, & Murnen, 2002). However, Internet material supportive of efforts to maintain a healthy lifestyle can also be effective in assisting a therapist who wants to use the Internet to his or her advantage. Recent studies indicate that Internet-based programs can be used to promote adaptive, healthy behaviors as well (Celio-Doyle et al., 2008).

In sum, although there are few methodologically rigorous studies of therapy for adolescents with eating disorders, evidence suggests that therapies that focus on changing eating-disordered behavior and symptom management up front are most effective. Additionally, studies to date that include cognitive-behavioral therapy for adolescents with BN appear very promising.

REFERENCES

Agras, W. S., Walsh, B. T., Fairburn, C, G., Wilson, G. T., & Kraemer, H. C. (2000). A multicenter comparison of cognitive-behavioral therapy and interpersonal psychotherapy for bulimia nervosa. *Archives of General Psychiatry, 57*, 459–466.

Ambrosini, P. J. (2000). Historical development and present status of the Schedule for Affective Disorders and Schizophrenia for School Age Children. *Journal of the American Academy of Child and Adolescent Psychiatry, 39*, 48–58.

American Academy of Pediatrics. (2003). Policy statement: Identifying and treating eating disorders. *Pediatrics, 111*, 204–211.

American Psychiatric Association. (2000). *Diagnostic and statistical manual of mental disorders* (4th ed., text rev.). Washington, DC: American Psychiatric Press.

Attie, I., & Brooks-Gunn, J. (1989). Development of eating problems in adolescent girls: A longitudinal study. *Developmental Psychology, 25*, 70–79.

Bardone-Cone, A. M., & Cass, K. A. (2007). What does viewing a pro-anorexia website do? An experimental examination of website exposure and moderating effects. *International Journal of Eating Disorders, 40,* 537–548.

Bellisle, F. (2004). Effects of diet on behavior and cognition in children. *British Journal of Nutrition, 92,* S227–S232.

Bostic, J. Q., Muriel, A. C., Hack, S., Weinstein, S., & Herzog, D. (1997). Anorexia nervosa in a 7-year-old girl. *Journal of Developmental and Behavioral Pediatrics, 18,* 331–333.

Bowers, W. A., & Ansher, L. S. (2000). Cognitions in anorexia nervosa: Changes at discharge from a cognitive therapy milieu inpatient treatment program. *Journal of Cognitive Psychotherapy, 14,* 393–401.

Bryant-Waugh, R., & Lask, B. (1995). Annotation: Eating disorders in children. *Journal of Child Psychology and Psychiatry, 36,* 191–202.

Bruch, H. (1973). *Eating disorders.* New York: Basic Books.

Bruch, H. (1995) *Conversations with anorexics.* New York: Basic Books.

Bulik, C. M., Sullivan, P. F., & Kendler, K. S. (2003). Genetic and environmental contributions to obesity and binge eating. *International Journal of Eating Disorders, 33,* 293–298.

Bulik, C. M., Sullivan, P. F., Carter, F. A., McIntosh, V. V., & Joyce, P. R. (1999). Predictors of rapid and sustained response to cognitive behavioral therapy for bulimia nervosa. *International Journal of Eating Disorders, 26,* 137–144.

Bulik, C. M., Sullivan, P. F., Tozzi, F., Furberg, H., Lichtenstein, P., & Pedersen, N. L. (2006). Prevalence, heritability, and prospective risk factors for anorexia nervosa. *Archives of General Psychiatry, 63,* 305–312.

Buzlaff, R. L., & Hooley, J. M. (1998). Expressed emotion and psychiatric relapse. *Archives of General Psychiatry, 55,* 547–552.

Celio-Doyle, A., Goldschmidt, A., Huang, C., Winzelberg, A. J., Taylor, C. B., & Wilfley, D. E. (2008). Reduction of overweight and eating disorder symptoms via the internet in adolescents: A randomized controlled trial. *Journal of Adolescent Health, 43,* 172–179.

Channon S., de Silva P., Hemsley D., & Perkins R. E. (1989). A controlled trial of cognitive-behavioural and behavioural treatment of anorexia nervosa. *Behaviour Research and Therapy, 27,* 529–535.

Coelho, J. S., Polivy, J., Herman, C. P., & Pliner, P. (2008). Effects of food cure exposure on dieting related goals: A limitation to counteractive control theory. *Appetite, 51,* 47–349.

Dare, C., Eisler, I., Russell, G., Treasure, J., & Dodge, L. (2001). Psychological therapies for adults with anorexia nervosa. *British Journal of Psychiatry, 178,* 216–221.

Eddy, K. T., Celio Doyle, A., Hoste, R., Herzog, D. B., & le Grange, D. (2008). Eating disorder not otherwise specified in adolescents. *Journal of the American Academy of Child and Adolescent Psychiatry, 47,* 156–164.

Eisler, I., Dare, C., Hodes, M., Russell, G., Dodge, E., & Le Grange, D. (2000). Family therapy for adolescent anorexia nervosa: The results of a controlled comparison of two family interventions. *Journal of Child Psychology & Psychiatry, 41,* 727–736.

Eisler, I., Dare, C., Russell, G. F. M., Szmukler, G. I., le Grange, D., & Dodge, E. (1997). Family and individual therapy in anorexia nervosa: A five-year follow-up. *Archives of General Psychiatry, 54,* 1025–1030.

Erikson, E. H. (1968). *Identity: Youth and crisis.* New York: Norton.
Fabian, L. J., & Thompson, J. K. (1989). Body image and eating disturbance in young females. *International Journal of Eating Disorders, 8,* 63–74.
Fairburn, C. G., Agras, W. S., Walsh, B. T., Wilson, G. T., & Stice, E. (2004). Prediction of outcome in bulimia nervosa by early change in treatment. *American Journal of Psychiatry, 161,* 2322–2324.
Fairburn, C. G., & Cooper, Z. (1993). The eating disorder examination. In C. G. Fairburn & G. T. Wilson (Eds.), *Binge eating: Nature, assessment, & treatment* (pp. 317–331. New York: Guilford Press.
Fairburn, C. G., Cooper, Z., Doll, H. A., Norman, P., & O'Connor, M. (2000). The natural course of bulimia nervosa and binge eating disorder in young women. *Archives of General Psychiatry, 57,* 659–665.
Fairburn, C. G., Cooper, Z., & Shafran, R. (2002). Cognitive behavioral therapy for eating disorders: A "transdiagnostic" theory and treatment. *Behavioral Research and Therapy, 41,* 509–528.
Fairburn, C. G., Jones, R., Peveler, R. C., Hope, R. A., & O'Connor, M. E. (1993). Psychotherapy and bulimia nervosa: Longer term effects of interpersonal psychotherapy, behavior therapy, and cognitive behavior therapy. *Archives of General Psychiatry, 50,* 419–428.
Fairburn, C. G., Kirk, J., O'Connor, M., & Cooper, P. J. (1986). A comparison of two psychological treatments for bulimia nervosa. *Behaviour Research and Therapy, 24,* 629–643.
Fairburn, C. G., Marcus, M. D., & Wilson, G. T. (1993). Cognitive-behavioral therapy for binge eating and bulimia nervosa: A comprehensive treatment manual. In C. G. Fairburn & G. T. Wilson (Eds.), *Binge eating: Nature, assessment, & treatment* (pp. 361–404). New York: Guilford Press.
Fairburn, C. G., Welch, S. L., Doll, H. A., Davies, B. A., & O'Connor, M. E. (1997). Risk factors for bulimia nervosa: A community based case control study. *Archives of General Psychiatry, 54,* 509–517.
Feldman, S., & Elliott, G. (1990). *At the threshold: The developing adolescent.* Cambridge, MA: Harvard University Press.
Fischer, S., & le Grange, D. (2007). Co-morbidity and high-risk behaviors in treatment seeking adolescents with bulimia nervosa. *International Journal of Eating Disorders, 40,* 751–753.
Groesz, L. M., Levine, M. P., & Murnen, S. K. (2002). The effect of experimental presentation of thin media images on body satisfaction: A meta-analytic review. *International Journal of Eating Disorders, 31,* 1–16.
Halmi, K. A., Agras, W. S., Crow, S., Mitchell, J., Wilson, G. T., Bryson, S. W., et al. (2005). Predictors of treatment acceptance and completion in anorexia nervosa: Implications for future study designs. *Archives of General Psychiatry, 62,* 776–781.
Herzog, D. B., Keller, M. B., Sacks, N. R., Yeh, C. J., & Lavori, P. W. (1992). Psychiatric comorbidity in treatment-seeking anorexics and bulimics. *Journal of the American Academy of Child and Adolescent Psychiatry, 31,* 810–818.
Hill, A. J., Weaver, C., & Blundell, J. E. (1990). Dieting concerns of 10 year old girls and their mothers. *British Journal of Clinical Psychology, 29,* 346–348.

Hodes, M., & le Grange, D. (1993). Expressed emotion in the investigation of eating disorders: A review. *International Journal of Eating Disorders, 13*, 279–288.

Hoek, H. (1993). Review of epidemiological studies of eating disorders. *International Review of Psychiatry, 5*, 61–74.

Holmbeck, G. N., Colder, C., Spaera, W., Westhoven, V., Kenealy, L., & Updegrove, A. (2000). Working with adolescents: Guides from developmental psychology. In P. Kendall (Ed.), *Child and adolescent therapy* (pp. 334–385). New York: Guilford Press.

Johnson, J. G., Cohen, P., Kasen, S., & Brook, J. S. (2002). Eating disorders during adolescence and the risk for physical and mental disorders during early adulthood. *Archives of General Psychiatry, 59*, 545–552.

Kent, A., Lacey, H., & McClusky, S. E. (1992). Pre-menarchal bulimia nervosa. *Journal of Psychosomatic Research, 36*, 205–210.

Killen, J. D., Taylor, C. B., Hayward, C., Haydel, K. F., Wilson, D. M., Hammer, L., et al. (1996). Weight concerns influence the development of eating disorders: A four year prospective study. *Journal of Consulting and Clinical Psychology, 64*, 936–940.

Killen, J. D., Taylor, C. B., Hayward, C., Wilson, D., Haydel, K., Hammer, L., et al., (1994). Pursuit of thinness and onset of eating disorder symptoms in a community sample of adolescent girls: A three year prospective analysis. *International Journal of Eating Disorders, 16*, 227–238.

Klump, K. L., Burt, S. A., McGue, M., & Iacono, W. G. (2007). Changes in genetic and environmental influences on disordered eating across adolescence: A longitudinal twin study. *Archives of General Psychiatry, 64*, 1409–1415.

Klump, K. L., McGue, M., & Iacono, W. G. (2000). Age differences in genetic and environmental influences on eating attitudes and behaviors in preadolescent and adolescent female twins. *Journal of Abnormal Psychology, 109*, 239–251.

Kotler, L. A., Cohen, P., Davies, M., Pine, D. S., & Walsh, B. T. (2001). Longitudinal relationships between childhood, adolescent, and adult eating disorders. *Journal of the American Academy of Child and Adolescent Psychiatry, 40*, 1434–1440.

Kreipe, R. E., Golden, N. H., Katzman, D. K., & Fisher, M. (1995). Eating disorders in adolescents: A position paper of the society for adolescent medicine. *Journal of Adolescent Health, 16*, 476–480.

Larsen, J. K., van Strien, T., Eisinga, R., Herman, C. P., & Engels, R. C. M. E. (2007). Dietary restraint: Intention versus behavior to restrict food intake. *Appetite, 49*, 100–108.

Lask, B., Bryant-Waugh, R., Wright, F., Campbell, M., Willoughby, K., & Waller G. (2005). Family physician consultation patterns indicate high risk for anorexia nervosa. *International Journal of Eating Disorders, 38*, 269–272.

le Grange, D., Binford, R., & Loeb, K. L. (2005). Manualized family-based treatment for anorexia nervosa: A case series. *Journal of the American Academy of Child and Adolescent Psychiatry, 44*, 41–46.

le Grange, D., Crosby, R. D., & Lock, J. (2008). Predictors and moderators of outcome in family based treatment for adolescent bulimia nervosa. *Journal of the American Academy of Child & Adolescent Psychiatry, 47*, 464–470.

le Grange, D., Crosby, R. D., Rathouz, P. J., Leventhal, B. L. (2007). A randomized controlled comparison of family-based treatment and supportive psychotherapy for adolescent bulimia nervosa. *Archives of General Psychiatry, 64*, 1049–1056.

le Grange, D., Eisler, I., Dare, C., & Russell, G. (1992). Evaluation of family treatments in adolescent anorexia nervosa: A pilot study. *International Journal of Eating Disorders, 12*, 347–357.

le Grange, D., Lock, J., & Dymek, M. (2003). Family based therapy for adolescents with bulimia nervosa. *American Journal of Psychotherapy, 57*, 237–251.

le Grange, D., & Schmidt, U. (2005). The treatment of adolescents with bulimia nervosa. *Journal of Mental Health, 14*, 587–597.

Lock, J. (2005). Adjusting cognitive behavior therapy for adolescents with bulimia nervosa: Results of a case series. *American Journal of Psychotherapy, 59*, 267–281.

Lock, J., Couturier, J., Bryson, S., & Agras, S. (2006). Predictors of dropout and remission in family therapy for adolescent anorexia nervosa in a randomized clinical trial. *International Journal of Eating Disorders, 39*, 639–647.

Lock, J., le Grange, D., Agras, W. S., & Dare, C. (2001). *Treatment manual for anorexia nervosa: A family-based approach.* New York: Guilford Press.

Lock, J., le Grange, D., & Crosby, R., (2008). Exploring possible mechanisms of change in family based treatment for adolescent bulimia nervosa. *Journal of Family Therapy, 30*, 260–271.

Lock, J., le Grange, D., Forsberg, S., & Hewell, K. (2006). Is family therapy useful for treating children with anorexia nervosa? Results of a case series. *Journal of the American Academy of Child and Adolescent Psychiatry, 45*, 1323–1328.

Loeb, K. L., Walsh, T., Lock, J., le Grange, D., Jones, J., Marcus, S., et al. (2007). Open trial of family based treatment for full and partial anorexia nervosa in adolescence: Evidence of successful dissemination. *Journal of the American Academy of Child and Adolescent Psychiatry, 46*, 792–800.

Lucas, A. R., Beard, C. M., O'Fallon, W. M., & Kurland, L. T. (1991). 50-year trends in the incidence of anorexia nervosa in Rochester, Minn: A population-based study. *American Journal of Psychiatry, 148*, 917–929.

McIntosh, V. W., Jordan, J., Carter, F. A., Luty, S. E., McKenzie, J. M., & Bulik, C. M. (2005). Three psychotherapies for anorexia nervosa: A randomized controlled trial. *American Journal of Psychiatry, 162*, 741–747.

Mitchell, J. E., Agras, S., & Wonderlich, S. (2007). Treatment of bulimia nervosa: Where are we and where are we going? *International Journal of Eating Disorders, 40*, 95–101.

NCCMH: National Collaborating Centre for Mental Health. (2004). *Eating disorders: Core interventions in the treatment and management of anorexia nervosa, bulimia nervosa and related eating disorders.* British Psychological Society and Gaskell, UK: Leicester & London.

Patton, G. C., Selzer, R., Coffey, C., Carlin, B., & Wolfe, R. (1999). Onset of adolescent eating disorders: Population based cohort study over three years. *British Medical Journal, 318*, 765–768.

Peebles, R., Wilson, J., & Lock, J. (2006). How do children and adolescents with eating disorders differ at presentation? *Journal of Adolescent Health, 39*, 800–805.

Pike, K. M., Walsh, B. T., Vitousek, K., Wilson, G. T., & Bauer, J. (2003). Cognitive behavior therapy in the post hospitalization treatment of anorexia nervosa. *American Journal of Psychiatry, 160*, 2046–2049.

Rome, E. S., & Ammerman, S. (2003). Medical complications of eating disorders: An update. *Journal of Adolescent Health, 33*, 418–426.

Russell, G. F. M., Szmukler, G. I., Dare, C., & Eisler, I. (1987). An evaluation of family therapy in anorexia and bulimia nervosa. *Archives of General Psychiatry, 44*, 1047–1056.

Rutter, M. (1990). Changing patterns of psychiatric disorders during adolescence. In J. Bancroft & J. M. Reinisch (Eds.), *Adolescence and puberty* (pp. 124–145). New York: Oxford University Press.

Safer, D. L., Telch, C. F., & Agras, W. (2001). Dialectical behavior therapy for bulimia nervosa. *American Journal of Psychiatry, 158*, 632–634.

Schapman-Williams, A. M., Lock, J., & Couturier, J. (2006). Cognitive-behavioral therapy for adolescents with binge eating syndromes: A case series. *International Journal of Eating Disorders, 39*, 252–255.

Schmidt, U., Lee, S., Beecham, J., Perkins, S., Treasure, J., Yim, I., et al. (2007). A randomized controlled trial of family therapy and cognitive behavior therapy guided self-care for adolescents with bulimia nervosa and related disorders. *American Journal of Psychiatry, 164*, 591–598.

Serfaty, M. A., Turkington, D., Heap, M., Ledsham, L., & Jolley, E. (1999). Cognitive therapy versus dietary counselling in the outpatient treatment of anorexia nervosa: Effects of the treatment phase. *European Eating Disorders Review, 7*, 334–350.

Shah, N., Passi, V., Bryson, S., & Agras, W. S. (2005). Patterns of eating and abstinence in women treated for bulimia nervosa. *International Journal of Eating Disorders, 38*, 330–334.

Shapiro, J. R., Berkman, N. D., Brownley, K. A., Sedway, J. A., Lohr, K. N., & Bulik, C. M. (2007). Bulimia nervosa treatment: A systematic review of randomized controlled trials. *International Journal of Eating Disorders, 40*, 321–336.

Steiger, H., & Seguin, J. R. (1999). Eating disorders: Anorexia and bulimia nervosa. In T. Millon & P.H. Blaney (Eds.), *Oxford textbook of psychopathology. Oxford textbooks in clinical psychology* (pp. 365–389). New York: Oxford University Press.

Steiner, H., & Lock, J. (1998). Anorexia nervosa and bulimia nervosa in children and adolescents: A review of the past 10 years. *Journal of the American Academy of Child and Adolescent Psychiatry, 37*, 352–359.

Szmukler, G. I., Eisler, I., Russell, G. F. M., & Dare, C. (1985). Anorexia nervosa, parental "expressed emotion" and dropping out of treatment. *British Journal of Psychiatry, 147*, 265–271.

Tchanturia, K., Campbell, I. C., Morris, R., & Treasure, J. (2005). Neuropsychological studies in anorexia nervosa. *International Journal of Eating Disorders, 37*, S72–S76.

Wilson, G. T., Fairburn, C. G., Agras, W. S., Walsh, B. T., & Kraemer, H. (2002). Cognitive behavioral therapy for bulimia nervosa: Time course and mechanisms of change. *Journal of Consulting and Clinical Psychology, 70*, 267–274.

Wilson, G. T., & Sysko, R. (2006). Cognitive behavioural therapy for adolescents with bulimia nervosa. *European Eating Disorders Review, 14*, 8–16.

Wonderlich, S. A., Mitchell, J. E., Peterson, C. B., & Crow, S. (2001). Integrative-cognitive therapy for bulimic behavior. In R. H. Striegel-Moore & L. Smolak (Eds.), *Eating disorders: Innovative directions in research and practice* (pp. 173–195). Washington, DC: American Psychological Association.

11

Assessment and Treatment of Child and Adolescent Sleep Disorders

CONNIE J. SCHNOES AND THOMAS M. REIMERS

Pediatric sleep problems, including problems with sleep onset and frequent night awakenings, are among the most common childhood concerns expressed by parents. It is estimated that 20 to 40% of children and adolescents experience some type of sleep disorder during their lifetime (Meltzer & Mindell, 2006; Mindell, Kuhn, Lewin, Meltzer, & Sadeh, 2006). Untreated pediatric sleep disorders persist over time (Kateria, Swanson, & Trevarthin, 1987) and the negative impact on development, emotion, and behavior has been well documented (Beebe & Gozal, 2002; Mindell & Owens, 2003).

Perhaps the most widely cited source as to how much sleep should be expected throughout childhood, between birth and 18 years, is provided by Ferber in his classic book, *Solve Your Child's Sleep Problems* (2006). In general, the younger a child is, the more sleep he or she needs. During the first 2 months of life, infants typically sleep for varying amounts of time off and on throughout the day and night, needing 16 hours of sleep during their first few weeks of life and 14 hours by 1 month of age. By 6 months of age, healthy infants are able to sleep through the night (approximately 9 hours) and nap about 3 more hours spread over two to three naps during the day. As children approach age 1, they are more likely to consolidate their sleep, sleeping nearly 10 hours at night with morning and afternoon naps occurring at more predictable times. However, this is also a time when parents initially report sleep difficulties, often expressing concern to pediatricians and other health care providers about difficulties with sleep onset and frequent night awakenings (Crowell, Keener, Ginsburg, & Anders, 1987; Minde, Faucon, & Falkner, 1994; Richman, 1981; Scott & Richards, 1990). By age 5 years, many children have outgrown the need for a nap and are typically sleeping 11 hours each night. During this time, sleep-onset concerns continue to be expressed by parents along with nighttime fears including fear of the dark (Blader, Koplewicz, Abikoff, & Foley, 1997). Throughout the elementary school years, it is recommended that children achieve at least 10 hours of sleep per night. Naps among this age group are very unusual. Sleep onset and frequent awakenings continue to be a concern within the population of children experiencing sleep disturbance. The causes of sleep disturbance in this age group may include factors related to anxiety and sleep-related apnea (Meltzer & Mindell, 2006). Throughout adolescence, 9 to 10 hours of sleep is recommended. Circadian rhythms tend to change during adolescence, often delaying sleep onset up to 2 hours. Many adolescents report difficulty falling asleep at night, as well as awakening in the morning. The early start time of most high schools, along with increased social and academic demands often places significant strain on adolescents sometimes leading to academic, behavioral, and emotional sequelae (Dahl & Lewin, 2002).

Sleep disturbance that occurs during childhood and adolescence takes on a variety of forms and affects both the quantity and quality of sleep. The purpose of this chapter is to provide an overview of the types of sleep disorders experienced by children and adolescents, methods of assessment of sleep disorders, evidence-based treatments for sleep disturbances, and, finally, factors that contribute to poor treatment response.

PEDIATRIC SLEEP DISORDERS

Sleep disorders are typically defined in two broad categories: *dyssomnias* and *parasomnias*. Both are found within the *Diagnostic and Statistical Manual of Mental Disorders, Fourth Edition, Text Revision* (*DSM-IV-TR*; American Psychiatric Association, 2000) and the *International Classifi-*

cation of Sleep Disorders (*ICSD*; American Academy of Sleep Medicine, 2005). Dyssomnias are typically characterized by insufficient, excessive, or inefficient sleep. As opposed to dyssomnias, parasomnias negatively affect sleep by engaging the autonomic nervous system, motor system, or cognition during sleep/wake transitions. Very broadly defined, dyssomnias affect the onset and process of falling sleep, whereas parasomnias tend to interrupt sleep once it has occurred.

It is important to refer to the *DSM-IV-TR* or *ICSD* for specific symptom, frequency, and duration criteria in diagnosing sleep disorders. In general, when diagnosing a specific sleep disorder, the symptoms must cause clinically significant distress or impairment in social, occupational, or other important areas of functioning, must not be caused by a medical condition, another sleep disorder, or mental health disorder.

Dyssomnias

Primary Insomnia

Primary insomnia typically refers to difficulty with initiating or maintaining sleep. Difficulty falling asleep, as well as intermittent wakefulness, is often commonly reported for individuals with primary insomnia. For children, primary insomnia typically takes on the form of either resisting going to sleep at bedtime, or of frequent awakenings during the night. The *ICSD* identifies two insomnia disorders that are specific to children: limit-setting sleep disorder, and sleep-onset association disorder. Primary insomnia is a diagnosis typically applied to adolescents and adults with sleep-onset or maintenance problems (American Psychiatric Association, 2000). The predominant complaint is difficulty initiating or maintaining sleep, or nonrestorative sleep, for at least 1 month.

Limit-Setting Sleep Disorder

Limit-setting sleep disorder is characterized by the child stalling or refusing to go bed or to follow appropriate bedtime regimens. The child's resistance usually occurs at the start of bedtime, but can also occur during awakenings in the middle of the night. Children who present with limit-setting sleep-disorder may be sleep deprived because of the disruptive bedtime behavior and resulting delayed sleep onset. However, these children ultimately fall asleep independently (American Academy of Sleep Medicine, 2005).

Sleep-Onset Association Disorder

Children who present with sleep-onset association disorder experience insomnia at bedtime and during night awakenings. With this disorder, sleep is normal when "certain conditions" are present and, when they are not, sleep is disrupted either at the onset of sleep or during night awakenings. The conditions that are necessary for sleep may include "normal" bedtime routines to more atypical associations such as the child falling asleep with a pacifier or bottle, being rocked by a parent, on a couch and then being carried to bed, and so on. As long as the conditions the child has associated with sleep are present, sleep onset usually happens fairly rapidly. However, when those conditions are not present, sleep is often either disrupted or does not occur within a reasonable time. Because this disorder involves associations with sleep onset, nighttime awakenings typically require the same sleep-onset conditions for sleep to be reinitiated. This disorder is most commonly found in children under the age of 3. The incidence decreases fairly rapidly after that age (American Academy of Sleep Medicine, 2005).

Primary Hypersomnia

Primary hypersomnia is characterized by excessive sleepiness, either through prolonged sleep or excessive sleepiness during the day. Hypersomnia is a common symptom among adolescents who exhibit major depression (Ryan et al., 1987). It is important to determine if youth who present with a mood disorder have a co-occurring sleep disorder. Children who present with excessive sleepiness during the day may be diagnosed with hyperactivity caused by irritability, impulsivity, and poor attention (Dahl, Pelham, & Wierson, 1991). Given the similar patterns, it is important to rule out other related sleep disorders, such as breathing-related sleep disorder and circadian rhythm sleep disorder, before making this diagnosis (American Psychiatric Association, 2000). The predominant complaint is excessive sleepiness for at least 1 month (or less if recurrent) as evidenced by either prolonged sleep episodes or daytime sleep episodes, which occur almost daily.

Narcolepsy

Narcolepsy is a relatively rare disorder that typically first presents during the late teens or early 20s. Estimates suggest a prevalence of .02 to .16% in the general population (Owens, 2005). There are several main features of narcolepsy that include excessive daytime sleepiness with irresistible sleep attacks, cataplexy (reversible loss of muscle tone that lasts from seconds to minutes most often in association with intense emotion), and/or recurrent intrusions of elements of rapid eye movement (REM) sleep into the transition between sleep and wakefulness, as manifested by either hypnopompic or hypnagogic hallucinations or paralysis of voluntary muscles at sleep onset. Individuals will often feel rested after a sleep attack, but begin to feel excessively sleepy several hours later. An individual must have daily attacks for a period of 3 months to qualify for a diagnosis. Individuals with narcolepsy may also have periodic cataplectic attacks, which include the loss of muscle tone during wakefulness. Individuals will often not lose consciousness and their memory remains intact. These attacks are usually brief, lasting no more than several minutes. The frequency can range from multiple attacks a day to several attacks per year. Narcolepsy is considered to be a lifelong, chronic condition even though the symptomology may decrease over time (American Psychiatric Association, 2000).

Breathing-Related Sleep Disorder

Breathing-related sleep disorder almost always includes apnea in children. Apnea takes on several forms, including obstructive, central, and mixed. The most common, by far, in children is obstructive sleep apnea. Apnea is defined as an interruption of breathing during sleep that exceeds 10 seconds. Hypopneas are shorter periods of reduced ventilation in which the oxygen saturation levels go below 50%. To have a diagnosis of sleep apnea, an individual has to have 5 apneas or 10 apnea–hypopnea combinations per hour while sleeping. A typical apnea lasts around 30 seconds, but can last several minutes. The most common cause of obstructive sleep apnea in children is enlarged tonsils or adenoids that obstruct the airway, causing increased effort by the individual to regain breathing. The individual will often complain of feeling tired the next day as a result of the frequency of the apneas and attempts to improve ventilation, causing increased arousal. Parents will also notice that their children are snoring, or engaging in open-mouth breathing while sleeping. The other forms of apnea, central and mixed, tend to be fairly unusual in children (American Psychiatric Association, 2000).

Circadian-Rhythm Sleep Disorder

Circadian-rhythm sleep disorder is found more commonly in the adolescent population (7%) than any other population (Owens, 2005). Circadian-rhythm sleep disorder typically falls within three subtypes; delayed sleep phase, jet lag, and shift work. Among adolescents, the most common is delayed sleep phase type, which is usually caused by prolonged periods of sleep deprivation or disruptions to normal sleep patterns. Adolescents who experience delayed sleep phase typically have difficulty falling asleep at a typical bedtime, and then want to sleep beyond what would be a reasonable morning wake time. During the school year, the time they need to be at school dictates the time they need to rise, thus creating challenges for many families. Because of this, they typically tend to shorten the amount of sleep they obtain. The lack of sleep has a variety of implications for adolescents, including impaired academic performance (Mitru, Millrood, & Mateika, 2002), depressive mood and sleep/wake behavior problems (Wolfson & Carskadon, 1998), difficulty staying awake while driving (Carskadon, 1990), and increased daytime sleepiness (Carskadon, 1990; Wolfson & Carskadon, 1998).

Parasomnias

As compared to dyssomnias, parasomnias do not affect sleep onset or the process of falling asleep. Rather, parasomnias involve disruption to the sleep process once sleep has occurred. For children and adolescents, the most common types of parasomnias are sleep terrors and sleepwalking (Mehlenbeck, Spirito, Owens, & Boergers, 2000). Sleep-related eating disorder is also a parasomnia.

Nightmare Disorder

Nightmares usually involve a lengthy dream sequence that includes frightening or anxiety-provoking sequences. They typically occur late in the sleep cycle, during REM sleep. REM sleep occurs during the last one third of the sleep period. Nightmares are typically well remembered, with the child or adolescent reaching alert wakefulness at some point during the nightmare and having very vivid recall of the dream. Nightmares do not always need to recount some actual event, but it is not uncommon, especially with children, for there to have been some precipitating event that elicited the nightmare (American Psychiatric Association, 2000).

Sleep Terror Disorder

Sleep terror disorders are partial-arousal parasomnias that are characterized by a child typically sitting up, screaming, and staring about with glassy eyes. Labored respiration and heart palpitations are quite noticeable. Children experiencing sleep terrors are relatively unresponsive to efforts of others to comfort them during the episode. To many parents, sleep terrors on the surface often look like nightmares. They are distinguishable from nightmares in that sleep terrors typically occur during the first one third of sleep (versus the last one-third of sleep for nightmares), during the transition from stage IV delta sleep to lighter stages of sleep. Children typically experience retrograde amnesia for the episode, that is, they have no recollection of the event when they awaken in the morning. Although night terrors can be triggered by insufficient sleep, stress, and illness, there is no know connection between night terrors and depression, anxiety, or other psychological problems. Most children will quickly outgrow the night terrors, with night terrors being very unusual by the onset of adolescence (American Psychiatric Association, 2000).

Sleepwalking Disorder

Sleepwalking disorder shares many of the same characteristics as sleep terror disorder. Sleepwalking is a partial arousal parasomnia; children who sleepwalk typically do so during the first one third of sleep and experience retrograde amnesia. While sleepwalking the child has a blank, staring face and is relatively unresponsive to the efforts of others to communicate with him or her, and can be awakened only with great difficulty. The sleepwalking typically includes purposeless walking that is generally poorly coordinated. Sleepwalking imposes a danger to children and adolescents and thus requires safety-proofing of the home. As with sleep terrors, there is no known connection between sleepwalking and anxiety, depression, or other mental health disorders. Both sleepwalking and sleep terrors are known to have a familial connection (American Psychiatric Association, 2000).

Sleep-Related Eating Disorder

Sleep-related eating is characterized by eating during arousal from sleep at least one time per week. A partial-arousal parasomnia, the individual has no recall of the event in the morning and the event typically occurs within the first third of the sleep cycle. This state of awareness differs from simple nocturnal eating, wherein the individual is fully alert. Individuals who present with sleep-related eating discover evidence of having eaten on awakening (e.g., candy wrappers in bed, food items out in the kitchen). Typically high-calorie foods and foods not usually consumed are eaten. Sleep-related eating disorder has a prevalence rate of 4.7%, is more common among females, and initially presents during adolescence (Winkelman, Herzog, & Fava, 1999). This disorder may be associated with daytime eating disorders and the occurrence of major life stressors as well as insufficient total sleep time (Winkelman et al., 1999).

ASSESSMENT

The factors related to sleep disturbance in children cover a wide range and typically include biological, behavioral, and environmental factors. As such, it is important to evaluate each of these factors to rule out and consider those variables that may be contributing to any particular child's sleep difficulties. We provide an overview of those factors that should be considered when evaluating a child's sleep difficulties.

Medical

In addition to behavioral and environmental factors, there are a variety of acute and chronic medical factors that could potentially contribute to a child's sleep difficulties. Considering a number of medical factors that may contribute to a child's sleep difficulties is important. A referral to the child's pediatrician or family practice physician should be considered, especially if the pediatrician and/or family practice physician is unaware of the sleep difficulties or has not seen the child recently. In many cases, parents' initial concerns of sleep difficulties have been made to the primary care provider and medical variables that may contribute to the sleep difficulties have already been ruled out. Sleep apnea is one of the more common medical factors associated with sleep difficulty. Most physicians are well trained in ruling out sleep apnea as a contributing factor to sleep difficulties (Coates & Thoreson, 1984).

Children who present with a very atypical sleep pattern, and/or who have failed to benefit from a thorough behavioral assessment and series of interventions may warrant more intensive medical examination. A common form of assessment is to conduct an all-night sleep study. Sleep studies include a continuous polysomnographic recording of the child's sleep cycles and brain-wave activity. Conducting this type of assessment allows for an examination of total sleep, time in bed, sleep efficiency, number of awakenings, oxygen levels, and brain activity. Abnormalities, outside of behavioral-based disruptions, can be determined and further medical assessment and/or intervention can be considered. Many major metropolitan areas have sleep labs and can facilitate this type of evaluation (Coates & Thoreson, 1984).

Behavioral

Behavioral assessment of sleep difficulties allows for a wide examination of a number of factors that can contribute to sleep difficulties. Because of the interpersonal, social, and environmental factors that often contribute to sleep difficulties, taking a fairly broad-based approach toward evaluating the environment, caretakers, and interpersonal characteristics of the child allows for a thorough behavior-analytic approach toward identifying those factors that are contributing to a child's sleep difficulties. Conducting a structured diagnostic interview, collecting standardized questionnaires, and obtaining ongoing data via a sleep diary are key components of a thorough behavioral assessment.

A *structured diagnostic interview* is warranted for all children presenting with sleep difficulties. This includes a comprehensive evaluation of not only the child's presenting problem, but also an understanding of the antecedents and consequences surrounding the behavior. The structured interview is a fairly inexpensive way to obtain a variety of information, including past approaches toward managing the problem, current efforts, interpersonal and behavioral characteristics of the child, and an examination of the child's current sleep pattern. Additionally, the child's past behavioral, medical, and mental health history warrant examination to determine if comorbid conditions exist that may be contributing to the existing sleep problem.

Examining all aspects of the child's sleep, including the bedroom environment, bedtime routine, and sleep schedule is a critical component of the structured interview. Obtaining a description of the home environment, including the location of the bedrooms in the home, the physical arrangement of the child's bedroom, as well as who sleeps in each bedroom, is important. Identifying what, if any, bedtime routine is in place, as well as the child's sleep schedule (e.g., what time he or she goes to bed, time he or she falls asleep, time of morning awakening) and the frequency and timing of nighttime awakenings, are also necessary. Examining the behavioral antecedents and consequences associated with sleep onset facilitates identifying the function of behavioral problems associated with sleep. Clinicians should examine activities (e.g., recreation, exercise) that occur prior to bedtime, dietary practices (e.g., snacks, caffeine) prior to bed, child behaviors (calling out, coming out, rumination, etc.) between bedtime and sleep onset, and specific conditions in place (e.g., who is present, objects present, lighting, location) once sleep onset occurs. Parents respond to children in a wide range of ways, and documenting parents' current and past responses to problematic bedtime behavior and sleep disruptions is important. Also obtaining a clear understanding of the various strategies—both behavioral and possibly medical—that are and have been implemented is important. Providing parents with homework assignments regarding collecting data on the frequency, duration, and intensity of sleep difficulties is prudent.

Having the parents complete *standardized questionnaires* is often useful. Normed behavior rating scales may prove to be very valuable, both in regard to concerns with sleep but also relating to other co-occurring behavioral difficulties that may be contributing to the child's sleep problems. These typically include questionnaires that allow parents to document a child's behavior during bedtime as well as the child's sleep behavior, which includes questions pertaining to the child's quality of sleep as well as frequency of awakenings, restlessness, and so on. The surveys also include information pertaining to the nature and

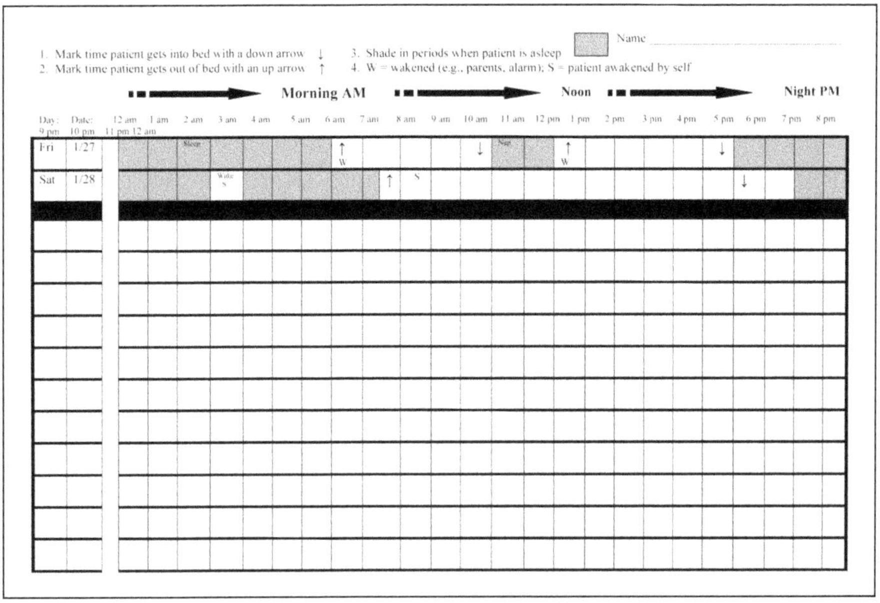

Figure 11.1 Two-week sleep record.

frequency of nighttime awakenings, the child's routine for waking up in the morning, as well as the nature of any daytime sleepiness.

Sleep diary data are critical to effective assessment and diagnosis, treatment-intervention planning, and treatment evaluation. Having parents complete a sleep diary is an essential component of any assessment. There are a variety of sleep diaries available. Probably the most commonly used sleep diary was provided by Ferber (1985; see Figure 11.1). A sleep diary allows parents to shade in those hours that their child is sleeping and to leave blank those times when the child awakens in the middle of the night and the periods of time the child is awake during the day. It also allows parents an opportunity to indicate the time that the child was put to bed. These data allow clinicians to assess the duration of sleep-onset latency, average total sleep time, total nighttime sleep, total daytime sleep, frequency, duration, and timing of nighttime awakenings, and sleep schedule. Thus, the structured interview allows for the clinician to not only gather thorough information about the problem but also develop hypotheses about those factors that may be initiating or maintaining the sleep difficulty.

TREATMENT

The range of treatments available for sleep problems is broad and ranges from dietary interventions to medical to behavioral interventions. Medical interventions include medication to aid in sleep onset or manage neurologically based sleep disorders, such as restless leg syndrome, narcolepsy, and periodic leg movement disorder; medical procedures (e.g., tonsillectomy, adenoidectomy) to address obstructive sleep apnea; and medical equipment, such as continuous positive air pressure (CPAP) machines for central sleep apnea. More detailed descriptions of pharmacologic treatment of sleep disorders are available (e.g., Dahl, 1992; Reed & Findling, 2002) as well as pediatric prescribing practices (e.g., Owens, Rosen, & Mindell, 2003; Schnoes, Kuhn, Workman, & Ellis, 2005). Given the nature and scope of this text, we will focus on the commonly employed behavioral interventions that are typically used to treat sleep problems in children.

Treatment Essentials

Treatment protocols for sleep disorders often combine several components in an effort to address identified contributing factors and to facilitate the efficiency of the treatment response (Mindell, 1999). Friman (2005) outlines a wide range of strategies that parents find useful for employing sleep essentials with their children. Strategies are combined to treat the central disorder and establish setting events that increase the likelihood of a positive response. There are a set of sleep intervention components that are fundamental to treating sleep disorders. These components address sleep hygiene, stimulus control, and sleep restriction. Children who present with sleep disturbance are often sleep deprived and/or the quality of their sleep is compromised. By attending to sleep hygiene, stimulus-control, and sleep-restriction, clinicians aid children and parents in achieving optimal sleep time and quality. For some disorders (e.g., parasomnias), increased total sleep time and enhanced sleep quality are recommended (Kuhn, 2001). By addressing these fundamental sleep components, clinicians also provide practical information of lifelong utility to parents and children alike. Central to diagnosing and treating sleep disorders is the monitoring of sleep patterns through methods such as a sleep diary.

Sleep hygiene refers to bedtime routines, sleep/wake schedules, dietary and exercise habits. Clinicians must ensure that sleep hygiene is addressed with children and adolescents who present with sleep disorders. Establishing a consistent bedtime routine and sleep/wake schedule promote efficient sleep onset and sufficient total sleep time. Bedtime routines should be initiated approximately 30 minutes before bedtime and include quiet relaxing activities like reading, bathing, and snuggling. It is important that consistent bedtime and morning wake time are established without significant variation on weekends. Limiting caffeine intake and vigorous exercise within 2 hours of bedtime will also facilitate falling asleep more readily.

Stimulus control refers to controlling what one does in bed. It is not uncommon for children and adolescents to engage in various activities (e.g., reading, watching TV, completing homework, etc.) from the comfort of their beds. The problem with these behaviors is related to the fact that falling asleep is a learned behavior. When children and adolescents engage in behaviors other than sleep while in bed, they learn to associate other activities besides sleep with being in bed (Durand, Mindell, Mapstone, & Gernert-Dott, 1998; Meltzer & Mindell, 2004) and experience increased sleep problems (Fehlings, Weiss, & Stephens, 2001; Owens et al., 1999). Stimulus control is about associating the bed as a stimulus for sleep. Therefore, treatment for sleep disorders must focus on limiting activities in bed to sleep. Ideally, TVs and computers would be removed from bedrooms to facilitate stimulus control and the bed being associated with sleeping. However, encouraging youth to sit anywhere but in their bed to watch TV or engage in any other activity while in their bedrooms may be a reasonable compromise. For youth who struggle with insomnia, the treatment protocol should include instructions to get out of bed if not asleep within 30 minutes. Once out of bed, the youth should read or draw (no TV or computer) until s/he feels sleepy. Upon feeling sleepy, the youth returns to bed. This procedure is repeated until the youth falls asleep within 30 minutes. For younger children, the time out of bed is predetermined and the parents are instructed to keep the child awake. This procedure is also known as faded bedtime with response cost (Ashbaugh & Peck, 1998; Piazza & Fisher, 1991). In addition to managing stimulus control, this procedure results in decreased negative interactions at bedtime between parents and young children (Adams & Rickert, 1989). As ready sleep onset is established, the bedtime is gradually moved to an earlier time to achieve optimal total sleep time as described under the topic of sleep restriction presented next.

Another aspect of stimulus control is related to the events children associate with falling asleep (i.e., what conditions must be present for the child to fall asleep). When external stimuli (e.g., parent, TV, music, light, etc.) must be present for the child to fall asleep, the child is likely exhibiting a sleep-onset association disorder. It is often recommended that a transitional object (e.g., blanket, stuffed animal) be introduced into the child's bedtime and napping routines (Ferber, 2006; Friman, 2005). The ultimate outcome is for the transitional object to acquire soothing or comforting properties for the child. The object becomes the sleep-onset association object and a stimulus for sleep. Pairing the identified object with holding, rocking, nurturing activities throughout the day will facilitate its acquisition of comforting properties for the child. Ultimately the transitional object replaces the maladaptive conditions previously required for sleep onset.

The child's sleep environment is another aspect of stimulus control. Providing a quiet environment not only around bedtime, but also well before bedtime is also likely to be helpful to most children. This includes eliminating access to high-action television shows, movies, and video games at least 60 to 90 minutes before bedtime. Keeping the house quiet and eliminating noisy distractions also makes logical sense. A quiet dark bedroom is recommended. If noise is preferred, white noise will enhance sleep over other types of noise like radios, movies, or CDs. White noise has been found to facilitate sleep onset and maintenance in infants, toddlers, and preschoolers (Borkowski, Hunter, & Johnson, 2001). A general rule concerning lighting is that if there is enough light to read a book by there is too much light. Light interferes with the body's natural response of producing melatonin when the environment becomes dark.

Sleep restriction facilitates a positive treatment response to intervention protocols for sleep disorders. Sleep restriction is about limiting the amount of time a child or adolescent spends in bed and napping to establish a high probability that he or she will fall asleep readily on getting into bed. Being tired is one of the three critical components identified by Christophersen (1998) as necessary for a child to be able to fall asleep at night. Sleep restriction limits total sleep time as well as time in bed. Sleep restriction is most commonly achieved by establishing a bedtime that takes into consideration actual time of sleep onset and morning wake time. The child's bedtime is pushed to a later time initially and parents withhold allowing the child to sleep later in the morning. This strategy increases the likelihood the child will fall asleep readily and squeezes his or her total sleep time, preventing make-up sleep in the morning. Initially the child achieves less than the recommended total sleep time. Restricting sleep achieves several effects. First, the youth gains experience and begins to establish a learning history of getting into bed and falling asleep readily, reducing bedtime refusal. Second, a child who is tired is naturally going to be more cooperative with the usual bedtime routine, thereby reducing disruptive behavior. Third, the youth is not catching up on sleep at other times of the day, thereby increasing sleepiness at the scheduled bedtime. Finally, sleepiness at bedtime decreases the duration of time that other sleep intervention strategies are needed, thereby reducing the demand on parents implementing additional strategies. Once ready, sleep onset is established (i.e., falling asleep within 20 minutes for 3 consecutive nights) and the bedtime is moved 15 minutes earlier. This procedure is followed until bedtime coincides with the child's usual bedtime. It may be necessary to educate parents about sleep–wake schedules and time in bed. If parents are striving for a schedule that results in the child being in bed for 12 hours and the child needs 10 hours of sleep, education on this issue will be necessary. Parents will need to evaluate their expectations and adjust them to meet the needs of their child.

Chronotherapy, another variation on sleep restriction, is an effective strategy for treating sleep-phase delay (Czeisler et al., 1981). Chronotherapy involves establishing a sleep–wake schedule based on the youth's current sleep-onset schedule. The youth's schedule is established based on 8 hours of sleep. Each subsequent night the youth's sleep-onset time is moved forward 3 hours (3 AM the first night, 6 AM the second, 9 AM the third, etc.) with the scheduled wake-up time 8 hours later. When implementing chronotherapy, it is important to ensure the youth does not nap during his or her 19-hour wake period and the bedtime routine is initiated prior to the scheduled sleep-onset time.

Treatment Protocols

In addition to the treatment essentials just described, there are several evidence-based protocols that are commonly used in the treatment of sleep disorders. The efficacy status of a variety of behavioral interventions for pediatric sleep disorders has been described (Kuhn & Elliott, 2003; Mindell, 1999; Mindell et al., 2006). Clinicians must consider the type of and function of the sleep disorder in establishing the treatment protocol. Children who are able to fall asleep independently after an extended sleep-onset latency require a different treatment approach than children who present with a sleep-onset association disorder. Components of the treatment essentials along with the treatment protocols must also be individualized to meet the needs and preferences of the child and parents.

Extinction is an effective intervention strategy (Kuhn & Elliott, 2003; Mindell, 1999; Mindell et al., 2006; Ramchandani, Wiggs, Webb, & Stores, 2000) that is typically referred to in the media of self-help books as the "cry it out approach." This strategy requires that parents ignore their child's crying, tantrums, whining, and so forth, from the time the child is put to bed until a designated time in the morning. Parents are expected to monitor for any illness, injury, and so forth, but for the most part are expected to ignore their child's negative behavior. The biggest challenge with this approach is the lack of parental consistency. It is extremely difficult for parents to ignore their child's crying, screaming, and so on from the onset of bedtime until the next morning. Parents who intervene after their children have been crying for a significant amount of time simply teach children to cry longer the next time. This standard extinction approach has been modified on some occasions by having parents present, but ignoring the child. Some parents find it more acceptable to be in the room so that they can monitor their child while ignoring the child's crying, screaming, and so forth. The parent's presence, with this type of intervention, usually leads to more intense and prolonged crying and pleading by the child. Because of the challenges associated with a standard extinction type process, the development of a graduated extinction (sometimes known as the Ferber Approach) was developed.

The *quick check* is an alternative to extinction. The quick check approach allows parents to briefly check on their crying child at predetermined intervals of time. The check is to ensure the child is not ill, hurt, or in danger. Parents are instructed to limit physical contact and verbal interaction while quickly inspecting their child's condition. The time between checks is determined with the parents and based on how long they are comfortable allowing their child to cry before conducting a visual inspection of the child. The object of the quick-check method is for the child to fall asleep independently when the parent is out of the room.

Graduated extinction is essentially identical to the quick-check method with the exception of the time between checks. Parents are instructed to ignore their child's crying and tantrums for specific periods of time. They are then allowed to check on their child, providing a minimal amount of interaction and contact. The interval between check-ins is gradually increased to a certain point. For example, parents might first check on their child after 5 minutes, then 10 minutes, and then every 15 minutes thereafter. The length of time between check-ins is established with the parents and is dependent on their comfort with ignoring the child's crying. This technique was first described by Van Houten and Rolider (1984) and by Ferber (1985). This technique limits parental contact while gradually extending the time between check-ins to allow the child to use his or her natural self-soothing skills to eventually fall asleep. This technique also allows parents to periodically check on their child, but to do so in a systematic and scheduled way. Although some might argue that the frequent check-ins will only serve to reinforce a child's crying and tantrums, the combination of very minimal verbal and/or physical contact on the part of the parent and gradually increasing the length of time between check-ins is often an effective combination to help facilitate children's sleep (Kuhn & Elliott, 2003; Mindell, 1999; Mindell et al., 2006).

The *Bedtime Pass* is a viable and effective strategy to employ for children who present with bedtime struggles but ultimately fall asleep independently (Freeman, 2006; Friman et al., 1999; Moore, Friman, Fruzzetti, & MacAleese, 2007). In practice, the child is encouraged to select or make an object to be designated as his or her bedtime pass. The pass is then "worth" one opportunity to come out of the bedroom after bedtime. Once the child uses the pass, no further opportunities to call out or come out are available and any attempts to do so are ignored by the parents. Research indicates the pass is highly effective. Children frequently fall asleep before using their pass. As a result limited disruptive behavior is exhibited at bedtime. One variation to this procedure is to identify with the child an incentive to be earned by not using the pass and simply remaining in bed at bedtime. Pairing the bedtime pass with the components described under treatment essentials facilitates a positive treatment response.

The *excuse me drill* is a protocol that has been useful in teaching children to fall asleep independently (Kuhn, Floress, & Newcomb, 2008). This protocol involves providing parental presence at bedtime. The parent may interact with the child (e.g., stroke his or her back, praise sleep-compatible behaviors) while sitting or lying next to the child. The excuse me drill involves the parent saying something like, "Excuse me, I need to check on something. I'll be right back." The parent then steps away from the child, returning to the child's bedside before the child engages in disruptive behavior. The procedure is repeated multiple times, with gradually increased duration of time away from the child's bedside. The parent is instructed to start with a very short (2 to 3 seconds) time away from the child and to return before the child is likely to call out or come out of the bedroom. On returning, the parent praises sleep-compatible behavior (lying still, eyes closed, quiet, etc.). If the child becomes disruptive, the parent is instructed to remain out of the bedroom and ignore the disruptive behavior and return only after the child quiets again. The excuse me drill is designed to facilitate the child falling asleep while the parent is absent from the room or, in other words, independently.

Motivation-based strategies are also of use in treating sleep disturbance. In developing and implementing a motivation-based strategy, the clinician works with the parent and child to assess current functioning around bedtime and sleep. This baseline data is used to establish goals and expectations for improved functioning. The clinician also identifies with the parents and child preferred and feasible reinforcers for achieving goals and meeting expectations. A reinforcement schedule is established and parents are encouraged to adhere to the plan. Such approaches seek to educate the child about acceptable bedtime and sleep behavior and the parents on the importance of contingent responding to positive and problematic bedtime and sleep-related behavior. Such approaches may be appropriate for addressing sleep disorders that include resistive behavior at bedtime as well as increasing adherence to recommended interventions such as CPAP. A packaged protocol exemplifying a motivation-based strategy is the Sleep Fairy (Peterson & Peterson, 2003). The Sleep Fairy protocol combines a social story with positive reinforcement to treat bedtime resistance and night waking (Burke, Kuhn, & Peterson, 2004).

Scheduled Awakenings

Some children present with spontaneous awakenings throughout the night. In these circumstances, parents are often asked to record the frequency and timing of the awakenings. If a pattern is established, parents are then asked to awaken their child 10 to 15 minutes before a typical spontaneous awakening, that is, creating a scheduled awakening. The child is awakened, soothed and comforted, and helped back to sleep with the least amount of interaction on the part of the parent. This prevents the child from awakening spontaneously and then crying, having a tantrum, and so forth, which eventually will require intervention on the part of the parent. If the scheduled awakenings are effective, they are gradually faded, with longer periods of time occurring between the awakenings, thus lengthening the amount of time the child is sleeping without parental intervention. Scheduled awakening has been determined to be probably efficacious (Kuhn & Elliott, 2003; Mindell, 1999; Mindell et al., 2006).

Factors Associated With Poor Treatment Response

Although sleep disturbances are amenable to effective treatment, there are a variety of factors associated with a poor treatment response. This section describes such potential barriers to treatment response. This discussion is organized in terms of barriers associated with the treatment protocol, parents, and the child. Clinicians and researchers alike are encouraged to be well informed regarding potential barriers in an effort to prevent interference with treatment response.

Treatment Protocol Factors

As was apparent in the previous section, treatment of sleep disorders involves establishing a comprehensive and thorough treatment protocol. Establishing an effective treatment protocol is central to successful resolution of sleep disturbance. Fundamental to an effective treatment protocol are intervention strategies that have been proven to work (Mindell, 1999). The effectiveness of a particular intervention strategy is likely related to the function or etiology of the sleep disturbance (Brophy, 2000; Mindell, 1999). It is important to ascertain why a child has difficulty falling asleep. Possible explanations for delayed sleep onset include an inability to fall asleep independently, securing reinforcing attention by resisting bedtime, or a delayed circadian rhythm. Each of these explanations indicates unique treatment strategies that if overlooked or misapplied would likely fail to produce the desired results. Another potential barrier is an incomplete treatment protocol. It is necessary to attend to all of the factors associated with a sleep disorder as well as those associated with its treatment.

Parent and Child Factors

Treatment *feasibility* is critical to effective implementation of sleep-disturbance intervention protocols. Treatment feasibility has been defined as encompassing acceptance and compliance (Chambless & Hollon, 1998) and is considered relevant to sleep disturbance (Mindell, 1999). In establishing a treatment protocol for children it is critical to enlist parent and child (depending on age) participation in the development process to minimize the likelihood that a component of the protocol is unacceptable. That is, it is essential to develop a protocol parents support and view feasible. If a toddler presents with a sleep-onset association disorder, one component of the treatment protocol must address how to teach the child to fall asleep independently. One strategy for doing so is the "cry it out" or extinction method. However, this approach is the least favored approach by parents (Kuhn & Elliot, 2003; Rickert & Johnson, 1988). Including this strategy for parents who cannot stand to hear their child cry will likely undermine the whole protocol. Feasibility may also come into play in multiple other contexts: establishing a later bedtime when the parents' schedule requires a very early (4 AM) wake-up for work; lack of funds or insurance when medical supplies/services are needed; getting a teenager whose day is scheduled with school, activities, and work, not to mention homework, to go to bed earlier.

Ensuring that children and parents *understand* the treatment protocol is also essential to effective treatment. Discussing strategy options, explaining them briefly, and outlining the protocol in detail will facilitate increased understanding. For example, it is important for parents to understand when and how to move the bedtime when sleep-restriction strategies are employed and during chronotherapy. Written instructions alone were found to be as effective as instructions delivered with additional therapist support in a study examining the efficacy of multicomponent treatment programs (Seymour, Brock, During, & Poole, 1989).

Child and parent *motivation*, or lack thereof, is a factor in treatment response. The characteristics of a sleep disorder a child presents with are maintained or reinforced by contingencies in place. For parents, negative reinforcement may be a factor. Parents are eager for their children to fall asleep. And they will go to great lengths to help their children do so. If the child cries or is disruptive at bedtime, parents find ways to seek relief from the crying and/or disruption. They may find they are able to relieve their child's crying and their own discomfort by rocking, feeding, or lying with the child. Putting a protocol in place that includes letting the child cry or call out may be difficult for parents to resist in established behavior that has historically eliminated these behaviors and served as an escape for the parents. It is important to reassure parents that negatively reinforcing problem behaviors at bedtime may work to alleviate their discomfort over the short term, however, in the long term, sleep disorders develop. Helping parents develop strategies for coping with their child's behavior as the sleep protocol is implemented is important. Cognitive-behavioral therapy (CBT) strategies like cognitive restructuring and self-talk are useful.

The very parental responses just described potentially serve as positive reinforcement for the child. When children who resist bedtime received additional attention, positive or negative, delay their bedtime, or obtain parental presence, these responses inadvertently serve to positively reinforce their problem behaviors. Developing strategies that will reduce the problem behaviors and simultaneously increase alternative positive behaviors is necessary. Parents are encouraged to reinforce sleep-compatible behaviors (e.g., lying still, being quiet, eyes closed, in bed) as well as cooperative behaviors at bedtime (e.g., engaging in the routine readily, following the schedule). Reinforcers might include verbal praise, physical touch, and prizes for young children and additional privileges, tokens, prizes for older children. Developing strategies that positively reinforce both parent and child behaviors consistent with implementing the recommended sleep protocol will enhance their motivation to implement the protocol with integrity. In time, ready, independent sleep onset by the child will serve as a positive reinforcer for parents. And children will learn that positive bedtime behavior is positively reinforced, whereas problem bedtime behavior is not.

Motivation is a critical factor for youth whose treatment requires use of CPAP. Research has shown the number-one barrier to CPAP effectiveness is use of the CPAP (Speer & Fayle 1997). That is, CPAP is very effective when individuals use it. However, individuals are reluctant to use CPAP for a variety of reasons, including discomfort of the mask, dry airways, strength of airflow, and noise. When these issues are barriers to CPAP use, youth fail to experience the benefits, thereby decreasing the likelihood that they will use it. Individuals who are reluctant and use the CPAP irregularly early on are much less likely to use it over time. Those individuals who get used to it gradually and work to titrate oxygen flow and humidity proactively are more likely to experience the benefits of the CPAP and use it consistently. Incorporating CBT strategies to increase motivation and willingness to use the CPAP is helpful.

The absence of parental *instructional control* is another factor that may lead to poor treatment response. Getting ready for bed, going to bed, and falling asleep are groups of behaviors that can be conceptualized as numerous individual commands. Parents who lack instructional control of the children, that is, their children fail to comply with the majority of instructions or commands throughout the day, may face increased challenges with obtaining compliance at bedtime. If lack of instructional control is a factor, it may be necessary to address and increase daytime compliance before focusing on bedtime problems. CBT strategies are useful in facilitating the parents' development of instructional control. Helping parents develop a personal sense of effectiveness will facilitate the establishment of bedtime expectations that parents will enforce.

A child who lacks *self-quieting skills* may have a poor response to treatment. Christophersen (1998) identified that being relaxed is critical for a child to be able to fall asleep. Finally, helping a child to relax requires that the child possess good self-quieting skills. Parents can promote children's self-quieting skills during naptime as well as during other times of the day when they have experienced some type of mild upset. Children who are dependent on their parents to help them fall asleep either by lying with them, rocking them, and so forth are not developing the type of self-quieting skills that another child might be developing through thumb-sucking, holding a favorite blanket, and so forth. Christophersen and Mortweet (2001) promote the use of self-quieting skills during the day to help address sleep problems at night.

This is especially effective for young children, especially those who are still napping. Many of the disruptive behaviors that occur during the night also occur for children during the day, especially when napping. By promoting self-quieting skills both at naptime and during other situations during the day, parents can help to promote similar types of self-quieting skills that are necessary for nighttime sleep.

Teaching children who are late-elementary-school age and older *relaxation strategies* may be useful. Combining a muscle relaxation strategy with mental imagery often helps to address both the behavioral and cognitive factors that sometimes affect sleep. Progressive muscle relaxation typically involves teaching children to systematically tighten and release individual muscle groups, starting with their feet and gradually working toward the neck and face. After completing progressive muscle relaxation, children are asked to imagine themselves in a relaxing event or location, either real or imagined. Some children prefer to imagine being a character in a favorite book or movie. The image is paired with the relaxed state to provide both a state of relaxation and cognitive redirection. This is especially helpful for those children and adolescents who focus on sounds in the house, review the day's events, or worry about upcoming events, causing them to delay sleep onset. Children are typically asked to practice this technique two or three times each night. Having parents practice this with them can also be helpful.

Medical problems among infants may influence parental support of sleep-disturbance interventions. It is not uncommon for parents to seek medical reasons, like gastroesophageal reflux, for an infant's frequent crying and night waking. It may be difficult for parents to discriminate the source of their child's sleep problem when the child has a medical condition or history of medical concerns (Ferber, 2006). Parents become accustomed to responding quickly to prevent pain, suffering, or even death. Treating sleep disturbance may involve allowing the child to be distressed for an extended period of time. As mentioned earlier, presenting parents with all available options, explaining the purpose of each sleep-intervention component, and enlisting the parents' endorsement of each component will increase the likelihood that they will implement the protocol with fidelity.

Co-occurring mental health problems may influence treatment adherence to sleep-disturbance interventions (Dahl et al., 1996; Ferber, 2006). Differentiating whether sleep disturbance is a symptom of a mental health problem (e.g., hypersomnia or insomnia associated with depression), is caused by a mental health problem (e.g., insomnia resulting from rumination associated with anxiety), or may lead to mental health problems (e.g., sleep deprivation in a young child resulting in hyperactivity) can be difficult. Although it may be helpful to define the relationship between sleep disturbance and mental health problems, doing so is not critical to establishing effective treatment protocols. In situations where co-occurring sleep disturbance and daytime mood and behavior problems exist, recommending treatment of both problems is considered best practice (Morgenthaler et al., 2006). For example, for a youth suffering from posttraumatic stress disorder and insomnia, treating both disorders is recommended, as treating one will not necessarily resolve the other (Bootzin & Chambers, 1990; Dahl, 1992). For young children who exhibit sleep disturbance at bedtime (e.g., sleep-onset association disorder, sleep terrors) and a disruptive behavior disorder, it may be more efficient, if not necessary, to achieve a treatment effect for daytime behavior through parent management training (Richman, Douglas, Hunt, Lansdown, & Kevere, 1985) before addressing bedtime struggles. Doing so increases the likelihood that parents will be able to implement a sleep-intervention protocol with increased fidelity and the child will be more responsive to parental management at bedtime.

CASE PRESENTATION

Tyler was a 15-year-old Caucasian male who lived with his birth parents in a small rural Midwestern community. Tyler and his parents presented to the sleep clinic because of Tyler's sleep problems and school absences. Tyler's medical history was unremarkable. His grades at treatment presentation were failing and represented a decline in his academic performance relative to previous years. In addition to frequent absences, his poor grades were attributed to Tyler's failure to complete assignments. Tyler reported he did not like school and often slept in his classes. Tyler reported having meaningful friendships and seeing his friends as the only positive aspect of attending school. Although Tyler reported playing sports in middle school and during his 9th-grade year, he no longer participated in extracurricular activities.

Tyler's parents reported that he was resistant to chores and frequently noncompliant with instructions. He also failed to follow family rules and expectations related to accessing privileges (e.g., watching TV or playing video games after bedtime). Tyler's late sleep onset was interfering with getting up in the morning and subsequently getting to school on time. Tyler's parents concluded during the clinical evaluation that the onset of Tyler's sleep problems coincided with his bedroom being moved to the basement in the family's home. Previously, his bedroom was on the second story along with his parents' and siblings' bedrooms. Tyler's room was moved to the basement to provide him and his brothers with their own bedrooms. Tyler's bedroom in the basement was next to the family/recreation room where a television and computer and video gaming systems were located. Tyler also had a TV and video gaming system in his bedroom. Tyler further shared that he consumed his favorite high-caffeine soda as late as midnight.

Baseline sleep diary data and the clinical interview revealed Tyler met diagnostic criteria for Delayed Sleep Phase. His bedtime was 10:30 PM, yet his sleep onset consistently occurred at 3:00 AM. Tyler reported he was unable to fall asleep before 3:00 AM. As his bedroom was in the basement of the family home, his parents were unaware of when Tyler fell asleep. Tyler stated he watched TV or played video games when he went to bed until feeling sleepy. Tyler's morning wake up was highly variable. On the infrequent days his parents were able to wake Tyler and get him to school, he was awakened at 7:00 AM. Tyler reported that on days he attended school in the morning he slept a majority of the morning and did not feel awake until approximately 11:00 AM. During weekday mornings, Tyler refused to get out of bed and on weekends he slept until at least 11:00 AM. Tyler's Total Sleep Time averaged 5.75 hours per night, with a sleep-latency-onset average of 4.5 hours. Tyler reported this sleep–wake pattern had been in place for several months.

Chronotherapy was recommended for the sleep-phase delay. Additional recommendations related to sleep hygiene and stimulus control were also made. Tyler and his parents established 10:30 PM as the weekday bedtime goal. Removing the TV and video games from his bedroom was recommended and his parents agreed to do so. Tyler was also encouraged to eliminate caffeinated soda within 3 hours of bedtime. He resisted this recommendation. However, his parents agreed to enforce this limit. Tyler's parents were encouraged to look at their and Tyler's schedules and to select a start date for the chronotherapy. They established bedtime at 3 AM the first night. They were to move bedtime ahead 3 hours each night until Tyler's bedtime fell at 10:30 PM. Tyler and his parents were instructed to follow the schedule closely with no napping. Tyler expressed reluctance to follow the protocol while his parents expressed determination to see it through.

Follow-up revealed that Tyler resisted chronotherapy, removing the TV and video games from his room, and reducing his caffeine intake. He was noncompliant with the procedures and refused to stay awake when he was not scheduled to be sleeping. The sleep diary revealed Tyler was still sleeping primarily from 3 AM to 10 AM with intermittent naps at school or after school. Tyler admitted that he did not want to change his sleep habits as he enjoyed his nighttime recreation and missing school.

His parents acknowledged they were unable to enforce the recommendations on personal authority alone and they continued to suggest medical causes for Tyler's sleep problem. Given this, additional strategies were implemented. During the next session, CBT strategies were introduced separately to Tyler and his parents. Cognitive restructuring was used to facilitate Tyler's parents viewing themselves as effective in parenting Tyler and understanding that the source of his sleep problems were behavioral. Specific strategies to positively reinforce desired behavior were defined along with negative consequences for resisting or failing to follow the protocol. Tyler's parents elected to make time with friends and access to video games contingent on following the sleep protocol. Tyler's parents were trained in delivering positive and negative consequences contingently, matter-of-factly, and confidently.

Cognitive restructuring was also used with Tyler to address his perceptions of school and his academic abilities. Problem solving related to attendance and high school credits earned was conducted. Tyler was involved in establishing goals related to sleep and school. Time was also spent helping Tyler grasp the relationship between his actions and subsequent consequences. His ability to decide to have access to his friends and video games via his decision to follow the sleep protocol was emphasized. Tyler also participated in identifying additional reinforcers for his success.

Subsequent follow-up revealed that Tyler had established a consistent bedtime of 10:30 PM with sleep onset within 20 minutes. His total sleep time averaged 8.5 hours. He was attending school consistently and on time. He was accessing his privileges daily as a result of his improved sleep habits and school attendance. Follow-up at 6 months posttreatment indicated that Tyler continued to have appropriate sleep onset and was sleeping at least 8 hours each night. He tried to convince his parents to return his electronics to his room, but to no avail. Both Tyler and his parents reported a more positive affect and interaction with others, once Tyler's sleep hygiene improved. Tyler and his parents have continued to follow treatment recommendations related to sleep hygiene, stimulus control, and sleep schedule.

FUTURE DIRECTIONS

The importance of sleep to healthy functioning has gained increased attention over recent years. The inclusion of this chapter in this book is just one example of the increased recognition of the role of sleep in healthy human functioning. Ideally, this trend will continue and become even more pervasive. As literature on sleep-related problems advances, we are discovering just how important sleep is to physical health, mental health, cognition, and learning as well as many other bodily functions and processes. The implications of impaired sleep combined with the prevalence of sleep disorders point to the needs for education, identification, and treatment. It is clearly in our best interest to encourage and pursue continued attention to sleep in terms of research, health care training curricula, and general public health education.

Continued research investigating the efficacy of treatment protocols for sleep disturbance is needed. As new protocols are developed and implemented, research demonstrating their efficacy is essential to establishing evidence for their applicability. Determining what intervention strategies or protocols are best suited for a given etiology, type of sleep disorder, and age of the child would be useful. Examining the extent to which public health education impacts/influences sleep habits and hygiene is another area of important research. Issues related to co-occurring sleep disturbance and behavioral or mental health disorders also warrant research attention. Specific areas of research might include: What are the outcomes of treating a sleep disorder first versus a behavior disorder in young children who present with co-occurring sleep and behavioral disorders? Will successful resolution of sleep disturbance resolve disruptive daytime behavior? Continued collaboration among researchers, clinicians, and the general public will lead, we hope, to answers to these and the many questions remaining within this important area.

REFERENCES

Adams, L. A., & Rickert, V. I. (1989). Reducing bedtime tantrums: Comparison between positive routines and graduated extinction. *Pediatrics, 84,* 756–761.

American Academy of Sleep Medicine. (2005). *International classification of sleep disorders* (2nd ed.). Westchester, IL: Author.

American Psychiatric Association. (2000). *Diagnostic and statistical manual of mental disorders* (4th ed., text rev.). Washington, DC: American Psychiatric Press.

Ashbaugh, R., & Peck, S. M. (1998). Treatment of sleep problems in a toddler: A replication of the faded bedtime with response cost protocol. *Journal of Applied Behavior Analysis, 31,* 127–129.

Beebe, D. W., & Gozal, D. (2002). Obstructive sleep apnea and the prefrontal cortex. Towards a comprehensive model linking nocturnal upper airway obstruction to daytime cognitive and behavioral deficits. *Journal of Sleep Research, 11,* 1–16.

Blader, J. C., Koplewicz, H. S., Abikoll, H., & Foley, C. (1997). Sleep problems of elementary school children. *Archives of Pediatric and Adolescent Medicine, 151,* 473–480.

Bootzin, R. R., & Chambers, M. J. (1990). *Childhood sleep disorders.* New York: Plenum.

Borkowski, M. M., Hunter, K. E., & Johnson, M. (2001). White noise and scheduled bedtime routines to reduce infant and childhood sleep disturbances. *Behavior Therapist, 24,* 29–47.

Brophy, G. (2000). Social work treatment of sleep disturbance in a 5-year-old boy: A single-case evaluation. *Research on Social Work Practice, 10,* 748–758.

Burke, R. V., Kuhn, B. R., & Peterson, J. L. (2004). A "storybook" ending to children's bedtime problems—The use of a rewarding social story to reduce bedtime resistance and frequent night waking. *Journal of Pediatric Psychology, 29,* 389–396.

Carskadon, M. A. (1990). Adolescent sleepiness: Increased risk in a high-risk population. *Alcohol, Drugs and Driving, 5,* 317–328.

Chambless, D. L., & Hollon, S. D. (1998). Defining empirically supported therapies. *Journal of Consulting and Clinical Psychology, 66,* 7–18.

Christophersen, E. R. (1998). *Beyond discipline.* Shawnee Mission, KS: Overland Press.

Christophersen, E. R., & Mortweet, S. L. (2001). *Treatments that work with children: Empirically supported strategies for managing childhood problems.* Washington, DC: American Psychological Association.

Coates, T. J., & Thoreson, C. E. (1984). Sleep disturbance in children and adolescents. In E. J. Mash & L.G. Terdal (Eds.), *Behavioral assessment of childhood disorders* (pp. 639–678). New York: Guilford Press.

Crowell, J., Keener, M., Ginsburg, N., & Anders, T. (1987). Sleep habits in toddlers 18 to 36 months old. *Journal of the American Academy of Child and Adolescent Psychiatry, 26,* 510–515.

Czeisler, C. A., Richardson, G. S., Coleman, R. M., Zimmerman, J. C., Moore-Ede, M. C., Dement, W. C., et al. (1981). Chronotherapy: Resetting the circadian clocks of patients with delayed sleep phase insomnia. *Sleep, 4,* 1–21.

Dahl, R. E. (1992). The pharmacologic treatment of sleep disorders. *Psychiatric Clinics of North America, 15,* 161–178.

Dahl R. E., & Lewin, D. S. (2002). Pathways to adolescent health sleep regulation and behavior. *Journal of Adolescent Health, 31,* 175–184.

Dahl, R. E., Ryan, N. D., Natty, M. K., Birmaher, B., Al-Schabbout, M., Williamson, D. E., et al. (1996). Sleep onset abnormalities in depressed adolescents. *Biological Psychiatry, 39,* 400–410.

Dahl, R. E., Pelham, W. B., & Wierson, M. C. (1991). The role of sleep disturbance in attention deficit disorder symptomatology. *Journal of Pediatric Psychology, 16,* 229–239.

Durand, V. M., Mindell, J. A., Mapstone, E., & Gernert-Dott, P. (1998). *Sleep problems.* New York: Plenum.

Fehlings, D., Weiss, S., & Stephens, D. (2001). Frequent night awakenings in infants and preschool children referred to a sleep disorder clinic: The role of nonadaptive sleep associations. *Children's Health Care, 30,* 43–55.

Ferber, R. (2006). *Solve your child's sleep problems* (2nd ed.). New York: Simon & Schuster.

France, K. G., & Hudson, S. M. (1993). Management of infant sleep disturbance: A review. *Clinical Psychology Review, 13,* 635–647.

Freeman, K. A. (2006). Treating bedtime resistance with bedtime pass: A systematic replication and component analysis with 3-year olds. *Journal of Applied Behavior Analysis, 39,* 423–428.

Friman, P. C. (2005). *Good night, sweet dreams, I love you.* Boys Town, NE: Boys Town Press.

Friman, P. C., Hoff, K. E., Schnoes, C., Freeman, K. A., Woods, D. W., & Blum, N. (1999). The bedtime pass: An approach to bedtime crying and leaving the room. *Archives of Pediatric and Adolescent Medicine, 153,* 1027–1029.

Kateria, S., Swanson, M., & Trevarthin, C. (1987). Persistence of sleep disturbances in preschool children. *Journal of Pediatrics, 110,* 642–646.

Kuhn, B. R. (2001). Behavioral treatment of sleep disorders: Pediatric parasomnias. *Sleep Review.* Retrieved from http://www.sleepreviewmag.com/issues/articles/2001-04_02.asp

Kuhn, B. R., & Elliott, A. J. (2003). Treatment efficacy in behavioral pediatric sleep medicine. *Journal of Psychosomatic Research, 54,* 587–597.

Kuhn, B. R., Floress, M. T., & Newcomb, T. C. (2008). *Strategic attention for children's sleep-compatible behaviors: Treatment outcome and acceptability of the "excuse-me drill."* Unpublished manuscript.

Mehlenbeck, R., Spirito, A., Owens, J., & Boergers, J. (2000). The clinical presentation of childhood partial arousal parasomnias. *Sleep Medicine, 1,* 307–312.

Meltzer, L., & Mindell, J. (2004). Nonpharmacologic treatments for pediatric sleeplessness. *Pediatric Clinics of North America, 51,* 135–151.

Meltzer, L. J., & Mindell, J. A. (2006). Sleep and sleep disorders in children and adolescents. *Pediatric Clinics of North America, 29,* 1059–1076.

Minde, K. K., Faucon, A., & Falkner, S. (1994). Sleep problems in toddlers: Effects of treatment on their daytime behavior. *Journal of the American Academy of Child and Psychiatry, 33,* 1114–1121.

Mindell, J. A. (1999). Empirically supported treatments in pediatric psychology: Bedtime refusal and night wakings in young children. *Journal of Pediatric Psychology, 24,* 465–481.

Mindell, J. A., Kuhn, B., Lewin, D.S., Meltzer, L. J., & Sadeh, A. (2006). Behavioral treatment of bedtime problems and night wakings in infants and young children. *Sleep, 29,* 1263–1276.

Mindell, J. A., & Owens, J. A. (2003). *A clinical guide to pediatric sleep: Diagnosis and management of sleep problems.* Philadelphia: Lippincott, Williams & Wilkins.

Mitru, G., Millrood, D. L., & Mateika, J. H. (2002). The impact of sleep on learning and behavior in adolescents. *Teachers College Record, 104,* 704–726.

Moore, B. A., Friman, P. C., Fruzzetti, A. E., & MacAleese, K. (2007). Evaluating the bedtime pass program for child resistance to bedtime—A randomized, controlled trial. *Journal of Pediatric Psychology, 32,* 283–287.

Morgenthaler, T. I., Owens, J., Alessi, C., Boehlecke, B., Brown, T. M., Coleman, J., et al. (2006). Practice parameters for behavioral treatment of bedtime problems and night wakings in infants and young children. *Sleep, 29,* 1277–1281.

Owens, J., Maxim, R., McGuinn, M., Nobile, C., Msall, M., & Alario, A. (1999). Television-viewing habits and sleep disturbance in school children. *Pediatrics, 104,* 27–39.

Owens, J. A. (2005). Epidemiology of sleep disorders during childhood. In S. H. Sheldon, R. Ferber, & M. H. Kryger (Eds.), *Principles and practices of pediatric sleep medicine* (pp. 27–33). Philadelphia: Elsevier Saunders.

Owens, J. A., Rosen, C. L., & Mindell, J. A. (2003). Medication use in the treatment of pediatric insomnia: Results of a survey of community-based pediatricians. *Pediatrics, 111,* 628–635.

Peterson, J., & Peterson, M. (2003). *The sleep fairy.* Omaha, NE: Behave'n Kids Press.

Piazza, C. C., & Fisher, W. (1991). A faded bedtime with response cost protocol for treatment of multiple sleep problems in children. *Journal of Applied Behavior Analysis, 24,* 129–140.

Ramchandani, P., Wiggs, L., Webb, V., & Stores, G. (2000). A systematic review of treatments for settling problems and night waking in young children. *British Medical Journal, 320,* 209–212.

Reed, M. D., & Findling, R. L. (2002). Overview of current management of sleep disturbances in children: I—Pharmacotherapy. *Current Therapeutic Research, 63,* B18–B37.

Richman, N. (1981). A community survey of characteristics of one- to two-year-olds with sleep disruptions. *Journal of the American Academy of Child Psychiatry, 20,* 281–291.

Richman, N., Douglas, J., Hunt, H., Lansdown, R., & Kevere, R. (1985). Behavioural methods in the treatment of sleep disorders—A pilot study. *Journal of Child Psychological Psychiatry, 26,* 581–590.

Rickert, V. I., & Johnson, C. M. (1988). Reducing nocturnal awakening and crying episodes in infants and a comparison between scheduled awakenings and systematic ignoring. *Pediatrics, 81,* 203–212.

Ryan, N. D., Puig-Antich, J., Rabinovich, H., Robinson, D., Ambrosdini, P. J., Nelson, B., & Iyengar, S. (1987). The clinical picture of major depression in children and adolescents. *Archives of General Psychiatry, 44,* 854–861.

Schnoes, C. J., Kuhn, B. R., Workman, E. F., & Ellis, C. R. (2005). Pediatric prescribing practices for clonidine and other pharmacologic agents for children with sleep disturbance. *Clinical Pediatrics, 45,* 229–238.

Scott, G., & Richards, M. P. M. (1990). Night waking in 1-year-old children in England. *Child Care, Health and Development, 16,* 283–302.

Seymour, F. W., Brock, P., During, M., & Poole, G. (1989). Reducing sleep disruptions in young children: Evaluation of therapist-guided and written information approaches: A brief report. *Journal of Child Psychology and Psychiatry and Allied Disciplines, 30,* 913–918.

Speer, T., & Fayle, R. (1997). The effects of systematic desensitization and sensory awareness training on adherence to CPAP treatment. *Sleep Research, 26,* 216.

Van Houten, R., & Rolider, A. (1984). The use of response prevention to eliminate nocturnal thumbsucking. *Journal of Applied Behavior Analysis, 17*, 509–520.

Winkelman, J. W., Herzog, D. B., & Fava, M. (1999). The prevalence of sleep-related eating disorder in psychiatric and non-psychiatric populations. *Psychological Medicine, 29,* 1461–1466.

Wolfson, A. R., & Carskadon, M. A. (1998). Sleep schedules and daytime functioning in adolescents. *Child Development, 69*, 875–887.

PART III

Externalizing Disorders

12

Adjunctive Cognitive-Behavior Therapy for Pediatric Bipolar Disorder

JEN KOGOS YOUNGSTROM, NORAH FEENY,
ERIC A. YOUNGSTROM, TYMESHA BUCKNER, AND
CARLA KMETT DANIELSON

Bipolar spectrum disorders (BPSDs) are characterized by cycles of extreme mood swings, often including periods of both depression and mania or hypomania. BPSDs include bipolar I (BP I), bipolar II (BP II), bipolar disorder not otherwise specified (BP NOS), and cyclothymia. Until recently, very little was known about the frequency of BPSD among youth, and it was rarely diagnosed in this population. Although still scant, the available data suggest that the prevalence of BPSD is likely to be similar in adolescents as in adults, and somewhat lower in children (see Youngstrom, 2007, for review).

In adults, BPSDs are typically recurrent (70 to 90%; Goodwin & Jamison, 1990; Kessing, Andersen, Mortensen, & Bolwig, 1998) and cause impairment across a wide range of areas, including marital, parental, occupational, and possibly neuropsychological functioning (Zarate, Tohen, Land, & Cavanagh, 2000). For children, the impact of BPSD can be even more severe, as the disorder may interfere with success in the classroom and mastery of important developmental tasks, such as emotion regulation and establishment of social relationships (Nottelmann & Jensen, 1995). Moreover, such difficulties in forming interpersonal relationships and becoming self-sufficient can significantly increase the risk for suicide (Craddock & Jones, 1999). The rate of completed suicide for individuals with BP I is 30 times that of the normal population. In fact, 19% of individuals with BP I die from suicide (Isometsa, 1993). Given these factors, BPSD has been ranked as the sixth most debilitating disorder across physical and psychiatric disorders (Lopez, Mathers, Ezzati, Jamison, & Murray, 2006).

LIMITED EMPIRICALLY SUPPORTED TREATMENTS AVAILABLE FOR PEDIATRIC BIPOLAR DISORDER

Given the severity and chronicity of BPSD, along with its impact on families and society, it is imperative that empirically validated interventions become available for youth diagnosed with these mood disorders. Although significant research has been dedicated to developing and evaluating treatments for adult bipolar disorder, interventions for pediatric BPSD have only begun to emerge in the literature over the past decade. There is consensus in the field that combined psychopharmacological and psychosocial interventions are optimal for treatment of adults with BPSD (American Psychiatric Association, 1994; Wilkinson, Taylor, & Holt, 2002), and pharmacological intervention with some adjunctive psychosocial treatment is optimal for children and adolescents with BPSD (Carlson et al., 2003; Kowatch et al., 2005).

As of the beginning of 2008, three medications have Food and Drug Administration (FDA) approval for the acute treatment of mania in adolescence and late childhood. Lithium has been "grandfathered" approval based on the extensive data available in adults. In addition, a large, double-blind randomized controlled trial (RCT) will soon be published comparing lithium to divalproex and placebo (Kowatch, Findling, Scheffer, & Stanton, 2007) further supporting the potential utility of lithium for youth populations. Risperdal has FDA approval based on efficacy from two large but unpublished, randomized controlled trials. Similarly, aripiprazole has FDA approval based on two large but as yet unpublished RCTs. For the moment, all other medication trials examining the efficacy of pharmacological interventions for pediatric BPSD are open-label studies. Many of these open-label trials have shown promising results. However, effect sizes from open studies are often much larger than the effect sizes yielded from RCTs (Straus, Richardson, Glasziou, & Haynes, 2005). When determining the efficacy of medications, RCTs conducted specifically with pediatric populations are crucial for three additional reasons: (a) metabolic differences in children versus adults can markedly change pharmacokinetics, also affecting a medication's efficacy and safety; (b) there are several examples of medications that are efficacious in adults but not children, and vice versa; and (c) it is unclear whether childhood onset of BPSD may reflect a different subtype or a different course of illness. Studies examining long-term medication maintenance (i.e., the ability to continue the consistent use of a medication regimen over an extended period of time) also are sorely needed to address questions such as the long-term risks and benefits of specific pharmacological treatments. Available evidence suggests that medication maintenance among individuals suffering from BPSD is a serious challenge, and relapse is a common outcome (Birmaher et al., 2006; Findling et al., 2005; Geller, Tillman, Craney, & Bolhofner, 2004). Maintenance may prove to be a vital niche for psychotherapeutic interventions (DelBello, Hanseman, Adler, Fleck, & Strakowski, 2007). A more extensive review of the medication evidence base is available (Kowatch et al., 2005).

Given the aforementioned challenges with research and maintenance of pharmacological interventions for individuals with BPSD, adjunctive psychosocial interventions, to be used in combination with medication, have been highlighted as an important component of comprehensive treatment for this population. Specifically, recent evidence for adjunctive psychosocial interventions looks promising in a variety of domains for adults with BPSD. Intensive psychotherapy (cognitive-behavior therapy [CBT], family-focused treatment, or interpersonal and social rhythm therapy) compared with collaborative, psychoeducational care for adults with BP I or BP II improved total functioning, relationship functioning, and life satisfaction in a sample of 152 outpatients (Miklowitz et al., 2007). In a review of RCTs examining psychosocial interventions for BPSD, Gutierrez and Scott (2004) reported that medication adherence, improved attitudes about treatment, decreased hospitalizations and relapses, and improved well-being and family functioning are all factors related to positive outcomes for adjunctive psychotherapy with adults with BPSD.

The severity of BPSD symptoms and outcomes and the promising outcomes associated with adjunctive psychosocial interventions with adults (e.g., Basco & Rush, 1996; Miklowitz, Frank, & George, 1996) have led to a demand for adjunctive psychosocial interventions for youth by clinicians, researchers, and families living with BPSD. However, to date, empirically supported psychosocial intervention for pediatric BPSD populations has been limited to multifamily psychoeducation groups for mood disorders (Fristad, Goldberg-Arnold, & Gavazzi, 2002; Lofthouse & Fristad, 2004). The results for the multifamily psychoeducation groups have been promising and provide a strong foundation for the utility of adjunctive psychosocial therapies for youth with BPSD. However, given that a group-therapy format is not likely amenable to all families or clinical settings, there is a clear need for evaluation of psychotherapies that could be delivered in an individual format as well. No RCTs examining the efficacy of individually administered psychosocial interventions for pediatric BPSD are published, although several projects are currently under way. Miklowitz and colleagues (2004) are currently examining family-focused treatment for adolescents based on their work with family-focused treatment for adults with BPSD. Also, a recent open trial of dialectical behavior therapy for adolescents with BPSD demonstrated feasibility and acceptability (Goldstein, Axelson, Birmaher, & Brent, 2007). At present, these psychotherapies have demonstrated tolerability and promising results in open trials, but it is unclear whether these interventions are superior to treatment as usual.

Cognitive-behavioral interventions have been shown to be effective in adults with BPSD in individual (Cochran, 1984; Lam et al., 2000) and group therapy format (e.g., Patelis-Siotis et al., 2001). The best candidates for CBT therapies appear to be those with relatively fewer episodes and in whom the effects of treatments are more marked on the depressive than manic symptoms. As noted previously, despite promising efficacy findings in adults, no RCTs have been published to date comparing the utility of CBT as an adjunctive intervention for youth with BPSD versus alternative conditions (e.g., other types of psychosocial interventions or no adjunctive intervention). Feeny, Danielson, Schwartz, Youngstrom, and Findling (2006) have conducted a pilot efficacy trial based on a CBT-based manual they developed (Danielson, Feeny, Findling, & Youngstrom, 2004; described in detail later in this chapter), demonstrating symptom reduction and good compliance in a small, open trial. In addition, Pavuluri and colleagues (2004) have developed a CBT manual that has demonstrated promising results with a pediatric BPSD population.

The majority of the research for unipolar depression has found CBT to be efficacious in adolescents (Asarnow, Jaycox, & Tompson, 2001; Birmaher, Ryan, Williamson, Brent, & Kaufman, 1996; Curry, 2001; Reinecke, Ryan, & Dubois, 1998; TADS, 2007; Weisz, McCarty, & Valeri, 2006). Despite the promising findings of psychosocial interventions for the treatment of unipolar depression, these treatments may not be sufficient for the treatment of BPSD because these disorders involve symptoms and other factors that are different from unipolar depression, such as hypomanic, manic, and mixed states. For example, an intervention targeted at treating BPSD in youth would require sessions/modules that addressed education regarding how to recognize manic episodes, the importance of medication compliance, and the substantial potential for substance abuse (Wilens et al., 2008).

A case study (Danielson et al., 2004) and a small efficacy trial with manualized CBT for youth showed that CBT as an adjunct to pharmacological treatment was feasible and associated with reductions in both manic and depressive symptoms in adolescents with bipolar spectrum disorders, including bipolar I, bipolar II, cyclothymia, and bipolar not otherwise specified (Feeny et al., 2006). Another group has found benefits for a psychosocial treatment involving CBT components in an open maintenance study (West, Henry, & Pavluri, 2007). Thus, the preliminary evidence supports that psychosocial interventions using CBT could be useful in the adjunctive treatment of mood disorders in youth.

At the time of this writing, the authors are in the midst of an effectiveness trial funded by the Ohio Department of Mental Health examining CBT versus treatment as usual for bipolar youth ages 7 through 18 years conducted at a large community mental health facility. The effectiveness trial of CBT treatment is based on the treatment manual successfully used in the Feeny et al. (2006) study and will be described in detail in the next section. Similarly, much of our experience with the refractory cases and thoughts about adaptations to the manual are based on our experience in this ongoing effectiveness trial with much diversity, comorbidity, family stressors, and low socioeconomic status in our sample.

It is an unusual decision to move directly from open trials and a small efficacy trial to an effectiveness study. However, there is a growing demand that research show the effectiveness and utility of empirically validated treatments in more typical, "real world" patients (Norquist,

Leibowitz, & Hyman, 1999). Indeed, the field of treatment outcome research has begun to expand its focus to examine whether interventions with demonstrated efficacy can affect meaningful outcomes, for "typical" patients, assessing a broader range of posttreatment outcomes, including functioning, disability, and quality of life (Street, Niederehe, & Lebowitz, 2000). In spite of the importance of establishing the external validity of treatments, most studies have been primarily concerned with the internal validity of their results (i.e., efficacy studies). Experts have called for research that examines the external validity of such empirically supported treatments (i.e., effectiveness research; Barlow, 1996; Howard, Moras, Brill, Martinovich, & Lutz, 1996; Seligman, 1995). There is an especially pronounced lack of effectiveness research in child settings (Hoagwood, Hibbs, Brent, & Jensen, 1995). Although significant research has been dedicated to developing and evaluating treatments for adult bipolar disorder, interventions for pediatric BPSD have only begun to emerge in the literature in the past decade. Our effectiveness trial is delivering intervention in a community mental health setting using broad inclusion criteria, including youth with multiple comorbidities, and comparing a manualized intervention to flexibly delivered treatment as usual. Given such broad inclusion criteria, we have a high percentage of complex and refractory cases in which we have used the CBT treatment manual described below. This is a strength if the results are to be applicable to most youths affected by BPSD, as few if any cases will present for treatment without meeting criteria for a comorbid disorder such as attention-deficit/hyperactivity disorder, anxiety, or oppositional behavior (Kowatch, Youngstrom, Danielyan, & Findling, 2005).

FACTORS ASSOCIATED WITH POOR TREATMENT RESPONSE

Although little is known about specific predictors of psychosocial treatment response among youth with BPSD (Davidson & Fristad, 2008; Miklowitz, Mullen, & Chang, 2008), research and clinical efforts indicate that this population is characterized by clinical complexity often associated with treatment refractoriness. Here we will highlight some of these complexities that are relevant to the case we will discuss later. First, youth with BPSD typically present with at least one, if not several, co-occurring disorders (Birmaher et al., 2006; Kowatch, Youngstrom et al., 2005; Youngstrom, Birmaher, & Findling, 2008) and, in particular, often externalizing disorders that can affect treatment compliance and progress (Perugi, 2008). Attention problems, for example, can limit how much information can be covered in one session and how quickly treatment progress can be made. Conduct problems often lead to crises (e.g., being arrested or kicked out of school) that must be attended to in treatment, but concomitantly dilute the focus on mood symptoms per se. Second, many youth with BPSD have parents who are struggling with their own mental health issues (Findling, Youngstrom, et al., 2005) and who may as a result have trouble complying with the demands of treatment; for example, bringing their children regularly for appointments or assisting their children with therapy homework assignments.

Third, a negative family environment, and high levels of family conflict in particular, are associated with worse treatment outcome across multiple disorders (Hooley, 1987) and is a common issue among families of youth with BPSD (e.g., Miklowitz, Wendel, & Simoneau, 1998). For example, Geller and colleagues (2002) conducted a 2-year prospective follow-up of youth (ages 7 to 16) with BPSD and found family environment to be associated with poorer outcome. Specifically, youth with intact families were over two times more likely to recover from their current episode. Likewise, in this study, participants' mothers reported to have low levels of maternal warmth were 4.1 times more likely to relapse during follow-up. These findings are not surprising, given that parents and other family members in the ecology of youth with BPSD play a significant role in the youth's treatment (e.g., by assisting with medication and sleep maintenance or by reinforcing coping strategies learned in therapy). Fourth and finally, all of these clinical complexities often occur together, not singly, which makes effective treatment delivery a challenge for therapists of all levels.

COGNITIVE-BEHAVIOR THERAPY TREATMENT MANUAL FOR BIPOLAR YOUTH

Danielson, Feeny, Findling, and Youngstrom (2004) performed a comprehensive literature review to gather empirical literature related to the identification, assessment, etiology, course, prognosis, and treatment of BPSD in adults and in youths. In addition, therapy strategies and techniques that had been shown to be useful in treating youth with

BPSD (Fristad, Gavazzi, & Soldano, 1998; Fristad, Goldberg-Arnold, & Gavazzi, 1999) and adults (Miklowitz & Goldstein, 1997) with BPSD were reviewed as a framework for developing a more comprehensive, cognitive-behavioral intervention for youth that specifically targeted many of the factors associated with poor response to treatment as described earlier. Because depressive episodes are a common element of BPSD clinical presentation, particular attention also was paid to treatments that have been found to be efficacious in treating youth with depression (e.g., Coping With Depression Course; Clarke, Rohde, Lewinsohn, Hops, & Seeley, 1999; G. N. Lewinsohn, Clarke, Rhode, Hops, & Seeley, 1996; P. M. Lewinsohn, Hops, Clarke, & Andrews, 1990).

This review yielded seven primary areas of focus, from which intervention components were developed. These components include (a) psychoeducation about mood disorders and their causes, as well as overview of components of treatment model (e.g., Peet & Harvey, 1991; Van Gent & Zwart, 1991); (b) medication compliance (e.g., Brondolo & Mas, 2001); (c) mood monitoring; (d) identification and modification of unhelpful thinking; (e) stressor/trigger identification (e.g., Gitlin, Swendsen, Heller, & Hammen, 1995); (f) sleep maintenance (e.g., Wehr, Wirz-Justice, & Goodwin, 1982); and (g) family communication (e.g., Miklowitz et al., 1996). In addition, optional modules devoted to other problems common among youth with BPSD (i.e., substance abuse, social skills, anger management, and contingency management) were developed. The treatment was designed to be delivered individually in a once-weekly format with flexible parental involvement, as such involvement has been shown to be particularly useful to families coping with BPSD (Miklowitz & Alloy, 1999; Miklowitz & Goldstein, 1997; Miklowitz et al., 1998). Thus, two sessions are co-joint sessions with the youth and parents, one session midway through treatment is with parents only, and 15-minute check-ins are offered to parents weekly. The check-ins are particularly useful in cases in which higher levels of family conflict exist, where issues related to family support, parental warmth in communication, and so on can be addressed in a consistent fashion. The treatment was initially formatted as a12-session acute treatment that incorporated all the modules/skills previously identified. This format is shown in Table 12.1. However, here we will describe the treatment as delivered in phases to emphasize concepts that need to be covered as opposed to a session-by-session description.

Table 12.1

SUGGESTED FORMAT FOR SESSION TOPICS

WEEK	SESSION NUMBER	LENGTH OF SESSION	WITH WHOM	TOPIC
1	1	60 minutes	Youth and Parent	Psychoeducation about BP (symptoms, causes, etc.) and medication, lay out what the sessions are going to be like, answer questions, set goals with parents and youth, provide reading and handouts to parents HW: Parents: read materials
1	2	30 minutes	Youth	Review psychoeducation material, answer questions, further develop treatment goals HW: take 1 step toward a goal
2	3	60 minutes	Youth	Medication compliance and mood monitoring HW: complete medication log and mood monitoring
3	4	60 minutes	Youth	Anticipating stressors and problem solving HW: mood monitoring, medication log
4	5	60 minutes	Parent	Catch-up and review what we have done so far, teach problem solving, go over vulnerability to mood swings HW: Document 3 situations when you used the new problem-solving techniques you learned, including what the situation was, what strategy was used, and what the outcome was; mood monitoring, medication log
5	6	60 minutes	Youth	Identifying and countering negative thinking HW: mood monitoring with "challenge to the thought" and "new feeling" columns added; medication log

(continued)

Table 12.1 (continued)

WEEK	SESSION NUMBER	LENGTH OF SESSION	WITH WHOM	TOPIC
6	7	60 minutes	Youth	Sleep regulation, relaxation HW: Maintain a regular sleeping schedule for the week; identify obstacles to maintaining a schedule and falling asleep; mood monitoring, medication log
7	8	60 minutes	Youth	Communication, assertiveness HW: Document an example of positive communication and negative communication over the week with a family member or close friend (address 'How could the negative communication have been handled differently?'); mood monitoring, medication log
8	9	60 minutes	Youth and Parent	Family communication; role-playing HW: Plan a one-hour family activity, mood monitoring, medication log
9	10	60 minutes	Youth	Optional Modules: Substance abuse or anger management HW: Substance abuse: Complete log of substance use, initiate positive activity with a friend who does not use drugs; HW: Anger: Document situation involving anger where assertiveness skills were applied
10	11	60 minutes	Youth or *Youth and parent management	Optional Modules: Social skills or *Contingency HW: Social skills: Assign social task in an area in which the adolescent has difficulty (e.g., social initiating, group activity, etc.) HW: Contingency management: Maintain a chart documenting frequency of target behaviors (as well as rewards and consequences)

(continued)

Table 12.1 (continued)

WEEK	SESSION NUMBER	LENGTH OF SESSION	WITH WHOM	TOPIC
11	12	60 minutes	Youth; Parent in last 15 min.	Wrap-up, review (What worked and what did not? What still needs to be addressed?), plans for maintenance phase HW: Anticipate upcoming stressors

Note. This acute phase of treatment is followed by a 6–10-session maintenance phase of biweekly meetings. Biannual follow-up "booster" sessions are recommended after the maintenance phase. The sessions will build on skills already taught and will be focused on the individual needs of each child. Optional: 15-minute check-in at the end of each session with parent.

PHASE I: PSYCHOEDUCATION AND GOAL SETTING

Education that involves family members and/or significant others of a client with BPSD also has been demonstrated to be useful in maintaining medication compliance (e.g., Van Gent & Zwart, 1991). Specific to youth, psychoeducation also has been shown to be advantageous for parents of hospitalized children with mood disorders (Fristad, Arnett, & Gavazzi, 1998; Fristad, Gavazzi, & Soldano, 1998). For the treatment of youth with BPSD, we recommend that initial educational sessions include both the youth and the parents, as parents are key participants in the youth's everyday life. It is important to note that parents are typically the ones who have sought treatment for their child, and they are responsible for ensuring session attendance. Also, as described earlier, they can play a pivotal role in the child's maintenance of treatment gains.

In this phase of treatment, the focus is on socializing the youth to treatment, educating him/her about BPSD, and establishing treatment goals. At the start of treatment, the youth is provided with a workbook, which contains all treatment handouts and homework assignments (divided by session). Parents also are provided with handouts of the introductory information, which includes information about five primary elements. First, the structure of the treatment is introduced. A table is provided (Table 12.1) that lists the estimated length of time of treatment, who will be participating, and skills/topics that will be addressed. Second, the youth and his/her parents are orientated to CBT. This discussion includes an overview of the treatment as active, time-limited, skills-oriented, and symptom-focused. Further, a model is provided that illustrates the connection among thoughts, feelings, and behaviors. The use and importance of "homework" in CBT (and this treatment in particular) should be explained as well. Third, education is provided that is specific to BPSD symptoms, possible etiologies, course, and treatment (e.g., importance of medication compliance). This is an opportunity to determine how much education the youth has received about BPSD and what his/her concerns are about having the disorder. Fourth, the therapist suggests strategies for how parents can assist the youth throughout the treatment, including being supportive, recognizing the child's strengths, attending the parent sessions of the treatment, helping the youth work on skills at home, and making sure the child gets to each treatment session. Fifth, these early sessions should involve setting initial treatment goals with both the child and the parents and providing parents with reading materials, including additional information on BPSD.

PHASE II: BASIC SKILL ACQUISITION

Medication Compliance

Medication is considered an essential frontline treatment for BPSD in children and adolescents (Kowatch, Fristad, et al., 2005; McClellan & Werry, 1997). As indicated overwhelmingly in the adult and emerging adolescent treatment literature, consistent medication use is crucial to the alleviation of BPSD symptoms (see Kafantaris, 1995; Prien & Potter, 1990) and, in some cases, in the prevention of future episodes (Strober, Morrell, Lampert, & Burroughs, 1990). The literature also indicates that even when an episode is in remission, it may be better for an individual to continue the medication rather than going off and on as needed (e.g., Sharma, Yatham, & Haslam, 1997). Thus, in the context of a psychosocial treatment, it is often important that BPSD symptoms be stabilized pharmacologically so that the youth is able to more fully comprehend and participate in the psychosocial component of the treatment.

This skill module is focused on emphasizing the important of compliance, tracking compliance, and troubleshooting problematic compliance. At the start of this module, the therapist asks the youth to rate his/her medication compliance on a scale of 1–10. Then the therapist helps the youth identify: (a) benefits of taking the medication (e.g., feeling more able to handle stressors, getting along better with family members); (b) obstacles that may tempt the youth to stop taking the medication (e.g., troublesome side effects, overwhelmed by daily regimen); and (c) consequences of noncompliance (e.g., becoming more irritable, getting in trouble). To improve medication compliance outside of the session, the therapist teaches the youth how to complete a daily medication log, which becomes a homework assignment for the remainder of treatment.

Mood Monitoring

Psychosocial interventions such as Lewinsohn and Clarke's (1986) Adolescents Coping With Depression (CWD) Course focus on teaching a basic skill early on in treatment, from which more complex skills can later be taught. The present treatment follows that model in attempting to alleviate affective symptoms of BPSD. Specifically, the skill "mood monitoring" is taught to the youths in the early sessions of treatment. Then, after several weeks of practicing this skill via homework assignments, the more complex skills of identifying negative thoughts and generating realistic counterthoughts are taught. To start, youth with BPSD are taught how to recognize and pay attention to these moods at the most basic level (e.g., "What are feelings and how do I recognize them?"). The therapist helps the youth point out the physical cues (e.g., "I have no energy"; "I feel tense") and emotional cues (e.g., "I feel overwhelming sadness"; "I'm incredibly irritable") associated with the mood states. An emotion thermometer is used to help the youth gauge situations in which he/she experiences different "degrees" of sadness, irritability, elation, happiness, and so on. The therapist and the youth discuss the concept of affect (e.g., "How does it feel to be manic?"), symptoms associated with the mood states (e.g., "I start to feel really good about myself"; "I talk faster than normal"), and changes in affective states (e.g., "What happens first when I start to move from really 'good' feelings to really 'bad' feelings?"). Specifically, youths are taught to monitor their mood daily using a three-column log (i.e., situation, thought, feeling).

Anticipating Stressors and Problem Solving

The role of life events in BPSD has not been investigated as thoroughly as it has with regard to other psychiatric illnesses (Hlastala, Frank, Kowalski, Sherrill, & Tu, 2000); however, research has indicated that stressful life events do indeed affect onset and recovery from manic and depressive episodes (Hammen, Ellicott, & Gitlin, 1992; Hunt, Bruce-Jones, & Silverstone, 1992; Johnson & Miller, 1997; Johnson & Roberts, 1995; Kennedy, Thompson, Stancer, Roy, & Persad, 1983; Reilly-Harrington, Alloy, Fresco, & Whitehouse, 1999). For example, high levels of stress are common triggers for episodes. In a 2-year follow-up of BPSD outpatients, individuals with high levels of life stress were more than four times as likely to experience a mood-disorder relapse than individuals with low levels of life stress (Ellicott, Hammen, Gitlin, Brown, & Jamison, 1990). Other examples of stressors identified in the literature that can serve as triggers for manic and depressive episodes include life events that disrupt the individual's daily social and circadian rhythms (Malkoff-Schwartz et al., 1998) and life events that involve striving for goal attainment (Johnson et al., 2000). Given these findings, a component of treatment addressing the anticipation of stressors has been incorporated into psychosocial interventions for adults with BPSD (e.g., Rothbaum & Astin, 2000). Helping youths identify what global and specific "stressors" or life events serve as triggers to certain mood states and/or episodes, while also instructing the youth on ways to alter negative cognitions, may provide a foundation from which the client can attempt to circumvent future episodes.

This module includes learning to "anticipate stressors" and to problem-solve in an attempt to provide the youth with structured opportunities to identify and learn to change or avoid those factors that may act as "triggers" for affective symptoms. Within this component of the treatment, the therapist addresses general stressful factors that affect all clients, such as striving to achieve life goals (Johnson et al., 2000; Lozano & Johnson, 2001), by demonstrating how to make goal setting and attainment less stressful and more manageable (e.g., by breaking goals down into manageable chunks). In conjunction with "anticipating stressors," it is important to teach the youth specific problem-solving skills. These skills can be useful when youths are faced with a specific trigger or when other conflicts are presented. Instead of becoming overwhelmed when faced with a problem, they can employ specific problem-solving tools heltp the youth break down conflicts into smaller, more manageable steps and slow down impulsive decision making that can lead to poor choices. The youth also is taught how to evaluate his/her choices and consequences when applying problem-solving skills to guide the way he or she handles problems and stressors in the future. As part of teaching problem solving, the therapist presents hypothetical vignettes of various minor and major problems on which to practice this new method of structured problem solving. After being presented with a vignette, the youth is asked to identify the problem, brainstorm possible solutions, evaluate consequences of each, choose a solution, and evaluate the decision outcome.

Parent Check-In

After teaching the youth several basic skills, an opportunity to check in with parents is provided. This "check-in" is conducted with parents only and includes a review of the material covered in Phase II. The therapist reviews with parents what topics and skills have been taught in treatment thus far and how parents can reinforce these skills at home. Conducting a session with parents only at this stage in the treatment also may help keep the parents engaged (and thus help to keep the youth in treatment) and can address questions and concerns that have arisen.

PHASE III: ADVANCED SKILLS

Learning to Identify and Fight Back Against Unhelpful Thoughts

Patterns of unhelpful thinking negatively influence emotions and behaviors in individuals with depressive disorders (Beck, 1995). In CBT, a primary focus is teaching clients to identify and challenge these cognitive errors/distortions. Distorted cognitions that may impede treatment progress, lead to increases in depressive or manic symptoms (e.g., Johnson & Tran, 2007), or augment risk of relapse include misconceptions about life events as they occur or about BPSD in general, catastrophic beliefs about the poor prognosis of treatment, and overgeneralizations about the presence of specific symptoms (Brondolo & Mas, 2001). Thus, it is essential to teach the youth how to counteract negative and/or irrational thinking that can lead to experiences of depression, irritability, and mania.

This is taught as three separate, but intertwined skills: mood monitoring, examining the role of thoughts in mood disturbance (identifying negative thoughts), and replacing distorted or overly negative thoughts with more realistic thoughts. At this point in treatment, the youth should have completed several weeks of monitoring his/her mood using the three-column mood log (in which the youth identified an event, a thought, and a feeling). Now, youth are taught how thoughts affect behavior and mood, common thinking errors, how to identify negative or unrealistic thinking, and how to challenge these cognitions. Ultimately, youth learn how the act of challenging negative and distorted thinking patterns can alter their mood. At this phase of treatment, it may be a good opportunity to begin to challenge thoughts and beliefs with regard to control over mood states and related behaviors, such as, "I can't stop myself from screaming and slamming doors because that's what happens during my BP episodes." The therapist demonstrates how replacing negative thoughts with positive ones helps the youth gain some control of his/her mood state and behaviors. After teaching this skill, the triple-column mood-monitoring log is replaced with a five-column mood-monitoring log, which asks the youth to also identify a thought countering the negative cognition and the subsequent change in feeling. After practice in session, the youth uses this log to begin to identify triggers and distorted cognitions that preceded the mood, and attempts to challenge the negative thinking.

Sleep Maintenance

Sleep disruption in youths has been linked with a range of deficits in functioning, including mood disturbance and suicidal ideation (Roberts, Roberts, & Chen, 2001). In fact, several community-based studies have found that sleep problems are robust risk factors for depressive episodes (see Ford & Cooper-Patrick, 2001). Specific to BPSD, research has indicated a close relationship between sleep loss and the onset of mania (Leibenluft, Albert, Rosenthal, & Wehr, 1996; Wu & Bunney, 1990). Investigations in this area have demonstrated that partial or total sleep deprivation for one night can induce "switching" into manic or hypomanic episodes in BPSD adults (Barbini, Bertelli, Colombo, & Smeraldi, 1996; Post, Kopin, & Goodwin, 1976; Stoddard, Post, & Bunney Jr., 1977; Wehr, 1992; Wehr et al., 1982). Wehr (1989) described a "vicious" cycle that can be established, in which mania disrupts sleep, and sleep disruption in turn provokes manic symptoms, causing the episode to become increasingly worse. Another rationale for addressing sleep with youths with BPSD is based on investigations of Interpersonal and Social Rhythm Therapy (IPSRT; see Frank et al., 1994), which have indicated the value of maintaining regular circadian rhythms. Taken together, such findings provide the basis of the rationale for addressing sleep regulation in the context of a psychosocial treatment of BPSD.

Delivery of this skill begins with a discussion about the importance of sleep and provides education about the research (noted earlier) indicating that sleep deprivation can lead to the onset of manic symptoms (and, in turn, can be an indicator of a manic episode). It is particularly important that youths, who may maintain irregular sleeping habits as a result of spending time with friends at sleepovers, doing schoolwork, talking on the phone, or playing video games late at night, be educated on the importance of regular sleep routines. The therapist then works with the youth to determine what are his/her specific obstacles to getting a "good night's rest." The therapist teaches two skills after the obstacles have been identified: relaxation techniques and developing and maintaining a regular sleep/wake schedule. Depending on the need of the youth and his/her ability to learn the relaxation techniques, the therapist may decide to make an audiotape of relaxation exercises within the session, with exercises such as progressive muscle relaxation and guided imagery. An example of a homework assignment following this session is a "Sleep Block Book," where the youth documents habits or events that disrupt or "block" sleep and, alternatively, strategies that help him or her follow a regular sleeping schedule. Other practical interventions in this module include removing the TV from the child's bedroom, setting consistent sleep and wake times and pre-bed routines, and/or negotiating with parents to limit access to TV or video games after a certain time in the evening.

Assertiveness and Family Communication

A major psychosocial factor that appears to affect the course of BPSD is interactions within the family (Miklowitz, Goldstein, Nuechterlein, Snyder, & Mintz, 1988). Specifically, certain styles of family communication and expression of emotion have been associated with relapse of BPSD (Miklowitz et al., 1998). High "expressed emotion" is the term applied to expressed negative feelings and interactions that exist in a family environment. High expressed emotion includes relatives' attributions about illness in the patient; these attributions often involve criticism, hostility, rejection, and/or emotional overinvolvement (Rothbaum & Astin, 2000). Thus, training the family in communication skills, including reducing the hostile attitudes and interactions and increasing positive communication, could be an important part of treatment in preventing future relapse. This part of the treatment also teaches parents to help their youths continue to develop the skills and strategies taught in the sessions, such as problem solving and affect regulation.

Given the importance of the role of assertiveness in family communication (e.g., teaching the youth how to express feelings and needs in an effective manner without being too passive or aggressive), assertiveness skills are taught as a precursor to the Family Communication module. The youth learns the importance of engaging in active listening and developing positive communication behaviors (and alternatively decreasing negative communication behaviors). Practicing these skills first with the youth alone allows time to prepare for possible disputes and problems that may arise when parents join the session at the next session. The youth and the parent meet jointly after this, and the family members identify current problems in communication styles, the parent learns the positive communication skills (e.g., active listening), and the youth and the parent together can practice the skills in role-playing exercises. The participants also are given situations to role-play at home, using the newly learned communication skills as homework.

PHASE IV: COMBINING SKILLS TO ADDRESS COMMON PROBLEMS—OPTIONAL MODULES

This treatment model includes four optional modules to meet the individual needs of the youths and to help them cope with additional stressors: Substance Abuse, Anger Management, Social Skills Training, and Contingency Management. The idea here is that skills developed and practiced earlier in treatment can be combined to address specific problems. Each of these modules is briefly discussed in more detail in the text that follows.

Substance Abuse

The first optional module is related to co-occurring substance-use problems, as it is well documented that those with BPSD are more likely than the general population, or patients with other psychiatric disorders, to have problems with substance use (Dunner, Hensel, & Fieve, 1979; Reiger, Farmer, & Rae, 1990; Winokur, Coryell, & Akiskal, 1995). Substance abuse can affect an individual's motivation for treatment. In addition, mood-altering substances can be used as "self-medication" by individuals suffering from psychological problems, and thus, can affect the course of BPSD. As a result, the inclusion of a module that educates adolescents with BPSD regarding the risks of substance use would be justified in a comprehensive psychosocial treatment. The Substance-Abuse module that is part of this treatment includes identification of high-risk or "trigger" situations and people at risk for substance abuse, revisiting skills learned earlier in the treatment that could serve as strategies to avoid or reduce substance use, including problem solving and assertiveness, and educating the youth about how substances impact mood and coping abilities.

Anger Management

The second optional module, Anger Management, is related to the common presence of irritability in youths with BPSD. Depending on the individual, this increased irritability can lead to anger, aggression, and even violence (Basco & Rush, 1996). In fact, conduct disorder has been identified as a common comorbid condition with BPSD (Bowring & Kovacs, 1992). As such, teaching anger management to youths who have exhibited extreme histories of "losing their tempers" and are experiencing consequences because of such reactions is suggested. This module includes helping the youth identify specific situations in which they have had difficulty managing feelings of anger and revisiting skills that may help them cope with such situations more appropriately. These skills include relaxation training, problem solving, and examining and challenging unhelpful thinking.

Social Support

The third module is related to the empirically demonstrated impact of social support on the course of BPSD (Johnson, Winnet, Meyer, Greenhouse, & Miller, 1999). Johnson and colleagues (1999) followed 59 individuals with BPSD and found that those with low social support took longer to recover from depressive episodes and had more depressive symptoms over time than those with higher levels of support. Receiving social support of self-esteem (i.e., both positive appraisal of self by others and positive self-comparison to others) also seems to play an important role in BPSD depression (Johnson, Meyer, Winett, & Small, 2000). In addition, a recent prospective investigation of the course of BP II symptoms found that poor previous social functioning predicted greater chronicity of BPSD symptoms (Judd et al., 2003). Thus, addressing behaviors that involve social interaction and support, such as social activity planning and fostering interpersonal problem solving, could be useful components of treatment for youths with BPSD. This module is offered to help youths learn basic social skills, including how to initiate and maintain conversations, how to use body language to convey interest, how to greet peers, and how to use problem-solving skills, which can be necessary in building and maintaining friendships.

Contingency Management

The fourth optional module, Contingency Management, is for families in which the youth with BPSD also displays defiant and oppositional behavior. This module may be most useful for children with BPSD, particularly those with co-occurring attention deficit hyperactivity disorder, which is commonly diagnosed concurrently with BPSD (Biederman, 1995). The format of this module includes the therapist specifically targeting the parent's strategies to elicit cooperation from the youth. The therapist then assists the family in setting up a contingency management system, in which the youth is rewarded for good behavior and receives consequences for defiant behavior. The target behaviors are defined in operational terms (e.g., improving school social behavior is defined as no reports of physical altercations with peers at school) and both the parent and the youth assist in determining the rewards and consequences.

PHASE V: WRAP-UP, RELAPSE PREVENTION, AND MAINTENANCE

The final phase of treatment is aimed at review, consolidation, generalization, and maintenance. During this session or sessions, the therapist reviews with the youth progress toward the goals set at the beginning of therapy. All of the skills taught in therapy are then summarized and the therapist helps the youth identify which techniques have been most helpful. Based on a discussion of anticipated challenges that may arise in the future, a relapse prevention plan is developed. Optimally, parents are involved to some extent in reviewing progress toward goals and developing their role in the relapse prevention plan. This role can include helping the youth practice skills learned in therapy, modeling and engaging in positive family communication, and supporting the youth during stressful situations.

The addition of maintenance phases to brief treatments have been identified as useful in the literature and are often recommended by experts in the field (Birmaher, Brent, & Benson, 1998; Clarke et al., 1999; Kroll, Harrington, Jayson, Fraser, & Gowers, 1996). A maintenance phase in which weekly sessions are replaced eventually with less frequent meetings can reinforce previously taught skills and can give a youth more independence in self-maintenance without breaking off the therapeutic relationship immediately following acute treatment. In addition, these sessions provide an opportunity to address any new or current stressors in the youth's life and possibly identify early symptoms of a mood episode onset.

CASE PRESENTATION

This case example demonstrates the skills covered by the CBT manual described previously and highlights many of the obstacles presented with refractory cases. The case described involves a participant in the effectiveness trial examining CBT versus treatment as usual. As part of the eligibility requirements, clients were enrolled if they were between ages 7 and 18 years, met the diagnostic criteria for a BPSD, and had not had any changes in medication for the month prior to the assessment. As part of the study, medication changes were allowed if it seemed necessary based on worsening mood or emergence of increased suicidal ideation. However, adding or changing medications was not encouraged during the 12-week acute trial prior to moving into the maintenance phase.

Presenting Problem

Ms. Smith sought treatment services at the community mental health center for her African American 9-year-old daughter, Tammy. According to intake records, Tammy was referred to treatment to address concerns of increased anger and aggression, hyperactivity, temper tantrums, difficulty sleeping, talking to herself, lying, and stealing. Tammy was described by her mother as a behavior problem at home and school. At home, Tammy was often irritable, refused to share with her two siblings and cousin who lived in the home, purposely annoyed others, initiated physical fights with siblings, screamed, threatened, and threw and destroyed things. Negative school behaviors included Tammy talking excessively, being easily distracted, and arguing with others. Ms. Smith reported being overwhelmed by having to manage Tammy's difficult emotions and behaviors. She was concerned with the safety of others in the household who consistently felt they were "walking on eggshells."

A semistructured diagnostic interview and questionnaires revealed that Tammy displayed symptoms consistent with cyclothymic disorder. Tammy's mood would shift several times throughout the day for brief periods. According to Ms. Smith, Tammy's mood did not appear related to circumstances or reactions to specific triggers. Depressive symptoms included depressed mood that occurred twice a week for much of the day, depressed appearance (looking visibly sad or withdrawn from others), crying, irritability, insomnia, and anhedonia. Manic symptoms included increased irritable mood that occurred at least three times a week, increased motor hyperactivity, decreased need for sleep, pressured speech, and flight of ideas. Specifically, Ms. Smith reported that Tammy could be full of energy and within several minutes, appeared sad and would begin crying for no apparent reason. Furthermore, shortly after crying, she would become angry and act aggressively toward others. When Tammy was described as "full of energy" she presented as more irritable, often purposely attacking others and destroying property, and engaged in threats to hurt others. When others attempted to restrain or calm her down, she became more angry and aggressive. These symptoms reportedly lasted from 30 minutes to several hours and were present for about 18 months prior to presentation to the clinic. In addition to cyclothymic disorder, Tammy also met diagnostic criteria for attention-deficit/hyperactivity disorder, combined type; oppositional defiant disorder; separation anxiety; and for rule-outs of psychotic disorder, not otherwise specified, and vocal tics.

Family History and Stressors

Tammy had a significant family history of mental illness. Ms. Smith reported that she herself is currently diagnosed with bipolar I disorder and is currently compliant with medications and counseling. Ms. Smith was previously diagnosed with major depressive disorder; anxiety disorder, not otherwise specified; posttraumatic stress disorder; and primary insomnia. Tammy's maternal grandmother was previously diagnosed with depression, her maternal aunt was diagnosed with bipolar diorder, and another maternal aunt was diagnosed with schizophrenia.

Course of Treatment

Psychoeducation and Goal Setting

Tammy and Ms. Smith attended the first CBT session jointly. Tammy was overly friendly, as evidenced by approaching the therapist with a hug and asking personal questions. Ms. Smith appeared overwhelmed and indicated that her child needed help. The therapist explained the treatment study, developed a no-harm contract, and provided psychoeducational information. Specific information was provided about symptoms associated with cyclothymic disorder and other BPSD. The therapist then provided Ms. Smith with additional information on how symptoms may present differently in children. It was increasingly evident that Ms. Smith was primarily interested in seeking pharmacological treatment as the sole intervention for Tammy's difficulties, and she expected progress to occur rapidly. The therapist encouraged Ms. Smith to try several sessions to learn skills before terminating with psychotherapy treatment and reassured Ms. Smith she would facilitate a psychiatric referral.

Ms. Smith had few questions and indicated that she was familiar with the disorder given her diagnosis. Tammy and her mother appeared to understand the content presented; however, both appeared preoccupied as attention shifted to unrelated topics. Ms. Smith demonstrated difficulty initially understanding her role in Tammy's treatment, and at first she did not want to accept the CBT handouts, as she stated she did not want responsibility to do more work or to fix the problems. Ms. Smith also reported that she felt as though Tammy needed immediate resolution and something to assist with controlling her aggression. This is an example of the treatment refractoriness issue discussed previously, in which Ms. Smith was clearly overwhelmed, struggling with her own mental health difficulties and life challenges. Thus, it was important to provide empathy and support to Ms. Smith regarding the many responsibilities and struggles she was juggling while also reframing the handouts as an additional source of support—and something that is intended to help her reach the treatment goals she would be setting for Tammy. Ms. Smith agreed to take home the CBT handouts once she understood they were a resource that she could use.

Thus, the next session was used to *identify and set goals for treatment*. Tammy and Ms. Smith agreed that their primary concern was to decrease aggressive acts and outbursts toward others. The therapist also encouraged and assisted the family with focusing more on underlying mood symptoms. This session appeared to engage Tammy and her mother as well as incorporate their concerns and various perspectives. Ms. Smith reported that she was extremely frustrated with Tammy's behavior throughout the week and seemed to focus only on negative behaviors. Tammy made several attempts to argue with her mother in session and to engage in power struggles. She also demonstrated limited ability to sustain attention and focus on content within the session. Ms. Smith was assigned to focus on positive behaviors and Tammy was assigned to identify various feelings she experiences throughout the week.

The following session deviated from the treatment manual somewhat by focusing on the critical role of Ms. Smith's engagement and of a positive family environment, given their association with treatment outcome. Thus, this session was used as an opportunity to align with the family by addressing the mother's concerns, reviewing symptoms, and discussing family stressors, because the therapist felt that this was crucial to maintaining the family's engagement with therapy. This deviation was conducted given Ms. Smith's initial reluctance to engage in therapy, her responses and reactions in sessions 1 and 2, as well as phone calls and messages between sessions indicating her feelings of being overwhelmed managing Tammy's emotions and behaviors. Additionally, when the family was greeted that day in the lobby, Ms. Smith responded, "You need to do something for her. She is not getting any better." During this supportive session, Tammy demonstrated fewer attention difficulties and contributed by providing more of her perspective regarding current mood difficulties she was experiencing. Both family members were praised for recent efforts.

Basic Skill Acquisition and Advanced Skills

At the next session, Ms. Smith reported that over the weekend Tammy threw a tantrum in the car, which involved hitting her brother and threatening to stab Ms. Smith with a pen. The therapist used part of the session time to discuss Ms. Smith's concerns. She reviewed a safety plan with the family, de-escalation techniques, and a plan to escort Tammy to the emergency room if risk to harm self or others increased. The remainder of the session was spent teaching and practicing *mood monitoring* skills with Tammy. She remained engaged and appeared to respond well to the handouts that reinforced the skills. Tammy also remained open to learning about different emotions other than "mad," "angry," and "sad," which she often referenced throughout the session. The therapist encouraged Tammy to continue to practice and use various emotions throughout the day, as well as to track experiences and thoughts related to emotions.

The next session proved to be challenging, as Ms. Smith expressed concerns about Tammy's aggressive behavior throughout the week. Ms. Smith requested an emergency session to discuss severe tantrums and noncompliant behavior. The session was used to assist Ms. Smith with learning skills to manage oppositional behavior, as well as to provide support for current feelings of frustration. Ms. Smith was taught skills to identify specific behaviors to address, establishing a monitoring system for these behaviors, and given assistance identifying rewards and consequences for Tammy's behaviors. As noted earlier, attention and oppositional problems are frequently comorbid with BPSD in youth and can serve as a risk factor for poor treatment outcome. Thus, by dedicating session time and effort to assist in coping with Tammy's comorbid oppositional behaviors, the therapist was increasing Tammy's likelihood of maintaining BPSD treatment gains over time.

During the next session, Tammy was again responsive and engaged while learning *problem-solving skills*. She appeared to respond well to the intervention as a result of the therapist assisting her with identifying her personal conflicts and situations that had caused her difficulty before (e.g. sharing with her siblings, fighting at school). Tammy was able to identify problems appropriately and admitted to often experiencing difficulty with stopping to consider alternative responses rather than reacting to a situation immediately and inappropriately. Tammy reported that the steps in problem solving (Stop, what's the problem? What can I do? What are good/bad things about the solution? and Make a choice) were helpful, and that she had not approached problems like this in the past.

Ms. Smith returned to the next session with a note from school indicating that Tammy had behaved aggressively toward a classmate. The session was also spent reviewing Tammy's *recent progress, addressing concerns, and reviewing previously learned skills*. Each skill was discussed to determine whether it might be helpful to employ in the school setting to prevent further concerns about aggression there.

Tammy and Ms. Smith attended the next session jointly and practiced *family communication skills*. Both demonstrated difficulty with active-listening skills, making eye contact, and accurately interpreting each other's message. Despite the difficulty, they demonstrated an ability to let the other person express her thoughts and not interrupt. Ms. Smith and Tammy were receptive toward feedback and agreed to practice communication skills daily at home. This module was moved to an earlier position in the sequence because of the intensity of conflict and negative communication between Ms. Smith and Tammy, especially Ms. Smith's focus on any negative behavior. In our experience, it often has been necessary to improve communication skills before making headway on mastering other CBT skills. Further, Tammy's success in treatment would likely be tied to successfully improving positive family communication and environment, given the previously reviewed research in this area.

At the following session, Ms. Smith reported that Tammy had attended a psychiatry appointment and was prescribed medication. *Medication compliance* was reviewed and the importance of consistency was discussed. The therapist *reviewed mood-monitoring skills* with Tammy, who admitted that she had not practiced the skills recently. The therapist also *introduced counterthinking and skills to alter negative thinking*. Despite adaptation worksheets, visual cues, and personal experiences, Tammy demonstrated difficulty separating thoughts, feelings, and behaviors. She also exhibited difficulty identifying alternative responses that were neutral or positive, as all of her responses reflected a negative view or experience. Additionally, Tammy was observed to demonstrate difficulty focusing her attention on questions posed by the therapist, as well as switching the subject frequently. The therapist also provided Tammy with feedback regarding her negative perspectives and assisted her with understanding how her current mood state is influenced by her views. Tammy reported that the thought bubbles to identify what several characters might be thinking were helpful cues that made it easier for her to understand the concepts.

Tammy attended the next session individually and there was no opportunity for the therapist to check-in with Ms. Smith because of child-care issues. The therapist introduced skills related to *sleep regulation and relaxation.* It was apparent that Tammy had difficulty understanding concepts associated with sleep maintenance and would require additional assistance from her mother. The therapist postponed the remaining associated concepts for the next session when Ms. Smith could be involved and provide additional information. Therefore, the therapist completed the session by focusing on relaxation skills. Tammy appeared to respond well to learning about relaxation skills and how this could also relate to anger difficulties. Tammy reported that she enjoyed the breathing exercises practiced in session.

The final session in our 12-week treatment addressed Ms. Smith's concerns regarding recent aggressive behavior. The therapist introduced *assertiveness skills* and taught and practiced skills during the session. Particular emphasis was placed on teaching Tammy the difference between assertiveness and aggressive skills. She demonstrated some difficulty with identifying examples of each during role plays. A review and discussion of previously learned skills was also conducted. Relapse prevention was discussed and the family provided limited information regarding which skills were most and least helpful. The therapist provided the family with feedback regarding maintenance and use of the skills in the future.

Positive Treatment Experiences

The manual included several developmental modifications—such as providing additional activities for younger children and using thought bubbles as a visual cue to think about cognitions. These appeared to assist Tammy with understanding more complex concepts. She was able to relate to a great deal of the information presented and often exhibited adequate insight into current difficulties. This was often evident when Tammy was able to appropriately identify problematic behaviors, mood, or feelings that occur in her daily functioning. Tammy responded well to skills that included goal setting, mood monitoring, problem solving, and relaxation. These skills required more of an individual effort and Tammy appeared motivated to complete tasks in which she perceived herself as having more control over the situation. Tammy appreciated the family communication skills and her mother's agreement to practice together at home. Tammy was consistently pleasant toward the therapist and responded favorably to praise received in session.

During the initial referral and intake, there had been concerns that Tammy initially presented to treatment with suicidal thoughts. However, she did not report such thoughts during the course of treatment and denied ever wanting to harm herself. It is not clear whether her behavior indicated a decrease in suicidal ideation in response to treatment, but suicidal ideation did not emerge and was no longer a concern by the end of therapy. Despite Ms. Smith's reports of Tammy's attempts to harm others, Tammy consistently denied any intent to harm others. Tammy also was characterized as being irritable frequently. Irritability symptoms appeared to decrease slightly, as Tammy was able to link emotions to stressors and thoughts, as well as to use communication skills to express thoughts and feelings appropriately. Specifically, the depressive irritability appeared to decrease significantly, whereas the mania irritability remained about the same.

Tammy's symptoms of anhedonia decreased significantly, if not subsided, during the course of treatment. Tammy was able to experience pleasure and was eager to engage in activities. The family also reported limited sleep difficulties and Ms. Smith reported that the sleep schedule and routine have been helpful for Tammy. The therapist also did not notice any depressed appearance at the end of treatment *or* throughout treatment and she consistently presented as euthymic. Tammy's mood and behavioral symptoms showed clinically significant reductions as measured by the General Behavior Inventory (both mania and depression) (Danielson et al., 2003; Youngstrom, Findling, Danielson, & Calabrese, 2001), Youth Mania Rating Scale (Young, Biggs, Ziegler, &

Meyer, 1978), and Child Behavior Checklist (Poznanski, Miller, Salguero, & Kelsh, 1984).

Barriers to Treatment

Often times, the therapist had to remain flexible and provide the family with additional behavior-management and crisis-management skills. Tammy frequently demonstrated difficulty in understanding her mood symptoms. Ms. Smith viewed and explained Tammy's difficulties as anger, rather than mood symptoms. Thus, several sessions were devoted to assisting the family with understanding (i.e., labeling, expressing, and addressing) mood symptoms.

Tammy received limited support from family members, which became an important focus of treatment, given its likely relation to Tammy's ultimate response to the intervention. It was often difficult to have Ms. Smith follow through at home and help Tammy to practice or encourage Tammy to use the skills outside of the session; it is important to note that many of the skills within this treatment regimen require frequent practice and use. However, Ms. Smith was often overwhelmed with parenting duties, logistical barriers (e.g., transportation), and her own mental health issues, which led to session cancellations. Given these stressors, additional session time was dedicated to providing support to Ms. Smith, so as to improve her engagement and positive feelings toward the treatment. Ms. Smith also had difficulty on many occasions identifying Tammy's positive behavior. Responsiveness and involvement in treatment also may have proved different with a parent who was more interested in adjunctive psychosocial and pharmacological treatment rather than solely interested in pharmacological treatment. However, Ms. Smith's preference for pharmacological treatment may be a reflection of her personal experience with medication, which she perceived as successful in decreasing her own mood symptoms.

Tammy frequently displayed limited attentional capacity and would become distracted while switching among multiple topics. She would often require redirection to remain on task. As a result, critical skills that would assist in decreasing mood difficulties were jeopardized. These skills included identifying thoughts and connecting them with feelings and behaviors, countering negative thinking, sleep maintenance, assertiveness, and family communication. It appears that most of these skills either involve more complex thinking ability or focuses on interactions with others. Those factors may serve to explain Tammy's problems with grasping new skills.

After the initial 12 sessions, despite Ms. Smith's initial strong hesitation to engage in a psychosocial treatment, she requested to stay in treatment with the study therapist. In the next phase of treatment, the therapist planned to review many of the CBT skills and then move to more of a maintenance model of less frequent sessions.

Overall, the therapist believed that the present treatment manual was a highly resourceful tool for therapy with a complex client. The therapist appreciated various content and skills that the manual addressed to target a range of disorders, with specific focus on those symptoms that are present for children with mood disorders. Given Tammy's age and challenges associated with limited attention, it was difficult to cover and master the target skills within a single session (even with brief reviews in the next session). Having the opportunity to focus on certain core or difficult skills for several weeks at a time may have proved more beneficial, particularly because it was evident that skills were not being practiced or maintained at home. Thus, we would recommend that clinicians flexibly implement the skills and content of the manual to allow for more review, repetition, and mastery of each skill before moving on to the next session. This could mean that some cases would complete the core content within 12 sessions, but many youth with BPSD may need 15 to 20 sessions to master these skills.

FUTURE DIRECTIONS

The need for psychosocial interventions for pediatric BPSD remains high. These disorders are becoming widely diagnosed, and the majority of the treatments with any RCT evidence are pharmacological interventions. Even the most well-researched drug treatments only have evidence of acute efficacy, not long-term maintenance, and long-term safety remains unknown. Psychotherapy would play several pivotal roles in the treatment portfolio: (a) offer adjunctive therapy combined with pharmacotherapy to promote adherence and improve acute outcomes; (b) enhance maintenance and relapse prevention; (c) promote positive social skills, academic achievement, and improved functioning and quality of life; (d) provide treatment options for those families unwilling to initiate pharmacological interventions because of cultural or personal considerations; and (e) provide low-risk interventions that could be used for early intervention or targeted prevention in at-risk youths.

On a broader level, clinicians using adjunctive psychosocial interventions have the ability to specifically address the very factors that are associated with poor outcomes for BPSD in youth (as reviewed previously). For example, clinicians can assist youth and their families in coping with attention or oppositional behaviors that often co-occur with mood symptoms—and help them understand how the mood symptoms impact the behaviors and vice versa. This would not easily be accomplished by medication alone. On a related note, even the most efficacious medication is unable to comprehensively target improving the family environment to create a warm, supportive ecology for both affected youth and their parents. Clinicians using psychosocial interventions can directly address family communication, problem solving, and support, all of which have been shown to increase positive outcomes for youth with BPSD. Similarly, clinicians working with families in which both the youth and a parent are struggling with mental health difficulties may actively collaborate with the parent's clinician so as to ensure repetition and support regarding common goals and skills acquisition.

Given these advantages to the utility of adjunctive psychosocial interventions, there is already evidence that psychotherapy, even at the level of "treatment as usual," is associated with statistically significant gains in outcome and maintenance with pediatric BPSD (DelBello et al., 2007). Thus, considerable progress has been made exporting treatment strategies with demonstrated efficacy in adults and adapting them for use with children and families. These interventions have succeeded in showing tolerability as well as promising results in open trials. Randomized trials are currently under way with several of the leading candidates for efficacious interventions. It is realistic that within the next 3 to 5 years there will be multiple therapies that can accumulate sufficient evidence to pass the threshold for consideration as an "empirically supported treatment" for BPSD. In the interim, the CBT approach described in this chapter offers an example of how one can use evidence-based strategies, guided by related findings and psychological theory, to craft interventions that can be flexible but also designed to meet the specific needs associated with pediatric BPSD.

ACKNOWLEDGMENTS

Research supported by grants from the Ohio Department of Mental Health (Co-PI: J.K. Youngstrom & N. Feeny) and National Institute of Health 5R01 MH066647 (PI: E. Youngstrom).

REFERENCES

American Psychiatric Association. (1994). American Psychiatric Association practice guideline for the treatment of patients with bipolar disorder. *American Journal of Psychiatry, 151* (Suppl.), 1–36.

Asarnow, J. R., Jaycox, L. H., & Tompson, M. C. (2001). Depression in youth: Psychosocial interventions. *Journal of Clinical Child Psychology, 30,* 33–47.

Barbini, B., Bertelli, S., Colombo, C., & Smeraldi, E. (1996). Sleep loss, a possible factor in augmenting manic episode. *Psychiatry Research, 65,* 121–125.

Barlow, D. H. (1996). Health care policy, psychotherapy research, and the future of psychotherapy. *American Psychologist, 51,* 1050–1058.

Basco, M. R., & Rush, A. J. (1996). *Cognitive-behavioral therapy for bipolar disorder.* New York: Guilford Press.

Beck, J. S. (1995). *Cognitive therapy: Basics and beyond.* New York: Guilford Press.

Biederman, J. (1995). Developmental subtypes of juvenile bipolar disorder. *Harvard Psychiatry Review, 3,* 227–230.

Birmaher, B., Axelson, D., Strober, M., Gill, M. K., Valeri, S., Chiappetta, L., et al. (2006). Clinical course of children and adolescents with bipolar spectrum disorders. *Archives of General Psychiatry, 63,* 175–183.

Birmaher, B., Brent, D., & Benson, R. S. (1998). Summary of the practice parameters for the assessment and treatment of children and adolescents with depressive disorders. *Journal of the American Academy of Child & Adolescent Psychiatry, 37,* 1234–1238.

Birmaher, B., Ryan, N. D., Williamson, D. E., Brent, D., & Kaufman, J. (1996). Childhood and adolecent depression: A review of the past 10 years. Part II. *Journal of the American Academy of Child & Adolescent Psychiatry, 35,* 1575–1583.

Bowring, M. A., & Kovacs, M. (1992). Difficulties in diagnosing manic disorders among children. *Journal of the American Academy of Child & Adolescent Psychiatry, 31,* 611–614.

Brondolo, E., & Mas, F. (2001). Cognitive-behavioral strategies for improving medication adherence in patients with bipolar disorder. *Cognitive and Behavioral Practice, 8,* 137–147.

Carlson, G. A., Jensen, P. S., Findling, R. L., Meyer, R. E., Calabrese, J., DelBello, M. P., et al. (2003). Methodological issues and controversies in clinical trials with child and adolescent patients with bipolar disorder: Report of a consensus conference. *Journal of Child Adolescent Psychopharmacology, 13,* 13–27.

Clarke, G. N., Rohde, P., Lewinsohn, P. M., Hops, H., & Seeley, J. R. (1999). Cognitive-behavioral treatment of adolescent depression: Efficacy of acute group treatment and booster sessions. *Journal of the American Academy of Child & Adolescent Psychiatry, 38,* 272–279.

Cochran, S. D. (1984). Preventing medical noncompliance in the outpatient treatment of bipolar affective disorder. *Journal of Consulting & Clinical Psychology, 52,* 873–878.

Craddock, N., & Jones, I. (1999). Genetics of bipolar disorder. *Journal of Medical Genetics, 36,* 585–594.

Curry, J. F. (2001). Specific psychotherapies for childhood and adolescent depression. *Biological Psychiatry, 49,* 1091–1100.

Danielson, C. K., Feeny, N. C., Findling, R. L., & Youngstrom, E. A. (2004). Psychosocial treatment of bipolar disorders in adolescents: A proposed cognitive-behavioral intervention. *Cognitive & Behavioral Practice, 11,* 283–297.

Danielson, C. K., Youngstrom, E. A., Findling, R. L., & Calabrese, J. R. (2003). Discriminative validity of the General Behavior Inventory using youth report. *Journal of Abnormal Child Psychology, 31,* 29–39.

Davidson, K.H., & Fristad, M. A. (2008). Psychoeducational psychotherapy. In B. Geller & M. DelBello (Eds.), *Treatment of bipolar disorder in children and adolescents* (pp. 184–201). New York: Guilford Press.

DelBello, M. P., Hanseman, D., Adler, C. M., Fleck, D. E., & Strakowski, S. M. (2007). Twelve-month outcome of adolescents with bipolar disorder following first hospitalization for a manic or mixed episode. *American Journal of Psychiatry, 164,* 582–590.

Dunner, D. L., Hensel, B. M., & Fieve, R. R. (1979). Bipolar illness: Factors in drinking behavior. *American Journal of Psychiatry, 136,* 583–585.

Ellicott, A., Hammen, C., Gitlin, M. J., Brown, G., & Jamison, K. (1990). Life events and the course of bipolar disorder. *American Journal of Psychiatry, 147,* 1194–1198.

Feeny, N. C., Danielson, C., Schwartz, L., Youngstrom, E. A., & Findling, R. L. (2006). CBT for bipolar disorders in adolescents: A pilot study. *Bipolar Disorders, 8,* 508–515.

Findling, R. L., McNamara, N. K., Youngstrom, E. A., Stansbrey, R., Gracious, B. L., Reed, M. D., et al. (2005). Double-blind 18-month trial of lithium versus divalproex maintenance treatment in pediatric bipolar disorder. *Journal of the American Academy of Child & Adolescent Psychiatry, 44,* 409–417.

Findling, R. L., Youngstrom, E. A., McNamara, N. K., Stansbrey, R. J., Demeter, C. A., Bedoya, D., et al. (2005). Early symptoms of mania and the role of parental risk. *Bipolar Disorders, 7,* 623–634.

Ford, D. E., & Cooper-Patrick, L. (2001). Sleep disturbances and mood disorders: An epidemiological perspective. *Depression and Anxiety, 14,* 3–6.

Frank, E., Kupfer, D. J., Ehlers, C. L., Monk, T. H., Corners, C., Carter, S., & Frankel, D. (1994). Interpersonal and social rhythm therapy for bipolar disorder: Integrating interpersonal and behavioral approaches. *Behavior Therapy, 17,* 143–149.

Fristad, M. A., Arnett, M. M., & Gavazzi, S. M. (1998). The impact of psychoeducational workshops on families of mood-disordered children. *Family Therapy, 25,* 151–159.

Fristad, M. A., Gavazzi, S. M., & Soldano, K. W. (1998). Multi-family psychoeducation groups for childhood mood disorders: A program description and preliminary efficacy data. *Contemporary Family Therapy: An International Journal, 20,* 385–402.

Fristad, M. A., Goldberg-Arnold, J. S., & Gavazzi, S. M. (1999, June). *Multifamily psychoeducation groups for families of children with bipolar disorder*. Presented at the Third International Conference on Bipolar Disorder, Pittsburgh, PA.

Fristad, M. A., Goldberg-Arnold, J. S., & Gavazzi, S. M. (2002). Multifamily psychoeducation groups (MFPG) for families of children with bipolar disorder. *Bipolar Disorders, 4,* 254–262.

Geller, B., Craney, J. L., Bolhofner, K., Nickelsburg, M.J., Williams, M., & Zimerman, B. (2002). Two-year prospective follow-up of children with a prepubertal and early adolescent bipolar disorder phenotype. *American Journal of Psychiatry, 159,* 927–933.

Geller, B., Tillman, R., Craney, J. L., & Bolhofner, K. (2004). Four-year prospective outcome and natural history of mania in children with a prepubertal and early adolescent bipolar disorder phenotype. *Archives of General Psychiatry, 61,* 459–467.

Gitlin, M. J., Swendsen, J., Heller, T. L., & Hammen, C. (1995). Relapse and impairment in bipolar disorder. *American Journal of Psychiatry, 152,* 1635–1640.

Goldstein, T. R., Axelson, D. A., Birmaher, B., & Brent, D. A. (2007). Dialectical behavior therapy for adolescents with bipolar disorder: A 1-year open trial. *Journal of the American Academy of Child & Adolescent Psychiatry, 46,* 820–830.

Goodwin, F. K., & Jamison, K. R. (1990). *Manic-depressive illness.* New York: Oxford University Press.

Gutierrez, M. J., & Scott, J. (2004). Psychological treatment for bipolar disorders: A review of randomized controlled trials. *European Archives of Psychiatry & Clinical Neuroscience, 254,* 92–98.

Hammen, C., Ellicott, A., & Gitlin, M. (1992). Stressors and sociotropy/autonomy: A longitudinal study of their relationship to the course of bipolar disorder. *Cognitive Therapy, 16,* 409–418.

Hlastala, S. A., Frank, E., Kowalski, J., Sherrill, J. T., & Tu, X. M. (2000). Stressful life events, bipolar disorder, and the "kindling model." *Journal of Abnormal Psychology, 109,* 777–786.

Hoagwood, K., Hibbs, E., Brent, D., & Jensen, P. (1995). Introduction to the Special Section: Efficacy and effectiveness in studies of child and adolescent psychotherapy. *Journal of Consulting & Clinical Psychology, 63,* 683–687.

Hooley, J. M. (1987). The nature and origins of expressed emotion. In K. Hahlweg & M. J. Goldstein (Eds.), *Understanding major mental disorder: The contribution of family interaction research* (pp. 176–194). New York: Family Process Press.

Howard, K. I., Moras, K., Brill, P. L., Martinovich, Z., & Lutz, W. (1996). Evaluation of psychotherapy: Efficacy, effectiveness, and patient progress. *American Psychologist,* 51, 1059–1064.

Hunt, N., Bruce-Jones, W., & Silverstone, T. (1992). Life events and relapse in bipolar affective disorders. *Journal of Affective Disorders, 25,* 13–20.

Isometsa, E. T. (1993). Course, outcome, and suicide risk in bipolar disorder: A review. *Psychiatric Fennica, 24,* 113–124.

Johnson, S. L., Meyer, B., Winett, C., & Small, J. (2000). Social support and self-esteem predict changes in bipolar depression but not mania. *Journal of Affective Disorders,* 58, 79–86.

Johnson, S. L., & Miller, I. (1997). Negative life events and time to recovery from episodes of bipolar disorder. *Journal of Abnormal Psychology, 106*, 449–457.

Johnson, S. L., & Roberts, J. E. (1995). Life events and bipolar disorder: Implications from biological theories. *Psychological Bulletin, 117*, 434–449.

Johnson, S. L., Sandrow, D., Meyer, B., Winters, R., Miller, I., Solomon, D., et al. (2000). Increases in manic symptoms after life events involving goal attainment. *Journal of Abnormal Psychology, 109*, 721–727.

Johnson, S. L., & Tran, T. (2007). Bipolar disorder: What can psychotherapists learn from the cognitive research? *Journal of Clinical Psychology, 63*, 425–432.

Johnson, S. L., Winnet, C. A., Meyer, B., Greenhouse, W. J., & Miller, I. (1999). Social support and the course of bipolar disorder. *Journal of Abnormal Psychology, 108*, 558–566.

Judd, L. J., Akiskal, H. S., Schettler, P. J., Coryell, W., Endicott, J., Maser, J. D., et al. (2003). A prospective investigation of the natural history of long-term weekly symptomatic status of Bipolar II Disorder. *Archives of General Psychiatry, 60*, 261–269.

Kafantaris, V. (1995). Treatment of bipolar disorder in children and adolescents. *Journal of the American Academy of Child & Adolescent Psychiatry, 34*, 732–741.

Kennedy, S., Thompson, R., Stancer, H. C., Roy, A., & Persad, E. (1983). Life events precipitating mania. *British Journal of Psychiatry, 142*, 398-403.

Kessing, L. V., Andersen, P. K., Mortensen, P. B., & Bolwig, T. G. (1998). Recurrence in affective disorder: I. Case register study. *British Journal of Psychiatry, 172*, 23–28.

Kowatch, R. A., Findling, R. L., Scheffer, R. E., & Stanford, K. E. (2007, October). *Placebo-controlled trial of divalproex versus lithium for bipolar disorder.* Poster presented at the American Academy of Child and Adolescent Psychiatry Meeting, Boston.

Kowatch, R. A., Fristad, M., Birmaher, B., Wagner, K. D., Findling, R., Hellander, M., et al. (2005). Treatment guidelines for children and adolescents with bipolar disorder. *Journal of American Academy of Child & Adolescent Psychiatry, 44*, 213–235.

Kowatch, R. A., Youngstrom, E. A., Danielyan, A., & Findling, R. L. (2005). Review and meta-analysis of the phenomenology and clinical characteristics of mania in children and adolescents. *Bipolar Disorders, 7*, 483–496.

Kroll, L., Harrington, R., Jayson, D., Fraser, J., & Gowers, S. (1996). Pilot study of continuation cognitive-behavioral therapy for major depression in adolescent psychiatric patients. *Journal of the American Academy of Child & Adolescent Psychiatry, 35*, 1156–1161.

Lam, D. H., Bright, J., Jones, S., Hayward, P., Schuck, N., Chisholm, D., et al. (2000). Cognitive therapy for bipolar illness: A pilot study of relapse prevention. *Cognitive Therapy & Research, 24*, 503–520.

Leibenluft, E., Albert, P. S., Rosenthal, N. E., & Wehr, T. A. (1996). Relationship between sleep and mood between patients with rapid-cycling bipolar disorder. *Psychiatry Research, 63*, 161–168.

Lewinsohn, G. N., Clarke, P., Rhode, H., Hops, H., & Seeley, J. (1996). A course in coping: A cognitive-behavioral approach to the treatment of adolescent depression.

In E. D. Hibbs & P. S. Jensen (Eds), *Psychosocial treatments for child and adolescent disorders: Empirically based strategies for clinical practice* (pp. 109–135). Washington, DC: American Psychological Association.

Lewinsohn, P. M., & Clarke, G. (1986). *The Coping with Depression Course—Adolescent version: Parent manual*. Unpublished manuscript, Oregon Research Institute, Eugene, OR. Press,

Lewinsohn, P. M., Clarke, G. N., Hops, H., & Andrews, J. (1990). Cognitive-behavioral treatment for depressed adolescents. *Behavior Therapy, 21*, 385–401.

Lofthouse, N., & Fristad, M.A. (2004). Psychosocial interventions for children with early-onset bipolar spectrum disorder. *Clinical Child & Family Psychology Review, 7*, 71–88.

Lopez, A. D., Mathers, C. D., Ezzati, M., Jamison, D. T., & Murray, C. J. (2006). Global and regional burden of disease and risk factors, 2001: Systematic analysis of population health data. *Lancet, 367*(9524), 1747–1757.

Lozano, B. E., & Johnson, S. L. (2001). Can personality traits predict increases in manic and depressive symptoms? *Journal of Affective Disorders, 63*, 103–111.

Malkoff-Schwartz, S., Frank, E., Anderson, B., Sherrill, J. T., Siegel, L., Patterson, D., et al.. (1998). Stressful life events and social rhythm disruption in the onset of manic and depressive bipolar episodes: A preliminary investigation. *Archives of General Psychiatry, 55*, 702–707.

McClellan, J., & Werry, J. (1997). Practice parameters for the assessment and treatment of children and adolescents with bipolar disorder. *Journal of the American Academy of Child & Adolescent Psychiatry, 36*, 138–157.

Miklowitz, D. J., & Alloy, L. Y. (1999). Psychosocial factors in the course and treatment of bipolar disorder: Introduction to the special section. *Journal of Abnormal Psychology, 108*, 555–566.

Miklowitz, D. J., Frank, E., & George, E. L. (1996). New psychosocial treatments for the outpatient management of bipolar disorder. *Psychopharmacology Bulletin, 32*, 613–621.

Miklowitz, D. J, George, E.L., Axelson, D.A., Kim, E.Y., Birmaher, B., Schneck, C., et al. (2004). Family-focused treatment for adolescents with bipolar disorder. *Journal of Affective Disorders, 82*, S113–S128.

Miklowitz, D. J., & Goldstein, M. J. (1997). *Bipolar disorder: A family-focused treatment approach*. New York: Guilford Press.

Miklowitz, D. L., Goldstein, M. J., Nuechterlein, K. H., Snyder, K. S., & Mintz, J. (1988). Family factors and the course of bipolar affective disorder. *Archives of General Psychiatry, 45*, 225–231.

Miklowitz, D. J., Mullen, K., & Chang, K. (2008). Family-focused treatment for bipolar disorder in adolescence. In B. Geller & M.Delbello (Eds.), *Treatment of child and adolescent bipolar disorder* (pp. 166–183). New York: Guilford Press.

Miklowitz, D. J., Otto, M. W., Frank, E., Reilly-Harrington, N. A., Kogan, J., Sachs, G. S., et al. (2007). Intensive psychosocial intervention enhances functioning in patients with bipolar depression: Results from a 9-month randomized controlled trial. *American Journal of Psychiatry, 164*, 1340–1347.

Miklowitz, D. J., Wendel, J. S., & Simoneau, T. L. (1998). Targeting dysfunctional family interactions and high expressed emotion in the psychosocial treatment of bipolar disorder. *In Session: Psychotherapy in Practice, 4*, 25–38.

Norquist, G., Leibowitz, B., & Hyman, S. (1999). Expanding the frontier of treatment research. *Prevention and Treatment, 2*, np.

Nottelmann, E. D., & Jensen, P. S. (1995). Comorbidity of disorders in children and adolescents: Developmental perspectives. In T. H. Ollendick & R. J. Prinz (Eds.), *Advances in clinical child psychology* (Vol. 17, pp. 109–155). New York: Plenum Press.

Patelis-Siotis, I., Young, T., Robb, J. C., Marriott, M., Bieling, P. J., Cox, L. C., et al. (2001). Group cognitive behavioral therapy for bipolar disorder: A feasibility and effectiveness study. *Journal of Affective Disorders, 65*, 145–153.

Pavuluri, M. N., Graczyk, P. A., Henry, D. B., Carbray, J. A., Heidenreich, J., & Miklowitz, D. J. (2004). Child- and family-focused cognitive behavioral therapy for pediatric bipolar disorder: Development and preliminary results. *Journal of the American Academy of Child & Adolescent Psychiatry, 43*, 528–537.

Peet, M., & Harvey, N. S. (1991). Lithium maintenance: I: A standard education program for patients. *British Journal of Psychiatry, 158*, 197–200.

Perugi, G. (2008). Comorbidity and treatment issues in juvenile bipolar disorder. *Annals of General Psychiatry*, 7(Suppl. 1), S43.

Post, R. M., Kopin, I. J., & Goodwin, F. K. (1976). Effects of sleep deprivation on mood and central amine metabolism in depressed patients. *Archives of General Psychiatry, 33*, 627–632.

Poznanski, E. O., Miller, E., Salguero, C., & Kelsh, R. C. (1984). Preliminary studies of the reliability and validity of the Children's Depression Rating Scale. *Journal of the American Academy of Child Psychiatry, 23*, 191–197.

Prien, R. F., & Potter, W. Z. (1990). NIMH workshop report on treatment of bipolar disorder. *Psychopharmacology Bulletin, 26*, 409–427.

Reiger, D. A., Farmer, M. E., & Rae, D. S. (1990). Comorbidity of mental disorders with alcohol and other drug abuse: Results from the Epidemiologic Catchment Area (ECA) Study. *Journal of the American Medical Association, 21*, 2549–2550.

Reilly-Harrington, N. A., Alloy, L. B., Fresco, D. M., & Whitehouse, W. G. (1999). Cognitive styles and life events interact to predict bipolar and unipolar symptomology. *Journal of Abnormal Psychology, 108*, 567–578.

Reinecke, M. A., Ryan, N. E., & DuBois, D. L. (1998). Cognitive-behavioral therapy of depression and depressive symptoms during adolescence: A review and meta-analysis. *Journal of the American Academy of Child & Adolescent Psychiatry, 37*, 26–34.

Roberts, R. E., Roberts, C. R., & Chen, I. G. (2001). Functioning of adolescents with symptoms of disturbed sleep. *Journal of Youth & Adolescence, 30*, 1–18.

Rothbaum, B. O., & Astin, M. C. (2000). Integration of pharmacotherapy and psychotherapy for bipolar disorder. *Journal of Clinical Psychiatry, 61*, 68–75.

Seligman, M. E. P. (1995). The effectiveness of psychotherapy: The Consumer Reports study. *American Psychologist, 50*, 965–974.

Sharma, V., Yatham, L. N., & Haslam, D. R. S. (1997). Continuation and prophylactic treatment of bipolar disorder. *Canadian Journal of Psychiatry, 42*, 92–100.

Stoddard, F. J., Post, R. M., & Bunney Jr., W. M. (1977). Slow and rapid psychobiological alterations in a manic depressive: Clinical phenomenology. *British Journal of Psychiatry, 130*, 72–78.

Straus, S. E., Richardson, W. S., Glasziou, P., & Haynes, R. B. (2005). *Evidence-based medicine: How to practice and teach EBM* (3rd ed.). New York: Churchill Livingstone.

Street, L. L., Niederehe, G., & Lebowitz, B. D. (2000). Toward greater public health relevance for psychotherapeutic intervention research: An NIMH workshop report. *Clinical Psychology: Science & Practice, 7*, 127–137.

Strober, M., Morrell, W., Lampert, C., & Burroughs, J. (1990). Relapse following discontinuation of lithium maintenance therapy in adolescents with bipolar I illness: A naturalistic study. *American Journal of Psychiatry, 147*, 457–461.

The TADS Team. (2007). The Treatment for Adolescents with Depression Study (TADS): Long-term effectiveness and safety outcomes. *Archives of General Psychiatry, 64*, 1132–1144.

Van Gent, E. M., & Zwart, F. M. (1991). Psychoeducation of partners of bipolar manic patients. *Journal of Affective Disorders, 21*, 15–18.

Wehr, T. A. (1989). Sleep loss: A preventable cause of mania and other excited states. *Journal of Clinical Psychiatry, 50*, 8–16.

Wehr, T. A. (1992). Improvement of depression and triggering of mania by sleep deprivation. *Journal of the American Medical Association, 267*, 548–551.

Weisz, J., McCarty, C. A., & Valeri, S. M. (2006). Effects of psychotherapy for depression in children and adolescents: A meta-analysis. *Psychological Bulletin, 132*, 132–149.

West, A. E, Henry, D. B., & Pavuluri, M. N. (2007). Maintenance model of integrated psychosocial treatment in pediatric bipolar: A pilot feasibility study. *Journal of the American Academy of Child & Adolescent Psychiatry, 46*, 205–212.

Wilens, T. E., Biederman, J., Adamson, J. J., Henin, A., Sgambati, S., Gignac, M., et al. (2008). Further evidence of an association between adolescent bipolar disorder with smoking and substance use disorders: A controlled study. *Drug and Alcohol Dependence, 95*, 188–198.

Wilkinson, G. B., Taylor, P., & Holt, J. R. (2002). Bipolar disorder in adolescence: Diagnosis and treatment. *Journal of Mental Health Counseling, 24*, 348–357.

Winokur, G., Coryell, W., & Akiskal, H. (1995). Alcoholism in manic-depressive (bipolar) illness: Familial illness, course of illness, and the primary-secondary distinction. *American Journal of Psychiatry, 152*, 365–372.

Wu, J. C., & Bunney, W. E. (1990). The biological basis of the antidepressant response to sleep deprivation and relapse; Review and hypothesis. *American Journal of Psychiatry, 147*, 14–21.

Young, R. C., Biggs, J. T., Ziegler, V. E., & Meyer, D. A. (1978). A rating scale for mania: Reliability, validity, and sensitivity. *British Journal of Psychiatry, 133*, 429–435.

Youngstrom, E. A. (2007). Pediatric bipolar disorder. In E. J. Mash & R. A. Barkley (Eds.), *Assessment of childhood disorders* (4th ed., pp. 253–304). New York: Guilford Press.

Youngstrom, E. A., Birmaher, B., & Findling, R. L. (2008). Pediatric bipolar disorder: Validity, phenomenology, and recommendations for diagnosis. *Bipolar Disorders, 10* (Suppl. 1), 194–214.

Youngstrom, E. A., Findling, R. L., Danielson, C. K., & Calabrese, J. R. (2001). Discriminative validity of parent report of hypomanic and depressive symptoms on the General Behavior Inventory. *Psychological Assessment, 13*, 267–276.
Zarate, Jr., C. A., Tohen, M., Land, M., & Cavanagh, S. (2000). Functional impairment and cognition in bipolar disorder. *Psychiatry Quarterly, 71*, 309–329.

13

Oppositional Defiant and Conduct Disorders

CLINT E. FIELD

Virtually every parent is occasionally challenged by his or her child's contentious or disruptive behavior. Such behavior is so common that the developmental period of toddlerhood is routinely referred to as the "terrible twos." Disobedience and temper tantrums are among the most common negative behaviors observed among young children. Display of these behaviors is typical during early childhood, yet their temporal persistence may be indicative of emerging clinical problems. Disruptive behavior concerns are the most common problems reported to pediatricians by parents (Arndorfer, Allen, & Aljazireh, 1999) and have increased as a treatment focus in primary care pediatric clinics over the past 20 years (Hoagwood, Kelleher, Feil, & Comer, 2000; Kelleher, McInerny, Gardner, Childs, & Wasserman, 2000), resulting in their being considered the "new morbidity" of pediatrics (Haggerty, Roughman, & Pless, 1975).

Parents are confronted with the task of recognizing developmentally typical disruptive behavior displayed by their children and responding in a manner that diminishes the likelihood of sustained negative behavioral displays in later childhood. The task of parsing that which is behaviorally typical from the atypical, relative to developmental stage, is increasingly being perceived as paramount. Recent research has suggested that a substantial portion of youth who display chronic and severe disruptive behavior during later childhood and adolescence also displayed significant behavior problems during early childhood, lending empirical support to the notion that early chronic disruptive behaviors may function as developmental precursors of subsequent antisocial or delinquent behavior (Campbell, 1995). Thus, it is not surprising to discover that the most common concerns brought to the attention of pediatricians persist as the most frequent referral concerns among older children and adolescents referred for mental health services (Kazdin, 1995b).

PRIMARY SYMPTOMS AND DIAGNOSTIC CRITERIA

Children may display a broad range of negative or disruptive behavior. Such behavior can appear simplistic, unsophisticated, and quite impulsive among young children. With age, disruptive behaviors are more likely to co-occur and are more complex given the child's social experience and developing cognitive abilities. Throughout this chapter, the term "conduct problems" (CP) will be adopted as a general reference for children's disruptive behaviors of all types (McMahon, Wells, & Kotler, 2006). Specific references to disruptive behavior diagnoses will be used when the distinction between these and CPs is noteworthy.

The American Psychiatric Association's (APA) *Diagnostic and Statistical Manual of Mental Disorders, Fourth Edition, Text Revision* (*DSM-IV-TR*; 2000) provides commonly accepted criteria for establishing a disagnosis of disruptive behavior disorder. Symptoms or behaviors are considered within a categorical classification framework wherein diagnostic criteria are counted as either present or absent. The *DSM-IV-TR* includes a section titled "Attention-Deficit and Disruptive Behavior Disorders" (pp. 85–103) (see also chapter 14, this volume) that specifies the diagnostic criteria of the disruptive behavior disorders that compose the diagnostic focus of this chapter: oppositional defiant disorder (ODD) and conduct disorder (CD).

Consistent with a categorical diagnostic approach to classification, these diagnostic classes require a cluster of CP to be present to establish a diagnosis. Thus, it can be assumed that when a diagnosis has been made, there are not only problems with sufficient frequency and intensity to cause concern, but there are also several problems co-occurring within a defined period of time. From a clinical perspective, it is important to note that most disruptive behaviors possess the potential to stand out to parents as problematic and worthy of clinical attention.

Thus, even though formal diagnostic criteria for a given disruptive behavior disorder may not be present, practitioners may be called on to provide clinical services. Consider as an example a youth who has developed a dishonesty problem. This behavior may cause a variety of social problems for the youth and generate serious concern among the youth's parents, yet dishonesty is not a diagnosable problem. However, dishonesty is a behavior that could contribute to a formal disruptive behavior diagnosis when it co-occurs with other CP. Regardless, dishonesty could function as the sole focus of clinical intervention. Following are the currently accepted diagnostic criteria for ODD and CD.

OPPOSITIONAL DEFIANT DISORDER

Oppositional defiant disorder may be expressed in a variety of ways, but generally requires a consistent pattern of negativity, hostility, or defiance directed toward authority figures such as parents and teachers. It is the frequency, intensity, and consistency with which such problems are displayed that typically trigger formal diagnosis. Specific diagnostic criteria require that at least four of eight problematic behaviors be present over the course of a 6-month period. Primary behaviors to be considered include: loss of temper, arguing with adults, refusing to comply with adult requests, deliberately annoying others or blaming others for one's mistakes, being easily annoyed by others, displaying anger or resentment toward others, and engaging in spiteful or vindictive behavior. The essence of this diagnosis is defiance or oppositionality, which often presents as noncompliance. In addition to the consistent display of the aforementioned behaviors, diagnostic criteria specify that functional impairment (typically social or academic) must be present. Further, the oppositional behaviors cannot be accounted for by an alternative psychological problem; and ODD can only be diagnosed if criteria are not met for the more severe disruptive behavior disorders such as CD (APA, 2000). Oppositional defiant disorder is most commonly observed among younger children (McMahon & Forehand, 2003).

CONDUCT DISORDER

In contrast to ODD, CD is viewed as a disorder of greater severity. It is not uncommon to see ODD symptomatology displayed among youth who qualify for a CD diagnosis. At the essence of CD is a repetitive pattern of behaving that violates the rights of others and contrasts with societal norms as they are generally accepted. In contrast to ODD, only 3 of 15 negative behaviors must be displayed during a single 12-month period, with at least one problem behavior having been displayed in the immediate past 6 months. Within the *DSM-IV-TR* framework, severe problem behaviors of CD are generally categorized as a type of aggression toward people or animals (e.g., fighting, weapon use, physical cruelty, forced sexual advances), destruction of property (e.g., fire setting, vandalism), deceitfulness or theft (e.g., breaking into other's property, purposeful dishonesty, theft without confrontation), or reflecting serious rule violations (e.g., curfew violations at an early age, running away from home, truancy prior to age 13 years). As with ODD, CD behaviors must cause significant impairment in social, academic, or occupational domains and cannot qualify for antisocial personality disorder (APA, 2000). Given the nature of the diagnostic criteria, CD is more likely to be diagnosed among older children and adolescents. The *DSM-IV-TR* makes a distinction between childhood-onset CD and adolescent-onset CD—a distinction that possesses implications for treatment and may also be useful in developing a clinical conceptualization of problem behavior.

CHARACTERISTICS OF DISRUPTIVE BEHAVIOR PROBLEMS

The display of mild CP by toddlers is very common and is likely linked to aspects of the child's development (e.g., inability to meet needs, inability to communicate, limited emotional control). Evidence suggests that CP occurs more commonly than any other type of problem among clinical and nonclinical samples of children (Quay, 1986). Depending on age and type of sample, ODD prevalence rate estimates have been observed to range from approximately 2% to as high as 15%. Prevalence rates of CD have similarly been described as ranging from approximately 1% to 16% (Costello, 1990; Loeber, Burke, Lahey, Winters, & Zera, 2000). Conduct problems have also been observed to vary according to gender. Generally speaking, boys are more often identified as displaying CP, with rates being as much as four times greater for boys than girls when assigning formal diagnoses. Another consistent gender-related finding has been that boys are more likely to engage in overt defiance and direct aggression than girls, who are more likely to engage in relational aggression (Anderson, Williams, McGee, & Silva, 1987; Crick & Grotpeter, 1995).

As alluded to previously, a significant degree of temporal stability has been observed for CP. The available data has suggested that problems which emerge and endure throughout early childhood are likely to linger into later childhood (Campbell, 1995). The stability of CP over time punctuates the need for early identification and early, effective intervention, even in the absence of formal diagnosis. The development of life-impairing health concerns (e.g., physical injury, addiction), life-altering circumstances (e.g., pregnancy, gang involvement), and altered social opportunity (e.g., criminal status) are potential long-term consequences of chronic CP (Keenan, Loeber, & Green, 1999; Maughan & Rutter, 2001; Zoccolillo, Paquette, & Tremblay, 2005).

The degree of temporal stability associated with CP may be partially accounted for through examination of data describing developmental course. Evidence suggests that a prominent subset of youth who exhibit CP may begin to do so early in life (e.g., during preschool years) and it may persist for years. This particular developmental pathway has been termed the "early-starter" pathway (Patterson, Capaldi, & Bank, 1991; Snyder, Reid, & Patterson, 2003) and is very consistent with accounts of temporal stability of CP. The "late-starter" pathway is an alternative account of development of CD, which posits that significant problems emerge primarily during adolescence. It is generally thought that the late-starter pathway accounts for a greater number of children exhibiting CP and has generally been associated with less chronic and less intense CP (Moffitt, Caspi, Dickson, Filva, & Stanton, 1996; Patterson, et al., 1991).

RISK AND CAUSAL FACTORS

A precise genetic account for CP has not yet been delineated. Nonetheless, it is plausible to believe that at least a subset of children with CP may have inherited an antisocial tendency (Kazdin, 1995b; Schroeder & Gordon, 2002). Some researchers have argued that CP subtypes may exist and that unique patterns of problem development and progression may be accounted for by differences in degree of heritability (Gjone,

Stevenson, Sundet, & Eilertsen, 1996; Rutter et al., 1990). Sufficient evidence has accumulated which suggests that child temperament is likely linked to the display of CP. Although the contribution of temperament to CP development has yet to be firmly established, it is clear that temperament can be associated with limited attachment, aggressive behavior, emotional reactivity, and resistance to being controlled by others (Bates, Pettit, Dodge, & Ridge, 1998; Caspi, Henry, McGee, Moffitt, & Silva, 1995; Greenberg, 1999; Snyder & Stoolmiller, 2002).

There are a host of environmental factors that have been implicated in the maintenance, if not the cause, of CP. In association with several decades of research they have conducted concerning children with CP and their families, Patterson and his colleagues have formulated an influential nonbiological theory of cause (Patterson, 2002; Patterson, Chamberlain, & Reid, 1982). This theory has been termed the coercive model and generally posits that CP may be primarily accounted for by chronic, negative, and intense parent–child interactions wherein each attempts to coerce or control the other. Central to this theory is data suggesting that both parents and children are unintentionally, yet effectively, reinforced for engaging in increasingly intense conflictual relations via the display of aversive behavior (e.g., tantrums, arguing, noncompliance, yelling, threats, physical force). The coercive model asserts that the onset of a CP is linked to the child's display of typical or developmentally appropriate misbehavior (e.g., noncompliance during preschool years) that parents respond to ineffectively. Over time, the class of inappropriate behavior expands while coercive strategies are practiced and modeled with consistency.

Within the coercive model, a number of factors have been identified that enhance the risk that children may develop CP. A thorough review of these factors is beyond the scope of this chapter, but several authoritative reviews are available to the interested reader (McGee & Williams, 1999; McMahon et al., 2006). Stated briefly, risk factors have generally been described as falling into one of three primary domains: (a) factors associated with the child (e.g., temperament, attachment, language impairment, problems with self-esteem), (b) problems in parenting (e.g., limited responsivity, poor parenting style, parental psychopathology), or (c) problems with the environment and social group (e.g., low socioeconomic status, family discord, peer rejection, dangerous neighborhoods/school).

EFFECTIVE TREATMENT FOR CONDUCT PROBLEMS

The most effective treatments for CP align closely with the prominent theories and factors thought to be involved in the development and maintenance of a CP. As described previously, etiological theories of CP posit that there is a complex interaction among child (e.g., temperament, learning and reinforcement history), parent (e.g., psychopathology, parenting strategies), and environmental (e.g., socioeconomic status, community influence, peer influence) variables that give rise to the initial display, maintenance, and increase in a CP over time. In short, the prevailing causal theories predict that a CP arises largely as a result of deficient skills—both on the part of the parent (e.g., identifying emergent problems, establishing or clarifying expectations, creating and maintaining structure, using effective consequences) and the child (e.g., poor problem-solving skills, limited emotional control, inability to communicate needs). The approaches to treatment that possess the greatest empirical support target these various factors directly. Eyberg, Nelson, and Boggs (2008) recently conducted an exhaustive review of the treatment literature to identify "best practices" or current evidence-based treatments for disruptive behavior problems, or CP. Three general conclusions can be drawn from their work.

First, there is little evidence indicating that medications can be used to effectively treat a CP. Medications have typically been used with CP to manage aggressive behaviors in children and not to address the underlying cause of the CP. To this end, the American Academy of Child and Adolescent Psychiatry has stated that medication may be integrated as a component of treatment for a CP, but is insufficient as an independent approach to treatment and should be used only if evidence-based psychosocial treatments have failed (Connor et al., 2006; Steiner, 1997). Second, there are a number of treatments that have been designed to treat children directly, most of which focus on social skill development or anger control, which qualify as "probably efficacious" or likely effective yet need additional evaluation (Chambless & Hollon, 1998). Third, there are a number of treatments that have been designed to target parenting skill deficits. These various treatment approaches are often referred to as behavioral parent training programs and generally overlap considerably in their approach to treatment. The primary goal of parent training is to enhance parent understanding of disruptive behavior and promote mastery in implementing basic behavioral management skills within the home environment. The majority of parent training programs have been established as probably efficacious in the treatment of CP. One approach to parent training, the Parent Management Training Oregon Model (PMTO), has attained "well-established" status as treatment for CP (Chambless & Hollon, 1998). Stated differently, sufficient data exists and has indicated that PMTO is more effective than comparison treatments in treating CP.

Many families referred for treatment of CP are initially offered behavioral parent training, since CP often emerges during early childhood and because behavioral parent training is considered the "first line approach" to treatment (Eyberg et al., 2008, p. 233). As indicated previously, there is a tremendous amount of overlap between behavioral parent training programs, yet only PMTO currently possesses well-established treatment status. This approach to treatment is reviewed in some detail to provide the reader with a general sense of behavioral parent training strategies.

Parent Management Training (Bernal, Klinnert, & Schultz, 1980; Patterson et al., 1982) is a behavioral parent training program used with the parents of children who have exhibited CP. Length of treatment varies but usually requires between 10 to 20 hours of direct therapeutic contact. PMTO assumes that the cause of a CP lies in the social environment, and this is the direct target of treatment. Within PMTO, parents are trained, often through the use of role playing, to (a) monitor their child's behavior, (b) use positive interactions (e.g., praise, attention, additional rewards) strategically to encourage display of prosocial behavior, (c) use positive and negative consequences (e.g., time-out) to alter environmental contingencies and teach new behavior, and (d) engage in family-based problem solving as needed, while (e) maintaining positive parental involvement in the child's life over time. Therapy is typically implemented in a step-wise fashion, wherein parents attend weekly therapy sessions, are trained to implement core strategies within the home environment, and are provided ample opportunity for practice and feedback within sessions. Parents then implement strategies within the home environment between sessions. A variety of data is collected to monitor treatment progress, and therapy typically concludes when core skills have been implemented and child behavior has markedly improved.

FACTORS ASSOCIATED WITH POOR TREATMENT RESPONSE

As mentioned previously, children who exhibit CP comprise the largest source of referrals to children's mental health services in the United States, accounting for up to half of all service requests (Sholevar & Sholevar, 1995). Unfortunately, not all children are treated successfully. Older children and adolescents who display severe CP are at risk of being removed from their home and community because of treatment needs (Friman, 1999). Although behavioral parent training has been recognized as effective in the treatment of CP (Eyberg et al., 2008), data have indicated that approximately one third of families fail to complete treatment (Forehand, Middlebrook, Rogers, & Steffe, 1983; Sanders, Markie-Dadds, Tully, & Bor, 2000), whereas another substantial subset of children fail to exhibit behavioral improvement despite completing treatment (Patterson, 1974; Webster-Stratton, Hollingsworth, & Kolpacoff, 1989). In sum, parent training appears to be consistently effective for less than 50% of targeted youth. The factors that contribute to this phenomenon are not fully understood and this is an important area of ongoing and needed research. Outlined below is a brief summary of factors that may be associated with negative treatment outcome. It should be noted, however, that primarily mixed results have emerged from efforts to replicate many factor-specific findings (Eyberg et al., 2008). McMahon and colleagues (2006) have conducted a detailed review of the treatment response literature for the interested reader.

Family Factors

Within parent training contexts, a significant amount of time may be devoted to addressing problems related to familial dysfunction (e.g., marital concerns, parent psychopathology; Patterson & Chamberlain, 1988). Allocating resources to address such factors is costly; however, this may represent an important aspect of successful CP treatment if obstacles are reduced. Research in this domain has illuminated a number of family and parent variables that may function as impediments to treatment success. Identified family factors that appear related to treatment outcome and should be carefully attended to and promoted include: (a) treatment-consistent shifts in parent behavior (Chamberlain & Moore, 1998; Reid, Webster-Stratton, & Hammond, 2003); (b) shifts in parental perception of child behavior that yield greater behavioral specificity and decreased reactivity (Wahler, Cator, Fleischman, & Lambert, 1993); and (c) decreased parental psychopathology (Kazdin, 1995a; McMahon, Forehand, Griest, & Wells, 1981). These variables are significant insofar as they reflect aspects of treatment designed to influence dynamics of the parent–child relationship (e.g., behaving differently during interactions, perceiving behavior with increased accuracy, preventing the child's exposure to dysfunction). Data have also suggested that single-parent and low socioeconomic status are variables that may increase the probability of dropout or result in limited treatment outcome because of the challenges that a single parent may face in managing the demands of home and family life without the support of a partner or because of limited ability to access needed services (Dumas & Albin, 1986; Kazdin, Mazurick, & Bass, 1993; McMahon et al., 1981; Kazdin, 2003; Strain, Steele, Ellis, & Timm, 1982).

Treatment Factors

Treatment characteristics may also affect outcome. For example, certain aspects of the therapist's style or behavior (e.g., empowering parents, warmth, directness, confidence) predict positive treatment outcome at least to some degree (Alexander, Barton, Schiavo, & Parsons, 1976; Sanders & Dadds, 1993; Webster-Stratton & Herbert, 1994). These findings reflect the fact that clients engage in treatment to a greater degree when the therapeutic relationship is rewarding and inviting. Similarly, degree of client engagement and therapist–client collaboration are also characteristics of the intervention that appear to positively influence outcomes (Kazdin, Holland, & Crowley, 1997; Patterson & Chamberlain, 1994; Prinz & Miller, 1996). Parental resistance to treatment (e.g., failed homework, refusal to implement treatment), especially early in treatment, may increase the risk of treatment failure, as important aspects of treatment may be neglected and attempts at treatment collaboration may be undermined (Chamberlain, Patterson, Reid, Kavanagh, & Forgatch, 1984; Patterson & Chamberlain, 1994). Finally, but not surprisingly, degree of treatment implementation and protocol adherence are also associated with positive treatment outcomes, as these directly mediate the potential impact of treatment (Forgatch, Patterson, & DeGarmo, 2005; Henggeler, Melton, Brondino, Scherer, & Hanley, 1997). Stated simply, treatment strategies that are not implemented have no opportunity to affect the child or family functioning.

Child Factors

There are factors unique to the child that may influence treatment outcome. Problem intensity prior to treatment onset may be linked to treatment dropout and outcome (Holden, Lavigne, & Cameron, 1990; Kazdin, 1990), although this finding has not been consistently replicated (Henggeler, Melton, & Smith, 1992; Kellam, Rebok, Ialongo, & Mayer, 1994). A high degree of intensity suggests a history of rehearsal and the presence of reinforcing contingencies that may be difficult to alter via typical treatment strategies. Engaging younger children in treatment may also be a factor that yields improved results; however, this finding has not been consistently replicated (Serketich & Dumas, 1996; Strain, Young, & Horowitz, 1981). This finding is not surprising, however, as younger children have not typically developed significantly entrenched problem behaviors and the behavior of younger children tends to be more malleable overall. Experiencing comorbid problems (e.g., attention-deficit/hyperactivity disorder (ADHD), anxiety, depression) in addition to CP has not reliably yielded negative outcomes; however, the extant data suggests that individually enhanced treatment (e.g., addition of needed treatment components) for the multiproblem youth may be optimal (Beauchaine, Webster-Stratton, & Reid, 2005). The experience of comorbid problems may suggest greater impairment, overall, or the presence of maladaptive processes that could interfere with treatment. For example, a youth with ADHD may struggle to attend to and monitor target behavior in a helpful manner, whereas a depressed child may seek social isolation that could preempt practice and feedback opportunities within social settings.

Kazdin (1995b) has suggested that five primary characteristics of parent training programs seem linked to successful outcomes. These include: (a) increased duration of treatment, (b) training in specific behavioral management techniques (e.g., how to give good instructions), (c) emphasizing social learning principles, (d) advanced therapist skills, and (e) targeting multiple childhood problems. Kazdin (1987) also concluded that limited success in parent training may be related to three factors: (a) low socioeconomic status, (b) social isolation, and (c) multiple familial problems. Consistent with this conclusion, the results from several studies have suggested that incorporating treatment strategies related to family need as an adjunct to parent training may yield improved treatment outcomes (Kazdin & Wassell, 2000; Sanders & McFarland, 2000; Taylor & Biglan, 1998).

Knowledge of the complex array of causal, maintaining, and moderating factors that are important in understanding and treating CP has evolved significantly over the past few decades. A direct result of this progress has been modifications in our approach to treatment. Although the primary tenets and tactics of parent training have not been abandoned, there has been acknowledgement that treatment must be modified if it is to be effective with the multiproblem familial context that is typical of youth who exhibit chronic disruptive behaviors (Griest & Wells, 1983; Miller & Prinz, 1990).

CASE PRESENTATION

The following case example illustrates an attempt to combine traditional parent training strategies with a number of adjunctive intervention strategies in treating the seemingly intractable disruptive behaviors of a child in a multiproblem familial context. It is likely that any practitioner who treats children with disruptive behavior problems will eventually encounter a difficult, multiproblem CP case. By their nature, such cases will be laden with refractory problems and saddled with a gloomy prognosis. This was such a case. Throughout this example, the name Tony will be used to reference the target child.

Tony was a youth at high risk for experiencing a lifetime of chronic problems related to the display of antisocial and aggressive behavior. A key factor in this case was the treatment context. Tony was referred by a pediatrician to a psychologist with whom he shared a long-standing mutually beneficial, professional relationship. The psychologist in this case was actively providing treatment in the context of a primary care pediatric outpatient setting. Although this model of practice may not always be feasible, it is optimal, as these circumstances facilitate referral flow, heighten trust between the pediatrician and psychologist, and eliminate barriers to treatment that otherwise may arise. As mentioned previously, the positioning of psychologists in close proximity to pediatricians is also advantageous given that disruptive behavior concerns are often initially reported to pediatricians by parents (Arndorfer et al., 1999) and have become a primary focus of treatment in primary care pediatric clinics over the past 20 years (Hoagwood et al., 2000; Kelleher et al., 2000)

Initial Contact

Tony was an 8-year-old, Caucasian youth referred because of concerns regarding extreme aggression. An initial interview conducted with Tony and his mother revealed behavioral concerns, including a history of multiple physical assaults on family members, multiple instances of police contact during the past month, an average of more than three daily intense tantrums, daily physical aggression, a high rate of noncompliance (over 80%), and school difficulties including diminishing grades, chronic tardiness, and absolute avoidance of homework. Diagnostic assessment was initiated during the first visit with the psychologist and continued over the first three sessions.

Treatment History

An initial interview revealed that Tony had previously received treatment for CP at the age of 5 years. Target behaviors included excessive noncompliance, physical aggression, and a "belligerent attitude." Tony's developmental and physical histories were negative. Legal history was negative prior to age 5 when a significant incident occurred that prompted police contact and, ultimately, resulted in the initial referral for services. The incident occurred during a community outing with his mother. Tony became frustrated when he did not get his way (i.e., wanted a toy that was being used) and displayed an extreme tantrum that included kicking, screaming, crying, and severe aggression toward a sibling while his mother was preoccupied driving the family car. Tony's mother pulled to the side of the road and attempted to separate Tony from his sister. This resulted in an enduring physical struggle between Tony and his mother along the roadside. An emergency cell phone call was made by a passing stranger that culminated with intervention by a dispatched police officer.

Tony's parents were referred to a university training clinic where they received treatment from an advanced graduate student. Tony was assigned a diagnosis of ODD and he and his mother participated in a total of seven parent training sessions. Tony's father did not participate in treatment, in part because of struggles with alcohol addiction. Based on the description provided in his record, the parent training intervention used overlapped considerably with the PMTO program described earlier. Records indicated that over the course of the seven sessions, four were missed or rescheduled, suggesting that problems with engagement/collaboration may have been present. The student-therapist concluded that Tony had progressed behaviorally although most of Tony's treatment goals were not realized. Further, termination of treatment was largely accounted for by family financial concerns.

In sum, the records review indicated the presence of significant CP at an early age; limited engagement in, and eventually failed treatment; and the presence of multiple family problems (e.g., parental psychopathology, limited parenting skills, financial hardship).

Assessment Summary and Diagnostic Impressions

Initial assessment of Tony included completion of standardized questionnaires (Eyberg Child Behavior Inventory [ECBI], Child Behavior Checklist [CBCL]), a semistructured diagnostic interview, records review, and home-based observation. The following details were revealed and diagnostic impressions developed.

Interview data indicated that aggression continued to be a significant concern for Tony. In recent months he had regularly assaulted his siblings with closed-fist punches that had caused bruising and bleeding. Such aggression typically occurred when he was frustrated. These physical attacks had prompted a series of police visits to Tony's home during the preceding months. Tony was responsive to police intervention and regularly displayed remorse following aggressive outbursts. Tony's mother also reported that he resisted arising from bed in the morning, avoided preparing for and typically arrived late to school. It was estimated that Tony completed only about 5% of assigned homework. Tony's father had a long history of alcohol abuse, which included an attempt at inpatient detoxification and outpatient treatment that had failed. Tony's mother had been treated for major depression and was currently prescribed antidepressant medication but often could not afford to fill her prescription. A significant degree of marital conflict and dissatisfaction was reported by each of Tony's parents. Financial concerns were significant as Tony's father was temporarily unemployed and his mother provided the family's primary income. However, her job required her to work most nights.

Home-based observation data indicated that intense tantrums (e.g., highly emotional and lasting for 10 minutes or longer) were occurring at a mean rate of four per day. It was not uncommon for tantrums to culminate in physical attack on a family member or displays of aggression in which Tony would break objects in the house. Verbal and physical aggression occurred multiple times per day. Across home and clinic observations, Tony was observed to comply with less than 10% of parent-delivered commands. Questionnaire data was consistent with interview data and indicated clinical concerns across all externalizing domains. Diagnostically, Tony easily met criteria for ODD and narrowly missed qualifying for a diagnosis of CD. Based on concerns expressed by his teacher and his history of academic struggles, ADHD (inattentive subtype) was retained as a rule-out diagnosis pending additional assessment of symptomatology.

Challenging Case Factors

As indicated previously, standard parent training at age 5 years resulted in mixed, short-term gains. A number of factors may have weakened the probability of treatment success, leaving Tony at risk for ongoing display and additional development of CP. As the target child, Tony possessed a number of characteristics thought to be associated with poor response to treatment. Among these was the extreme aggression that Tony displayed prior to intervention and at an early age, his early contact with legal authorities, and the potential presence of comorbid symptomatology associated with ADHD.

Also present were parent factors that increased Tony's risk for treatment failure. Each of his parents had struggled with psychopathology or addictions, possessed limited ability to discriminate prosocial from antisocial behavior, generally reacted impulsively and in a harsh manner to inappropriate behavior, possessed underdeveloped communication and problem-solving skills, used ineffective behavior management strategies, and expressed marital and familial dissatisfaction.

Environmental factors associated with poor treatment outcome were also present. Financial concerns were a significant, long-term stressor that had negatively impacted family functioning. Tony's family was in receipt of minimal social support, which was a significant concern given that Tony's mother worked nights and struggled to find time to sleep as she was needed in a parenting role during daytime hours.

Standard Treatment

Previous parent training yielded minimal gains despite being delivered in the absence of paternal involvement and for a brief number of sessions. Somewhat surprisingly, Tony's parents were optimistic about participating in additional parent training sessions. It was determined that treatment would be comprised of a number of carefully constructed parent training sessions designed to provide a review of basic parenting skills while targeting variables that could undermine treatment progress. Additionally, Tony was asked to concurrently participate in Problem-Solving Skills Training (PSST).

Parent training sessions generally followed the PMTO program outlined previously. Tony's parents reviewed strategies for monitoring his behavior, developed their ability to parse appropriate from inappropriate behavior, and practiced implementing differential reinforcement strategies. Behavioral expectations and house rules were clarified, and parents practiced implementing aversive consequences such as time-out. A simple token economy was developed in which Tony could complete a sticker chart contingent on the display of appropriate behavior.

In addition to parent training, PSST was provided for Tony. Over the course of several sessions, Tony was taught to identify problems and their associated negative consequences; brainstorm potential solutions; assess the likely effectiveness of each solution; and, finally, decide on, implement, and evaluate the effectiveness of a solution. A variety of strategies including discussion, role play, modeling, and feedback were used to shape Tony's problem-solving skills over time.

Adjunctive Treatment Strategies

Several adjunctive treatment strategies were employed to minimize treatment barriers and promote eventual success. Functional Behavioral Assessment (FBA) is a strategy used to facilitate understanding of the function or utility of behavior (Wacker, Cooper, Peck, Derby, & Berg, 1999). This approach to assessment prioritizes discerning antecedents and consequences contingently linked to target behaviors thereby suggesting the presence of controlling variables. Functional Behavioral Assessment has not been used extensively in traditional parent training contexts historically; however, it is an assessment strategy worthy of consideration when confronted with complex disruptive behaviors. An

FBA was conducted for Tony's tantrums and aggressive behavior. Results suggested that Tony was much more likely to tantrum when his parents displayed negative affect (e.g., displaying anger, using reprimands, yelling). Further, Tony was most likely to become aggressive when the gain or loss of a tangible reinforcer was at stake. These results yielded modifications in the focus of parent training. Specifically, parents were trained to carefully monitor their behavior and explicitly disengage in interaction with Tony when their behavior could not be neutral or positive. Considerable session time was committed to practicing positive engagement tactics and the timing of disengagement strategies. This culminated in the absence of parental harsh responding, which removed potent reinforcers (e.g., parental attention, escape of aversive stimulus) from the target context.

A preference assessment (Ivancic, 2000) was used to identify preferred tangible reinforcers that could be incorporated into the token economy. Subsequently, the token economy and the philosophy of positive engagement/disengagement were combined as a prevention strategy for addressing tantrums and aggressive behavior. Tony and his parents were taught to discern high-risk situations (monitoring), label them as such, and collaborate in using problem-solving skills to identify appropriate actions. Degree of parent support was gradually faded to promote Tony's independent skill practice. Effort and success in solving problems resulted in access to preferred tangible rewards (e.g., candy, small toys) via the token economy. Tony's parents indicated that these strategies were effective in preventing most negative interactions and the display of aggression.

Lengthening the duration of treatment was another adjunctive strategy applied in this case. Parent Management Training is typically conducted over the course of 10 to 20 therapy sessions. Problem Solving Skills Training may be conducted in 20 sessions or less, depending on treatment progress. It was anticipated that treatment may need to extend beyond these typical parameters and Tony's parents were prepared for this possibility. In fact, Tony and his parents ultimately completed 32 therapy sessions spanning a period of 41 weeks. Multiple telephone contacts occurred between therapy sessions, and a generalization plan was developed wherein session frequency faded to three sessions over a 9-week period at the conclusion of treatment. Additional changes were made at the level of case management. At the outset of treatment, Tony's case was assigned to an experienced practitioner with specialization in the treatment of disruptive behavior. Additionally, consent was gained to allow Tony's provider to consult with another psychologist who possessed extensive experience in the treatment of CP. These strategies were implemented to ensure that subtle, yet important, aspects of the case would not be overlooked.

Factors related to social support were also addressed. Tony and his parents were encouraged to identify a trusted neighbor who could provide child care during the afternoon hours while Tony's mother was asleep because of night-shift employment. As a result, Tony would immediately go to his neighbor's house following school and complete homework with appropriate adult monitoring, support, and encouragement. This provided Tony with adequate adult monitoring, facilitated completion of homework, which had been a chronic challenge, and provided respite for his mother who was often unable to obtain needed rest as a result of her night job and daytime family demands.

The family's socioeconomic status and limited insurance benefits also reflected a significant concern. Inquiry was made and it was determined that Tony and his parents qualified for an alternative clinic fee arrangement making the cost of therapy more feasible. Additionally, Tony's family actively participated in a community church, and it was discovered that a percentage of therapy fees could be covered through a social support fund managed by the church. These strategies removed a significant barrier to treatment for Tony's family and provided the added benefit of not further burdening the family financially.

A number of parent factors were also addressed adjunctively. Specifically, Tony's mother was aided in identifying and inquiring about an employee assistance program available to her. Through this program she was able to obtain a current medical evaluation, an updated prescription for an alternative antidepressant, and individual psychotherapy to address mood concerns. Session time was also used to identify factors that had precluded involvement of Tony's father in treatment. Barriers to his participation were addressed and he agreed to attend all therapy sessions. Finally, development of family communication skills was prioritized as a treatment target and all family members participated in sessions with a communication focus.

In addition to these adjunctive strategies, additional assessment was conducted to determine the presence of ADHD symptomatology. ADHD (inattentive subtype), which was originally retained as a rule-out diagnosis, was formally diagnosed and Tony's pediatrician prescribed stimulant medication as an additional aspect of treatment. Tony's parents reported that his ability to concentrate and understand school-based instruction improved as a result. Combined with the home token economy, which rewarded timely arrival at school and homework completion, Tony's teacher indicated that most of his academic concerns had resolved.

Treatment Outcome

Treatment progress was monitored in a variety of ways. Weekly communication with Tony's teacher was established through the use of a school communication card. Thus, his academic progress was monitored throughout treatment. At treatment conclusion, Tony had completed 100% of homework and had arrived to school on time on 98% of days over the previous 2 months. Card data suggested that the after-school homework arrangement with Tony's neighbor largely resolved homework concerns. Likewise, linking the time of school arrival to tangible reinforcers within the home token economy seemed to produce increased cooperation. Tony's parents anecdotally indicated that stimulant medication was most helpful in altering Tony's attitude about school.

Tony's parents collected data on a weekly basis as participant observers in the home. This data indicated that, over the course of treatment, tantrums had decreased from four per day (very intense) to one per week (mild). Further, nearly all aggression had ceased with the exception of occasional minimal contact (e.g., push, grab object), which typically occurred in the context of sibling disagreement. Home data also indicated that Tony was compliant with 80% of commands delivered at home. In contrast, compliance data collected in the clinic yielded a 98% compliance rate. Perhaps most important, over the course of treatment there had been no need for police contact.

CONCLUSIONS AND FUTURE DIRECTIONS

Although very common, CP concerns may not be readily resolved and can prove to be among the most challenging of clinic cases. The paramount need for effective services for these cases is made clear by the fact that CP remains the primary referral concern for the majority of children requiring mental health services. Our understanding of CP and the factors that contribute to their development have progressed significantly over the last several decades. Nonetheless, our most effective treatments retain "probably efficacious" status suggesting that further research remains necessary. Minimal information is currently available regarding the most reliable predictors, moderators, and mediators of treatment effects associated with CP. The overwhelming theme present in this body of research is inconsistency in findings. Efforts to identify the factors that contribute to the development of refractory CP cases will continue to be stymied until this research domain is prioritized.

Prevention strategies will likely prove to be critical in quelling the development of chronic CP cases. However, prevention of CP is a domain of research that remains significantly underdeveloped (McMahon et al., 2006). Noticeably absent from the CP prevention literature are clearly delineated prevention strategies driven by identification of early risk factors that could be implemented with very young children. The development of such strategies may prove to play a prominent role in the primary prevention of CP. This approach to addressing CP is highly consistent with currently available data suggesting that the developmental origin of such problems likely resides in the innocent stages of early childhood and may be significantly influenced by environmental, parental, and child factors that are measurable and malleable.

REFERENCES

Alexander, J. F., Barton, C., Schiavo, R. S., & Parsons, B. V. (1976). Systems-behavioral intervention with families of delinquents: Therapist characteristics, family behavior, and outcome. *Journal of Consulting and Clinical Psychology, 44*, 656–664.

American Psychiatric Association. (2000). *Diagnostic and statistical manual of mental disorders* (4th ed., text rev.). Washington, DC: American Psychiatric Press.

Anderson, J. C., Williams, S., McGee, R., & Silva, P. A. (1987). DSM-III disorders in preadolescent children. *Archives of General Psychiatry, 44*, 69–76.

Arndorfer, R. E., Allen, K. D., & Aljazireh, L. (1999). Behavioral health needs in pediatric medicine and the acceptability of behavioral solutions: Implications for behavioral psychologists. *Behavior Therapy, 30*, 137–148.

Bates, J. E., Pettit, G. S., Dodge, K. A., & Ridge, B. (1998). Interaction of temperamental resistance to control and restrictive parenting in the development of externalizing behavior. *Developmental Psychology, 34*, 982–995.

Beauchaine, T. P., Webster-Stratton, C., & Reid, M. J. (2005). Mediators, moderators, and predictors of 1-year outcomes among children treated for early-onset conduct problems: A latent growth curve analysis. *Journal of Consulting and Clinical Psychology, 73*, 371–388.

Bernal, M. E., Klinnert, M. D., & Schultz, L. A. (1980). Outcome evaluation of behavioral parent training and client-centered parent counseling for children with conduct problems. *Journal of Applied Behavior Analysis, 13*, 677–691.

Campbell, S. B. (1995). Behavior problems in preschool children: A review of recent research. *Journal of Child Psychology and Psychiatry, 36*, 113–149.

Caspi, A., Henry, B., McGee, R. O., Moffitt, T. E., & Silva, P. A. (1995). Temperamental origins of child and adolescent behavior problems: From age three to age fifteen. *Child Development, 66*, 55–68.

Chamberlain, P., & Moore, K. J. (1998). Models of community treatment for serious juvenile offenders. In J. Crane (Ed.), *Social programs that really work* (pp. 258–276). New York: Russell Sage Foundation.

Chamberlain, P., Patterson, G., Reid, J., Kavanagh, K., & Forgatch, M. (1984). Observation of client resistance. *Behavior Therapy, 15*, 144–155.

Chambless, D. L., & Hollon, S. D. (1998). Defining empirically supported therapies. *Journal of Consulting and Clinical Psychology, 66*, 7–18.

Connor, D. F., Carlson, G. A., Chang, K. D., Daniolos, P. T., Ferziger, R., Findling, R. S., et al. (2006). Juvenile maladaptive aggression: A review of prevention, treatment, and service configuration and a proposed research agenda. *Journal of Clinical Psychiatry, 67*, 808–820.

Costello, E. J. (1990). Child psychiatric epidemiology: Implications for clinical research and practice. In B. B. Lahey & A. E. Kazdin (Eds.), *Advances in clinical child psychology* (Vol. 13, pp. 53–90). New York: Plenum Press.

Crick, N. R., & Grotpeter, J. K. (1995). Relational aggression, gender, and social-psychological adjustment. *Child Development, 66*, 710–722.

Dumas, J. E., & Albin, J. B. (1986). Parent training outcome: Does active parental involvement matter? *Behaviour Research and Therapy, 24*, 227–230.

Eyberg, S. M., Nelson, M. M., & Boggs, S.R. (2008). Evidence-based psychosocial treatments for children and adolescents with disruptive behavior. *Journal of Clinical Child & Adolescent Psychology, 37*, 215–237.

Forehand, R., Middlebrook, J., Rogers, T. R., & Steffe, M. (1983). Dropping out of parent training. *Behaviour Research and Therapy, 21*, 663–668.

Forgatch, M. S., Patterson, G. R., & DeGarmo, D. S. (2005). Evaluating fidelity: Predictive validity for a measure of competent adherence to the Oregon model of parent management training. *Behavior Therapy, 36*, 3–13.

Friman, P. C. (1999). Family-style residential care really works: Scientific findings demonstrating multiple benefits for troubled adolescents. In J. E. Carr & J. Austin (Eds.), *Handbook of applied behavior analysis* (pp. 187–209). Reno, NV: Context Press.

Gjone, H., Stevenson, J., Sundet, J. M., & Eilertsen, D. E. (1996). Changes in heritability across increasing levels of behavior problems in young twins. *Behavior Genetics, 26*, 419–426.

Greenberg, M. T. (1999). Attachment and psychopathology in childhood. In J. Cassidy & P. Shaver (Eds.), *Handbook of attachment: Theory, research, and clinical applications* (pp. 469–496). New York: Guilford Press.

Griest, D. L., & Wells, K. C. (1983). Behavioral family therapy with conduct disorders in children. *Behavior Therapy, 14*, 37–53.

Haggerty, R. J., Roughman, K. J., & Pless, I. B. (1975). *Child health and the community*. New York: John Wiley.

Henggeler, S. W., Melton, G. B., Brondino, M. J., Scherer, D. G., & Hanley, J. H. (1997). Multisystemic Therapy with violent and chronic juvenile offenders and their families: The role of treatment fidelity in successful dissemination. *Journal of Consulting and Clinical Psychology, 65*, 821–833.

Henggeler, S., W., Melton, G. B., & Smith, L. A. (1992). Family preservation using Multisystemic Therapy: An effective alternative to incarcerating serious juvenile offenders. *Journal of Consulting and Clinical Psychology, 60*, 953–961.

Hoagwood, K., Kelleher, K. J., Feil, M., & Comer, D. M. (2000). Treatment services for children with ADHD: A national perspective. *Journal of the American Academy of Child and Adolescent Psychiatry, 39*, 198–206.

Holden, G. W., Lavigne, V. V., & Cameron, A. M. (1990). Probing the continuum of effectiveness sin parent training: Characteristics of parents and preschoolers. *Journal of Clinical Child Psychology, 19*, 2–8.

Ivancic, M. T. (2000). Stimulus preference and reinforcer assessment applications. In J. Austin & J. E. Carr (Eds.), *Handbook of applied behavior analysis* (pp. 19–38). Reno, NV: Context Press.

Kazdin, A. E. (1987). Treatment of antisocial behavior in children: Current status and future directions. *Psychological Bulletin, 102*, 187–203.

Kazdin, A. E. (1990). Premature termination from treatment among children referred for antisocial behavior. *Journal of Child Psychology and Psychiatry, 31*, 415–425.

Kazdin, A. E. (1995a). Child, parent and family dysfunction as predictors of outcome in cognitive-behavioral treatment of antisocial children. *Behaviour Research and Therapy, 33*, 271–281.

Kazdin, A. E. (1995b). *Conduct disorder in childhood and adolescence* (2nd ed.). Thousand Oaks, CA: Sage.

Kazdin, A. E. (2003). Problem-solving skills training and parent management training for conduct disorder. In A. E. Kazdin & J. R. Weisz (Eds.), *Evidence-based psychotherapies for children and adolescents* (pp. 241–262). New York: Guilford Press.

Kazdin, A. E., Holland, L., & Crowley, M. (1997). Family experience of barriers to treatment and premature termination from child therapy. *Journal of Consulting and Clinical Psychology, 65*, 453–463.

Kazdin, A. E., Mazurick, J. L., & Bass, D. (1993). Risk for attrition in treatment of antisocial children and families. *Journal of Clinical Child Psychology, 22*, 2–16.

Kazdin, A. E., & Wassell, G. (2000). Therapeutic changes in children, parents, and families resulting from treatment of children with conduct problems. *Journal of American Academy of Child and Adolescent Psychiatry, 39*, 414–420.

Keenan, K., Loeber, R., & Green, S. (1999). Conduct disorder in girls. *Clinical Child and Family Psychology Review, 2*, 3–20.

Kellam, S. G., Rebok, G. W., Ialongo, N., & Mayer, L. S. (1994). The course and malleability of aggressive behavior from early first grade into middle school: Results of a developmental epidemiologically-based preventive trial. *Journal of Child Psychology and Psychiatry, 35*, 259–281.

Kelleher, K. J., McInerny, T. K., Gardner, W. P., Childs, G. E., & Wasserman, R. C. (2000). Increasing identification of psychosocial problems. *Pediatrics, 105*, 1313–1321.

Loeber, R., Burke, J. D., Lahey, B. B., Winters, A., & Zera, M. (2000). Oppositional defiant and conduct disorder: A review of the past 10 years, Part I. *Journal of the American Academy of Child and Adolescent Psychiatry, 39*, 1468–1484.

Maughan, B., & Rutter, M. (2001). Antisocial children grown up. In J. Hill & B. Maughan (Eds.), *Conduct disorders in childhood and adolescence* (pp. 507–552). Cambridge, UK: Cambridge University Press.

McGee, R., & Williams, S. (1999). Environmental risk factors in oppositional-defiant disorder and conduct disorder. In H. C. Quay & A. E. Hogan (Eds.), *Handbook of disruptive behavior disorders* (pp. 419–440). New York: Kluwer Academic.

McMahon, R. J., & Forehand, R. L. (2003). *Helping the noncompliant child: Family-based treatment for oppositional behavior* (2nd ed.). New York: Guilford Press.

McMahon, R. J., Forehand, R., Griest, D. L, & Wells, K. C. (1981). Who drops out of treatment during parent behavioral training? *Behavioral Counseling Quarterly, 1*, 79–85.

McMahon, R. J., Wells, K. C., & Kotler, J. S. (2006). Conduct problems. In E. J. Mash & R. A. Barkley (Eds.), *Treatment of childhood disorders* (3rd ed., pp. 137–268). New York; Guilford Press.

Miller, G. E., & Prinz, R. J. (1990). Enhancement of social learning family interventions for childhood conduct disorder. *Psychological Bulletin, 108*, 291–307.

Moffitt, T. E., Caspi, A., Dickson, N., Silva, P., & Stanton, W. (1996). Childhood-onset versus adolescent-onset antisocial conduct problems in males: Natural history from ages 3 to 18 years. *Development and Psychopathology, 8*, 399–424.

Patterson, G. R. (1974). Interventions for boys with conduct problems: Multiple settings, treatments, and criteria. *Journal of Consulting and Clinical Psychology, 42*, 471–481.

Patterson, G. R. (2002). The early development of coercive family process. In J. B. Reid, G. R. Patterson, & J. Snyder (Eds.), *Antisocial behavior in children and adolescents: A developmental analysis and model for intervention* (pp. 25–44). Washington, DC: American Psychological Association.

Patterson, G. R., Capaldi, D., & Bank, L. (1991). An early starter model for predicting delinquency. In D. J. Pepler & K. H. Rubin (Eds.), *The development and treatment of childhood aggression* (pp. 139–168). Hillsdale, NJ: Erlbaum.

Patterson, G. R., & Chamberlain, P. (1988). Treatment process: A problem at three levels. In L. C. Wynne (Ed.), *The state of the art in family therapy research: Controversies and recommendations* (pp. 189–223). New York: Family Process Press.

Patterson, G. R., & Chamberlain, P. (1994). A functional analysis of resistance during parent training therapy. *Clinical Psychology: Science and Practice, 1*, 53–70.

Patterson, G. R., Chamberlain, P., & Reid, J. B. (1982). A comparative evaluation of a parent training program. *Behavior Therapy, 13*, 638–650.

Prinz, R. J., & Miller, G. E. (1996). Parental engagement in interventions for children at risk for conduct disorder. In R. D. Peters & R. J. McMahon (Eds.), *Preventing childhood disorders, substance abuse, and delinquency* (pp. 161–183). Thousand Oaks, CA: Sage.

Quay, H. C. (1986). Conduct disorders. In H. C. Quay & J. S. Werry (Eds.), *Psychopathological disorders of childhood* (3rd ed., pp. 35–72). New York: John Wiley.

Reid, M. J., Webster-Stratton, C. H., & Hammond, M. (2003). Follow-up of children who received the Incredible Years intervention for oppositional defiant disorder: Maintenance and prediction of a 2-year outcome. *Behavior Therapy, 34*, 471–491.

Rutter, M., MacDonald, H., LeCouteur, A., Harrington, R., Bolton, P., & Bailey, A. (1990). Genetic factors in child psychiatric disorders: II. Empirical findings. *Journal of Child Psychology and Psychiatry, 31*, 39–83.

Sanders, M. R., & Dadds, M. R. (1993). *Behavioral family intervention*. Boston: Allyn & Bacon.

Sanders, M. R., Markie-Dadds, C., Tully, L., & Bor, B. (2000). The Triple P-Positive Parenting Program: A comparison of enhanced, standard, and self-directed behavioral family intervention for parents of children with early onset conduct problems. *Journal of Consulting and Clinical Psychology, 68*, 624–640.

Sanders, M. R., & McFarland, M. (2000). Treatment of depressed mothers with disruptive children: A controlled evaluation of cognitive behavioral family intervention. *Behavior Therapy, 31*, 89–112.

Schroeder, C. S., & Gordon, B. N. (2002). *Assessment and treatment of childhood problems: A clinician's guide* (2nd ed.). New York: Guilford Press.

Serketich, W. J., & Dumas, J. E. (1996). The effectiveness of behavioral parent training to modify antisocial behavior in children: A meta-analysis. *Behavior Therapy, 27*, 171–186.

Sholevar, G. P., & Sholevar, E. H. (1995). Overview. In G. P. Sholevar (Ed.), *Conduct disorders in children and adolescents* (pp. 3–26). Washington, DC: American Psychiatric Press.

Snyder, J., Reid, J., & Patterson, G. (2003). A social learning model of child and adolescent antisocial behavior. In B. B. Lahey, T. E. Moffitt, & A. Caspi (Eds.), *Causes of conduct disorder and juvenile delinquency* (pp. 27–48). New York: Guilford Press.

Snyder, J., & Stoolmiller, M. (2002). Reinforcement and coercion mechanisms in the development of antisocial behavior: The family. In J. B. Reid, G. R. Patterson, & J. Snyder (Eds.), *Antisocial behavior in children and adolescents: A developmental analysis and model for intervention* (pp. 65–100). Washington, DC: American Psychological Association.

Steiner, H. (1997). Practice parameters for the assessment and treatment of children and adolescents with conduct disorder. *Journal of the American Academy of Child and Adolescent Psychiatry, 36* (Suppl. 10), 122S–139S.

Strain, P. S., Steele, P., Ellis, T., & Timm, M. A. (1982). Long-term effects of oppositional child treatment with mothers as therapists and therapist trainers. *Journal of Applied Behavior Analysis, 15*, 163–169.

Strain, P. S., Young, C. C., & Horowitz, J. (1981). Generalized behavior change during oppositional child training: An examination of child and family demographic variables. *Behavior Modifications, 5*, 15–26.

Taylor, T. K., & Biglan, A. (1998). Behavioral family interventions for improving child-rearing: A review of the literature for clinicians and policy makers. *Clinical Child and Family Psychology Review, 1*, 41–60.

Wacker, D. P., Cooper, L. J., Peck, S. M., Derby, K. M., & Berg, W. K. (1999). Community-based functional assessment. In A. C. Repp & R. H. Horner (Eds.), *Functional analysis of problem behavior: From effective assessment to effective support* (pp. 32–56). Belmont, CA: Wadsworth.

Wahler, R. G., Cartor, P. G., Fleischman, J., & Lambert, W. (1993). The impact of synthesis teaching and parent training with mothers of conduct-disordered children. *Journal of Abnormal Child Psychology, 21*, 425–440.

Webster-Stratton, C. H., & Herbert, M. (1994). *Troubled families—problem children.* Chichester, UK: Wiley.

Webster-Stratton, C. H., Hollinsworth, T., & Kolpacoff, M. (1989). The long-term effectiveness and clinical significance of three cost-effective training programs for families with conduct-problem children. *Journal of Consulting and Clinical Psychology, 57*, 550–553.

Zoccolillo, M., Paquette, D., & Tremblay, R. (2005). Maternal conduct disorder and the risk for the next generation. In D. J. Pepler, K. C. Madsen, C. Webster, & K. S. Levene (Eds.), *The development and treatment of girlhood aggression* (pp. 217–221). Mahwah, NJ: Erlbaum.

14

Treatment of Refractory Cases of Attention-Deficit/Hyperactivity Disorder in Children

ERIN L. GIRIO, LAUREN RICHERSON, AND JULIE SARNO OWENS

Children with attention-deficit/hyperactivity disorder (ADHD) display frequent and disruptive behaviors (e.g., noncompliance, interrupting) across multiple settings. There is evidence that these disruptive behaviors are particularly stressful for teachers, classmates, parents, and siblings (Greene, Beszterczey, Katzenstein, Park, & Goring, 2002; Johnson & Reader, 2002; Mikami & Pfiffner, 2008; Sterling-Turner, Robinson, & Wilczynski, 2001). Because the effects of ADHD extend far beyond the individual child, multiple evidence-based interventions may be required to adequately treat the disorder. A comprehensive treatment plan often includes evidence-based psychosocial and pharmacological interventions that focus on several domains of child functioning (e.g., behavioral, academic, social) as well as the many environments in which the child functions (i.e., home, classroom, peer group). Although evidence-based treatments have empirical support in reducing symptoms and impairment associated with ADHD, a significant minority of children do not show the intended response to treatment.

This chapter provides an introduction to ADHD, a description of evidence-based treatments for elementary-school-aged youth with this disorder, and a review of factors associated with poor treatment outcome. In addition, we present an example of a difficult-to-treat or refractory case of ADHD. More specifically, we describe the evidence-based treatments that were initially applied, the child's less than adequate response to these treatments, and his eventual positive response in the context of a supplemental cognitive-behavioral treatment. This case illustrates the importance of data-driven decision making, the process of adjusting the treatment plan to address the unique needs of the child and family, and the importance of ongoing coordination of care to adequately treat refractory cases.

ADHD: DIAGNOSIS, PREVALENCE, AND ASSOCIATED IMPAIRMENTS

Attention-deficit/hyperactivity disorder is a neuropsychological disorder affecting 2 to 9% of children (American Academy of Child & Adolescent Psychiatry [AACAP], 2007). According to the *Diagnostic and Statistical Manual of Mental Disorders, Fourth Edition, Text Revision* (*DSM-IV-TR*; American Psychiatric Association [APA], 2000), ADHD is diagnosed when both parent and teacher endorse the presence of six or more symptoms of inattention and/or six or more symptoms of hyperactivity/impulsivity that are developmentally inappropriate and that interfere with the child's daily functioning. The *DSM-IV-TR* indicates that the symptoms must have persisted for at least 6 months, with some having been present before age 7 years. Inattentive symptoms include, but are not limited to, difficulty attending to details, sustaining attention in tasks, and following instructions, as well as forgetfulness and poor organization in activities. Impulsive and hyperactive symptoms include excessive talking, interrupting, and fidgeting; inappropriate running and climbing; difficulty remaining seated; and difficulty engaging in tasks quietly.

Some children experience predominantly inattentive symptoms, others experience predominantly hyperactive/impulsive symptoms, and some display a combination of these two dimensions. These symptom combinations are represented by the three subtypes of ADHD: predominantly inattentive type (IA), predominantly hyperactive-impulsive type (HI), and combined type (C), respectively (APA, 2000). Data from school and community samples suggests that IA is more common (prevalence rates range from 46 to 56%) than C (rates range from 23 to 33%) or HI (rates range from 21 to 23%; Carlson, Shin, & Booth, 1999).

In contrast, data from clinic-based samples suggests that C is more common (rates range from 45 to 61%) than IA (rates range from 19 to 51%) or HI (rates range from 3 to 18%; Carlson et al. 1999). Data from exploratory factor, confirmatory factor, and latent class analyses provide consistent evidence for the two distinct dimensions of HI and IA (Lahey & Willcutt, 2002). These studies also show that symptoms co-occur more often than not, providing justification for C being the more common type.

Children with ADHD experience challenges in multiple areas of their lives. In the classroom, they often have deficient study skills, poor test performance, disorganized notebooks and desks, as well as difficulty completing independent seatwork, attending to lectures, and participating cooperatively in group activities (DuPaul & Stoner, 2003). In addition, approximately one out of every three children with ADHD also suffers from a comorbid learning disability (DuPaul & Stoner, 2003). Given these academic difficulties, it is not surprising that children with ADHD also experience difficulties in their relationships with teachers and peers. Teachers have reported that having children with ADHD in the classroom is stressful, as they create disruptions in the classroom process and require additional support (Greene et al., 2002). With regard to peer relationships, children with ADHD often experience high rates of peer rejection, have difficulty overcoming this rejection, and tend to have fewer dyadic relationships than typical children (see Hoza, 2007 for a review). Interestingly, research shows that children with ADHD often experience peer rejection from others even following brief interactions.

At home, the manifestation of ADHD significantly affects interactions with caregivers (C. Johnston & Mash, 2001). Children with ADHD require more supervision and instruction, as they are less likely to follow directions, play quietly, and stay on task. Research has shown mothers to be less rewarding, more directive, and more negative with children with ADHD than with those without the disorder (C. Johnston & Mash, 2001). Similarly, having a child with ADHD is associated with significantly greater parenting stress (Gupta, 2007; Johnson & Reader, 2002) and higher levels of parental depression (Cunningham & Boyle, 2002; Harrison & Sofronoff, 2002). Reportedly, parenting stress is exacerbated not only by the children's undesirable behaviors, but also by the consequences of these behaviors (e.g., receiving calls from the child's school while at work; not being able to maintain a babysitter; Johnson & Reader, 2002).

Of further concern are the comorbid conditions also experienced by children with ADHD. Approximately two thirds of children with ADHD meet criteria for oppositional defiant disorder (ODD) and one third for conduct disorder (CD; Carlson, Tamm, & Gaub, 1997; Loeber, Green, Lahey, Frick, & McBurnett, 2000). Indeed, ADHD-HI is one of the most reliable predictors of ODD and CD (Burns & Walsh, 2002; Hinshaw & Lee, 2006). Further, of children with ADHD-approximately one fourth experience comorbid anxiety, one fourth experience comorbid depression, and one third experience a learning disability (Jensen & Cooper, 2002). Thus, given these possible diagnostic complexities, a comprehensive treatment plan must include the use of empirically supported treatments for ADHD and the comorbid conditions.

Finally, ADHD is a chronic condition, as studies show that the majority of those diagnosed with ADHD in childhood experience marked symptoms of ADHD into adulthood (e.g., Barkley, Fischer, Smallish, & Fletcher, 2002). Indeed many children with ADHD experience a host of aversive outcomes, including grade retention, suspensions/expulsions, early school dropout, substance abuse, and risky sexual behavior (e.g., Barkley, Fischer, Smallish, & Fletcher, 2004; 2006; Loe & Feldman, 2007).

EMPIRICALLY SUPPORTED TREATMENTS FOR ADHD

Many treatments for ADHD have been proposed, including, but not limited to, behavioral interventions, cognitive interventions, pharmacological interventions, elimination diets, electroencephalograph biofeedback, and play therapy. However, only a few treatments have substantial empirical support for their efficacy in reducing ADHD symptoms and associated functional impairments. Those treatments include: (a) psychoactive medications such as central nervous system stimulants (i.e., methylphenidate, amphetamines) or atomoxetine (Strattera); (b) behavioral interventions, including parent training, classroom management, and intensive peer interventions; and (c) some combination of these interventions (Pelham, Wheeler, & Chronis, 1998; Pelham & Fabiano, 2008). These treatments have been categorized as "well established," empirically supported treatments by the American Psychological Association (APA; Lonigan, Elbert, & Johnson, 1998) and are often referred to as "evidence-based" treatments.

Pharmacotherapy

The literature on stimulant medication for the treatment of ADHD spans decades and has been reviewed extensively. In an attempt to synthesize this research, Swanson and colleagues (1993) produced a "review of reviews," which included 341 reviews on this topic with combined reference lists of over 9,000 articles from 1966 to 1990. Reviews showed stability over time, as stimulant medication consistently demonstrated temporary management of the diagnostic symptoms of ADHD (i.e., improvement in on-task behavior and compliance, reduction of classroom disruption) with a 60 to 80% response rate. These reviews also provide strong empirical support for the beneficial effects of stimulant medication on reducing comorbid aggressive and defiant behaviors. More recent articles confirm the potent short-term effects of stimulant medication and also document the positive short-term effects of the nonstimulant atomoxetine (e.g., Spencer et al., 1996; Waxmonsky, 2005).

Although pharmacotherapy can be a critical component in a multimodal treatment program, it is not without limitations. In fact, 10 to 30% of children show either iatrogenic effects or no response to stimulants (Swanson, McBurnett, Christian, & Wigal, 1995). The most common side effects of stimulant medications are insomnia and loss of appetite; other side effects include irritability, nausea, headaches, stomachaches, dizziness, increased blood pressure, rapid heart rate, lip smacking, cheek chewing, and tics. In addition to these disturbing side effects, pharmacotherapy does not normalize the behavior of all children with ADHD (Swanson et al., 2001) and does not seem to produce benefits once the medication has worn off. Finally, many parents are less satisfied with pharmacotherapy than with behavioral interventions (MTA Cooperative Group, 1999a). Parent dissatisfaction may be a function of the possible negative side effects just listed and/or because pharmacotherapy alone does not provide social or collaborative support to the parents and family, as behavioral interventions often do.

Behavioral Interventions

Over the last 25 years, a rich literature describing the implementation of behavior modification for children with ADHD has developed. One of the most prominent reviews of psychosocial treatments for children with ADHD (Pelham, Wheeler, & Chronis, 1998) concluded that behavioral parent training and behavioral management in the classroom were the only two treatments with sufficient evidence to meet the APA criteria of "well established" (see Lonigan et al., 1998). In addition, treatments that have met some, but not all of the criteria for "well established" have been labeled "probably efficacious" (Pelham et al., 1998). Those that currently meet this status include peer tutoring, social skills training, self-reinforcement, and computer-assisted instruction (e.g., Raggi & Chronis, 2006; Waschbusch & Hill, 2003).

Theories guiding most behavioral parenting programs propose that parental attention, although it may not be the cause of the disruptive behavior, serves to reinforce and maintain disruptive behavior. Thus, behavioral parent training programs typically involve 8 to 16 sessions in which parents learn strategies to enhance positive attention to appropriate behaviors, decrease attention to disruptive behaviors, and consistently use prudent consequences and limit setting (e.g., Barkley, 1997). Strategies discussed often include the use of praise, effective instructions, active ignoring, contingent application of time-out, and use of token systems. Parenting programs have been shown to improve child compliance, reduce impulsivity and aggression, and improve parent–child interactions (see Chronis, Chacko, Fabiano, Wymbs, & Pelham, 2004, for a review). Pelham and Fabiano (2008) recently provided an updated review, describing an additional 23 studies on behavioral parent training that have been conducted since the Pelham et al. (1998) review. These studies further confirm the efficacy of behavioral parent training for children with ADHD.

Consistent with behavioral parent training, teachers can apply the same strategies to increase positive behaviors and extinguish negative behaviors in the classroom. Behavioral classroom treatments such as daily report cards, token reinforcement programs, response-cost, and time-out procedures have produced marked reductions in off-task and disruptive behavior, as well as marked improvements in academic productivity in children with ADHD (e.g., DuPaul & Eckert, 1997). Pelham et al.'s (1998) review described 23 studies and Pelham and Fabiano's updated review (2008) described an additional 23 studies that demonstrate the efficacy of behavioral interventions in the classroom.

One commonly studied classroom intervention is the daily report card (DRC). Several studies document the positive effects of the DRC in improving the academic and behavioral functioning of children with behavior problems (see Kelley, 1990, for review). For the DRC intervention, teachers, often in consultation with parents and a mental health professional, identify and define behaviors in need of improvement (e.g., stay in seat, improve math productivity). The child must meet an established criterion (e.g., in seat with fewer than three rule violations, complete 75% of math work) to earn privileges provided by parents (ideally) or by the teacher. As the criterion is consistently met, the DRC is altered to continue shaping appropriate behaviors. The DRC provides consistent communication between home and school and allows for reinforcement in multiple settings. Several studies document teachers' preference of the DRC procedure over other treatments (e.g., Girio & Owens, 2008; Power, Hess, & Bennett, 1995).

Finally, several recent studies suggest that intensive peer interventions that apply behavior modification principles in the context of a social and recreational setting (e.g., summer day camp) also meet the criteria for "well-established" treatments (Pelham & Fabiano, 2008). The Summer Treatment Program (STP), established by Pelham and colleagues (Pelham & Hoza, 1996), involves approximately 200 to 400 hours of treatment over 5 to 8 weeks. This intervention involves teaching children social and recreational skills and providing opportunities to demonstrate these skills during recreational activities, while simultaneously applying contingency management programs (i.e., point system, time-out; Pelham & Fabiano, 2008). This intensity and reinforcement of skill development at the point of performance may be responsible for the positive outcomes in the STP, as compared to traditional social skills programs in which children may only receive 15 to 20 hours of intervention (e.g., 1- to 2-hour group sessions across several months) and may not be reinforced for the use of social skills.

Although pharmacotherapy and the previously described behavioral interventions have demonstrated efficacy as stand-alone treatments for ADHD, the literature suggests the combination of pharmacotherapy and behavior modification may lead to optimal outcomes for many children (e.g., Carlson, Pelham, Milich, & Dixon, 1992; Conners et al., 2001; Swanson et al., 2001). However, despite the benefits described above, no one treatment has been shown to 'cure' ADHD (Rapport, 1992), normalize the behavior of all children with ADHD (Swanson et al., 2001), produce long-term benefits on adolescent or adult outcomes (e.g., Loe & Feldman, 2007), or produce consistent results across individuals and settings (Pelham & Smith, 2000).

COGNITIVE-BEHAVIORAL TREATMENTS FOR ADHD

Given the limitations of pharmacotherapy and behavioral modification, researchers and clinicians have considered other alternatives, such as cognitive-behavioral treatments (CBT), for the treatment of ADHD. Several approaches within the broad domain of CBT have been considered, such as self-instruction, cognitive modeling, self-reinforcement, interpersonal problem solving, and social skills. Training children to self-regulate their behavior through CBT may seem like an intuitive choice for children with poor attention and behavioral control. Reviews examining the effect of cognitive training on cognitive functioning, academic performance, and behavior have concluded that these interventions have little empirical support for children with ADHD (AACAP, 2007; Abikoff, 1991). Many studies within the CBT-for ADHD-literature have several limitations (e.g., a lack of control or comparison group, small sample sizes, "nonclinical" samples; Greene & Ablon, 2001); however, recent studies that have improved on these limitations continue to show poor results for CBT as a stand-alone treatment for children with ADHD (e.g., Antshel & Remer, 2003).

Some have asserted that a child with complex behavior patterns may benefit from cognitive-behavioral modification (CBM). Cognitive-behavior modification includes the application of traditional behavioral methods used jointly with strategies to modify underlying cognitions and thought processes (e.g., Meichenbaum, 1977). A meta-analysis of 17 studies of CBM in the school setting examined 136 effect-size measures for children with behavior problems (Robinson, Smith, Miller, & Brownell, 1999). Results showed that the mean weighted ES score was .79. It is important to note, however, that in any given CBM study it is unclear which intervention components lead to improved outcomes—the behavior therapy elements or the cognitive techniques. Given the above-described evidence, the current recommendation is to use CBT approaches only in conjunction with a well-established treatment for ADHD (AACAP, 2007).

PREDICTORS OF POOR TREATMENT RESPONSE

Despite the documented benefits of the well-established treatments for ADHD, some children do not make anticipated gains and may be considered refractory cases. Several factors that may contribute to the refractory nature of particular cases have been identified. In the pages that follow, factors associated with poor treatment response will be reviewed, highlighting variables that pertain to the child, the familial environment, and the treatment process.

Child Variables

Intellectual Functioning

Although many have hypothesized that children who have lower than average intellectual functioning (IQ) are at a disadvantage in treatment, the literature on this topic is equivocal. Some studies involving children with disruptive behavior have revealed a positive relationship between IQ and treatment outcome (e.g., Conduct Problems Prevention Research Group [CPPRG], 2002), some have found a positive relationship only when other variables are present (e.g., parental depression and child symptom severity; E. B. Owens et al., 2003), some have found a negative relationship (e.g., Grizenko, Sayegh, & Papineau, 1994), and some have found no relationship (e.g., Kazdin & Crowley, 1997).

With regard to treatment of ADHD specifically, there is some evidence to suggest that IQ can moderate treatment outcome. In the context of the Multimodal Treatment Study of Children with ADHD (MTA), IQ moderated the effects of treatment for participants in the intensive Medication Management (MED) and the Combined Intensive Medication and Behavioral Treatment (COMB) conditions who met specific criteria (E. B. Owens et al., 2003). Namely, children with severe ADHD symptoms whose parents were experiencing symptoms of depression and who had at least average intellectual functioning had a much better chance of responding positively to MED or COMB treatment (i.e., 48% were "excellent responders") as compared to children with similar characteristics but lower IQs (only 10% were "excellent responders"). Thus, there is some evidence that below average intellectual functioning is worthy of consideration as a potential contributing factor to the refractory nature of any individual case.

Symptom Severity

More consistent results have been found for the role of pretreatment symptom severity as a predictor of poor treatment outcome. For example, higher initial severity of externalizing symptoms has been found to predict poorer treatment outcomes when outcome is defined as children's posttreatment externalizing behavior or behavioral improvement (e.g., CPPRG, 2002; Kazdin & Crowley, 1997). Data from the MTA study suggest that this appears to hold true for ADHD symptoms specifically. For example, among children with more depressed parents, only 29% of the children who presented with higher baseline ADHD symptoms were "excellent responders" to MED or COMB treatments, compared to 59% of those with less severe baseline symptoms. Among those with less depressed parents, only 41% who presented with higher ADHD symptoms were excellent responders, compared to 73% of those with lower ADHD symptom scores. Therefore, although children with severe pretreatment symptoms of ADHD may make significant gains in treatment, their absolute symptom level following treatment may remain in the clinical range and may be considered refractory.

Comorbid Symptomatology

Another child characteristic to consider when faced with a difficult-to-treat child with ADHD is comorbidity. Interestingly, evidence from several studies suggests that comorbid aggressive disorders (i.e., ODD and CD) do not moderate treatment outcome (Kazdin & Whitley, 2006; MTA Cooperative Group, 1999b). However, studies involving school-based and inpatient treatments for ADHD provide some evidence that comorbid externalizing behaviors may be associated with worse treatment outcome for children with ADHD (Beauchaine & Gartner, 2003; Richerson, 2004). The impact of comorbid anxiety disorders on treatment outcome for children with ADHD is also noteworthy, as results suggest that behavioral treatments may be particularly helpful for children with this comorbid profile. For example, moderation analyses conducted with the MTA dataset revealed that children with high levels of comorbid anxiety received incremental benefit in the reduction of hyperactive/impulsive symptoms from COMB treatment relative to MED treatment (MTA Cooperative Group, 1999b). Similarly, children with comorbid anxiety received incremental benefit in the reduction of internalizing symptoms and improvement of social skills from the BEH treatment, as compared to the community control treatment (in which the majority of children received medication). Finally, although not consistent across all studies (e.g., Diamond, Tannock, & Schachar, 1999) some medication studies have found that the presence of comorbid anxiety problems decreases the likelihood of a positive medication response (e.g., DuPaul, Barkley, & McMurray, 1994).

Familial Environment Variables

Parental Psychopathology and Stress

Although ADHD represents a disorder with substantial evidence of neurological and genetic causes (Jensen & Cooper, 2002), research indicates that the familial environments of children with ADHD are not only disrupted by but also can contribute to the maintenance and exacerbation of behavioral symptoms (C. Johnston & Mash, 2001). Thus, working with parents to structure the child's environment, avoid negative parent–child interactions, and reinforce positive behavior is an integral component of well-established treatment for ADHD (Pelham et al., 1998). As such, parents' ability to meet the demands of such interventions is related to child treatment outcomes.

In particular, parental psychopathology and stress may interfere with parents' abilities to meet such demands. For example, parental depression and parental ADHD are risk factors for poorer treatment response for children receiving well-established treatments for ADHD (E. B. Owens et al., 2003; Sonuga-Barke, Daley, & Thompson, 2002). Further, even if the child's parents are not experiencing clinically significant levels of psychopathology, parenting stress may interfere with positive treatment outcomes through its association with parents' use of ineffective discipline and their attributions about the causes of child behavior (e.g., attributing noncompliance to the child's lack of effort), both of which predict worse treatment outcome (Hoza et al., 2000).

Parent Divorce

Although there is significant variation in children's reactions to divorce, research has indicated that divorce has a small, but significant, impact on children's functioning (Amato & Keith, 1991). A review of several studies showed that children, especially boys, from families of high-conflict divorces, where verbal and physical aggression, overt hostility, and mistrust occurred, were significantly more likely to have emotional and behavioral disturbances when compared to national norms (J. R. Johnston, 1994). More specifically, Kasen and colleagues (Kasen, Cohen, Brook, & Hartmark, 1996) found that children from stepfamilies were at four times greater risk for ADHD and CD than children from intact families.

However, results across studies are inconsistent and suggest that confounding variables may play a large role in study outcomes. For example, one study found that marital status alone was not a significant risk factor for adolescent psychopathology; yet, there was an interaction between physical abuse and marital status in adolescents diagnosed with lifetime ADHD (Cohen, Adler, Kaplan, Pelcovitz, & Mandel, 2002). In fact, the risk for a lifetime diagnosis of ADHD increased 15-fold for children who experienced both physical abuse and marital disruption, compared to children who had not. This study serves as a reminder that additional factors should be considered in the interpretation of results in these studies, as well as in future study designs. Finally, some have noted that parent behaviors may be more influential than parent marital status in determining child outcomes (Ellwood & Stolberg, 1991, 1993). Thus, how these factors are defined and interpreted is critical to future research that attempts to understand the direct and indirect effects of divorce and its potential impact on ADHD.

Socioeconomic Status

Another characteristic of the familial environment that may contribute to poorer treatment outcomes is lower socioeconomic status (SES). Research has demonstrated that lower SES is associated with treatment attrition and worse treatment outcomes for children whose parents participate in behavioral parent training (e.g., Chronis et al., 2004; Webster-Stratton, 1990). To maximize treatment participation and outcome when working with low-income families, it may be necessary to address the SES-related barriers (e.g., transportation, financial barriers, child care, literacy) before participation in treatment or as a critical part of treatment throughout the process.

Treatment Process Variables

Factors directly pertaining to the process of treatment itself may also contribute to child treatment outcomes. For example, despite the impressive data documenting the effectiveness of behavioral parent training programs (Pelham & Fabiano, 2008), many parents choose not to attend, or do so only sporadically. Factors associated with parents' lack of participation include busy family schedules, single-parent status, lower educational status, and minimization of child symptom severity. These factors likely interfere with the number of parent training sessions attended and the integrity with which parents implement the recommended parenting skills. Similarly, the outcomes of behavioral classroom interventions are likely affected by the degree to which the teacher implements the intervention with integrity (Durlak & DuPre, 2008). Thus, intervention integrity and factors affecting treatment integrity should be examined as possible contributors to refractory cases.

Kazdin and colleagues (Kazdin, Holland, Crowley, & Breton, 1997) have identified five factors representing barriers to parent involvement in treatment. These are: practical obstacles (e.g., transportation), treatment demands (e.g., child refusal to participate), parent's perceptions of treatment, parent's relationship with the therapist, and stressful life events. Families with higher barrier scores had higher rates of cancellations and missed appointments and were more likely to have dropped out of treatment than families with lower barrier scores. Barriers were also stronger predictors of treatment dropout than were family, parent, and child factors such as maternal age, child aggression, and family environment. Most important, barrier scores predicted the degree to which children improved in treatment (Kazdin & Wassell, 1999). These data suggest that if barriers to treatment participation are not surmounted, child outcomes will suffer.

Summary of Factors Associated With Poorer Outcome

Taken together, the aforementioned findings indicate that children with ADHD who might be most at risk for poor treatment outcomes are those who present with lower than average IQs, higher baseline symptomatology including comorbid aggression or anxiety, parents with psychopathology or high parenting stress, low SES, teachers who have not demonstrated strong acceptability or integrity for the classroom intervention, and/or parents who experience many barriers to participation in treatment. Thus, these are factors to consider evaluating and addressing in the treatment of refractory cases of ADHD.

CASE PRESENTATION

Referral Information

At the time of referral, Brandon was an 8-year-old Caucasian male in 3rd grade, living in a rural, Appalachian community. He was initially referred to the intervention assistance team at his school by his 3rd grade teacher, who reported that Brandon was inattentive, easily distracted, impulsive, had difficulty transitioning between tasks, and frequently refused to complete written work. Brandon's mother and father described that Brandon was unorganized, forgetful, and required constant redirection to complete tasks at home. Brandon's mother reported that his behavior problems had been a concern since he was 5 years old and that he had been attending weekly counseling during the last year. Brandon's mother acknowledged that the counseling, designed to address Brandon's "delayed ego development," was not resulting in improvement. Thus, she provided consent for Brandon to participate in a school-based mental health program.

School-Based Mental Health Program

Brandon was referred to The Youth Experiencing Success in School (Y.E.S.S.) Program, a school mental health program designed to increase access to evidence-based services for children and families in rural communities (see J. S. Owens et al., 2005; J. S. Owens, Girio, Abbott, & Himawan, 2008; J. S. Owens, Murphy, Richerson, Girio, & Himawan, 2008 for details). The program provides comprehensive assessment, behavioral parenting sessions (Barkley, 1997), a classroom-based daily report card (DRC) intervention (Kelley, 1990), and year-long collaborative teacher consultation (Sheridan, Kratochwill, & Bergan, 1996). Children's academic and behavioral functioning is evaluated three times during the year (fall, winter, spring). Brandon participated in the Y.E.S.S. Program for 3 years (during 3rd, 4th, and 5th grade). Figure 14.1 depicts parent and teacher ratings across these 3 years. The initial assessment results, as well as Brandon's response to treatment across these 3 years, are described in the following section.

Assessment and Background Information

The assessment process included a diagnostic interview with Brandon's mother, interviews with Brandon and Brandon's teacher, parent and

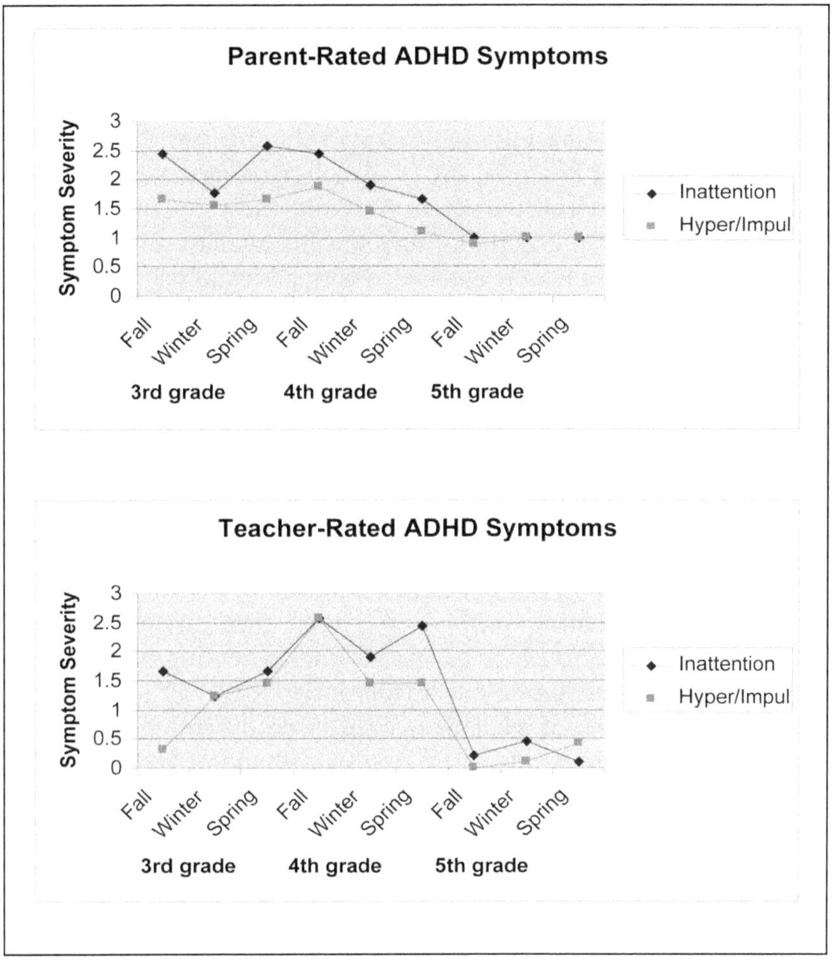

Figure 14.1 Parent and teacher ratings of inattentive and hyperactive/impulsive symptoms over 3 years.

Note. Scores are from the Disruptive Behavior Disorders Rating Scale and range from 0 to 3.

From: Pelham, W. E., Gnagy, E. M., Greenslade, K. E., & Milich, R. (1992). Teacher ratings of DSM-III-R symptoms for the disruptive behavior disorders. *Journal of the American Academy of Child and Adolescent Psychiatry, 31*, 210–218.

teacher rating scales, review of school records, and an observation of Brandon in the classroom. Data from this process provided evidence that Brandon was displaying clinically significant symptoms of inattention and at-risk levels of hyperactivity/impulsivity at home and at school, as well as significant impairment in academic and social functioning. A diagnosis of ADHD, inattentive type was made (see *DSM-IV-TR*; APA, 2000). Further, parent and teacher ratings indicated that Brandon was also experiencing above-average levels of anxiety (T-scores > 65) on the Child Behavior Checklist (CBCL) and the Teacher Report Form (TRF) (Achenbach & Rescorla, 2001). Although rating scale scores were elevated, information from the parent and child interviews indicated that Brandon did not meet criteria for any specific anxiety disorder; most of his anxiety symptoms were associated with perfectionism and a rigid, inflexible personality style. A secondary diagnosis of anxiety disorder, not otherwise specified was made. Based on the Wechsler Abbreviated Scales of Intelligence (WASI; Psychological Corporation, 1999), Brandon's Full Scale IQ was estimated to be 129 and his achievement scores were not significantly discrepant from his cognitive ability.

In terms of the family environment, Brandon's parents divorced when he was 3 years old. Both parents had earned a college degree and were of middle-class SES. Brandon's mother had remarried and his father had not. His parents had a joint-custody arrangement in which Brandon spent alternating weeks at each home. The parents seemingly had an amicable relationship. In terms of her parenting practices, his mother stated that in response to inappropriate behavior she typically would talk to him about what he needed to do differently. Brandon's father also reported lecturing and taking away Brandon's television. His father noted that he experienced some of the same symptoms that Brandon was displaying when he was a child. All three caregivers reported experiencing significant stress related to Brandon's noncompliant behaviors and his failure to achieve his academic potential; all three were willing to attend behavioral parenting sessions with the clinician.

Treatment Implementation and Response

3rd Grade

Following the assessment, the clinician and the teacher established bi-weekly meetings to discuss monitoring and modifying Brandon's behavior. Brandon's teacher agreed to increase her use of positive reinforcement of Brandon whenever he was displaying appropriate behaviors in her classroom. Further, she identified the primary behaviors to target through a daily report card intervention. Target behaviors included Brandon's independent initiation of seatwork and percentage of work completed during his writing period, as these were times when Brandon was most distracted and noncompliant. Brandon's teacher tracked his completion of writing assignments on DRCs that went home to his parents, who subsequently provided privileges, contingent on whether Brandon had met his daily goal. During this year, each biological parent met with the program clinician for eight behavioral parenting sessions during which strategies such as the privilege system for the DRC, time-out, active ignoring, and praise were discussed. It was the clinician's perception that the parents implemented the DRC privilege system with reasonable integrity; however, their between-session practice and subsequent implementation of other parenting skills was variable and inconsistent within each home and across homes. In addition, a medication evaluation was recommended and discussed with the parents on two occasions during this year; however, both biological parents voiced strong objections to this.

Brandon made significant progress in completing written work over the course of 3rd grade (see Figure 14.2). Although his performance was still variable, he was completing at least 75% of his writing on most days. However, in terms of his symptoms of ADHD (see Figure 14.1) and anxiety, Brandon's behavior remained stable or deteriorated across 3rd grade. Further, on return to school in 4th grade, his parents and teachers described him as more immature relative to his peers. In fact, during the assessment process in 4th grade, Brandon's teacher reported that, in addition to displaying symptoms of ADHD, Brandon was frequently argumentative and excessively emotional. Reportedly, when Brandon became frustrated, he had temper tantrums and hid under his desk. Given that Brandon presented with these symptoms despite having already undergone 1 year of evidenced-based behavioral treatment, he was determined to be a refractory case.

4th Grade

An analysis of Brandon's poor treatment response ruled out many of the aforementioned risk factors. For example, Brandon had a high IQ and did not present with extremely severe baseline symptoms; his parents were educated, of middle-class SES, and did not have current

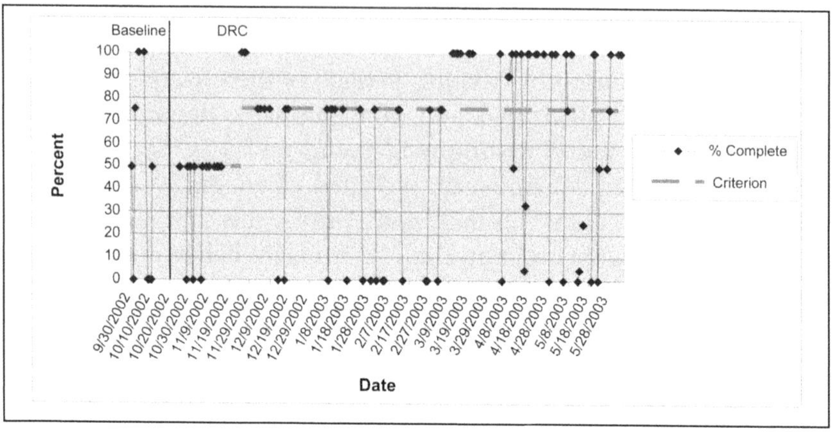

Figure 14.2 Percentage of writing assignments completed during 3rd grade.

mental health issues of their own; and his teachers were implementing the classroom intervention with respectable integrity. The two factors that were then considered as contributing to the lack of treatment response were the inconsistent adoption and use of effective parenting strategies within and across the homes of his parents and Brandon's comorbid anxiety. Observations of Brandon's behavior in the classroom suggested that he had inadequate coping skills to deal with selected academic challenges (e.g., translating his ideas into written products) and with constructive feedback from his teachers. Brandon was very critical of himself and his work and engaged in a significant amount of negative self-talk. Not being aware of Brandon's negative self-talk, his 4th-grade teacher simply observed inattention, noncompliance, oppositional behavior, and moodiness. She indicated that she was at a loss as to how to address his classroom behavior and experienced significant stress as a result. During Brandon's 4th-grade year, consultation sessions with his teacher focused on (a) enhancing the teacher's understanding of the complexity of Brandon's behaviors (e.g., inadequate coping skills, anxiety related to perfectionism, as well as ADHD), and (b) providing opportunities for collaborative problem solving to improve Brandon's behavior and reduce the teacher's stress, both of which led to an increase in the teacher's willingness to adopt and implement the DRC intervention. Thus, during this year, the teacher learned how to encourage Brandon's initiation and completion of work

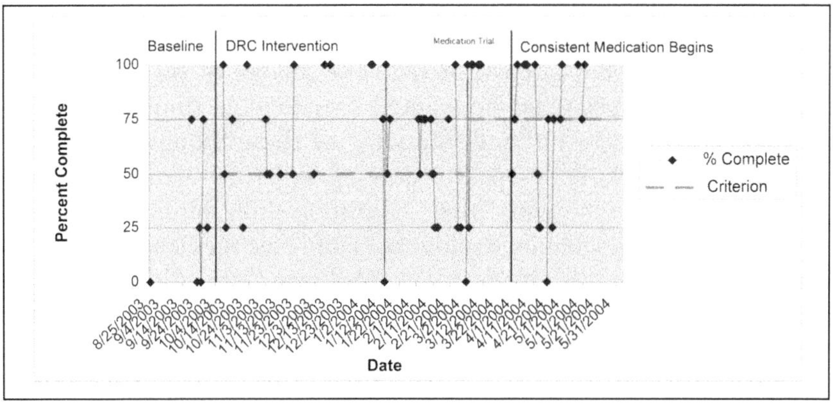

Figure 14.3 Percentage of writing assignments completed in 4th grade.

Note. DRC Graphs for Reading, Math, Science, and Social Studies reveal similar or better work productivity in response to intervention.

through supportive interactions and positive reinforcement (in the context of the DRC intervention) rather than through threats and abrasive interactions. Subsequently, Brandon's tantrums began to decrease and his classroom productivity improved. Indeed, according to his DRC data, his work completion had improved from an average of 25% during baseline to 75% by the end of the year across all subjects (see Figure 14.3). Similarly, between the first quarter and the last quarter of the school year, his grades had improved from "Ds" to "Bs" in writing and spelling and from an "F" to a "C" in social studies, with an "A" and a "B" in science and reading, respectively.

In addition, during this time the clinician began to meet with Brandon for weekly individual therapy in which cognitive-behavioral (C-B) techniques for anxiety were applied. It is possible that Brandon's above-average intellectual functioning contributed to his positive response; specifically, he responded very well to the use of metaphors (e.g., "rocks and balloons" to represent negative and positive self-talk, viewing a situation through black versus rosy-colored glasses) when identifying, analyzing, and modifying his negative self-talk. Brandon also created his own metaphor ("train thoughts") to describe his cognitive experience when approaching writing assignments. Specifically,

Brandon's momentum in writing was halted by his negative "train thoughts" (as if he has to stop and wait for the train to pass by). These "train thoughts" were often related to the quality of his writing and caused him to forget what he wanted to write. As Brandon became more sophisticated in his understanding of these thoughts and their impact on his work, he learned to develop skills that would help him overcome his "train thoughts" (e.g., relaxation skills, building a "thinking bridge" that allowed him to move over and past the "train thought"). Moreover, Brandon was able to adapt these new skills to the classroom setting, as evidenced by improvements in his completion of daily routines and assignments. In addition, according to the TRF (Psychological Corporation, 1999), his teacher witnessed a decrease in his anxiety-related behaviors (T-scores dropped from 65 to 55 on teacher ratings between the first and third grading periods).

With regard to the parenting intervention, the clinician directly yet sensitively discussed a new approach to parenting sessions with the parents. Namely, the new approach would involve some individual sessions with each parent and some sessions that included all three caregivers. The individual sessions focused on each parent's stress and the effect of that stress on their parenting. The joint sessions focused on (a) enhancing consistency within each home and across homes, (b) informing the parents about the strategies that Brandon was acquiring in the C-B individual sessions, and (c) engaging in discussions about the possible advantages and disadvantages of supplemental pharmacotherapy. The parents were gradually receptive to all of these modifications. Their in-home and across-home implementation and consistent use of praise, time-out, and response-cost procedures improved, as did communication among the three parents. Brandon's parents adopted some of the metaphor language that Brandon had created in individual therapy and began to use these terms as cues for Brandon to implement his coping strategies (e.g., positive self-talk, relaxation skills). Finally, although hesitant about long-term medication use because of concerns about unnecessary medication use and possible negative side effects, Brandon's parents began to see the value of a medication assessment. Thus, in collaboration with Brandon's pediatrician, a medication trial was conducted in which Brandon ingested a low dose of Concerta on half of the school days during this period and his teacher (blind to the medication condition) completed ratings scales about his behavior and possible side effects. Incremental benefits of the medication were observed in Brandon's behavior toward peers and teachers, and in work completion. As seen in Figure 14.1, Brandon's ADHD symptoms continued to decrease in the context of combined treatments throughout 4th grade and during the summer before 5th grade.

5th Grade

During Brandon's 5th-grade year, he remained in the program for maintenance and monitoring. He continued to have a DRC intervention targeting work completion and following teacher instructions, and he continued to meet with the program clinician for individual cognitive-behavioral therapy (on a biweekly basis in the fall, faded to as needed in winter and spring). His parents continued to implement a home-based privilege system for the DRC and continued to use praise, time-out, and privilege loss at home to manage Brandon's behavior. Figure 14.1 demonstrates that treatment gains were maintained over the summer between 4th and 5th grade, as well as throughout the 5th-grade academic year.

CONCLUSIONS

Although well-established treatments have been identified and thoroughly studied for elementary-school youth with ADHD, their existence does not ensure successful treatment implementation or treatment outcomes. Well-established treatments for ADHD require intensive and consistent participation from parents, educators, and health and mental health providers, as well as coordination among these adults. Like Brandon, many children with ADHD present with additional factors that must be considered when planning and implementing these treatments.

Brandon's case highlights several critical factors in addressing refractory cases of ADHD. First, a multimodal, multiinformant assessment should precede treatment planning and implementation. This assessment process should consider not only diagnostic possibilities, but also other child (e.g., IQ, symptom severity, comorbidity), family (e.g., parent psychopathology, SES), and treatment process factors (e.g., treatment acceptability, treatment integrity, barriers to treatment) prior to intervention and at various points throughout the treatment process.

Second, Brandon's case underscores the importance of ongoing assessment and data-driven decision making. At the end of his first year of treatment, improvements were observed on his DRC targets; however, Brandon's symptoms of ADHD and anxiety as well as his impairment in peer and teacher relationships had not changed. Without the ongoing multidomain, multiinformant ratings, the improvement on the DRC may have been viewed as an indicator of successful treatment; subsequently, treatment intensity, as well as coordination of care, may have plateaued or declined for Brandon. As the data suggest, this would not have been an appropriate treatment decision.

Third, the case example demonstrates the incremental benefits of supplemental CBT for children with ADHD and comorbid anxiety. The use of CBT was perhaps particularly successful in Brandon's case because of his higher intellectual capacity. This process provided him with additional understanding of his strengths and weaknesses, as well as coping skills for overcoming impediments to his academic and social success. This exemplifies how capitalizing on a child's strengths can bolster the effectiveness of a given treatment. It also highlights the importance of applying treatments to both ADHD and co-occurring conditions (e.g., cognitive-behavioral therapy for depression; academic intervention for comorbid learning disability).

Fourth, the importance of teacher and parent involvement in the child's treatment cannot be understated. Informing Brandon's 4th-grade teacher of the complexities of his challenges provided her with insight and empathy and seemed to facilitate her willingness to implement the DRC. In addition, ongoing consultation helped her understand that, although improvements could be made, variability in student performance was still likely to occur. Similarly, although Brandon's parents had participated in behavioral parent training in Brandon's first year of treatment, their use of the skills produced only modest benefits. To achieve maximal benefits, treatment modifications had to be made (e.g., joint parenting sessions, supplemental cognitive-behavioral therapy, and continued education about the possible advantages and disadvantages to medication). This case also demonstrates the value of continued discussions with parents at critical junctures in treatment about the possible benefits of a medication trial.

Finally, it is also critical to note that this process of intervention, documentation, evaluation, and modification occurred over 3 years. We must educate parents and teachers about the chronic nature of the disorder and about the importance of ongoing monitoring, booster sessions, and intervention modification at each subsequent stage of child development. Clearly, the evidenced-based-practice process is a journey that requires patience and persistence. Tailoring interventions to the individual needs and preferences of the child and his or her family, evaluating the outcomes, and making adjustments are critical to the process of evidence-based practice (APA, 2006). We believe that Brandon's case illustrates this process.

In recent decades, researchers have turned their attention toward large, clinical trials of treatments for children with ADHD (e.g., MTA Cooperative Group, 1999b). Although beneficial in documenting the positive outcomes of multiple treatments, this process has only begun to examine factors associated with refractory cases. Too often researchers are not reinforced for publishing seemingly unsuccessful treatment cases, yet there are rich data to be gleaned from cases that fail to respond to well-established treatments, particularly when treatments were implemented with high fidelity. We must embrace research involving case studies that inform and guide the treatment of refractory cases. In this process, it will be important to highlight child, family, and environmental factors that contributed either to the refractory nature of the case or the eventual positive outcomes achieved. Over time, this process may render well-established treatments more useful when applied to complex cases, and will highlight for both research and practice communities the science of the decision-making process that integrates current research evidence with the unique needs of each individual child and family (APA, 2006).

REFERENCES

Abikoff, H. (1991). Cognitive training in ADHD children: Less to it than meets the eye. *Journal of Learning Disabilities, 24,* 205–209.

Achenbach, T. M., & Rescorla, L. A. (2001). *Manual of the ASEBA School Age Forms & Profile.* Burlington, VT: University of Vermont, Research Center for Children, Youth & Families.

Amato, P. R., & Keith, B. (1991). Parent divorce and the well-being of children: A meta-analysis. *Psychological Bulletin, 110,* 26–46.

American Academy of Child and Adolescent Psychiatry. (2007). Practice parameters for the assessment and treatment of children and adolescents with attention-deficit/hyperactivity disorder. *Journal of the American Academy of Child and Adolescent Psychiatry, 46,* 894–921.

American Psychiatric Association. (2000). *Diagnostic and statistical manual of mental disorders* (4th ed., text rev.). Washington, DC: American Psychiatric Press.

American Psychological Association. (2006). Evidenced-based practice in psychology. *American Psychologist, 61*, 271–285.

Antshel, K. M., & Remer, R. (2003). Social skills training in children with attention deficit hyperactivity disorder: A randomized-controlled clinical trial. *Journal of Clinical Child and Adolescent Psychology, 32*, 153–165.

Barkley, R. A. (1997). *Defiant children: A clinician's manual for assessment and parent training* (2nd ed.). New York: Guilford Press.

Barkley, R. A., Fischer, M., Smallish, L., & Fletcher, K. (2002). The persistence of attention-deficit/hyperactivity disorder into young adulthood as a function of reporting source and definition of disorder. *Journal of Abnormal Psychology, 111*, 279–289.

Barkley, R. A., Fischer, M., Smallish, L., & Fletcher, K. (2004). Young adult follow-up of hyperactive children: Antisocial activities and drug use. *Journal of Child Psychology and Psychiatry, 45*, 195–211.

Barkley, R. A., Fischer, M., Smallish, L., & Fletcher, K. (2006). Young adult outcomes of hyperactive children: Adaptive functioning in major life activities. *Journal of the American Academy of Child & Adolescent Psychiatry, 45*, 192–202.

Beauchaine, T. P., & Gartner, J. (2003). A linear growth curve analysis of inpatient treatment response by conduct-disordered, ADHD, and comorbid preadolescents. *Aggressive Behavior, 29*, 440–456.

Burns, G. L., & Walsh, J. A. (2002). The influence of ADHD-hyperactivity/impulsivity symptoms on the development of oppositional defiant disorder symptoms in a 2-year longitudinal study. *Journal of Abnormal Child Psychology, 30*, 245–256.

Carlson, C. L., Pelham, W. E., Milich, R., & Dixon, M. J. (1992). Single and combined effects of methylphenidate and behavior therapy on the classroom performance of children with attention-deficit hyperactivity disorder. *Journal of Abnormal Child Psychology, 20*, 213–232.

Carlson, C. L., Shin, M., & Booth, J. (1999). The case for DSM-IV subtypes in ADHD. *Mental Retardation and Developmental Disabilities Research Reviews, 5*, 199–206.

Carlson, C. L., Tamm, L., & Gaub, M. (1997). Gender difference in children with ADHD, ODD, and co-occuring ADHD/ODD identified in a school population. *Journal of the American Academy of Child & Adolescent Psychiatry, 36*, 1706–1714.

Chronis, A., Chacko, A., Fabiano, G., Wymbs, B., & Pelham, W. (2004). Enhancements to the behavioral parent training paradigm for families of children with ADHD: Review and future directions. *Clinical Child and Family Psychology Review, 7*, 1–27.

Cohen, A. J., Adler, N., Kaplan, S. J., Pelcovitz, D., & Mandel, F. S. (2002). Interactional effects of marital status and physical abuse on adolescent psychopathology. *Child Abuse & Neglect, 26*, 277–288.

Conduct Problems Prevention Research Group. (2002). Predictor variables associated with positive Fast Track outcomes at the end of third grade. *Journal of Abnormal Child Psychology, 30*, 37–52.

Conners, C. K., Epstein, J. N., March, J. S., Angold, A., Wells, K. C., Klaric, J., et al. (2001). Multimodal treatment of ADHD in the MTA: An alternative outcome analysis. *Journal of the American Academy of Child and Adolescent Psychiatry, 40*, 159–167.

Cunningham, C. E., Boyle, M. H. (2002). Preschoolers at risk for attention-deficit hyperactivity disorder and oppositional defiant disorder: Family, parenting, and behavioral correlates. *Journal of Abnormal Child Psychology, 30,* 555–569.

Diamond, I. R., Tannock, R., & Schachar, R. J. (1999). Response to methylphenidate in children with ADHD and comorbid anxiety. *Journal of the American Academy of Child & Adolescent Psychiatry, 38,* 402–409.

DuPaul, G. J., Barkley, R. A., & McMurray, M. B. (1994). Response of children with ADHD to methylphenidate: Interaction with internalizing symptoms. *Journal of the American Academy of Child and Adolescent Psychiatry, 33,* 894–903.

DuPaul, G. J., & Eckert, T. L. (1997). The effects of school-based interventions for attention deficit hyperactivity disorder: A meta-analysis. *School Psychology Review, 26,* 5–27.

DuPaul, G. E. & Stoner, G. (2003). *ADHD in the schools: Assessment and intervention strategies* (2nd ed.). New York: Guilford Press.

Durlak, J. A., & DuPre, E. P (2008). Implementation matters: A review of research on the influence of implementation on program outcomes and the factors affecting implementation. *American Journal of Community Psychology, 32,* 345–357.

Girio, E. L., & Owens, J. S. (2008). *Teacher acceptability of evidence-based and promising treatments for children with attention deficit/hyperactivity disorder.* Unpublished manuscript.

Ellwood, M. S., & Stolberg, A. L. (1991). A preliminary investigation of family systems' influence on individual divorce adjustment. *Journal of Divorce, 15,* 157–174.

Ellwood, M. S., & Stolberg, A. L. (1993). The effects of family composition, family health, parenting behavior, and environmental stress on children's divorce adjustment. *Journal of Child and Family Studies, 2,* 23–26.

Greene, R. W., & Ablon, J. S. (2001). What does the MTA study tell us about effective psychosocial treatment for ADHD? *Journal of Clinical Child Psychology, 30,* 114–121.

Greene, R., Beszterczey, S. K., Katzenstein, T., Park, K., & Goring, J. (2002). Are students with ADHD more stressful to teach? Patterns of teacher stress in an elementary school sample. *Journal of Emotional and Behavioral Disorders, 10,* 79–89.

Grizenko, N., Sayegh, L., & Papineau, D. (1994). Predicting outcome in a multimodal day treatment program for children with severe behaviour problems. *Canadian Journal of Psychiatry, 39,* 557–562.

Gupta, V. B. (2007). Comparison of parenting stress in different developmental disabilities. *Journal of Developmental and Physical Disabilities, 19,* 417–425.

Harrison, C., & Sofronoff, K. (2002). ADHD and parental psychological distress: Role of demographics, child behavioral characteristics, and parental cognitions. *Journal of the American Academy of Child & Adolescent Psychiatry, 41,* 703–711.

Hinshaw, S. P., & Lee, S. S. (2006). Predictors of adolescent functioning in girls with attention deficit hyperactivity disorder (ADHD): The role of childhood ADHD, conduct problems, and peer status. *Journal of Clinical Child and Adolescent Psychology, 35,* 356–368.

Hoza, B. (2007). Peer functioning in children with ADHD. *Journal of Pediatric Psychology, 32,* 655–663.

Hoza, B., Owens, J. S., Pelham, W. E., Swanson, J. M., Conners, C. K., Hinshaw, S. P., et al. (2000). Parent cognitions as predictors of child treatment response in attention-deficit/hyperactivity disorder. *Journal of Abnormal Child Psychology, 28,* 569–583.

Jensen, P. S., & Cooper, J. R. (Eds.) (2002). *Attention deficit hyperactivity disorder: State of the science best practices.* Kingston, NJ: Civic Research Institute.

Johnson, J. H., & Reader, S. K. (2002). Assessing stress in families of children with ADHD: Preliminary development of the Disruptive Behavior Stress Inventory. *Journal of Clinical Psychology in Medical Settings, 9,* 51–62.

Johnston, C., & Mash, E. J. (2001). Families of children with attention-deficit/hyperactivity disorder: Review and recommendations for future research. *Clinical Child and Family Psychology Review, 4,* 183–207.

Johnston, J. R. (1994). High-conflict divorce. *Future of Childen: Children and Divorce, 4,* 165–182.

Kasen, S., Cohen, P., Brook, J. S., & Hartmark, C. (1996). A multiple-risk interaction model: Effects of temperament and divorce on psychiatric disorders in children. *Journal of Abnormal Child Psychology, 24,* 121–150.

Kazdin, A. E., & Crowley, M. J. (1997). Moderators of treatment outcome in cognitively based treatment of antisocial children. *Cognitive Therapy and Research, 21,* 185–207.

Kazdin, A. E., & Whitley, M. K. (2006). Comorbidity, case complexity, and effects of evidence-based treatment for children referred for disruptive behavior. *Journal of Consulting and Clinical Psychology, 74,* 455-467.

Kazdin, A. E., & Wassell, G. (1999). Barriers to treatment participation and therapeutic change among children referred for conduct disorder. *Journal of Clinical Child Psychology, 28,* 160–172.

Kelley, M. L. (1990). *School-home notes: Promoting children's classroom success.* New York: Guilford Press.

Lahey, B. B., & Willcutt, E. G. (2002). Validity of the diagnosis and dimensions of attention deficit hyperactivity disorder. In P. Jensen & J. Cooper (Eds.), *Attention deficit hyperactivity disorder: State of the science* (pp. 1–21). Kingston, NJ: Civic Research Institute.

Loe, I. M., & Feldman, H. M. (2007). Academic and educational outcomes of children with ADHD. *Journal of Pediatric Psychology, 32,* 643–654.

Loeber, R., Green, S. M., Lahey, B. B., Frick, P. J., & McBurnett, K. (2000). Findings on disruptive behavior disorders from the first decade of the Developmental Trends Study. *Clinical Child and Family Psychology Review, 3,* 37–60.

Lonigan, J., Elbert, J. C., & Johnson, S. B. (1998). Empirically supported psychosocial interventions for children: An overview. *Journal of Clinical Child Psychology, 27,* 138–145.

Meichenbaum, D.H. (1977). *Cognitive-behavior modification: An integrative approach.* New York: Plenum Press.

Mikami, A. Y., & Pfiffner, L. J. (2008). Sibling relationship among children with ADHD. *Journal of Attention Disorders, 11,* 482–492.

MTA Cooperative Group. (1999a). 14-month randomized clinical trial of treatment strategies for attention deficit hyperactivity disorder. *Archives of General Psychiatry, 56,* 1073–1086.

MTA Cooperative Group. (1999b). Moderators and mediators of treatment response for children with attention-deficit/hyperactivity disorder: The multimodal treatment study of children with ADHD. *Archives of General Psychiatry, 56,* 1088–1096.

Owens, E. B., Hinshaw, S. P., Kraemer, H. C., Arnold, L. E., Abikoff, H. B., Cantwell, D. P. et al. (2003). Which treatment for whom for ADHD? Moderators of treatment response in MTA. *Journal of Consulting and Clinical Psychology, 71*, 540–552.

Owens, J. S., Murphy, C. E., Richerson, L., Girio, E., & Himawan, L. (2008). Science to practice in underserved communities: The effectiveness of school mental health programming. *Journal of Clinical Child and Adolescent Psychology, 37*, 434–447.

Owens, J. S., Richerson, L., Beilstein, E. A., Crane, A., Murphy, C. E., & Vancouver, J. B. (2005). School-based mental health programming for children with inattentive and disruptive behavior problems: First-year treatment outcome. *Journal of Attention Disorders, 9*, 261–274.

Pelham, W. E., & Fabiano, G. A. (2008). Evidence-based psychosocial treatment for attention deficit/hyperactivity disorder: An update. *Journal of Clinical Child and Adolescent Psychology, 37*, 184–214.

Pelham, W. E., & Hoza, B. (1996). Intensive treatment: A summer treatment program for children with ADHD. In E. D. Hibbs & P. S. Jensen (Eds.), *Psychosocial treatments for child and adolescent disorders: Empirically based strategies for clinical practice* (pp. 311–340). Washington, DC: American Psychological Association.

Pelham, W. E., & Smith, B. H. (2000). Prediction and measurement of individual responses to Ritalin by children and adolescents with ADHD. In L. Greenhill & B. P. Osman (Eds.), *Ritalin: Theory and practice* (2nd ed., pp. 193–217). New York: Mary Ann Liebert.

Pelham, W. E., Wheeler, T., & Chronis, A. (1998). Empirically supported psychosocial treatments for attention deficit hyperactivity disorder. *Journal of Clinical Child Psychology, 27*, 190–205.

Power, T. J., Hess, L. E., & Bennett, D. S. (1995). The acceptability of interventions for attention-deficit hyperactivity disorder among elementary and middle school teachers. *Developmental and Behavioral Pediatrics, 16*, 238–243.

Psychological Corporation. (1999). *Wechsler Abbreviated Scale of Intelligence (WASI) manual*. San Antonio, TX: Author.

Raggi, V. L., & Chronis, A. M. (2006). Interventions to address the academic impairment of children and adolescents with ADHD. *Clinical Child and Family Psychology Review, 9*, 85–111.

Rapport, M. D. (1992). Treating children with attention-deficit/hyperactivity disorder. *Behavior Modification, 16*, 155–163.

Richerson, L. (2004). *Child, family, and school predictors of outcome of a school-based intervention for children with disruptive behavior problems*. Retrieved April 11, 2008, from Ohio University library http://www.ohiolink.edu/etd/view.cgi?ohiou1090939935

Robinson, T. R, Smith, S. W., Miller, D. M., & Brownell, M.T. (1999). Cognitive behavior modification of hyperactivity-impulsivity and aggression: A meta-analysis of school-based studies. *Journal of Educational Psychology, 91*, 195–203.

Sheridan, S. M., Kratochwill, T. R., & Bergan, J. R. (1996). *Conjoint behavioral consultation: A procedural manual*. New York: Plenum Press.

Sonuga-Barke, E. J., Daley, D., & Thompson, M. (2002). Does maternal ADHD reduce the effectiveness of parent training for preschool children's ADHD? *Journal of the American Academy of Child & Adolescent Psychiatry, 41*, 696–702.

Spencer, T., Biederman, J., Wilens, T., Harding, M., O'Donnell, D., & Griffin, S. (1996). Pharmacotherapy of attention-deficit hyperactivity disorder across the life cycle. *Journal of the American Academy of Child and Adolescent Psychiatry, 35,* 409–432.

Sterling-Turner, H. E., Robinson, S. L., & Wilczynski, S. M. (2001). Functional assessment of distracting and disruptive behaviors in the school setting. *School Psychology Review, 30,* 211–226.

Swanson, J. M., Kramer, H. C., Hinshaw, S. P., Arnold, L. E., Conners, C. K., Abikoff, H. B., et al. (2001). Clinical relevance of the primary findings of the MTA: Success rates based on severity of ADHD and ODD symptoms at the end of treatment. *Journal of the American Academy of Child and Adolescent Psychiatry, 40,* 168–179.

Swanson, J. M., McBurnett, K., Christian, D. L., & Wigal, T. (1995). Stimulant medications and the treatment of children with ADHD. *Advances in Clinical Child Psychology, 17,* 265–322.

Swanson, J. M., McBurnett, K., Wigal, T., Pfiffner, L. J., Lerner, M. A., Williams, L., et al. (1993). Effect of stimulant medication on children with attention deficit disorder: A "review of reviews." *Exceptional Children, 60,* 154–161.

Waschbusch, D. A., & Hill, G. P. (2003). Empirically supported, promising, and unsupported treatments for children with attention-deficit/hyperactivity disorder. In S. Lilienfield, S. Lynn, & J. Lohr (Eds.), *Science and pseudoscience in clinical psychology* (pp. 333–362). New York: Guilford Press.

Waxmonsky, J. G. (2005). Nonstimulant therapies for attention-deficit hyperactivity disorder (ADHD) in children and adults. *Essential Psychopharmacology, 6,* 262–276.

Webster-Stratton, C. (1990). Enhancing the effectiveness of self-administered videotape parent training for families with conduct-problem children. *Journal of Abnormal Child Psychology, 18,* 479–492.

15

The Challenges of Working With Young People Diagnosed With Asperger Syndrome

KATE SOFRONOFF AND RENAE BEAUMONT

Since the seminal paper by Wing (1981) introduced the term "Asperger syndrome" there has been controversy over the validity of the diagnosis and interest in clarifying the boundaries of the condition. A recent review of the research literature on Asperger syndrome suggests that it is not substantively different from autism (Frith, 2004). The primary distinction between a diagnosis of high-functioning autism (HFA) and Asperger syndrome is based on whether the child demonstrated a significant language delay before 3 years of age. There is now evidence that casts doubt over the use of early language delay as a differential criterion between autism and Asperger syndrome. Mayes and Calhoun (2001) demonstrated that using a large sample of children with normal IQ and diagnoses of autism or Asperger syndrome and the criteria of the *Diagnostic and Statistical Manual of Mental Disorders, Fourth Edition, Text Revision* (*DSM-IV-TR*; American Psychiatry Association [APA], 2000), none met criteria for Asperger syndrome because they all met the criterion of communication impairment, resulting in a necessary diagnosis of autism. This has also been the finding of previous studies (e.g., Eisenmajer et al., 1996; Miller & Ozonoff, 1997). There is, however, a popular view among clinicians that, contrary to *DSM-IV* diagnostic hierarchy, if a child meets criteria for both autism and Asperger syndrome, the child should be given the diagnosis of Asperger syndrome

(Mahoney et al., 1998). As a result of this interest and controversy, there are many clinicians who prefer to give a diagnosis of autism spectrum disorder (ASD), reflecting a diagnosis that is part of a spectrum of disorders rather than being categorical, as is reflected in the current *DSM-IV-TR*.

There is no doubt that young people diagnosed with an ASD encounter difficulties in everyday living that can make them vulnerable to a wide range of mental health problems. Difficulties with emotional understanding and social interaction lie at the heart of ASDs and are important prognostic indicators for this population (Mackay, Knott & Dunlop, 2007). Indeed, these young people are likely to experience high levels of anxiety (Sofronoff, Attwood, & Hinton, 2005); are at significantly increased risk of depression (Kim, Szatmari, Bryson, Streiner, & Wilson, 2000); often have severe anger-management issues (Sofronoff, Attwood, Hinton, & Levin, 2007); and, as children, demonstrate numerous and frequent challenging behaviour problems (Einfeld & Tonge, 1996). Some of these problems are exacerbated by significant ineptitude in social interaction and by a lack of capacity to understand the motivations, feelings, and actions of others (i.e., Theory of Mind).

The social impairments that characterize high-functioning individuals with ASD (i.e., those without intellectual impairment) include difficulties interpreting and reacting appropriately to the nonverbal communication of others, a tendency to invade other people's personal space, and a proclivity to dictate activities in joint play and engage in long-winded monologues about their obsessive interests (Attwood, 2007). With respect to the emotional dimension of transactions, high-functioning individuals with ASD often have problems seeking or offering comfort in times of distress, and may fail to spontaneously share enjoyment with others (APA, 2000). Difficulties identifying and/or responding appropriately to one's own thoughts and feelings and those of others are typical, and can create the impression of insensitivity and disregard for other people (Klin & Volkmar, 1995).

As a result of the social skill impairments and deficits in emotional recognition and regulation just described, children with HFA and Asperger syndrome (AS) face many challenges at home and school, including conflict with family and teachers, rejection and bullying by peers, social isolation, and impaired academic performance (Bauminger & Kasari, 2000). Long-term effects of social skill deficits include the onset of affective disorders in many individuals during adolescence (~65%; Attwood, 2004) and limited prospects for independent living, college education, or employment in adulthood (Howlin, 2000; Venter, Lord & Schopler, 1992).

When evaluating interventions for this population, there is little in the way of accepted empirically supported interventions or heuristics for treatment. The behavioural interventions of Lovaas and colleagues (Lovaas, Koegel, Simmons, & Long, 1973) have formed the basis for the strategies used to increase skills and to manage noncompliant behavior in children with a more severe expression of autism. The method involves a detailed functional analysis of a child's dysfunctional behavior in a specific setting to inform specific interventions to remediate that behavior. It also involves breaking tasks and skills into very small incremental components and rewarding successive approximations to the task or skill. This is still suggested as particularly helpful in early intervention to increase skills and manage aggressive and disruptive behaviours (Matson & Smith, 2008).

For those children with higher functioning presentations there has, until recently, been little available with regard to managing problem behaviors, emotional problems, or social problems. In the following pages, we outline two programs that have demonstrated the use of cognitive-behavioral strategies with children diagnosed with Asperger syndrome.

MANAGING ANXIETY

The estimated prevalence rate of anxiety in young people with ASD is high, ranging from 47 to 84% (Gillot, Furniss, & Walter, 2001; Muris, Steerneman, Merkelbach, Holdrinet, & Meesters, 1998). One study found that of their sample of 65 children diagnosed with AS, the participants were comparable with a clinically anxious sample and the rate of anxiety was significantly higher than the comparison clinical sample on overall anxiety, obsessive-compulsive symptoms, and physical injury fears (Russell & Sofronoff, 2005). Attwood (2007) suggests, on the basis of extensive clinical experience, that anxiety arises in individuals diagnosed with AS over a wide range of issues, but that it should be possible to work with the population using cognitive-behavioral (CBT) treatment.

An intervention for children with ASD and anxiety was developed incorporating both a CBT framework and strategies such as Social Stories (Gray, 1998), designed originally for children with more severe autism. As outlined by Attwood (2004), it is necessary to accommodate the cognitive profile of the child with AS when using CBT, and to modify the approach to achieve this. The program is called "Exploring Feelings: Cognitive Behaviour Therapy to Manage Anxiety" (Attwood, 2004) and incorporates many elements specifically designed to overcome the known difficulties of working with children with AS. Children worked in groups of three, with two therapists per group. The reason for this ratio was so that each child would have the experience of being a part of an inclusive group; but if a child found this too difficult to manage for an entire session, then it was still possible to offer individual attention.

For one experimental condition a larger parent group was also run at the same time as the child sessions in which parents were taught the strategies offered in the program, encouraged to assist their child with home projects, to reinforce use of strategies, and given an opportunity to share experiences with the larger group. For another condition this parent intervention did not occur, parents were simply asked to help their child with home tasks. It was found that the parent training component produced significantly better results for the children and the parents preferred the involvement. In subsequent programs we have always included the parent training.

The program was designed to be engaging to children with a diagnosis of AS and is highly structured while maintaining specific approaches to engage the child. Each child receives a workbook and additional materials for six 2-hour sessions. The sessions include information about being happy, relaxed, and anxious, and the workbook provides space for individual comments and responses. At the end of each session participants are asked to complete a 'project' with the help of parents and this is then discussed at the beginning of the next session. A metaphor was created within the program, depicting the child as scientist or astronaut exploring a new planet, to align with common special interests—science and science fiction.

PROGRAM OUTLINE

Session one explores two positive emotions, happiness and relaxation, with a range of group and individual activities to measure and compare emotions in specific situations. The session incorporates games to engage the children and uses concrete examples to illustrate the range of happiness and increase the child's ability to describe degrees of the emotion. Many of the children enjoy the relaxation activities and do go on to use them for themselves at home and school. The home project from this session offers a wide variety of tasks so that each child can choose a project that suits him or her. Session two involves an exploration of anxiety and recognition of the changes that occur in physiology, thinking, behavior, and speech. The concept of a "toolbox" with different types of "tools" to "fix the feeling" is explained, with a focus in this session on physical tools that provide a constructive release of emotional energy (e.g., jumping on a trampoline), and relaxation tools that lower heart rate (e.g., listening to music).

Sessions three to six explore more of the "tools" that can be used and also the idea of using tools that work for other people. Throughout the sessions each child is encouraged to try out strategies in situations that she or he has nominated as "anxiety provoking." Graded-exposure activities are developed for each child and explained to parents so that the child can be encouraged to practice at home. Each child compiles an individual "toolbox" with strategies that he or she has selected and tried to see if they work. In the final session, the participants worked together designing a program for each participant to improve her or his management of anxiety. This session encourages each participant to use several different strategies to help manage anxiety and to think about different situations with a little more flexibility.

BARRIERS TO TREATMENT

To reduce the occurrence of typical issues that would need to be addressed for the children, ground rules were established for the group. These rules were determined in session one by consensus and were then reinforced consistently by therapists. Several important barriers to treatment implementation are described in the following text.

Reluctance to Speak

Some children refused to speak or to contribute to sessions for several weeks, whereas some had difficulty not speaking constantly. We addressed this issue by gaining information about the very quiet children from parents and using this in the early sessions, and also through positive reinforcement (i.e., rewards such as stickers, sweets, and collector cards) of approximations of interaction such as nodding or pointing. The very talkative children were similarly reinforced for listening to others and on occasion taken aside and engaged individually. This was done by one therapist spending 5 minutes working through an exercise or role-play with the child before encouraging him/her to rejoin the group and share the experience with the others.

Listening and Maintaining Attention

Many children were restless when it was someone else's turn to share information. This was managed by invoking the ground rules, reinforcing polite listening, and using diversion through games with small prizes for compliance. Sessions were also broken up with games so that children did not become restless and bored by solely working on the program. Some favorites were a treasure hunt (set up quickly before the session) for a sweet or token in which each child was given a clue to follow or a game that involved physical activity such as the therapist-led "put your nose on something blue," "put your knee on something green," and so on.

Child's Denial of Anxiety

Several children denied experiencing anxiety at all for several sessions and in these cases we used information gained from parents to work with the children. In most cases, after these children had listened to others talk about anxiety, they were able to participate for themselves with continued encouragement. For those who were not able to identify the anxiety, we relied on parents to introduce strategies to manage the child's anxiety. This involved first evaluating how parents currently responded to and managed the child's anxious behaviors and then providing education for the parents within the parent group. It was explained to the child in his/her session that Mom and Dad would also be trying out some strategies from the program to see how well they worked at home or school.

For example, we had one child who could not admit to anxiety regarding her mother being late to collect her from school. Both parent and teacher reported that if the child did not immediately see her mother she would become very distressed and begin to panic. We introduced this situation within the group as one that could cause anxiety and developed strategies to cope. We also engaged the child in role-plays of this situation and we developed a graded-exposure hierarchy for the child and parent that was put into practice. The parent then reinforced the child for successive brave behaviors.

Therapist Challenges

The therapists found working with the groups challenging and needed to consistently and continually find creative ways to engage the children, to keep the mood and motivation high, to cover the material, and to check that strategies were understood by the child and the parent. Therapists met with each child's parent/s both before the session and after to gather information from parents and also relate information from sessions. These meetings with parents are considered essential to the therapist's capacity to learn quickly about individual children, to be aware of any disruptive events likely to affect the child's ability to function in the group, and to keep parents aware of how the child is responding to the program. It was very important for the therapists to have regular supervision in small groups so that they could share their experiences, share their successes and failures, and brainstorm possible approaches for individual children.

Parental Factors and Generalization of Treatment Gains

The outcome data from the trial provided support for the program, with children able to demonstrate knowledge of strategies to manage anxiety at a much greater level than before the intervention (see Figure 15.1), and parent report of reduced anxiety in specific situations targeted by the program for a particular child (see Figure 15.2). The ability to generalize the gains made to other settings and situations was not always successfully achieved and depended very much on the parent's ability to continue to coach the child. For example, one boy, aged 11 years, who did very well in using his "toolbox" of strategies to manage his anxiety about spiders, refused to use any of the strategies he had learned to manage his fear of the dark. His mother reported this to the therapists, with the explanation that as far as Steven was concerned those strategies

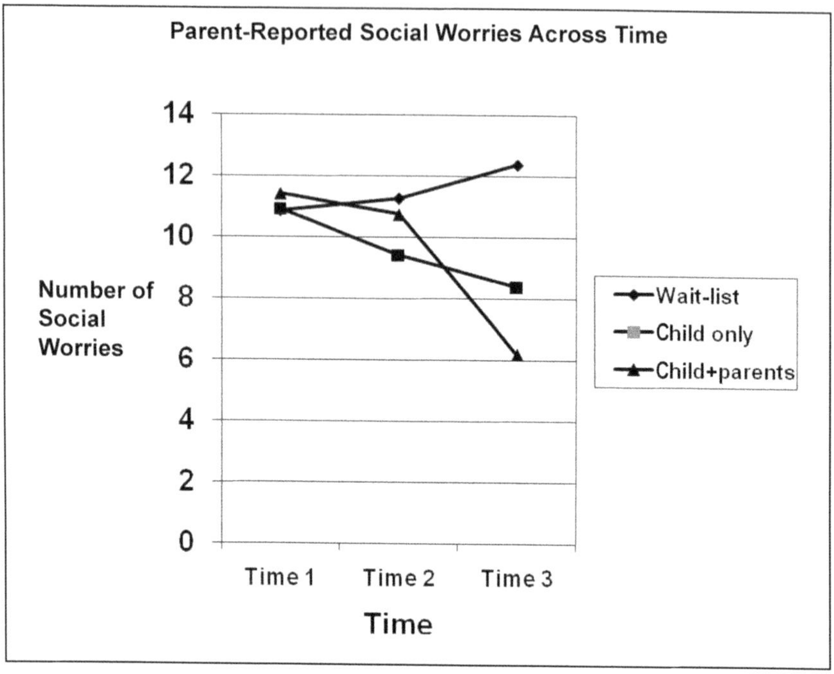

Figure 15.1 Number of strategies generated by children preintervention, postintervention and at follow-up.

were for "anxiety" and his night-time problems were about "fear" and this was entirely different and would not be helped by similar strategies.

We also found that it was quite difficult to assess exactly how many of the strategies the children were adopting in day-to-day life. Each child often would choose only one or two strategies without gaining the flexibility to adopt different strategies for different situations despite coaching. The children were able to generate strategies to manage anxiety in a hypothetical situation, as demonstrated by Figure 15.1, and were able to use strategies to manage anxiety in a specific setting, as reflected in lower scores on anxiety measures (Figure 15.2). Parents often reported, however, that they felt they needed ongoing help with each new situation that arose. This was addressed specifically in the final group session, when parents were encouraged to generate other problems and settings in which they could encourage their child to use strategies learned in the program.

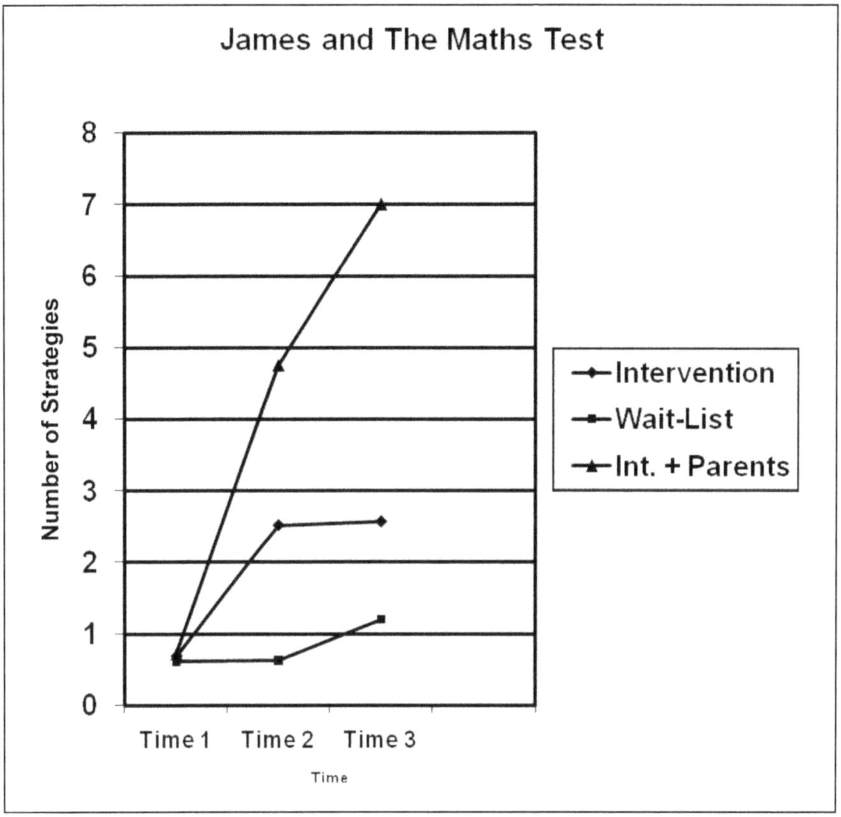

Figure 15.2 Parent ratings of social worries in their children across time.

IMPROVING CHILDREN'S SOCIAL FUNCTIONING

Given the profound impact that social skill deficits have on the lives of children with HFA/AS, the development and evaluation of interventions designed to remediate these impairments is crucial. However, until recently, few treatment programs for improving social competence have been specifically designed for children with HFA/AS. Social skills curricula designed for children with other psychological disorders are likely to be ineffective for this population, as they often have insufficient coverage of skills such as nonverbal communication, perspective taking, and emotion regulation and the constituent steps of prosocial behaviours (e.g., how to start, maintain, and end a conversation). Furthermore, they do not address some of the unique social challenges that children with HFA/AS face, including distinguishing friendly joking from mean teasing and coping with making mistakes.

Beaumont (2008) developed a social skills curriculum to address the unique social challenges of 8- to 11-year-old children with HFA/AS entitled the Junior Detective Training Program.[1] This eight-session intervention comprised a computer game, small-group therapy sessions, concurrent parent training sessions, and weekly teacher handouts. A more detailed description of the program is provided.

Program Description

The Junior Detective computer game was designed to teach children skills in emotion recognition, emotion regulation, and social interaction. The user assumes the role of a junior detective who completes specialist training at the International Junior Detective Training Headquarters to become a "Controlled Remote Viewer" (i.e., a mind reader). In Level one of the game, the user learns how to recognize complex emotions (e.g., embarrassment, confusion) from characters' facial expressions, body postures, and prosody of speech, and calibrates physiological and thought scales to detect emotions in themselves. In Level two, the user decodes how computer-animated characters are feeling from nonverbal and environmental clues. In Level three, skills from levels one and two of the game are integrated and applied to confront social challenges such as trying a new activity, dealing with bullying, and playing with others. Computers were considered to be a highly effective teaching medium for children with HFA/AS, as they capitalize on a common special interest (Gray, 1998), allow for self-paced learning through a visual modality—a relative learning strength for this population (Charlop-Christy & Daneshvar, 2003), provide immediate feedback on response accuracy and minimize the need for "real-world" social interactions for the initial acquisition of information—a common source of anxiety for individuals with ASD (Golan & Baron-Cohen, 2006). Frequent repetition of the program was envisioned to help children with AS to rote learn social rules in a controlled context before attempting to apply them to real-world situations.

[1]This program is to be commercially released as the "Secret Agent Society."

To facilitate children's generalization of computer game content and to teach additional social and problem-solving skills, weekly 1- to 2-hour small-group therapy sessions were conducted. A group intervention was considered important for many reasons, including allowing several children to receive services at one time, providing interactive partners with whom children could practice learned skills, and enhancing children's motivation to interact with peers outside of the therapeutic setting by creating an enjoyable learning environment (Kroeger, Schultz, & Newsom, 2007).

Concurrent parent training sessions were conducted during child sessions to teach parents how to support their children in applying skills to real-life challenges. Parent session material paralleled child session content and was taught via didactic presentation, role plays, and discussion. Weekly teacher handouts were also forwarded to children's school teachers in an effort to facilitate the generalization of treatment gains to the school environment. These one- to two-page tip-sheets summarized weekly session content and provided teachers with suggestions for how they could support children in applying learned skills at school (e.g., prompting them to refer to pocket-sized "code cards" summarizing skill steps; setting up a "chill-out zone" in the classroom). Teachers were also provided with practitioner contact details to discuss program content if desired.

Results from an initial efficacy trial showed that, relative to children in a wait-list control group (n = 23), children who participated in the Junior Detective Training Program (n = 26) showed greater improvements on parent-report measures of social functioning from pre- to posttreatment (Beaumont & Sofronoff, 2008). Teacher-report data suggested that treatment gains also generalized to the school environment. Treatment group participants were better able to suggest appropriate emotion-management strategies for story characters at postintervention than at preintervention relative to controls, and follow-up data indicated that treatment gains were maintained up to 5 months postintervention (Beaumont & Sofronoff, 2008). Seventy-six percent of children who displayed clinically significant impairments in social functioning at the beginning of the program improved to within normal range on parent-report measures by 5-month follow-up (Beaumont & Sofronoff, 2008). Several challenges were faced in delivering the Junior Detective Training Program, however, as will be described.

Challenges in Program Delivery

Frustration With the Computer Game

Within the context of the intervention trial, parents assisted children in completing assigned sections of the computer game at the beginning of weekly therapy sessions. Although children reported enjoying the computer game, they became easily frustrated when they failed to complete a game module successfully or when they experienced technical difficulties.

To minimize children's frustration and to maximize their success in progressing through the program in a time-efficient manner, the program provided clues after an initial incorrect response. If a child answered incorrectly on his/her second attempt, the game provided an explanation of the correct response. Parents were also encouraged to support children in using the relaxation strategies or "gadgets" that they learned in the program to calm down, and then to resume game play. These strategies included slow breathing (the "O_2 regulator"), thinking helpful thoughts ("helpful thought missiles"), and/or taking a break and having a drink of water. Parents were advised to provide descriptive praise and/or other rewards (e.g., stickers, an after-session treat) to acknowledge children's efforts at staying calm and completing assigned sections of the computer game each session.

Children's Lack of Insight Into Their Social Difficulties

One of the challenges faced by group facilitators at the outset of the program was that several children failed to acknowledge experiencing any difficulties with making and keeping friends, a finding that was in stark contrast to the social problems reported by their parents. To motivate these children to continue attending the program, group facilitators explained how they may be able to use their "social expertise" to help other group members to make friends. When introducing a new social skill in session, group facilitators typically asked group members what the Junior Detective character in the computer game or a friend from school could do to manage a social challenge. Group members also assumed the roles of different characters during in-session role-play games. By initially introducing new skills and concepts in this detached manner, group facilitators noted that over the course of the program, children's awareness of and willingness to acknowledge their own social difficulties increased.

Children's Anxiety Regarding Group Attendance

It is well documented that children with AS often become anxious in unfamiliar social situations (e.g., Attwood, 2007). To reduce children's anxiety about program participation, the rationale, content, and structure of the Junior Detective Training Program were clearly explained to participants at the beginning of the first session. Each child group session was structured in a similar manner: presentation of the agenda, review of previous session content and home "missions, " implementation of group activities, and discussion of home missions for the coming week. To optimize predictability and consistency, children were also given warnings prior to transitions in group activities, and every effort was made to ensure that children attended weekly sessions in the same room and with the same group facilitators. Practitioners were encouraged to be aware of early-warning signs that indicated a child was becoming distressed and to prompt the child to use his/her relaxation strategies to calm down. Children were rewarded with tokens and descriptive praise for their efforts at implementing these relaxation techniques in session.

Maintaining Children's Focus on Session Content

As there is a high level of comorbidity between AS and symptoms of attention-deficit/hyperactivity disorder (Ke, Zou, & Jia, 2007), maintaining children's focus on session content was anticipated to be a challenge when implementing the social skills curriculum. This challenge was largely overcome by keeping the duration of session activities brief (typically 15 to 20 minutes); encouraging therapists to be energetic and to have a sense of humor when delivering program content; and using fun, active games to teach skills and behaviors. For example, children practiced inferring emotions from people's voice tone by playing the "Secret Agent Transmission Device" game, which involved taking turns saying and listening to "secret messages" through a walkie-talkie and guessing how the speaker was feeling from the pitch, pace, and volume of his/her voice. Visually engaging materials such as card games, posters, and a board game were also used to maximize children's attention to and retention of program content. Practitioners were encouraged to avoid engaging in lengthy monologues when discussing program content with children and to encourage their active involvement wherever possible. As fine-motor skill deficits are common in individuals with AS (Klin, Volkmar, Sparrow, Cicchetti, & Rourke, 1995), children were provided with weekly session handouts to minimize their need to take within-session notes.

Another challenge that practitioners faced was the proclivity of children with AS to interrupt session activities to discuss their own special interests. To manage this behavior, group facilitators used descriptive praise and tokens to reward children for listening to others and making comments that were relevant to the topic of conversation. Time was allocated during breaks and at the end of sessions for children to discuss their special interests.

Managing Children's Noncompliance in Session

To create a safe, conducive learning environment, ground rules were negotiated with children at the outset of the program. These included: one person speaking at a time, using a friendly voice and friendly words, and keeping your hands and feet to yourself. To motivate children to participate in group activities, clear rationales were provided for all skills taught within the program. A token economy system was also implemented, whereby children were awarded tokens for following group rules, demonstrating prosocial behaviors, participating in activities, and demonstrating individualized goal behaviors that were chosen on the basis of each group member's behavioral profile (e.g., answering questions for quieter group members, versus keeping comments brief and on-topic for overtalkative children). Group members were informed of how many tokens they needed to earn at the beginning of each session, and the token value of rewards increased as the program progressed and prosocial behaviors became established.

In Session one, children nominated up to five rewards that they would like to receive over the course of the program and the appropriateness of these items was checked with children's parents. Rewards included tangible items such as stickers/pictures relating to a special interest, action figurines, Lego™ and collector cards, or activity-based rewards such as going to a favorite restaurant after session. The individualized nature of these rewards was believed to be crucial to motivating children to participate in group activities, as generic rewards and/or descriptive praise alone were considered to be insufficient. Every time that a token was awarded, the group facilitator praised the child for the target behavior displayed (e.g., "Well done for acting out that scene. Here is a token to add to your pile."). To minimize within-session distractions, children's tokens were kept in a place that was clearly visible to them, but out of reach. Children were provided with a reward each session if they earned the prerequisite number of tokens, and extra tokens were counted toward the next session's reward.

When a child was disruptive, practitioners initially ignored the disruptive behavior and rewarded other group members with tokens for behaving appropriately. Because of concerns about children losing motivation in the token-economy system, tokens were not removed for inappropriate behavior. However, as soon as the target child displayed an appropriate behavior, descriptive praise and token reinforcement were provided. In the event that a child's behavior escalated, s/he was prompted to sit away from other group members and to implement a relaxation strategy or "gadget" where necessary. Once the child was calm, s/he was permitted to rejoin the group.

In the event that a child became angry or aggressive, practitioners were advised to stay calm and to refrain from reasoning with the child or attempting to impose a consequence for his/her behavior. This was anticipated to fuel the child's anger and aggression. Instead, one practitioner accompanied the child outdoors and prompted him/her to do a physical activity (e.g., walk or run around) to burn up energy, while the other practitioner continued delivering program content. Practitioners were advised to allow sufficient time for the child to calm down after an outburst before discussing it with him/her and developing a coping plan for the future. This protocol was shown to work very well when group members had unexpected anger outbursts. However, it was only possible because of the high staff-to-child ratio employed (i.e., two facilitators and three children per group).

Facilitating Skill Generalization

To facilitate the generalization of children's treatment gains to real-world contexts, children were asked to complete weekly home missions that involved practicing their emotion recognition, emotion regulation, and social interaction skills both at home and school. Children reviewed their completion of these activities in a computerized "Secret Agent Journal" section of the computer game by using words and/or pictures from a "picture library." Group members brought printouts of their journal entries to weekly sessions for review and were rewarded for their efforts with descriptive praise and tokens. Parents were encouraged to assist group members to complete home missions and to provide additional home-based rewards if necessary. Over the course of the program, children were also given pocket-sized "code-cards" that featured the key steps for each learned skill. Children were encouraged to refer to these cards in secret at school to remind them how to stay calm, feel happy, and make friends.

Concurrent Family Stressors at the Time of Program Entry

Many parents who participated in the intervention were experiencing several concurrent stressors, including breakdown in couple relationships, family relocation, personal adjustment difficulties, limited financial resources, concerns about their child being suspended or expelled from school, and the demands of caring for additional offspring. Where possible, the parent group facilitator advised parents where they could access advice and support to assist with these challenges. However, a significant amount of time was also spent problem-solving these obstacles to enable parents to support their children in practicing therapeutic skills at home and in the community. By prompting parents to identify obstacles to home-mission completion in advance, developing plans for how these challenges could be overcome, and adapting or reducing home-mission requirements where necessary, the majority of parents were able to assist their children in completing between-session tasks. Practitioner acknowledgement of these successes improved parents' confidence in their ability to support their children's future social skills development.

Parental ASD Symptomatology

Consistent with evidence that there is a genetic contribution to ASD symptomatology (Baron-Cohen et al., 2006), several parents who participated in the intervention presented with features of ASD themselves, including dominating group discussions, interrupting others, and being resistant to topic changes during group meetings. These challenges were managed by setting clear ground rules at the outset of the group program and reminding parents of these as the program progressed, setting an agenda at the beginning of each session, providing warnings prior to topic transitions, and clearly communicating how long group members should speak during activities. Role-plays were a very effective teaching tool for boosting parents' confidence in their capacity to support their children in completing weekly home missions.

Parental Resistance to Program Recommendations

A minority of parents who participated in the Junior Detective Training Program initially expressed negative attitudes toward the strategies presented in the intervention, claiming that they did not work for their child. The group facilitator addressed this resistance by initially acknowledging the parent's concerns, seeking further clarification regarding what specific aspects of the skill or strategy the parent considered to be inappropriate or ineffective, and providing corrective information if necessary. The group facilitator also encouraged other parents to share their personal experiences in applying a strategy or technique and to suggest appropriate alternatives where possible. If a child regularly failed to complete home missions or a parent reported no improvements in the child's social functioning, the group facilitator offered the parent individualized support through follow-up telephone consultations and/or after-group discussions.

Variable Teacher Support of the Program

Within the context of a clinic-based social skills intervention, it was difficult to determine the extent to which teachers supported children's skill usage in the school environment. Parent feedback suggested that this was highly variable, with 12.2% of parents stating that their child's teacher did not support the program at all at school, 20.4% reporting that their child's teacher was a "little bit" supportive, 38.8% reporting a moderate amount of teacher support, and 28.6% indicating that their child's teacher was very supportive of the program. To gain a better understanding of the social challenges faced by group members at school and to encourage teachers to implement program recommendations, it is highly recommended that practitioners make contact with children's teachers at the beginning of a social skills program.

Barriers to Program Implementation by Teachers

Challenges faced by teachers in supporting children to apply their social skills at school included parents not providing them with the weekly teacher handouts and a perceived lack of time and/or capacity to read and implement the recommendations provided. In some cases, these challenges were overcome by forwarding handouts directly to teachers via e-mail, and contacting them at the mid- and end-points of the program to problem-solve barriers to strategy implementation (e.g., tailoring relaxation strategies to a child's special interest and the specific classroom and school environment). On occasion, teachers did not return the group facilitator's phone calls, making engagement difficult. In these instances, the group facilitator attempted to confer with other school staff who had direct contact with the child (e.g., teacher aide, behavior-support teacher).

CASE PRESENTATION

"George" was a 9-year-old boy diagnosed with AS who presented with anger-management difficulties, problems adjusting to changes in routine, and social and academic challenges at school. George lived with his mother, "Kathy," and 3-year-old sister. Kathy reported that George had been suspended from school on two occasions in the past year because of aggressive outbursts toward other children. The principal had indicated that if George's behavior did not improve, he would be asked to leave the school.

At presentation, George scored in the clinical range on the parent- and teacher-report versions of the Spence (1995) Social Skills Questionnaire and was estimated to have a Full Scale IQ score of 105 from an abbreviated version of the Wechsler Intelligence Scale for Children—Third edition (WISC-III). Kathy's scores on the Autism Spectrum Quotient (Baron-Cohen, Wheelwright, Skinner, Martin, & Clubley, 2001) and the Depression Anxiety Stress Scales—21 Item Version (DASS-21; Lovibond & Lovibond, 1995) suggest that although her level of ASD symptomatology was within normal range, she experienced moderate levels of stress and depression.

Kathy and George attended all sessions of the Junior Detective Training Program and Kathy met with George's classroom teacher on a weekly basis to deliver teacher handouts and to discuss George's progress. Although he became frustrated at times, George was able to successfully complete the Junior Detective computer game and actively participated in small-group activities by Session 4 of the program. By the 5-month follow-up, George had improved to within the normal range on the parent- and teacher-report versions of the Spence (1995) Social Skills Questionnaire. Kathy reported that he showed greater awareness of his emotions and implemented the anxiety- and anger-management strategies that he learned in the program at home and at school.

As suggested in the teacher handouts, George's classroom teacher educated George's peers about AS and informed them how they could help George to stay calm and have fun at school. The teacher also implemented the recommended classwide buddy system and points-based reward system. By the end of the intervention, George had made two friends at school and one friend in the program with whom he socialized outside of school/session time. George, Kathy, and George's teacher faced several barriers to program participation, however, as summarized below.

George was easily frustrated with the Junior Detective computer game, and would yell, hand-flap, and hide in the corner when he became distressed. To help her son successfully complete the computer game, Kathy provided George with additional hints and the correct answers where necessary. She also encouraged George to only play the game for brief periods of time (10–15 minutes) before taking a break, and offered a reward (pocket-sized Lord of the Rings™ figurine) if George successfully completed all of the assigned computer game activities for a given session.

George was very anxious during the initial small-group therapy sessions and was reluctant to participate in group activities. A group facilitator tried to engage him by providing individualized support and discussing his special interest (medieval architecture) before commencing therapy activities in session. If George became distressed, he demonstrated a secret hand signal to the group facilitator, who silently supervised him as he ran around a courtyard area and talked to himself to calm down. As George became familiar with the session structure and group members, he began to participate enthusiastically in group activities, with minimal practitioner support.

George's mother initially found it difficult to support her son in completing weekly home missions because of her low mood and competing demands on her time (i.e., full-time work and caring for George's younger sister). She reported feeling uncomfortable discussing these challenges in parent group sessions because she felt "like a failure." The group facilitator telephoned Kathy after the first four group sessions to problem-solve challenges to George's home-mission completion (e.g., scheduling 10 minutes at a regular time each day to practice learned skills, implementing a reward chart to encourage skill usage). It was also recommended that Kathy talk to her family doctor about her low mood and stress levels. As George's anger outbursts decreased in intensity and frequency, Kathy felt more confident in asking neighbors and friends to care for George to give her some personal relaxation time.

By Session 6, Kathy reported that George was expressing his anxiety and anger in more appropriate ways at home, although there were ongoing challenges with him hurting other children at school and running away when he became distressed. A meeting was scheduled with George's classroom teacher and school principal to discuss these behavioral concerns. In accordance with George's special interest in medieval architecture, it was recommended that George and his art teacher construct a large, cardboard castle in the corner of his classroom. When George or his teacher noticed that he was becoming distressed, a "chill-out" card would be displayed to signal that George needed to go to his castle to calm down. A smiley chart was used to reward George for going to the castle, using appropriate strategies to calm down (e.g., drawing, squeezing a stress ball) and then continuing with his schoolwork. This approach was reported to be effective in reducing the frequency and intensity of George's anger outbursts and in making them easier to manage. As a result of George's improved classroom behavior, his capacity to complete assigned academic tasks also improved.

CONCLUSIONS AND FUTURE DIRECTIONS

In conclusion, children with AS can successfully be taught cognitive behavioral skills such as emotion recognition, emotion regulation, problem solving, and prosocial behaviors when interventions are tailored to their unique interests and learning style. Program modifications may include using an interactive computer game for instructional purposes, implementing a small-group therapy curriculum involving visually engaging, interactive games and applying an individualized reward system. To optimize the generalization of learned skills to real-world contexts, strategies such as setting and reviewing home-practice activities, providing children with visual prompts for learned skills, and supplementing child group therapy sessions with parent training and teacher handouts and consultations may be worthwhile. Future research needs to determine which of these program components is/are most crucial to treatment outcome in an effort to improve the cost-effectiveness and time-efficiency of interventions for children with AS.

Results from the initial randomized controlled trial of the Junior Detective Training Program showed that when the computer game, child group therapy sessions, parent training sessions, and teacher handouts were implemented as a comprehensive therapy package, the intervention was equally effective for children with AS irrespective of their IQ, age, severity of AS symptoms, level of comorbidity, use of psychotropic medication, and primary caregiver psychopathology. The only significant predictor of treatment outcome was the number of home missions completed by children. These findings, together with those from evaluations of CBT anxiety- and anger-management programs for children with AS (e.g., Sofronoff et al., 2005, 2007), suggest that combining several instructional and generalization-enhancement strategies into a structured intervention optimizes treatment responsiveness among program participants.

REFERENCES

American Psychiatric Association (2000). *Diagnostic and statistical manual of mental disorders* (4th ed., text rev.). Washington, DC: American Psychiatric Press.

Attwood, T. (2004). Cognitive behaviour therapy for children and adults with Asperger's syndrome. *Behaviour Change, 21,* 147–161.

Attwood, T. (2007). *The complete guide to Asperger's syndrome.* London: Jessica Kingsley.

Baron-Cohen, S., Ring, H., Chitnis, X., Wheelwright, S., Gregory, L., Williams, S., et al. (2006). fMRI of parents of children with Asperger Syndrome: A pilot study. *Brain and Cognition, 61,* 122–130.

Baron-Cohen, S., Wheelwright, S., Skinner, R., Martin, J., & Clubley, E. (2001). The autism-spectrum quotient (AQ): Evidence from Asperger syndrome/high-functioning autism, males and females, scientists and mathematicians. *Journal of Autism and Developmental Disorders, 31,* 5–17.

Bauminger, N., & Kasari, C. (2000). Loneliness and friendship in high-functioning children with autism. *Child Development, 71,* 447–456.

Beaumont, R. (2008). *The Secret Agent Society Facilitator's Manual.* Unpublished manuscript.

Beaumont, R., & Sofronoff, K. (2008). A multi-component social skills intervention for children with Asperger Syndrome: The Junior Detective Training Program. *Journal of Child Psychology and Psychiatry, 49,* 743–753.

Charlop-Christy, M., & Daneshvar, S. (2003). Using video modeling to teach perspective taking to children with autism. *Journal of Positive Behavior Interventions, 5,* 12–21.

Einfeld, S. L., & Tonge, B. J. (1996). Population prevalence of psychopathology in children and adolescents with intellectual disability: II epidemiological findings. *Journal of Intellectual Disability Research, 40,* 99–109.

Eisenmajer, R., Prior, M., Wing, L., Gould, J., Welham, M., et al., (1996). Comparison of clinical symptoms in autism and Asperger's disorder. *Journal of the American Academy of Child and Adolescent Psychiatry, 35,* 1523–1531.

Frith, U. (2004). Emanuel Miller lecture: Confusions and controversies about Asperger syndrome. *Journal of Child Psychology and Psychiatry, 45,* 672–686.

Gillot, A., Furniss, F., & Walter, A. (2001). Anxiety in high functioning children with autism. *Autism, 5,* 277–286.

Golan, O., & Baron-Cohen, S. (2006). Systemizing empathy: Teaching adults with Asperger syndrome or high-functioning autism to recognize complex emotions using interactive multimedia. *Development and Psychopathology, 18,* 591–617.

Gray, C. A. (1998). Social stories and comic strip conversations with students with Asperger Syndrome and high functioning autism. In E. Schopler, G. Mesibov, & L. Kunce (Eds.), *Asperger syndrome or high functioning autism? Current issues in autism* (pp. 167–198). New York: Plenum Press.

Howlin, P. (2000). Outcome in adult life for more able individuals with autism or Asperger Syndrome. *Autism, 4,* 63–83.

Ke, X., Zou, B., & Jia, J. (2007). Attention deficit and hyperactivity symptoms in school children with Asperger Syndrome. *Chinese Mental Health Journal, 21,* 86–89.

Kim, J. A., Szatmari, P., Bryson, S. E., Streiner, D. L., & Wilson, F. J. (2000). The prevalence of anxiety and mood problems among children with autism and Asperger syndrome. *Autism, 4,* 117–132.

Klin, A., & Volkmar, F. R. (1995). Autism and the pervasive developmental disorders. *Child and Adolescent Psychiatric Clinics of North America, 4,* 617–630.

Klin, A., Volkmar, F.R., Sparrow, S.S., Cicchetti, D.V., & Rourke, B.P. (1995). Validity and neuropsychological characterization of Asperger syndrome: Convergence with nonverbal learning disabilities syndrome. *Journal of Child Psychology and Psychiatry, 36,* 1127–1140.

Kroeger, K.A., Schultz, J.R., & Newsom, C. (2007). A comparison of two group-delivered social skills programs for young children with autism. *Journal of Autism and Developmental Disorders, 37,* 808–817.

Lovaas, O. I., Koegel, R., Simmons, J. Q., & Long, J. S. (1973). Some generalization and follow-up measures on autistic children in behavior therapy. *Journal of Applied Behavior Analysis, 6,* 131–166.

Lovibond, S. H., & Lovibond, P. F. (1995). *Manual for the Depression Anxiety Stress Scales* (2nd ed.). Sydney: Psychological Foundation of Australia.

Mackay, T., Knott, F., & Dunlop, A. (2007). Developing social interaction and understanding in individuals with autism spectrum disorders: A groupwork intervention. *Journal of Intellectual and Developmental Disability, 32,* 279–290.

Mahoney, W. J., Szatmari, P., MacLean, J. E., Bryson, S. E., Bartolucci, G., Walter, S. D., et al. (1998). Reliability and accuracy of differentiating pervasive developmental

disorder subtypes. *Journal of the American Academy of Child and Adolescent Psychiatry, 37*, 278–285.
Matson, J. L., & Smith, K. R. M. (2008). Current status of intensive behavioural interventions for young children with autism and PDD-NOS. *Research in Autism Spectrum Disorders, 2*, 60–74.
Mayes, S. D., & Calhoun, S. L. (2001). Non-significance of early speech delay in children with autism and normal intelligence and implications for DSM-IV Asperger's disorder. *Autism, 5*, 81–94.
Miller, J. N, & Ozonoff, S. (1997). Did Asperger's cases have Asperger disorder? A research note. *Journal of Child Psychology and Psychiatry, 38*, 247–251.
Muris, P., Steerneman, P., Merckelbach, H., Holdrinet, I., & Meesters, C. (1998). Comorbid anxiety symptoms in children with Pervasive Developmental Disorders. *Journal of Anxiety Disorders, 12*, 387–393.
Russell, E., & Sofronoff, K. (2005). Anxiety and social worries in children with Asperger syndrome. *Australian and New Zealand Journal of Psychiatry, 39*, 633–638.
Sofronoff, K., Attwood, T., & Hinton, S. (2005). A randomized controlled trial of a CBT intervention for anxiety in children with Asperger Syndrome. *Journal of Child Psychology and Psychiatry, 46*, 1152–1160.
Sofronoff, K., Attwood, T., Hinton, S., & Levin, I. (2007). A randomized controlled trial of a cognitive behavioral intervention for anger management in children diagnosed with Asperger Syndrome. *Journal of Autism and Developmental Disorders, 37*, 1203–1214.
Spence, S. H. (1995). Social skills questionnaire. In *Social skills training: Enhancing social competence with children and adolescents: Photocopiable resource book*. Windsor, UK: NFER-Nelson.
Venter, A., Lord, C., & Schopler, E. (1992). A follow-up study of high-functioning autistic children. *Journal of Child Psychology and Psychiatry and Allied Disciplines, 33*, 489–507.
Wing, L. (1981). *Psychological Medicine, 11*, 115–129.

16

Nocturnal Enuresis and Encopresis: Empirically Supported Approaches for Refractory Cases

MARY L. KEELEY, PAULO GRAZIANO, AND GARY R. GEFFKEN

The elimination disorders include enuresis and encopresis. Both enuresis and encopresis are disorders for which psychological research has demonstrated empirically supported treatments (Mikkelsen, 2001). Although research on psychological treatments based on principles of learning theory are efficacious for most youth with these disorders, there remain a substantial minority of children, estimates range from 11 to 20% (Cendron, 1999; Devlin & O'Cathain, 1990; Mellon, 2000; Skoog, 1998), who show a refractory response to these treatments. This chapter explicates various reasons that children and adolescents do not respond to these empirically supported treatments. In reviewing reasons for treatment failure for youth with this disorder, it is hoped that some direction and understanding may be gained to help an increasing number of these children and their families find relief from the interference and distress resulting from these disorders.

INTRODUCTION TO ENURESIS

As defined by the *Diagnostic and Statistical Manual of Mental Disorders, Fourth Edition, Text Revision* (*DSM-IV-TR*; American Psychiatric Association [APA], 2000), enuresis is manifested by the repeated voiding of urine during the day or at night into bed or clothes for at least 3 consecutive months that must not be entirely attributed to a general medical condition or the effects of a substance. If enuretic problems lead to clinically significant distress or impairment, the frequency and/or duration criteria may be waived (APA, 2000). Although there is cultural variation for the age at which nocturnal enuresis or bedwetting is considered psychopathology or a developmental deviance, the *DSM-IV-TR* has selected a chronological age of 5 years (or a mental age of 5 years for children with developmental delays) as a threshold for diagnosis. Subtypes of enuresis include nocturnal only, diurnal only, and nocturnal and diurnal (mixed daytime and nighttime wetting). Children are considered to have primary enuresis if they have never been consistently dry, whereas children are considered to have secondary enuresis in instances in which they have achieved continence for at least 6 months but then subsequently lost it (APA, 2000).

There are a number of etiological factors implicated in the development and maintenance of enuresis, including genetic contributions (von Gontard, Eiberg, Hollmann, Rittig, & Lehmkuhl, 1999); dysfunctional sleep arousal system (Neveus et al., 1999; Wolfish, 1999); physiological factors, such as low levels of the antidiuretic hormone (ADH) vasopressin (Butler, 1994) or reduction in functional bladder capacity (Kawauchi et al., 2003; Yeung, Chiu, & Sit, 1999); and psychological factors, such as trauma (Eidlitz-Markus, Shuper, & Amir, 2000) or behavioral disturbances (von Gontard, Mauer-Mucke, Pluck, Berner, & Lehmkuhl, 1999). Given these multiple etiological factors, a comprehensive assessment, including a clinical interview gathering personal and family history as well as enuresis-specific history, a physical examination, and a 2-week baseline record of wet and dry nights, is warranted (Fritz et al., 2004; Mikkelsen, 2001). Treatment planning should be tailored to specific assessment findings and should take into account the willingness of the child and his or her parent to participate in treatment.

TREATMENT OF ENURESIS

Based on empirical support across numerous research studies, the treatment of choice for nocturnal enuresis is the moisture alarm system—

referred to as bell-and-pad method, urine alarm system, or bed alarm system (Vogel, Young, & Primck, 1996)—with an average treatment success rate of approximately 65 to 75% and an average treatment duration between 5 and 12 weeks (Butler, 2004; Glazener, Evans, & Peto, 2005; Mellon & McGrath, 2000; Mikkelsen, 2001).[1] Based on the Mowrer two-step process, using a combination of classical conditioning and operant principles, the moisture alarm system is designed to initially condition nighttime awakening (through an alarm[1]) to the sensation of a full bladder, which is presumed to be cued by a contraction of the smooth bladder muscle known as the detrussor (Mowrer & Mowrer, 1938). Some devices rest between the child and his or her mattress, whereas other devices are portable transistorized alarms that use a sensor that can be attached to the child's underwear. The devices operate such that the first few drops of urine moisten the fabric separating the device's two electrodes, thereby completing an electrical circuit and triggering an alarm to sound. Under most circumstances, the sound awakens the child, who is then directed to go to the bathroom to finish emptying his or her bladder into the toilet. With repeated use, the child gradually becomes conditioned to awaken earlier and earlier until he or she learns to awaken to the sensation of a full bladder prior to wetting. A treatment component routinely used with the moisture alarm is cleanliness training; this involves cleaning the body after an accident, changing nighttime clothing, and stripping and remaking the bed. It is also important to use a plastic mattress cover with the alarm.

Although the initial conditioning of waking to bladder cues after several trials of the alarm is conceptualized as classical in nature, it is thought that the operant principle of negative reinforcement eventually supercedes classical processes in maintaining the response of learning to become dry with the moisture alarm system. Learning an initial response through classical conditioning in which the response is maintained by negative reinforcement is known as the Mowrer two-step process (Mowrer & Mowrer, 1938). Classical conditioning is known to go through extinction if the conditioned stimulus (i.e., the bladder cues) is not regularly paired with the unconditioned stimulus (i.e., the alarm), which is known in classical conditioning as reinforcement. Without reinforcement between the conditioned stimulus and the un-

[1]Variations on the alarm include a bell, buzzer, light, or vibration.

conditioned stimulus, the conditioned response (i.e., waking to the bladder cues) is lost through extinction. Hence, negative reinforcement in the form of avoidance learning, which is known to be highly resistant to extinction, is the hypothesized mechanism for maintaining the response of being dry through the night. That is, to avoid the alarm, which is aversive, the child feels the bladder cues and either wakes up or learns a new response (i.e., bladder sphincter contraction to prevent a wetting accident while being able to continue sleeping). Geffken and colleagues (Geffken, Johnson, & Walker, 1986; Geffken et al., 2007) have explicated a hypothesis about the role of bladder capacity size in determining the primary mode of accomplishing sustained dryness. The child with relatively smaller functional bladder capacity will most often continue waking to bladder cues as the mechanism of maintaining dryness. Children with relatively larger bladder capacity may alternatively be more likely to learn a new response of a bladder sphincter contraction in response to the bladder cue (i.e., presumably the detrusor contraction), and hence maintain sleeping throughout the night without awakening.

Once the child has been conditioned via the moisture alarm system to awaken prior to wetting, with treatment "success" consisting of at least 14 consecutive dry nights (Butler, 1991), additional techniques are employed before discontinuing treatment to prevent relapse. Overlearning is a procedure in which the child is instructed to increase the amount of liquid consumed before bedtime to cause additional stress to the detrusor muscles in the bladder so that the child achieves enhanced bladder control. A second relapse prevention procedure entails using an intermittent reinforcement schedule with the moisture alarm system (through setting the device to sound for only 50–75% of wetting episodes), given that such reinforcement schedules are assumed to optimize learning (Doleys, 1977).

When discussing the moisture alarm system with families, it is critical to provide thorough instruction regarding how to use the system and to encourage frequent parental monitoring of the device to ensure that it is operating adequately (*JAACAP*, 2004). Caveat: in the beginning stages of treatment, parental involvement is critical to treatment implentation, as few children awaken to the alarm easily on their own. Parents must assist in awakening the child, directing him or her to finish urinating in the toilet, and helping him or her put on dry underwear before returning to bed. In some cases, this level of parental involvement may be considered by parents to be too overwhelming or unfeasible. In situations in which parents are resistant or unable to participate in treatment, it is likely that the moisture alarm system will not be successful, and the therapist should consider other methods of treating the child's enuresis. (See the following text for discussion of additional behavioral techniques.)

Although the moisture alarm system is the most empirically supported intervention for nocturnal enuresis, there are additional behavioral methods that have been found to be more effective than no treatment at all (Glazener & Evans, 2004). These relatively simple behavioral methods may be considered prior to the use of a moisture alarm system as initial attempts at treating the problem, or some may be used in combination with the moisture alarm system to possibly enhance treatment success. One method that may be used first without the alarm is scheduled awakening (Azrin, Sneed, & Foxx, 1974). This entails having parents wake their child and encourage him or her to urinate at specific times during the night. Schedules may vary in terms of frequency of awakenings, with some programs recommending rigorous schedules during the first several nights of treatment (e.g., waking the child every hour throughout the night) and then gradual fading of awakenings over time (Azrin et al., 1974). This method should not be used in combination with the alarm, as it would decrease learning trials with the alarm.

A second method is positive reinforcement, in which parents are taught to reward their child (e.g., with praise or sticker charts) for specific positive toileting behaviors and/or dry nights (Houts, Peterson, & Whelan, 1986). In the initial stages of positive reinforcement, parents should consider combining positive reinforcement with scheduled awakenings, to enhance opportunities for the child to achieve the targeted behavior and be reinforced. Punishment for wet nights is not recommended, as this method typically results in negative parent–child interactions and increased distress surrounding toileting issues. Another behavior intervention concerns lifting, in which a parent is instructed to pick up the sleeping child from his or her bed and bring him or her to the toilet to urinate.

More complex treatment approaches have also been developed that are aimed at comprehensively addressing enuretic problems (Glazener, Evans, & Peto, 2004). Although the main and essential component of these regimens is the moisture alarm system, they also include supplemental components aimed at enhancing treatment response. One example of a complex treatment is dry-bed training (Azrin et al., 1974), which includes scheduled awakening, positive practice (i.e., child repeatedly practices getting out of bed, walking to the bathroom, and going to the toilet), cleanliness training (i.e., cleaning the body after an accident, changing clothing, and stripping and remaking the bed), and the moisture alarm system. Full-spectrum home training (Houts et al., 1986) is another complex treatment approach for nocturnal enuresis in which a moisture alarm system is combined with cleanliness training, retention-control training (i.e., teaching the child to retain progressively larger amounts of urine in their bladders during the day to enhance bladder capacity and/or sensitize the child to bladder cues), and overlearning.

Several family-related variables have been found to be associated with poor treatment outcome with moisture alarm systems, including levels of family stress and discord (Devlin & O'Cathain, 1990; Dische, Yule, Corbett, & Hand, 1983), parental intolerance (Wagner & Johnson, 1988), and poor housing conditions (Dische et al., 1983). Additionally, research has indicated that a lack of motivation to change (Butler, Forsythe, Devlin, & O'Cathain, 1990) and child behavioral problems (Moffatt & Cheang, 1995) negatively impact treatment success. When such factors are present, therapists may consider augmenting treatment with individual or family interventions that target identified child or family problems.

REFRACTORY RESPONSES TO TREATMENT OF PEDIATRIC NOCTURNAL ENURESIS WITH THE MOISTURE ALARM

As reviewed previously, the moisture alarm has a substantial history in the psychology literature of demonstrated efficacy for childhood nocturnal enuresis. For example, a review conducted by Mellon (2000) indicated that the implementation of a basic moisture alarm system obtains a treatment success rate of 78%. In a study comparing the standard moisture alarm system to modified dry training, findings revealed that both treatments had a 70% success rate following 4 weeks of treatment (Butler, Brewin, & Forsythe, 1988) and there were no differences between groups in number of wet nights following treatment. In another study comparing the moisture alarm system plus cleanliness training with imipramine or a waitlist control condition, 83% of the participants in the moisture alarm system condition were successfully treated, compared to 33% in the imipramine condition, and 8% in the waitlist control condition (Wagner, Johnson, Walker, Carter, & Wittner, 1982). However, this leaves a significant number of children who do not respond optimally to this treatment. There are a wide range of reasons for the poor response. Below we have reviewed reasons children with nocturnal enuresis have a poor response to the moisture alarm.

Parental Factors

Parental Adherence to Recommendations for Psychological Treatment

Among the reasons for a poor response to the moisture alarm for nocturnal enuresis are a variety of factors related to the parents of these children. As described earlier, there is a consensus among psychological practitioners who use the alarm, that parental involvement and assistance in the procedures are necessary. Unfortunately, there is a lack of parental adherence to mental health provider recommendations that is not restricted to nocturnal enuresis (Geffken, Keeley, Kellison, Storch, & Rodrigue, 2006). Behavioral treatment is one of the most likely categories of recommendations for which there is parental noncompliance. The moisture alarm is a behavioral treatment that is relatively labor-intensive for parents. Parents must arise on the alarm sounding during the night while both parents and children are asleep and ensure that their child adheres to the procedures for treatment with the moisture alarm. When children with nocturnal enuresis are questioned during the day while they are awake, the overwhelming majority of them respond that they want to stop wetting the bed (Wagner & Geffken, 1986). However, as psychologists who work with families with an enuretic child will tell you, many children do not maintain their resolve after a nighttime accident, and parents experience difficulty and resistance when working with their children on the moisture alarm procedures. Further, stated intentions often do not match behavioral intentions, particularly in children.

Parental Intolerance of Enuresis

Implementing the moisture alarm system is a particular challenge for parents who are especially bothered by enuresis problems (Morgan &

Young, 1975; Wagner et al., 1982). Although at first this may seem counterintuitive, two out of three studies examining this issue (Geffken et al., 1986; Morgan & Young, 1975; Wagner et al., 1982) found that higher scores on the Parental Tolerance Scale (indicative of high intolerance and frustration with enuresis) were predictive of an increased likelihood of premature termination of treatment with the moisture alarm. This is consistent with an interpretation that parents who lack patience and commitment to this treatment, and who have a tendency not to delay gratification of their frustration with their children's bedwetting, are likely to prematurely drop out of this treatment or to negatively interfere with treatment progress. There a couple of ways in which these parents may interfere with treatment. First, parents who lack patience may quickly become frustrated with the lack of initial success, as treatment does not occur overnight. This may lead parents to lose confidence in the treatment and consequently begin to implement the behavioral components that are necessary for success inconsistently. Second, parents who have difficulty regulating their own frustrations may overtly express their feelings to their child. The expression of such frustration may be counterproductive to the treatment, as the child may internalize the parent's frustration. The child's internalization of such frustration may lead him or her to lose motivation in the treatment and/or engage in behavior that will likely interfere with the treatment. Lastly, parents' own level of frustration and need for immediate results may lead them to revert back to putting diapers or Pull-ups on the child to avoid engaging in the initially difficult, and in their eyes negative, aspects of the treatment. One clinically anecdotal example of parental intolerance pertains to a case in which the parents of an enuretic teenager refused to participate in treatment. In part because of the parents' lack of participation, the case lasted 11 months, a period of time much longer than the average treatment duration of 5 to 12 weeks.

Parents With an Infant

Some constellations of family characteristics may contribute to the lack of parental support for this type of behavioral treatment for their children's nocturnal enuresis. These characteristics are based on the clinical experience of the third author (GG) in using the moisture alarm for many years with hundreds of children and their families. Parents with infants have a competing need of higher priority to arise during their sleep to attend to their baby; hence, the motivation to comply with moisture alarm procedures that require arising from sleep are compromised.

Comorbid Diagnoses

Comorbid Mental Retardation

It has also been reported based on numerous clinical trials that children with a diagnosis of mental retardation (MR; Johnson, 1980) have a treatment response rate 10 to 15% lower than children without mental retardation. Our own clinical experience suggests that rates of diurnal and nocturnal enuresis are higher among children diagnosed in the severe and profound ranges of MR. Furthermore, in these cases, we have found that nocturnal bedwetting is usually accommodated by the use of diapers, and that diurnal wetting is treated with frequently scheduled breaks to urinate.

Comorbid Type 1 Diabetes

Some childhood chronic illnesses such as type 1 diabetes are associated with higher rates of nocturnal enuresis (Geffken et al., 2007). The high blood and urine glucose levels of children with diabetes are associated with more frequent urination in many children. During sleep, this is associated with higher rates of nocturia, arising to urinate, and nocturnal enuresis. The diagnostic criterion that there is no demonstrable organic basis to bedwetting is blurred by factors such as comorbid type 1 diabetes. Although most children with diabetes do not have enuresis, the greater prevalence among this group of children is contributed to by organic factors.

Multiple Comorbidities

Another clinical observation is that children referred from child and adolescent psychiatrists and pediatricians in a medical school with a tertiary population tend to have numerous comorbidities. The effect of several comorbid medical and/or psychiatric diagnoses is that other diagnostic conditions, depending on their acuity and severity, compete for attention by the families, both parents and children. Often this may result in enuresis and its labor-intensive behavioral treatment receiving lower priority. For example, when an enuretic child has a disruptive behavior disorder, mental retardation, and poor reality testing, these factors could present barriers to a labor-intensive treatment like the moisture alarm, which may exceed perceived benefits. Another example in which barriers might exceed perceived benefits could be an enuretic child with autistic spectrum disorder imposing high caretaker burden on a family with several children and a highly stressed and depressed single mother.

Age

Developmental considerations are important when choosing treatment options for enuresis. The treating clinician should take into consideration the physical, cognitive, and emotional level of the child when determining the best treatment approach. For example, cognitive limitations in youngsters, such as difficulties with future-oriented thinking, may prove to be an obstacle in motivating the young child to withstand aversive treatment components in the short term. Other possible developmental considerations are explicated below.

Young Children

Clinical experience has found that young children (e.g., children under 5 years of age) may be too immature for the moisture alarm system. Although age is somewhat arbitrary as a criterion for starting the alarm, the child should be physically and emotionally capable of awakening and going through the nighttime procedures, including cleanliness training. Clinical experience with young children has been complicated by crying, apparent lack of understanding, and/or cooperation on awakening and being asked to engage in the nighttime procedures. The size and development of a young child limits his or her participation in cleanliness training components, such as stripping the bed and remaking it. The typical young child's understanding of the treatment and level of emotional development may combine to make for an unpleasant and unsuccessful experience, for child and parent alike. Consequently, it may be worthwhile to wait until the child is developmentally ready prior to initiating treatment, as clinical experience, rather than empirical studies, suggests that an additional year of maturation results in a positive and successful experience for a greater percentage of children. Although it is often difficult to define what constitutes being developmentally ready, the child should at least demonstrate an awareness of his or her bodily functions and perhaps an intent to communicate such functions, via either verbal or nonverbal means.

Older Adolescence and Adulthood

Likewise, epidemiological data indicates that there is an enuresis prevalence rate of 2–3% among individuals ranging in age from adolescence until late adulthood, when incontinence in seniors increases (Ali & Snape, 2004). It may be that emotional stigmatization and resignation to bedwetting precludes initiatives to treat the problem. This is not to suggest that individuals over 15 years of age could not be successfully treated by the moisture alarm or some other method of treatment. The prevalence rates may suggest that individuals fall into learned helplessness in large numbers. These individuals may possibly be making erroneous assumptions about the inevitability of their bedwetting and consequently cease their efforts to stop wetting the bed.

Hypothetical Obstacles Based on Individual Differences and/or Etiological Factors

Bladder Capacity

Functional bladder capacity is a variable that has been studied by many researchers investigating nocturnal enuresis (Butler, 1998; Geffken et al., 1986; Rushton, Belman, Zaontz, Skoog, & Sihelnik, 1996). Functional bladder capacity is measured by having a child drink a prescribed amount of water (i.e., 12 ounces) and to have the child wait as long as he or she can before urinating. When the child urinates, it is in a container that allows the measurement of volume. Following this, the child's urine volume is compared to a normative database based on the child's sex and age, and classification of the functional bladder capacity is determined (Starfield, 1967); this is generally classified as "large" or "small" for the sex and age. Functional bladder capacity has been studied in relation to treatment with the moisture alarm versus the combination of the moisture alarm plus retention control training (Geffken et al., 1986). Geffken and colleagues (1986) found that retention-control training appeared to sensitize children with smaller bladder capacity to bladder cues, such that these children woke up more often and achieved dryness more quickly. Conversely, children with larger bladder capacity achieved arrest of wetting more quickly with the moisture alarm alone as they learned to sleep through the night; when retention-control training was added, the children with large bladder capacity were slower to achieve dryness. Hence, treatment response was in part a function of bladder capacity, such that the moisture alarm alone was a relative obstacle to achieve arrest for small-bladder children, whereas the addition of retention-control training to the moisture alarm represented an obstacle for children with large bladder capacity.

Vasopressin Levels

There has been recent research on use of the medication DDAVP or desmopression—a synthetic antiduretic hormone—for nocturnal enuresis, as well as vasopressin, an endogenous antiduretic hormone, in nocturnal enuresis (Butler, 1998; Katz, Spivak, Mester, Grinshpoon, & Weizman, 1997). Children were found to have a circadian rhythm for vasopressin: during the night, when most children do not wet the bed, there are on average higher circulating levels of vasopressin; and during the day, when children urinate more frequently, there are on average lower levels of vasopressin. Further, researchers found that the groups of children who had nocturnal enuresis had lower mean levels of circulating vasopressin at night than nonenuretic children (Rittig, Schaumburg, Siggaaro, Schmidt, & Djurhuus, 2008). Hence, it was postulated that low levels of vasopressin at night in children was an etiological factor in nocturnal enuresis. Although this is a reasonable hypothesis, scatterplots showing the specific levels of nocturnal vasopressin for individual children indicated that there was overlap in the levels of vasopressin between the groups of children with enuresis and those without. Hence, there was no absolute level of vasopressin that predicts incontinence at night versus continence. It is possible that other hormones or electrolytes interacting with vasopressin determine who is continent at night and who is not. It is also possible that the ratio of daytime to nighttime vasopressin levels in an individual may predict continence or incontinence. Hence, questions remain about the etiological contribution of vasopressin to bedwetting. However, the circadian rhythm of vasopressin and the mean difference between nighttime levels of vasopressin in children with enuresis and those without allow one to postulate that vasopressin level plays a role in nocturnal enuresis.

INTRODUCTION TO ENCOPRESIS

The *DSM-IV-TR* defines encopresis as the repeated passage of feces into inappropriate places (e.g., clothing, floor) in a child at least 4 years of age (or equivalent developmental level) that must not be entirely attributed to a general medical condition or the effects of a substance (APA, 2000). The *DSM-IV-TR* duration criterion requires that the child must have at least one encopretic event each month for at least 3 months. Subtypes of encopresis include the designation of either (a) "with constipation and overflow incontinence" (i.e., retentive encopresis) or (b) "without constipation and overflow incontinence" (i.e., nonretentive encopresis). As with enuresis, primary encopresis refers to children who have never achieved appropriate bowel control, whereas secondary encopresis refers to children who develop encopresis following a period of fecal continence (APA, 2000).

In most cases of encopresis, the development of the disorder is largely caused by both physiological and behavioral factors associated with constipation (McGrath, Mellon, & Murphy, 2000). One physiological factor implicated in the development and maintenance of the disorder is external anal sphincter (EAS) dysfunction, such as in instances in which the EAS fails to relax during defecation. Another physiological factor relates to poor rectal sensation, either because of dysfunction in neural pathways that signal sensation (such as in spina bifida), stretching of the area (megarectum), or habituation to chronic rectal fullness (McGrath et al., 2000). A third physiological factor pertains to dysfunction in digestive processes. Behavioral factors associated with encopresis include dietary behaviors that interfere with proper digestion and appropriate defecation, the ability and willingness to respond to bodily cues signaling the need to defecate, the social knowledge of understanding "appropriate" places and ways to defecate, and the learned fear associated with constipation problems (McGrath et al., 2000). Additionally, secondary encopresis may develop as a response to stressful life events (Brazzelli & Griffiths, 2006). Because encopresis generally involves both physiological and behavioral factors, a proper evaluation should include both (a) a medical assessment aimed at obtaining a thorough history of the child's stooling and dietary habits as well as physical examination, and (b) a behavioral assessment aimed at gathering information related to the behavioral responses of the child, parents, and peers to encopretic events as well as an inquiry into events surrounding the onset of the disorder.

Given that most cases of encopresis involve or result from constipation, a major aspect of encopresis treatment pertains to medical interventions aimed at softening the stool and emptying the intestine (Cox, Sutphen, Ling, Quillian, & Borowitz, 1996; Stark et al., 1997). Standard medical management strategies include use of enemas, laxatives, or mineral oil for "clean outs" and increased dietary intake of fiber and water. These strategies are typically accompanied by daily toilet-sitting schedules, in which the child is instructed to sit on the toilet at regularly scheduled intervals (including a scheduled morning sitting as well as sittings after all meals).

Research has highlighted the beneficial effects of augmenting medical interventions with behavioral treatment approaches (Brazzelli & Griffiths, 2006). One study comparing medical management to medical management-plus-behavioral approaches found that the combined group had a 76% treatment success rate, compared to a 21% success rate in the medical management-only group (Cox, Sutphen, Borowitz, Kovatchev, & Ling, 1998). In another study, a group of children with unsuccessful prior medical treatment-only intervention participated in a medical management-plus-behavioral intervention treatment (Stark, Owens-Stively, Spirito, Lewis, & Guevrement, 1990). Results indicated that 89% of treatment participants had no soiling problems at the end of treatment. Behavioral treatment approaches generally focus on using behavioral modification techniques (e.g., differential attention, contingency management, behavioral contracting) as well as monitoring of toilet-sitting scheduling (Cox et al., 1998; Stark et al., 1997). Additionally, parental psychoeducation and support have been shown to have positive effects on treatment outcome (Stark et al., 1997).

Behavioral modification techniques primarily involve reinforcing the child with positive attention (e.g., praise) or tangible reinforcers for positive toileting behaviors (e.g., making independent trips to the bathroom) or successfully emptying his or her bowel in the toilet. Additionally, positive reinforcement can be a successful technique for improving adherence to the child's toilet-sitting schedule or fiber intake recommendations through the use of sticker charts to monitor and reinforce adherence. Punishment techniques, such as time-out or response-cost, may be considered in instances in which standard medical management and positive reinforcement strategies are not successful.

Cleanliness training, as described in the enuresis treatment section, involves having the child clean his or her body, clothing, and sheets as well as redress and remake the bed (O'Brien, Ross, & Christophersen, 1986). In some cases, encopretic children attempt to hide soiled underwear in an effort to avoid aversive consequences or to prevent teasing. In these situations, underwear marking is considered a useful strategy. Using this approach, each pair of the child's underwear may be marked with the day of the week (or some other distinguishing label, such as a number), and the child is instructed to show his or her parent at the beginning and end of the day the specified day's underwear. Behavioral modification strategies may be implemented to reward compliance with this approach and to punish hiding (Kronenberger & Meyer, 2001).

Parent education about encopresis may be important for parents who do not adequately understand the medical and psychological aspects of the disorder or who perceive the child's encopretic behaviors to be manipulative. Understanding the nature of the disorder as well as the rationale for the chosen medical and behavioral interventions will likely increase the parent's participation in the treatment process and decrease parental criticism or blame surrounding the child's encopresis. One treatment program that uses a group format for parent education has demonstrated effectiveness in reducing encopresis symptoms in children (Stark et al., 1997). The developers of the program argued that using a group format allows parents to receive support from others experiencing similar difficulties and permits the normalization of encopresis and associated problems (Stark et al., 1990).

Several treatment programs have been developed that combine standard medical interventions with additional behavioral interventions (see McGrath et al., 2000 for a review). Generally, these treatment programs include a parent involvement component that focuses on behavior modification techniques. Researchers have highlighted that the selection of behavioral interventions should be tailored to the specific presenting problems and associated characteristics of the child and family (Brazzelli & Griffiths, 2006). Of note, although several treatment programs incorporate biofeedback training, an intervention aimed at teaching children how to control their sphincter muscles, a recent review of the literature concluded that biofeedback training has yet to be considered a clinically effective or cost-effective intervention for encopresis (Brazzelli & Griffiths, 2006). Empirical support for biofeedback training has been mixed, with some studies indicating that adding biofeedback components to traditional medical management has resulted in enhanced treatment success (Cox et al., 1994; Loening-Baucke, 1990), whereas others have failed to demonstrate any significant additive effects of biofeedback (Nolan, Catto-Smith, Coffey, & Well, 1998; van der Plas, Benninga, Redekop, Taminiau, & Buller, 1996).

There is a dearth of research investigating predictors of poor outcome in treatments for encopresis. One study examining long-term follow-up of 45 cases treated for encopresis between 1986 and 1994 found that previous encopresis treatment and/or nonretentive encopresis were risk factors for poor treatment outcome (Rockney, McQuade, Days, Linn, & Alario, 1996). Another study of 67 children with encopresis found that good school performance, high levels of parental education, and absence of constipation were related to better outcome (Unal & Pehlivanturk, 2005).

REFRACTORY RESPONSES TO THE TREATMENT OF PEDIATRIC ENCOPRESIS

Parental Factors

As is the case in children with enuresis, evidence-based treatment of childhood encopresis is dependent on parental involvement. In some cases, there is a clear issue of parental readiness for treatment. In other cases, there are situational constraints on parents that place limitations on their level of involvement in the treatment. Behavioral treatments are frequently labor intensive and time-consuming. This section elaborates on these issues.

Low Priority on Treatment of Child's Encopresis

As in pediatric nocturnal enuresis, the priority a parent puts on the treatment of his or her child's encopresis is highly significant with respect to treatment outcome. Contrary to what might be expected, clinical experience suggests encopretic children are frequently not highly motivated to address encopresis. With a very behaviorally oriented treatment, like the treatment of pediatric encopresis, it is essential that the parent be highly motivated. This is not a diagnosis in which a parent can drop a child off at the psychologist, expecting the psychologist to "fix it."

Unfortunately, there are many reasons that a parent may give a low priority to the treatment of his or her child's encopresis. There may be exasperation and limited hope of successful treatment after enduring years of this problem. The parent may have other priorities that interfere with adherence to this behavioral treatment. A parent may be working a shift in the afternoon and evening, which can be very limiting to his or her involvement in treatment. The parent may have other children with more intensive treatment regimens and significant health consequences; or the child may have other more demanding conditions with serious health consequences that demand the parent's attention. The parent may have a misconception about the child's encopresis, such as the child is being manipulative or "lazy" and that it is the child's responsibility to take care of the problem. There are myriad reasons for a parent to give a low priority to involving him or herself with the behavioral treatment of the child's encopresis. Psychologists who treat a sufficient number of children with encopresis will likely face the situation when one of the treatment obstacles is a parent who places a low priority on helping in the treatment of the child's encopresis. In general, unless the psychologist can successfully address that obstacle, the prognosis for that treatment is poor.

Single Parent

The implementation of behavioral principles to the treatment of encopresis is time-consuming and adds an aspect of stress to the family structure because of the various components (e.g., constant monitoring, toilet-scheduling time, implementation of rewards). Although empirical evidence may not be available, clinical experience suggests the challenges of adhering to the treatment may increase when it is a single-parent household. First, a single parent may not have the necessary time to implement the treatment, as he or she may work two jobs or may be constantly providing transportation services for his or her children. This may also result in the family being late for therapy appointments or completely missing appointments because of an unexpected errand that has to be done. Second, a single-parent household is often economically disadvantaged. Thus, although the parent may be motivated for treatment, his or her insurance may not cover mental health services, or it may be simply too expensive to pursue treatment. Lastly, but perhaps the most significant factor, is the stress of being the sole provider. The parent's own stress level may make it difficult for him or her to consistently implement the treatment. For example, after a long stressful day at work it may be easier for the parent to let the child play after dinner instead of adhering to the toilet-sitting time after meals. A parent may also feel stressed about the impact that implementing the treatment may have on his or her parent–child relationship. For example, oftentimes in a two-headed household, either the father or mother will take a role of disciplinarian or use a good cop/bad cop approach. A single parent, on the other hand, will have to implement the treatment while balancing his or her other roles with the child.

Multiple Children

Adherence to treatment may also suffer as a function of multiple children. When more than one child is present in the home, caretakers must balance the needs of all children. A parent's focus on treating encopresis becomes particularly difficult should any of the other children have more significant health concerns, such as asthma, which may entail more intensive treatment because of the potentially more dangerous consequences. Even when the other children are healthy, implementing the treatment may create feelings of jealousy among siblings as the parent inevitably ends up spending more time with the child suffering from encopresis. Over time, the parent may start to feel guilty and withdraw some attention, eventually leading to inconsistent treatment adherence.

Child Factors

Comorbid Mental Retardation

The treatment of encopresis may be particularly challenging for children with lower levels of intellectual functioning. Despite its challenges, our own clinical experience along with limited research via case studies (see Lancioni, O'Reilly, & Basili, 2001) has indicated that successful implementation of behavioral principles in a lower functioning population, specifically MR, is possible. The major barrier to overcome to successfully treat children with comorbid MR is the various aspects of treatment that are affected by children's lower cognitive functioning. In children with severe MR, verbal communication may be limited, making it difficult for the child to indicate that he or she needs to go to the bathroom. A child with MR may also have a more difficult time understanding why he or she is receiving rewards, especially if there is a significant time lag between the child's behavior and the reward (e.g., receiving a reward in the morning following a dry night). In a similar fashion, limited cognitive abilities may make it more difficult for the child to understand the connection between certain physiological signals and going to the bathroom.

Comorbid Autism Spectrum Disorder

Although exact prevalent rates are lacking, it has been noted that encopresis is overrepresented in the population of children with autism spectrum disorders. Clinical observations along with limited studies have suggested that as much as 20% of children diagnosed with autism suffer from encopresis (Radford & Anderson, 2003). Treating pediatric encopresis in a child diagnosed with an autism spectrum disorder presents various challenges, especially given the high comorbidity between autism and MR. Although a thorough review of such challenges is outside the scope of this chapter, some of the challenges include: (a) overcoming communication deficits (often present in children with autism spectrum disorders and MR), in terms of the child being able to express when he or she wants to go to the bathroom; (b) teaching the child the social awareness of when and where to go the bathroom; and (c) learning how to understand one's physiological signals that indicate a need to go to the bathroom.

Other Comorbidities

The treatment of encopresis may also be more challenging for children with a difficult temperament and/or attention difficulties. In fact, higher rates of encopresis are reported in children with significant attentional difficulties such as attention-deficit/hyperactivity disorder (ADHD) as well as disruptive behavior problems (Cox, Morris, Borowitz, & Sutphen, 2002; Joinson et al., 2006). A child's hyperactivity and distractibility may affect his or her ability to detect bodily signals that indicate that a bowel movement is ready to occur. In addition, successful implementation of some behavioral components of encopresis treatment, such as scheduling toilet-sitting time, has been found to be more difficult for toddlers who were rated by their mothers as temperamentally difficult (Blum, Taubman, & Osborne, 1997). For example, children with a difficult temperament, who have lower frustration tolerance, may be easily discouraged when initial success is not attained in treatment, such as when sitting on the toilet but not immediately succeeding in having a bowel movement. Perhaps the main challenge in treating encopresis in children with ADHD and/or disruptive behavior problems is overcoming a potentially stressful parent–child relationship.

Children with ADHD and/or disruptive behavior problems often have stressful interactions with their caretakers, as they are frequently preoccupied with managing their primary symptoms (e.g., making sure they are staying attentive to complete their homework, not fighting with siblings) (Johnston & Mash, 2001; Lange et al., 2005). The caretaker's frustration with managing his or her child's disruptive behaviors may generalize to the treatment of encopresis. For example, the caretaker may not take the child's encopresis seriously, as he or she may think that the child is "acting out." In addition, the caretaker may be so overwhelmed in dealing with his or her child's ADHD and/or disruptive behavior problems that the treatment of encopresis will be seen as secondary and thus not be given the proper attention. Lastly, children with ADHD and/or disruptive behavior problems may themselves be resistant to treatment. For example, as part of their oppositional behaviors children with disruptive behavior problems may not want to comply with a set toilet-training time. The child's ADHD symptoms (e.g., his or her hyperactivity levels) may also make it more difficult to practice sitting still on a toilet.

CASE PRESENTATION

The patient, whom we will refer to as John, is an 8-year-old Caucasian male who was referred by his pediatrician because of chronic difficulties suggestive of encopresis. John was soiling his pants on a near daily basis, during the day as well as at night. John's encopresis was significantly impairing his social and family life. For example, he was getting teased at school so much that he started to avoid going to school by complaining that he was sick. John had recently had a physical examination. Other than the hypothetical possibilities of anal neural pathway signal detection and undetected digestive problems, there were no demonstrable organic bases that could be medically treated or that were found to be the cause of his encopresis. John did not have megacolon or impacted feces. A clinical background interview with the patient's mother indicated that he had never had a significant period of time since birth without a soiling episode. In fact, she indicated that the frequency of soiling (nearly every day) had remained about the same since he was a toddler. Thus, after the clinical interview it became apparent that the patient met criteria for primary encopresis.

The clinical interview also revealed that John had been diagnosed with autism spectrum disorder when he was 4 years of age because of significant language delays as well as significant social difficulties. Findings from a recent intellectual evaluation, using the Wechsler Intelligence Scale for Children –Fourth Edition (WISC-IV; Wechsler, 2003), revealed that John's Full Scale IQ was a 65. John also had significant deficits across adaptive functioning areas (e.g., communication, self-help skills). Thus, John also met criteria for mild mental retardation.

In terms of his family functioning, John was the youngest of four children. His parents had divorced 1 year prior to the initiation of treatment and all four of the children were in the primary custody of their single mother. His oldest brother was 14 years old and was diagnosed with Asperger syndrome. John's mother was financially stressed and depressed. She was a graduate student at a local university, where she was striving to obtain advanced skills to earn a better income after her divorce.

The treatment approaches used with John were monitoring and reinforcing scheduled sitting on the toilet plus increased fiber consumption. Psychoeducation explaining the behavioral basis of the treatment was provided by the psychologist to the mother as well as to the patient in the first session, and as deemed necessary throughout treatment. This treatment approach with a child with these special needs requires a high degree of adherence to treatment strategies by the mother. Many challenges were encountered throughout the treatment that unfortunately contributed to the unsuccessful treatment of John's encopresis.

The first factor that contributed to the unsuccessful treatment was inconsistent therapy attendance. After the first session, John and his mother missed two consecutive weeks of treatment for various reasons (e.g., the mother's babysitter fell through or she forgot the appointment time). After troubleshooting these issues (e.g., allowing the mother to bring the other children with her as well as providing her with a reminder call), attendance improved, although coming late to therapy appointments continued throughout treatment. Nevertheless, after a couple of weeks the psychoeducational component of the treatment was implemented successfully. However, the next major challenge faced in treatment was implementing the monitoring component. Although monitoring forms were provided, John's mother would often forget to bring them back to therapy or would provide an excuse for not filling them out. Some of her excuses seemed to be related to her stress levels as a single parent such as having to work overtime unexpectedly or transporting her other children to a school function.

Adhering to the next phase of the treatment, scheduling toilet time, also proved difficult. As a single parent, John's mother was in charge of getting all the children ready for school as well as cleaning up after dinner. Thus, during important scheduling times (e.g., after breakfast and dinner), John's mother seemed overwhelmed in trying to balance John's needs and the needs of her other children. This was particularly challenging because of John's older sibling also needing special attention as a result of his recent diagnosis of Asperger syndrome. Consequently, the implementation of toilet time was inconsistent. Even when toilet time was implemented, John's mother reported several barriers to providing rewards for her son. First, financially she could not afford giving the child even small prizes. Second, and most important, John's comorbid diagnosis of autism eliminated many natural reinforcers such as praise and/or general affection. Finally, her son's lower cognitive functioning frustrated her. For example, she cried in session on several occasions over how even when she finds time to implement the treatment John does not seem to respond as she expected as he does not seem to understand why he is getting rewards. Unfortunately, despite the therapist's best efforts to help John's mother navigate all of these challenges, she stopped coming to treatment, after about 10 sessions. After numerous attempts to contact John's mother the therapist finally talked to her and asked why she terminated therapy. Her response was that "right now everything is so stressful" that "I don't have the energy" to come to treatment, as she has a "lot of other problems to deal with," including her older son who was recently diagnosed with Asperger syndrome.

This case illustrates most of the reasons for a failed response to a generally successful behavioral treatment as described in the preceding sections of this chapter. The patient was a special-needs child who, in addition to having encopresis, had been diagnosed as meeting criteria for mild mental retardation as well as autism spectrum disorder. This child would present any parent with a heavy caretaker burden. However, the caretaker burden of this mother was incredibly compounded, given that she was single, having divorced 1 year prior to beginning treatment. It is not clear how much this mother could have resolved her emotional issues related to the divorce. In addition to having custody of the patient who presented a heavy caretaker burden, she was also the mother of three other children of whom she had primary custody. Moreover, her oldest son was diagnosed with Asperger syndrome, another autism spectrum disorder that necessitates a high level of care from the parent.

All the described aspects of the mother's life competed with her attention to the behavioral treatment of her youngest son's encopresis. In addition to the therapist directing treatment of the child's encopresis, significant therapeutic attention was aimed at providing support and cognitive-behavioral strategies for the mother's depression. With a highly behavioral treatment of a special-needs child, it is essential to develop a therapeutic alliance with a parent, which usually is the mother. It was the mother who had to ensure compliance with the behavioral strategies of the treatment of this child's encopresis, which had a very poor prognosis from the beginning of this case.

CONCLUSIONS AND FUTURE DIRECTIONS

Research and clinical experience have demonstrated the effectiveness of several behavioral treatments for childhood elimination disorders. For enuresis, the empirically supported treatment with the most evidence base is the moisture alarm system. Several additional treatments, including cleanliness training, retention control training, and general behavioral modification techniques (e.g., positive reinforcement), have also been shown to be beneficial in the treatment of enuresis. In the case of encopresis, augmenting the standard medical treatment with behavioral approaches has been shown to enhance treatment outcome in many cases. Common behavioral approaches include the monitoring and reinforcement of daily toilet-sitting, cleanliness training, and parent education.

Although an evidence base exists for behavioral treatments for childhood enuresis and encopresis, we have identified and discussed multiple reasons for poor treatment response. Many of the factors contributing to treatment-refractory cases may be amenable to intervention, and future research within these areas should examine how additional or adjunctive treatment approaches may augment treatment response. For example, research incorporating the Transtheoretical Model of Behavior change (TTM; Prochaska, 1995; Prochaska & DiClemente, 1992) may help address issues related to poor motivation and nonadherence both in children and their parents. Including an assessment of issues related to TTM, such as perceived barriers to successful implementation of the recommended treatment or acceptability of the treatment to the family, may help to prompt the therapist to include motivational interviewing techniques or additional problem-solving methods to target potential obstacles to participation in treatment.

An additional area deserving of future research attention pertains to cases in which comorbidity complicates the clinical presentation. As discussed earlier, comorbid mental retardation with enuresis or encopresis represents a risk factor for poor treatment response. Future research should begin to explore whether treatments that are more tailored to the developmental level of the child may enhance treatment response. Furthermore, it will be worthwhile to investigate whether enuretic or encopretic children with other comorbid conditions (e.g., disruptive behavior disorders, anxiety disorders) may benefit from treatment tailored to their unique clinical presentation.

The cost-effectiveness of treatments will likely be a future area of concern. We have reviewed several treatment packages that have demonstrated effective results for children with elimination disorders. It is not entirely clear, however, which treatment components are essential for successful treatment outcome. In today's society, in which the influence of health maintenance organizations (HMOs) has resulted in limits placed on treatment duration for children, the importance of condensing treatments into their most effective form is paramount. Therefore, dissecting treatment packages to identify the essential treatment processes that will result in the most potent therapeutic changes will help to advance the field in developing cost-effective treatment packages that can be implemented in real-world settings (Weersing & Weisz, 2002).

Finally, acquiring information regarding the child's coping skills will help to identify specific targets for intervention. It is important to obtain information regarding the frequency with which the child uses specific coping strategies and how well the selected coping strategies are implemented. Examples of coping strategies include problem-solving, acceptance, distraction, social support seeking, escape, denial, and emotional expression. Despite finding a consistent relation between family dysfunction and treatment response, research has not consistently indicated that involvement of family members enhances treatment response. Looking at research with one pediatric condition, specifically pediatric obsessive-compulsive disorder (OCD), this latter finding may largely be a consequence of the fact that almost all studies of pediatric OCD include family members in treatment but do not measure how the extent of family involvement affects treatment outcome (Barrett, Healy-Farrell, & March, 2004; Storch et al., 2007). Future studies should investigate the level, as well as the nature (i.e., positive/supportive versus critical/hostile), of family involvement in treatment outcome studies.

REFERENCES

Ali, A., & Snape, J. (2004). Nocturia in older people: A review of causes, consequences, assessment and management. *International Journal of Clinical Practice, 58*, 366–373.

American Psychiatric Association. (2000). *Diagnostic and statistical manual of mental disorders* (4th ed., text rev.). Washington, DC: American Psychiatric Press.

Azrin, N. H., Sneed, T. J., & Foxx, R. M. (1974). Dry-bed training: Rapid elimination of childhood enuresis. *Behaviour Research and Therapy, 12*, 147–156.

Barrett, P., Healy-Farrell, L., & March, J. (2004). Cognitive-behavioral family treatment of childhood obsessive-compulsive disorder: A controlled trial. *Journal of the American Academy of Child & Adolescent Psychiatry, 43*, 46–62.

Blum, N., Taubman, B., & Osborne, M. (1997). Behavioral characteristics of children with stool toileting refusal. *Pediatrics, 99*, 50–53.

Brazzelli, M., & Griffiths, P. (2006). Behavioural and cognitive interventions with or without other treatments for the management of faecal incontinence in children. *Cochrane Database of Systematic Reviews*, Issue 2.

Butler, R. J. (1991). Establishment of working definitions in nocturnal enuresis. *Archives of Disease in Childhood, 66*, 267–271.

Butler, R. J. (1994). *Nocturnal enuresis. The child's experience*. Oxford, UK: Butterworth-Heinemann Ltd.

Butler, R. (1998). Annotation: Night wetting in children: Psychological aspects. *Journal of Child Psychology and Psychiatry, 39,* 453–463.
Butler, R. J. (2004). Childhood nocturnal enuresis: Developing a conceptual framework. *Clinical Psychology Review, 24,* 909–931.
Butler, R. J., Brewin, C. R., & Forsythe, W. I. (1988). A comparison of two approaches to the treatment of nocturnal enuresis and the prediction of effectiveness using pre-treatment variables. *Journal of Child Psychology and Psychiatry and Allied Disciplines, 29,* 501–509.
Butler, R. J., Forsythe, W. I., Devlin, J. B., & O'Cathain, C. (1990). Predicting treatment outcome in nocturnal enuresis. *Archives of Disease in Childhood, 65,* 1158–1161.
Cendron, M. (1999). Primary nocturnal enuresis: Current. *American Family Physician, 59,* 1205–1214.
Cox, D. J., Morris, J. B., Borowitz, S., & Sutphen, J. (2002). Psychological differences between children with and without chronic encopresis. *Journal of Pediatric Psychology,* 27, 585–591.
Cox, D. J., Sutphen, J., Borowitz, S., Dickens, M. N., Singles, J., & Whitehead, W. E. (1994). Simple electromyograhpic biofeedback treatment for chronic pediatric constipation/encopresis: Preliminary report. *Biofeedback and Self Regulation, 19,* 41–50.
Cox, D. J., Sutphen, J., Borowitz, S., Kovatchev, B., & Ling, W. (1998). Contribution of behavior therapy and biofeedback to laxative therapy in the treatment of pediatric encopresis. *Annals of Behavioral Medicine, 20,* 70–76.
Devlin, J. B., & O'Cathain, C. (1990). Predicting treatment outcome in nocturnal enuresis. *Archives of Disease in Childhood, 65,* 1158–1161.
Dische, S., Yule, W., Corbett, J., & Hand, D. (1983). Childhood nocturnal enuresis: Factors associated with outcome of treatment with an enuresis alarm. *Developmental Medicine and Child Neurology, 25,* 67–80.
Doleys, D. M. (1977). Behavioral treatments for nocturnal enuresis in children: A review of the recent literature. *Psychological Bulletin, 84,* 30–54.
Eidlitz-Markus, T., Shuper, A., & Amir, J. (2000). Secondary enuresis: Post-traumatic stress disorder in children after car accidents. *Israel Medical Association Journal, 2,* 135–137.
Fritz, G., Rockney, R., Bernet, W., Arnold, V., Beichtman, J., Benson, R., et al. (2004). Practice parameter for the assessment and treatment of children and adolescents with enuresis. *Journal of the American Academy of Child and Adolescent Psychiatry, 43,* 1540–1550.
Geffken, G. R., Johnson, S. B., & Walker, D. (1986). Behavioral interventions for childhood nocturnal enuresis: The differential effect of bladder capacity on treatment progress and outcome. *Health Psychology, 5,* 261–272.
Geffken, G. R., Keeley, M., Kellison, I., Storch, E. A., & Rodrigue, J. R. (2006). Parental adherence to child mental health providers' recommendations. *Professional Psychology: Research and Practice, 37,* 599–505.
Geffken, G. R., Williams, L. B., Silverstein, J. H., Monaco L., Rayfield, A., & Bell, S. K. (2007). Metabolic control and nocturnal enuresis in children with type 1 diabetes. *Journal of Pediatric Nursing, 22,* 4–8.

Glazener, C. M. A., & Evans, J. H. C. (2004). Simple behavioural and physical interventions for nocturnal enuresis in children. *Cochrane Database of Systematic Reviews*, Issue 2.

Glazener, C. M. A., Evans, J. H. C., & Peto, R. E. (2004). Complex behavioural and educational interventions for nocturnal enuresis in children. *Cochrane Database of Systematic Reviews*, Issue 1.

Glazener, C. M. A., Evans, J. H. C., & Peto, R. E. (2005). Alarm interventions for nocturnal enuresis in children. *Cochrane Database of Systematic Reviews*, Issue 2.

Houts, A. C., Peterson, J. K., & Whelan, J. P. (1986). Prevention of relapse in full spectrum home training for primary enuresis: A component analysis. *Behaviour Therapy, 17*, 462–469.

Johnson, S. B. (1980). Enuresis. In R. Daitzman (Ed.), *Clinical behavior therapy and behavior modification* (Vol. 1, 81–142). New York: Garland Press.

Johnston, C., & Mash, E. (2001). Families of children with attention-deficit/hyperactivity disorder: Review and recommendations for future research. *Clinical Child and Family Psychology Review, 4*, 183–207.

Joinson, C., Heron, J., Butler, U., von Gontard, A., & Avon Longitudinal Study of Parents and Children Study Team. (2006). Psychological differences between children with and without soiling problems. *Pediatrics, 117*, 1575–1584.

Katz, G., Spivak, B., Mester, R., Grinshpoon, A., & Weizman, A. (1997). Desmopressin (DDAVP) treatment in adult sleep-related enuresis. *Human Psychopharmacology: Clinical and Experimental, 12*, 505–507.

Kawauchi, A., Tanaka, Y., Naito, Y., Yamao, Y., Ukimura, O., Yoneda, K., et al. (2003). Bladder capacity at the time of enuresis. *Urology, 61*, 1016–1018.

Kronenberger, W. G., & Meyer, R. G. (2001). *The child clinician's handbook* (2nd ed.). Needham Heights, MA: Allyn & Bacon.

Lancioni, G., O'Reilly, M., & Basili, G. (2001). Treating encopresis in people with intellectual disabilities: A literature review. *Journal of Applied Research in Intellectual Disabilities, 14*, 47–63.

Lange, G., Sheerin, D., Carr, A., Dooley, B., Barton, V., Marshall, D., et al. (2005). Family factors associated with attention deficit hyperactivity disorder and emotional disorders in children. *Journal of Family Therapy, 27*, 76–96.

Loening-Baucke, V. A. (1990). Modulation of abnormal defecation dynamics by biofeedback treatment in chronically constipated children with encopresis. *Journal of Pediatrics, 116*, 214–222.

McGrath, M. L., Mellon, M. W., & Murphy, L. (2000). Empirically supported treatments in pediatric psychology: Constipation and encopresis. *Journal of Pediatric Psychology, 25*, 225–254.

Mellon, M. (2000). Empirically supported treatments in pediatric psychology: Nocturnal enuresis. *Journal of Pediatric Psychology, 25*, 193–214.

Mikkelsen, E. J. (2001). Enuresis and encopresis: Ten years of progress. *Journal of the American Academy of Child and Adolescent Psychiatry, 40*, 1146–1158.

Moffatt, M. E. K., & Cheang, M. (1995). Predicting treatment outcome with conditioning alarms. *Scandinavian Journal of Urology and Nephrology, 173* (Suppl.), 119–122.

Morgan, R. T., & Young G. C. (1975). Parental attitudes and the conditioning treatment of childhood enuresis. *Behavior Research and Therapy, 13*, 237–239.

Mowrer, O. H., & Mowrer, W. M. (1938). Enuresis—A method for its study and treatment. *American Journal of Orthopsychiatry, 8*, 436–459.
Neveus, T., Hetta, J., Cnattingius, S., Tuvemo, T., Lackgren, G., Olsson, U., et al. (1999). Depth of sleep and sleep habits among enuretic and incontinent children. *Acta Paediatrica, 88*, 748–752.
Nolan, T., Catto-Smith, T., Coffey, C., & Well, J. (1998). Randomised controlled trial of biofeedback training in persistent encopresis with anismus. *Archives of Diseases in Childhood, 79*, 131–135.
O'Brien, S., Ross, L. V., & Christopherson, E. R. (1986). Primary encopresis: Evaluation and treatment. *Journal of Applied Behavior Analysis, 19*, 137–142.
Prochaska, J. O. (1995). An eclectic and integrative approach: Transtheoretical therapy. In A. S. Gurman & S. Messer (Eds.), *Essential psychotherapies* (pp. 403–440). New York: Guilford Press.
Prochaska, J. O., & DiClemente, C. C. (1992). The transtheoretical approach. In J. C. Norcross & M. R. Goldfried (Eds.), *Handbook of psychotherapy integration* (pp. 300–334). New York: Basic Books.
Radford, J., & Anderson, M. (2003). Encopresis in children on the autistic spectrum. *Early Child Development and Care, 173*, 375–382.
Rittig, S., Schaumburg, H.L., Siggaaro, C., Schmidt, F., & Djurhuus, J.C. (2008). The circadian defect in plasma vasopression and urine output is related to desmopressin response and enuresis status in children with nocturnal enuresis. *Journal of Urology, 179*, 2389–2395.
Rockney, R. M., McQuade, W. H., Days, A. L., Linn, H. E., & Alario, A. J. (1996). Encopresis treatment outcome: Long-term follow-up of 45 cases. *Journal of Developmental and Behavioral Pediatrics, 17*, 380–385.
Rushton, H., Belman, A., Zaontz, M., Skoog, S., & Sihelnick, S. (1996). The influence of small functional bladder capacity and other predictors on the response to desmopressin in the management of monosymptomatic nocturnal enuresis. *Journal of Urology, 156*, 651–655.
Skoog, S. J. (1998). Primary nocturnal enuresis: An analysis of factors related to its etiology. *Journal of Urology, 159*, 1338–1339.
Starfield, B. (1967). Functional bladder capacity in enuertic and nonenuretic children. *Journal of Pediatrics, 70*, 777–781.
Stark, L. J., Opipari, L. C., Donaldson, D. L., Danovsky, M. B., Rasile, D. A., & DelSanto, A. F. (1997). Evaluation of a standard protocol for retentive encopresis: A replication. *Journal of Pediatric Psychology, 22*, 619–633.
Storch, E. A., Geffken, G. R., Merlo, L. J., Mann, G., Duke, D., Munson, M., et al. (2007). Cognitive-behavioral therapy for pediatric obsessive-compulsive disorder: Comparison of intensive and weekly approaches. *Journal of the American Academy of Child and Adolescent Psychiatry, 46*, 469–478.
Unal, F., & Pehlivanturk, B. (2005). Encopresis: Long-term clinical outcome of 67 cases. *Turkish Journal of Pediatrics, 47*, 53–57.
van der Plas, R. N., Benninga, M. A., Redekop, W. K., Taminiau, J. A., & Buller, H. A. (1996). Randomized trial of biofeedback training for encopresis. *Archives of Diseases in Childhood, 75*, 367–374.

Vogel, W., Young, M., & Primack, W. (1996). A survey of physician use of treatment methods for functional enuresis. *Journal of Developmental and Behavioral Pediatrics, 17*, 90–93.

von Gontard, A., Eiberg, H., Hollmann, E., Rittig, S., & Lehmkuhl, G. (1999). Molecular genetics of nocturnal enuresis: Linkage to a locus on chromosome 22. *Scandinavian Journal of Urology and Nephrology, 202,* 76–80.

von Gontard, A., Mauer-Mucke, K., Pluck, J., Berner, W., & Lehmkuhl, G. (1999). Clinical behavioral problems in day- and night-wetting children. *Pediatric Nephrology, 13,* 662–667.

Wagner, W. G., & Geffken, G. R. (1986). Enuretic children: How they view their wetting behavior. *Child Study Journal*, 16(1), 13–18.

Wagner, W. G., & Johnson, J. T. (1988). Child nocturnal enuresis: The prediction of premature withdrawal from behavioral conditioning. *Journal of Abnormal Child Psychology, 16,* 687–692.

Wagner, W. G., Johnson, S. B., Walker, D., Carter, R., & Wittner, J. (1982). A controlled comparison of treatments for nocturnal enuresis. *Journal of Pediatrics, 101*, 302–307.

Wechsler, D. (2003). *WISC-IV technical and interpretive manual.* San Antonio, TX: Harcourt Assessment.

Weersing, V. R., & Weisz, S. R. (2002). Mechanisms of action in youth psychotherapy. *Journal of Child Psychology and Psychiatry, 43*, 3029.

Wolfish, N. (1999). Sleep arousal function in enuretic males. *Scandinavian Journal of Urology and Nephrology, 202* (Suppl.), 24–26.

Yeung, C. K., Chiu, H. N., & Sit, F. K. (1999). Bladder dysfunction in children with refractory monosymptomatic primary nocturnal enuresis. *Journal of Urology, 162,* 1049–1054.

17

Cognitive-Behavioral Therapy for Children and Adolescents With Difficult-to-Treat Substance-Use Disorders

LISA J. MERLO AND AMANDA M. STONE

Substance-use disorders (SUDs) are increasingly being considered diseases of pediatric origin, because of the fact that most individuals who develop substance abuse or dependence begin using substances (e.g., alcohol, tobacco, marijuana, and/or other drugs) during childhood or adolescence. As a result, substance abuse remains an important topic for mental health professionals who specialize in working with children and teens. This chapter provides an overview of treatment strategies for youth with SUDs, focusing on the use of cognitive-behavioral therapy (CBT) with difficult-to-treat members of this population. Specifically, the chapter will introduce the reader to substance use disorders among pediatric patients, describe factors associated with treatment response, and describe recommended methods of treatment for children and teens who suffer from an SUD. A case description is included to illustrate the use of CBT with adjunctive treatments in a difficult-to-treat patient.

Several disorders are included under the heading of substance-related disorders (e.g., substance-induced psychosis, amnesia, mood disorders, etc.); however, the term "SUD" is used to describe problems typically referred to as "addiction" by the general population. Specifically, the SUDs include the diagnoses of substance abuse and substance dependence. Substance-use disorders can result from misuse of illicit drugs, prescription drugs, over-the-counter drugs, and/or other legal drugs such as alcohol and tobacco. In addition, polysubstance abuse is common among individuals with SUDs (Spooner, Mattick, & Noffs, 2000).

Though substance abuse and dependence are often confused, it is important to distinguish the two disorders. The *Diagnostic and Statistical Manual of Mental Disorders, Fourth Edition, Text Revision* (*DSM-IV-TR;* American Psychiatric Association, 2000) criteria for substance *abuse* are met if at least one of the following has occurred in the past 12 months: (a) recurrent failure to meet major responsibilities (e.g., at home, school, or work) because of substance use, (b) continued substance use when it may be physically dangerous, (c) legal problems arising from substance use, and/or (d) use of substances even when they frequently cause social or interpersonal problems. The *DSM-IV-TR* definition of substance *dependence* includes meeting at least three of the following criteria in a 12-month period: (a) tolerance (manifested as either a need for more of a substance to sustain the same effect or notably decreased effects of a substance while continuing to use the same amount); (b) withdrawal (manifested as the characteristic physical withdrawal symptoms for the substance or the continued use of the substance or a closely related substance to avoid experiencing such symptoms); (c) use of the substance in larger amounts and/or over a longer period of time than was initially planned; (d) desire to quit, or unsuccessful efforts to cut down on substance use; (e) large amounts of time spent obtaining, using, and/or recovering from the effects of a substance; (f) neglect of responsibilities and/or social life because of substance use; and/or (g) continued use of a substance, even though the user recognizes that it is causing or intensifying a psychological or physical problem.

It is noteworthy that an individual cannot be diagnosed with both substance abuse and substance dependence for the same drug at the same time. Rather, once criteria for substance dependence are met, that diagnosis supercedes the substance-abuse diagnosis. However, individuals can meet criteria for abuse of one substance and dependence on another. For example, a teen may exhibit alcohol dependence with concurrent marijuana abuse. In addition, the *DSM-IV-TR* does not distinguish separate criteria for youth with SUDs. Rather, the diagnostic criteria for both substance abuse and substance dependence are the same for children/adolescents as they are for adults. Despite this, the symptom presentation and associated features may differ somewhat among children and teens compared to adults. As a result, SUD symptoms are often mistaken for developmentally appropriate "experimentation" or other common pediatric problems, including depression, anxiety, oppositional behavior, and school failure.

DETECTION OF SUBSTANCE-USE DISORDERS IN PEDIATRIC PATIENTS

A four-item questionnaire (i.e., "Have you ever felt you ought to Cut down on your drinking? Have people Annoyed you by criticizing your drinking? Have you ever felt bad or Guilty about your drinking? Have you ever had a drink first thing in the morning to steady your nerves or to get rid of a hangover [Eye Opener]?) which is commonly referred to as the CAGE questionnaire (Ewing, 1984) is the most common quick-screening device for detecting alcohol abuse in adults. However, its efficacy in children and adolescents is questionable. Further, CAGE does not screen for drug abuse. As a result, separate questions were developed to be used as a brief screen for drug and alcohol abuse in adolescents (i.e., Have you ever ridden in a Car driven by someone [including yourself] who was high or had been using alcohol or drugs? Do you ever use alcohol/drugs to Relax, feel better about yourself, or fit in? Do you ever use alcohol/drugs while you are by yourself or Alone? Do you ever Forget things that you did while you are using alcohol/drugs? Do your Family or Friends ever tell you that you should cut down on your drinking or drug use? Have you ever gotten into Trouble while you were using drugs or alcohol?). Similar to CAGE, this CRAFFT questionnaire (Knight et al., 1999) consists of six items that comprise the acronym of its name. The CRAFFT can be administered in either interview format or as a self-report questionnaire. Items are scored as 1 = "yes" or 0 = "no." A score of 2 or higher indicates a potential substance-abuse problem and suggests that further assessment is warranted. Using this cut-off, the CRAFFT has a 92% sensitivity rating (Knight et al., 1999).

When adolescent alcohol misuse is suspected, the Rutgers Alcohol Problem Index (RAPI; White & Labouvie, 1989) is an additional effective screening measure. The RAPI consists of 23 self-report items. It focuses on negative consequences of alcohol abuse, such as problems in school and fighting, and has an internal consistency of $\alpha = .92$ (White & LaBouvie, 1989). Sample items include, "How many times have you gone to work or school high or drunk?" and "How many times have you missed out on other things because you spent too much money on alcohol?" Responses range from 0 = "never" to 4 = "more than 10 times," with higher scores indicating more severe alcohol abuse. The RAPI has demonstrated acceptable temporal stability and correlates moderately with measures of drinking intensity (White & LaBouvie, 1989).

If a youth screens positive on one of the aforementioned measures, or other evidence suggests the presence of an SUD, the clinician should conduct a full assessment or refer the patient to an addiction specialist for an evaluation. In general, in-depth assessments will include a clinical interview with the patient, as well as the collection of collateral information from parents, siblings, school, and friends. Additional psychological testing may also be indicated. In addition, urine drug screening is recommended to assess for recent drug use, as this method is more sensitive than blood or breath testing (Preston, Silverman, Schuster, & Cone, 1997). Urine screening will only identify drug *use* and cannot verify the presence of a substance-use disorder. However, such screening can verify recent use, and may be a powerful deterrent to future use.

PREVALENCE OF SUBSTANCE-USE DISORDERS AMONG CHILDREN AND ADOLESCENTS

Rates of substance use among children and adolescents peaked during the 1980s and have shown a significant decrease since that time (Johnston, O'Malley, Bachman, & Schulenberg, 2008). Unfortunately, however, adolescent substance use remains a relatively common phenomenon. In the 2006 National Survey on Drug Use and Health, 27.6% of adolescents between the ages of 12 and 17 years reported having used illicit drugs in their lifetime and 9.8% reported using in the past month. In addition, 19% of those aged 12 to 20 years reported binge drinking in the past month. It was estimated that about 6% of youth aged 12 to 17 years are in need of treatment for an alcohol-use disorder, and 5.5% need treatment for an illicit-drug-use disorder. Similarly, results of the annual Monitoring the Future surveys indicate that half of all 12th graders, 36% of 10th graders, and 21% of 8th graders reported illicit drug use at some time in their lives (Johnston, O'Malley, Bachman, & Schulenberg, 2007). Within the primary care population, Knight et al. (2007) found that approximately 15% of patients between the ages of 12 and 18 screened positive for a substance-use disorder using the CRAFFT screening method, with higher incidence rates for sick visits (23.2%) than well visits (11.4%). Among this sample, 43.5% of patients reported lifetime substance abuse.

Among children and adolescents who use drugs, rates of alcohol use are historically the highest (82%), followed by tobacco use (64%: Johnston, O'Malley, & Bachman, 1998). Marijuana is the most frequently used illicit drug, with 42% of high school seniors reporting lifetime use (Johnston et al., 2007). Rates of other illicit drug use have remained relatively stable in recent years (Johnston, O'Malley, Bachman, & Schulenberg, 2008). However, adolescent nonmedical use of prescription drugs is a growing phenomenon (Hertz & Knight, 2006). Misuse of prescription opioids, benzodiazepines, and stimulants are becoming particularly problematic. Significant factors hypothesized to contribute to the increased use of these substances include relatively easy access (i.e., prescription drugs are frequently available in medicine cabinets of family or friends, prescription "sharing" is common among friends, and these drugs can be purchased via the Internet), and lower perceived risk (i.e., teens view these drugs as "safe" because they are prescribed by a physician).

FACTORS ASSOCIATED WITH DEVELOPMENT OF SUBSTANCE-USE DISORDERS

Presence of a psychiatric disorder appears to be among the top risk factors associated with development of a substance-use disorder in youth. Research has consistently demonstrated a strong correlation between prior mental health problems and the onset of substance abuse. For example, rates of substance abuse are almost three times higher among teenage girls with depression than among their nondepressed peers (Rao, Daley, & Hammen, 2000). Similarly, adolescents who regularly smoke tobacco or drink alcohol in combination with marijuana use are four to five times more likely to be diagnosed with a depressive disorder (Boys et al., 2003). Anxiety disorders are also commonly comorbid with adolescent substance abuse, with one study indicating that 44% of their substance-abusing teenage sample met criteria for an anxiety disorder, with posttraumatic stress disorder (PTSD) being the most prevalent at 27% (Lubman, Allen, Rogers, Cementon, & Bonomo, 2007). Youth with attention-deficit/hyperactivity disorder (ADHD), particularly those with significant hyperactivity/impulsivity symptoms, display higher rates of substance abuse for illicit drugs, nicotine, and alcohol. This association is observed for both males and females (Elkins, McGue, & Iacono, 2007). However, the risk appears to decline with successful ADHD treatment (Wilson & Levin, 2005). Further research suggests that adolescents who display high reward sensitivity and low punishment sensitivity also show higher levels of substance use (Genovese & Wallace, 2007). Perhaps as a result, youth with comorbid substance-abuse and psychiatric disorders are also more likely to have problems with family and school and show higher levels of criminal involvement (Grella, Hser, Joshi, & Rounds-Bryant, 2001).

Other risk factors that are strongly associated with substance abuse are related to the child's social environment and interactions. For example, Boys et al. (2003) reported that youth from one-parent households are twice as likely to use marijuana, whereas youth who have a stay-at-home parent are half as likely to smoke tobacco. Similarly, Hill, Shen, Lowers, and Locke (2000) found that family history of alcoholism predicted earlier onset of alcoholism and other substance-use problems. In addition, peer influences are also strongly associated with substance use. In fact, a 2008 review of teen tobacco use found the most common reason for initiation of smoking was peer pressure (Lenney & Enderby, 2008). Additionally, a 2001 study found that difficulty resisting the pressure to smoke during the early teens was associated with increased risk for alcohol misuse later in adolescence (Ellickson, Tucker, Klein, & McGuigan, 2001). In a sample of adolescents calling in to a cocaine helpline, almost all (88%) described their initiation of illicit drug use to be peer influenced, with the top three reasons specifically cited as (a) it was "cool, " (b) everyone else used alcohol or drugs, and (c) peer *pressure* (Dupre, Miller, Gold, & Rospenda, 1995). In the 2006 National Survey on Drug Use and Health, 15.3% of teens aged 12 to 17 reported being approached by someone selling drugs (Substance Abuse and Mental Health Services Administration, 2007), but most teens who initiate substance use are initially introduced to the substance by a friend. Peer influence does appear to weaken over time, decreasing in a linear fashion between the ages of 14 and 18 (Steinberg & Monahan, 2007). As a result, this risk factor may be a more prominent concern for younger patients.

Finally, age of initial substance use strongly predicts future development of a substance-use disorder, with earlier use of virtually all substances predicting a higher likelihood of later abuse or dependence. For example, use of alcohol before the age of 14 is a strong predictor of later alcohol dependence, and the risk of developing alcohol dependence or abuse are decreased by 14% and 8%, respectively, for every year that onset of drinking is delayed (Grant & Dawson, 1997).

COURSE OF THE SUBSTANCE-USE DISORDERS

Among virtually all individuals who develop a substance-use disorder, there is a progression from experimentation with the substance, to problematic/excessive use, to abuse, and for some, to dependence. The trajectory varies greatly from one individual to another, with some individuals progressing quickly to substance abuse/dependence, and others using substances "recreationally" for some time before a more serious problem develops. Various factors can influence this process, including the drug(s) of choice, genetic vulnerability, social factors, and access to the drugs.

Gateway Drug Hypothesis

Tobacco use (and particularly cigarette smoking) has often been cited as a risk factor for later drug use. For example, one study showed that smoking is associated with later alcohol abuse (Chen et al., 2002). Similarly, marijuana is often referred to as a "gateway drug" because its use is associated with an increased risk of abusing other drugs, becoming dependent on other drugs, and abusing a wider variety of other drugs in the future (Fergusson, Boden, & Horwood, 2006). A 1999 study by Brook, Balka, and Whiteman (1999) found that those who had used marijuana in early adolescence were significantly less likely to believe that drugs are harmful in later adolescence, and were more likely to have an increased tolerance for risky behavior. However, the prevalence of these attitudes decreased with older age of onset for substance use (Fergusson et al., 2006). Recently, other drugs have been explored as gateway drugs. Consistent with the increasing prevalence of prescription-drug misuse, one study demonstrated that OxyContin abuse is associated with later abuse of other opioids, including heroin (Grau et al., 2007).

Neurobiological Sensitivity Hypothesis

In addition to changing attitudes, early drug exposure (whether in utero, via secondhand exposure, or through experimentation during childhood/adolescence) also appears to change the brain (Andersen & Navalta, 2004). The neurobiological reward system is particularly sensitive to pleasurable substances and experiences during adolescent development (Bjork et al., 2004). Indeed, animal models have demonstrated that rats who are administered THC (tetrahydrocannabinol) during adolescence self-administer opioids at higher rates during adulthood than rats who were not exposed to THC (Ellgren, Spano, & Hurd, 2007). Similarly, physicians who used marijuana or tobacco during adolescence appear to be particularly vulnerable to the development of addictions later in life (Merlo, Goldberger, Kolodner, Fitzgerald, & Gold, 2008). Finally, longitudinal studies of human twins have shown that marijuana use during adolescence is a strong predictor of illicit drug use during adulthood (Agrawal, Neale, Prescott, & Kendler, 2004; Lynskey et al., 2003). Though more research is needed to confirm the neurobiological sensitivity hypothesis, it may be advisable to address *any* substance use during adolescence as a significant risk factor for future addiction.

Consequences of Substance Abuse in Youth

As with adults who suffer from substance abuse or dependence, there are (by definition) several negative consequences of SUDs for youth. Perhaps most important, suicide and accident-related deaths are significant risks associated with substance abuse. Adolescents with alcohol dependence are approximately three times more likely to experience suicidal ideation and/or suicide attempts (Esposito-Smythers, Spirito, Uth, & LaChance, 2006). In addition, the odds of *completed* suicide are 5 to 13 times greater among adolescents diagnosed with an alcohol- or drug-use disorder (Esposito-Smythers et al., 2006). Driving under the influence accounts for 1 in 5 teenage deaths and is a leading cause of adolescent mortality (Julien, 1998).

Adolescents who abuse substances are also more likely to engage in other risky behaviors. For example, teens who abuse alcohol or drugs engage in more violent behaviors and are more likely to suffer violence-related injuries than teens who abstain from drug use (Sege, Stringham, Short, & Griffith, 1999; Borowsky & Ireland, 2004). Dating violence and rape are also strongly associated with substance use (Slaughter, 2000). In addition, adolescents with substance-abuse problems are more likely to engage in risky sexual behaviors such as early sexual activity, multiple partners, and inconsistent or lack of condom use (Tapert, Aarons, Sedlar, & Brown, 2001; Yan, Chiu, Stoesen, & Wang, 2007). This increased likelihood of sexual-risk behavior persists through adolescence for as long as the substance abuse continues. As a result, rates of sexually transmitted infections (including human immunodeficiency virus [HIV]) and unwanted pregnancies are typically higher among this population (De Genna, Cornelius, & Cook, 2007; Flanagan & Kokotailo, 1999). Increased sex education and screening for sexually transmitted infections should be considered important additions to adolescent substance-abuse treatment and prevention programs.

Finally, adolescent substance use is also associated with academic problems and school dropout. One study found regular marijuana use during early adolescence to be a risk factor for leaving high school before completion (Lynskey, Coffey, Degenhardt, Carlin, & Patton, 2003). Similarly, results of a study on teen inhalant use demonstrated that adolescents who had abused inhalants during their lifetime were significantly more likely than those who had not to have suffered a variety of school-related problems (e.g., disciplinary action taken at school, increased truancy, or earning grades of "D" or below: McGarvey, Canterbury, & Cohn, 1996).

COGNITIVE-BEHAVIORAL THERAPY FOR CHILDREN AND ADOLESCENTS WITH SUBSTANCE-USE DISORDERS

Given its demonstrated efficacy and effectiveness, CBT is widely accepted as the leading treatment for adolescent SUDs. In general, sessions include a mixture of psychoeducation, motivational enhancement, instruction in self-monitoring, coping skills training, cognitive restructuring, problem solving, substance refusal, and relapse prevention. In the first phase of treatment, the therapist focuses mainly on developing rapport with the patient and providing psychoeducation regarding the conceptualization of addiction as a disease. If the patient does not demonstrate motivation for treatment, then encouraging motivation will be an additional focus of the sessions.

Once the therapist and patient are "on the same page" with regard to their views of addiction and treatment, the focus of sessions will shift to the patient's own present situation, past experiences, and overall views. The patient and therapist will explore specific factors in the patient's life that contribute to or maintain substance use, identifying high-risk individuals and situations. They will explore both cognitive triggers (e.g., dysfunctional cognitions) and behavioral triggers (e.g., exposure to substance-using friends), and discuss alternative responses to employ in place of using substances. Problem-solving strategies are introduced by the therapist and practiced extensively in session. In addition, the therapist and clinician will practice other useful skills (e.g., substance-refusal strategies, eliciting social support, etc.).

After the patient has achieved an acceptable level of substance use (typically, abstinence), the therapist and patient will transition to relapse-prevention strategies. In this phase of treatment, more psychoeducation is provided regarding the nature of a "lapse" as compared to a "relapse" (which may be interpreted as failure by the patient). Planning ahead to prevent temptation and to have a back-up plan in times of trouble is emphasized. The therapist and patient will typically work together to develop an "emergency contacts" list for the patient to call if he or she is tempted to use substances. Often, if the patient is participating in a 12-step fellowship program (e.g., Alcoholics Anonymous or Narcotics Anonymous), the patient's sponsor will be placed at the top of such a list. In the final phase of treatment, associated problems may be addressed. These issues might include comorbid psychiatric or psychological disorders (e.g., depression, anxiety, etc.), social skills deficits, educational or occupational problems, relationship difficulties, anger management, or any other difficulty that may contribute to substance use in the future.

Each CBT session for substance-use disorders generally begins with a brief period of supportive therapy and a review of the previous session (including homework assignments). As treatment progresses, new material and skills are presented. The therapist gives the rationale for each new skill before presenting it to the patient. After brief instruction and discussion, the therapist elicits the patient's reaction and reviews any questions or concerns. Role-play is used for each skill to ensure that the patient has achieved a basic level of competency. Patients are encouraged to role-play using these new skills in response to common situations in their own lives. Finally, homework is assigned for the patient to complete before the next session. A comprehensive manual of CBT for alcohol-use disorders, which was used in Project Matching Alcoholism Treatments to Client Heterogeneity (Project MATCH), is available online at http://pubs.niaaa.nih.gov/publications/match.htm. It can be adapted for use with other SUDs and with younger patients.

Though more research has assessed the use of CBT in adult patients with SUDs, several studies have also shown positive outcomes in adolescent patients. For example, CBT has been compared to interactional treatment (IT) and/or psychoeducational therapy in three separate studies (Kaminer & Burleson, 1999; Kaminer, Burleson, Blitz, Sussman, & Rounsaville, 1998; Kaminer, Burleson, & Goldberger, 2002). Group CBT was compared to group psychoeducation or a group IT intervention, which consisted of a present-centered group therapy designed to help patients gain insight, improve interpersonal interactions, facilitate self-care, and promote positive self-esteem. Patients treated with CBT demonstrated improved outcome, compared with IT in only the first study (Kaminer et al., 1998). However, though subsequent studies suggested that all interventions were effective in reducing rates of substance use among adolescents, CBT showed an earlier and more robust treatment response across studies. Similarly, another study compared the effectiveness of a behavioral outpatient treatment program to that of a supportive counseling program (Azrin, McMahon, et al., 1994). In the behavioral program, the number of adolescents using drugs by the end of treatment decreased by 73%, compared to a decrease of only 9% for those receiving the comparison treatment (Azrin, McMahon, et al., 1994). In addition, in a review of the literature, Waldron and Kaminer (2004) found group CBT to be equally as effective as individual CBT in reducing adolescent substance use.

FACTORS ASSOCIATED WITH POOR TREATMENT RESPONSE

Substance-use disorders can be very difficult to treat, even without complicating factors. To be successful, long-term treatment is generally required, preferably with a significant follow-up period. In addition, relapse is common, even among those who have a successful treatment experience. However, certain factors, when present, frequently detract from the efficacy of treatment and are associated with worse outcome.

Substance(s) of Abuse

Though more research is needed in this area, there is some evidence to suggest that substances with a quicker onset of effects and shorter lasting effects are more likely to lead to abuse or dependence (APA, 2000). For example, anecdotal evidence suggests that crack cocaine and heroin are particularly problematic for this reason. In addition, substances that result in unpleasant withdrawal symptoms (e.g., opioids) may be more difficult to quit, as early efforts at abstaining from use have significant negative consequences (Renzelli & Capretto, 2006). Use of multiple substances typically complicates treatment as well. However, it is noteworthy that recovery is possible, no matter the substance(s) of abuse, if high-quality treatment is attained.

Comorbid Psychiatric Conditions

Among many teens, comorbid psychiatric conditions can lead to difficulties in both the initiation of treatment and continued participation. As noted earlier, symptoms of teenage substance abuse are similar in nature to symptoms of other common psychological disorders (e.g., depression, anxiety, disruptive behavior disorders). As a result, the SUD may initially be overlooked or hidden from family and health care providers. This delay in identification may allow the SUD to worsen, potentially creating the need for more intensive or longer term treatment than would have been necessary with earlier identification. In addition, research has indicated that, even after treatment for an SUD, adolescent patients with a dual diagnosis are significantly more likely than those with no psychiatric comorbidities to use marijuana and/or hallucinogens, and to engage in illegal activity during the 12-month period that follows their discharge from treatment (Grella et al., 2001).

Family History

Research has demonstrated that a family history of substance abuse is strongly associated with the presence of multiple complicating factors in the treatment of SUDs. For example, teens with a family history of substance abuse typically present with more concurrent medical problems, a larger number of drugs of choice, and increased psychiatric symptoms such as asocial behavior (Coviello, Alterman, Cacciola, Rutherford, & Zanis, 2004). However, despite the fact that each of these factors can make the provision of treatment more difficult for the clinician, results of the same study found that these barriers did not cause a significant difference in treatment response at the 6-month follow-up.

Family and Social Factors

Adolescents' quality of parenting and family life also appear to play a crucial role in the outcome of their substance-abuse treatment. Research has shown that teens with increased parental and/or family involvement during substance-abuse treatment have better overall treatment outcomes at 6- and 12-month follow-ups (Hsieh, Hoffmann, & Hollister, 1998). In addition, Dakof, Tejeda, and Liddle (2001) found that the recognition of a serious substance-abuse problem by parents, as well as a parental expectation for the attainment of higher education, leads to a greater likelihood that the adolescent will remain in treatment. Waldron, Kern-Jones, Turner, Peterson, and Ozechowski (2007) found one-parent families to have a lower rate of engaging in family-based treatment than two-parent families. As a result, it may be worthwhile for the clinician to focus extra attention on encouraging parental involvement with these families. With regard to social factors, Hsieh and colleagues (1998) found that school problems, legal problems, and lack of religious involvement at pretreatment were all associated with significantly poorer treatment outcomes at the 6-month follow-up. This trend continued at the 12-month follow-up; however, the results were no longer statistically significantly.

ADJUNCTIVE TREATMENTS TO IMPROVE TREATMENT RETENTION AND OUTCOME

To maximize the likelihood of treatment success, additional interventions are frequently combined with CBT to encourage motivation for treatment and participation in therapy, to address associated problems, and/or to facilitate behavior change. These adjunctive interventions may be implemented in either an outpatient or residential setting, and can be tailored to the specific needs of each patient. As a result, patients may receive any combination of the following interventions in conjunction with their standard CBT intervention.

Motivational Interviewing

Motivational interviewing (MI) is a client-centered, goal-directed therapy that focuses on enhancing the patient's motivation for change by resolving ambivalence and increasing self-efficacy (Miller & Rollnick, 2002). Based on the transtheoretical Stages of Change model (Prochaska & DiClemente, 1983), MI approaches are designed to facilitate the patient's progression from the precontemplation stage (i.e., denial of the problem), through the contemplation (i.e., problem recognition) and preparation (i.e., taking steps toward behavior change) stages, and into the action (i.e., active behavior change) and maintenance (i.e., sustained behavior change) stages. It is understood that patients do not always progress in a linear fashion through these stages, and therapists remain vigilant to signs of an impending lapse. However, the focus of the session is predicated on the patient's current stage of change. For example, a patient in the precontemplative stage would work with the therapist to examine the pros and cons of her or his behavior, and the goal of the session might be to encourage the patient to consider making a change at some point in the future. A patient in the action stage would work with the therapist to develop a plan to quit substance use successfully, and the goal of the session might be for the patient to initiate abstinence from the substance.

Benefits of motivational interviewing include the fact that it is generally brief in nature and that it can be used to encourage acceptance of other empirically supported treatments. In addition, MI can be used to reach individuals who may not otherwise seek treatment, such as homeless populations or patients being treated in the emergency department (Dunn, Droesch, Johnston, & Rivara, 2004; Peterson, Baer, Wells, Ginzler, & Garrett, 2006; Tevyaw & Monti, 2004). It also can be useful for engaging adolescents who are initially resistant to participating in treatment. MI interventions focus on personal responsibility and view the patient's participation in creating the treatment plan as vital to its success. In a study of brief interventions for substance use in adolescents, Grenard and colleagues (2007, p. 191) reported an improvement in "readiness to change drug use" in 64% of those receiving MI versus 0% in those receiving the control treatment. Individuals receiving MI also displayed reduced frequency of using club drugs, hard drugs, and alcohol, as well as reduced RAPI scores. However, use of MI alone has demonstrated mixed results in the literature. Although Walker and colleagues (2006) found their voluntary, school-based motivational enhancement therapy (MET) program to be a useful method of treatment to attract adolescents, they found no difference in end-of-treatment marijuana use between the MET group and the control 3-month delay condition. As a result, it may be more beneficial to use MI interventions to encourage participation in other established treatment programs.

Contingency Management

Contingency management (CM) is another technique that may be particularly useful when treating adolescents who have difficulty initiating abstinence from substance use (Higgins, Silverman, & Heil, 2008). The CM approach involves using an additive reward system for patients that is contingent on verification of a negative urine drug screening. Typically, monetary, voucher-based, or raffle-type rewards are provided to create an external reward that can compete with the natural dopamenergic rewards experienced following drug use. Patients generally earn increasing rewards for achieving longer periods of sobriety; lapses back to drug use result in withholding of the reward, as well as a reset of the reward value to baseline. In a randomized trial, CM was found to significantly reduce illegal drug use in 76% of their adolescent sample, compared with only 9% of their control group (Azrin, Donohue, Besalel, Kogan, & Acierno, 1994). Although shown to be effective alone, CM is usually used for adolescent patients in conjunction with one or more other treatments (e.g., CBT). For example, a 2006 study looking at smoking cessation in adolescents found CBT and CM to be significantly more effective than CBT alone, with 53% and 0% 1-month abstinence rates, respectively (Krishnan-Sarin et al., 2006).

Family Therapy

Multidimensional Family Therapy (MDFT) is a family-based, manualized, outpatient treatment for adolescent substance abuse. Though structured in nature, it was designed to be flexible to each family's needs, and can be modified for intensity of treatment, length of treatment, method of delivery, and a number of other factors (Liddle, 2004). Treatment typically lasts 16 to 24 weeks and covers four domains: the adolescent domain, the parent domain, the interactional domain (in which parents and their adolescent attend treatment together), and the extrafamilial domain (which focuses on establishing healthy relationships and alliances with those in social situations in which the adolescent is involved: Hogue, Dauber, Samoulis, & Liddle, 2006). In a 2001 randomized clinical trial, Liddle and colleagues compared MDFT to group therapy and multifamily education intervention (MEI). MDFT saw the lowest dropout rate, as well as the highest amount of participants who had clinically significant reductions in drug use (Liddle et al., 2001).

Community Reinforcement and Family Training (CRAFT) is another way of treating difficult-to-engage adolescents with SUDs by involving the family. The CRAFT method is a parent-focused intervention designed to assist parents with engaging their treatment-resistant child in an efficacious treatment. In addition, the CRAFT intervention focuses on teaching parents how to support the changes that their child makes during treatment, as well as how to improve their family life overall. Specifics of the program include: (a) helping to identify the negative consequences of substance use and possible benefits of participation in treatment; (b) using contingency management techniques to support the teen's attempts at abstinence or a reduction in substance use; (c) communication training among the family members; (d) coping skills training, including identifying competing reinforcers; (e) enhancing reinforcing activities that involve the parents; (f) planning to avoid risky situations; and (g) preparing for formal treatment entry. Waldron et al. (2007) found this method to be superior to other family-based treatments, with others resulting in a treatment engagement rate of 13% to 30% and CRAFT resulting in a treatment engagement rate ranging from 59% to 74%.

12-Step Programs

In general, 12-step programs are directed by the group members, rather than a mental health professional. Thus, unlike most formal substance-use treatment programs attended by adolescents, 12-step programs are generally not modified for adolescent participants. Rather, expectations for teen participants are the same as those for adult participants. Many teens can benefit from the identification of a sponsor as part of participation in a 12-step program. This provides them with an adult role model to whom they can turn in times of difficulty, without fear of being disciplined (as they might if turning to a parent, teacher, or coach). Successful recovery following participation in 12-step programs as the primary treatment modality is generally seen in adolescents who are motivated to remain abstinent from substances, regularly attend meetings, and to become actively involved in the program (Kelly, Myers, & Brown, 2002). However, Hsieh et al. (1998) found that Alcoholics Anonymous (AA) and Narcotics Anonymous (NA) attendance after formal substance-abuse treatment greatly improved the likelihood of drug abstinence at 6-month and 12-month follow-ups.

Residential or Partial Hospitalization Programs

In some cases, participation in outpatient therapy or mutual-support groups will not be sufficient for successful treatment. In such cases, participation in a specialized inpatient, residential, or partial hospitalization treatment program may be indicated. Such programs are typically based in a cognitive-behavioral therapy approach, but combine additional components of care. For example, introduction to the 12-step method, recreational therapy, group counseling sessions, milieu therapy, contingency management, and so on may all be included. In general, decisions regarding the treatment modality of choice should be based on a comprehensive evaluation conducted by an addiction specialist or other mental health professional with adequate expertise. The American Society of Addiction Medicine has published recommended guidelines for assigning the appropriate level of care (American Society of Addiction Medicine, 2001).

Pharmacotherapy

Recent advances in understanding the neurobiology of addiction have resulted in the development of a variety of pharmacological agents that can assist with the management of substance-use disorders. Medications have been approved for use in adult patients to assist with detoxification, help control cravings, manage withdrawal symptoms, decrease the rewarding effects of drugs, and for emergency use in the case of overdose. Each medication is typically effective for only one or two classes of drugs; however, medications are now available to manage abuse of alcohol, nicotine, opioids, cocaine, and other stimulants (Merlo, Gold, Campbell, Omli, & Gold, in press). Among adolescent substance-use-disorder patients, use of pharmacotherapy is rare. Patients are generally evaluated on a case-by-case basis, but use of medication tends to be limited to assisting with management of opioid withdrawal in patients with a significant history of opioid use or comparable situations (e.g., Marsch et al., 2005).

CBT FOR DIFFICULT-TO-TREAT CASES

In general, all patients suffering from an SUD might be considered "difficult-to-treat" cases because of the significant behavioral and neurobiological factors involved in the disorder. Indeed, among patients being treated for an SUD, the experience of at least one episode of relapse is the rule, rather than the exception. However, CBT can be particularly effective with these difficult-to-treat patients because it can be effectively modified to treat multiple specific issues that are most relevant in each case. In fact, modified CBT interventions have been developed for specific populations with comorbid problems. For example, Curry and colleagues (Curry, Wells, Lochman, Craighead, & Nagy, 2003) developed a CBT program to treat substance-abusing adolescents with comorbid depression. Similarly, a CBT program was developed for alcohol-abusing adolescents with concurrent suicidality (Esposito-Smythers et al., 2006).

For all patients, CBT sessions are structured, but they are individualized to the patient and address specific barriers to treatment success. For example, patients review people, places, and situations that might tempt them to use substances either as a method of coping or escape, as a way to fit in, or because of boredom or other factors. They also spend significant time during sessions evaluating their contribution to their problems, practicing new skills, and using cognitive restructuring to change their thinking related to substance use and its (positive and negative) consequences. Finally, training in relapse prevention is included as an integral part of treatment. This component is crucial for difficult-to-treat patients, as they often have low self-efficacy for abstinence, and are in need of skills to use following discharge from treatment to retain their treatment gains.

CASE PRESENTATION

Dominic was a 17-year-old African American male from an inner-city environment. He was an emancipated minor living with older friends, and was referred for treatment by his primary care physician. Since being diagnosed with HIV at the age of 15, Dominic had been followed by a pediatric HIV specialist at a large children's hospital. On arrival for his first session, Dominic indicated that he did not feel the appointment was necessary, as his substance use "wasn't a problem." Given his precontemplative state, motivational interviewing strategies were used to assess Dominic's current view of his drug use and elicit motivation for change. For example, after being given the chance to describe his current drug use in his own words, Dominic was asked to talk about the "good" and "not-so-good" things about his substance use. The therapist then reflected Dominic's own reasons for change (e.g., benefits of reduced substance use and potential consequences of continued use), rather than lecturing Dominic on accepted medical reasons to avoid substance use. This resulted in a visible improvement in Dominic's comfort level during the session and promoted the development of rapport.

During the session, Dominic described a history in which he began experimenting with alcohol at the age of 13 and started occasionally smoking cigarettes a few months later. He reported that he began experimenting with marijuana at the age of 15, and continued to smoke cigarettes. Dominic further reported that his drinking later escalated and that he began to engage in binge drinking episodes two to three times per week. Dominic described his substance use as an "escape" from his life, and noted that he began smoking marijuana much more frequently after learning of his HIV diagnosis. He described experiencing some depressed mood with suicidal ideation after diagnosis, but denied any clear plan or attempts. Dominic indicated that he currently smoked cigarettes very infrequently, but continued to drink heavily and smoked marijuana every day. He noted that he often became nauseous and lost his appetite (as a result of his regimen of antiretroviral medications), and that marijuana helped to ease these symptoms and allow him to eat. He also indicated that being drunk, or especially high, helped him to "get through the day" and to connect with friends. When asked about the not-so-good things about his substance use, Dominic stated that it sometimes got in the way of accomplishing tasks, that he sometimes felt bad after "a lot of partying," and that he had heard that it could make him get sicker more quickly. After further discussion, Dominic agreed to think about making some changes and to return for another session.

In the next session, Dominic indicated a willingness to talk more about his substance use. This provided an opportunity for the therapist to transition to more CBT-based intervention strategies. After asking permission to provide Dominic with some information, the therapist offered psychoeducation regarding the nature of addiction and how substance use is often triggered by irrational thoughts and environmental cues. Working together, Dominic and the therapist identified situations in which Dominic was tempted to use drugs, as well as specific triggers for use (e.g., substance-using friends, nausea, feeling depressed, etc.). The therapist empathized with the difficult decision that Dominic had when choosing whether or not to use substances, particularly given these contributing factors. The two agreed to problem-solve solutions to these situations in a future session. They also began to discuss ways to cope with cravings (e.g., engaging in a distracting activity, talking it through with a supportive person, etc.). The therapist assigned homework for the next session.

Over the next few sessions, the therapist worked with Dominic on ways to manage dysfunctional thinking related to substance use (e.g., "I can't get through this if I'm not high," "There's nothing else to do," "I'll be miserable if I'm sober"). They worked together on cognitive techniques to counteract his distorted beliefs. In addition, as previously discussed, they spent a great deal of time problem-solving solutions to seemingly unmanageable problems. For example, given Dominic's comorbid medical condition and side effects of his complicated pharmacological regimen, they discussed alternative ways to manage his nausea (and Dominic was given a homework assignment to talk to his physician about a prescription for Marinol, as well as the potential negative effects of alcohol and marijuana use on his health, considering his HIV status). Given Dominic's comorbid depressive symptoms, the therapist taught him several methods for coping with negative mood symptoms (and later in treatment, additional time was devoted to using CBT strategies to manage the residual depressive symptoms). Finally, given his particularly challenging social situation (i.e., being estranged from his family of origin and living with substance-abusing friends), the therapist and Dominic also discussed alternative activities he could engage in while friends were using substances.

Dominic expressed significant concern about his ability to refrain from using substances in the home, so motivational interviewing techniques were used to help increase his feelings of self-confidence. For example, the therapist reviewed with Dominic previous challenges that he had successfully navigated. The therapist also reflected qualities and strengths that Dominic had previously demonstrated, which could be used in this situation as well. From a CBT perspective, extra time was spent practicing substance-refusal techniques. The therapist elicited very specific descriptions of challenging situations, asked about arguments for substance use that his friends would give, and discussed potential positive and negative consequences of substance refusal for Dominic. The two practiced responses for each situation until Dominic's confidence was sufficiently strengthened. The therapist also helped Dominic to challenge dysfunctional cognitions (e.g., catastrophizing) regarding the consequences of not using substances with his friends.

Although the goal of CBT treatment for SUDs is generally abstinence, Dominic remained hesitant about setting such a stringent goal for himself. As a result, in the spirit of motivational interviewing, the therapist worked with Dominic to determine a goal that fit with his own values and interests. Dominic decided to work on cutting down his alcohol and marijuana use, to maintain his sobriety during the day and be able to awake the next day without feeling hungover. Over the course of treatment, Dominic gradually began cutting down his marijuana use and frequency of binge drinking, though he continued to smoke cigarettes and drink moderate amounts. To encourage motivation for abstinence, the therapist began to address Dominic's self-reported goal of finishing high school and getting a job. Dominic described this as a major accomplishment that he hoped to achieve one day. As a result, they reviewed job-seeking skills and discussed how substance use might interfere with his success (e.g., not passing a preemployment drug screening, making it difficult to get to school/work, etc.). Dominic also noted that he enjoyed having less financial stress since he was no longer spending as much of his monthly governmental stipend on drugs, and expressed excitement about the possibility of receiving an additional paycheck.

As noted earlier, later sessions focused on Dominic's comorbid symptoms of depression. Cognitive-behavioral techniques for managing dysfunctional cognitions and negative mood symptoms were reviewed and practiced during the session. In addition, the therapist worked with Dominic in the area of enhancing his social support networks. Dominic was able to identify an acquaintance who abstained from substance use, and they worked together on ways to develop that relationship. He was also encouraged to begin participating with a local chapter of Alcoholics Anonymous (AA). Over time, Dominic expressed interest in eventually restoring contact with his parents. He and the therapist worked together to help Dominic develop conflict-resolution skills and improve communication skills to facilitate this reunion. As he continued to cut down on his substance use and began to feel more comfortable with his new lifestyle, the focus of sessions shifted to relapse prevention. The therapist worked with Dominic to identify risky situations, plan for dealing with such situations, and create an emergency list of phone contacts to carry with him at all times. Dominic's AA sponsor remained a valuable resource in this effort. Discussion supporting Dominic's self-efficacy to maintain a drug-free lifestyle became an additional focus of the sessions; Dominic and the therapist then began to plan for termination.

CONCLUSIONS AND FUTURE DIRECTIONS

Substance-use disorders are relatively prevalent among youth, and they are associated with long-standing problems that extend into adulthood. Though "experimentation" with substances of abuse during childhood and adolescence are sometimes written off as developmentally normative behaviors, there is evidence that such early exposure can sensitize the brain's reward system and create a disease (i.e., addiction) where none would otherwise have been (Andersen & Navalta, 2004). However, recovery from addiction is possible, and individuals who obtain high-quality treatment are able to achieve sobriety and live productive lives.

In general, treatment of SUDs in pediatric patients involves participation in CBT. Sessions can be adapted to meet the specific needs of the patient, including addressing comorbid psychiatric conditions. Adjunctive therapies, such as MI and family therapy, often contribute to treatment success. However, pharmacotherapy is usually not used with children and teens who suffer from an SUD. In some cases, participation in a residential treatment or partial hospitalization program may be warranted. Participation in a 12-step fellowship (e.g., AA, NA) may help to solidify gains made during CBT and provide the patient with ongoing support.

Unfortunately, treatment for SUDs varies greatly in quantity and quality, depending on the treatment program or center. Not all individuals who suffer from SUDs benefit completely from treatment, and relapse is common, even after successful participation in treatment. As a result, more research is needed to identify factors associated with treatment success and those that are associated with long-term recovery. In addition, studies assessing the benefit of combining CBT with adjunctive treatments may provide more support for this method of treatment.

REFERENCES

Agrawal, A., Neale, M. C., Prescott, C. A., & Kendler, K. S. (2004). A twin study of early cannabis use and subsequent use and abuse/dependence of other illicit drugs. *Psychological Medicine, 34*, 1227–1237.

American Psychiatric Association. (2000). *Diagnostic and statistical manual of mental disorders* (4th ed., text rev.). Washington, DC: American Psychiatric Press.

American Society of Addiction Medicine. (2001). *ASAM PPC-2R-ASAM patient placement criteria for the treatment of substance-related disorders* (2nd ed.). Chevy Chase, MD: Author.

Andersen, S. L., & Navalta, C. P. (2004). Altering the course of neurodevelopment: A framework for understanding the enduring effects of psychotropic drugs. *International Journal of Developmental Neuroscience, 22*, 423–440.

Azrin, N. H., Donohue, B., Besalel, V.A., Kogan, E. S., & Acierno, R. (1994). Youth drug abuse treatment: A controlled outcome study. *Journal of Child & Adolescent Substance Abuse, 3*, 1–16.

Azrin, N. H., McMahon, P. T., Donohue, B., Besalel, V. A., Lapinski, K. J., Kogan, E. S., et al. (1994). Behavior therapy for drug abuse: A controlled treatment outcome study. *Behaviour Research and Therapy, 32*, 857–866.

Bjork, J. M., Knutson, B., Fong, G. W., Caggiano, D. M., Bennett, S. M., & Hommer, D. W. (2004). Incentive-elicited brain activation in adolescents: Similarities and differences from young adults. *Journal of Neuroscience, 24*, 1793–1802.

Borowsky, I. W., & Ireland, M. (2004). Predictors of future fight-related injury among adolescents. *Pediatrics, 113*, 530–536.

Boys, A., Farrell, M., Taylor, C., Marsden, J., Goodman, R., Brugha, T., et al. (2003). Psychiatric morbidity and substance use in young people aged 13-15 years: Results from the Child and Adolescent Survey of Mental Health. *British Journal of Psychiatry, 182*, 509–517.

Brook, J. S., Balka, E.B., & Whiteman, M. (1999). The risks for late adolescence of early adolescent marijuana use. *American Journal of Public Health, 89*, 1549–1554.

Chen, X., Unger, J. B., Palmer, P., Weiner, M. D., Johnson, C. A., Wong, M. M., et al. (2002). Prior cigarette smoking initiation predicting current alcohol use: Evidence for a gateway drug effect among California adolescents from eleven ethnic groups. *Addictive Behaviors, 27*, 799–817.

Coviello, D. M., Alterman, A. I., Cacciola, J. S., Rutherford, M. J., & Zanis, D. A. (2004). The role of family history in addiction severity and treatment response. *Journal of Substance Abuse Treatment, 26*, 303–313.

Curry, J. F., Wells, K.C., Lochman, J. E., Craighead, W. E., & Nagy, P. D. (2003). Cognitive-behavioral intervention for depressed, substance-abusing adolescents: Development and pilot testing. *Journal of the American Academy of Child and Adolescent Psychiatry, 42*, 656–665.

Dakof, G. A., Tejeda, M., & Liddle, H. A. (2001). Predictors of engagement in adolescent drug abuse treatment. *Journal of the American Academy of Child and Adolescent Psychiatry, 40*, 274–281.

De Genna, N. M., Cornelius, M. D., & Cook, R. L. (2007). Marijuana use and sexually transmitted infections in young women who were teenage mothers. *Women's Health Issues, 17*, 300–309.

Dunn, C., Droesch, R. M., Johnston, B. D., & Rivara, F. P. (2004). Motivational interviewing with injured adolescents in the emergency department: In-session predictors of change. *Behavioural and Cognitive Psychotherapy, 32*, 113–116.

Dupre, D., Miller, N., Gold, M., & Rospenda, K. (1995). Initiation and progression of alcohol, marijuana, and cocaine use among adolescent abusers. *American Journal on Addictions, 4*, 43–48.

Elkins, I. J., McGue, M., & Iacono, W. G. (2007). Prospective effects on attention-deficit/hyperactivity disorder, conduct disorder, and sex on adolescent substance use and abuse. *Archives of General Psychiatry, 64*, 1145–1152.

Ellgren, M., Spano, S. M., & Hurd, Y. L. (2007). Adolescent cannabis exposure alters opiate intake and opiod limbic neuronal populations in adult rats. *Neuropsychopharmacology, 32*, 607–615.

Ellickson, P. L., Tucker, J. S., Klein, D. J., & McGuigan, K. A. (2001). Prospective risk factors for alcohol misuse in late adolescence. *Journal of Studies on Alcohol, 62*, 773–782.

Esposito-Smythers, C., Spirito, A., Uth, R., & LaChance, H. (2006). Cognitive behavioral treatment for suicidal alcohol abusing adolescents: Development and pilot testing. *American Journal on Addictions, 15*, 126–130.

Ewing, J. A. (1984). Detecting alcoholism: the CAGE questionnaire. *Journal of the American Medical Association, 252*, 1905–1907.

Fergusson, D. M., Boden J. M., & Horwood, L. J. (2006). Cannabis use and other illicit drug use: Testing the cannabis gateway hypothesis. *Addiction, 101*, 556–569.

Flanagan, P., & Kokotailo, P. (1999). Adolescent pregnancy and substance use. *Clinics in Perinatology, 26*, 185–200.

Genovese, J. E., & Wallace, D. (2007). Reward sensitivity and substance abuse in middle school and high school students. *Journal of Genetic Psychology, 168*, 465–469.

Grant, B. F., & Dawson, D. A. (1997). Age at onset of alcohol use and its association with DSM-IV alcohol abuse and dependence: Results from the National Longitudinal Alcohol Epidemiologic Survey. *Journal of Substance Abuse, 9*, 103–110.

Grau, L. E., Dasqupta, N., Harvey, A. P., Irwin, K., Givens, A., Kinzly, M. L., et al. (2007). Illicit use of opiods: Is OxyContin a "gateway drug"? *American Journal on Addictions, 16*, 166–173.

Grella, C. E., Hser, Y., Joshi, V., & Rounds-Bryant, J. (2001). Drug treatment outcomes for adolescents with comorbid mental and substance use disorders. *Journal of Nervous and Mental Disease, 189*, 384–392.

Grenard, J. L., Ames, S. L., Wiers, R. W., Thush, C., Stacy, A. W., & Sussman, S. (2007). Brief intervention for substance use among at-risk adolescents: A pilot study. *Journal of Adolescent Health, 40*, 188–191.

Hertz, J. A., & Knight, J. R. (2006). Prescription drug misuse: A growing national problem. *Adolescent Medicine Clinics, 17*, 751–769.

Higgins, S. T., Silverman, K., & Heil, S. H. (2008) *Contingency management in substance abuse treatment*. New York: Guildford Press.

Hill, S. Y., Shen, S., Lowers, L., & Locke, J. (2000). Factors predicting the onset of adolescent drinking in families at high risk for developing alcoholism. *Biological Psychiatry, 48*, 265–275.

Hogue, A., Dauber, S., Samuolis, J., & Liddle, H. A. (2006). Treatment techniques and outcomes in multidimensional family therapy for adolescent behavioral problems. *Journal of Family Psychology, 20*, 535-543.

Hsieh, S., Hoffmann, N. G., & Hollister, C. D. (1998). The relationship between pre-, during-, post-treatment factors, and adolescent substance abuse behaviors. *Addictive Behaviors, 23*, 477–488.

Johnston, L. D., O'Malley, P. M., & Bachman, J. G. (1998). *National survey results on drug use from monitoring the future study, 1975-1997: Volume I. Secondary school students*. Rockville, MD: National Institute on Drug Abuse.

Johnston, L. D., O'Malley, P. M., Bachman, J. G., & Schulenberg, J. E. (2007). *Monitoring the future national survey results on drug use, 1975–2006: Volume I. Secondary school students* (NIH Publication No. 07-6205). Bethesda, MD: National Institute on Drug Abuse.

Johnston, L. D., O'Malley, P. M., Bachman, J. G., & Schulenberg, J. E. (2008). *Monitoring the Future national results on adolescent drug use: Overview of key findings, 2007* (NIH Publication No. 08-6418). Bethesda, MD: National Institute on Drug Abuse.

Julien, R. M. (1998). *A primer of drug action* (8th ed.). San Francisco: Freeman.

Kaminer, Y., & Burleson, J. A. (1999). Psychotherapies for adolescent substance abusers: 15-month follow-up of a pilot study. *American Journal on Addictions, 8*, 114–119.

Kaminer, Y., Burleson, J. A., Blitz, C., Sussman, J., & Rounsaville, B. J. (1998). Psychotherapies for adolescent substance abusers: A pilot study. *Journal of Nervous and Mental Disease, 186*, 684–690.

Kaminer, Y., Burleson, J. A., & Goldberger, R. (2002). Cognitive-behavioral coping skills and psychoeducation therapies for adolescent substance abuse. *Journal of Nervous and Mental Disease, 190*, 737–745.

Kelly, J. F., Myers, M. G., & Brown, S. A. (2002). Do adolescents affiliate with 12-step groups? A multivariate process model of effects. *Journal of Studies on Alcohol, 63*, 293–304.

Knight, J. R., Shrier, L. A., Bravender, T. D., Farrell, M., Vander Bilt, J., & Shaffer, H.J. (1999). A new brief screen for adolescent substance abuse. *Archives of Pediatrics & Adolescent Medicine, 153*, 591–596.

Krishnan-Sarin, S., Duhig, A. M., McKee, S. A., McMahon, T. J., Liss, T., McFetridge, A., et al. (2006). Contingency management for smoking cessation in adolescent smokers. *Experimental and Clinical Psychopharmacology, 14*, 306–310.

Lenney, W., & Enderby, B. (2008). "Blowing in the wind": A review of teenage smoking. *Archives of Disease in Childhood, 93*, 72–75.

Liddle, H. A. (2004). Family-based therapies for adolescent alcohol and drug use: Research contributions and future research needs. *Addiction, 99*, 76–92.

Liddle, H. A., Dakof, G. A., Parker, K., Diamond, G. S., Barrett, K., & Tejeda, M. (2001). Multidimensional family therapy for adolescent drug abuse: Results of a randomized clinical trial. *American Journal of Drug and Alcohol Abuse, 27*, 651–688.

Lubman, D. I., Allen, N. B., Rogers, N., Cementon, E., & Bonomo, Y. (2007). The impact of co-occuring mood and anxiety disorders among substance-abusing youth. *Journal of Affective Disorders, 103*, 105–112.

Lynskey, M. T., Coffey, C., Degenhardt, L., Carlin, J. B., & Patton, G. (2003). A longitudinal study of the effects of adolescent cannabis use on high school completion. *Addiction, 98*, 685–692.

Lynskey, M. T., Heath, A. C., Bucholz, K. K., Slutske, W. S., Madden, P. A., Nelson, E. C., et al. (2003). Escalation of drug use in early-onset cannabis users vs co-twin controls. *Journal of the American Medical Association, 289*, 427–433.

Marsch, L. A., Bickel, W. K., Badger, G. J., Stothart, M. E., Quesnel, K. J., Stanger, C., et al. (2005). Comparison of pharmacological treatments for opioid-dependent adolescents: A randomized controlled trial. *Archives of General Psychiatry, 62, 1157–1164.*

McGarvey, E. L., Canterbury, R. J., & Cohn, W. F. (1996). Adolescent inhalant use and school problems. *School Counselor, 43*, 181–186.

Merlo, L. J., Gold, K., Campbell, K., Omli, M., & Gold, M. S. (in press). Pharmacological therapeutics for relapse reduction in addictive diseases. In N.S. Miller & M.S. Gold, *Addictions in medicine: Principles and practice*. Indianapolis, IN: Wiley.

Merlo, L. J., Goldberger, B., Kolodner, D., Fitzgerald, K. & Gold, M. S. (2008). Fentanyl & propofol exposure in the operating room: Sensitization hypotheses and further data. *Journal of Addictive Diseases, 27*, 67–76.

Miller, W. R., & Rollnick, S. (2002). *Motivational interviewing: preparing people for change*. Guilford Press: New York.

Peterson, P. L., Baer, J. S., Wells, E. A., Ginzler, J. A., & Garrett, S.B. (2006). Short-term effects of a brief motivational intervention to reduce alcohol and drug risk among homeless adolescents. *Psychology of Addictive Behavior, 20*, 254–264.

Preston, K. L., Silverman, K., Schuster, C. R., & Cone, E. J. (1997). Comparison of self-reported drug use with quantitative and qualitative urinalysis for assessment of drug use in treatment studies. *NIDA Research Monograph, 167*, 130–145.

Prochaska, J. O., & DiClemente, C. C. (1983). Stages and processes of self-change of smoking: Toward an integrative model of change. *Journal of Consulting and Clinical Psychology, 51*, 390–395.

Rao, U., Daley, S. E., & Hammen, C. (2000). Relationship between depression and substance use disorders in adolescent women during the transition to adulthood. *Journal of the American Academy of Child and Adolescent Psychiatry, 39*, 215–222.

Renzelli, C. M., & Capretto, N. A. (2006). Less pain, more gain: Buprenorphine-naloxone and patient retention in treatment. *Journal of Addictive Diseases, 25,* 97–104.

Sege, R., Stringham, P., Short, S., & Griffith, J. (1999). Ten years after: Examination of adolescent screening questions that predict future violence-related injury. *Journal of Adolescent Health, 24,* 395–402.

Slaughter, L. (2000). Involvement of drugs in sexual assault. *Journal of Reproductive Medicine, 45,* 425–430.

Spooner, C., Mattick, R. P., & Noffs, W. (2000). A study of the patterns and correlates of substance use among adolescents applying for drug treatment. *Australian and New Zealand Journal of Public Health, 24,* 492–502.

Steinberg, L., & Monahan, K. C. (2007). Age differences in resistance to peer influence. *Developmental Psychology, 43,* 1531–1543.

Substance Abuse and Mental Health Services Administration. (2007). *Results from the 2006 National Survey on Drug Use and Health: National findings* (Office of Applied Studies, NSDUH Series H-32, DHHS Publication No. SMA 07-4293). Rockville, MD:Author.

Tapert, S. F., Aarons, G. A., Sedlar, G. R., & Brown, S. A. (2001). Adolescent substance use and sexual risk-taking behavior. *Journal of Adolescent Health, 28,* 181–189.

Tevyaw, T. O., & Monti, P. M. (2004). Motivational enhancement and other brief interventions for adolescent substance abuse: foundations, applications and evaluations. *Addiction, 99,* 63–75.

Waldron, H. B., & Kaminer, Y. (2004). On the learning curve: The emerging evidence supporting cognitive-behavioral therapies for adolescent substance abuse. *Addiction, 99,* 93–105.

Waldron, H. B., Kern-Jones, S., Turner, C. W., Peterson, T. R., & Ozechowski, T. J. (2007). Engaging resistant adolescents in drug abuse treatment. *Journal of Substance Abuse Treatement, 32,* 133–142.

Walker, D. D., Roffman, R. A., Stephens, R. S., Wakana, K., Berghuis, J., & Kim, W. (2006). Motivational enhancement therapy for adolescent marijuana users: A preliminary randomized controlled trial. *Journal of Consulting and Clinical Psychology, 74,* 628–632.

White, H. R., & Labouvie, E. W. (1989). Towards the assessment of adolescent problem drinking. *Journal of Studies on Alcohol, 50,* 30–37.

Wilson, J. J., & Levin, F. R. (2005). Attention-deficit/hyperactivity disorder and early-onset substance use disorders. *Journal of Child and Adolescent Psychopharmacology, 15,* 751–763.

Yan, A. F., Chiu, Y. W., Stoesen, C. A., & Wang, M. Q. (2007). STD-/HIV-related sexual risk behaviors and substance use among U.S. rural adolescents. *Journal of the National Medical Association, 99,* 1386–1394.

18

Treatment of Disorders Related to Feeding in Pediatric Populations

WENDY N. GRAY AND DAVID M. JANICKE

The treatment of pediatric obesity and feeding disorders poses a unique challenge to health care professionals because of the heterogeneous nature of these conditions. Pediatric obesity and feeding disorders generally occur at the extreme ends of the food-intake spectrum. They include disorders of insufficient, excessive, and/or inappropriate food intake that can be maintained by various medical and environmental factors. Left untreated, pediatric obesity or a feeding disorder can result in severe medical and psychosocial consequences. Because the current chapter's focus is on the treatment of intractable cases of obesity and feeding disorders in children, it is not meant to be a comprehensive review. For additional information on pediatric obesity, the reader is referred to Jelalian and Mehlenbeck (2003). For comprehensive information on feeding disorders, Linscheid (2006) and Iwata, Riodian, Wohl, and Finney (1982) are excellent resources.

PEDIATRIC OBESITY

Pediatric obesity is a major public health concern. As many as 33% of all children and adolescents in the United States are overweight (above

85th weight percentile for age and gender) or obese (above the 95th percentile; Ogden et al., 2006), representing a threefold rate increase over the past 20 years (G. Wang & Dietz, 2002). Relative to their peers, children from racial and ethnic minority backgrounds, lower socioeconomic backgrounds, and underserved medical settings are at greatest risk for obesity (Danielzik, Czerwinski-Mast, Langnäse, Dilba, & Müller, 2004; McMurray, Harrell, Bangdiwala, & Deng, 1999; Ogden et al., 2006).

Childhood obesity is associated with significant medical and psychosocial consequences. Obese children are at greater risk for the development of type 2 diabetes (Fagot-Campagna, 2000; Strauss, 1999), are two times more likely to develop cardiovascular disease and hypertension (Mossberg, 1989), and are at greater risk for the development of metabolic syndrome (Weiss et al., 2004). From a psychosocial standpoint, children who are obese are at greater risk for weight-based teasing, social marginalization, and physical aggression from peers (Eisenberg, Neumark-Sztainer, & Story, 2003; Puhl & Latner, 2007; Schwimmer, Burwinkle, & Varni, 2003; Strauss & Pollack, 2003). Such negative social interactions are associated with lower quality of life, more negative body image, and increased emotional problems such as depression and anxiety (French, Story, & Perry, 1995; Pesa, Syre, & Jones, 2000; Schwimmer et al., 2003; Zametkin, Zoon, Klein, & Munson, 2004). The fact that obese children are up to four times more likely to become obese adults (Freedman et al., 2005) further increases children's risk for severe health and psychosocial consequences (Ferraro, Thorpe, & Wilkinson, 2003).

The rapid increase in rates of obesity over the past 20 years suggests that environmental factors, rather than changes in our gene pool, are responsible for the current epidemic (J. Miller, Rosenbloom, & Silverstein, 2004). Reduced consumption of fruits and vegetables and increased consumption of unhealthy foods have been associated with obese status (Lin & Morrison, 2002; Raja'a & Bin Mohanna, 2005). Children are spending less time engaged in physical activity and more time engaged in sedentary activities such as watching television (Andersen, Crespo, Bartlett, Cheskin, & Pratt, 1998; Gortmaker et al., 1996). Although most children are not meeting expert recommendations of 60 minutes engaged in moderate to vigorous activity each day (U.S. Department of Human Services and U.S. Department of Agriculture, 2005; Strong et al., 2005), obese children are even less likely to reach this goal (Ball, Marshall, & McCarger, 2005; Levin, Lowry, Brown, & Dietz, 2003). Compared to their normal-weight peers, obese children walk an average of 3,000 fewer steps per day and identify more barriers to being physically active (Tudor-Locke et al., 2004; Zabinski, Saelens, Stein, Hayden-Wade, & Wilfley, 2003). Because changes in dietary intake and physical activity have coincided with increased rates of obesity in children, these two areas are often the most targeted in treatment.

Effective Treatment of Pediatric Obesity

The most effective interventions reported in the research literature use behavior-modification strategies to target dietary intake and activity levels in children (Jelalian & Saelens, 1999; C. K. Miller et al., 2001). Common targets of dietary intake include: (a) decreasing the consumption of high-fat, high-calorie foods; (b) increasing the consumption of fruits and vegetables; and (c) increasing children's awareness of appropriate food-portion size. With regard to activity levels, decreasing time spent in sedentary activities (e.g., watching television) and increasing time spent in physical activity are major treatment goals.

Although many children and families know that healthy dietary intake and physical activity are needed to treat and prevent obesity, many either do not translate this knowledge into behavior change or are unable to sustain these changes over time (Epstein, Roemmich, & Raynor, 2001). Behavioral approaches provide patients with the skills needed to successfully modify and maintain positive health behaviors through their focus on altering environmental factors promoting an unhealthy lifestyle.

Results from existing behavioral pediatric weight intervention programs are promising. Repeatedly they have shown to be superior to waitlist control and education-only interventions (Janicke et al., 2008; Wilfley et al., 2007), with some researchers reporting maintenance of treatment effects up to 5 and 10 years posttreatment (Epstein, McCurley, Wing, & Valoski, 1990; Epstein, Valoski, Wing, & McCurley, 1990). For a comprehensive review of the efficacy of pediatric weight interventions, the reader is referred to Jelalian and Saelens (1999) and Spear et al. (2007).

Pediatric weight programs use many common behavior-modification principles to facilitate weight loss (Epstein et al., 2001). Unfortunately, many health care professionals report low levels of proficiency with behavioral approaches because of limited training opportunities in counseling and behavior-management techniques (Story et al., 2002). As an aid to the practicing clinician, the behavioral principles most commonly used in the treatment of childhood obesity will be briefly reviewed. Most, if not all, of the principles to be discussed require some form of parental involvement and consistent enforcement to successfully target weight loss in children.

Self-Monitoring

Self-monitoring requires patients to record all of the food they eat and drink and their caloric content (Saelens et al., 2002). It serves as a rough measure of adherence to dietary recommendations, can track the maintenance of changes, and may help to increase children's awareness of portion size and the caloric densities of the foods they eat (Barlow & Dietz, 1998). It has been positively associated with weight change (Baker & Kirschenbaum, 1993; Epstein, McCurley, et al., 1990) and may be useful in helping individuals minimize weight gain during high-risk periods of excess food intake such as the holiday season (Boutelle, Kirschenbaum, Baker, & Mitchell, 1999). Monitoring logs may also reveal unhealthy dietary intake patterns that may be counterproductive to weight loss such as skipping breakfast or cycles of overly restrictive food consumption followed by compensatory high caloric intake (Spear et al., 2007). Activity levels such as steps taken per day and time spent watching television can also be tracked via monitoring logs (Carels et al., 2005; Robinson, 1999).

Stimulus Control

Many environmental stimuli serve as triggers for food consumption or inactivity. When desirable energy-dense foods are visible and readily available (e.g., cookies on the kitchen counter), children are more likely to consume them, even when they are not hungry (Birch, Fisher, & Davison, 2003). Similarly, children with greater access to cues for sedentary activity (e.g., a television in their bedroom) are more likely to be less active than children with limited exposure to such cues (Dietz & Gortmaker, 1985; Gortmaker et al., 1996). Behavior therapy alters environmental cues of food consumption and inactivity that promote and maintain obesity by making healthy choices readily available and unhealthy choices difficult to obtain (Saelens et al., 2002; Varni & Banis, 1985). Examples of such alterations include: limiting children's access to energy-dense foods by keeping them outside of the home, restricting eating to the dining room table only (e.g., not while watching television), keeping low-fat nutritious foods such as fruits and vegetables in easily accessible locations, enforcing limits on time spent engaged in sedentary activity, and providing children with opportunities for physical activity (e.g., sports equipment, trips to recreation facilities).

Contingency Contracting

Contingency contracting serves as an agreement among providers, parents, and children regarding behavior change (Epstein & Wing, 1984). Although specific guidelines for the design of behavioral contracting are outlined elsewhere (Epstein & Wing, 1984), briefly, contracting consists of a written agreement that clearly operationalizes treatment goals, states a timeline for goal attainment, includes a detailed plan describing each individual's (e.g., parent, child) specific responsibility for reaching those goals, and outlines the contingencies that are in place to promote behavior change (Varni & Banis, 1985). Because reinforcement is contingent on goal attainment, all elements of the contract (e.g., treatment goals, strategies for reaching goals) must be clear, detailed, and objective (e.g., eat three servings of fruits and vegetables per day) rather than vague and subjective (e.g., eat more fruits and vegetables).

Appropriate reinforcement used in a contingency contract is desirable to the child and acceptable to the parent (Schwimmer et al., 2003). Rewards may include privileges such as being allowed to stay up 1 hour past bedtime, having a friend over for a play date, or other rewards to which the child normally does not have access. The use of social reinforcement, such as praise and parental attention (e.g., special time with a parent), are encouraged as they are often more reinforcing than material rewards (Varni & Banis, 1985). Children should not be rewarded with food (Barlow & Dietz, 1998).

Successive Approximation/Gradual Shaping

Dramatic changes in diet or activity are not recommended, as they are difficult to maintain and, ultimately, are unsuccessful at maintaining weight loss (Barlow & Dietz, 1998). Gradual changes are advocated through the reinforcement of successive approximations to targeted behaviors. The gradual shaping of behaviors over time is less likely to be met with resistance and therefore more likely to be sustained (Varni & Banis, 1985). For example, when working to increase fruit and vegetable intake, setting a goal of an average of one fruit/vegetable more than what is typically consumed per day may be appropriate. When the child is able to consistently meet this amount, the goal for reinforcement can be increased to two servings per day, and so on, until the ultimate goal for daily consumption is reached. The same can be done with other dietary targets or physical activity, such as adding small increments of time spent in exercise or steps taken per day to reach treatment goals.

Parent Training

Interventions that have been the most successful at producing both short- and long-term weight loss have used parent participation as a key component of treatment (Golan & Crow, 2004). Parents play a key role in the successful application of the behavioral principles previously described. Because changing ingrained unhealthy lifestyle habits can be challenging, special attention should be given to helping parents motivate and support their child. Parents should be taught how to reinforce child efforts for change through praise, differential attention, and the use of contingent rewards. Parent modeling of healthy lifestyle choices should also be encouraged.

The behavioral techniques previously described are often used together to promote weight loss. When applying these behavioral principles, it is important to meet the patient where he or she is in terms of his or her goals, resources, and current dietary and physical activity practices. Failure to take these factors into consideration by adhering to a rigid treatment protocol ignores each patient's unique situation and increases the likelihood of treatment failure.

Factors Leading to Poor Treatment Response

Despite the relative success of behavioral interventions helping children lose weight, treating childhood obesity has been described as "one of the most frustrating and difficult diseases to treat" (Barlow & Dietz, 1998). Numerous factors can negatively affect treatment responsiveness by interfering with a patient's ability to adhere to treatment recommendations. Adherence is a key factor in promoting weight loss. Patients who are most adherent to treatment (e.g., attending treatment sessions, engaging in self-monitoring) show greater improvements in weight status and greater maintenance of treatment gains over time (Israel, Silverman, & Solotar, 1988; Wrotniak, Epstein, Paluch, & Roemmich, 2005). In general, maintaining flexibility is critical in overcoming barriers to adherence. Treatment rigidity fails to acknowledge the unique circumstances of each patient, which may interfere with treatment responsiveness. To maximize the likelihood of treatment success, it is important to meet the patient where she or he is in terms of diet and physical activity levels, as well as her or his motivation and ability to use behavioral-change strategies, so that treatment recommendations can be tailored to her or his unique needs and resources. The following paragraphs are offered as important factors to consider when trying to maximize treatment responsiveness in obese children.

Financial Stressors

Although the prevalence of obesity is highest among children from lower socioeconomic backgrounds (Danielzik et al., 2004), attrition rates from pediatric weight management are highest among this group (Zeller et al., 2004). Limited finances may interfere with a family's ability to adhere to treatment recommendations in many ways. Families from lower socioeconomic backgrounds may experience social inequalities in health care, eat a diet that is higher in fat, and have fewer opportunities for physical activity (Danielzik et al., 2004; Hanson & Chen, 2007; Y. Wang, 2001). For families that cannot afford reliable transportation or adequate child care for other children, attending treatment sessions may serve as a significant challenge. Families with limited financial resources may also struggle with the cost of healthier food options. When working with families that report financial barriers, it is important to acknowledge their concerns while focusing on strategies to make healthy foods less expensive, such as purchasing natural fruits and vegetables instead of processed, prepackaged foods, comparing prices across vendors, and finding creative alternatives (e.g., canned fruit) when preferred foods are less affordable or not in season. By having a good understanding of the resources available in the local community, clinicians may help increase patient access to healthier options.

Motivation

Lack of motivation, or readiness to change, is one of the most frequently reported barriers encountered by clinicians in the treatment of pediatric obesity (Kolagotla & Adams, 2004; Story et al., 2002). Motivation can be lacking at the family level or at the individual child level. In either case those who are unmotivated to change are unlikely to be adherent to treatment recommendations, thereby increasing the likelihood of treatment failure (Barlow & Dietz, 1998; Bender, 2002). Failed attempts at weight loss may negatively impact child self-esteem and may decrease willingness to participate in future weight-loss interventions (Barlow & Dietz, 1998).

Exploring factors affecting patient motivation is critical before attempting to intervene. Some families are not motivated because they do not view obesity as a concern. Alternatively, less than optimal participation or follow-through on treatment recommendations may be caused by other factors, but incorrectly attributed to a lack of motivation. Some families may not appear motivated because they are either overwhelmed by treatment demands, have low self-efficacy regarding their ability to change, or have incorrect assumptions about behavioral weight-loss programs. For families that do not view obesity as problematic, interventions might be limited to providing education on the health and psychosocial consequences of obesity. With families that are overwhelmed, the clinician must consider the possibility that they are asking too much from the family at this point in time. When working with an overwhelmed family, the clinician must tailor treatment to the client's abilities such that a balance is struck between what families can realistically do and what is necessary to promote meaningful change over time. Adhering to rigid treatment protocols (e.g., daily self-monitoring) ignores each client's strengths and weaknesses and increases the likelihood of treatment failure. Based on clinical judgment, changes can be made to the regimen (e.g., less frequent or comprehensive self-monitoring) without significantly compromising treatment effectiveness. Motivational interviewing (W. Miller & Rollnick, 2002) may be used when working with patients reporting low self-efficacy and a health-education approach can be used to clear up misconceptions about treatment.

Children who are motivated for change can play an active role in their treatment by setting goals and making healthy choices. However, it is not uncommon to come across families in which a parent is motivated to change but the child is not. Though it is still possible to intervene in such a situation by focusing mainly on environmental changes (Barlow & Dietz, 1998), the clinician should assess for and try to address factors affecting child motivation. Oftentimes, children are resistant to intervention because they hold unrealistic beliefs about what treatment involves and their degree of control over what happens. Addressing treatment misconceptions with both parents and children is critical. To increase child motivation, it is important that parents work to create a positive environment for change. This involves allowing children a certain degree of control over the foods they eat and the activities they choose. Rather than giving their children unlimited choices, parents should provide their children with a variety of healthy options to choose from (Barlow & Dietz, 1998). For example, a parent may give a child the choice between a granola bar and a banana for an after-school snack instead of choosing between a granola bar and potato chips. Providing children with the ability to choose gives them a sense of control and minimizes the extent to which they will be unhappy with their choice (Barlow & Dietz, 1998). Though less researched among pediatric populations, motivational interviewing strategies may also be used to help children identify the benefits of making lifestyle changes (e.g., I won't get as tired when I run; the kids at school won't make fun of me for my weight).

Occasionally, the clinician will come in contact with overly motivated families who are eager to make immediate, drastic changes to their current lifestyle to lose weight. Such dramatic lifestyle changes often cannot be sustained for the long term. Patients who are unable to reach their ambitious goals can become discouraged and give up their health behavior change efforts altogether. When working with highly motivated families, clinicians need to strike a careful balance between reinforcing motivation for change and setting patients up for success by agreeing on more reasonable and attainable goals. Explaining the rationale for taking a gradual approach while at the same time praising participants for their motivation may help increase patient acceptance for more moderate goals.

Inappropriate Expectations

Misconceptions regarding treatment responsibility should be addressed at the beginning of treatment to improve compliance. Families looking for a "quick fix" as a viable treatment option may be unaware of the degree of careful planning and self-monitoring needed to promote and sustain long-term behavior change. We have noted that many families initially come into our program and address goal achievement as something beyond their control and a result of chance rather than assume personal responsibility and treatment-goal achievement as an active, ongoing process. That is, they evaluate their progress at one point in time (e.g., at the end of the day or week), note whether they reached their goal (e.g., Oops! I didn't make it), but do not internalize the need for active planning and budgeting within each day and within each week to reach their goals. For example, if a family is planning to consume a high-fat, high-calorie dessert later on in the day, they can budget their consumption of high-calorie foods at other times in the day by planning on eating healthier foods so that they can reach their dietary goals.

Our clinical experience has also shown us that inappropriate parental expectations regarding child responsibility for treatment may also interfere with treatment recommendations. Some parents may assign all responsibility for behavior change to the child, believing that the child is fully capable of managing his or her weight on his or her own. Although such an approach may be beneficial in acknowledging autonomy when working with older adolescents, disengagement may interfere with treatment by depriving children of necessary support when attempting to make and maintain positive behavior changes. Similarly, parents may defer all aspects of treatment to the clinician, believing that he or she will be fully responsible for their child's weight loss.

Co-occurring Psychological Conditions

Psychological conditions may interfere with treatment for pediatric obesity. Symptoms of depression may make it difficult for a child to limit

tion of unhealthy foods and engage in physical activity. In children who display symptoms characteristic of an eating disorder (e.g., binging, purging), weight-loss treatment may inadvertently exacerbate disordered eating behavior and unhealthy weight-control practices by placing an emphasis on dietary intake. Special consideration should be taken when deciding to intervene with a child who has a mood disorder, eating disorder, is experiencing physical or sexual abuse, is engaging in substance use or abuse, or has significant behavior problems that may interfere with treatment. Moreover, parent psychopathology can influence lifestyle change efforts through modeling or a lack of emotional or logistical support. To optimize the likelihood of treatment success, it is recommended that children, and if possible parents, receive treatment for these conditions before participating in a behavioral weight-control program.

PEDIATRIC FEEDING DISORDERS

The term "pediatric feeding disorder" is used to describe a variety of behaviors associated with food refusal, avoidance, and selectivity. Up to 45% of healthy children, and between 64 and 80% of developmentally delayed children, present with some difficulty consuming adequate oral nutrition (Bentovim, 1970; Field, Garland, & Williams, 2003; Manikam & Perman, 2000). A feeding disorder may be limited to a specific food type (e.g., vegetables), texture (e.g., "slimy" food), or consistency (e.g., pureed vs. solid food). In other cases, a feeding disorder can be more general (e.g., all solid food refusal, only liquid intake). Although most children present with feeding difficulties (e.g., crying, food refusal) at some point in their lives, such problems are usually transitory and arise when children are introduced to a new food or are presented with new demands for feeding (e.g., learning to self-feed using utensils, consuming increasing amounts of food). Such feeding difficulties typically resolve spontaneously without need for professional care (O'Brien, Repp, Williams, & Christophersen, 1991).

When feeding problems become chronic and so severe that a child is unable to meet his or her nutritional needs for physical growth and development, then medical care should be sought (Bernard-Bonnin, 2006; O'Brien et al., 1991). Without appropriate medical intervention, chronic feeding aversions may have severe consequences on a child's physical functioning. Children with long-lasting feeding problems are at higher risk of malnutrition. This may lead to an increased risk of cognitive, motor, and behavioral impairment, compromised immune functioning, and growth retardation (Martorell, 1999). Children with feeding aversions may be diagnosed with failure to thrive because of their persistent inability to reach critical growth parameters and developmental milestones. In very severe cases, a pediatric feeding disorder may result in death (Martorell, 1999).

Feeding disorders and their treatment are best conceptualized using a biopsychosocial approach. Such an approach acknowledges the role of biological/physiological, psychological/behavioral, and social factors interacting to promote and maintain feeding problems. Biological contributors to a feeding disorder may include sensory problems, oral–motor abnormalities, anatomical abnormalities, and disorders of digestion (Fischer & Silverman, 2007; Manikam & Perman, 2000; Stevenson, 1995). Psychological/behavioral factors that may contribute to a feeding disorder include inappropriate mealtime behaviors and food phobias. Social factors may include problematic parent–child interactions and inappropriate socialization of food. Over half of all child feeding disorder cases have mixed etiologies (Budd et al., 1992). An understanding of the complex factors causing and maintaining a feeding disorder is necessary to provide effective treatment.

Effective Treatment of Pediatric Feeding Disorders

A full assessment by a multidisciplinary team comprised of a physician (e.g., gastroenterologist, endocrinologist, etc.), a dietician, a speech pathologist, an occupational therapist, and a behavioral psychologist is recommended to determine the nature and severity of the presenting problem (C. K. Miller et al., 2001). As experts in their respective fields, each member can offer unique insight as to the complex factors that may be contributing to or exacerbating a child's specific feeding difficulties (Fischer & Silverman, 2007). Once a full assessment has determined the presenting problem and identified medical and environmental contributors to the feeding difficulty, a functionally determined treatment plan can be devised.

Treatment can occur on either an inpatient or an outpatient basis. Benefits of inpatient treatment include more frequent and intense feeding sessions than would be provided in an outpatient setting and 24-hour medical supervision (Fischer & Silverman, 2007). Generally, inpatient treatment is most beneficial for children who are highly resistant to treatment, who have severe or complex medical and feeding needs, or whose parents are unable or unwilling to effectively implement behavioral strategies in an outpatient setting (Fischer & Silverman, 2007). Generally, outpatient treatment is preferred for feeding disorders, as it is more cost-effective and generalizable to other settings. The remainder of the chapter will focus exclusively on the outpatient treatment of pediatric feeding disorders.

Although each treatment plan is crafted to the specific needs of each individual child and family, general goals of treatment include: (a) increasing amount and variety of oral intake, (b) decreasing inappropriate mealtime behaviors, (c) reducing negative parent–child feeding interactions and increasing positive interactions, (d) decreasing parent stress, and (e) improving mealtime structure and routines (Fischer & Silverman, 2007).

Of the many existing treatments for feeding disorders, only behavioral approaches have met the criteria for an empirically supported treatment set forth by the 1995 Task Force on Promotion and Dissemination of Psychological Procedures and modified by the Society for Pediatric Psychology (for review, see Kerwin, 1999). Common behavioral techniques across intervention studies will now be discussed. Though the principles that will be described may be effective when used individually, clinicians often use a combination of behavioral principles based on each families' needs and resources. As such, the behavioral treatment of feeding disorders is considered to be both "an art and a science" that requires great clinical skill (Linscheid, 2006, p. 6).

Improving Mealtime Structure

An important step in promoting oral intake begins with the reintroduction of structure into the feeding environment (Fischer & Silverman, 2007). This structure applies to mealtime locations, meal timing and duration, child positioning, and other environmental factors known to affect feeding. In general, all feedings should be limited to the dining table. Ideally, children should not be allowed to eat in any other location or carry food with them throughout the home. Children should be kept seated throughout the entire meal in a chair that is appropriate for their height and physical limitations. Children who get out of their chairs should be guided back to a seated position by a parent. Meal and snack times should be scheduled and consistently implemented to help the child adjust to routines. Though food should only be offered during regularly scheduled meal and snack times, children should be allowed access to water between meals. Mealtime duration should be determined based on the child's development (Fischer & Silverman, 2007). However, it is generally recommended that meals not be allowed to go beyond 30 minutes (Bernard-Bonnin, 2006). It is typically recommended that televisions be turned off and any other form of distraction be removed during mealtimes to allow parents and children to direct their undivided attention to the purpose of feeding. However, there may be occasions when the television may be used as a reward for acceptance of presented food. A functional analysis can help determine the costs and benefits of various contingencies associated with mealtime behaviors.

Shaping of Behavior

The gradual shaping of behavior is also relevant in the treatment of pediatric feeding disorders. It is unrealistic to expect that children with long-standing feeding aversions will immediately transform into nonselective individuals with perfect mealtime behaviors. Just as in the treatment of pediatric obesity, ingrained behaviors do not change overnight! When working with families dealing with a feeding aversion, it is important to identify major problem areas and break them down into small steps so that they can gradually be resolved over time. For example, if working with a child who refuses to engage in any sort of appropriate mealtime behaviors (including sitting down for meals), reinforcing sitting at the table for short periods of time may be needed before food is introduced. As the child is able to tolerate sitting at the table, perhaps placing a food item in front of the child, but not requiring him or her to eat it, may be the next step to work on before the child is ready to progress toward feeding. Future steps may include having the child touch or mix the food with a utensil, bringing the food to the child's lips for brief moments, accepting one spoonful of food, and so on. Treatment should progress in such a stepwise approach until an adequate amount of the food is consumed. This may take several trials over time, with each successful approximation bringing the child closer to the target goal.

Contingent Reinforcement

The use of contingent reinforcement has been used effectively to promote intake in children with feeding disorders (Kerwin, 1999). The immediate reinforcement of desirable child-feeding behaviors helps to increase the likelihood of these behaviors occurring in the future. Reinforcement can include parent attention, praise, and access to preferred toys and activities that are normally not available to children. Among the most commonly used form of contingent reinforcement in the treatment of pediatric feeding disorders is differential social attention.

Differential Social Attention

Parents may engage in a variety of behaviors such as comforting, bribing, threatening, and bargaining to coax their children to eat. Often times, such behaviors are ineffective at promoting food intake in the long term, may reinforce negative mealtime behavior, and may prolong mealtime duration beyond acceptable limits (Field et al., 2003; Manikam & Perman, 2000). When applying differential attention to the feeding environment, parents are taught not to attend to such negative behaviors. For example, when the child is engaging in a nondesired behavior, parents are taught to turn away from the child and to not interact with the child until he or she engages in the desired behavior. The parent must pay close attention to the child so that positive attention can be provided as soon as the child engages in the desired behavior. Although often successful in the long run, this strategy takes patience. It is not uncommon for a child to receive long or successive periods of ignoring before a desirable behavior (e.g., sitting upright in the chair, accepting a spoonful of food) is obtained. The return of parent attention, combined with specific praise for positive child behaviors, helps to promote positive feeding behaviors.

Escape Extinction

Parents will often describe their attempts to feed their child as a "battle of will." When parents offer food, they are met with child resistance.

Oftentimes, such "battles" end with the parent giving in to the child's resistance by taking the food away or allowing the child to leave the feeding environment. In either situation, the end result is limited-to-no food intake. After repeated pairings of food refusal followed by food removal/escape, children's negative behaviors of resistance become reinforced (Hoch, Babbitt, Coe, Krell, & Hackbert, 1994). This may serve to maintain feeding problems rather than minimize them (Piazza, Patel, Gulotta, Sevin, & Layer, 2003).

The principle of escape extinction disrupts the negative reinforcement of child food refusal by altering its typical consequence, food removal/escape. With escape extinction, different procedures may be implemented to prevent children from escaping the feeding situation. Over time, children learn that resistance will no longer serve as a mechanism for escape. Typically, food is not removed from the child's presence until it is accepted. In a classic application of escape extinction to promote food intake, a spoonful of food is held at the child's lips until the child accepts the food into her or his mouth (Coe et al., 1997). Children may also be provided with verbal prompts to accept and swallow the food. The spoon is not removed from in front of the child's lips until the child opens his or her mouth and accepts the food (Linscheid, 2006). If children try to turn their heads away, the food follows so that it is always in front of them. When the child accepts the food offered, he or she is immediately rewarded with parent attention, praise, or another salient reward. The pairing of escape extinction with positive reinforcement has been found to successfully promote food intake in children with chronic food refusal (Cooper et al., 1995; Hoch et al., 1994, Piazza et al., 2003).

A more intense form of escape extinction is sometimes invoked in children who express high levels of resistance and are nonresponsive to the other behavioral techniques previously described. Sometimes called "force feeding," this form of escape extinction involves physically prompting the child to accept food offered by inserting food into the child's mouth. Though force feeding has been used in some case reports, it is generally a nonpreferred strategy because of the risk of aspiration (Linscheid, 2006). The medical risks of force feeding, combined with its negative impact on parent–child interactions, makes this a last-resort strategy that should be considered only in severe and recalcitrant cases (Linscheid, 2006). In general, positive-reinforcement strategies should be attempted before negative strategies/punishment are considered (Fischer & Silverman, 2007).

Parent Training

Parent training is essential in promoting treatment success (Fischer & Silverman, 2007). Parents are responsible for children's nutritional intake and thus are in an excellent position to serve as the primary interventionist in a behavioral feeding program. Parent training has been found to be effective in improving child dietary intake and increasing positive parent–child mealtime interactions (Turner, Sanders, & Wall, 1994). It also helps to promote the generalization of skills outside of the treatment setting (Babbitt et al., 1994).

Therapist modeling of behavioral principles can help parents understand how these principles can be applied to their child. As parents gain an understanding of the skills being taught, they are given the opportunity to practice them with their child while being coached by the therapist. Live coaching can help to reinforce parent skill acquisition by praising correct and shaping inaccurate applications of the skills being taught. The use of modeling and coaching in parent training increases the likelihood that parents will correctly understand and apply the technique learned in settings outside of treatment sessions (Fischer & Silverman, 2007).

In addition to general behavior-management principles, parents should also be provided with information on nutrition, normal child development, and general feeding skills. These areas have been linked to feeding problems in children, and education in these areas may help improve child oral intake (Manikam & Perman, 2000).

Factors Leading to Poor Treatment Response

Lack of Appetite

Hunger provides children with intrinsic motivation to consume food (Linscheid, 2006). Without such motivation, children may express no interest in addressing a problem (e.g., calorie deprivation) that is not salient for them. When working with a child who does not appear to have an appetite, it is important to identify underlying causes. Does the child not have an appetite because of delayed gastric emptying syndrome? Is the child not hungry because all of his or her nutritional needs are being met with gastrostomy tube feedings or high-calorie liquids (e.g., nutritional supplements) or because the child is allowed to graze on foods throughout the day? Depending on the cause of the lack of appetite, interventionists may take different approaches to address the child's hunger. In children fed by gastrostomy tube, families may work under the supervision of a nutritionist to promote hunger by decreasing the amount of food delivered by tube feedings (Fischer & Silverman, 2007). Other families may cut back on the amount of calories children are provided through nutritional supplements. A moderate way to manipulate hunger is to limit child access to food only to scheduled meal and snack times. Sometimes it is necessary for children to skip a meal before they begin to experience hunger (Fischer & Silverman, 2007). In severe cases in which children do not respond to the appetite-manipulation strategies jst described, physicians may prescribe an appetite stimulant.

Parent Anxiety/Unwillingness to Adhere to Treatment

It is important to gauge the parent's ability and willingness to effectively implement treatment. Many parents are uncomfortable placing their child in temporary distress to obtain a future positive outcome (Linscheid, 2006). Because parents of children who have feeding disorders are usually very concerned about their child's limited intake, some may not agree that withholding or limiting access to food will promote food intake. Parents may also be concerned about compromising their child's health by restricting food and may doubt their ability to do so (Linscheid, 2006).

Parents who are unable or unwilling to follow through with treatment recommendations may inconsistently implement behavioral techniques. Indeed, lack of parent follow-through is among the most common causes of treatment failure (Linscheid, 2006). To promote adherence to treatment recommendations, it is important to explore and identify parental factors that may interfere with outpatient treatment. Parents may display high levels of distress or anxiety associated with their child's food intake and medical state. These parents tend to struggle with limiting access to food and implementing differential social attention. Brief discussion of their concerns in an accepting manner (with a focus on normalizing) and then hands-on guidance in implementing the behavioral strategies are often helpful in overcoming this anxiety. In parents expressing high levels of anxiety, individual psychotherapy may be needed, as feeding problems in children may be linked with parent symptoms of anxiety (Fischer & Silverman, 2007).

With both parents participating in outpatient feeding therapy, brief phone calls in-between scheduled sessions are recommended, as they can be very helpful and reassuring to parents. In addition to providing support, phone calls also give parents the opportunity to consult with the therapist regarding any problems that may have arisen since the last session.

Medical and Developmental Factors

Child physical development and medical state may negatively affect treatment responsiveness. Behavioral feeding programs operate on the assumption that the child has mastered basic feeding skills (e.g., physical ability to chew and swallow food). Some children may not have the physical capability to chew, swallow, and/or accommodate food as a result of structural anomalies (Field et al., 2003; Manikam & Perman, 2000). Other children may have the correct anatomical structure for feeding but may not have developed the skills needed to feed because of sensory issues or lack of experience with oral intake (Fischer & Silverman, 2007). Many medical conditions may also interfere with the effectiveness of a behavioral feeding program. Children with gastroenterological disorders such as gastroesophageal reflux, dysphagia, or constipation may experience discomfort and pain associated with feeding or the elimination of food (Fischer & Silverman, 2007).

Though both child physical development and medical conditions can pose as significant challenges for behavioral feeding programs, treatment is possible when a multidisciplinary assessment approach is used to identify and target underlying factors. Children with structural deficiencies may need surgical intervention to correct problems with chewing and swallowing. Those with sensory problems and/or feeding skill deficits may need treatment from an occupational therapist before behavioral treatment can begin. A physician can prescribe medications to aid in digestion; dieticians can recommend calorie-dense, low-volume foods for children who struggle with the digestion/absorption of nutrients (Manikam & Perman, 2000).

CASE PRESENTATIONS

Pediatric obesity and feeding disorders are heterogeneous and can be maintained by numerous biological, psychological, and social factors. Rigidly adhering to a single treatment protocol increases the likelihood of treatment failure. The behavioral techniques described throughout this chapter must be applied in a flexible, consistent, and skillful manner to be effective. When treatment response is less than desired, the clinician must be able to take a step back and reexamine his or her treatment approach and goals. The following case examples illustrate the critical role of maintaining flexibility when facing adversity and attempting to overcome treatment obstacles.

Case Example #1: Pediatric Obesity

Patient is a 12-year-old obese male (BMI above the 95th percentile) and his mother self-referred to a community-based weight-loss program. No medical or psychological contraindications for treatment were reported. Initial assessment data revealed that patient consumed many high-fat, high-calorie foods (e.g., pizza, soda) on a regular basis and had limited physical activity (4,000 steps per day as measured by a pedometer).

The Traffic Light System (Epstein, Wing, & Valoski, 1985) was used to classify foods according to their nutrient and caloric content. Both the patient and his mother appeared highly motivated and eager to set aggressive goals (e.g., five fewer "red" foods and 1,500 more steps per day). After discussing the rationale for gradual change over time, the patient and his mother agreed to more moderate goals of eating one less "red" food per day and increasing daily steps by 1,000. Full-monitoring logs, in which participants record the type and amount of food and drinks consumed (including caloric content), were used to track progress.

The family did not attend their next session and were contacted by telephone. The family admitted skipping the session because they were embarrassed. They had been unable to meet their goals, had not completed the monitoring logs, and felt that they had "failed." The patient's mother reported that her son had become resistant to her attempts to regulate his food intake and was sneaking food. She expressed high levels of frustration with her son, stating, "It's like he doesn't care that he's obese." After empathizing with the patient's mother, normalizing her experiences over the past week (e.g., "A lot of families struggle when making changes"), and instilling hope for positive change, the family agreed to attend the next session.

At the next session, reasons for the patient's apparent resistance were explored. The patient's resistance appeared to be in reaction to his mother's high expectations for change in his dietary intake and weight loss. Whenever the patient made a less than optimal food choice, his mother would respond in a critical manner (e.g., "You're never going to lose weight if you keep eating things like that"). Such negative interactions served to decrease the patient's willingness to comply with treatment. His mother, who reported feeling overwhelmed by her son's resistance and his total deferment of treatment-related tasks (e.g., filling out monitoring logs) to her, expressed the desire for her son to assume more responsibility for his treatment.

Several factors increasing the likelihood for treatment failure were identified and addressed by the interventionists. Because the patient's resistance appeared to be, in part, related to his mother's high expectations and punitive style of interaction surrounding his food choices, the therapist focused on helping the patient's mother minimize resistance by creating a positive environment for change. This included avoiding negative and critical comments, allowing her son to choose among several healthy options, keeping unhealthy foods outside of the home, and using praise to reinforce healthy choices and child efforts to change.

Treatment goals were also reevaluated. Rigid application of the treatment protocol had failed to acknowledge how the family's needs and resource limitations might affect their ability to adhere to treatment recommendations. The family's report of being overwhelmed, along with their inability to reach any of the goals set in the previous session, suggested that the clinicians were asking too much of the family. Instead of setting numerous goals, the family agreed to focus on only one goal for the week (eating one less "red" food per day). Contingency contracting was used to clearly specify each individual's responsibility for reaching the goal, strategies for reaching the goal (e.g., having juice instead of soda with dinner), and rewards/consequences for goal attainment. The patient also agreed to assume more responsibility for recording his food intake. Abbreviated monitoring logs, which only tracked red food and fruit/vegetable consumption, were introduced to minimize the patient's burden of recording his food intake.

Over time, the implementation of these changes led to treatment success. As the patient was able to meet his "red" food goal successfully on a regular basis, goals for physical activity and fruit/vegetable intake were added. Continued coaching and problem solving by the therapist helped to address treatment challenges. Through this individualized approach and flexible application of treatment, child resistance decreased and responsibility for treatment increased. Parent–child interactions became more positive and by the end of treatment the patient had made a number of positive lifestyle changes. Relative to the beginning of treatment, the child experienced a 5% decrease in his overweight percentage by the end of the intervention. Assessment of the child's weight status 6 months posttreatment found continued improvement in weight status (15% decrease in percentage overweight from pretreatment).

Case Example #2: Feeding Aversion

Patient was a 3-year-old female with a history of congenital heart disease, developmental delay, and a long-standing history of feeding aversion or limited oral intake. A full multidisciplinary assessment ruled out any current underlying structural anomalies that precluded oral intake. Feedings were predominantly delivered by gastrostomy tube (g-tube). Oral intake was selective (only pureed sweet potatoes) and minimal (700 calories). Her oral caloric intake was well below the recommended value (1,400 calories) set forth by her nutritionist. Caloric intake was supplemented via three cans of Pediasure daily through the g-tube. Mealtime duration was excessive (1 1/2 hours). Attempts at oral feedings were sometimes followed by patient gagging and vomiting. In-vivo observation of a feeding session, in combination with other assessment information, suggested a behaviorally maintained feeding problem. When presented with a spoonful of food, the patient would engage in a variety of refusal behaviors such as crying, turning her head away, gagging, pinching her mother, and attempting to leave her chair. The patient's mother, who was distraught about her daughter's weight and overall health status, displayed high levels of distress throughout the session and used numerous unsuccessful strategies (threatening, pleading, and bribing) to coax her daughter into eating. After 15 minutes of failed attempts, the mother became tearful and allowed the child to leave the table to play with her toys.

Treatment began by increasing structure in the feeding environment and using differential attention to shape appropriate mealtime behaviors. Initially, the patient was reinforced for sitting at the table for brief periods. Over time, receipt of reinforcement was made contingent on successive approximations to the target goal of sitting at the table for longer periods and with food present. The patient's mother struggled with implementing differential attention in response to patient escalation of negative behaviors. In-vivo coaching was used to support the mother, and the patient's grandmother was included in treatment to provide at-home support for the mother. Brief phone calls in-between sessions were also conducted. Though differential attention was successful at increasing the child's willingness to sit at the table for extended periods of time and decreasing negative behaviors, oral intake did not improve. The patient expressed no apparent hunger or interest in consuming food. Review of dietary records suggested that gastrostomy tube feedings kept the patient in a perpetual state of fullness. When the clinician, after consultation with the medical team, suggested reducing the amount of food delivered via gastrostomy tube to promote hunger, the patient's mother stated that she was not willing to compromise her child's health and weight by withholding food. Though the rationale for appetite manipulation was provided, the patient's mother continued to express high levels of concern regarding its safety. Consultation with the child's pediatrician and nutritionist provided the patient's mother with an individualized "safety" plan that outlined the many steps team members would take to closely monitor the child's health and weight during appetite manipulation, including weekly weight checks and careful monitoring of the patient's caloric consumption. Given the mother's high level of anxiety about food restriction, the plan first focused on the timing of meals rather than reducing the amount of food delivered. Morning tube feedings were delayed until after scheduled feeding sessions to maximize the likelihood of child hunger during the session. Child access to preferred toys was only granted during the feeding session and was contingent on acceptance of food. Outpatient therapy feeding sessions were increased to two times per week to provide the parent with additional guidance and support during this challenging time. These alterations to the treatment plan were successful in promoting food intake. As the child's weight slowly began to increase and the parent developed mastery and confidence in the application of behavioral techniques taught, foods of different tastes and textures were introduced. Treatment sessions were gradually faded out. After 3 months of participating in our behavioral feeding program, the child had exhibited significant increase in the type and amount of foods consumed. Over time, her daily oral caloric intake increased from 700 to 1,200 calories per day. Her mother felt comfortable in applying the behavior strategies learned to promote continued improvement in caloric intake and address typical feeding challenges as they arose.

CONCLUSIONS AND FUTURE DIRECTIONS

Though the efficacy of behavioral approaches in the treatment of pediatric obesity and feeding disorders has been well documented (Jelalian & Saelens, 1999; Kerwin, 1999; Spear et al., 2007), less attention has been dedicated to the treatment of refractory cases. Factors negatively affecting treatment responsiveness, and how to address them, have been largely ignored in the research literature. To our knowledge, this is the first chapter solely dedicated to the treatment of refractory cases of obesity and feeding disorders in children. The current chapter provides clinicians with guidance on the treatment of these cases by discussing the most commonly encountered factors that lead to poor treatment response. The treatment of pediatric obesity and feeding disorders is a slow and arduous process for both the clinician and the patient. When dealing with a challenging case, clinicians should keep in mind the importance of flexibility in overcoming obstacles. The initial treatment plan is often only a starting point. Treatment approaches and goals often need to be modified to reflect the unique needs and circumstances of each patient. An understanding of the commonly encountered barriers to treatment can greatly increase a clinician's ability to adapt interventions to the presenting needs of each family.

In addition to the focus on the treatment of refractory cases, increasing emphasis is now being placed on the dissemination of interventions outside of research settings and into the community. To accomplish this, researchers are now focusing on the delivery of behavioral treatments in diverse populations (e.g., rural vs. urban, high vs. low socioeconomic status, ethnic minorities, comorbid conditions), and settings (e.g., schools, county health departments). To maximize generalizability and treatment outcome in pediatric obesity and feeding disorders, it is imperative that clinical research identify the mechanisms of change underlying behavioral treatment. This may allow for more cost-effective and less burdensome interventions. Unfortunately, mechanisms of change have been understudied in pediatric obesity and feeding disorders. Dismantling designs are needed to identify essential treatment components, with an emphasis on addressing issues related to the typical challenges noted in this chapter. Once critical mechanisms of change have been identified, treatments can be streamlined and made more acceptable for community settings.

REFERENCES

Andersen, R. E., Crespo, C. J., Bartlett, S. J., Cheskin, L. J., & Pratt, M. (1998). Relationship of physical activity and television watching with body weight and level of fatness among children. *Journal of the American Medical Association, 279,* 938–942.

Babbitt, R. L., Hoch, T. A., Coe, D. A., Cataldo, M. F., Kelly, K. J., Stackhouse, C., et al. (1994). Behavioral assessment and treatment of pediatric feeding disorders. *Journal of Developmental and Behavioral Pediatrics, 15,* 278–291.

Baker, R. C., & Kirschenbaum, D. S. (1993). Self-monitoring may be necessary for successful weight control. *Behavior Therapy, 24,* 377–394.

Ball, G. D., Marshall, J. D., & McCarger, L. J. (2005). Physical activity, aerobic fitness, self-perception, and dietary intake in at risk of overweight and normal weight children. *Canadian Journal of Dietetic Practice & Research, 66,* 162–169.

Barlow, S. E., & Dietz, W. H. (1998). Overweight evaluation and treatment: Expert committee recommendations. *Pediatrics, 102,* e29.

Benard-Bonnin, A. (2006). Feeding problems of infants and toddlers. *Canadian Family Physician, 52,* 1247–1251.

Bender, B. G. (2002). Overcoming barriers to nonadherence in asthma treatment. *Journal of Allergy and Clinical Immunology, 109,*554–559.

Bentovim, A. (1970). The clinical approach to feeding disorders of childhood. *Journal of Psychosomatic Research, 14,* 267–276.

Birch, L. L., Fisher, J. O., & Davison, K. K. (2003). Learning to overeat: Maternal use of restrictive feeding practices promotes girls' eating in the absence of hunger. *American Journal of Clinical Nutrition, 78,* 215–220.

Boutelle, K. N., Kirschenbaum, D. S., Baker, R. C., & Mitchell, M. E. (1999). How can obese weight controllers minimize weight gain during the high risk holiday season? By self-monitoring very consistently. *Health Psychology, 18,* 364–368.

Budd, K. S., McGraw, T. E., Farbisz, R., Murphy, T. B., Hawkins, D., Heilman, N., et al. (1992). Psychosocial concomitants of children's feeding disorders. *Journal of Pediatric Psychology, 17,* 81–94.

Carels, R. A., Darby, L. A., Rydin, S., Douglass, O. M., Cacciapaglia, H. M., & O'Brien, W. H. (2005). The relationship between self-monitoring, outcome expectancies, difficulties with eating and exercise, and physical activity and weight loss treatment outcomes. *Annals of Behavioral Medicine, 30,* 182–190.

Coe, D. A., Babbitt, R. L., Williams, K. E., Hajimihalis, C., Snyder, A. M., Ballard, C., et al. (1997). Use of extinction and reinforcement to increase food consumption and reduce expulsion. *Journal of Applied Behavior Analysis, 30,* 581-583.

Cooper, L. J., Wacker, D. P., McComas, J. J., Brown, K., Peck, S. M., Richman, D., et al. (1995). Use of component analysis to identify active variables in treatment packages for children with feeding disorders. *Journal of Applied Behavior Analysis, 28,* 139–153.

Danielzik, S., Czerwinski-Mast, M., Langnäse, K., Dilba, B., & Müller, M.J. (2004). Parental overweight, socioeconomic status and high birth weight are the major determinants of overweight and obesity in 5-7 y-old children: Baseline data of the Kiel Obesity Prevention Study (KOPS). *International Journal of Obesity, 28,* 1494–1502.

Dietz, W. H., & Gortmaker, S. L. (1985). Do we fatten our children at the television set? Overweight and television viewing in children and adolescents. *Pediatrics, 75,* 807–812.

Eisenberg, M. E., Neumark-Sztainer, D., & Story, M. (2003). Associations of weight-based teasing and emotional well-being among adolescents. *Archives of Pediatrics & Adolescent Medicine, 157,* 733–738.

Epstein, L. H., McCurley, J., Wing, R. R., & Valoski, A. (1990a). Five-year follow-up of family-based behavioral treatments for childhood overweight. *Journal of Consulting and Clinical Psychology, 58,* 661–664.

Epstein, L. H., Roemmich, J. N., & Raynor, H. A. (2001). Behavioral therapy in the treatment of pediatric overweight. *Pediatric Clinics of North America, 48,* 981–993.

Epstein, L. H., Valoski, A., Wing, R. R., & McCurley, J. (1990b). Ten-year follow-up of behavioral, family-based treatment for obese children. *Journal of the American Medical Association, 264,* 2519–2523.

Epstein, L. H., & Wing, R. R. (1984). Behavioral contacting: Health behaviors. In C. Franks (Ed.), *New developments in behavioral therapy from research to clinical application* (pp. 409–449). New York: Haworth Press.

Epstein L. H., Wing R. R., & Valoski A. (1985). Childhood obesity. *Pediatrics Clinics of North America, 32,* 363–379.

Fagot-Campagna, A. (2000). Emergence of type 2 diabetes mellitus in children: Epidemiological evidence. *Journal of Pediatric Endocrinology and Metabolic Disorders, 13,* 1395–1402.

Ferraro, K. F., Thorpe, R. J., & Wilkinson, J. A. (2003). The life course of severe overweight: Does childhood overweight matter? *Journals of Gerontology, 58,* S110–119.

Field, D., Garland, M., & Williams, K. (2003). Correlates of specific childhood feeding problems. *Journal of Paediatrics & Child Health, 39,* 299–304.

Fischer, E., & Silverman, A. (2007). Behavioral conceptualization, assessment, and treatment of pediatric feeding disorders. *Seminars in Speech and Language, 28,* 223–231.

Freedman, D. S., Khan, L. K., Serdula, M. K., Dietz, W. H., Srinivasan, S. R., & Berenson, G. S. (2005). The relation of childhood BMI to adult adiposity: The Bogalusa Heart Study. *Pediatrics, 115*, 22–27.

French, S., Story, M., & Perry, C. (1995). Self-esteem and overweight in children and adolescents: A literature review. *Obesity Research, 3*, 479–490.

Golan, M., & Crow, S. (2004). Parents are key players in the prevention and treatment of weight-related problems. *Nutrition Reviews, 62*, 39–50.

Gortmaker, S. L., Must, A., Sobol, A. M., Peterson, K., Colditz, G. A., & Dietz, W. H. (1996). Television viewing as a cause of increasing overweight among children in the United States, 1986-1990. *Archives of Pediatrics & Adolescent Medicine, 150*, 356–362.

Hanson, M. D., & Chen, E. (2007). Socioeconomic status, race, and body mass index: The mediating role of physical activity and sedentary behaviors during adolescence. *Journal of Pediatric Psychology, 32*, 250–259.

Hoch, T. A., Babbitt, R. L., Coe, D. A., Krell, D. M., & Hackbert, L. (1994). Contingency contracting: Combining positive reinforcement and escape extinction procedures to treat persistent food refusal. *Behavior Modification, 18*, 106–128.

Israel, A. C., Silverman, W. K., & Solotar, L. C. (1988). The relationship between adherence and weight loss in a behavioral treatment program for overweight children. *Behavior Therapy, 19*, 25–33.

Iwata, B. A., Riordian, M. M., Wohl, M. K., & Finney, J. W. (1982). Pediatric feeding disorders: Behavioral analysis and treatment. In P. J. Accardo (Ed.), *Failure to thrive in infancy and early childhood: A multidisciplinary approach* (pp. 163–182). Chicago: University of Chicago Press.

Janicke, D. M., Sallinen, B. J., Perri, M. G., Lutes, L. D., Silverstein, J. H., Huerta, M., et al. (2008). Comparison of parent-only versus family-based interventions for overweight children in underserved rural settings: Outcomes from Project STORY. *Archives of Pediatrics and Adolescent Medicine, 162*, 1119–1125.

Jelalian, E., & Mehlenbeck, R. (2003). Pediatric obesity. In M.C. Roberts, (Ed.), *Handbook of pediatric psychology* (3rd ed., pp. 529–543). New York: Guilford Press.

Jelalian, E., & Saelens, B. (1999). Empirically supported treatments in pediatric psychology: Pediatric overweight. *Journal of Pediatric Psychology, 24*, 223–248.

Kerwin, M. E. (1999). Empirically supported treatments in pediatric psychology: Severe feeding problems. *Journal of Pediatric Psychology, 24*, 193–214.

Kolagotla, L., & Adams, W. (2004). Ambulatory management of childhood overweight. *Obesity Research, 12*, 275–283.

Levin, S., Lowry, R., Brown, D. R., & Dietz, W. H. (2003). Physical activity and body mass index among US adolescents: Youth Risk Behavior Survey, 1999. *Archives of Pediatrics & Adolescent Medicine, 157*, 816–820.

Lin, B. H., & Morrison, R. M. (2002). Higher fruit consumption linked with lower body mass index. *Food Review, 25*, 28–32.

Linscheid, T. R. (2006). Behavioral treatment for pediatric feeding disorders. *Behavior Modification, 30*, 6–23.

Manikam, R., & Perman, J.A. (2000). Pediatric feeding disorders. *Journal of Clinical Gastroenterology, 30*, 34–46.

Martorell, R. (1999). The nature of child malnutrition and its long-term implications. *Food Nutrition Bulletin, 20*, 288–292.

McMurray, R. G., Harrell, J. S., Bangdiwala, S. I., & Deng, S. (1999). Cardiovascular disease risk factors and obesity of rural and urban elementary school children. *Journal of Rural Health, 15,* 365–374.

Miller, C. K., Burklow, K. A., Santoro, K., Kirby, E., Mason, D., & Rudolph, C. D. (2001). An interdisciplinary team approach to the management of pediatric feeding and swallowing disorders. *Children's Health Care, 30,* 201–218.

Miller, J., Rosenbloom, A., & Silverstein, J. (2004). Childhood overweight. *Journal of Clinical Endocrinology & Metabolism, 89,* 4211–4218.

Miller, W., & Rollnick, S. (2002). *Motivational interviewing: Preparing people for change* (2nd ed.). New York: Guildford Press.

Mossberg, H. O. (1989). 40-year follow-up of overweight children. *Lancet, 2,* 491–493.

O'Brien, S., Repp, A. C., Williams, G. E., & Christophersen, E. R. (1991). Pediatric feeding disorders. *Behavior Modification, 15,* 394–418.

Ogden, C. L., Carroll, M. D., Curtin, L. R., McDowell, M. A., Tabak, C. J., & Flegal, K. M. (2006). Prevalence of overweight and obesity in the United States, 1999–2004. *Journal of the American Medical Association, 295,* 1549–1555.

Pesa, J. A., Syre, T. S., & Jones, E. (2000). Psychosocial differences associated with body weight among female adolescents: The importance of body image. *Journal of Adolescent Health, 26,* 330–337.

Piazza, C. C., Patel, M. R., Gulotta, C. S., Sevin, B. M., & Layer, S. A. (2003). On the relative contributions of positive reinforcement and escape extinction in the treatment of food refusal. *Journal of Applied Behavior Analysis, 36,* 309–324.

Puhl, R. M., & Latner, J. D. (2007). Stigma, obesity, and the health of the nation's children. *Psychological Bulletin, 133,* 557–580.

Raja'a, Y. A., & Bin Mohanna, M. A. (2005). Overweight and obesity among schoolchildren in Sana'a City, Yemen. *Annals of Nutrition and Metabolism, 49,* 342–345.

Robinson, T. N. (1999). Reducing children's television viewing to prevent obesity: A randomized controlled trial. *Journal of the American Medical Association, 282,* 1561–1567.

Saelens, B. E., Sallis, J. F., Wilfley, D. E., Patrick, K., Cella, J. A., & Buchta, R. (2002). Behavioral weight control for overweight adolescents initiated in primary care. *Obesity Research, 10,* 22–32.

Schwimmer, J. B., Burwinkle, T. M., & Varni, J. W. (2003). Health-related quality of life of severely obese children and adolescents. *Journal of the American Medical Association, 289,* 1813–1819.

Spear, B. A., Barlow, S. E., Ervin, C., Ludwig, D. S., Saelens, B. E., Schetzina, K. E., et al. (2007). Recommendations for treatment of child and adolescent overweight and obesity. *Pediatrics, 120,* 254–288.

Stevenson, R. D. (1995). Feeding and nutrition in children with developmental disabilities. *Pediatric Annals, 24,* 255–260.

Story, M. T., Neumark-Stzainer, D. R., Sherwood, N. E., Holt, K., Sofka, D., Trowbridge, F. L., et al. (2002). Management of child and adolescent obesity: Attitudes, barriers, skills, and training needs among health care professionals. *Pediatrics, 110,* 210–214.

Strauss, R. S. (1999). Childhood obesity. *Current Problems in Pediatrics, 29,* 5–29.

Strauss, R. S., & Pollack, H. A. (2003). Social marginalization of overweight children. *Archives Pediatrics and Adolescent Medicine, 157,* 746–752.

Strong, W. B., Malina, R. M., Blimkie, C. J. R., Daniels, S. R., Dishman, R. K., Gutin, B., et al. (2005). Evidence-based physical activity for school-age youth. *Journal of Pediatrics, 146*, 732–737.

Tudor-Locke, C., Pangrazi, R. P., Corbin, C. B., Rutherford, W. J., Vincent, S. D., Raustorp, A., et al. (2004). BMI-referenced standards for recommended pedometer-determined steps/day in children. *Preventive Medicine, 38,* 857–864.

Turner, K. M., Sanders, M. R., & Wall, C. R. (1994). Behavioural training versus dietary education in the treatment of children with persistent feeding difficulties. *Behaviour Change, 11,* 242–258.

U.S. Department of Human Services and U.S. Department of Agriculture. (2005). *Dietary guidelines for Americans 2005*. Accessed January 31, 2008, from http://www.healthierus.gov/dietaryguidelines

Varni, J. W., & Banis, H. T. (1985). Behavior therapy techniques applied to eating, exercise, and diet modification in childhood obesity. *Journal of Developmental & Behavioral Pediatrics, 6,* 367–372.

Wang, G., & Dietz, W. H. (2002). Economic burden of obesity in youths aged 6 to 17 years: 1979–1999. *Pediatrics, 109,* e81.

Wang, Y. (2001). Cross-national comparison of childhood obesity: The epidemic and the relationship between obesity and socioeconomic status. *International Journal of Epidemiology, 30,* 1129–1136.

Weiss, R., Dziura, J., Burgert, T. S., Tamborlane, W. V., Taksali, S. E., Yeckel, C. W., et al. (2004). Obesity and the metabolic syndrome in children and adolescents. *New England Journal of Medicine, 350,* 2362–2374.

Wilfley, D. E., Tibbs, T. L., Van Buren, D. J., Reach, K. P., Walker, M. S., & Epstein, L. H. (2007). Lifestyle interventions in the treatment of childhood overweight: A meta-analytic review of randomized controlled trials. *Health Psychology, 26,* 521–532.

Wrotniak, B. H., Epstein, L. H., Paluch, R. A., & Roemmich, J. N. (2005). The relationship between parent and child self-reported adherence and weight loss. *Obesity Research, 13,* 1089–1096.

Zabinski, M. F., Saelens, B. E., Stein, R. I., Hayden-Wade, H. A., & Wilfley, D. E. (2003). Overweight children's barriers to and support for physical activity. *Obesity Research, 11,* 238–246.

Zametkin, A. J., Zoon, C. K., Klein, H. W., & Munson, S. (2004). Psychiatric aspects of child and adolescent obesity: A review of the past 10 years. *Journal of American Child and Adolescent Psychiatry, 2,* 625–641.

Zeller, M., Kirk, S., Claytor, R., Khoury, P., Grieme, J., Santangelo, M., & Daniels, S. (2004). Predictors of attrition from a pediatric weight management program. *Journal of Pediatrics, 144,* 466–470.

19

Tourette's Syndrome

CHRISTINE A. CONELEA, MICHAEL R. WALTHER, AND
DOUGLAS W. WOODS

Tourette's syndrome (TS) is a neurological disorder characterized by the presence of tics, which are "sudden, rapid, recurrent, nonrhythmic, stereotyped motor movements or vocalizations" (*Diagnostic and Statistical Manual of Mental Disorders Fourth Edition, Text Revision [DSM-IV-TR]* American Psychiatric Association, 2000). Additional *DSM-IV-TR* criteria include: the presence of multiple motor tics and one or more vocal tics that occur many times a day or intermittently for a period of longer than 1 year, with no tic-free periods lasting more than 3 consecutive months. In addition, the onset of tics must occur prior to 18 years of age, and the tics cannot be the result of the physiological effects of a substance or resulting from a medical condition.

The *DSM-IV-TR* outlines other tic disorders, such as chronic tic disorder, transient tic disorder, and tic disorder not otherwise specified, which vary from TS and from each other in terms of the presence of only motor or vocal tics and the length of time the tics have been present.

PREVALENCE AND DEMOGRAPHICS

TS was once thought to be a relatively rare disorder, but recent prevalence estimates suggest it is more common than previously thought.

Robertson (2003) estimated that TS occurs in about 1% of 5- to 16-year-old students in mainstream schools. Prevalence rates of 0.6% have been found in Swedish child samples (Khalifa & von Knorring, 2003) and 0.5% in Taiwanese child samples (Wang & Kuo, 2003). Prevalence rates of chronic tic disorder and transient tic disorder are believed to be higher (Findley, 2001). For example, Kurlan et al. (2002) reported that 21% of children in a school community sample had tics. TS is more common in children than in adults, and TS occurs more frequently in males than females, with a gender ratio of about 3:1 or 4:1 (Robertson & Stern, 2000).

AGE OF ONSET AND COURSE

By definition, symptoms of TS must begin before the age of 18 years. Median age of onset is 6 to 7 years (Findley, 2001) and the peak of symptom intensity occurs in late childhood to early adolescence (Leckman et al., 1998). Although symptoms often decrease or remit in later adolescence and adulthood, some individuals continue to experience symptoms of TS throughout the lifespan. In fact, some of the most severe cases of TS are seen in adulthood (Leckman, King, & Cohen, 1999).

Tics are usually classified as being simple or complex. Simple tics are sudden movements, brief in duration, and appear more "meaningless" than complex tics. Complex tics, on the other hand, may appear more purposeful and are longer in duration. Initially, tics are often simple and transient. Later in the course of development, TS symptoms may become more complex (Leckman et al., 1999). Though not true for every child with TS, an anatomical progression of tics may occur, with tics first developing in the head and facial region (e.g., eye-blinking, head jerking) and later moving into the extremities (Jagger et al., 1982). Vocal tics tend to develop after motor tics.

FUNCTIONAL IMPAIRMENT

Tourette's syndrome is associated with impairment in a number of domains (Storch et al., 2007). Because those with TS are often affected by comorbid conditions (e.g., attention-deficit/hyperactivity disorder [ADHD]; obsessive-compulsive disorder [OCD]), it can be difficult to tease out the relative contribution of TS and each comorbid condition with respect to impact on functional impairment.

Tics can produce physical complications such as nerve and spinal damage, broken bones, contusions, inflammation, joint pain, and infection (Messiha & Carlson, 1983; Moon, Price, & Campbell, 1998; Shimberg, 1995). Individuals with TS may also experience impairment in the academic and occupational domains. Consistent with findings that individuals with TS have deficits in visual–motor integration and fine-motor skills (Schultz, Carter, Scahill, & Leckman, 1999), children with TS often have difficulty with writing (Comings & Comings, 1987). Studies indicate that those with TS also may have difficulty in arithmetic, reading, and retaining information. Those with TS and comorbid ADHD are also more likely to be placed into special classrooms as a result of academic difficulties (Comings & Comings, 1987). In addition to the possible academic complications, the unemployment rate in those with TS may be higher than average (Meyers, 1988) and those with TS report circumstances in which they have been fired or denied a job or promotion because of their symptoms (Shady, Broder, Staley, Furer, & Papadopolos, 1995).

Those with TS may also experience difficulty in social functioning. Tics can lead peers to view them negatively (Woods, 2002) and lead to misattributions about the person's behavior. Likewise, children with TS may be at greater risk of exhibiting poor social skills (Dykens et al., 1990) and, as a result, may have trouble making or keeping friends. Multiple explanations for the exhibition of poor social skills are possible. The frequent presence of co-occurring psychiatric conditions can contribute to more negative social behavior (e.g., Carter et al., 2000), and being perceived negatively because of the tics (e.g., Woods, 2002) may lead to repeated social alienation, which could establish more negative social interaction patterns. There is evidence that peer education about TS can improve social acceptability (Woods, 2002; Woods & Marcks, 2005).

ETIOLOGY

Genetics

Tourette syndrome is a neurobehavioral disorder with an underlying genetic basis. One study found TS concordance rates of 53% for monozygotic (MZ) twins and 8% for dyzygotic (DZ) twins, and when concordance criteria were loosened to include just the presence of tics, MZ rates rose to 77% and DZ rates rose to 23% (Pauls, Raymond, Leckman, & Stevenson, 1991). Although the SLITRK 1 region (Abelson et al., 2005) and other chromosomal areas have been implicated in TS (Merette et al., 2000), results have not often been replicated (Swain, Scahill, Lombroso, King, & Leckman, 2007). Current consensus is that TS is likely polygenetic (Swain et al., 2007).

Neurobiology

The neurotransmitter dopamine has long been suspected to be involved in TS. An increase in dopamine activity in those with TS compared to controls has been demonstrated (Swain et al., 2007) and psychopharmacological agents that block dopamine receptors have been proven effective in reducing tic frequency (e.g. haloperidol; Ross & Moldofsky, 1978; risperidone; Scahill, Leckman, Schultz, Katsovich, & Peterson, 2003).

In addition, a number of brain regions are believed to play a key role in TS symptom expression. The basal ganglia, a set of structures within the corticostriatalthalamocortical (CSTC) circuit have been most widely implicated, as they form the basis for motor selection and inhibition (Lerner et al., 2007; Singer & Minzer, 2005). Other areas that have been implicated include the corpus callosum (i.e., larger volume in TS population; e.g., Baumgardner et al., 1996), supplementary motor cortex (Karp, Porter, Toro, & Hallett, 1996; Obseo, Rothwell, & Marseden, 1981), cerebellum (Lerner et al., 2007), and hippocampus (B. S. Peterson et al., 2007).

Environmental Variables

A variety of environmental variables are believed to play a role in TS symptom expression. These include both biologically based events and events occurring in day-to-day life. With respect to biologically based environmental factors, it has been speculated that some cases may be explained as a negative reaction to streptococcal infection. Although pediatric autoimmune neuropsychiatric disorder associated with streptococcal infections (PANDAS) may be a cause of some cases of TS (Giovannoni, 2006), the topic has created considerable controversy, with opinions differing on whether or not infections are a cause of TS or if infections simply exacerbate symptoms of a preexisting condition. Other biochemical variables hypothesized to affect TS include stress, perinatal risks, and exposure to stimulants (Findley, 2001).

Research in the field of behavior analysis has yielded information on the impact of day-to-day life events on TS symptoms. Much of this work has focused on isolating variables in the environment (e.g., antecedent and consequence variables) and identifying the direct impact they have on tic expression. Examples of antecedents that may increase tics include anxiety, boredom, and situations like watching television or playing videogames. Examples of consequences may include attention from parents and teachers as well as escaping from demands like completing homework (Findley, 2001). In addition, some have hypothesized that the reduction of the premonitory urge contingent on tics may serve to maintain the occurrence of tics via a negative reinforcement process (Himle, Woods, Conelea, Bauer, & Rice, 2007; Woods & Miltenberger, 1996).

COMORBIDITY

TS is associated with a number of co-occurring psychiatric conditions. Attention-deficit/hyperactivity disorder is the most common co-occurring disorder, with published comorbidity rates ranging from 50 to 90% (Walkup et al., 1999). Obsessive-compulsive disorder is also commonly associated with TS, but reported comorbidity rates have been highly variable, ranging from as low as 25% to as high as 80% (Walkup et al., 1999).

Those with TS may also experience elevated rates of anxiety and mood disorders (Coffey et al., 2000; King, Leckman, Scahill, & Cohen, 1999; Kurlan et al., 2002). An established time sequence between TS and the mood and anxiety disorders has not been well established, but it is thought that some individuals with TS experience mood difficulties and anxiety as a result of having TS (e.g., social anxiety resulting from fear of evaluation that is exacerbated by having tics, etc.).

ASSESSMENT AND DIFFERENTIAL DIAGNOSIS

To accurately diagnose TS and obtain a clear clinical picture of the presenting individual, the following steps should be taken. If there is confusion or uncertainty with respect to the presence of tics, a medically competent professional, such as a neurologist or psychiatrist specializing in movement disorders, should conduct a thorough assessment. In addition, the medical professional should rule out stereotypies present in developmental delays.

After confirming a tic disorder diagnosis, a semistructured diagnostic interview such as the Semi-structured Clinical Interview for *DSM-IV-TR* Axis-I disorders (SCID; First, Spitzer, Gibbon, & Williams, 2002) should be conducted for co-occurring psychiatric conditions. If the patient is a child, diagnostic interviews such as the Anxiety Disorders Interview Schedule (ADIS; Silverman & Albano, 2002) or the National Institutes of Mental Health Diagnostic Interview Schedule for Children, version IV (NIMH DISC IV; Shaffer, Fisher, Lucas, Dulcan, & Schwab-Stone, 2000) may be used instead.

Differential diagnosis in individuals with TS can be difficult. One particularly confusing distinction occurs between TS and OCD, as some behaviors share characteristics of both tics and compulsions. A few suggestions can be made to assist in differentiating between TS and OCD. First, it is often helpful to investigate the functional relationship between the identified behavior (the tic or compulsion) and environmental variables, such as physiological states, emotions, and consequences, because simply looking at topography of behavior often does not resolve the situation. For example, assume a patient has to repeatedly touch a table with one hand if the other hand touched it. Compulsions in OCD are often performed in response to cognitive phenomena, such as obsessions or intrusive thoughts, or physiological phenomena (e.g., anxiety), whereas tics are often preceded by sensory phenomena (Miguel et al., 1995). With compulsions, there may be a particular consequence that is being avoided if one completes the behavior (e.g., "My mother will get into a car accident if I don't touch the table"), whereas the consequences of not engaging in a tic are more vague and sensory in nature (e.g., "I'll just feel uncomfortable if I don't do it" or "I don't know, I just feel like I have to do it"). The clinician should also take into account the presence of tics and compulsions outside of the behavior in question. For example, if it has been established that the client has many tics and other than the behavior in question the client exhibits no other OCD symptoms, a diagnosis of TS only and not OCD is more likely. The converse is also true.

In addition to confirming the tic disorder diagnosis, the clinician should assess severity of TS symptoms. Various methods can be used, including clinician ratings, parent-report scales, and direct observation. The gold standard in TS assessment is the Yale Global Tic Severity Scale (YGTSS; Leckman et al., 1989), a semistructured clinician rating scale that includes a tic checklist, ratings on five dimensions of tic characteristics (number, frequency, intensity, complexity, and interference), and an overall rating of impairment. Storch and colleagues (2005) reported that the YGTSS demonstrated good internal consistency, stability, and divergent validity in a sample of children and adolescents with TS.

A useful questionnaire that overlaps with the YGTSS is the Parent Tic Questionnaire (PTQ; Chang, Himle, Tucker, Woods, & Piacentini, 2008). The PTQ is a quick, convenient measure that includes parent reports on the presence of certain tics as well as the frequency and intensity of those tics. In addition, the Premonitory Urge for Tics Scale (Woods, Piacentini, Himle, & Chang, 2005) is useful in measuring the intensity of urges that precede an individual's tics.

Direct observation of tics is also possible. Some have raised the concern that direct observation in clinical settings may not generalize to real-life settings, but clinic-based observations of tics have corresponded well to home-based observations, and direct observation has been found to be relatively stable over time (Himle et al., 2006). Nevertheless, some may find self-monitoring or caregiver observation to be more feasible options, but such strategies should only be used in those who have developed adequate awareness of their (or their child's) tics (Carr & Rapp, 2001).

Finally, obtaining functional assessment data is a critical component of a thorough assessment, especially if the assessment data are being gathered to inform treatment. Functional assessment involves systematically gathering information about the antecedent and consequence variables that may be associated with fluctuations in tic frequency or intensity. For example, variables such as stress, parental attention, and escape from demands have all been cited as variables that affect the occurrence of tics (Findley, 2001). A functional assessment serves to give important information about the types of function-based interventions a clinician chooses to implement, which will be discussed in the "treatment" section of this chapter.

TREATMENT

A variety of treatments exist for individuals with TS. This section will briefly cover psychopharmacological interventions, followed by a discussion about nonpharmacological treatment options for those with TS.

Psychopharmacology

As noted previously, pharmacological agents such as typical and atypical neuroleptics have been shown to reduce tic frequency in those with TS. Tests of these agents in randomized controlled trials (RCTs) have generally demonstrated significant pre–post change in tic frequency or severity, as well as superiority over placebo (Ross & Moldofsky, 1978; Scahill et al., 2003, Shapiro, Shapiro, Fulop, & Hubbard, 1989). However, concerns about side effects, which may include tardive dyskinesia, dystonia, parkinsonism, sedation, nervousness, cognitive dulling, depression, and electrocardiogram abnormalities (Robertson & Stern, 2000), have been noted. That being said, a wide array of medications exist that can be valuable in the treatment of TS.

Psychotherapy

General Overview

Effective nonpharmacological treatments in TS are predominantly behavioral. Such treatments involve altering environmental variables that impact tic expression and teaching specific self-management skills to reduce tic frequency. Various behavioral treatment packages have been created, and each will be described.

Habit Reversal Training

In addition to its use for TS, habit reversal training (HRT; Azrin & Nunn, 1973) has been used in treating numerous repetitive-behavior disorders, including trichotillomania (hair pulling), skin picking, thumb sucking, and nail biting (Woods & Miltenberger, 1996). Habit reversal training is comprised of three main components: awareness training, competing-response training, and social support training. Awareness training is designed to enhance the client's ability to predict when a tic occurs. This is accomplished through describing each tic in detail (e.g., what it looks like, what it feels like right before, etc.), and having the client practice "catching the tic" and any premonitory urges or sensations in session.

Competing-response training involves teaching the client to implement, contingent on awareness of the tic or its premonitory sensations, a movement that is incompatible with the targeted tic. For example, a competing response for a throat-clearing tic may include diaphragmatic breathing. A good competing response should be (a) physically incompatible with the tic, (b) able to be performed in multiple contexts (e.g., standing up or sitting down), and (c) less noticeable or more socially acceptable than the tic. The competing response should be done for 1 minute or until the urge to tic goes away (whichever is longer).

Finally, social support involves having a person close to the client prompt the use of exercises taught in therapy and reward the client for properly implementing the treatment techniques. Social support is seen as particularly important in the treatment of children, with a parent typically serving in the role.

Function-Based Interventions

After obtaining information about the specific antecedent and consequence variables associated with tics (see Assessment section earlier in the chapter), the clinician may develop treatment strategies designed to eliminate or decrease the impact of these tic-controlling variables. For example, if a child is often asked to leave the classroom during periods of high tic frequency (e.g., a consequence to having tics), the teacher may be inadvertently reinforcing the occurrence of tics. In this scenario, it would be helpful for the clinician to discuss this possibility with the teacher and devise an alternative to classroom dismissal. Also, suppose that playing videogames and watching television exacerbates tics in a child. A function-based intervention targeting these antecedents may include limiting time spent playing videogames and watching television. In addition, the clinician should remind the client to use strategies learned in treatment (e.g., use competing responses) during these high-risk activities.

Exposure and Response Prevention

Exposure and response prevention (ERP) is a cognitive-behavioral treatment traditionally used to treat OCD. However, it has recently been applied to TS. In TS, ERP involves the systematic exposure to uncomfortable bodily sensations (e.g., the premonitory urge) while abstaining from engaging in tics. It is thought that over time, if the client is able to abstain from engaging in tics, the intensity of the premonitory urge will decrease or will cease altogether. Thus, ERP is an intervention designed to manipulate the functional relationship between the tic and the premonitory urge.

Efficacy

Several RCTs have been conducted evaluating behavior therapy for TS. In the first, Azrin, Nunn, and Frantz (1980) compared HRT and massed negative practice (MNP) in 22 individuals and concluded that HRT was superior to MNP. In the HRT group, tic frequency decreased by an average of 99% at 6 months posttreatment and by 97% at 18-month follow-up. However, tic frequency was assessed via patient report, which may be unreliable in comparison to more objective measures, such as the YGTSS or direct observation.

Azrin and Peterson (1989) compared HRT to wait-list control in 10 adults using direct observation in the clinic and at home. Although no follow-up data were collected, posttreatment data for the HRT group showed a 93% reduction in tic frequency, which was superior to the reductions found in the wait-list group. Similarly, HRT was found to be superior to supportive psychotherapy in 30 adults with TS, reducing YGTSS severity scores by 37.5% at posttreatment (Deckersbach, Rauch, Buhlmann, & Wilhelm, 2006). Wilhelm and colleagues (2003) also found HRT to be superior to supportive psychotherapy in 32 patients with TS.

O'Connor and colleagues (2001) evaluated a cognitive-behavioral therapy (CBT) treatment package based on HRT in 47 participants with chronic tic disorder. CBT was found to be superior to wait-list control and reduced tic frequency by 65% at posttreatment according to participants' daily diary. Likewise, in an RCT comparing HRT to ERP in 43 participants with TS, results showed that both HRT and ERP significantly and equally reduced tic frequency, and that treatment gains were maintained at 3-month follow-up (Verdellen, Keijsers, Cath, & Hoogduin, 2004).

A number of studies using single-subject experimental designs have also evaluated the efficacy of HRT. Results of these studies have generally shown that HRT effectively reduces tic frequency (Azrin & Peterson, 1989; Carr & Bailey, 1996; Miltenberger, Fuqua, & McKinley, 1985; Woods, Miltenberger, & Lumley, 1996).

In sum, available data indicate that behavioral treatments, especially HRT, are effective in the treatment of TS. A recent review by Cook and Blacher (2007) named HRT a *well-established treatment* and ERP a *probably efficacious treatment* (see chapter 2) according to the American Psychological Association's Division 12 Task Force on Promotion and Dissemination of Psychological Procedures.

FACTORS RELATED TO POOR RESPONSE TO HRT

Treatment Noncompliance

As is the case with most cognitive-behavioral interventions, patient compliance often plays a large role in response to HRT and function-based interventions (A. L. Peterson, 2007). Habit reversal therapy is a time-consuming treatment that requires the client to engage in treatment outside of the therapy room in the form of weekly homework assignments and incidental practice. Homework typically consists of practicing the competing response at least three times per week during "planned practice sessions" in which the parent implements social support procedures. In addition, children are encouraged to use their competing responses as much as possible during other situations, such as school.

Child noncompliance can occur when the child does not participate during treatment sessions or does not fully complete homework assignments. Implementation of reward systems can often help resolve these problems. For example, the therapist can reward the child for in-session attendance and participation using a point system in which points can be exchanged for a small reward. Similarly, parents can implement a home-based reward system to encourage the child to complete homework assignments. Given the biological nature of TS, we recommend that reward systems be based on the child's effort rather than on actual reductions in tic frequencies.

It is also important for the therapist to assess the nature of the child's noncompliance to ensure that it is not attributable solely to motivation. For example, a child may not be using a competing response because it feels uncomfortable or is difficult to implement in some situations (e.g., while conversing, walking, or swimming). In these cases, modification of competing responses may help increase the likelihood that the child will use them.

Habit reversal training for children typically necessitates the involvement of parents and family members. In addition, parents are relied on to implement function-based interventions and the social support component of HRT. Parents may have difficulty adhering to treatment procedures for a variety of reasons, such as a chaotic family environment, parenting stress, needs of other children in the family, marital strain, and parental psychopathology. In these cases, treatment response may be improved with therapist-guided problem solving, the use of evidence-based parent training programs (e.g., Barkley, 1997), or a referral to outside resources and services to address familial concerns. It may also be beneficial to instruct other family members, family friends, babysitters, and teachers in treatment procedures so that the parent and child both have increased treatment support.

In adults with TS, compliance may be enhanced by focusing on client motivation. For example, the therapist could implement Motivational Interviewing (Miller & Rollnick, 2002), an evidence-based approach used to elicit behavior change by helping the client resolve his/her ambivalence about treatment and move toward his/her desired outcome. Adults may also benefit from greater involvement on the part of a social support person, such as a spouse, family member, friend, or roommate.

Finally, when faced with potential noncompliance, it is important for the clinician to assess whether the client's social, academic, and/or occupational environments are complicating treatment adherence. School-based interventions and accommodations (Kepley & Conners, 2007; Packer, 2005), occupational accommodations (Taubert, 1999), and peer education (Woods & Marcks, 2005) may help to reduce stress-related tic exacerbations and help the client feel more supported in his/her treatment efforts.

ADHD/Attention Problems

Although the outcome of HRT for individuals with and without comorbid ADHD has not been specifically examined in the literature, research suggests that attention and impulsivity problems may contribute to a poorer treatment response.

In a study comparing HRT to supportive psychotherapy for adults with TS, Deckersbach et al. (2006) found that individuals with greater response inhibition deficits showed less improvement following HRT. Research examining voluntary tic suppression has found significant negative correlations between measures of attention and tic suppressability (Himle & Woods, 2005; Woods et al., 2007), suggesting that increasing attention problems are related to poorer suppressability. Neuroimaging research also supports the idea that attentional processes are involved in tic suppression (B. S. Peterson et al., 1998).

Although specific modifications to HRT for individuals with co-occurring ADHD have not yet been proposed, it may be the case that coupling HRT with behavior therapy for ADHD (Barkley, 1997) will improve treatment outcome. Stimulant medication may also be used to improve ADHD symptoms. Concerns have been raised regarding the use of stimulants for children with TS and ADHD tics (Borcherding, Keysor, Rapoport, Elia, & Amass, 1990), but placebo-controlled studies suggest that, in general, stimulant mediation does not cause a permanent increase in tics in this population (Castellanos et al., 1997; Kurlan et al., 2002).

OCD

When OCD and TS occur together, they often have phenomenological similarities that can make case conceptualization and treatment selection difficult. Often referred to as "Tourettic OCD" or tic-related OCD, individuals with this overlap present with a higher rate of touching, tapping, evening out, and repeating behaviors; premonitory experiences that include vague psychological distress rather than just somatic sensations; and unelaborated obsessional themes (Mansueto & Keuler, 2005). Mansueto and Keuler (2005) proposed that these patients are more difficult to treat and may be more likely to be designated treatment-refractory cases. It is thought that a modified treatment approach involving exposure with response prevention and cognitive therapy (e.g., Woods, Hook, Spellman, & Friman, 2000; Piacentini, Langley, & Roblek, 2007) can be beneficial for these individuals. In general, it is recommended that a thorough assessment of TS and OCD symptoms be conducted prior to treatment selection. In those with both TS and OCD, particular attention should be paid to isolating the events preceding the tic-like behavior and the perceived consequences of not engaging in the behavior. It is likely that repetitive behaviors that are preceded by cognitions or images and/or physiological anxiety, rather than a vague somatic feeling, would be better addressed using an ERP-based treatment (Mansueto & Keuler, 2005).

Other Comorbid Conditions

Anxiety and mood difficulties may also complicate HRT. Tourette syndrome has been described as a stress-reactive disorder based on data suggesting that tic frequency and severity increase in the presence of stressful or anxiety-inducing events for many individuals (Findley et al., 2003; Silva, Munoz, Barickman, & Friedhoff, 1995). Because of this, it is possible that individuals who experience frequent daily life stressors and/or heightened anxiety will have greater difficulty in HRT. Functional assessments should be used to determine whether these particular emotional states are associated with tic exacerbations and to identify particular contextual variables that may evoke these emotions. Based on these results, adjunctive interventions could be implemented, such as CBT for anxiety or social phobia, relaxation training, and other function-based interventions. In addition, particular emphasis could be placed on having the client practice competing responses in identified "high-risk for tic" situations.

Patients with TS may also present with symptoms of depression. Similarly, the impact of depressive symptoms on tics and the client's ability to comply with treatment should be thoroughly assessed. Adjunctive interventions could then be added to bolster treatment outcome, such as behavioral activation (Martell, Addis, & Jacobson, 2001), coping and skills training (Hops & Lewinsohn, 1995), and family therapy.

Finally, disruptive behavior can contribute to functional impairment and may weaken response to HRT. Beyond simple treatment noncompliance, disruptive behaviors reportedly occur in 25–70% of individuals with TS and include explosive anger or "rage attacks," aggression, temper tantrums, oppositional-defiant behaviors, bullying, and extreme irritability (Budman, Rockmore, & Stokes, 2003). Options for patients with these behaviors include pharmacological treatment and/or psychosocial interventions. For example, Scahill et al. (2006) found that parent management training was significantly better than treatment as usual in producing short-term improvement in disruptive behaviors in children with TS, and Sukholdolsky et al. (2009) examined the use of an anger-control treatment for this population. It is likely that treating disruptive behavior prior to implementing HRT would help promote compliance during HRT, although this has yet to be examined empirically.

Young Children and Individuals With Developmental Disabilities

Some research has suggested that HRT and function-based interventions may be effective for young children (Azrin & Peterson, 1989; Watson & Sterling, 1998) and individuals with developmental disabilities (Richman & Lindauer, 2002; Roane, Piazza, Cercone, & Grados, 2002). However, the impact of these client factors on the efficacy of HRT for tics has not been evaluated systematically. Although some function-based interventions, such as removal of positive reinforcement in the form of social or parental attention, may help decrease tic frequencies for these populations, it is thought that HRT is generally not as effective for these populations (Miltenberger, Fuqua, & Woods, 1998). HRT may be ineffective in these populations because of motivational and compliance problems, skill deficits, or reduced awareness of social consequences related to tics. Furthermore, HRT relies on the client's ability to implement the competing response contingent on premonitory-urge sensations. It has been found that children below the ages of 8–10 years inconsistently recognize urge sensations (Woods et al., 2005), so it is likely that younger children would have greater difficulty implementing competing responses correctly.

If behavioral interventions are to be used with young children or individuals with developmental disabilities, it is recommended that treatment largely focus on function-based intervention strategies. In addition, greater involvement on the part of a parent or caregiver may also bolster treatment outcome. For example, parents and caregivers could spend more time implementing function-based procedures so that they occur throughout the child's day. In addition, if competing-response training is used, it is less likely that children in these populations can be relied on to use the competing response independently.

Therefore, it may be beneficial for parents to have "planned practice" sessions daily and to implement social support procedures more frequently.

CASE PRESENTATION

Ethan was an 11-year-old Caucasian male who lived with his biological parents and his siblings. He was the youngest child of three and was enrolled in sixth grade at a public elementary school. The primary presenting complaints involved concerns about involuntary movements and vocalizations, distress related to intrusive thoughts and images, and a strong need to touch things until they felt "even."

Developmental history revealed a pregnancy and birth without complications and typical progress through developmental milestones. Ethan's parents did not report any concerns related to Ethan's academic performance, noting that he generally performed in the above-average range across all subjects. Social history revealed that Ethan had struggled with peer relations related to being teased for having tics, although he reported close friendships with a couple of same-age classmates. The family reported close and warm relationships with each other. Family history revealed a diagnosis of TS in Ethan's paternal uncle and a diagnosis of OCD in Ethan's paternal grandfather.

Ethan's parents first noticed the onset of hard eye blinking and subtle facial tics at 6 years of age. Throughout childhood, Ethan demonstrated a heightened sensitivity to tactile sensations, such as the texture of rough fabrics. At approximately age 7 years, Ethan began to exhibit repeated coughing and throat clearing. Both Ethan's pediatrician and allergist could determine no clear medical cause for these symptoms and referred him to a neurologist, who diagnosed Ethan with TS. Ethan's parents considered pharmacotherapy, but decided to pursue behavioral treatment at our clinic first because of concerns about medication side effects.

Ethan and his parents reported several motor tics during intake: arm jerking, in which one or both arms moved out to the side and snapped out once from the elbow joint; head shaking, in which the head moved rapidly from side to side; and leg jerking, in which one leg swung out from the knee and kicked forward. Vocal tics were also reported and included a loud, high-frequency yelping sound and coughing. For these simple tics, Ethan reported several premonitory-urge sensations, including pressure inside of his body, tingling in his arms and legs, and an itchy feeling in his throat. Several complex tics were also reported, including evening-out behaviors, in which Ethan repeatedly touched both ends of an object until it felt "right," and oral repetition of words that Ethan felt sounded "incorrect" when spoken. Ethan indicated that his complex tics were usually preceded by uncomfortable somatic sensations. He reported that he often felt tingling or pressure in his fingertips before his evening-out behavior. When asked about his oral word repetition, Ethan reported no feared consequence or physiological anxiety for saying an "incorrect" word only once but rather a strong urge that he "just has to do it."

Shortly after tic onset, Ethan began to complain of obsessive symptoms that continue to persist. Ethan reported seeing intrusive images several times per day. These included vivid images of his parents being physically harmed as well as vague images in the form of darkly colored shapes that Ethan perceived as somewhat frightening. When asked about compulsive behaviors, Ethan reported trying to eliminate these images by either visualizing a positive image or by "ticcing it away." In particular, Ethan reported that his loud yelping sound removed images of his parents by "drowning them out." He indicated that his arm and leg jerking could "move" shape images farther away from his body. Ethan said that his head shaking could "clear his mind" of both intrusive images. Ethan reported that approximately 50% of his tics were associated with intrusive images, and the other 50% were associated with his bodily premonitory-urge sensations.

During the intake, tic severity was assessed using the YGTSS. Ethan's total tic score was a 26 (out of 50), placing him in the moderate range. Ethan obtained a score of 17 on the Children's Yale-Brown Obsessive-Compulsive Scale (CY-BOCS; Scahill et al., 1997), suggestive of clinically significant OCD symptoms.

Based on information gathered during the intake, it was determined that Ethan met criteria for TS and OCD. Ethan and his parents reported more functional impairment related to the TS symptoms, so HRT was initially implemented to address Ethan's tics. Given that Ethan was neutralizing some of his obsessions with tics (such as the yelping sound and arm jerk), it was thought that use of competing responses might incidentally provide some reduction in OCD-related premonitory experiences. Ethan reported that his head-shaking tic bothered him the most, so awareness training was implemented and a competing response was chosen (tensing the neck muscles and focusing the eyes on a spot). He was instructed to implement the competing response contingent on the head-shaking tic or its warning signs, which included pressure at the back of his neck or intrusive images.

Ethan and his parents reported no notable reductions in the frequency of the head shaking tic in the following week. Ethan's parents said that they tried to prompt use of the competing response during planned practice times. At the beginning of practice sessions, Ethan was compliant, but after about 10 minutes he became very frustrated, complained that it "wasn't working," and asked to stop practicing. Ethan's parents were asked to implement a reward system. It was agreed that Ethan would earn points toward a desired reward for every 20 minutes of practice time in which he exerted good effort. Ethan's motivation for improving was discussed and he was encouraged to remind himself of these motivations at times when treatment seemed difficult. Ethan was asked to continue practicing the competing response with the help of his parents and to try using it on his own while at school.

Habit reversal training procedures were then implemented for Ethan's next most distressing tic, his loud yelp. Ethan was asked to purse his lips together and breathe through his nose for the competing response. After another week, Ethan and his parents again reported no changes in either his head-shaking or yelping tics. They indicated that the reward system helped to lengthen the time that Ethan remained compliant with practice sessions. His parents decided to also reward Ethan when they "caught him" using his competing responses on his own, which they reported greatly improved his compliance at home. However, they reported that Ethan frequently seemed to be visibly distressed while holding his competing responses. When asked about this, Ethan said that his intrusive images bothered him greatly during these times. He noted that it was hard to focus on holding his competing response because he was trying instead to make the images "go away" by using thought-distraction strategies.

At this point, it was decided to reevaluate the overlap between Ethan's tic and obsessive-compulsive symptoms. Although it initially seemed that Ethan's noncompliance was hindering progress, this information led us to believe that Ethan's OCD symptoms were interfering with his ability to use his competing responses as directed. To determine whether this was the case, Ethan's parents were asked to help him complete a self-monitoring form to track how often Ethan's head-shaking and yelping tics were preceded by either a premonitory urge or an intrusive image. The family completed this task over the course of 1 week. The form indicated that these tics were preceded by intrusive images much more frequently than Ethan had originally estimated.

Based on this information, we decided to implement cognitive-behavioral therapy for OCD (Piacentini et al., 2007; see chapter 4, this volume). Exposure hierarchies were created for Ethan's intrusive images and included items such as drawing out the images and telling detailed stories about image content. If Ethan had difficulty suppressing a tic during exposure exercises, competing-response strategies were suggested. Cognitive restructuring was used to help Ethan recognize and distance himself from his obsessive thoughts and feelings. In addition to the intrusive images, Ethan's complex tics were targeted using this approach. Following treatment, Ethan and his parents reported some notable reductions in the frequencies of obsession-related tics, as well as in Ethan's distress related to his intrusive images. At termination, Ethan's total tic score on the YGTSS had fallen to an 11, and his CY-BOCS score was a 10.

In Ethan's case, deviation from the standard HRT protocol to an exposure-based treatment directed specifically at obsessional content appeared to be beneficial in terms of treatment response for TS and obsessive-compulsive symptoms. Ethan's case highlights the importance of a thorough assessment of the association between tics and obsessions for children who present with a profile of "Tourettic OCD." It is likely that gathering self-monitoring data in these cases will assist with the assessment and case conceptualization, as clients may not initially be able to accurately report the occurrence or frequency of particular tic-preceding phenomena. For children who present with both obsession-related tics and typical tics, it may be helpful to divide symptoms into these categories and implement CBT for OCD or HRT for TS as needed.

CONCLUSIONS AND FUTURE DIRECTIONS

Treatment outcome research has demonstrated the efficacy of cognitive-behavioral approaches for TS, including HRT and ERP (Cook & Blacher, 2007). However, to date, studies examining the efficacy of these treatments have generally used small sample sizes, which have precluded our ability to closely examine client variables that predict treatment response. In addition, these efficacy studies often exclude individuals with prominent comorbid psychopathology or with below average cognitive functioning, making the efficacy of HRT in these populations unclear.

A limited research literature, coupled with anecdotal clinical observations, suggests that client variables such as the presence of comorbid conditions, client motivation and compliance, and client age and cognitive ability may play a role in the outcome of HRT. This chapter provides some initial suggestions for improving treatment outcome for these populations; however, it is important to note that these suggestions are largely based on clinical experience rather than on empirical data. As we move toward examining the efficacy of cognitive-behavioral therapies in nonresponders to traditional HRT or ERP protocols or to those who have traditionally been excluded from outcome research, it will be important to test the efficacy of particular treatment modifications. For example, research should examine the impact of adjunctive treatments (e.g., Motivational Interviewing, CBT for OCD) on HRT response. It would also be beneficial to know whether adjunctive treatment procedures produce better outcomes when applied before, after, or simultaneously with HRT. More research examining psychosocial or neuropsychological predictors of treatment response, such as the Deckersbach et al. (2006) study, would also help us to target particular variables associated with poor outcome, so that treatment can be appropriately modified. Future research aimed at improving HRT and ERP for treatment-refractory children and adults will help clinicians make treatment decisions based on empirical support and, we hope, improve the overall benefit of CBT approaches for this population.

REFERENCES

Abelson, J. F., Kwan, K. Y., O'Roak, B. J., Baek, D. Y., Stillman, A. A., Morgan, T. M., et al. (2005). Sequence variants in SLITRK1 are associated with Tourette's syndrome. *Science, 310*, 317–320.

American Psychiatric Association. (2000). *Diagnostic and statistical manual of mental disorders* (4th ed., text rev.). Washington, DC: American Psychiatric Press.

Azrin, N. H., & Nunn, R. G. (1973). Habit-reversal: A method of eliminating nervous habits and tics. *Behaviour Research and Therapy, 11*, 619–628.

Azrin, N. H., Nunn, R. G., & Frantz, S. E. (1980). Habit reversal vs. negative practice treatment of nervous tics. *Behavior Therapy, 11*, 169–178.

Azrin, N. H., & Peterson, A. L. (1989). Reduction of an eye tic by controlled blinking. *Behavior Therapy, 20*, 467–473.

Barkley, R. A. (1997). *ADHD and the nature of self-control.* New York: Guilford Press.

Baumgardner, T. L., Singer, H.S., Denckla, M. B., Rubin, M. A., Abrams, M. T., Colli, M. J., et al. (1996). Corpus callosum morphology in children with Tourette syndrome and attention deficity hyperactivity disorder. *Neurology, 47,* 477–482.
Borcherding, B. G., Keysor, C. S., Rapoport, J. L., Elia, J., & Amass, J. (1990). Motor/vocal tics and compulsive behaviors on stimulant drugs: Is there a common vulnerability? *Psychiatry Research, 33,* 83–94.
Budman, C. L., Rockmore, L., & Stokes, J. (2003). Clinical phenomenology of episodic rage in children with Tourette syndrome. *Journal of Psychosomatic Research, 55,* 59–65.
Carr, J. E., & Bailey, J. S. (1996). A brief behavior therapy protocol for Tourette syndrome. *Journal of Behavior Therapy and Experimental Psychiatry, 27,* 33–40.
Carr, J. E., & Rapp, J. T. (2001). Assessment of repetitive behavior disorders. In D. W. Woods & R. G. Miltenberger (Eds.). *Tic disorders, trichotillomania, and other repetitive behavior disorders.* New York: Springer Science + Business Media.
Carter, A. S., O'Donnell, D. A., Schultz, R. T., Scahill, L., Leckman, J. F., & Pauls, D. L. (2000). Social and emotional adjustment in children affected with Gilles de la Tourette's syndrome: Associations with ADHD and family functioning. *Journal of Child Psychology and Psychiatry, 41,* 215–223.
Castellanos, F. X., Giedd, J. N., Elia, J., Marsh, W. L., Ritchie, G. F., Hamburger, S. D., et al. (1997). Controlled stimulant treatment of ADHD and comorbid Tourette's syndrome: Effects of stimulant and dose. *Journal of the American Academy of Child and Adolescent Psychiatry, 36,* 589–596.
Chang, S. C., Himle, M. B., Tucker, B. T. P., Woods. D. W., & Piacentini, J. (2008). *Initial psychometric properties of a brief parent-report instrument for assessing tic severity in children with chronic tic disorders.* Unpublished manuscript.
Coffey, B. J., Biederman, J., Smoller, J. W., Geller, D. A., Sarin, P., Schwartz, S., & Kim, G. S. (2000). Anxiety disorders and tic severity in juveniles with Tourette's disorder. Journal of the *American Academy of Child & Adolescent Psychiatry, 39,* 562–568.
Comings, D. E., & Comings, B. G. (1987). A controlled study of Tourette syndrome. I. Attention-deficit disorder, learning disorders, and school problems. *American Journal of Human Genetics, 41,* 701–741.
Cook, C. R., & Blacher, J. (2007). Evidence-based psychosocial treatments for tic disorders. *Clinical Psychology: Science and Practice, 14,* 252–267.
Deckersbach, T., Rauch, S., Buhlmann, U., & Wilhelm, S. (2006). Habit reversal versus supportive psychotherapy in Tourette's disorder: A randomized controlled trial and predictors of treatment response. *Behaviour Research and Therapy, 44,* 1079–1090.
Dykens, E., Leckman, J., Riddle, M., Hardin, M., Schwartz, S., & Cohen, D. (1990). Intellectual, academic, and adaptive functioning of Tourette syndrome children with and without attention deficit disorder. *Journal of Abnormal Child Psychology, 18,* 607–615.
Findley, D., Leckman, J., Katsovich, L., Lin, H., Zhang, H., Grantz, H., et al. (2003). Development of the Yale Children's Global Stress Index (YCGSI) and its application in children and adolescents with Tourette's syndrome and obsessive-compulsive disorder. *Journal of the American Academy of Child and Adolescent Psychiatry, 42,* 450–457.

Findley, D. B. (2001). Characteristics of tic disorders. In D. W. Woods & R. G. Miltenberger (Eds.), *Tic disorders, trichotillomania, and other repetitive behavior disorders: Behavioral approaches to analysis and treatment* (pp. 53–71). New York: Springer Science + Business Media.

First, M. B., Spitzer, R. L., Gibbon, M., & Williams, J. B. W. (2002). *Structured clinical interview for DSM-IV-TR axis 1 disorders—Patient edition* (SCID-I/P, 11/2002 revision). New York: Biometrics Research Department.

Giovannoni, G. (2006). PANDAS: Overview of the hypothesis. In J. T. Walkup, J. W. Mink, & P. J. Hollenbeck (Eds.), *Advances in neurology, Volume 99, Tourette syndrome* (pp. 159–165). Philadelphia: Lipincott, Williams, & Wilkins.

Himle, M. B., Chang, S., Woods, D. W., Pearlman, A., Buzzella, B., Bunaciu, L., et al. (2006). Establishing the feasibility of direct observation in the assessment of tics in children with chronic tic disorders. *Journal of Applied Behavior Analysis, 39*, 429–440.

Himle, M. B., & Woods, D. W. (2005). An experimental evaluation of tic suppression and the tic rebound effect. *Behaviour Research and Therapy, 43*, 1443–1451.

Himle, M. B., Woods, D. W., Conelea, C. A., Bauer, C. C., & Rice, K. A. (2007). Investigating the effects of tic suppression on premonitory urge ratings in children and adolescents with Tourette's syndrome. *Behaviour Research and Therapy, 45*, 2964–2976.

Hops, H., & Lewinsohn, P. M. (1995). A course for the treatment of depression among adolescents. In K. D. Craig & K. S. Dobson (Eds.), *Anxiety and depression in adults and children* (pp. 230–245). Thousand Oaks, CA: Sage.

Jagger, J., Prusoff, B. A., Cohen, D. J., Kidd, K. K., Carbonari, C. M., & John, K. (1982). The epidemiology of Tourette's syndrome: A pilot study. *Schizophrenia Bulletin, 8*, 276–278.

Karp, B. I., Porter, S., Toro, C., & Hallett, M. (1996). Simple motor tics may be preceded by a premotor potential. *Journal of Neurology, Neurosurgery, and Psychiatry, 61*, 103–106.

Kepley, H. O., & Conners, S. (2007). Management of learning and school difficulties in children with Tourette syndrome. In D. W. Woods, J. C. Piacentini, & J. T. Walkup (Eds.). *Treating Tourette syndrome and tic disorders* (pp. 242–264). New York: Guilford Press.

Khalifa, N., & von Knorring, A.-L. (2003). Prevalence of tic disorders and Tourette syndrome in a Swedish school population. *Developmental Medicine & Child Neurology, 45*, 315–319.

King, R. A., Leckman, J. F., Scahill, L., & Cohen, D. J. (1999). Obsessive-compulsive disorder, anxiety, and depression. In J. F. Leckman & D. J. Cohen (Eds.), *Tourette's syndrome: Developmental psychopathology and clinical care* (pp. 43–62). New York: John Wiley.

Kurlan, R., Como, P. G., Miller, B., Palumbo, D., Deeley, C., Andersen, E. M., et al. (2002). The behavioral spectrum of tic disorders: A community-based study. *Neurology, 59*, 414–420.

Leckman, J. F., King, R. A., & Cohen, D. J. (1999). Tics and tic disorders. In J. F. Leckman & D. J. Cohen (Eds.), *Tourette's syndrome: Developmental psychopathology and clinical care* (pp. 23–42). New York: John Wiley.

Leckman, J. F., Riddle, M. A., Hardin, M. T., Ort, S. I., Swartz, K. L., Stevenson, J., et al. (1989). The Yale Global Tic Severity Scale (YGTSS): Initial testing of a clinical-rated scale of tic severity. *Journal of the American Academy of Child & Adolescent Psychiatry, 28,* 566–573.

Leckman, J. F., Zhang, H., Vitale, A., Lahnin, F., Lynch, K. Bondi, C., et al. (1998). Trajectories of tic severity in Tourette's syndrome: The first two decades. *Pediatrics, 102,* 14–19.

Lerner, A., Bagic, A., Boudreau, E. A., Hanakawa, T., Pagan, F., Mari, Z. et al. (2007). Neuroimaging of neuronal circuits involved in tic generation in patients with Tourette syndrome. *Neurology, 68,* 1979–1987.

Mansueto, C. S., & Keuler, D. J. (2005). Tic or compulsion?: It's Tourettic OCD. *Behavior Modification, 29,* 784–799.

Martell, C. R., Addis, M. E., & Jacobson, N. S. (2001). *Depression in context: Strategies for guided action.* New York: W. W. Norton.

Merette, C., Brassard, A., Potvin, A., Bouvier, H., Rousseau, F., Bisonnette, L., et al. (2000). Significant linkage for Tourette syndrome in a large French Canadian family. *American Journal of Human Genetics, 67,* 1008–1013.

Messiha, F. S., & Carlson, J. C. (1983). Behavioral and clinical profiles of Tourette's disease: a comprehensive overview. *Brain Research Bulletin, 11,* 195–204.

Meyers, A. S. (1988). Social issues of Tourette's syndrome. In D. J. Cohen, R. D. Bruun, & J. F. Leckman (Eds.), *Tic and tic disorders: Clinical understanding and treatment* (pp. 257–264). New York: John Wiley.

Miguel, E. C., Coffey, B. J., Baer, L., Savage, C. R., Rauch, S. L., & Jenike, M. A. (1995). Phenomenology of intentional repetitive behaviors in obsessive-compulsive disorder and Tourette's disorder. *Journal of Clinical Psychiatry, 56,* 246–255.

Miller, W. R., & Rollnick, S. (2002). *Motivational interviewing: Preparing people for change.* New York: Guilford Press.

Miltenberger, R. G., Fuqua, R. W., & McKinley, T. (1985). Habit reversal with muscle tics: Replication and component analysis. *Behavior Therapy, 16,* 39–50.

Miltenberger, R. G., Fuqua, R. W., & Woods, D. W. (1998). Applying behavior analysis to clinical problems: Review and analysis of habit reversal. *Journal of Applied Behavior Analysis, 31,* 447–469.

Moon, B. S., Price, C. T., & Campbell, J. B. (1998). Upper extremity and rib distress fractures in a child. *Skeletal Radiology, 27,* 403–405.

Obseo, J. A., Rothwell, J. C., & Marsden, C.D. (1981). Simple tics in Gilles de la Tourette's syndrome are not prefaced by normal premovement EEG potential. *Journal of Neurology Neurosurgery, and Psychiatry, 44,* 735–738.

O'Connor, K. P., Brault, M., Robillard, S., Loiselle, J., Borgeat, F., et al. (2001). Evaluation of a cognitive-behavioural program for the management of chronic tic and habit disorders. *Behaviour Research and Therapy, 39,* 667–681.

Packer, L. E. (2005). Tic-related school problems: Impact on functioning, accommodations, and interventions. *Behavior Modification, 29,* 876–899.

Pauls, D. L., Raymond, C. L., Leckman, J. F., & Stevenson, J. M. (1991). A family study of Tourette's syndrome. *American Journal of Human Genetics, 48,* 154–163.

Peterson, A. L. (2007). Psychosocial management of tics and intentional repetitive behaviors associated with Tourette syndrome. In D. W. Woods, J. C. Piacentini, &

J. T. Walkup (Eds.). *Treating Tourette syndrome and tic disorders* (pp. 154–184). New York: Guilford Press.

Peterson, B. S., Choi, H. A., Hao, X., Amat, J. A., Zhu, H., Whiteman R., et al. (2007). Morphologic features of the amygdale and hippocampus in children and adults with Tourette syndrome. *Archives of General Psychiatry, 64,* 1281–1291.

Peterson, B. S., Skudlarski, P., Anderson, A. W., Zhang, H., Gatenby, J. C., Lacadie, C. M., et al. (1998). A functional magnetic resonance imaging study of tic suppression in Tourette syndrome. *Archives of General Psychiatry, 55,* 326–333.

Piacentini, J., Langley, A., & Roblek, T. (2007). *Cognitive-behavioral treatment of childhood OCD.* New York: Oxford University Press.

Richman, D. M., & Lindauer, S. E. (2002). Identifying operant functions for tics in children with mental retardation. *Behavioral Interventions, 17,* 179–190.

Roane, H. S., Piazza, C. C., Cercone, J. J., & Grados, M. (2002). Assessment and treatment of vocal tics associated with Tourette's syndrome. *Behavior Modification, 26,* 482–498.

Robertson, M. M. (2003). Diagnosing Tourette syndrome: Is it a common disorder? *Journal of Psychosomatic Research, 55,* 3–6.

Robertson, M. M., & Stern, J. S. (2000). Gilles de la Tourette Syndrome: Symptomatic treatment based on evidence. *European Child & Adolescent Psychiatry, 9,* 160–175.

Ross, M. S., & Moldofsky, H. (1978). A comparison of pimozide and haloperidol in the treatment of Gilles de la Tourette's syndrome. *American Journal of Psychiatry, 135,* 585–587.

Scahill, L., Leckman, J. F., Schultz, R. T., Katsovich, L., & Peterson, B. S. (2003). A placebo-controlled trial of risperidone in Tourette syndrome. *Neurology, 60,* 1130–1135.

Scahill, L., Riddle, M. A., McSwiggin-Hardin, M., Ort, S. I., King, R. A. Goodman, W. K., et al. (1997). Children's Yale-Brown obsessive compulsive scale: Reliability and valididty. *Journal of the American Academy of Child and Adolescent Psychiatry, 36,* 844–852.

Scahill, L., Sukhodolsky, D. G., Bearss, K., Findley, D., Hamrin, V., Carroll, D. H., et al. (2006). Randomized trial of parent management training in children with tic disorders and disruptive behavior. *Child Neurology, 21,* 650–656.

Schultz, R. T., Carter, A. S., Scahill, L., & Leckman, J. F. (1999). Neuropsychological findings. In J. F. Leckman & D. J. Cohen (Eds.), *Tourette's syndrome: Developmental psychopathology and clinical care* (pp. 80–103). New York: John Wiley.

Shady, G., Broder, R., Staley, D., Furer, P., & Papadopolos, R. B. (1995). Tourette syndrome and employment: Descriptors, predictors, and problems. *Psychiatric Rehabilitation Journal, 19,* 35–42.

Shaffer, D., Fisher, P., Lucas, C. P., Dulcan, M. K., & Schwab-Stone, M. E. (2000). NIMH Diagnostic Interview Schedule for Children Version IV (NIMH DISC-IV): Description, differences from previous versions, and reliability of some common diagnoses. *Journal of the American Academy of Child and Adolescent Psychiatry, 39,* 28–38.

Shapiro, E., Shapiro, A. K., Fulop, G., & Hubbard, M. (1989). Controlled study of haloperidol, pimozide, and placebo for the treatment of Gilles de la Tourette's syndrome. *Archives of General Psychiatry, 46,* 722–730.

Shimberg, E. F. (1995). *Living with Tourette syndrome*. New York: Simon & Schuster.

Silva, R. R., Munoz, D. M., Barickman, J., & Friedhoff, A. J. (1995). Environmental factors and related fluctuation of symptoms in children and adolescents with Tourette's disorder. *Journal of Child Psychology and Psychiatry, 36*, 305–312.

Silverman, W. K., & Albano, A. M. (2002). *The anxiety disorders interview schedule for DSM-IV, research and lifetime version for children and parents (ADIS-RLV)*. New York: Columbia University. Unpublished manuscript.

Singer, H. S., & Minzer, K. (2005). Neurobiological issues in Tourette's syndrome. In R. Kurlan (Ed.), *Handbook of Tourette's syndrome and related tic and behavioral disorders* (2nd ed., pp. 273–317). New York: Marcel Dekker.

Storch, E. A., Lack, C. W., Simons, L. E., Goodman, W. K., Murphy, T. K., & Geffken, G. R. (2007). A measure of functional impairment in youth with Tourette's syndrome. *Journal of Pediatric Psychology, 32*, 950–959.

Storch, E. A., Murphy, T. A., Geffken, G. R., Sajid, M., Allen, P., Roberti, J. W., & Goodman, W. K. (2005). Reliability and validity of the Yale Global Tic Severity Scale. *Psychological Assessment, 17*, 486–491.

Sukhodolsky, D. G., Scahill, L., Zhang, H., Peterson, B. S., King, R. A., Lombroso, P. J., et al. (2009). *Randomized controlled study of anger control training for adolescents with Tourette syndrome and disruptive behavior*. Unpublished manuscript.

Swain, J. E., Scahill, L, Lombroso, P. J., King, R. A., & Leckman, J. F. (2007). Tourette syndrome and tic disorders: A decade of progress. *Journal of the American Academy of Child and Adolescent Psychiatry, 46*, 947–968.

Taubert, K. A. (1999). Role of voluntary organizations in clinical care, research, and public policy. In D. J. Cohen, R. D. Bruun, & J. F. Leckman (Eds.), *Tic and tic disorders: Clinical understanding and treatment* (pp. 399–413). New York: John Wiley.

Verdellen, C. W. J., Keijsers, G. P. J., Cath, D. C., & Hoogduin, C. A. L. (2004). Exposure with response prevention versus habit reversal in Tourette's syndrome: A controlled study. *Behaviour Research and Therapy, 42*, 501–511.

Walkup., J. T., Khan, S., Schuerholz, L., Paik, Y.-S., Leckman, J. F., & Schultz, R. T. (1999). Phenomenology and natural history of tic-related ADHD and learning disabilities. In J. F. Leckman & D. J. Cohen (Eds.), *Tourette's syndrome: developmental psychopathology and clinical care* (pp. 63–79). New York: John Wiley.

Wang, H.-S., & Kuo, M.-F. (2003). Tourette's syndrome in Taiwan: An epidemiological study of tic disorders in an elementary school at Taipei County. *Brain & Development, 25*, S29–S31.

Watson, T. S., & Sterling, H. E. (1998). Brief functional analysis and treatment of a vocal tic. *Journal of Applied Behavior Analysis, 3*, 471–474.

Wilhelm, S., Deckersbach, T., Coffey, B. J., Bohne., A., Peterson, A. L., & Baer, L. (2003). Habit reversal versus supportive psychotherapy for Tourette's disorder: A randomized controlled trial. *American Journal of Psychiatry, 160*, 1175–1177.

Woods, D. W. (2002). The effect of video-based peer education on the social acceptability of adults with Tourette's syndrome. *Journal of Developmental and Physical Disabilities, 14*, 51–62.

Woods, D. W., Himle, M. B., Miltenberger, R. G., Carr, J. E., Osmon, D. C., Karsten, A. M., et al. (2007). Durability, negative impact, and neuropsychological predictors of tic suppression in children with chronic tic disorder. *Journal of Abnormal Child Psychology, 36,* 234–245.

Woods, D. W., Hook. S. S., Spellman, D. F., & Friman, P. C. (2000). Case study: Exposure and response prevention for an adolescent with Tourette's syndrome and OCD. *Journal of the American Academy of Child and Adolescent Psychiatry, 39,* 904–907.

Woods, D. W., & Marcks, B. A. (2005). Controlled evaluation of an educational intervention used to modify peer attitudes and behavior toward persons with Tourette's syndrome. *Behavior Modification, 29,* 900–912.

Woods, D. W., & Miltenberger, R. G. (1996). A review of habit reversal with childhood habit disorders. *Education & Treatment of Children, 19,* 197–214.

Woods, D. W., Miltenberger, R. G., & Lumley, V. A. (1996). Sequential application of major habit-reversal components to treat motor tics in children. *Journal of Applied Behavior Analysis, 29,* 483–493.

Woods, D. W., Piacentini, J. C., Himle, M. B., & Chang, S. (2005). Premonitory urge for tics scale (PUTS): Initial psychometric results and examination of the premonitory urge phenomenon in youths with tic disorders. *Journal of Developmental & Behavioral Pediatrics, 26,* 397–403.

20

Charting a Course for the Future: Empirically Supported Procedures, Translational Approaches, and Models for Complex Cases

ERIC A. STORCH AND DEAN McKAY

As detailed in the varied chapters of this text, the fields of child psychology and psychiatry have undergone significant advancements with regard to the understanding and treatment of child psychiatric diagnoses. For virtually all of the disorders covered in this volume, methodologically rigorous data exist that support the superiority of cognitive-behavioral therapy (CBT) against placebo-controlled conditions, nonspecific interventions, and, in some cases, pharmacotherapy alone (e.g., obsessive-compulsive disorder [OCD]). Although these data are very encouraging, a number of issues remain to be addressed to improve patient outcomes, as not all youth respond to cognitive-behavioral interventions, residual symptoms often remain after treatment, and dissemination remains limited. Further, although effective treatments exist, many conditions require ongoing clinical management (e.g., Asperger syndrome, bipolar disorder), suggesting that there are still additional treatment avenues to explore aside from complicating factors for our existing treatment programs. Thus, important next steps must be taken to refine existing treatments so as to maximize treatment outcome and disseminate findings to the masses. We conclude the text by reflecting on several areas that we highlight as particularly promising in this regard.

TAILORING TREATMENT TO THE INDIVIDUAL

Currently, we have generally good empirical data on which treatments work for which disorders. For example, the recent Child/Adolescent Anxiety Multimodal Study (CAMS, 2008) showed that both CBT and sertraline were effective in reducing anxiety severity across several childhood anxiety disorders (response rates of 59.7 and 54.9%, respectively), with a combination approach having the greatest efficacy (80.7%). However, as shown across the chapters in this book, multiple confounding factors can affect CBT outcome and require adjustments to established approaches. Given this, and consistent with the National Institutes of Health mission of tailoring evidence-based interventions to the individual, treatments must be tailored for each child and his or her clinical presentation to maximize efficacy. For example, several comorbid conditions (e.g., disruptive behavior disorders, depression, attention-deficit/hyperactivity disorder) negatively impact CBT for pediatric OCD (Storch et al., 2008), thereby requiring alternative strategies for treating these youth (e.g., combine parent management training and CBT for comorbid OCD and disruptive behavior disorders). Similarly, parental psychopathology must be considered in the child's clinical presentation and may require adaptations in how the case is conceptualized and treated. Considering instances such as these, it is critical to move beyond simple efficacy studies and begin considering how to adapt and empirically test treatments that address the myriad mediating and moderating variables that can affect outcome.

In some ways, it is interesting that tailoring treatment to individual needs must be mandated by a grant-issuing government agency. A central tenet of empirically supported practice (under different headings such as psychological clinical science [Treat, Bootzin, & Baker (2007)], or transdiagnostic CBT [Harvey, Watkins, Mansell, & Shafran (2004)]), involves the application of established treatment approaches within the context of specific symptom presentations. This allows one to escape the tight restrictions established by empirically supported treatment protocols whereby therapy programs are formulated for specific diagnoses, not necessarily specific individuals who happen to suffer from the diagnosis.

We appear to be at a critical juncture in the dissemination of effective treatment procedures for youth. As of 2004, it was clear that the existing empirically supported treatments that were designed expressly for specific diagnoses in children lagged behind those for adult disorders (Herschell, McNeil, & McNeil, 2004). Although Herschell et al. (2004) do not expressly call for the application of empirically supported practice, they do note that greater emphasis must be placed on idiographic factors, and that prognostic signs associated with poorer outcome, especially treatment adherence and noncompletion, require greater attention. Further, an increasing number of researchers are making the call for better dissemination of empirically supported approaches, including suggestions for complicating factors and for conducting further research on complicating factors (i.e., mediational analyses) (Kendall & Beidas, 2007).

TRANSLATIONAL RESEARCH

By nature, translational research involves scientific discoveries occurring at the basic science level that are "translated" to the clinical setting. Over the years, a multitude of advancements in psychiatry have been a reflection of this process (e.g., development of effective and more tolerable antidepressants and other medications); however, there have been fewer instances of translational research affecting psychological treatments, particularly among youth. Yet, one recent translational success has involved the use of basic science to suggest the exposure-treatment-enhancing effects of D-Cycloserine (DCS) (Norberg, Krystle, & Tolin, 2008). Medication augmentation strategies in childhood anxiety disorders are limited, have little empirical support, and may have undesirable side effects (e.g., metabolic effects associated with atypical antipsychotics); thus, improving the efficacy of exposure-based treatments with DCS, which seemingly has few side effects when administered for this purpose, has significant clinical benefit.

The presumed efficacy of DCS is based on evidence suggesting that the *N*-methyl-D-aspartate (NMDA) system plays a primary role in the neural processes underlying learned associations and fear extinction, which are core theoretical underpinnings of exposure therapy for anxiety disorders. Because NMDA receptor antagonists block or inhibit extinction (Walker, Ressler, Lu, & Davis, 2002), DCS, a partial agonist that acts at the strychnine-insensitive glycine-recognition site of the NMDA receptor complex, may enhance the acquisition and/or consolidation processes that occur during associative learning (Ledgerwood,

Richardson, & Cranney, 2003). And, as the extinction training inherent to exposure therapy is a form of associative learning, pharmacological agents like DCS that enhance extinction learning may improve behavioral therapies.

Following the accumulation of nonhuman animal data (Ledgerwood et al., 2003; Ledgerwood, Richardson, & Cranney, 2004, 2005; Walker et al., 2002), several trials in adult humans have been conducted with positive findings for adults with acrophobia (Ressler et al., 2004), social phobia (Hofmann et al., 2006), and OCD (Wilhelm et al., 2008). Currently, one of the authors (EAS) is completing a double-blind placebo-controlled trial of DCS augmentation in youth with OCD. Children receive either 25 mg or 50 mg DCS/placebo (depending on weight) 1 hour prior to seven exposure-and-response prevention sessions. Notably, these studies are critical in the use of basic science data to inform clinical intervention with the ultimate goal of improving patient outcome. The National Institutes of Health have funded a number of translational centers (http://nihroadmap.nih.gov/clinicalresearch/overview-translational.asp) to advance this effort; however, few have centers that focus on mental health in general and even fewer on child mental health specifically. Thus, translational efforts in this realm are sorely needed, to investigate ways of developing interventions and/or ways to augment response to effective psychological therapies.

DISSEMINATION

With knowledge about what treatments are effective, dissemination efforts are desperately required. In some instances, such as depression, federally funded trials have been or are being conducted with this in mind. As well, numerous publications, including the present one, have detailed evidence-based programs for specific disorders. Taking OCD as an example, there are several CBT protocols published for youth with OCD (e.g., Freeman & Garcia, 2009; March & Mulle, 1996) as well as multiple parent-oriented CBT guides (e.g., Chansky, 2001; Wagner, 2002). In addition to empirical scholarship, such books help "spread the word" about effective psychological treatments for childhood disorders and make the therapy more available for providers. Despite these positive advances, there is limited consistency among psychological providers in the community in the type of psychotherapy provided—although an increasing number are conducting evidence-based practice, many are providing non-evidence-based care. Unfortunately, such approaches convey the inaccurate notion that psychotherapy is ineffective, drain important resources (e.g., insurance), and instill a sense of hopelessness in many child and adult clients who have had limited response to non-evidence-based treatments. For such reasons, dissemination efforts that encourage the use of evidence-based interventions in clinical settings are highlighted as an area for future focus.

There are some impediments to dissemination that must be overcome. One prominent barrier involves the ready application of the empirically supported approach to the condition being treated—including all the complications—in a manner that can be easily implemented. This criticism of empirically supported treatment protocols has been described elsewhere (Herschell et al., 2004). In fact, it has been suggested that some mixed results in treatment trials with empirically supported approaches stem from the assumption that the protocol may be applied intact irrespective of other known factors that interfere with outcome. Another barrier to implementation comes at the training level. Students are often trained in researcher's labs where the empirically supported protocols are developed. This provides a unique opportunity to train with "the master." But an important shortcoming involves the disconnect between what is valued in the research design (i.e., purity of cases, complete integrity of protocol adherence) and the application to cases that do not "fit the mold" (i.e., have comorbid conditions, cannot follow the strict demands of the protocol). To the extent that more clinicians are trained in a science of clinical practice, whereby additional factors may be acknowledged and integrated into the treatment plan, the adequacy of future treatment models (Wilson, 2007) will be predicted.

CONCLUSION

It is our great hope that the reader is left with a sense of direction regarding the state of the literature on issues related to CBT nonresponse and methods of addressing such presentations. Clearly, there is much work that remains to be done to tailor evidence-based treatments to meet the needs of the many presentations that clinicians encounter. We hope that the collection of chapters contained within this volume provides a starting point in this regard to help improve clinical outcome and guide researchers in their clinical academic pursuits.

REFERENCES

Chansky, T. (2001). *Freeing your child from obsessive-compulsive disorder: A powerful, practical program for parents of children and adolescents*. New York: Crown Publishing Group.

Freeman, J. B., & Garcia, A. M. (2009). *Family-based treatment for young children with OCD*. Oxford, UK: Oxford University Press.

Harvey, A., Watkins, E., Mansell, W., & Shafran, R. (2004). *Cognitive behavioural processes across psychological disorders: A transdiagnostic approach to research and treatment*. Oxford, UK: Oxford University Press.

Herschell, A. D., McNeil, C. B., & McNeil, D. W. (2004). Clinical child psychology's progress in disseminating empirically supported treatments. *Clinical Psychology: Science and Practice, 11*, 267–288.

Hofmann, S. G., Meuret, A. E., Smits, J. A., Simon, N. M., Pollack M. H., & Eisenmenger, K. (2006): Augmentation of exposure therapy for social anxiety disorder with D-Cycloserine. *Archives of General Psychiatry, 63*, 298–304.

Kendall, P. C., & Beidas, R. S. (2007). Smoothing the trail for dissemination of evidence-based practices for youth: Flexibility within fidelity. *Professional Psychology: Research and Practice, 38*, 13–20.

Ledgerwood, L., Richardson, R., & Cranney, J. (2003). Effects of D-cycloserine on extinction of conditioned freezing. *Behavioral Neuroscience, 117*, 341–349.

Ledgerwood, L., Richardson, R., & Cranney, J. (2004). D-cycloserine and the facilitation of extinction of conditioned fear: consequences for reinstatement. *Behavioral Neuroscience, 118*, 505–513.

Ledgerwood, L., Richardson, R., & Cranney, J. (2005). D-cycloserine facilitates extinction of learned fear: Effects on reacquisition and generalized extinction. *Biological Psychiatry, 15*, 841–847.

March, J., & Mulle, K. (1996). Banishing obsessive-compulsive disorder. In E. Hibbs & P. Jensen (Eds.), *Psychosocial treatments for child and adolescent disorders* (pp. 82–103). Washington, DC: American Psychological Press.

Norberg, M. M., Krystle, J. H., & Tolin, D. H. (2008). A meta-analysis of d-cycloserine and the facilitation of fear extinction and exposure therapy. *Biological Psychiatry, 63*, 1118–1126.

Ressler, K. J., Rothbaum, B. O., Tannenbaum, L., Anderson, P. Graap, K., Zimand, E., et al. (2004). Cognitive enhancers as adjuncts to psychotherapy: Use of D-cycloserine in phobic individuals to facilitate extinction of fear. *Archives of General Psychiatry, 61*, 1136–1144.

Storch, E. A., Merlo, L. J., Larson, M., Geffken, G. R., Lehmkuhl, H. D., Jacob, M. L., et al. (2008). The impact of comorbidity on cognitive-behavioral therapy response in pediatric obsessive compulsive disorder. *Journal of the American Academy of Child and Adolescent Psychiatry, 47*, 583–592.

Treat, T. A., Bootzin, R. R., & Baker, T. B. (2007). *Psychological clinical science: Papers in honor of Richard M. McFall*. New York: Taylor & Francis.

Wagner, A. P. (2002). *What to do when your child has obsessive-compulsive disorder: Strategies and solutions*. New York: Lighthouse Press.

Walker, D. L., Ressler, K. J., Lu, K. T., & Davis, M. (2002). Facilitation of conditioned fear extinction by systemic administration or intra-amygdala infusions of D-cycloserine as assessed with fear-potentiated startle in rats. *Journal of Neuroscience, 22*, 2343–2351.

Wilhelm, S., Buhlmann, U., Tolin, D. F., Meunier, S. A., Pearlson, G. D., Reese, H. E., et al. (2008). Augmentation of behavior therapy with D-cycloserine for obsessive-compulsive disorder. *American Journal of Psychiatry, 165*, 335–341.

Wilson, G.T. (2007). Manual-based treatment: Evolution and evaluation. In T. A. Treat, R. R. Bootzin, & T. B. Baker (Eds.), *Psychological clinical science: Papers in honor of Richard M. McFall* (pp. 105–132). New York: Taylor & Francis.

Index